International Investment Law

To: Ellen, Elizabeth, Franz, Julian, Lily, Mark, Pierre, and Thomas – in thanks for your constant support.

International Investment Law

TEXT, CASES AND MATERIALS, SECOND EDITION

Krista Nadakavukaren Schefer

Senior Fellow, World Trade Institute, Bern, Switzerland

Edward Elgar
PUBLISHING

Cheltenham, UK • Northampton, MA, USA

Published by
Edward Elgar Publishing Limited
The Lypiatts
15 Lansdown Road
Cheltenham
Glos GL50 2JA
UK

Edward Elgar Publishing, Inc.
William Pratt House
9 Dewey Court
Northampton
Massachusetts 01060
USA

A catalogue record for this book
is available from the British Library

Library of Congress Control Number: 2016938604

ISBN 978 1 78536 007 7 (cased)
ISBN 978 1 78536 009 1 (paperback)
ISBN 978 1 78536 008 4 (eBook)

Typeset by Servis Filmsetting Ltd, Stockport, Cheshire
Printed and bound in Great Britain by TJ International Ltd, Padstow, Cornwall

Contents in brief

Full contents

Preface

The effort involved in keeping up with the changes to international investment law are witness to my conviction that the law of international investment protection remains one of international law's most dynamic fields of both research and practice. The recent years have seen a steady increase in the number of disputes being brought and in the complexity of the questions being faced by arbitrators. Although some of the substantive issues have become more settled (which is not to say we have anything approaching consensus on many of the questions that were pressing in 2013, but the arguments on them are settling to a handful of core positions) many have remained highly contentious (such as the standards of arbitrator ethics and the correct level of transparency in arbitral proceedings). Moreover, new issues are arising which had not been given much attention before: multiple claimant complaints, third-party funding, and the relationship between treaty regimes, just to mention a few. The growth in non-ICSID dispute settlement adds further complexity to the system as different arbitral rules begin to compete with each other.

Perhaps the most striking characteristic of investment law's recent past, however, has been its move onto the mainstream political stage. At time of writing, demonstrations against the Transatlantic Trade and Investment Partnership (TTIP) negotiations have just been expressing Europeans' skepticism about closer economic relations with the United States. A major part of this skepticism stems from the TTIP's planned inclusion of investment protections backed up by an investor-State dispute settlement mechanism (ISDS). Distrust of, or resentment toward, ISDS-backed investment protections has also led to broad governmental efforts at revising bilateral investment agreements. The 'right to regulate' has become a firm fixture in the related discussions—even as governments continue to liberalize their foreign investment regimes nationally and offer incentives to attract foreign investors.

What is the relationship between the increasing complexity of the legal framework and the increasing public interest in investment policy? At this point it seems that each is a response to the rapid developments of the past. They can be seen as a maturing of the system. The future direction of investment law's growth, however, is less clear than ever. This, I think, makes it more, rather than less worthy of study than ever before.

This second edition continues to be primarily focused on introducing university-level students to the legal regime of investment protection. Intended to serve as a stand-alone text for a typical one-semester course, I have made the book as condensed as possible without omitting anything fundamental to the understanding the system of international investment law as a whole.

For those with more time and interest, I have provided Discussion notes to bring out some of the more intricate points of law, or to provide thought-provoking questions. The Q&A pages are also intended to introduce perspectives that extend beyond the basics of the rules. These short pieces are written by some of the most experienced practitioners and researchers in the field and will give the reader insights that no amount of pure studying can lend.

Once again, the text is aimed at providing a neutral view of international investment law. I want readers to have the basic tools for considering how the system works without telling them how I think it should work. If the book can achieve that, my own goals in writing it will have been fulfilled.

Acknowledgements

Once again I am highly indebted to many people for the completion of this work. My students at the University of Basel, the World Trade Institute, and the Indian Institute of Foreign Trade were an inspiration as well as a source of valuable comments on the text itself. Edward Elgar's publishing team and their anonymous reviewers' critiques helped me think about what needed adjustment and what should be retained in the second edition.

Once again, however, my thanks go most of all to my research assistants. Pablo Arnaiz and Julian Powell were tirelessly thorough in their research as well as true examples of Swiss precision in the organization of their findings. Their comments were thought-provoking and their attitude constructively critical, Pablo and Julian encouraged me to continue trying to make the book better as well as more current—and to do it with a smile. If the future of investment law lies in hands as intellectually able, creative, and just plain fun as theirs are, we can only welcome our tomorrows.

Krista Nadakavukaren Schefer
Basel, May 2016

Table of cases

International

National

European Court of Human Rights

Table of legal instruments[1]

1 The bilateral investment treaty names are shortened to refer only to the Parties to the agreements and the year. The full citations are given in the footnotes.

National

Regional

1

Introduction to the study of international investment law

1.1 Introduction

International investment law has rapidly become one of the most vibrant sub-jects of international law. Its popularity among legal scholars and law students was already firmly established by 2012—in part because of its sheer scope: the Investment Policy Hub of the United Nations Conference on Trade and Development (UNCTAD) indicates that there are over 3000 international investment agreements (IIAs) in existence today, with over 2500 in force.[1] A general term, IIA refers to any bilateral investment treaty (BIT), regional investment treaty (the ASEAN Comprehensive Investment Agreement is an example), or the investment protection provisions of a preferential trade agreement (such as NAFTA's Chapter 11, or MERCOSUR's Colonia Protocol for the Promotion and Reciprocal Protection of Investments) or of a sectoral agreement with investment protection provisions (such as the Energy Charter Treaty). While many of the provisions contained within these different types of treaties are similar, they vary enough to supply a wide set of legal issues to be considered and debated.

More important than the number of investment agreements in the growing attention to this area of law, however, is the fact that investors are using these IIAs to challenge foreign states' sovereign actions. International investment agreements, that is, may (and generally do) offer private persons access to binding dispute settlement procedures against foreign sovereign govern-ments on the international plane. Utilizing the so-called investor-State dispute settlement (ISDS) mechanisms found in most IIAs, investors can go

---

1 UNCTAD, International Investment Agreements Navigator. Available at: http://investmentpolicyhub.unctad.org/IIA. UNCTAD, Bilateral Investment Treaties 1959–1999, iii (United Nations: New York and Geneva, 2000).

to arbitration to enforce the rights host states owe to them and their investments, claiming cash compensation for any violations the investors may have
suffered. As investors have been taking advantage of this possibility more
frequently and more openly, these ISDS actions have spurred responses from
those outside legal circles, as well as from lawyers. With procedures that have
scrutinized governmental regulation of the environment, public health, and
the rights of indigenous peoples, and with awards that have reached as high
as $50 billion,[2] enforcing the obligations of international investment law is
effecting legal changes domestically. This, in turn, has attracted the attention
of governments, specialized non-governmental organizations (NGOs), the
press, and the general public.

This book is designed to introduce readers to the basic principles of investment law. It answers the questions of what is an investment, what is an expropriation, and what obligations a state has toward foreign investors—in short,
the typical public international law aspects of investment protection. Given
the centrality of the enforcement of investment protection to lawyers' interest in the field, the rules and procedures of the settlement of investors' disputes with host states are the subject of extended treatment. Finally, a chapter
on investment insurance offers a further perspective on protecting an investor's financial exposure to governmental actions.

1.2 Why investment law is different from other areas of economic law

The law of foreign direct investment (FDI) has as its goal the protection of
foreign property by the government of the state in which it is found. We talk
then about the 'host state', or the state in which the investment is made in
opposition to the 'home state', or the state of which the investor is a national.[3]

The hallmark of investment law is that it applies to commercial activities
that are different from domestic business activities as well as from other international commercial activities. The structure of a foreign investment is
characterized by a long-term relationship between a private person and a
government in which the negotiating power of the parties shifts between the
negotiating stage and the project implementation stage. For the government,
this relationship means that it must attract the private party to put money,

---

2 *Yukos Universal Ltd (Isle of Man) v. The Russian Federation*, UNCITRAL, PCA Case No. AA 227, Final
Award p. 564, para. 1827 (July 18, 2014).
3 We will see that a 'legal home' can mean a variety of things, including: citizenship, incorporation, majority
ownership, etc.

time, and effort into the relationship with its country. As money, time, and effort are scarce resources, the private party will normally have to choose a single country with which to have this relationship. Thus, the would-be host has to market its location.

For the investor, the long-term nature of the relationship means that it must spend money immediately (to put up a factory or to buy production facilities, for example) with the hope of making a profit in the future. This entails a risk that something will occur between the putting in of financial resources, and the return of financial profits. The profit-making potential of the factory or production facilities, however, is not just contingent on the normal risks of business (such as changing customer tastes, the risks of poor business decisions, or hiring mistakes) but also on the official or unofficial actions of the government that is the host of the investment. Such governmental actions often are, and even cannot be, foreseen at the time the investor makes its decision to invest.

For the parties to the investment relationship, there are thus two critical stages: negotiations and implementation. The negotiating positions of the parties change between these two stages. The investor often has the negotiating advantage during the negotiations, as the government has an interest in attracting the investor's assets into the country.[4]

For the investor, the problems normally arise after the investment has been made, when it wants to implement its investment project. During the implementation stage, then, the bargaining power shifts in favor of the host government. Once the investor has put money into the country, it will face a problem if the host starts taking actions that take away or minimize the profit flows.[5] As a sovereign, the host has the right to regulate all of the resources within its territory—including foreign capital. If it chooses to limit the investor's access to the capital, or tax the profits, or take away the property entirely, the host's right to regulate will provide a possible reason to see the act as within the bounds of international law. Yet, even when a host's actions are taken in good faith (and they may not be), from the investor's point-of-view,

---

4 Governments, often faced with competing states, may make numerous promises to the investor during the negotiations—perhaps they offer infrastructure (building access roads), or tax exemptions; perhaps they ensure administrative assistance (e.g. promising licences), or the possibility of repatriating profits. Not yet well-regulated, the legal questions relating to such 'investment incentives' are numerous and important, but cannot be covered in this text. For more on this topic, *see*, e.g. Kenneth P. Thomas, *Investment Incentives and the Global Competition for Capital* (Palgrave Macmillan, 2011).

5 The government might decide to seize a production plant or to withhold mining rights; it might impose a special tax on profits or even prohibit a certain activity entirely.

the hopes of profit are crushed. What can the investor do legally against the state? This is the question for the law of FDI, or international investment law.

1.3 An overview of the history of investment and investment protection

1.3.1 The evolution of international investment law

Laws protecting investors have a long history. Even though scholarly attention to investment law was in abeyance for much of the twentieth century, there are centuries of development that have gone into investment law, and over a millennium during which laws relevant to foreign investment activities have existed.[6]

Studying the historical development of laws protecting investors in any jurisdiction mainly relies on looking at how the law treated foreigners.[7] While not all of the Ancient Greek city-states welcomed aliens, at least in Athens, foreign businessmen were welcomed and encouraged to engage in the economy of the city. As a result, there were treaties guaranteeing reciprocal treatment of citizens (a principle of national treatment) and court procedures to ensure the enforcement of commercial contracts. Similar arrangements are found under Roman law. Both systems, notably, were based in bilateral treaties rather than any sort of more generally applicable principles of law, yet the concepts are still found in today's IIAs to protect foreign investors, albeit in a somewhat altered form.

During the Middle Ages, early thinking about international law led to the evolution of general principles to govern the treatment of foreigners as individuals. Vittoria proposed national treatment for aliens in trade matters and Grotius supported a most favored nation obligation (treating all foreigners equally) for the state toward its resident aliens. Neither, however, questioned the general practice of the *droit d'aubain*, denying aliens any rights to property.[8]

---

6 R. Doak Bishop, James Crawford and W. Michael Reisman eds., *Foreign Investment Disputes: Cases, Materials, and Commentary* 2 (2005) (noting the probability of investment in Ancient Egypt and the Mediterranean empires. The amount of trade between the Ancient empires of what is today China, India, and the Middle East suggests the existence of formal investment protection agreements in these regions as well).

7 In many of the early civilizations, the ownership of real property was forbidden to aliens, as the laws determining citizenship were generally based on religion, itself a local institution. *See* Carmen Tiburcio, *The Human Rights of Aliens under International and Comparative Law*, 23–5 (2001).

8 Id. at 105.

It was Emer de Vattel who elaborated upon the idea of diplomatic protection for alien property. In developing his argument in *The Law of Nations*, de Vattel posited that once a state has admitted a foreigner, it must treat that person as it would its own citizen, while recognizing that the individual is still a citizen of his or her home state.[9]

> §108. The state has no right over the person of a foreigner; the state, which ought to respect the rights of other nations, and in general those of all mankind, cannot arrogate to herself any power over the person of a foreigner, who, though he has entered her territory, has not become her subject. The foreigner cannot pretend to enjoy the liberty of living in the country without respecting the laws . . . but he is not obliged to submit, like the subjects, to all the commands of the sovereign: and if such things are required of him as he is unwilling to perform, he may quit the country. He is free at all times to leave it; nor have we a right to detain him . . . This [would be] at once a violation of the rights of individuals, and of those of the state to which they belong.[10]

Given the acceptance of the Roman law concept whereby property was considered an extension of the person possessing it, de Vattel therefore elaborated a principle for the treatment of aliens *and their property* as governed by sovereign courtesy—because citizens were considered the 'property' of their home state's government, equal protection of them was a sign of courtesy to the home government by the host:

> §109. The property of an individual does not cease to belong to him on account of his being in a foreign country; it still constitutes a part of the aggregate wealth of his nation [. . .]. Any power, therefore, which the lord of the territory might claim over the property of a foreigner, would be equally derogatory to the rights of the individual owner, and to those of the nation of which he is a member.[11]

Consequently, a violation of the foreigner's property rights was a violation of the rights of the home state. Such a violation, then, would incur the international responsibility of the host to the home state rather than to the foreigner as an individual. Typical state-to-state dispute resolution was the logical response.[12,13]

---

9 Emerich de Vattel, *The Law of Nations or Principles of Natural Law*, Book 2, Ch 8, §§ 99–115 (1798).
10 Id. § 108.
11 Id. § 109.
12 Id. § 109. Bishop et al., *supra* note 6, at 2.
13 Dispute settlement is discussed in Chapter 6.

The protective concepts of foreign investment protection were further developed as the major European states (and the United States, following its independence) accepted reciprocal obligations to protect foreigners and their property in treaties with each other. Further abroad, however, the protection of foreign investment lacked this equality. True, colonization was well under way in European states by the late eighteenth century and great sums were being 'invested' abroad, but the imperial relationships were such that the mother country investors remained subject to mother country laws. In uncolonized areas, where there was truly 'foreign' investment, the European rules of protection were established in a context of: 'few reciprocal relationships, considerably more coercion, and constrained bargaining among radically unequal states'.[14]

The result was a mixture of forms of what were essentially trading privileges for investors: 'capitulation treaties', providing national treatment for foreign traders as well as reciprocal promises to protect endangered sailors and merchandise; the creation of special areas within a state in which property protection would be ensured (and enforced either by means of diplomacy or through military force); or simply by the extraterritorial application of the foreigner's domestic legal protections.[15]

By the mid-nineteenth century, the level of FDI began to expand rapidly.[16] This was due in part to the technological developments that made increasingly larger-scale projects feasible: projects such as mineral mining, export-oriented agricultural, and the newly-developing transportation and communication technologies which necessitated large infrastructure. In part, the expansion was made possible by legal developments to ensure sufficient financing of such projects by private companies. The development of the corporation as a new form of legal person permitted entrepreneurs to raise capital sufficient to cover the enormous financial demands of the new types of foreign investment—and to spend it without personal liability.[17]

1.3.2 The Calvo Doctrine's challenge to international investment law

The European nations of the nineteenth century widely adhered to the view that their citizens enjoyed a right to property. The set of treaties they had

---

14 Charles Lipson, *Standing Guard: Protecting Foreign Capital in the Nineteenth and Twentieth Centuries* 12 (Berkeley/Los Angeles/London: University of California Press, 1985).

15 Id., pp. 13–14

16 Bishop et al., *supra* note 5, at 2–3.

17 Id., pp. 2–3.

established with each other also led to a general acceptance of the idea that governments would protect foreign property owners on the same level as they protected their own.

As a result, in Europe, foreign investors could be secure in knowing that their property would enjoy the protections from unreasonable governmental interference with their assets.[18]

Nevertheless, many non-European countries that were receiving European investments—particularly the newly independent South American states—began to want control over their infrastructure development. Thus, besides defaulting on debts held by European investors, governments began to take over the investors' property directly. Without offers of compensation, such expropriations were considered unacceptable breaches of accepted breaches of international law to the European powers. This obvious challenge to the existing international system led to political tensions, which themselves sometimes escalated into military skirmishes.

The frequency of home states' use of military force to protect citizens' investments overseas led to rising resentment among host states. While the Drago–Porter Treaty eventually outlawed the use of force for investment protection,[19] one of the challenges to home states' involvement in their citizens' foreign activities was more fundamental than the complaint about methods of protection. In 1868 Argentine scholar Carlos Calvo wrote that the treatment owed foreign investors should be one of pure national treatment. The treatment a foreign investor should receive, Calvo argued, should be the same treatment as the treatment the host offers its own citizens' property, no matter what the level of protection. Calvo added that home states should not be able to interfere in another state's treatment of its nationals, and that foreign investors—like national investors—should be limited to national courts when in search of remedies. International law, in short, would be substantially removed from investment law.

The investment law debates regarding Calvo's ideas only began post-1918. Why? Because this was the year in which the Bolshevik leaders of the Russian Revolution proclaimed the triumph of communist ideas about property—namely, that there should be no protection of private property.[20] The

---

18 Lipson, *supra* note 14, at p. 8.
19 Hague Convention II—Limitation of Employment of Force for Recovery of Contract Debts (Drago–Porter Treaty), Oct. 18, 1907, art. 1(1).
20 *See* Samuel Kucherov, *Property in the Soviet Union*, 11(3) Am. J. Comp. L. 376 (1962).

international legal implications of Lenin's abolishment of private property were particularly strong for the contemporary law of international investment protection, because if citizens enjoyed no right to property, the principle of national treatment no longer offered foreign investors an assured standard of protection of their property.

Soviet Russia's defence of its expropriations of foreign properties (on the basis of national treatment) was adopted by other hosts, quickly dividing world opinion on the level of investor protection required by international law. In what would become the forerunner to a line of arguments put forward throughout the twentieth century by various host state governments around the world, Mexico's revolutionary governments of the 1920s relied on national treatment *à la* Calvo. In the *Harry Roberts* case (1926) the national treatment doctrine was put to the test in a human rights context: Harry Roberts, a US citizen, was arrested for murder in Mexico and held by the Mexican police for 19 months. Delays in the prosecution of Roberts were noted by the Mexican government (admittedly unconstitutional under the then-constitution of Mexico) but no action was taken. While in prison, Roberts was also subjected to 'rude and cruel treatment'. The US brought a case on his behalf against Mexico before an arbitral tribunal. The tribunal reasoned that: 'Aliens of course are obliged to submit to proceedings properly instituted against them in conformity with local laws'.[21] Because Mexico had 'ample grounds to suspect' Roberts' guilt, the arrest itself was not illegal. The second question, however, was whether he had been treated legally. Here, Mexico argued that as Roberts was treated no differently than Mexican prisoners, the government should not be found responsible for violating any norms of treatment. The Commission, however, made the following remarks: 'such equality is not the ultimate test of the propriety of acts of authorities in light of international law. The test is, broadly speaking, whether aliens are treated in accordance with ordinary standards of civilization'.[22] A minimum standard—not the national treatment principle—was the measure of Mexico's acts, and on this measure, the government had failed.

Soon the debate over minimum standards/national treatment reached international investment law. When Mexico nationalized US oil investments in 1938, US Secretary of State Cordell Hull wrote a diplomatic note acknowledging the Mexican right to expropriate, but stating that any

---

21 *Harry Roberts (USA) v. United Mexican States*, Decision of 2 November 1926, 4 RIAA 77, 79 at para. 6 [hereinafter '*Harry Roberts*'].
22 Id. at para. 8.

expropriation must be accompanied by 'prompt, adequate, and effective' compensation.[23] The so-called 'Hull Formula', still the widely used measure of compensation, encapsulated the idea of a minimum standard: hosts must at least protect investors to the extent that expropriations are compensated fully, whether or not citizens have such a right.

Discussions as to whether the minimum standard or pure national treatment was the correct standard to grant investors continued for several decades, but it was not until the early post-World War II years that the investment debates became significant again. The general thrust of the arguments was clear: the right to compensation for expropriations was asserted by the commercially dominant European governments and the United States against the insistence of new states, created out of the wave of de-colonization, on their sovereign right to expropriate without offering the foreign investors payments—at least full payments— for the value of their properties.[24]

The reasoning behind the denial of a minimum standard of protection was less theoretical than practical. With much of the natural resource wealth in the newly independent countries owned by private companies from the former colonial mother, the new governments were left with few possibilities to finance themselves. Using the concept of permanent sovereignty over natural resources, the governments thus asserted their rights to such properties and denied the prerequisite of compensation.[25]

1.3.3 From the New International Economic Order to the present: FDI as curse, blessing, or simply a fact of global economic life?

By the late 1960s, growing wealth and development gaps between the industrialized and developing countries prompted the latter to start questioning the global economic system's basic structures. Under the label New International Economic Order (NIEO) developing countries (with the assistance of UNCTAD, the Commonwealth, and the non-aligned movement) began a concerted effort to steer the post-war economic

---

23 Green Hackworth, 3 *Digest of International Law* 658–9 (1942) (reprinting the statement of Cordell Hull addressed to the Government of Mexico on August 22, 1938).

24 For an extensive discussion of the development of international economic policies from the 1940s through to the 1970s, *see* Lipson, *supra* note 20.

25 Notably, even in the politicized context of the North–South debates, the industrialized countries generally supported the right to expropriate. This recognition, though, was underlain by the condition that the expropriation was for a public purpose, non-discriminatory, and compensated fully.

system away from the domination of Western capitalist, liberal ideas. The concept set out formally in UN General Assembly resolutions[26] and the Charter of Economic Rights and Duties of States[27] was based on the belief that the Bretton Woods economic system was set up to rebuild Europe's economic capacity and that the developing world was ignored during the planning. As a result, the NIEO argued, the structures in place not only did not foster growth and development in the poorer nations, but the liberalizations and grants of conditional aid actually worsened poverty in the global South. The NIEO goals therefore included a fair allocation of the world's resources, technology transfer to developing countries, preferential trade conditions, and a reformation of the international monetary system.[28]

In investment law, the NIEO fostered the development of the 'dependency' theory.[29] This warns that FDI causes the host to enter into a harmful, dependent relationship on the 'centre', where transnational corporations' and their home states' interests coincide. The periphery— where the subsidiaries of corporations, but not their headquarters, are located—is left to serve the home state's interests. The dependency theory led to severe restrictions being placed on the entry and domestic activities of foreign investors. Where foreign investment was allowed at all, policies such as minimum local ownership, required transfers of technology, and restricted repatriation of profits were used as conditions of governmental approval.

As the 1970s gave way to the 1980s, developing economies' attitudes toward investment changed, and they began to regard foreign capital as an instrument to finance economic development. Adopting the 'classical' theory of investment promoted by the multilateral financial institutions and the main home states, hosts began actively trying to attract investment. Hosts began to offer tax credits, subsidies, low regulatory burdens, and—significantly— promises of investor protection to bring in foreign capital in an attempt to reap the technology and local jobs promised by investment.

In the early years of this attitude, a dichotomy thus arose: in international fora, developing countries continued arguing for national treatment stand-

---

26 Declaration on the Establishment of a New International Economic Order, GA Res. 3201, UN Doc. A/RES/S-6/3201 (May 1, 1974); Programme of Action on the Establishment of a New International Economic Order, GA Res. 3202, UN Doc. A/RES/S-6/3202 (May 1, 1974).

27 GA Res. 3281, UN Doc. A/RES/29/3281 (Dec. 12, 1974).

28 GA Res. 3201, *supra* note 26, para. 4.

29 *See* Muthucumaraswamy Sornarajah, *The International Law on Foreign Investment* 53–5 (third edn, 2010).

ards of investment protection, while in the BIT negotiating rooms, these same governments were agreeing to bind themselves to promises of even more-than-minimum commitments to protect foreign property.

Today, attitudes toward FDI are more sophisticated than the binary view of good or bad. Investment is widely regarded as a necessary ingredient for enhancing growth, but it is recognized as only one from a palette of potential inputs. Binding commitments to protect foreign investment are valued, not only as a means of attracting capital, but also as a tool for binding governments to standards of good governance that benefit citizens as well as foreign investors. Whilst some foreign investors continue to view host territories as simply low-cost production platforms, others have had an undeniably beneficial impact on the local societies in which they operate. A welcoming but watchful attitude toward FDI seems the dominant approach among the world's FDI hosts.

1.4 The future of investment law

The current investment environment is more complex than before, with huge FDI flows going in all directions—developing economies are increasingly senders as well as receivers of FDI, while industrialized countries are also recipients of FDI from developing countries; and while investment is recognized as beneficial to the economy, fears have been voiced about too much foreign control of certain sectors (energy, in particular) and the influence of private foreign corporations (most investors today are corporations rather than individuals) on governments.

Moreover, most IIAs contain dispute settlement provisions allowing private investors to sue a government for breach of the treaty. Such ISDS mechanisms have come under intense scrutiny, and are the focus of many current debates regarding the future of international investment law.

The influence of these contextual changes is certain to influence future investment law. While expropriations will probably continue to require compensation, the actions that are considered to be an expropriation may be narrowed to protect the state's policy space. As the Internet allows for more cross-border trade in services, protection of investment might need to respond to limitations on electronic access by citizens, even where the provider remains physically located in the home state. The development of other areas of international law, too, are having an influence on investment law—questions of environmental protection, labor rights, and corporate social responsibility are already being addressed in some treaties.[30] Is it only a matter of time before legal rules in these different areas find their way into the mainstream of international investment agreements?

With these potential legal changes in mind, let us now turn to the basics of existing international investment law.

---

30 Besides hortatory language on the aims of sustainable development in the preambles of some investment treaties, Belgium and the United States, among others, have included provisions on the environment and labor in their Model investment agreements, and Canada and Peru have placed corporate social responsibility (CSR) within the substantive text of their Free Trade Agreement's investment chapter. *See*, e.g. 2002 Belgium Model Bilateral Investment Treaty, arts. 5–6; 2012 US Model Bilateral Investment Treaty United States, arts. 12–13. Available at: http://www.state.gov/documents/organization/188371.pdf; Agreement Between the United Arab Emirates, on the one hand, and the Belgian-Luxembourg Economic Union, on the other hand, on the Reciprocal Promotion and Protection of Investments, Articles 5–6 (2004); Treaty Between the Government of the United States of America and the Government of the Republic of Rwanda Concerning the Encouragement and Reciprocal Protection of Investment, arts. 12–13 (2008); Canada–Peru Free Trade Agreement, art. 810 ('Each Party should encourage enterprises operating within its territory or subject to its jurisdiction to voluntarily incorporate internationally recognized standards of CSR in their internal policies').

Question to an expert: Piero Bernardini

Piero Bernardini is Of Counsel in the law firm Ughi e Nunziante in Rome and holds the chair in international arbitration at the LUISS University. He was formerly the General Counsel as well as a Member of the Board and Executive Committee to the Eni Group. Having been an arbitrator, president of the tribunal, or counsel in over 300 commercial and investment treaty cases, under the rules of ICSID, ICC, LCIA, NAI, Cairo Centre, UNCITRAL, CAM, AIA, VIAC, SCC, Mr. Bernardini is the President of the Italian Arbitration Association, a member of the ICCA Advisory Board, and one of Italy's appointments to the ICSID panel of conciliators and arbitrators. He is also a frequent speaker and a prolific author.

How has international investment law changed in light of the changing international investment business environment?

The experience of international investment agreements in force worldwide (currently over 3000) has encouraged the progressive development of new rules governing investment. An increasing number of states, both capital-importing and capital-exporting, are publicly reconsidering their participation in trade and investment protection agreements in order to reclaim their regulatory space. This process has been favored by the growing interconnectedness of global markets and the experience gained from investment treaty decisions.

The key challenge for this development is the need to ensure that the goal of protecting and encouraging investment does not affect the ability of states to pursue public policy objectives by the exercise of regulatory power. There is now a move to recognize that 'investment flows are not an end in themselves and [the] well-being of ordinary citizens . . . and customers . . . are the benchmarks' for an agreement (see European Parliament Resolution of 8 July 2015).

This view of citizen well-being as a benchmark for investment law is reflected by a number of recent free trade agreements, such as the EU–Canada Comprehensive Economic and Trade Agreement (CETA) (2014), the Trans–Pacific Partnership 2015 (TPP 2015) between the US and 11 Asia–Pacific States, and the EU–US Transatlantic Trade and Investment Partnership (TTIP) (under negotiation at time of writing).

The rules that have been developed in these and other negotiations have generated intense debate in particular as regarding transparency, the host state's regulatory powers, and the settlement of disputes.

Transparency of the arbitration process requires making publicly available parties' submissions and tribunal's decisions, as reflected by the new UNCITRAL Arbitration Rules on Transparency (2013) and the UN Convention on Transparency in Treaty-based Investor-State Arbitration (2014) and allowing the filing of *amicus curiae* briefs by interested third parties (e.g. NGOs and trade unions) in further development of the ICSID Convention provision.

QUESTION TO AN EXPERT: PIERO BERNARDINI *(continued)*

States' power to regulate has been reaffirmed by the inclusion of exceptions provisions in a number of recent free trade agreements. States intend these to help allow them to achieve legitimate public policy objectives, such as public health, safety, environment, public morals, and the promotion and protection of cultural diversity.

New rules have also been introduced to prevent the parties' 'forum shopping', to limit the arbitrators' powers by defining key concepts such as 'fair and equitable treatment', and 'indirect expropriation', and by introducing a code of conduct for arbitrators ensuring high ethical and professional standards. As noted by the European Parliament's rapporteur for the TTIP, governments must: 'insist that the right of lawmakers . . . to legislate must not be undermined by private arbitration courts', given that 'private interests cannot undermine public policy objectives'.

Globalized business, it seems, has underscored, rather than undermined, the role of the state.

2

Sources of international investment law

2.1 Introduction

This chapter gives an overview of the study of sources of international investment law. First, it sets out an explanation of general international law's sources. Second, it turns to particular sources of investment law. The explanation of the general legal sources is concise, as there is a significant amount of literature available that addresses the topic thoroughly.[1] Thus, for readers familiar with international law, those sections may be considered optional. The brief description of the sources of law specific to international investment protection law is vital however, as the reader will need to recognize the various types and understand their relationship to each other and to the sources of other areas of law.

2.1.1 Definition of 'sources' of law

Law is commonly thought of as consisting of rules to which we must adjust our behaviour. Local laws set out where commercial buildings can be placed and how elections for local officials will be run. National laws determine who may enter the country and how much an individual pays in income taxes. Regional law may indicate the information required on the label of goods sold within its members' territories. International law can determine whether an import tariff can be levied. All of these types of laws are considered *primary rules*—rules giving the substance of the law. To know the obligations and rights of natural or legal persons, one must know where such primary rules can be found. One also must know the relationship of primary rules to one another. Hierarchies and interactions of legal provisions determine the applicability of particular rules in different contexts.

---

1 *See*, e.g. Hilary Charlesworth, 'Law-Making and Sources', *in Cambridge Companion to International Law* 187, 187–202 (James Crawford and Martti Koskenniemi eds., 2012); Martii Koskenniemi, ed., *Sources of International Law* (2000); Malcolm N. Shaw, *International Law* 49–91 (seventh edn, 2014); Hugh Thirlway, 'Sources of International Law', in: Malcolm D. Evans, ed., *International Law* 91–117 (fourth edn, 2014).

But the study of any system of laws also needs to take into account the law-making process: that 'process whereby rules of international law emerge'.[2] Thirlway describes the process as determined by 'secondary rules', or rules that govern *how* or *from where* the primary rules come and become binding.[3] The idea common to all is that there are rules behind the substantive or procedural primary rules that contribute to the development of the body of law—there is an evolutionary process of legal system-building consisting of ideas and beliefs about what is and what should be law, state practice, judicial decision-making, and scholarly analysis, as well as the basic laws as written. This is of great importance because it is the process of making the laws that —to a large degree—determines the legitimacy of the primary rules.

The location, relationships, interactions, and the process of creation and evolution of laws are all included in the domain known as 'sources of law'. We now turn to this area of legal study.

2.1.2   Importance of sources for the study of investment law

It is important to know where one can look for the law in order to study law. Thus, on the basic level, the study of sources is necessary to know what the law is and whether it is applicable in a particular case. In studying international law, however, sources analysis holds an added interest because questions are often more complicated than in national law: whether a particular document is really a 'source' (or was a source when the disputed subject matter originated) may be in question; whether a state had an obligation under that source may need investigation, since not all states are obliged under the same legal source; the relationship of different sources of law is also complicated, as hierarchies are less clear in international law than in domestic legal regimes.

It is also interesting to realize that there are so many actors influencing sources. These questions mainly stem from the fact that states in the international system are not presumed to have entered into any type of social contract with other states—they are sovereign and equally so. Thus, the international system was often regarded as being a situation in which states were only bound to do, or not do, that to which assent was given. This is changing, but slowly.

For non-specialists in the field of legal sources, the most important reason to study sources is to gain an appreciation of the evolutionary aspect of international law—the international legal regime is a framework housing a process

---

2 Shaw, *supra* note 1, at 50.
3 Thirlway, *supra* note 1, at 92.

that itself is characterized by the influence of various actors creating restrictions on themselves, combined with a temporal dimension and underlain by a requirement of belief in the rules as ones of law. In investment law, this evolutionary process is currently occurring with great speed—and with it, the shuffling of sources. This makes sources of particular importance for our study.

2.2 Sources of international law

International law scholars often subdivide 'sources' of international law into categories.[4] As our purpose is to understand the instruments of international investment law, this chapter simplifies the categorization, examining: (1) the types of instruments that are 'law'; and (2) the international law-making process.

2.2.1 What instruments are 'law'?

For all the scholarly activity surrounding sources, most authors come back to the same point in their discussions: the one firm statement on what exactly count as sources, the Statute of the International Court of Justice (ICJ), Article 38.

Basically reproducing the statute of the Permanent Court of International Justice, the ICJ Statute indicates *upon* what the ICJ judges may decide cases brought to them.

Article 38, paragraph 1 says that the judges may rely on international law as set out in:

(a) international *conventions* as: 'rules expressly recognized by the contesting states';
(b) international *customary law* 'as evidence of a general practice accepted as law'; and
(c) *general principles* of law 'recognized' by states; supplemented by
(d) *judicial decisions* and *teachings* by scholars around the world, as *subsidiary* sources.

---

4 Among the many divisions of sources are the two basic types: formal and material. With the term *formal sources* we mean 'the question of the authority for the rule as a rule of law' (Thirlway, *supra* note 1, at 92). That is, the *kind* of law that is a 'source' includes the sources enumerated in Article 38 of the Statute of the ICJ. The term *material source* is more difficult to describe. Thirlway defines it as: 'the place [. . .] in which the terms of the rule are set out' (Thirlway, *supra* note 1, at 92) while the legal authority/binding-qualities of the instrument is unimportant. As Fitzmaurice stated, material sources are whose 'to which the lawgiver goes, so to speak, in order to obtain ideas, or to decide what the law is to consist of [. . .]'. Sir Gerald G. Fitzmaurice, 'Some Problems Regarding the Formal Sources of International Law' in: Koskenniemi, *supra* note 1, at 153.

Article 38, paragraph 2 adds that the judges can rely on decision-making *ex aequo et bono*, that is, on the basis of what is fair under the circumstances. As such decision-making is independent of the legal rights of the parties, the parties must agree to the court's use of this tool.

The provisions thus set out general types of *sources* available to the judges: *primary sources, subsidiary sources*, and *equity*. Most of the teaching on sources looks at the primary sources: conventions (or, treaties), customary international law, and general principles of law. Subsidiary sources, however, can also generate important questions, as can the possibility of the usage of equitable solutions to international legal disputes.

? **DISCUSSION NOTES**

1 Why did the drafters of the ICJ Statute feel the need to say what law the judges could rely on? How do international arbitral tribunals compare with the ICJ decision-makers in this respect?
2 Sources of law differ between jurisdictions. Many states divide sources into legislative and administrative law. The recognition of judicial decisions as an additional source of law is one of the features distinguishing the common law from the civil law.

2.2.2   Primary sources of law

a   *International conventions*

The *prime source* of current international law, and the focus of the present study, is *treaty law*, or the law of international conventions/agreements.[5] A 'treaty' is an agreement between states, setting out relations and/or obligations of the parties to be performed in the future.

a.i   *International law governing treaties*

The law of treaties is to a great extent customary international law (recognized by states as binding) but it is also largely set out in a 'Treaty on Treaties': the Vienna Convention on the Law of Treaties 1969.

---

5 Treaties have not always been the prime source of law—in fact, throughout history and up until the mid-nineteenth century, customary law was a much more prominent source of international law. General principles and the teachings (or writings) of scholars were also much more heavily considered than treaties. This was no doubt in part due to the fact that treaties were relatively few in number, and relatively limited in content. Increasingly, however, treaties have come to dominate the regulation of legal relations on the international level.

The Vienna Convention on the Law of Treaties (VCLT) was drafted as one of the first assignments given to the International Law Commission (ILC) upon its formation, as an attempt to codify what was recognized international law. Although some states have not ratified the VCLT, most of its terms are usually accepted by them as customary international law (CIL).

The label

Article 2, VCLT defines a 'treaty' as a written agreement between two or more states that is governed by international law.[6] The label of the document containing the obligations is irrelevant. An agreement between states can be called a treaty, convention, protocol, covenant, charter, statute, act, declaration, concordat, exchange of notes, memorandum of agreement (MoA) or sometimes even a memorandum of understanding (MoU) and still be considered a 'treaty'. Alternatively, however, such labels may be used for non-treaty documents. A 'treaty', however, cannot be an agreement that is governed solely by national law. A lease or purchase agreement, for instance, is not a treaty even if it is inter-state.

Treaties can be on any subject matter, and can reflect the wishes of the parties to a very large extent, although there are some limits to what can be agreed upon. No states could, for example, bind themselves to ensuring the conditions for slave trade, as slavery is prohibited by *jus cogens* norms.

Breach of a treaty

The violation of a treaty provision is considered a 'wrongful' act in international law, and results in 'responsibility' for the violating state. The exact consequences, however, depend on the terms of the treaty.

Other laws on treaties

Other sources of treaty law include two further Vienna Conventions: one is the draft Vienna Convention on the Law of Treaties between States and International Organizations (21 March 1986), the other is the Vienna Convention on the Succession of States in Treaties (23 August 1978). Both are still subject to great disagreement, although the Convention on the Succession of States is in force. Its basic principle, as set forth in Article 16, is that of relieving the new government of the former government's treaty commitments. This is supplemented, however, with an option of choosing to continue the treaty obligations.[7] In the Vienna Convention on Treaties

---

6 The form of the treaty is irrelevant to the existence of the parties' obligations, but an oral agreement, for example, is not subject to the VCLT, but rather to the provisions of the VCLT as rules of CIL.

7 Vienna Convention on Succession of States in Respect of Treaties art. 17, Aug. 23, 1978, 1946 UNTS 3

between States and International Organizations, there is too much disagreement for sufficient numbers of organizations and states to sign, so it is not in effect. The rules, although very similar to the Vienna Convention on the Law of Treaties (between states) would, for example, allow for dispute settlement claims between a state and an international organization. This has led to only a few international organizations signing the Convention's text, a fact that itself makes non-signatory states more reluctant to sign.

a.ii   *Treaty-making*

Treaty-making is the one way that states can consciously act to create immediately (or at least relatively immediately) binding law. The treaty-making process has been described as being composed of four/five steps.

1. *Negotiation phase*
    The text of an agreement is worked out among the parties to the agreement. 'Full powers' (Article 2(1)(c) VCLT) show authority resides with person to negotiate, sign, and seal a treaty, to bind a government. This is often no longer required outside the UN context.
2. *Signature phase*
    The negotiating states' signing of a treaty draft authenticates its text.[8] If ratification is necessary, the signature indicates an intent to move toward ratification and it puts an obligation of good faith on the signator not to act in a way that is meant to frustrate the object of the treaty. If ratification is not necessary, signature indicates consent to be bound and a good faith obligation not to act in a way that is meant to frustrate the object of the treaty.
3. *Ratification phase*
    The formal deposition with the official depository of an instrument committing to bind one's state. It may require a national constitutional process to precede the deposition.
4. *Accession/acceptance/approval phase*
    Indication by a non-signatory to be bound to a treaty.
5. *Entry into force phase*
    Provisions become effective for all states that have given their consent to be bound; upon coming into force. The agreement is registered and published by the UN Secretariat (with a backlog of up to ten years, however).

(entered into force 6 Nov. 1996). In fact, most state successions rely on special regimes for taking over treaty obligations. Such regimes are negotiated with the affected states.

8 Alternatively, the drafters may incorporate the draft text into a final act, or provide for the initialing of the draft to achieve the stabilization of the text.

b   Custom (customary international law)

Custom, or customary international law, is another formal source of international law mentioned in Article 38, ICJ Statute. Paragraph (b) states:

> 'international custom, as evidence of a general practice accepted as law'.

The source of international law known as customary law is called that because its authority arises out of actual state practice, or 'custom'. This means, in other words, that that which states have always done becomes the law, even if it is nowhere written down and even if states have not intentionally agreed to it. Historically, customary law has been the main source of international law and it continues to be an important force in developing the law: it remains of particular importance where the old becomes out-of-date or where there are gaps in treaty-made law.

Customary law, however, is a complex source to study because practice alone— doing something over and over—is not enough to create it. That is because in the specific sense of sources, *custom* refers to a general recognition among states that a certain practice is obligatory (on its own, practice, for instance, a state just doing something, is *not* the *same* as an obligation). Thus, to be customary international law, a rule (1) requires consistent, widespread, and long-term practice; and (2) requires that this consistent, widespread, and long-term practice is combined with *opinio juris sive necessitatis*. The first element is objective, measuring the extent of state practice as observable. The second is subjective, looking at qualitative evidence of states' belief in the rule as implied by their statements and behaviour. We examine these two basic parts to custom, the *objective* elements and the *subjective* elements, one at a time.

b.i   Objective custom: state practice

To be considered a source of international law, the practice of states must exhibit several characteristics, or elements.

Even the definition of 'practice' has been the focus of differing opinions, but generally speaking, state practice is that which a state does or does not do, as well as what a state says, or does not say. Thus, actions taken (for example: a state allows its fishers to fish in seas that are 10nm from the coast of another state), statements made in regards to a particular situation (for example: recognizing the independence of Ossetia), statements made in regard to a general concept (for example: the ministry of health expressing support for a precautionary principle), arguments formulated in a dispute settlement context, or the lack of expressing any opinion (for example: upon the invasion of a land by another state), can all be considered state practice. Practice, therefore, has unilateral, as well as multilateral aspects.

What is not state practice is, perhaps, easier to define—those acts or omissions that are not carried out by a state, as, for example, a corporate decision to issue dividends. Yet even there one must be careful as the reaction of the state to such actions *is* practice.

Consistent practice

The acts or omissions that count as state practice, of course, do not all become international law. First, that practice must be consistent over states and time. That is, similar actions need to occur repeatedly and contrary practices must not be so common as to destroy the practice's claims to emerging law. It is helpful here to notice the contrary actor's treatment of the action—is it justified as an exception (therefore supporting the CIL claim) or is it a clear attempt to alter or disregard the old practice (undermining CIL). An example to think about, arose when the US administration promoted the idea of 'pre-emptive strikes' against enemies. Many international lawyers were worried, because the prohibition of aggression has been the cornerstone of international law since the UN system was put in place. Was this a turning point, allowing aggression? The way the US categorized it, however, fitted it into the privilege of self-defence—something that exists alongside the prohibition of aggression. Thus, there was not a denial of the customary norm of non-aggression.

Furthermore, there is required 'substantial' uniformity, and only isolated cases of disregarding the norm (where there should be a reaction by other states to the breach). Here, it is important to determine reasons for a lack of adherence (e.g., dissent or disinterest).

Widespread practice

The practice must also be general, accepted, and carried out by a number of states, and not just one. This does not mean that all states must adhere to the practice, but the idea that the status as a 'superpower' can substitute for widespread adherence remains unaccepted. That said, the ICJ has held that 'specially affected' states' practice matters more than others', in determining whether a rule of CIL has come into being. In the *North Sea Continental Shelf* cases,[9] the court therefore determined that the practice of marine powers is

---

9 In the *North Sea* cases, the Court signaled that ten years was not a sufficient period of time for custom to evolve. *See North Sea Continental Shelf* cases (*Federal Republic of Germany v. Denmark/Federal Republic of*

more important than the practice of landlocked states in determining the laws of the sea.

Consider, however, the problems the practice element poses for countries that are not in a position to take particular actions—such as space exploration.[10] Should the rules on uses of space be left to those countries with space programs? There are a couple of treaties, but these do not answer all of the questions regarding the rules of outer space use, yet most states have no technical capability of actually *practising* in space.

It seems that, for the moment, widespread practice is still required to develop a norm of CIL, even if not all states are able to participate in it (conservative force). Scholars have proposed two modifications to 'widespread practice' to liberalize CIL creation. One would count the practice of *specially affected* states more than the practice of other states. This proposal would still require adherence to the rule by states from various regions and cultures, but would lower the numerical threshold for norms to emerge. A second proposal is to recognize *'regional custom'*. This would entail accepting norms that are consistently followed by states in a certain geographical region as CIL for all states in the region.[11]

Long-term practice
The time element is also questionable, because classic international law would require years of consistent practice before a customary rule would be considered a legal source. The problem of delay, however, severely limits the flexibility of this as a source of new rules, so some have argued for the recognition of 'instant custom'.[12] The ICJ has not directly set out a minimum time period, but rather suggested that the requirement would vary by subject matter. That said, the tendency is to allow for *more rapid concretization* of custom, although this is most often the case where there is much practice (in the Law of the Sea Convention, the 200nm exclusive economic zone was first proposed in 1973, and by 1978 the exclusive economic zone was considered customary

---

Germany v. Netherlands), Judgment, 1969 ICJ Rep. 3, paras. 60–82 (Feb. 20). Available at: http://www.icj-cij.org/docket/files/51/5535.pdf.

10 *See* Bin Cheng, United Nations Resolutions on Outer Space: 'Instant' International Customary Law?, 5 Indian J. Int'l L. 23 (1965); Niels Petersen, Customary Law without Custom? Rules, Principles, and the Role of State Practice in International Norm Creation, 23 Am. U. Int'l L. Rev. 275, 281–2 (2008).

11 *See generally*, Tullio Treves, *Customary International Law, in* Max Planck Encyclopedia of Public International Law, paras. 35–40, Oxford Public International Law (explaining the scholarship and jurisprudence on the generality of practice needed to consider a norm customary law. Available at: http://www.mpepil.com/sample_article?id=/epil/entries/law-9780199231690-e1393&.

12 Shaw, *supra* note 1, at 57.

international law). The proposed idea of 'instant custom' (suggested, for instance, in the context of the Moon Treaty) however, has been criticized.[13]

b.ii   *Subjective custom: opinio juris*

Opinio juris et necessitatis, or *opinio juris*, as it is generally abbreviated, is the conviction that the state is acting because the law requires it. Evidence of it must demonstrate that the state is acting on the belief that it is required to by law rather than morality or courtesy (as would, for instance, dipping the flag on the high seas). This *evidence* can come from press releases, policy statements, diplomatic correspondence, official manuals, judicial decisions, comments on drafts, treaty provisions, or UN General Assembly resolutions, for example.

Opinio juris
This is one of the hardest legal elements to demonstrate, as it requires that a state acts in such a way as to demonstrate its belief in the legal bindingness of what it is doing in the absence of the actual existence of a legal obligation. If a state merely acts in a way that it thinks is a good idea, its behaviour cannot be qualified as a statement of *opinio juris* (practice can act as evidence of *opinio*, but cannot substitute for it). On the other hand, if a state acts in a way that it believes is in accordance with a legal obligation and the legal obligation actually exists, such behaviour will not count toward the development of custom.

 DISCUSSION NOTES

1   Consider the following case: State Argentia has not signed the Vienna Convention on the Law of Treaties, and it signs a treaty with State Bolthan in which it agrees to allow for labour migrations during harvests. Let's assume that one year the crops are very poor, and Argentia's agricultural workers do not have enough work, and to make matters worse, Bolthanese workers continue to come in, because harvests were poor in their country too. Argentia closes the borders. Bolthan complains that migrations during harvests are to be free. Argentia claims 'harvests' do not exist this year. Bolthan responds that 'harvests' refers to a calendar season. A case is brought to the ICJ, which has to interpret the treaty. What difference does the fact that Argentia has not signed the Vienna Convention make?

2   The ICJ has held that states may opt out of customary international

---

13 The precise status of the claim is questionable. While Thirlway, e.g. writes that it has been 'implicitly rejected' by the ICJ (Thirlway, *supra* note 1, at 100), Shaw is more ambivalent (Shaw, *supra* note 1, at 56).

law while it is forming.[14] This is possible if the state has been a 'persistent objector' to the rule's development into a customary norm. Persistent objection, however, must be expressed during the emergence of the rule—there is no support for a 'subsequent objector' rule. See International Law Association's Committee on Formation of Customary Law, *Statement of Principles Applicable to the Formation of General Customary International Law*, Principle 15 and Commentary at 27–8 (2000). Not all authors, however, agree with the concept of a persistent objector rule. For some, the rule is highly problematic, threatening not just the coherence of the international legal system, but even challenging its moral integrity. Luigi Condorelli, for example, says:

> Must it, for instance, be asserted that South Africa is not bound by the rule banning apartheid . . . because it has always, consistently and continuously, disputed that rule? Is one really to believe that a State may exempt itself from a principle of international law by its attitude as a 'permanent objector', when all other States regard this principle as perfectly in existence? . . .
>
> In my opinion, permanent objection to a customary practice by an interested State is quite certainly an element to be taken into account and carefully weighed when verifying whether a general custom has in fact been able to emerge in these circumstances . . . But if, despite isolated objection, the norm in question actually corresponds to truly general practice and opinion juris, it is then binding on all, including, in my view, the 'permanent objector'.[15]

3 How important is the *opinio juris* element to customary international law? Goldsmith and Posner theorize that states act in accordance with their interests and then label such action custom rather than acting according to a legal 'pull' of custom.[16]

c *General principles of law*

Another primary source of law is the set of general principles of law. Despite some commentators who do not recognize principles as true sources of law,[17] the mention of general principles in the ICJ Statute's Article 38 confirms

---

14 *See Fisheries Case (U.K. v. Norway)*, 1951 I.C.J. 116 (judgment of 18 December 1951).

15 Luigi Condorelli, *Discussion*, *in* Change and Stability in International Law-Making 108, at 120 (Antonio Cassese and Joseph H.H. Weiler eds., 1988).

16 Jack L. Goldsmith and Eric A. Posner, A Theory of Customary International Law, 66(4) Univ. Chicago L. Rev. 1113 (1999).

17 M. Cherif Bassiouni, A Functional Approach to 'General Principles of International Law', 11 Mich. J. Int'l L. 768, 775 (1989–90).

their importance in judicial searches for legal answers. The concept of general principles can cover the following definitions:

1. *General principles as natural law*

   The first possibility is that general principles are sort of 'natural law' elements—concepts that exist independently of the state's desire for them to exist. Here, a principle of no-harm to the environment or protection of human rights would be applicable to states regardless of a lack of obligations in any treaties or the non-existence of CIL.

2. *General principles as systemic essentials*

   Another view is that general principles are principles that international law needs by virtue of the fact that it is a legal *system*. As concepts or rules inherent in the practice of interpreting and applying rules, i.e. these principles would include good faith and state responsibility.[18]

3. *General principles as internationalized national rules*

   Finally, there is a view that general principles means the use of elements of legal thought that are common throughout national (municipal) legal systems. Insofar as they are applicable to inter-state relations,[19] these would include legal reasoning and private law analogies, but also principles such as estoppel or acquiescence.[20]

Whatever the indefiniteness of scope, reliance on general principles as a source is important above all to ensuring that cases can be decided even in the absence of an applicable treaty norm or customary law. When the incomplete development of international law leaves judges without a basis to make a legal finding, they can rely on claims of general principles to prevent a situation of declaring a claim *non liquet*.[21]

There may be other uses for general principles, however. Bassiouni finds four functions of general principles of law as a source of international law, all of which are 'complementary to' those provided by the other sources:

(1) a source of interpretation for conventional and customary international law;

(2) a means for developing new norms of conventional and customary international law;

---

18 For example, *Nuclear Test Case (Australia v. France)*, Judgment, 1974 ICJ 253, at 268 para. 46 (Dec. 20). Available at: http://www. icj-cij.org/docket/files/58/6093.pdf ('One of the basic principles governing the creation and performance of legal obligations, whatever their source, is the principle of good faith. Trust and confidence are inherent in international co-operation'.

19 Alfred Verdross and Bruno Simma, Universelles Völkerrecht 383–4 (third edn, 1984).

20 *See generally* Jörg Paul Müller and Luzius Wildhaber, Praxis des Völkerrechts 39–56 (third edn, 2001).

21 Shaw, *supra* note 1, at 70.

(3) a supplemental source to conventional and customary international law; and

(4) a modifier of conventional and customary international rules.[22]

While the first and third of these functions are not controversial, recognizing the evolutionary potential of general principles might be novel for many international lawyers.

d Secondary sources of law

The ICJ Statute's Article 38 mentions further instruments to which the judges can look to determine the legal rules to apply. Such sources, however, are to be 'secondary'. This means that these do not create rights, but in the absence of definitive answers yielded by treaty, custom, or general principles, they can aid decision makers in determining the content or application of a rule of law. These secondary sources are most often used to support a decision or to emphasize the correctness of a claim.

Specifically, the judges may look to:

Judicial decisions—Very often other courts' decisions will be regarded as a pool of ideas. Note, however, that in international law there is no principle of *stare decisis*. International adjudicators in most fora are not required to adhere to an earlier analysis of a particular law. There is, however, still a norm of practice that fosters consistency among cases even where there is no legal requirement to do so.

Teachings of highly regarded academics—Though no longer as vital to the creation of international law as in the days of e.g., Grotius, Gentili, or de Vattel, scholarly opinion is still important to the development of new directions of international law. Academic writings can be referred to in international judicial opinions, although the extent or reliance on scholarly works varies with the tribunal concerned.

e Equity

A final source of international law is that of equity. Decision-making on the basis of equity resolves legal questions so as to achieve fairness rather than to protect legal rights. Developing as a legal principle out of English monarchs' residual judicial power to grant petitions from legal decisions, equity is now

---

22 Bassiouni, *supra* note 17, at 775–6.

divided into legal equitable procedures and the extra-legal aspects of equity. While legal equity grew out of a separation of court systems and consists of principles (such as clean hands or equity delights in equality) and special remedies (including injunction, special performance, estoppel), equity in ICJ Statute, Article 38 is of the extra-legal type known as *ex aequo et bono decision making*.

Ex aequo et bono decision making means that the court may decide the result of a case on the basis of what it deems the good, or fair, solution to a problem. Although it is recognized as available to the judges, Article 38.2 of the Statute stipulates that the availability is dependent on the parties' agreement to its use in the dispute resolution process. The ICJ has never officially relied upon it, although it has frequently invoked equity as legal principle.[23] This is presumably due to the international tribunal's fears of critique based on accusations relating to judicial activism.

2.2.3 Sources beyond the International Court of Justice Statute

There is more 'law' regarded by courts and lawyers than just those sources enumerated in Article 38, ICJ Statute. We will discuss these other possible sources of international law only briefly, not because they are not important in international law, but because their application in international investment law is underdeveloped.

a   Soft law

Soft law is the term given to non-binding norms. Debated in international law circles, the idea that soft law could give rise to obligations or rights is not a majority view.[24] Still, soft law is clearly an area of intense interest as suggestions, encouragements, guidelines, or programs clearly shape state (and non-state) behaviour on the international level despite the absence of legal sanctions in case of a state's non-adherence to such instruments, and can influence non-state actors' expectations.

---

23 Borzu Sahabi, Compensation and Restitution in Investor-State Arbitration 186–7 (2011). Sahabi notes the difficulty in distinguishing legal equity from *ex aequo* decision making: 'Considering the inherent proximity of the two concepts it is difficult to determine with precision when a tribunal has applied equity as part of the law and when it has decided *ex aequo et bono*'. This is supported by the court's judgment in the North Sea Continental Shelf Cases *supra* note 9, at para. 88 (Feb. 20). *See* Wolfgang Friedmann, *The North Sea Continental Shelf Cases—A Critique*, 64 AJIL 229, 236 (1970) (saying that, in effect, the ICJ decided the case *ex aequo et bono*).

24 *See*, e.g. Shaw, *supra* note 1, at 83–4 ('"Soft law" is not law. That needs to be emphasised ').

The main benefit of soft law rules is the flexibility left states upon their conclusion. It may be faster to gain consensus on divisive or sensitive issues if the discussions leading to it are clearly aimed at achieving a non-legally binding statement of agreement rather than to a treaty. The non-binding effect may also provide for more innovations in legal norms—soft law as a step toward hard law—as creative norm development via soft law does not need to be subject to the formalities of treaty-making or the time constraints of custom. Finally, the non-formal nature of soft law's development means that non-state actors can be directly involved in the norm creation process. Corporations, NGOs, and even influential individuals can ensure that soft law norms are acceptable and suitable for implementation for those most directly affected by them if they are included in the development of such norms—something that the state-driven creation of hard international law often fails to do.

Among the most notable soft law instruments are the numerous non-binding statements from the United Nations General Assembly. The Declaration on Human Rights, the Stockholm Declaration on the Human Environment, and the Guiding Principles on Business and Human Rights are all considered soft instruments, despite their undoubted influence on states' and non-state actors' behaviour and expectations. Outside the UN, soft law rules emerge from a variety of organizations and bodies, among them the OECD's various sets of Guidelines, the Bank of International Settlement's Basel Committee rules, and the International Standard Organization's quality measures. Non-binding, such norms often influence the way states and corporations approach problems as much as traditional hard legal rules do.

b Unilateral acts

When a state makes a declaration or promise or otherwise performs an action that is not reciprocal, we speak of a unilateral act. The law on how to treat such acts is in development, but it is established that if a unilateral act is 'publically made and manifesting the will to be bound', it may create legal obligations for that state.[25] As explained by the ICJ, because the obligation arises out of the principle of good faith, decision-makers must determine

---

25 The International Law Commission has a Working Group on Unilateral Acts of States. These experts have produced Guidelines and commentaries on various aspects of unilateral acts that were adopted by the General Assembly. ILC, *Guiding Principles applicable to unilateral declarations of States capable of creating legal obligations*, Principle 1, 58th Sess., UN Doc. A/61/10, at 370 (2006). The Principle reflects the ICJ's finding in the Nuclear Tests case. *See Nuclear Tests Case (New Zealand v. France)*, *supra* note 18 at para. 46.

whether the state made the declaration with an intent to bind itself before it finds an obligation arising from it:

> Of course, not all unilateral acts imply obligation; but a State may choose to take up a certain position in relation to a particular matter with the intention of being bound—the intention is to be ascertained by interpretation of the act. When States make statements by which their freedom of action is to be limited, a restrictive interpretation is called for.[26]

The court continues:

> Trust and confidence are inherent in international co-operation, in particular in an age when this co-operation in many fields is becoming increasingly essential. Just as the very rule of *pacta sunt servanda* in the law of treaties is based on good faith, so also is the binding character of an international obligation assumed by unilateral declaration. Thus interested States may take cognizance of unilateral declarations and place confidence in them, and are entitled to require that the obligation thus created be respected.[27]

c   *Jus cogens*

Jus cogens are fundamental principles to which states must adhere. Also called 'peremptory norms' of international law, these rules are defined by the Vienna Convention on the Law of Treaties (VCLT) by reference to their hierarchical superior position in relation to other sources of international law. Article 53 VCLT provides:

> [. . .] a peremptory norm of general international law is a norm accepted and recognized by the international community of States as a whole as a norm from which no derogation is permitted and which can be modified only by a subsequent norm of general international law having the same character.

There exist no exceptions to justify a departure from a norm of *jus cogens*. Unless the state can demonstrate the existence of an opposing norm of the same quality, state responsibility will apply if a *jus cogens* norm is breached. Such responsibility, too, is of particular weight, placing obligations on the international community as well as on the responsible state itself. The Articles on State Responsibility set forth the consequences of a serious breach of a peremptory norm of international law. Article 41 states:

---

26 *Nuclear Tests Case (New Zealand v. France), supra* note 18, at 47.
27 *Id.* at para. 49.

1. States shall cooperate to bring to an end through lawful means any serious breach . . .
2. No State shall recognize as lawful a situation created by a serious breach . . . nor render aid or assistance in maintaining that situation.
3. This article is without prejudice to the other consequences referred to in this part and to such further consequences that a breach to which this chapter applies may entail under international law.

The ICJ has named eight examples of *jus cogens*: aggression, war crimes, crimes against humanity, torture, racial discrimination, slavery and slavery-like practices, piracy, and genocide. There may be other norms of *jus cogens*, but there is no agreement on which norms these may be.

2.2.4 Hierarchy of sources

The foregoing discussion on the different sources of international law has shown that while there does exist a hierarchy in international law due to the eminent rule of *jus cogens* over all other sources, the flatness of other sources *vis-à-vis* each other is characteristic of the system. Nevertheless, given rules about specificity and the requirements of a functioning relationship among sources, general reasoning about state intentions permit an informal deduction of the following 'hierarchy':

1. *Jus cogens*

As set out above, norms of *jus cogens* are superior to all other law. Any treaty that would purport to violate a norm of *jus cogens* would be void *ab initio*.

2. Hierarchy of other international law sources

Structurally, non-*jus cogens* sources of international law are equal, so in case of conflict the decision as to which is the applicable law will be based on content. There are general rules for determining such content-based superiority:

a. If the treaties are about the same subject matter, apply the treaty that:
   i. is more specific than the other on a particular rule or
   ii. the treaty that was concluded after the other.

The general principles on treaty conflict address a narrow set of international law problems: those of unavoidably contradictory obligations of states. The rules of *lex specialis* (the more specific rule applies) and the *lex posterior* rule (the most recently created rule applies) assume that the parties knew of the existence of both relevant treaties and knowingly added the provision of the others. Thus, their agreement on the more specific regulation or on the more recently concluded provision can be implied.

b. If a treaty provision contradicts a general principle, apply the treaty.

Treaties usually trump general principles because their provisions are often more specific. Because general principles are mainly used as gap-fillers for non-existing treaty law, such conflicts do not occur very often.

c. If a treaty provision conflicts with customary international law, apply the treaty.

Usually treaties trump custom because they are more specific. However, this general rule is weak, as a new norm of custom may override an older treaty provision.

d. If a norm of customary international law conflicts with a general principle, apply the customary international law norm.

This rule, which is more theoretical than practical, continues the idea of applying more the specific rule to a particular situation.

DISCUSSION NOTES

The structure of international legal sources in Article 38, ICJ Statute seems relatively simple, with its two tiers of hierarchically equal sets. The application of the sources in a particular context is much more complex, however. While there is often more than one substantive rule that applies to a particular dispute, decision-makers must give attention to which source within the hierarchy should be given precedence in the particular context. Specificity of obligation and temporal considerations may influence which treaty or customary obligation is given greater emphasis, while general principles often act more as background concepts or gap-fillers than as trumping law. The secondary sources, moreover, act as interpretive assistance to a greater or lesser extent, depending on the decision-maker.

International investment law sources, discussed below, are yet more complex. While the primary-secondary source rules are similar, there are more sources of authoritative rules and the influence of the interpretive authorities is differently weighed than in general international law. Figures 2.1 and 2.2 illustrate one possible way of viewing the differences between the theory and application of general international law (Figure 2.1) and the sources of international investment law (Figure 2.2).

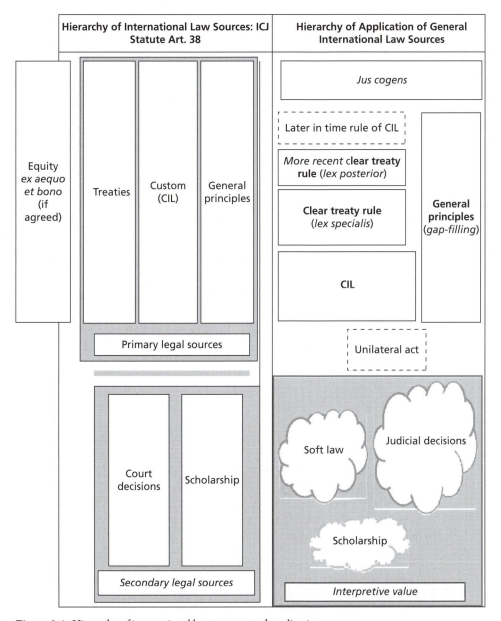

Figure 2.1 Hierarchy of international law: sources and application

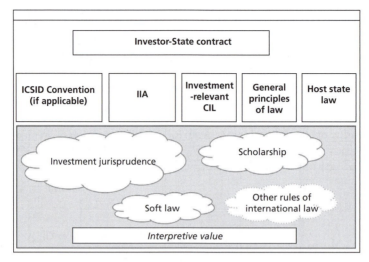

Figure 2.2 Hierarchy of international investment law: application of sources

2.3   Sources of investment law

Investment law is a specialized area of international economic law, and international economic law is a specialized area of international law. Thus, the general international law sources discussion is valid for investment, but there are some specificities that need to be mentioned to present a fuller picture of the system.

The following will illustrate certain sources of international law that are of particular importance for investment law and particular types of legal instruments that are specific to investment law.

2.3.1   Treaties

Today, by far the main source of international investment law is treaty law. The thousands of bilateral investment treaties and various sectorial, regional, or multilateral agreements contain specific obligations of the party states. Of particular significance is the fact that investment treaties contain numerous third-party benefits. That is, while the parties to the treaty are states, many of the obligations contained in the agreement are owed to investors rather than to the other party or parties.

a   Bilateral investment treaties

Bilateral investment treaties (BITs) are the most prevalent source of host state investment protection obligations. It is important to remember that

while the BITs contain obligations that the host has as regards foreign investors, it is two states that conclude the treaty. Thus, it is primarily state-to-state
relations that are governed by BITs. As international treaties, BITs are subject
to general international law rules on interpretation, applicability, conflicts,
and withdrawal if these issues are not specifically regulated by the parties'
agreement to create their own rules.

a.i   *Structure of bilateral investment treaties*

While each bilateral treaty is drafted to take into account the particular
context of the parties' relationship, most BITs are similar in form and basic
content. (Hence the usefulness of model BITs developed by many governments as a basis for negotiating BIT texts.)

Preamble
The first section of the BIT is generally a preamble, setting out the parties'
goal in concluding the agreement. The interesting aspect of BIT preambles
is the heavy emphasis on two related aims: protection of the investor and
the stimulation of economic activity in the host. Given international law
principles of treaty interpretation, these aims can colour the extent of party
obligations.

Definitions
The first several treaty articles will often be devoted to providing key definitions. The scope of 'investment' and the qualifications for being an 'investor
of a party' are often set out in detail.

Scope
The BIT will circumscribe the application of its provisions to investors and
investments of the parties. The scope provisions may expand upon terms
included in the definitions by explaining the conditions under which an
investment or an investor will benefit from the Agreement's protections.
Covered investments, for example, are often limited to those that were established in accordance with the host's laws.

Another aspect of scope that is of great importance is the determination of
when the protections contained in the treaty take effect. Most BITs only secure
'post-establishment' protection of investments. That is, the governments may
not be bound to afford the investor any particular treatment until the investment project has been initiated. Thus, governments may be able to discriminate among potential investors or offer differing conditions of entry. There are
some IIAs, however, that offer 'pre-entry' protection to investors. Still mainly

found in the investment chapters of comprehensive free trade agreements, pre-entry obligations may grant market access rights to investors or ensure that party investors are subject to non-discriminatory treatment.

Market access
Some BITs contain a statement about the admission of investments from the other party's investors. While most IIAs do not set out a firm obligation of market access, the text may include calls for the parties to 'promote' investment and to admit investment 'in accordance with' national legislation. Relying on hortatory language, these statements maintain the parties' ability to continue to screen foreign investments and limit them according to what is in the national interest.

Protection standards
Provisions setting out the treatment hosts are to accord the other party's covered investors or investments can be found in several forms. While some states separate each obligation into a distinct article, others combine them. The standards themselves, however, are generally the same: obligations of full protection and security, non-arbitrariness, non-discrimination (national treatment and most favoured nation treatment) fair and equitable treatment, expropriation only with compensation, and free transfers of payments.

Dispute settlement
Nearly all BITs also will contain provisions on the procedures to be invoked in case of dispute between the parties. These processes can either be in the interest of the state itself or in the interest of an investor whose claim has been espoused by the home state. Such state-to-state dispute settlement will usually call for consultations prior to the invocation of legal proceedings.

Most BITs include a separate provision providing investors of one party with the possibility of bringing a claim against the other party government before an arbitral tribunal. These investor-State dispute settlement proceedings are an important characteristic of international investment law.

The BIT arbitration clauses may or may not contain the host's consent to arbitration and they may limit the consent even if given directly. Nevertheless, the provision will indicate the forum or fora available and, often, the procedures for establishing a tribunal.

Final provisions
BITs, like any other international treaty, also specify the ratification requirements, the effective date of the obligations, and amendment and withdrawal procedures. The interaction of these provisions has become the focus

of growing attention as governmental efforts to limit exposure to investor claims have brought up the question of the precise temporal scope of the individual treaty obligations.

a.ii Problems with BIT proliferation

With nearly 3000 IIAs in effect, some observers have voiced their concern that the investment system is becoming hopelessly intransparent and complicated. Using the 'spaghetti bowl' metaphor developed in the trade agreement context to describe the multiple treaty regimes placing investment protection obligations on hosts, two authors list 'fragmentation', 'regulatory competition', and 'treaty shopping' as the undesired results of the individualized negotiation of investment protection agreements.[28]

Despite such fears, states continue to negotiate investment protection agreements bilaterally.

b Sectoral agreements

The first multilateral investment protection agreement entered into force in 1998 in the form of a sectoral agreement—a treaty regulating a particular economic industry. This was the 1994 Energy Charter Treaty (ECT) between Russia, the EU Member States, and the Eastern European and Central Asian states.

Covering trade, investment, and transit of energy resources, the ECT aims to spur exploration and development of hydrocarbon fuels. The investment provisions include a multi-fora dispute settlement provision (ICSID, UNCITRAL, Stockholm Chamber of Commerce), along with the usual protection standards: fair and equitable treatment standard (FET), constant protection and security, non-discrimination and minimum standard. The ECT's importance to international investment law has been growing as the invocation of its provisions becomes more frequent. By 2015, the ECT had surpassed the NAFTA to be the most-invoked IIA for arbitration claims.[29]

---

28 Stefan D. Amaransinha and Juliane Kokott, *Multilateral Investment Rules Revisited, in* The Oxford Handbook of International Investment Law 119, at 121 and 124 (Peter Muchlinski, Federico Ortino and Christoph Schreuer eds., 2008).

29 UNCTAD, IIA Issues Note: Recent Trends in IIAs and ISDS, No. 1, p. 7 (February 2015).

One notable aspect of the ECT is that there is a hortatory provision for pre-establishment non-discrimination. Article 10(2) says: 'Each Contracting Party shall endeavour to accord to Investors of other Contracting Parties [most favored nation or national treatment], as regards the Making of Investments in its Area'. This extension of non-discrimination to treatment of prospective investors is an indication that the ECT takes a more comprehensive view of the parties' relationship with private investors than do most BITs, which generally only apply once an investor has been permitted to enter the territory of the host.

Another ECT feature is its provisional application provision. Highlighted in the *Yukos v. Russia* arbitration, provisional application was found to allow an investor to claim a violation of his rights by a host government which has only signed (but not ratified) the treaty.[30]

c   *Regional agreements*

Plurilateral treaties, such as regional free trade agreements, also may contain investment protection provisions. Increasing rapidly in number, regional (or 'preferential') trade agreements allow a group of like-minded states to pursue an agenda of economic integration that is deeper than could be achieved on the multilateral level. As a result, such agreements may have both investment protection provisions and investment liberalization obligations. Some may also have separate dispute settlement mechanisms providing for investor-State claims to be brought to arbitration.

The North American Free Trade Agreement's Chapter 11 was the first free trade agreement to include investment protection provisions. Since then, a number of other regional trade and investment agreements have followed. While the liberalization of trade and strong investment protection are clearly compatible, the extent of market liberalization entailed by a combination of both sets of provisions can lead to vigorous opposition to the overall agreement. Among the most fiercely debated regional agreements are the Transatlantic Trade Partnership (TTP) and the Transatlantic Trade and Investment Partnership (TTIP). Still under negotiation, at time of writing, each proposed agreement has been heavily criticized for offering foreign investors non-discriminatory investment protection and access to investor-State dispute settlement mechanisms. In response to public outcry, the negotiating governments have reformulated a number of protection provisions

---

30 *See Yukos Universal Ltd. (Isle of Man) v. Russian Federation*, PCA Case No. AA227, Interim Award on Jurisdiction and Admissibility, paras. 388, 390 (Nov. 30, 2009).

and suggested procedural safeguards to the investment chapters' dispute settlement provisions.

d   A multilateral investment treaty?

There is no multilateral framework treaty on international investment law. Attempted several times, the negotiations of such an agreement have failed to draft a broadly acceptable statement of the substantive rules that should govern states in all of their actions toward foreign investors and their direct investments.

Recounted elsewhere in detail,[31] the last serious attempt to garner agreement on multilateral rules on investment protection were the negotiations of the Multilateral Agreement on Investment (MAI), held between September 1995 and Fall 1998 under the auspices of the Organisation for Economic Co-operation and Development (OECD). Those negotiations aimed to put in place a set of 'multilateral rules which set high standards and a balanced and equitable framework for dealing with investment issues'.[32] Given the ideologies of the forum, it is not surprising that such an agreement was to include 'rules on liberalisation and investor protection, with dispute settlement, thereby underpinning the continued removal of barriers to market access and encouraging economic growth'.[33] The negotiations were suspended in April 1998, and the negotiating parties' withdrawal of support (starting with France in October 1998) effectively ended them.

The failure of the MAI is the subject of a large literature. It appears to have been due to a combination of factors internal to the negotiating process and factors external to it, including efforts by NGOs to discredit the negotiations and the planned result. Whether it was the lack of transparency and fears of non-democratic dispute settlement processes that sealed the fate of the MAI (as the civil society movements claimed) or the basic differences among the negotiators over the substance of the treaty (as officials propose) is open to speculation. Most likely, both had their effects.

---

31 *See,* e.g. Katia Tieleman, *The Failure of the Multilateral Agreement on Investment (MAI) and the Absence of a Global Public Policy Network* 8–13 (UN Vision Project on Global Public Policy Networks). Available at: http://www.gppi.net/fileadmin/gppi/Tieleman_MAI_GPP_Network.pdf.

32 OECD, *Report by the Committee on International Investment and Multinational Enterprises (CIME)/ and the Committee on Capital Movements and Invisible Transactions (CMIT)*, OECDDoc. DAFFE/CMIT/CIME(95)13/FINAL (May 5, 1995). Available at: http://www1.oecd.org/daf/mai/htm/cmitcime95.htm.

33 *Id.*

Currently, there seems to be no enthusiasm for re-initiating multilateral negotiations for an investment agreement. For some observers, creating a multilateral framework for investment protection should remain an aim of the international system. For others, however, the individualized context of investment is best left to bilateral or regional agreements.

2.3.2 Customary investment law

While investment treaties cover a substantial number of issues that arise in investor-State disputes, there remains room for tribunals to invoke other sources of law. Customary rules, then, maintain their significance even in the midst of a burgeoning number of IIAs.

a   *Customary rules on treaty interpretation*

Among the most frequently invoked norms of customary international law are those of treaty interpretation. The provisions on treaty interpretation contained in the Vienna Convention on the Law of Treaties are widely recognized as a codification of customary international law, and are cited by nearly every investment tribunal as a basis of the analysis even where the IIA parties have not ratified the VCLT.[34]

Vienna Convention Articles 31–33 set forth the basic rule of interpretation of international treaties between states. The provisions state:

Article 31 General rule of interpretation

1. A treaty shall be interpreted in good faith in accordance with the ordinary meaning to be given to the terms of the treaty in their context and in the light of its object and purpose.
2. The context for the purpose of the interpretation of a treaty shall comprise, in addition to the text, including its preamble and annexes:
    (a) any agreement relating to the treaty which was made between all the parties in connection with the conclusion of the treaty;
    (b) any instrument which was made by one or more parties in connection with the conclusion of the treaty and accepted by the other parties as an instrument related to the treaty.
3. There shall be taken into account, together with the context:

---

34 For example, *Hesham Talaat M. Al-Warraq v. the Republic of Indonesia*, UNCITRAL arbitration, Award on Respondent's Preliminary Objections to Jurisdiction and Admissibility of the Claims, para. 70 (June 21, 2012) (noting that the fact that the disputing parties both relied on the VCLT as well as the character of the VCLT rules on interpretation as customary law allow the tribunal to apply Articles 31–3 VCLT to the dispute).

(a) any subsequent agreement between the parties regarding the interpretation of the treaty or the application of its provisions;

(b) any subsequent practice in the application of the treaty which establishes the agreement of the parties regarding its interpretation;

(c) any relevant rules of international law applicable in the relations between the parties.

4. A special meaning shall be given to a term if it is established that the parties so intended.

Article 32 Supplementary means of interpretation

Recourse may be had to supplementary means of interpretation, including the preparatory work of the treaty and the circumstances of its conclusion, in order to confirm the meaning resulting from the application of article 31, or to determine the meaning when the interpretation according to article 31:

(a) leaves the meaning ambiguous or obscure; or

(b) leads to a result which is manifestly absurd or unreasonable.

Article 33 Interpretation of treaties authenticated in two or more languages

1. When a treaty has been authenticated in two or more languages, the text is equally authoritative in each language, unless the treaty provides or the parties agree that, in case of divergence, a particular text shall prevail.

2. A version of the treaty in a language other than one of those in which the text was authenticated shall be considered an authentic text only if the treaty so provides or the parties so agree.

3. The terms of the treaty are presumed to have the same meaning in each authentic text.

4. Except where a particular text prevails in accordance with paragraph 1, when a comparison of the authentic texts discloses a difference of meaning which the application of articles 31 and 32 does not remove, the meaning which best reconciles the texts, having regard to the object and purpose of the treaty, shall be adopted.

The applicability of the VCLT Articles to international investment agreements is not in dispute.[35] As one tribunal noted:

---

35 *See,* e.g. Christoph Schreuer, *Diversity and Harmonization of Treaty Interpretation in Investment Arbitration, in* Treaty Interpretation and the Vienna Convention on the Law of Treaties: 30 Years 129, 130–31 (Malgosia Fitzmaurice, Olufemi Elias and Panos Merkouris eds., 2010).

> All three instruments [the Energy Charter Treaty, the relevant BIT, and the ICSID Agreement] are treaties under international law; and their interpretation is governed by rules of international law, expressed in Articles 31 and 32 of the Vienna Convention on the Law of Treaties of 1969 [. . .] Under Article 31(1), the general rule requires a treaty to be interpreted in good faith in accordance with the ordinary meaning to be given to the terms of the treaty in their 'context' and in the light of the treaty's 'object' and 'purpose'; Article 31(2) defines 'context'; and the remaining provisions of Articles 31 and 32 provide further means of interpretation as applicable:[36]

Generally, tribunals' invocation of the VCLT indicates a commitment to determining the content of parties' obligations from the written text of the agreement. Arbitrators' strict reliance on the words of the treaty not only is supposed to foster predictability and foreseeability in what the parties' obligations and rights are, the plain meaning approach provides legitimacy to arbitrators' decisions.[37] Textual interpretations allow the tribunal to do its 'duty . . . to discover and not to create meaning',[38] thus keeping the parties' agreement as the sole basis of the decision.

In an international system based on the voluntariness of states' acceptance of obligations, this reasoning makes some sense. How else are states to know that what they think they oblige themselves to will actually be the extent of their international obligations?

If, however, one views the international legal system as one that should impose particular values on its states as members of a community or if one questions the concept that there can ever be an 'objective' definition given to treaty terms, the reliance on the VCLT articles would appear to be more of a cover than a rigorous analytical method. Indeed, while nearly all parties and tribunals claim to be applying the 'plain language in context' method of interpretation, the results of this application can be far from uniform.

---

36 *Emilio Augustín Maffezini v. Kingdom of Spain*, ICSID Case No. ARB/97/7, Decision on Objections to Jurisdiction, para. 27 (Jan. 25, 2000). Available at: http://italaw.com/sites/default/files/case-documents/ita0479.pdf.

37 *Plama Consortium Ltd. v. Republic of Bulgaria*, ICSID Case No. ARB/03/24, Decision on Jurisdiction, para. 117 (Feb. 8, 2005). Available at: http://italaw.com/sites/default/files/case-documents/ita0669.pdf.

38 Claus-Dieter Ehlermann, *Reflections on the Appellate Body of the WTO*, 6(3) J. Int'l Econ. L. 695, 699–701 (2003); Isabelle Van Damme, *Treaty Interpretation by the WTO Appellate Body*, 21(3) Eur. J. Int'l L. 605, 621–2 (2010).

The objective meaning, for example, must be determined at a particular time—should the parties' original understanding of the terms be applied or should the terms be interpreted in their contemporary meaning?[39]

In the *Al-Warraq* dispute, for example, the respondent argued that the IIA's drafters' understanding of the disputed terms should govern the result. The tribunal disagreed:

> [. . .] [I]n the opinion of the Tribunal, the VCLT requires interpretation of the *mens legis*, not the *mens legislatoris*. What the [negotiators] did or did not visualise when sponsoring the Treaty has not been established on the evidence; [. . .] but the Tribunal considers this as irrelevant; what is relevant is not the intention of anyone [. . .], but what the language used [. . .] means on an interpretation of the words used. The Tribunal considers that the language of [the IIA provision] can and should be interpreted from a contemporary perspective.[40]

The VCLT approach requires decision-makers to take the context of a term into consideration when interpreting. For a tribunal, this often means that the preamble to the IIA gains significance. As most traditional IIAs have short preambles that stress the parties' intention to promote flows of investments between their territories, the use of context to interpret IIA terms has often resulted in a preference being given to investor-friendly interpretations rather than ones that preserve the host's policy space. As a result, there have been suggestions to include specific language in IIA preambles to voice the goal of protecting the states' policy space.[41]

 DISCUSSION NOTES

1 Should all provisions of an IIA be interpreted with the same level of scrutiny? The drafters of the VCLT had debated whether all treaties should be interpreted in the same way, with some committee members proposing special rules for human rights treaties. Similar questions arise in investment law. Some tribunals approach the interpretation of IIA provisions that allegedly contain the state's consent to arbitrate more rigorously than they do other provisions, refusing to find consent without unambiguous words to demonstrate it. Other tribunals main-

39 *Renta 4 SVSA et al. v. The Russian Federation*, SCC No. 24/2007, Award on Preliminary Objections, para. 93 (May 20, 2009), Available at: http://italaw.com/documents/Renta.pdf.

40 *Al-Warraq, supra* note 34 at para. 81.

41 For example, Model Text for the Indian Bilateral Investment Treaty (2015); Howard Mann, Konrad von Moltke, Luke Eric Peterson, and Aaron Cosbey, *IISD Model International Agreement on Investment for Sustainable Development* (April 2005).

tain that consent provisions are just like all other provisions, and should be interpreted with the same standard, which allows for inferences to be drawn. Compare the majority opinion and the dissent in the decision on jurisdiction in the *Garanti Koza v. Turkmenistan* dispute.[42]

2 Sometimes a tribunal must interpret national investment legislation. Should the interpretation of national laws that offer protection to foreign investors be conducted under VCLT rules or under the rules of interpretation used in the host's national legal system? The tribunal in *OPIC Karimun v. Venezuela* analysed this question. To do so, the arbitrators reviewed a number of prior tribunals' decisions and the International Court of Justice's findings in the *Fisheries Jurisdiction* case.[43] The arbitrators determined that Venezuela's legislation for foreign investment protection should be treated as a unilateral act of the state and interpreted using the approach international law sets out for such acts. This approach emphasizes the legislator's intent. In the Venezuelan context, the tribunal determined that such intent was absent. Interestingly, the tribunal distinguished the drafter's personal intent to include consent from the legislator's overall intent to refrain from consenting to the arbitration.

b   State responsibility

Among the most firmly entrenched customary norms of international law are the rules on *state responsibility*. The norms of state responsibility have been set out to a great extent in the Articles on Responsibility of States for Internationally Wrongful Acts, a document drafted over a time-span of approximately 50 years and adopted by the International Law Commission in 2001.[44] These Articles are based on the fundamental principle that a state incurs international 'responsibility' for breaches of any international legal obligation.

As states clearly have obligations arising from international laws on investment protection, there are several aspects of state responsibility that should be highlighted.

---

42 *Garanti Koza v. Turkmenistan*, ICSID Case No. ARB/11/20, Decision on Objection to Jurisdiction for Lack of Consent (July 3, 2013).

43 *OPIC Karimun v. Venezuela*, ICSID Case No. ARB/10/14, paras. 70–76 (May 28, 2013) (citing *Fisheries Jurisdiction Case (Spain v. Canada)*, Jurisdiction of the Court, Judgment, ICJ Reports 1998).

44 Responsibility of States for Internationally Wrongful Acts (2001). Available at: http://untreaty.un.org/ilc/texts/instruments/english/draft%20articles/9_6_2001.pdf [hereinafter ASR].

b.i   *The definition of the state and state actions*

Public international investment obligations generally rest on the state. Yet, due to the nature of investment activities, the state's typical role as regulator is often intermingled with its role as a commercial actor, either as contractor or as business partner. This complicates the identification of whether 'state' action is involved despite the formal recognition that the activities were undertaken by the government. Moreover, the frequent use of private companies of which the state owns a majority and/or manages to oversee large infrastructure projects requires an analysis of whether actions or omissions by the company can be attributed to the state.

The answer to such questions can be extracted from the International Law Commission's (ILC) Articles on the Responsibility of States for Internationally Wrongful Acts (Articles on State Responsibility). The Articles on State Responsibility provisions define the scope of 'the state' and set out the rules on the attribution of acts of private persons to the state. For the former, the Articles set out a *structural test*. All executive, legislative, and judicial offices, whether at the national, state, or local level, are considered to be 'the state' for purposes of state responsibility. Thus, local zoning boards' decisions to halt a construction project can be challenged by a foreign investor.[45]

The actions of individual officials of the government are equally deemed as 'state' acts. Such is true even if an official acted illegally or without proper authorization when breaching an international obligation.

For the question of attribution, international law generally does not deem private entities to be part of 'the state'. There are exceptions, however, the detection of which relies on a *functional test*. According to the ILC, if a person or entity is 'empowered by the law of that State to exercise elements of the governmental authority' and acts in that capacity, the conduct will be attributable to the state.[46] Similarly, if a person or group is acting at the instruction of the state in carrying out some conduct, that conduct will be attributable to the state.[47]

---

45 *See*, e.g. *Metalclad Corporation v. United Mexican States*, ICSID Case No. ARB(AF)/97/1, Award, para. 73 (Aug. 30, 2000). Available at: http://italaw.com/sites/default/files/case-documents/ita0510.pdf (supporting a finding that the acts of the Municipality of Guadalcazar's Town Council in denying a construction permit was a legitimate ground for investor's complaint with the rules of state responsibility as set forth by the ILC).
46 ASR art. 5.
47 ASR art. 8.

For investment law, the question of attribution of private entity actions to a state is highly relevant. Recent privatizations of governmental functions—that is, the handing over of traditionally state-provided services to private companies—have spurred a need to think carefully about how to treat conduct of private actors when such actors are acting for the state *or in lieu of* the state. Can a state absolve itself of its international responsibility if the wrongful act was perpetrated by a company? The short answer is no—not if that company was:

- 'in fact acting on the instructions of, or under the direction of control of' the state;[48]
- 'in fact exercising elements of the governmental authority';[49] or
- such conduct is accepted by the state 'as its own'.[50]

Referring to norms of state responsibility, investment tribunals have assessed questions of attribution using a combination of testing both   and function. The first step in attributing actions is to look at the formal structure of the entity. If it is wholly owned by the government or if the government controls the entity, a presumption arises that the entity is structurally governmental.

A second step looks at the function of the entity. The tribunal might ask if 'an entity's purpose or objectives is the carrying out of functions which are governmental in nature or which are otherwise normally reserved to the State, or which by their nature are not usually carried out by private businesses or individuals'.[51] If the answer to such questions is yes, a presumption will exist that the state can be held accountable for the wrongful acts of the company.

Finally, even if the entity is deemed to not be attributable to the government and its functions are not governmental in nature, the government may have accepted the entity's decision or conduct as its own. In such a case as well, the tribunal may hold the state responsible for the detrimental impacts on the investor.

---

48 ASR art. 8.

49 ASR art. 9. This responsibility only applies if there is 'the absence or default of the official authorities and in circumstances such as to call for the exercise of those elements of authority'. *Id.*

50 ASR art. 11.

51 *Maffezini v. Spain, supra* note 36, para. 77.

CASE

Gustav F.W. Hamester GmbH and Co KG v. Republic of Ghana[52]

Claimant Hamester is a German company that processes and trades cocoa and cocoa products. As legal successor to a company that had entered a joint venture with the Ghanaian cocoa board, Cocobod, it had a contract to cooperate on a project to modernize and rejuvenate Wamco, an old cocoa processing factory. By the end of 1993, Wamco was operating successfully, and soon was able to purchase another plant. During the time of operations, Cocobod was supplying the raw materials to Wamco, which eventually resulted in the plant's indebtedness. After several years of disagreements as to the pricing of Cocobod's supply of beans to Wamco, during which time Wamco became further indebted, Cocobod stopped supplying the plant. Hamester then decided to withdraw from the joint venture, and brought a claim to the ICSID against Cocobod for its actions that led to Wamco's insolvence.

The tribunal first had to determine whether Cocobod's actions could be considered those of Republic of Ghana (ROG).

> 181. As already noted, the Claimant asserts that Cocobod is either an organ *de jure* or *de facto* under Article 4 of the ILC Articles or an entity qualifying under Article 5 of the ILC Articles, or that the acts of Cocobod are attributable to the ROG because they were performed on the instructions of, or under the direction or control of that State, under Article 8 of the ILC Articles. The Respondent denies that Cocobod can be considered a State organ, either *de jure* or *de facto*, and does not consider either that its acts can be attributed to Ghana on the basis of Article 8, as there is no evidence of any effective control of the Government over the acts performed by Cocobod in its dealings with Hamester. According to the Respondent, it cannot be doubted that Cocobod is a State entity under Article 5 of the ILC Articles, but the acts complained of cannot be attributed to Ghana on the basis of Article 5 in this case. Faced with these conflicting views, the Tribunal has therefore to ascertain the status of Cocobod.

> ### A. Is Cocobod a state organ under article 4 of the ILC articles?

> 182. An organ is part of the structure of the State itself, whether its central organisation (*i.e.* its legislative, executive or judicial structures), or decentralised

52 *Gustav F.W. Hamester GmbH and Co KG v Republic of Ghana*, ICSID Case No. ARB/07/24, Award (June 18, 2010); footnotes omitted; http://italaw.com/documents/Hamesterv.GhanaAward.pdf.

organisation. (*e.g.* territorial entities such as federated States; provinces; municipalities; etc.). In the present case, it is clear that the Tribunal has jurisdiction over the acts of the Ministers and over the acts of the police, which are part of the executive power of the Ghanaian State. The question is whether Cocobod is a State organ, as the Claimant contends.

183. In order to ascertain whether Cocobod is an organ of the Ghanaian State, the Tribunal must first look at Ghanaian law, as Article 4 of the ILC Articles provides that '(a)n organ includes any person or entity which has that status in accordance with the internal law of the State.'

184. Cocobod was created by the GCB Law [. . .]. It appears that the Ghana Cocoa Board is not classified as a State organ under Ghanaian law, but was created as a 'corporate body', which can be 'sued in its corporate name' [. . .]. Cocobod is a commercial corporation whose principal purpose is to trade in cocoa beans and generate a profit for the Government, as provided for in Section 6(1):

> 'It shall be the duty of the Board to conduct its affairs on sound commercial lines and in such a manner as to ensure a reasonable return on its capital.'

185. Moreover, Cocobod, as a public entity, can hold assets and open bank accounts. Section 11 provides that 'the Board of Directors shall be charged with the management of the property, business and finances [of Cocobod] . . .'. Section 24(1), provides for Cocobod to open its own bank accounts, stating '[Cocobod] may have bank accounts in such banks as the Board of Directors may determine'. Section 37(2) vests the Ghana Cocoa Marketing Board's assets—which was the body existing before the creation of Cocobod—in Cocobod.

186. Most likely in recognition of Law 1984, the Claimant's main focus is on Cocobod's status as State organ *de facto*. The Claimant relies in this regard on the case of *Eureko v. Poland*. The Tribunal does not consider this decision pertinent here. The contract in that case was signed by 'the State Treasury of the Republic of Poland represented by the Minister of the State Treasury,' which is quite different from the situation of the JVA which was signed by the Claimant and Cocobod, and did not involve any Minister of Ghana. The award in *Eureko* discussed the status of the State Treasury because under Polish Law the State Treasury had a separate personality. In fact, however, the tribunal did not expressly decide on the status of the State Treasury, but rather canvassed a range of possible analyses. It suggested that the State Treasury could be classified as a State organ (citing Professor Crawford, that the State is responsible for acts of 'all the organs, instrumentalities and officials which form part of its organisation and act in that capacity, whether or not they have separate legal personality under its internal law.') However, the tribunal also suggested that acts of the State Treasury could be attributed to the State under Article 5 or 8:

'Professor Crawford further observed that the principles of attribution are cumulative so as to embrace not only the conduct of any State organ but the conduct of a person or entity which is not an organ of a State but which is empowered by the law of that State to exercise elements of governmental authority. It embraces as well the conduct of a person or group of persons if he or it is in fact acting on the instructions of, or under the direction or control of, that State.'

In other words, the decision in *Eureko* does not, in itself, support the Claimant's contention that Cocobod is a State organ: first, because the situation of the State Treasury was very different from the situation of Cocobod; and second, because even if it were the same, the tribunal did not actually decide that the State Treasury was a State organ. The tribunal indeed concluded:

'In brief, *whatever may be the status of the State Treasury* in Polish law, in the perspective of international law, which this Tribunal is bound to apply, the Republic of Poland is responsible for the actions of the State Treasury.' [*Emphasis added*]

187. Another argument advanced by the Claimant to the effect that Cocobod is an organ of the State *de facto*, is Article 32 of Law 1984. This provides as follows:

'The P.N.D.C. [Provisional National Defence Council] Co-ordinating Secretary may, after consultation with the Board of Directors or the Management, give the Board in writing directions of a general character not being inconsistent with the provisions of this Law or with the contractual or other legal obligations of the Board relating to the exercise of the Board of its functions under this Law and the Board shall give effect to such directions.'

The Tribunal does not accept the conclusion drawn by the Claimant from this provision. First, Article 32 provides that the Government can only give 'directions of a general character' and not specific instructions to Cocobod. Second, these general policy directions can only be made 'after consultation with the Board of Directors or the Management' of Cocobod. Third, these directions of a general character cannot be 'inconsistent with the contractual and other obligations' of Cocobod, which means that the commitments of Cocobod, accepted in contracts and dealings with other economic actors, prevail over the Government's directions.

188. Having analysed all the circumstances put forward by both parties, the Tribunal concludes that Cocobod can by no means be considered an organ of the Ghanaian State, either *de jure* or *de facto*.

B. Is Cocobod a State entity under Article 5 of the ILC Articles?

189. It is obvious, in the Tribunal's view, that Cocobod has a whole range of objects and functions, as detailed in Section 2 of the Law 1984. This provides as follows

(the Tribunal having underlined those objects and functions which are essentially commercial, the remaining objects and functions being essentially governmental in nature):

'2. Objects and Functions of the Board.

(a) to encourage the production of cocoa, coffee and shea nuts;

(b) *to undertake the cultivation* of cocoa, coffee and shea nuts;

(c) to initiate programmes aimed at controlling pests and diseases of cocoa, coffee and shea nuts;

(d) *to purchase, import, undertake* and encourage *the manufacture* in Ghana of, and *distribute and market inputs* used in the production of cocoa, coffee and shea nuts;

(e) to undertake, promote and encourage scientific research aimed at improving the quality and yield of cocoa, coffee, shea nuts and other tropical crops;

(f) to regulate the marketing and export of cocoa, coffee and shea nuts;

(g) to secure the most favourable arrangements for the purchase, inspection, grading, sealing and certification, *export and sale* of cocoa, coffee, and shea nuts;

(h) *to purchase, market and export* cocoa produced in Ghana which is graded under the Cocoa Industry (Regulation) (Consolidation) Decree, 1968 [...] or any other enactment as suitable for export;

(i) *to establish* or encourage the establishment of *industrial processing factories* for the processing of cocoa and cocoa waste into marketable cocoa products;

(j) *to purchase, market and export* cocoa, cocoa products, coffee, shea nuts and shea butter produced in Ghana;

(k) to assist in the development of the cocoa, coffee and shea nuts industries of Ghana; and to promote the general welfare of cocoa, coffee and shea nuts farmers in Ghana.'

[*Emphasis added*]

190. From this section, it appears to the Tribunal that Cocobod is indeed entrusted with governmental functions. Among others, it has the mission to regulate the marketing and export of cocoa, coffee and shea nuts; to encourage the development of all aspects of cocoa production and transformation; and to fight diseases of cocoa beans. In order to fulfil these functions, Cocobod was granted governmental powers. Section 34(1) is quite clear when it states that '(t)he Board of Directors may, *by legislative instrument*, make such regulations as it may see fit for the purpose of giving effect to the provisions of this Law' (Emphasis added). The purpose of these regulations can be to 'prescribe the form of all licences or permits to be issued under this Law,' and to 'regulate the control of the issue of such licences or permits

and determine the conditions under which they may be used, produced, revoked or returned' (Section 34(2)). Moreover, if the regulations enacted by Cocobod are violated, it can impose penalties. All these entitlements make it clear that, besides its economic and commercial objects, Cocobod was endowed with elements of *'puissance publique'*.

191. The Tribunal, however, agrees with the Respondent's statement, referring to *UPS v. Canada Post*:

> 'Like Canada Post and the Suez Canal Authority, the GCB is a public corporation, dominates a particular economic activity, and has some governmental powers (such as the power to make regulations). But that does not, and cannot, lead to the conclusion that all of its conduct, including purely commercial business decisions in relation to a joint venture for processing agricultural commodities, are governmental in nature.'

192. The Tribunal concludes from the preceding analysis that Cocobod is an entity exercising elements of governmental authority, as described in Article 5 of the ILC Articles.

193. Having found that Cocobod is a public entity empowered with some *'prérogatives de puissance publique'*, this in itself clearly does not resolve the issue of attribution. The distinction between a State organ and a separate public entity is fundamental in this context. As 'organs' participate in the structural setting of the State, all their acts are attributed to the State, whether commercial or not. In contrast, it is well established that for an act of a separate entity exercising elements of governmental authority to be attributed to the State, it must be shown that the precise act in question was an exercise of such governmental authority and not merely an act that could be performed by a commercial entity. This approach has been followed in national as well as international case law.

194. National precedents include the famous case of *Rolimpex*, which concerned the status of a Polish state trading organisation (called Rolimpex). Although Rolimpex was under the strict control of the State in a centralized economy—much more dependent on the State than Cocobod—Lord Denning did not consider that *all* its acts could be attributed to the State:

> 'I do not think that Rolimpex can be considered to be a department of the Government of Poland . . . Rolimpex is a State trading agency.'

195. Another case to the same effect is *Trendtex v. Central Bank of Nigeria*, where a distinction was made between the activities performed by the Bank as a central monetary authority, and the act of buying cement for the construction of offices, which could not be attributed to the State.

196. This approach has also been adopted by numerous ICSID tribunals. A good example of the rationale to be applied can be found in the *Maffezini v. Spain* case,

where the different acts performed by a separate State entity (SODIGA), having been entrusted with some governmental powers, were analysed:

'In dealing with these questions, the Tribunal must again rely on the functional test, that is, *it must establish whether specific acts or omissions are essentially commercial rather than governmental* in nature or, conversely, whether their nature is essentially governmental rather than commercial. Commercial acts cannot be attributed to the Spanish State, while governmental acts should be so attributed.'

'At the time EAMSA was established, SODIGA was in the process of transforming itself from a State-oriented to a market-oriented entity. While originally a number of SODIGA's functions were closer to being governmental in nature, they must today be considered commercial in nature. But at the time of transition, there was in fact a combination of both, some to be regarded as functions essentially governmental in nature and others essentially commercial in character. As mentioned above, this is the *dividing line between those acts or omissions that can be attributed to the Spanish State and those that cannot*. The Tribunal must accordingly categorize the various acts or omissions giving rise to the instant dispute.' (*Emphasis added*)

197. The conclusion that flows from these decisions is that only the acts of Cocobod utilizing State prerogatives are attributable to the State for the purpose of international responsibility, and that the Tribunal therefore only has jurisdiction over acts of Cocobod that would have been performed in the exercise of elements of governmental authority. This, in turn, requires an inquiry into the nature of each and every act of which the Claimant complains.

198. At the same time, for all the acts complained of, in case they are not attributable to the State under Article 5, the Tribunal must also determine whether they are attributable under Article 8, the attribution or non-attribution under Article 8 being independent of the status of Cocobod, and dependent only on whether the acts were performed 'on the instructions of, or under the direction or control' of that State. Such acts could therefore be attributable not because they are the result of the use of governmental power, but because they are under the direct command or effective control of the State.

199. As a general remark, the Tribunal notes that it has not seen in the evidence any compelling sign of such a strong control by the State, as would be required by Article 8. It is not denied that the Government was informed, mainly at the initiative of the Claimant, of the developments taking place in the last phase of the dispute, before the departure of Mr. Holzäpfel from Ghana. However, being informed and discussing the case with the parties—both the Claimant and Cocobod—does not mean that the latter was under the effective control of the Government, and that the acts of Cocobod could be attributed to the State of Ghana, on the basis of Article 8 of the ILC Articles.

200. The Tribunal therefore concludes, as a starting point, that the acts of Cocobod do not appear to have been exercised under the direct command of the ROG, and do not appear to be attributable to the Government under Article 8 of the ILC Articles. This general conclusion, however, requires to be verified in relation to each of the acts complained of, where the Claimant has denounced an intervention of the Government.

201. Therefore, as will be examined in the next Section, and by way of summary:

(i)   Under Article 5 of the ILC Articles, if the acts of Cocobod which are the subject of complaint were performed in the exercise of governmental power, they will be attributed to the State. If they were performed in the fulfillment of commercial relations, they will not be attributable on that basis to the State.

(ii) In so far as acts are not attributable under Article 5, they could also be attributed to the State under Article 8 of the ILC Articles, if they can be shown as having been performed 'on the instructions of, or under the direction or control' of the State.

IX. The Tribunal's analysis on attribution: are the acts of Cocobod attributable to the State under ILC Articles 5 or 8?

202. In considering the application of Article 5 of the ILC Articles, the Tribunal has carefully assessed whether, in its dealings with Hamester in relation to the JVA, Cocobod acted like any contractor/shareholder, or rather as a State entity enforcing regulatory powers. It must be observed that this analysis has necessarily concentrated on the utilisation of governmental power. It is not enough for an act of a public entity to have been performed in the general fulfilment of some general interest, mission or purpose to qualify as an attributable act. In this regard, the Tribunal shares the view expressed by the tribunal in *Jan de Nul*, when it stated that:

> '(w)hat matters is not the "*service public*" element, but the use of "*prérogatives de puissance publique*" or governmental authority'.

203. In so far as any act of Cocobod has been found not attributable to the State because it is an act *de jure gestionis*, the Tribunal has then considered whether it has been performed under the direct command of the State, such as to be attributable by application of Article 8 of the ILC Articles.

204. The first task in this enquiry is to identify the Claimant's exact claims, and the individual acts which are said to be the basis for each claim. [. . .]

The tribunal continued its inquiry by asking whether the specific acts complained of could be found to be acts taken under governmental command. It determined that none of the acts were, thus disposing of the claimant's arguments.

The case of *Clayton/Bilcon v. Canada* demonstrated the application of the Articles of State Responsibility, Article 11.[53] That provision provides for a state's responsibility for actions that it accepts as its own:

> *Article 11: Conduct acknowledged and adopted by a State as its own*
> *Conduct which is not attributable to a State under the preceding articles shall neverthe-*
> *less be considered an act of that State under international law if and to the extent that*
> *the State acknowledges and adopts the conduct in question as its own.*

In *Clayton/Bilcon*, the Respondent argued that a review panel's determination that the Claimant's mining project should not be permitted was not attributable to the government. After analyzing the panel itself on the basis of control and function, the tribunal noted that even if the panel were not governmental in structure or function, the government's reliance upon the panel's actions made it responsible for the findings and their effects:

> 321. Even if [the panel] were not, by its nature, a part of the apparatus of the Government of Canada, the fact would remain that federal Canada and Nova Scotia both adopted its essential findings in arriving at the conclusion that the project should be denied approval under their environmental laws. [. . .]
> 322. It is possible to imagine a case in which a government arrives at the same conclusion as a recommendatory body, but in which the government does so by pursuing investigations and reasoning that are so distinctly its own that it might not be viewed as acknowledging and adopting the conduct of the recommendatory body. On the facts of the present case, however, Article 11 would establish the international responsibility of Canada even if the JRP were not one of its organs.

? **DISCUSSION NOTES**

Does governmental shareholding suffice to permit a company's actions to be attributed to the state? If the holding does not lend control of the company, the mere holding of shares will not make the government responsible for the company's decisions or acts. See *Lao Holdings NV v. Lao Peoples Democratic Republic*, ICSID Case No. ARB(AF)/12/6, Decision on the Merits, para. 81 (10 June 2015).

---

53 *William Ralph Clayton, William Richard Clayton, Douglas Clayton, Daniel Clayton and Bilcon of Delaware, Inc. v. Government of Canada*, UNCITRAL (NAFTA tribunal), PCA Case No. 2009-04, Award on Jurisdiction and Liability (Mar. 17, 2015).

b.ii   *Definition of a wrongful act*

Another principle from the Articles of State Responsibility of importance to investment law is that states can wrongly fail to act as well as act wrongfully.[54] Omissions to protect an investor by failing to pay for contracted activities or failing to compensate expropriated property, for example, will be found to be wrongful, even if the act of taking property was not.

b.iii   *Consequences of a wrongful act*

Despite the fact that most investment treaties provide for dispute settlement, IIAs rarely set out treaty-specific remedies for violations of their provisions. Thus, the international customary rules are the primary source of determining the consequences of investment responsibility. Tribunals have consistently recognized this fact, and often refer to the customary norms set out in the Articles on State Responsibility.

Under the Articles on State Responsibility, any wrongful act of a state makes the state 'responsible'. The particular consequences of responsibility will depend on the primary rules that have been breached, but the general consequences, customary international law, are a requirement for the state:

(1) to continue to abide by its obligations;[55]
(2) to stop acting wrongfully;[56] and
(3) to 'make full reparation for the injury caused'.[57]

The term 'full reparation' is further defined as consisting of one or more of three elements: restitution;[58] compensation;[59] and satisfaction.[60] As restitution (re-establishing the situation to be as it would have been in the absence of the wrongful act) is rarely feasible in the investment context and satisfaction will rarely satisfy the financially deprived investor, compensation for damages is heavily relied upon by arbitral tribunals. Important, then, is the Articles on State Responsibility's explicit reference to compensation for 'loss of profits'[61]—a consideration that looms large in many disputes

---

54 ASR art. 2 (defining a wrongful act as 'conduct consisting of an act or omission').
55 ASR art. 29.
56 ASR art. 30.
57 ASR art. 31.
58 ASR art. 35.
59 ASR art. 36.
60 ASR art. 37.
61 ASR art. 36(2).

over the consequences of host state failures to protect the investment of foreigners.

? **DISCUSSION NOTES**

1 The PCIJ's comments as to the suitability of the international rules on reparations for disputes between a state and a private person are interesting, but little commented upon in the investment literature:

> [. . .] The reparation due by one State to another does not however change its character by reason of the fact that it takes the form of an indemnity for the calculation of which the damage suffered by a private person is taken as the measure. The rules of law governing the reparation are the rules of international law in force between the two States concerned, and not the law governing relations between the State which has committed a wrongful act and the individual who has suffered damage. Rights or interests of an individual the violation of which rights causes damage are always in a different plane to rights belonging to a State, which rights may also be infringed by the same act. The damage suffered by an individual is never therefore identical in kind with that which will be suffered by a State; it can only afford a convenient scale for the calculation of the reparation due to the State.[62]

See also Articles on State Responsibility, Article 33, clearly separating the applicability of the rules as between states (para. 1) and as between a state and a private entity (para. 2).

An IIA may have specific rules on the attribution of state responsibility for state-owned enterprises (SOE). The investment chapter of the US–Oman Free Trade Agreement, for example, limits attribution of SOE acts to those which are taken by the enterprise '*when it exercises any regulatory, administrative, or other governmental authority delegated to it by that Party*.' (Agreement between the Government of the United States of America and the Government of the Sultanate of Oman on the establishment of a Free Trade Area, (1 January 2009), Art. 10.1.2).

The tribunal in *al Tamimi v. Oman* held that such language can be regarded as *lex specialis* by arbitral tribunals and thus override the customary rule of Article 5, Articles on State Responsibility. The Articles on State Responsibility were not made irrelevant, but their influence was to be as an aid to interpretation of the IIA. In the words of the tribunal:

---

62 *The Factory at Chorzów (Germany v. Poland)*, Claim for Indemnity/Merits, 1928 PCIJ (ser. A) No. 17, at 28 (Sept. 13). Available at: http://www.worldcourts.com/pcij/eng/decisions/1928.09.13_chorzow1.htm.

322. The effect of Article 10.1.2 of the US–Oman FTA is to limit Oman's responsibility for the acts of a state enterprise such as OMCO to the extent that: (a) the state enterprise must act in the exercise of *'regulatory, administrative or governmental authority'*; and (b) that authority must have been delegated to it by the State. The Respondent is therefore correct in its submission that, whether or not the Ministry of Oil and Minerals exercised *'effective control'* over OMCO through its 99% shareholding, or through influence over its directors or managers, as the Claimant submits, this is not relevant to the test for attribution under Article 10.1.2 of the US–Oman FTA.

323. The US–Oman FTA does not define what is meant by *'regulatory, administrative or governmental authority'*. The Respondent has submitted, however, that in this respect the *'requirement for attribution in the FTA closely parallels that in Article 5 of the ILC Articles'*. Under Article 5 of the ILC Articles, a person or entity which is not an organ of the State must be empowered by the law of that State to *'exercise elements of the governmental authority'* and must act *'in that capacity in the particular instance'*. The conduct at issue must be *'governmental'* or sovereign in nature (*acta jura imperii*). Purely commercial conduct (*acta jure gestionis*) cannot be attributed to the State under Article 5.

324. Given the specific test laid out by the State parties under Article 10.1.2, the criteria of Article 5 of the ILC Articles are not directly applicable to the present case. Indeed, there may be points of divergence between the test under Article 5 and the test under Article 10.1.2 of the US–Oman FTA: Article 10.1.2 refers to the exercise of *'regulatory'* and *'administrative'* authority in addition to *'governmental'* authority. But Article 5 nevertheless provides a useful guide as to the dividing line between sovereign and commercial acts.

Adel al Hamadi al Tamimi v. Sultanate of Oman, ICSID Case No ARB/11/33 (3 November 2015).

c   *Investment protection as customary international law?*

Beyond looking at specific customary rules of international law that apply to investment, one can legitimately ask if foreign investment protection standards set out in nearly all treaties have themselves become 'customary'.

Several scholars are of the view that, given the growing number of substantively similar treaties, the provisions of BITs themselves constitute existing (or at least emerging) customary law.[63] Others counter that the obligations

---

63 José E. Alvarez, *A BIT on Custom*, 42(1) J. Int'l L. & Pol. 17 (2009) (*see particularly* at 17, footnote 1, citing Andreas F. Lowenfeld, *Investment Agreements and International Law*, 42 Colum. J. Transnat'l L. 123 (2003);

accepted by states are accepted as treaty obligations precisely because they do not have the *opinio juris* necessary for customary law.[64] Discussion of these issues will be taken up in the relevant chapters.

2.3.3 General principles of law

There are some investment law cases that have relied on general principles of law. One interesting arbitration that demonstrates the importance of general principles to investment law is the 1984 *Amco v. Indonesia* award.

 CASE

Amco Asia Corporation and others and the Republic of Indonesia[65]

American investor Amco invested in the Indonesian company P.T. Wisma to build, lease, and manage a hotel in Jakarta. Amco received a foreign investment licence from the government, and proceeded with its plans. During the hotel's construction, Amco and P.T. Wisma fell into a dispute which ended with Wisma's taking ownership and control from Amco with the help of Indonesia's military and police forces. Wisma also persuaded the government to revoke Amco's licence.

Amco initiated arbitration in 1981 alleging it had been the victim of an illegal expropriation and that Indonesia had been unjustly enriched. Agreeing with the claimant, the tribunal had to calculate the damages owed Amco. Because the expropriation had been illegal, the tribunal looked to general principles of law rather than to the treaty's terms for guidance.

> 266. The principles governing damages for contractual liability hardly leave room for discussion.
> In Indonesian law, like in all systems of civil law, damages are to compensate the whole prejudice, whose two classical components are the loss suffered (*damnum emergens*) and the expected profits which are lost (*lucrum cessans*).
> Indeed, Article 1246 of the Indonesian Civil Code (Cl. Statement of Law

Stephen M. Schwebel, *The Influence of Bilateral Investment Treaties on Customary International Law*, 98 Am. Soc'y Int'l L. 27 (2004) as sharing this opinion).

64 For example, Patrick Dumberry, *Are BITs Representing the 'New' Customary International Law in International Investment Law?*, 28(4) Penn St. Int'l L. Rev. 675 (2009); Tarcisio Gazzini, *The Role of Customary International Law in the Field of Foreign Investment*, 8(5) The Journal of World Investment & Trade 691 (2007).

65 *Amco Asia Corporation and others and the Republic of Indonesia*, ICSID Case No. ARB/81/1, Award (Nov. 21, 1984), 24 ILM 1022 (1985).

Documents, Doc. R) provides as follows: 'Cost, losses and interest which a claimant may claim shall consist of, in general, losses already suffered and profit which he would otherwise enjoy, subject to the exceptions and qualifications set forth below.' Such exceptions and qualifications concern mainly the contractual limitation of liability (which is of course not met in the instant case), and the requirement of directness and foreseeability of the prejudice, which will be taken into account in the calculation of the damages (see hereunder, para. 268, 269ff.).

Likewise, Article 1149 of the French Civil Code—which has been used as a model by many other civil law systems—reads as follows:

> 'The damages due to the creditor amount in general to the loss which he has sustained and the profit of which he has been deprived, except as provided in the exceptions and qualifications below'.

In this respect, the Tribunal can only adhere to the enlightening explanations presented by Professor Bernard AUDIT in the legal opinion he delivered to counsel for Respondent (Resp.Leg.App., Vol. VIII, 2-2), at pages 6 to 10. Indeed, 'the loss sustained must be ascertainable'; 'a future loss can be ascertained'; 'a loss of profits constitutes a remediable loss'; 'the loss must be foreseeable'.

The same basic principles are met in common law. The rule of English law is that 'where a party sustains a loss by reason of a breach of contract, he is, so far as money can do it, to be placed in the same situation with respect to damages, as if the contract had been performed' (*Robinson v. Harman* (1848) 1 Exch. 850, at 855; and in particular as to loss of profits: *Anson's Law of Contract*, 25th (Centenary) edition, by A.G. Guest, Oxford 1982, at 553). In the law of the United States, the Courts or arbitral tribunals attempt to put the injured party in as good a position as he would have been in if the contract had been performed (Restatement Second on Contracts § 344; Uniform Commercial Code § 1-106 (1)).

267. Thus, the full compensation of prejudice, by awarding to the injured party the *damnum emergens* and the *lucrum cessans* is a principle common to the main systems of municipal law, and therefore, a general principle of law which may be considered as a source of international law.

Moreover, the same principle has been applied, in cases of breach of contract by a State (and in particular, in cases of breach of a concession contract which are closely comparable to an unjustified revocation of a license to invest) by a number of authoritative international judicial decisions and awards.

One could say that the basic precedent in this respect is to be found in the decision *Chorzow Factory* (Germany v. Poland), (1928 P.C.I.J., Ser. A, no. 17) where the Permanent Court of International Justice stated as follows:

> 'The essential principle contained in the actual notion of an illegal act—a principle which seems to be established by international practice and in particular by the decisions of arbitral tribunals—is that reparation must, as far as possible,

> wipe out all the consequences of the illegal act and re-establish the situation which would, in all probability, have existed if that act had not been committed. Restitution in kind, or, if this is not possible, payment of a sum corresponding to the value which a restitution in kind would bear; the award, if need be, of damages for loss sustained which would not be covered by restitution in kind or payment in place of it—such are the principles which should serve to determine the amount of compensation due for an act contrary to international law.
>
> [...]
>
> 268. Applying the same principles, the Tribunal will grant, in the instant case, damages calculated to fully compensate the prejudice suffered by the Claimant. Before proceeding to this calculation, the Tribunal has to state that here again, according to principles and rules common to the main national legal systems and to international law, the damages to be awarded must cover only the *direct* and *foreseeable* prejudice. The requirement of *directness* is but a consequence of the requirement of a causal link between the failure and the prejudice; and the requirement of *foreseeability* is met practically everywhere ([...]).

2.3.4 Other sources of investment law

a Contracts

Another source of investment law is agreements negotiated directly between investors and the host country. Contracts laying down allocation of rights, risks, responsibilities of each party as well as dispute settlement provisions (forum and choice of law), sometimes termed 'state contracts', are frequently used for large investment projects and can be relied upon by tribunals in analysing disputes.

The types of contracts investors and states enter have changed over time. The most common forms through history include:

1. *Concessions*—Most prevalent prior to the mid-twentieth century, concessions are long-term investor contracts between an investor and the host state in which the investor receives a right to develop natural resource (often mineral or oil) production facilities in exchange for an initial 'bonus' payment and subsequent royalty payments. The investor held that title to the resource, and had no obligations to research or even to produce a particular amount.[66] Concessions negotiated more recently

---

66 Kevin T. Jacobs and Matthew G. Paulson, *The Convergence of Renewed Nationalization, Rising Commodities, and 'Americanization' in International Arbitration and the Need for More Rigorous Legal and Procedural Defenses,*

are generally more balanced, with the host retaining control over the exploited material and the term of the contracts.[67]

2. *Production sharing agreements*—These agreements came into use beginning in the mid-twentieth century to replace concession agreements as resource-rich hosts began to demand more control over their natural wealth. Mainly found in the petroleum sector, production sharing agreements generally gave the foreign investor a right to explore and drill in a specified area, but left it with the risk of failed exploration.[68] The title to the resources remained with the host, following the permanent sovereignty over natural resources concept, one arising out of the New International Economic Order movement. The investor benefited by recovering its profits for the initial years of the contract, and receiving a specified (usually decreasing) percentage of the profits in the subsequent years.

3. *Licences*—A licence is a general administrative right to explore or use a resource or operate an enterprise for a specified period of time under specified conditions. While licence grants are often subject to the investor fulfilling certain criteria, the granting of a licence may remain discretionary for the government.

4. *Service contracts*—A service contract is an agreement between an investor and the host that grants the investor a possible payment for its expertise in locating and developing the production of oil and gas deposits. Because the payment will occur (and the investor's costs be recovered) only if the investor locates such deposits, service contracts are sometimes referred to as 'risk contracts' or 'risk service contracts'.[69] Significantly, the host retains ownership of the production and may tax the fees the investor receives.[70]

5. *Build, operate and own* (BOO)—As privatization of public infrastructure and utility networks increased beginning in the 1990s, build, operate and own contracts gained prominence among investors and hosts. The BOO contracts often require the parties to form a joint venture where the foreign partner contributes by taking the financial risk of putting its money into improving upon existing (or creating new) investments in

---

43 Tex. Int'l L.J. 359, 370 (2008).

67 Jan Ole Voss, *The Impact of Investment Treaties on Contracts between Host States and Foreign Investment* 17–21 (2011).

68 Klaus Peter Berger, *Renegotiation and Adaptation of International Investment Contracts: The Role of Contract Drafters and Arbitrators*, 36 Vand. J. Transnat'l L. 1347–8 (2003).

69 R. Doak Bishop, James Crawford and W. Michael Reisman eds., *Foreign Investment Disputes: Cases, Materials, and Commentary* 222 (2005) (excerpt from Daniel Johnston, *International Petroleum Fiscal Systems and Production Sharing Contracts* (Penn Well, 1994)).

70 *Id.*

the public sector. The costs are to be recovered in the later phases of the investment when they split the income from the investment with the host-owner and then when the ownership is transferred to the investor alone.

6. *Build, operate and transfer* (BOT)—These contracts are similar to the BOOs, but in the final stage the investment is handed over to the host.[71]

Besides the description of the obligations of each party, investment contracts may contain other provisions relevant to investment protection: a dispute settlement clause specifying a forum with jurisdiction; an arbitration clause containing the host's consent; choice of law provisions—often the domestic law of the host, but possibly another jurisdiction's or international rules; a clause excusing non-performance on particular grounds, such as inability due to *force majeure*; a stabilization clause that freezes the investor's obligations to those existing in the host's national legal system at the time of the contract conclusion; and renegotiation clauses.

? DISCUSSION NOTES

One of the difficult questions facing tribunals is what is the relationship between investment contracts and IIAs. Where violations of the IIA are alleged, it is accepted that the investor can make a claim on the basis of the treaty even if there is also a contract with the government: 'A state cannot rely on an exclusive jurisdiction clause in a contract to avoid the characterisation of its conduct as internationally unlawful under a treaty'.[72] While both are applicable, however, which should the tribunal prefer in case of a conflict between their provisions? What if, for example, a contract provides for disputes to be settled exclusively in national courts and the IIA permits arbitration in a different forum, should a claim brought to the latter forum be allowed? While one could find the contract to be *lex specialis*,[73] some tribunals have determined that the IIA's provisions are equally available to investors that have specific contracts with their host governments.[74]

---

71 *Id.* at 223–4 (excerpt from Muthucumaraswamy Sornarajah, *The Settlement of Foreign Investment Disputes* (*Kluwer Law International*, 2000)). *See also* Voss, *supra* note 67, at 24.

72 *Compañía de Aguas del Aconquija and Vivendi Universal v. Argentine Republic*, ICSID Case No. ARB/97/3, Decision on Annulment, para. 103 (July 3, 2002). *See also*, e.g. Jörn Griebel, *Internationales Investitionsrecht* 105 (Verlag C.H. Beck, 2008).

73 *See SGS Société Générale de Surveillance v. Republic of the Philippines*, ICSID Case No. ARB/02/6, Decision of the Tribunal on Objections to Jurisdiction, para. 141 (Jan. 29, 2004).

74 The chain of cases starting with *Lanco v. Argentina* follow this reasoning. These include *Lanco International Inc. v. The Argentine Republic*, ICSID Case No. ARB/97/6, Preliminary Decision on the Jurisdiction of the Arbitral Tribunal (Dec. 8, 1998), the *Vivendi* case (*see supra* note 72) and *CMS Gas Transmission Company v. Argentine Republic*, ICSID Case No. ARB/01/8, Decision of the Tribunal on Objections to Jurisdiction, para.

> See S.I. Strong's discussion of the multiple open legal questions that can arise from arbitration waiver provisions contained in State contracts. S.I. Strong, Note: Contractual Waivers of Investment Arbitration: Wa(i)ve of the Future? 29:3 ICSID Review 690 (2014).

b Jus cogens

Principles of *jus cogens* have not been addressed by investment tribunals. Their superior status to IIA provisions, however, is unlikely to be challenged by arbitrators if a future dispute would require an analysis of such a principle's application where it conflicted with an investment protection provision. At the same time, tribunals are likely to strive to interpret investment treaty provisions to be consistent with *jus cogens*, and only take up the issue where there is a direct and explicit conflict.

It is not unforeseeable that issues of *jus cogens* norms arise in the investment context.[75] Host state attempts to abolish slavery or slave-like practices, piracy, or even torture, may infringe on foreign investors' expected profits or deprive them of the use of their investment. Indeed, the prohibition on racial discrimination was implicated in the case of *Piero Foresti v. South Africa*, although the tribunal did not discuss the *jus cogens* nature of discriminatory practices.[76] While the *Foresti* claimants contended that aspects of South Africa's Black Economic Empowerment program's divestiture requirements violated their investment rights, the respondent's goal of remedying the unequal distribution of property that was the result of the apartheid system would have required the tribunal to address the requirements on the state to counter *jus cogens* violations. The case was discontinued, however, leaving such discussions for a future tribunal.

2.3.5 Teachings and writings of scholars

Although the use of scholarly teachings and writings is rarely directly cited by most international courts, investment tribunals often look to what experts say

---

76 (July 17, 2003).

75 Moshe Hirsch, *Sources of International Investment Law, in* International Investment Law and Soft Law 9–38, 33 (Andrea K. Bjorklund and August Reinisch eds., 2012).

76 *Piero Foresti, Laura de Carli and others v. Republic of South Africa*, ICSID Case No. ARB(AF)/07/1, Award (Aug. 4, 2010). Available at: http://icsid.worldbank.org/ICSID/FrontServlet?requestType=CasesRH&actionVal=showDoc&docId=DC1651_En&caseId=C90.

about the legal issues in dispute.[77] This practice began in the early phase of investor-State arbitrations under the ICSID Convention, when the thoughts of Aaron Broches[78] and Christoph Schreuer[79] were the notable exceptions to the dearth of international investment law scholarship.[80] Arbitral tribunals, facing legally novel questions in a context where individual investors were challenging state actions on an international plane and unable to rely on an extensive body of jurisprudence, were eager to bolster the acceptance of their analysis through reference to academic writings.

Since that time, the number of commentators on investment law has grown exponentially. Parties and arbitrators now have a wide range of authors from whom to choose when developing their opinions. It remains to be seen whether the growth in the quantity of scholarly materials (and the accompanying increase in availability of diverging opinions on what is a 'correct' interpretation) will result in a decline in tribunals' readiness to use them.

2.3.6 Awards by other tribunals: precedential or not?

In keeping with general international law, international investment law has no formal rule of *stare decisis*, or precedent. Each dispute is settled for the purposes of the particular parties and for the questions relating to the particular context that they have placed before the tribunal. The lack of precedential effect is set out explicitly for the awards of arbitrators deciding on the basis of certain treaties, such as the North American Free Trade Agreement's Investment Chapter,[81] while, for instance, the International Centre for the Settlement of Investment Disputes (ICSID) Convention's reference to the

---

77 Moshe Hirsch, *Sources of International Investment Law, in* International Investment Law and Soft Law 9–38, 33 (Andrea K. Bjorklund and August Reinisch eds., 2012).

78 For example, Aaron Broches, *The Convention on the Settlement of Investment Disputes between States and Nationals of Other States*, 135 Hague Rec. des Cours 331 (1972). *See*, e.g. *Fedax NV v. Republic of Venezuela*, ICSID Case No. ARB/96/3, Decision of the Tribunal on Objections to Jurisdiction, para. 21 (July 11, 1997), 31 ILM 1378 (1998); *Tokios Tokelés v. Ukraine*, ICSID Case No. ARB/02/18, Decision on Jurisdiction, paras. 25 and 46 (Apr. 29, 2004), 20 ICSID Rev.–FILJ 205 (2005).

79 *See* Christoph H. Schreuer, *Commentary on the ICSID Convention: Article 25*, 11 ICSID Rev–FILJ 441 (1996); ibid., The ICSID Convention: A Commentary (2001). The volume, first published in 2001, appeared in a second edition in 2009, with the addition of Loretta Malintoppi, August Reinisch, and Anthony Sinclair as co-authors. *See*, e.g. *Emilio Agustín Maffezini v. Kingdom of Spain*, ICSID Case No. ARB/97/7, Decision of the Tribunal on Objections to Jurisdiction, paras. 28, 31, 74, and 94 (Jan. 25, 2000), 5 ICSID Rep. 396 (2002); *SGS Société Générale de Surveillance S.A. v. Republic of the Philippines*, ICSID Case No. ARB/02/6, Decision on the Tribunal on Objections to Jurisdiction, para. 141 (Jan. 29, 2004), 8 ICSID Rep. 518 (2005).

80 Tribunals also frequently referred to scholarship on international law or commercial law issues where applicable. *See*, e.g. *Salini Costruttori SpA v. Kingdom of Morocco*, ICSID Case No. ARB/00/4, Decision on Jurisdiction, paras. 31 and 54 (July 23, 2001), 42 ILM 609 (2003).

81 NAFTA art. 1136(1) ('An award made by a Tribunal shall have no binding force except between the disputing parties and in respect of the particular case').

award's binding effect on 'the parties' implies the exclusion of *stare decisis*.[82] Other investment agreements are silent on the topic of precedent, but the differing texts of the provisions upon which the awards are frequently made, combined with the heavily textual approach of many tribunals to interpretation, supply a justification to keep awards specific to the dispute settled.

Nevertheless, like most adjudicatory decision-makers, arbitral tribunals often give significant weight to the findings of earlier panels that examined the same general issue of law. Given the similarity of BIT language, the interest of systemic consistency has a large, if informal, weight in the minds of tribunal members. This was the subject of great attention in the mid- to late-2000s, when the number of awards was increasing rapidly.[83] The newly created body of materials from which arbitrators and counsel could draw inspiration stimulated thinking about whether investment law could be said to have a rule of precedent as well as a practice. Professor and arbitrator Gabrielle Kaufmann-Kohler's declaration of a 'moral obligation' on investment arbitrators to follow precedent, based on the values of predictability, consistency, and ultimately credibility, goes further than many would venture.[84]

In the *Quiborax v. Bolivia* decision on jurisdiction, the majority of the tribunal (including Professor Kaufmann-Kohler) promoted the obligation view of precedent, but co-arbitrator Professor Brigitte Stern disagreed:

> The Tribunal considers that it is not bound by previous decisions. At the same time, it is of the opinion that it must pay due consideration to earlier decisions of international tribunals. Specifically, it deems that, subject to compelling contrary grounds, it has a duty to adopt solutions established in a series of consistent cases. It further deems that, subject to the specifics of the Treaty and of the circumstances of the actual case, it has a duty to contribute to the harmonious development of investment law, with a view to meeting the legitimate expectations of the community of States and investors towards the certainty of the rule of law. Arbitrator Stern does not analyze the arbitrator's role in the same manner, as she considers it her duty to decide each case on its own merits, independently of any apparent jurisprudential trend.[85]

---

82 ICSID Convention art. 53(1) ('The award shall be binding on the parties').
83 *See*, e.g. Tai-Heng Cheng, *Precedent and Control in Investment Treaty Arbitration*, 30 Fordham Int'l L.J. 1014 (2007); Gabriela Kaufmann-Kohler, *Arbitral Precedent: Dream, Necessity or Excuse?*, 23 Arbitration Int'l 357 (2007); 3 *Transnational Dispute Review, Special Issue: Precedent in Investment Arbitration* (2008); W. Mark C. Weidemaier, *Toward a Theory of Precedent in Arbitration*, 51 William & Mary L. Rev. 1895 (2010).
84 Kaufmann-Kohler, *Arbitral Precedent, supra* note 83, at 374.
85 *Quiborax SA, Non Metallic Minerals SA and Allan Fosk Kaplún v. Plurinational State of Bolivia*, ICSID Case No. ARB/06/2, Decision on Jurisdiction, para. 46 (Sept. 27, 2012).

Nevertheless, it remains true that most tribunals align themselves with the international legal framework in which investment law finds itself. Their awards may not be binding on other tribunals, but they are undoubtedly highly persuasive. This was explained by the *Daimler Financial Services* tribunal, in its jurisdictional findings:

> [. . .]The Tribunal agrees with the parties in noting that there is no system of precedent in investor-State arbitration, nor indeed could there be, given the large and diverse set of treaties presently applicable to various investor-State claims. Each case must be decided on the basis of the applicable treaty texts and in the light of the relevant facts. On the other hand, the Tribunal acknowledges that it is a fundamental principle of the rule of law that 'like cases should be decided alike', unless a strong reason exists to distinguish the current case from previous ones. This latter consideration will weigh more or less heavily depending upon: a) how 'like' the prior and present cases are, having regard to all relevant considerations; b) the degree to which a clear *jurisprudence constante* has emerged in respect of a particular legal issue; and c) the Tribunal's independent estimation of the persuasiveness of prior tribunals' reasoning.[86]

---

86 *Daimler Financial Services AG v. The Argentine Republic*, ICSID Case No. ARB/05/1, Award, para. 52 (Aug. 22, 2012). Available at: http://italaw.com/sites/default/files/case-documents/ita1082.pdf (footnotes omitted; citing Suez, Sociedad General de Aguas de Barcelona S.A., and *Vivendi Universal S.A. v. The Argentine Republic*, ICSID Case No. ARB/03/19 and *AWG Group v. The Argentine Republic* (UNCITRAL) (jointly decided), Decision on Liability (July 30, 2010), para. 189).

Question to an expert: Baiju S. Vasani

Baiju S. Vasani is a Partner in Jones Day's Global Disputes Practice in London and Washington D.C. He is a Fellow of the Chartered Institute of Arbitrators and is on the arbitrator panels of various institutions worldwide. He previously served as an Adjunct Professor of Law at Georgetown University and also has given visiting lectures at, among other universities, Harvard, Northwestern, Vanderbilt, Columbia and SOAS. He is currently a Visiting Lecturer on Investor-State Arbitration at the University of Bedfordshire. He was named to Global Arbitration Review's '45 under 45' leading arbitration practitioners worldwide at the age of 36, and has regularly been ranked by Chambers USA, Chambers UK, Who's Who of International Commercial Arbitration, Guide to the World's Experts in Commercial Arbitration, Reuters' Super Lawyers and Latin American Corporate Counsel Association. In 2015, he was named to the Best Lawyers in America list for international arbitration.

Do energy companies need arbitration clauses in their host government agreements if they are established in an Energy Charter Treaty member territory?

The Energy Charter Treaty (ECT) is—by design—a powerful tool for investors in the energy industry seeking to add several extra layers of protection from governmental interference for their foreign investments. This is not only in terms of the substantive protections the ECT offers over and above domestic law, such as the guarantee of fair and equitable treatment, but also the right to international arbitration before a tribunal under the auspices of the International Centre for Settlement of Investment Disputes (ICSID) and the attendant benefits that process brings. As a result, the most sophisticated of investments will seek to ensure that the ECT is engaged—properly and fully—at the moment the investment is made. But there is a palpable danger in seeing the ECT, or any such treaty for that matter, as a panacea for all ills. This would be particularly so if an investor were to forgo the opportunity to negotiate an arbitration clause in its agreement with the host government on the notion that it may already be adequately protected by the ECT (assuming jurisdictional prerequisites are met). This is for several reasons.

First, from a purely philosophical perspective, treaty-based protections should be viewed as secondary or even tertiary rights, and certainly ones of last resort. Treaties in and of themselves protect against the most egregious of government conduct. They require delicts of international proportion. To rely on them as a first port of call would be to misunderstand their purpose and nature. Second, and intimately related to the first, there is a certain line that is crossed when an investor commences a treaty arbitration against a host state. The arbitration is public, listed on the ICSID website, weighed against the state in assessing its attractiveness to foreign investment, and discussed amongst international commentators. As a gambit by an investor, it is to 'bring out the big guns' or 'initiate the nuclear option' and,

QUESTION TO AN EXPERT: BAIJU S. VASANI *(continued)*

depending on the host state involved, may have serious repercussions for the investor's standing, reputation and relationships in the host country going forward. Third, again related to the first two points, ECT arbitration is long and expensive as a general proposition.

Considering then the nature of treaty rights, the potential stigma and message associated with bringing a treaty action, and the time and expense in seeing it through, it would make little sense to bring any and all breaches of an agreement with a host state to the level of an ECT claim. Many violations may not even rise to the level of a treaty breach, and certainly if one considers the ECT's umbrella clause in Article 10 as limited to breaches of a purely governmental, non-commercial character. Still others may do so, but there may be advantages in not seeking to elevate the matter to an ECT violation, from time and costs considerations to commercial and political imperatives at a particular time in the lifecycle of an investment.

Finally, except with the possibility of the ECT's umbrella clause, simply having an arbitration clause in the agreement with the host state does not preclude any treaty action before an ICSID tribunal. From a purely 'belts and suspenders' perspective then, there is no downside. Moreover, while jurisdiction under the ECT may be properly planned in advance, there is no guarantee that an arbitral tribunal will accept jurisdiction for any number of given reasons. This may leave the investor with no recourse other than the domestic courts. It is thus during those times when a procedure under a contractual arbitration clause is preferable to an ECT action—whether for legal, commercial, political or other considerations—an investor that leaves itself without an alternative avenue may well regret its reliance on international treaties as a primary means of the enforcement of rights.

3

Definitions

3.1 Introduction

In this chapter, we will be looking at some of the basic definitions that are central to the law of investment protection. We start out with the very essential question of *what* is an investment and then move on to examine *who* is an investor. These are critical elements in ensuring investment protection, because only investors and investments are able to call upon the protective laws, whether customary norms or treaty provisions.

3.2 What is an investment in international investment law?

3.2.1 The concept of 'an investment'

The concept of an investment in international law is a key area of international investment law study. Referred to as part of the *ratione materiae* element of a claim, determining the existence of an 'investment' is a jurisdictional issue for investment dispute adjudicators. Quite simply, if there is no investment, the arbitrators will not have the competence to address the case.

The traditional approach to investment protection was to view it as the protection of 'property, rights, and interests'.[1] Customary international law on the protection of alien property had given this term a clearly defined legal meaning which was not subject to much discussion.[2] By the 1960s, however, the term 'property, rights and interests' was being replaced by the more general 'investment'—an economic concept that has been transposed into law.

Economists consider investment activities to be those in which someone purchases assets in the hope of creating future wealth or generating future

---

1 Rudolf Dolzer and Christoph Schreuer, Principles of International Investment Law 60 (second edn, 2012).
2 Id.

income.[3] The aspect of a creation of wealth keeps speculative portfolio investments and pure sales contracts outside the coverage of investment protection.[4] If this definition was applied to the law of investment protection, hosts may face national claims for breach of contract for actions that hindered wealth or income creation, but they would not be liable under the rules of an international investment protection treaty.

In investment law, an understanding of 'foreign investment' developed to describe projects that were tacitly accepted as investments. This kept questions regarding whether a particular project was an investment to a minimum until the late 1990s, thus precluding many disputes. Since then, however, there have been numerous discussions of precisely what activities the protections of IIAs should cover.

3.2.2 Definition of investment

The legal advent of investment protection was popularized by its flexibility: states could define the term 'investment' themselves in their investment treaty texts, and, in doing so, expand the scope of their foreign investors' property protection.[5] Where the term was ambiguous, tribunals could step in to interpret the precise extent of the host's obligations. IIAs, however, tended to define investment explicitly and broadly, through a general definition plus illustrative list of activities that the parties consider to be investments. The ICSID Convention, on the other hand, does not define the term at all. Thus, ICSID tribunals are faced with the challenge of determining whether the investor's activity satisfies both the IIA and the Convention terms. They therefore must make a decision as to whether the ICSID's use of the word 'investment' has a determined content and how it might relate to 'investment' as defined in the IIA.

a *International Investment Agreements (IIAs)*

The term 'investment' is explicitly defined by most IIAs by one of two basic approaches, the 'asset-based' approach, or the 'enterprise approach'. As the terms indicate, the asset-based definitions safe-guard foreigners' property and rights while the enterprise-based definition looks to the foreigner's ownership of or control over a business entity or portion thereof.[6]

---

3 Kevin D. Hoover, Applied Intermediate Macroeconomics 36 (Cambridge Univ. Press, 2012).
4 Id. at 181.
5 Dolzer and Schreuer, *supra* note 1.
6 UNCTAD, Scope and Definition: UNCTAD Series on Issues in International Investment Agreements II 21–2 (New York/Geneva, 2011).

The definitions of investment found in most existing bilateral investment protection agreements are asset-based. Similar to one another, these definitions are very broad, generally stating that investment can apply to all of the assets of the investor, including equity, debt, contracts, property, stocks, rights to mortgages and liens, as well as to pledges or licenses granted by the host government. The list of examples, moreover, is illustrative and open, rather than exclusive. Thus, a large range of activities falls within the scope of the definition—a much broader range, in particular, than had traditionally been understood by the term 'investment'.

Enterprise definitions are more limited. These define investments to be businesses or shares of a business—a more traditional way of considering 'investment'. Found originally in free trade agreements (FTAs), enterprise-based definitions can ensure that the host's obligations will only attach to projects that have been established in accordance with certain procedures.[7] In a pure form, these definitions would also exclude the ownership of real estate and portfolio shares from the scope of protection.[8]

While the approach can indicate the extent to which the treaty parties are willing to cede their sovereign prerogative regarding foreign properties, it is the text of the individual provisions that are of real significance for determinations of what obligations a host has toward the investor's activities in its territory.

Some commentators would have tribunals rely on the wording of the IIA alone to determine whether the investor's challenge is within the scope of the relevant treaty's protection. The state parties to the treaty, they argue, agreed to consider certain programs 'investments' and the textual language is clear, so it would be against the rules of treaty interpretation to restrict the scope of the treaty's protection merely on the grounds that the tribunal members believe the definition should be narrower.[9]

The following case demonstrates an early analysis of a tribunal which based its interpretation of 'investment' on the language of the IIA. Notice how expansive the tribunal is in its approach.

---

7 Id. at 22.

8 OECD Negotiating Group on the Multilateral Agreement on Investment (MAI), Note by the Chairman: Definition of Investor and Investment, DAFFE/MAI (95)2 (Oct. 13, 1995).

9 Barton Legum, Of Definitions and Disregard: An Editorial, 30:2 ICSID Review 281, 281–2 (2015).

CASE

Fedax NV v. Republic of Venezuela[10]

Fedax is a Dutch corporation operating in Venezuela. Having performed services for a creditor of the Venezuelan government, the corporation was paid by means of the creditor's endorsing its debt instruments to Fedax. As possessor of the promissory notes, Fedax objected to Venezuela's refusal to pay either the interest or the principal on the notes. Fedax instigated an arbitration in 1996, claiming that their right to the value of the notes had been expropriated by the government's actions. Venezuela objected to jurisdiction on the grounds that the promissory notes did not qualify as an investment. The tribunal had to analyse whether financial instruments—not an economic activity—nevertheless fulfil the characteristics of the term 'investment' and whether the text of the treaty otherwise limits the scope of the term.

31. . . . [T]he definition of 'investment' is controlled by consent of the Contracting Parties, and the particular definition set forth in Article 1 (a) of the Agreement is the one that governs . . . :
'[T]he term Investments' shall comprise every kind of asset and more particularly though not exclusively:

. . .

(ii) rights derived from shares, bonds, and other kinds of interests in companies and joint ventures;
(iii) titles to money, to other assets or to any performance having an economic value . . .'.

32. This definition evidences that the Contracting Parties to the Agreement intended a very broad meaning for the term 'investment.' The Tribunal notes in particular that titles to money in this definition are not in any way restricted to forms of direct foreign investment or portfolio investment, as argued by the Republic of Venezuela. [. . .]
33. The Tribunal has also undertaken a close examination of other provisions of the Agreement which are related to the definition of an investment, including Article 5 of the Agreement, under which the Contracting Parties guarantee the transfer of payments related to an investment. . . . The conclusion that the definition of 'investment' and the meaning of 'titles to money' under the Agreement include loans and related credit transactions is thus reinforced. [. . .].

10 *Fedax NV v. Republic of Venezuela*, ICSID Case No. ARB/96/3, Decision of the Tribunal on Objections to Jurisdiction (July 11, 1997), 37 ILM 1378 (1998); footnotes omitted.

34. A broad definition of investment such as that included in the Agreement is not at all an exceptional situation. On the contrary, most contemporary bilateral treaties of this kind refer to 'every kind of asset' or to 'all assets,' including the listing of examples that can qualify for coverage; claims to money and to any performance having a financial value are prominent features of such listings. This broad approach has also become the standard policy of major economic groupings such as the European Communities. In providing for the protection of investments the EC have included 'all types of assets, tangible and intangible, that have an economic value, including direct or indirect contributions in cash, kind or services invested or received.' Among the transactions listed as investments are 'stocks, bonds, debentures, guarantees or other financial instruments of a company, other firm, government or, other public authority or an international organization; claims to money, goods, services or other performance having economic value.' [. . .].

35. A similar trend can be identified in the context of major multilateral instruments. It has been rightly noted that the World Bank Guidelines on the Treatment of Foreign Direct Investment are not at all restricted to 'direct' investments. The explanatory Report makes clear that there are no restrictions in this context as to the nature of covered investments and that the Guidelines are applicable to 'indirect, as well as to direct, investments and to modern contractual and other forms of investment.' The Energy Charter Treaty and Mercosur Protocols have included 'every kind of asset,' the former listing 'claims to money and claims to performance pursuant to certain contracts,' and the latter referring to 'claims to performance having an economic value.' Again only exceptionally has a multilateral treaty strictly related the listing of given assets such as interests to equity investments, or excluded claims to money that arise solely from commercial contracts for the sale of goods or services.

36. The Tribunal has also examined the practice of the Republic of Venezuela as to the various investment treaties it has made with other countries and the definition of investment therein included. While this practice is varied, it is possible to conclude that every time the Republic of Venezuela has wished to exclude investments that are not manifestly direct, it has done so in unequivocal terms. [. . .].

37. The Tribunal being satisfied that loans and other credit facilities are within the jurisdiction of the Centre under both the terms of the Convention and the scope of the bilateral Agreement governing consent in this case, it must now examine the specific situation of the six promissory notes issued by the Republic of Venezuela. A promissory note is by definition an instrument of credit, a written recognition that a loan has been made. In this particular case the six promissory notes in question were issued by the Republic of Venezuela in order to acknowledge its debt for the provision of services under a contract signed in 1988 with Industrias Metalúrgicas Van Dam C.A.; Venezuela had simply received a loan for the amount

of the notes for the time period specified therein and with the corresponding obligation to pay interest.

38. The Tribunal notes first that there is nothing in the nature of the foregoing transaction, namely the provision of services in return for promissory notes, that would prevent it from qualifying as an investment under the Convention and the Agreement. Specifically, the Tribunal has raised the question whether if Fedax N.V., as a Netherlands company, had been doing business in Venezuela at the time in question and had entered into exactly the same arrangement with the Republic of Venezuela as Industrias Metalúrgicas Van Dam C.A. did, such transaction would have involved an 'investment' or whether, in Venezuela's view, the transaction would be excluded from that category. The record shows that Venezuela does not contend that such an exclusion would be appropriate. It follows that the issue for decision is focused not in the nature of the underlying service transaction but in whether the subsequent endorsement of the notes to foreign holders somehow requires the Tribunal to treat the matter as one falling outside the concept of foreign investment.

39. The claimant has rightly argued that promissory notes of this kind have a legal standing of their own, separate and independent from the underlying transaction. It is not disputed in this case that the Government of Venezuela foresaw the possibility that the promissory notes would be transferred and endorsed to subsequent holders, since they explicitly allow for such a possibility. [. . .]

40. In such a situation, although the identity of the investor will change with every endorsement, the investment itself will remain constant, while the issuer will enjoy a continuous credit benefit until the time the notes become due. To the extent that this credit is provided by a foreign holder of the notes, it constitutes a foreign investment which in this case is encompassed by the terms of the Convention and the Agreement. While specific issues relating to the promissory notes and their endorsements might be discussed in connection with the merits of the case, the argument made by the Republic of Venezuela that the notes were not purchased on the Venezuelan stock exchanges does not take them out of the category of foreign investment because these instruments were intended for international circulation. Nor can the Tribunal accept the argument that, unlike the case of an investment, there is no risk involved in this transaction: the very existence of a dispute as to the payment of the principal and interest evidences the risk that the holder of the notes has taken.

41. [. . .]

42. The nature of the transactions involved in this case, and the fact that they qualify as a foreign investment for the purposes of the Convention and the Agreement, serves to distinguish them from an ordinary commercial transaction. In this connection, however, there is one additional element that the Tribunal has to take into consideration. The promissory notes were issued by the Republic of Venezuela under the terms of the Law on Public Credit (the Law), which specifi-

cally governs public credit operations aimed at raising funds and resources 'to undertake productive works, attend to the needs of national interest and cover transitory needs of the treasury.' It is quite apparent that the transactions involved in this case are not ordinary commercial transactions and indeed involve a fundamental public interest. [. . .]

43. The status of the promissory notes under the Law of Public Credit is also important as evidence that the type of investment involved is not merely a short-term, occasional financial arrangement, such as could happen with investments that come in for quick gains and leave immediately thereafter—i.e. 'volatile capital.' The basic features of an investment have been described as involving a certain duration, a certain regularity of profit and return, assumption of risk, a substantial commitment and a significance for the host State's development. The duration of the investment in this case meets the requirement of the Law as to contracts needing to extend beyond the fiscal year in which they are made. The regularity of profit and return is also met by the scheduling of interest payments through a period of several years. The amount of capital committed is also relatively substantial. Risk is also involved as has been explained. And most importantly, there is clearly a significant relationship between the transaction and the development of the host State, as specifically required under the Law for issuing the pertinent financial instrument. It follows that, given the particular facts of the case, the transaction meets the basic features of an investment.

Not every tribunal will use a plain-text approach when analysing an IIA's definition of 'investment'. The case of *Romak v. Uzbekistan* illustrates how an examination of the context and purpose of the applicable IIA may affect the determination of whether a particular program should be considered an investment or not.

 CASE

Romak SA v. the Republic of Uzbekistan[11]

Romak is a grain seller incorporated in Switzerland. In 1996, Romak and the State Joint-Stock company of Uzbekistan (Uzkhleboproduct) signed a Protocol of Intention that set out their plans for a 'long-term and mutually profitable cooperation'. The Protocol set forth Romak's promise to help Uzkhleboproduct study cereals markets and to give them advice on prices

---

11 *Romak Switzerland v. the Republic of Uzbekistan*, PCA Case No. AA280, UNCITRAL, Award (Nov. 26, 2009). Available at: http://italaw.com/documents/ROMAK-UZBEKISTANAward26November2009_000. pdf; footnotes omitted.

and on grain import possibilities. In return, Uzkhleboproduct agreed to give preference to Romak in bids for the 1996/97 import-export quotas.

Between July and November 1996, Romak sent five deliveries of grain, totalling 50 000 tons of wheat, to Uzbekistan. Uzkhleboproduct did not pay for these shipments. Romak brought a successful investment claim under the Grain and Feed Trade Association, but Uzkhleboproduct refused to pay this award.

In 2006, Romak instituted separate arbitral proceedings pursuant to the UNCITRAL Arbitration Rules based on the 1993 Switzerland–Uzbekistan BIT. Uzbekistan objected to jurisdiction, claiming Romak had made no 'investment'.

B. The term 'Investments' under the BIT

173. At issue in this case is the meaning of the term 'investments' as it is used in the BIT, particularly in Articles 1 and 9—the alleged basis for this Tribunal's jurisdiction.

174. Article 1 ('Definitions') of the BIT states:

> 'For the purpose of this Agreement:
>
> . . .
>
> 2. The term 'investments' shall include every kind of assets and particularly:
>   a) movable and immovable property as well as any other property rights in rem, such as servitudes, mortgages, liens, pledges;
>   b) shares, parts or any other kinds of participation in companies;
>   c) claims to money or to any performance having an economic value;
>   d) copyrights, industrial property rights (such as patents, utility models, industrial designs or models, trade or service marks, trade names, indications of origin), technical processes, know-how and goodwill;
>   e) concessions under public law, including concessions to search for, extract or exploit natural resources as well as all other rights given by law, by contract or by decision of the authority in accordance with the law.'

175. The Parties disagree as to the meaning and relevance of the enumeration found in Article 1(2) of the BIT. Both Parties agree that the list is not exhaustive which is confirmed by a straightforward reading of the introductory expression 'and particularly'. Uzbekistan argues that the 'term "include" indicates that the ensuing enumeration is only part of the definition of the term investment,' and that the enumeration 'can constitute part of an investment but is not sufficient on its own as a definition of an investment.' For its part, Romak contends that the expression 'every kind of asset' is a broad one which, pursuant to its plain meaning, covers the rights underlying its claims. Specifically, Romak submits that it owned an investment under Article 1(2), letters (c) and (e).

176. The Arbitral Tribunal is therefore required to interpret the term 'investments' as found in Article 1(2) of the BIT. In order to do so, it shall resort to the *'ordinary meaning'* of the terms of the BIT *'in their context and in the light of its object and purpose'*.

177. The *'ordinary meaning'* of the term 'investments' is the commitment of funds or other assets with the purpose to receive a profit, or 'return,' from that commitment of capital. The term 'asset' means property of any kind.

178. Romak alleges that the Arbitral Tribunal should simply confirm that the Claimant's assets fall within one or more of the categories listed in Article 1(2) of the BIT, thus sponsoring a construction of the BIT that puts special emphasis on the literal words in the list of Article 1(2).

179. The Arbitral Tribunal disagrees with this approach.

180. First, the approach advanced by Romak deprives the term 'investments' of any inherent meaning, which is contrary to the logic of Article 1(2) of the BIT. Indeed, as already mentioned, the categories of investments enumerated in Article 1(2) of the BIT are not exhaustive, and do not constitute an all-encompassing definition of 'investment'. Both Parties agree that this is the case. Therefore, there may well exist categories different from those mentioned in the list which, nevertheless, could properly be considered investments protected under the BIT. Accordingly, there must be a benchmark against which to assess those non-listed assets or categories of assets in order to determine whether they constitute an 'investment' within the meaning of Article 1(2). The term 'investment' has a meaning in itself that cannot be ignored when considering the list contained in Article 1(2) of the BIT.

181. Second, such literal application of the terms of the BIT effectively ignores the second sentence of Article 31(1) of the Vienna Convention, which requires the interpreter to take into account, together with the 'ordinary meaning' of the terms of the treaty, their context and the object and purpose of the treaty. The BIT's object and purpose is reflected in its preamble, which declares that the Contracting Parties entered into the BIT *'[r]ecognizing the need to promote and protect foreign investments with the aim to foster the economic prosperity of both States'* and *'[d]esiring to intensify economic cooperation to the mutual benefit of both States'*.

182. Furthermore, and shedding more light on the 'context' of the list contained in Article 1(2) of the BIT and on the 'object and purpose' of the BIT, on the same day the BIT was signed, the Swiss Confederation and the Republic of Uzbekistan also entered into an Agreement on Trade and Economic Cooperation. This treaty specifically regulates the two States' mutual rights and obligations in relation to contracts for the sale of goods between parties established in the two States [. . .]. The Arbitral Tribunal is therefore persuaded that the Contracting Parties to the BIT adopted a distinction—also drawn in international practice—between trade and investment, and that a special and discrete treaty was concluded with respect to investment.

183. The Arbitral Tribunal therefore considers that a construction based solely

on the 'ordinary meaning' of the terms of the list contained in Article 1(2) of the BIT, as advocated by Romak, is inconsistent with the given context and ignores the object and purpose of the BIT.

184. In addition, for a number of reasons the Arbitral Tribunal finds that a mechanical application of the categories listed in Article 1(2) of the BIT would produce '*a result which is manifestly absurd or unreasonable*'. Such an outcome is contrary to Article 32(b) of the Vienna Convention.

185. First, said interpretation would eliminate any practical limitation to the scope of the concept of 'investment'. In particular, it would render meaningless the distinction between investments, on the one hand, and purely commercial transactions, on the other. As the *Joy Mining* tribunal explained:

> . . . *if a distinction is not drawn between ordinary sales contracts, even if complex, and an investment, the result would be that any sales or procurement contract involving a State agency would qualify as an investment. International contracts are today a central feature of international trade[. . .]. Yet, those contracts are not investment contracts, except in exceptional circumstances, and are to be kept separate and distinct for the sake of a stable legal order. Otherwise, what difference would there be with the many State contracts that are submitted every day to international arbitration in connection with contractual performance, at such bodies as the International Chamber of Commerce and the London Court of International Arbitration?*

[. . .]

187. Finally, the approach that Romak advances would mean that every contract entered into between a Swiss national and a State entity of Uzbekistan (regardless of the nature and object of the contract), as well as every award or judgment in favor of a Swiss national (irrespective of the nature of the underlying transaction), would constitute an investment under the BIT. This in turn would mean that, by entering into the BIT, Switzerland and Uzbekistan have renounced, in respect of every contract entered into with a national of the other Contracting Party, the application of domestic [. . .] law, and surrendered the jurisdiction of their own domestic courts [. . .].

188. Based on the above considerations, Romak's proposed literal construction of Article 1(2) of the BIT is untenable as a matter of international law. The Arbitral Tribunal must therefore explore the meaning of the word 'investments' contained in the introductory paragraph of that Article. As stated above at paragraph 180, the categories enumerated in Article 1(2) are not exhaustive and are clearly intended as illustrations. Thus, for example, while many 'claims to money' will qualify as 'investments', it does not follow that all such assets necessarily so qualify. The term 'investments' has an intrinsic meaning, independent of the categories enumerated in Article 1(2). This meaning cannot be ignored.

189. In construing the term 'investments', the Arbitral Tribunal will have due regard to the object and purpose of the BIT which, by referring to '*economic cooperation to the mutual benefit of both States*' and to the '*aim to foster the economic prosperity of*

both States', suggests an intent to protect a particular kind of assets, distinguishing them from mere ordinary commercial transactions. However, it is also plain that the BIT's stated object and purpose sheds little light on the meaning of the term 'investments', and *'leaves [it] ambiguous or obscure'*.

[...]

205. There is some debate as to whether, from a purely subjective perspective—and by analogy to the freedom of contract normally enjoyed by private parties—an investment will consist of whatever the contracting States have decided to label as such in the treaty they have concluded. [...] However, we are of the view that contracting States are free to deem any kind of asset or economic transaction to constitute an investment as subject to treaty protection. Contracting States can even go as far as stipulating that a 'pure' one-off sales contract constitutes an investment, even if such a transaction would not normally be covered by the ordinary meaning of the term 'investment'. However, in such cases, the wording of the instrument in question must leave no room for doubt that the intention of the contracting States was to accord to the term 'investment' an extraordinary and counterintuitive meaning. As explained above, the wording of the BIT does not permit the Arbitral Tribunal to infer such an intent in the present case.

[...]

207. The Arbitral Tribunal therefore considers that the term 'investments' under the BIT has an inherent meaning [...] entailing a *contribution* that extends *over a certain period of time* and that involves some *risk*. The Arbitral Tribunal is further comforted in its analysis by the reasoning adopted by other arbitral tribunals ([...]) which consistently incorporates contribution, duration and risk as hallmarks of an 'investment'. By their nature, asset types enumerated in the BIT's non-exhaustive list may exhibit these hallmarks. But if an asset does not correspond to the inherent definition of 'investment', the fact that it falls within one of the categories listed in Article 1 does not transform it into an 'investment'. In the general formulation of the tribunal in *Azinian*, *'labelling . . . is no substitute for analysis'*.

208. It is on the basis of the plain meaning of the term 'investment' that the Arbitral Tribunal will now consider whether Romak owns an investment under the BIT.

c. The existence of an 'investment' under the BIT

[...]

212. The Arbitral Tribunal will therefore address the issue of whether what Romak refers to as *'contracts and economic relations entered into with Uzbek public entities'* constitute an investment under the BIT; that is, whether they involved a contribution that extended over a certain period of time and entailed some risk.

1. Contribution

[...]

214. The Arbitral Tribunal interprets the term 'contribution' in broad terms. Any dedication of resources that has economic value, whether in the form of financial obligations, services, technology, patents, or technical assistance, can be a 'contribution'. In other words, a 'contribution' can be made in cash, kind or labor.

215. As alleged by Romak, its expenditure encompassed, on the one hand, the performance of the Romak Supply Contract (which involved the transfer of title over 40 581.58 tons of milling wheat) and, on the other, the performance of Romak's obligations under the Protocol of Intention [. . .] which, in the words of Romak, *'institutes true cooperation between the OUZKHLEBOPRODUCT State Group and ROMAK'*. With respect to the supply of wheat itself, this can hardly be considered a contribution, given that immediate payment at a market rate was envisaged under the Romak Supply Contract.

[. . .]

219. The Arbitral Tribunal notes that the Protocol of Intention in essence envisages that: (i) Romak will provide technical and marketing assistance, (ii) Uzkhleboproduct will give preference to Romak when presenting bids for the future supply of *'grain products'*, and (iii) the Parties will meet twice a year to *'discuss the current matters and exchange experiences'*. The Protocol creates no binding obligation for the Uzbek parties to enter into future contracts with Romak, whether for the supply of wheat or otherwise.

220. No evidence has been submitted that substantiates the performance of any of the undertakings contained in the Protocol of Intention. . . .

221. The Arbitral Tribunal finds that Romak made no contribution in furtherance of the Protocol of Intention, which—as its title suggests—seems never to have evolved from the status of a mere statement of aspiration, and was never acted upon by the Parties.

222. The only possible contribution established in the evidentiary record is the actual transfer of title over the 40 581.58 tons of wheat, the delivery of which has never been contested. However, as noted above, there is a difference between a contribution in kind and a mere transfer of title over goods in exchange for full payment. Romak's delivery of wheat was a transfer of title in performance of a sale of goods contract. Romak did not deliver the wheat as contribution in kind in furtherance of a venture. Accordingly, the Arbitral Tribunal does not consider that Romak made a contribution in relation to the transaction in question.

2. Duration

223. Romak has alleged that *'the supply agreement entered into by ROMAK was duly performed, and it solely consisted of a first order'*, and—with reference to the Protocol of Intention—that *'it would seem that the commercial relationship was intended to last for several years, with ROMAK enjoying a preferential right with regard to future grain imports'*.

224. The Arbitral Tribunal has found that the Protocol of Intention was never implemented, and that no expenditure was incurred in connection with it. The only potentially relevant event that has been borne out by the evidence is the delivery of wheat, which took place between July and November 1996.

225. The Arbitral Tribunal does not consider that, as a matter of principle, there is some fixed minimum duration that determines whether assets qualify as investments. Short-term projects are not deprived of 'investment' status solely by virtue of their limited duration. Duration is to be analyzed in light of all of the circumstances, and of the investor's overall commitment.

226. In the instant case, Romak's wheat deliveries spanned a five-month period. [. . .] Romak had no history of a prior, let alone continuing, economic relationship with Uzbekistan. [. . .]

227. In light of the facts before it, the Arbitral Tribunal considers that the duration of Romak's wheat deliveries does not reflect a commitment on the part of Romak beyond a one-off transaction, and is not of the sort normally associated with 'investments' according to the common understanding of the term.

3. Assumption of Risk

228. Romak considers that by accepting to engage in a contractual relationship with '*public entities of a state in relation to which international observers have alerted foreign investors to the absence of true financial security,*' Romak assumed a risk that ultimately materialized, and was fatal to its investment.

229. All economic activity entails a certain degree of risk. As such, all contracts including contracts that do not constitute an investment—carry the risk of non-performance. However, this kind of risk is pure commercial, counterparty risk, or, otherwise stated, the risk of doing business generally. It is therefore not an element that is useful for the purpose of distinguishing between an investment and a commercial transaction.

230. An 'investment risk' entails a different kind of *alea*, a situation in which the investor cannot be sure of a return on his investment, and may not know the amount he will end up spending, even if all relevant counterparties discharge their contractual obligations. Where there is 'risk' of this sort, the investor simply cannot predict the outcome of the transaction.

231. It is clear from the evidence in the record of this arbitration that, at the time it entered into the wheat supply transaction, Romak knew that its exposure was limited to the value of the wheat to be delivered. Indeed, Romak sought to avoid even this risk by providing, in the Romak Supply Agreement, for payment by means of a '*letter of guarantee*' or '*letter of credit*' . . .

232. On this basis, the Tribunal considers that Romak's economic activity did not involve the risk normally associated with an investment.
[. . .]

> **?** | **DISCUSSION NOTES**
>
> **1** The tribunal in *Malicorp v. Egypt*, referring to a typical IIA definition of 'investment', noted that 'This definition does not so much stress the contributions made by the party acting, as the rights and assets that such contributions have generated for it'.[12] Does this imply that the definition of investment is intended to primarily benefit the claimant?

---

b *International Centre for the Settlement of Investment Disputes*

The International Centre for the Settlement of Investment Disputes (ICSID) is one of the main fora for resolving disputes between foreign investors and host states. For arbitral tribunals established within its aegis, jurisdiction depends on the existence of a dispute arising out of 'an investment'. Article 25(1) of the ICSID Convention states:

> The jurisdiction of the Centre shall extend to any legal dispute arising directly out of an investment, between a Contracting State (or any constituent subdivision or agency of a Contracting State designated to the Centre by that State) and a national of another Contracting State, which the parties to the dispute consent in writing to submit to the Centre. When the parties have given their consent, no party may withdraw its consent unilaterally.

What is not clear is what precisely is meant by 'investment' in the ICSID Convention: the Convention contains no definition of this term. Does this mean that the drafters wanted to leave it up to states to determine for themselves—through an IIA negotiation—what activities would fall within its scope? Or does it indicate that the Convention's use of the term 'investment' has a meaning independent of any IIA, one that is inherent to the concept of investment?

The relationship between IIA and ICSID definitions of 'investment' has given rise to a rich jurisprudence and scholarship. Because so many IIAs have such a broad definition of 'investment', the basic question is whether a program must fulfil both definitions, or whether the ICSID tribunal can rely solely on the IIA's definition.

---

12 *Malicorp Limited v. The Arab Republic of Egypt*, ICSID Case No. ARB/08/18, Award, para. 108 (Feb. 7, 2011). Available at: http://italaw.com/documents/MalicorpvEgyptAward_7Feb2011.pdf.

The majority view of this question seems to have settled on the applicability of both sets of requirements. Thus, ICSID arbitrators must determine not only if an activity is an 'investment' for purposes of the IIA at issue, but also for purposes of their jurisdiction as ICSID decision-makers. This so-called *double keyhole approach* (or, '*double-barrelled approach*') requires the claimant to demonstrate the qualification of the investment under both treaties. If it fails to do so on either, the claim will be rejected as a jurisdictional matter.

? DISCUSSION NOTES

1 The double-keyhole approach is not universally thought to be correct. For one author, limiting the IIA parties' agreed-upon definition of 'investment' by a subjectively determined interpretation of the ICSID Convention's term is akin to 'an irretrievably irrational violation of the parties' freedom to contract'.[13] What relevant differences are there for interpreting the terms of a private contract and interpreting international treaties differently?

2 While the double-keyhole approach originated in the context of ICSID arbitrations, tribunals from other arbitration fora sometimes also consider the term 'investment' independently from its definition in the applicable IIA. The Romak tribunal, for example, explained its reasons for doing so as avoiding arbitrary differences of result depending on the forum in which a claim is brought:

> 196. [. . .] The Arbitral Tribunal cannot ignore the fact that Article 9(3) of the BIT provides for the possibility to resort to ICSID Arbitration. Romak has suggested that the definition of the term 'investment' may vary depending on the investor's choice between UNCITRAL or ICSID Arbitration, and has suggested that the definition of 'investment' in UNCITRAL proceedings (i.e., under the BIT alone) is wider than in ICSID Arbitration.
>
> 197. The Arbitral Tribunal does not share this view, which could lead to '*unreasonable*' results. This view would imply that the substantive protection offered by the BIT would be narrowed or widened, as the case may be, merely by virtue of a choice between the various dispute resolution mechanisms sponsored by the Treaty. This would be both absurd and unreasonable. [. . .] There is no basis to suppose that this word had a different meaning in the context of the ICSID Convention than it bears in relation to the BIT. Indeed, the drafters appear to have excluded any specific definition from the ICSID Convention precisely to accord contracting parties a great deal of flexibility in their designation of transactions or disputes as investment-related in their instruments of consent.

---

13 Barton Legum, Of Definitions and Disregard: An Editorial, 30:2 ICSID Review 281 (2015).

> 198. On this basis, it would be unreasonable to conclude that the Contracting Parties contemplated a definition of the term 'investments' which would effectively exclude recourse to the ICSID Convention and therefore render meaningless—or without *effet utile*—the provision granting the investor a choice between ICSID or UNCITRAL Arbitration. [. . .]
>
> The same reasoning led the *Nova Scotia Power v. Venezuela Tribunal* to determine that the term 'investment' found in the applicable IIA had an 'inherent' meaning which could limit its scope even when an activity was included in the enumerated list set forth by the treaty parties.[14]

While the double keyhole approach is widely accepted, there is still a need for determining the ICSID's meaning of 'investment'. ICSID tribunals have generally taken one of two basic approaches to this issue: an objective approach, in which criteria for consideration as an investment are set forth and then the challenged activity judged against the criteria; and a conceptual, or 'inherent meaning' approach, whereby 'investment' is taken to have a set meaning.

b.i   *Objective approach*

An objective view of determining what an 'investment' is relies on considering whether a particular activity demonstrates a set group of elements that defines 'investment'. The particular elements to be considered are therefore of particular importance. The tribunal in *Salini v. Morocco* applied a four-element test that has become known as the '*Salini* test'. This test, developed within the ICSID framework, has been widely relied upon by ICSID[15] and non-ICSID[16] tribunals alike.

---

14 *See Nova Scotia Power Incorporated (Canada) v. Bolivarian Republic of Venezuela*, ICSID Case No. ARB(AF)/11/1, Award, para. 80 (April 30, 2014).

15 *See,* e.g. *Joy Mining Machinery Limited v. The Arab Republic of Egypt*, ICSID Case No. ARB/03/11, Award on Jurisdiction, paras. 53–63 (July 30, 2004). Available at: http://www.italaw.com/sites/default/files/case-documents/ita0441.pdf; *Bayindir Insaat Turizm Ticaret Ve Sanayi A.Ş. v. Islamic Republic of Pakistan*, ICSID Case No. ARB/03/29, Decision on Jurisdiction, paras. 130–38 (Nov. 14, 2005). Available at: http://www.italaw.com/sites/default/files/case-documents/ita0074.pdf. *See also Alpha Projektholding GmbH v. Ukraine*, ICSID Case No. ARB/07/16, Award, paras. 316–23 (Nov. 8, 2010). Available at: http://www.italaw.com/sites/default/files/case-documents/ita0026.pdf (assuming that the BIT and ICSID definitions overlap, but addressing the *Salini* elements because the disputants had argued them).

16 *See,* e.g. *White Industries Australia Limited v. the Republic of India*, UNCITRAL Arbitration, Final Award, paras. 7.4.9–7.4.19; *Mytilineos Holdings SA v. the State Union of Serbia and Montenegro and Republic of Serbia*, UNCITRAL Arbitration, Partial Award on Jurisdiction, paras. 112–25 (Sept. 8, 2006). Available at: http://italaw.com/documents/MytilineosPartialAward.pdf. *See also Romak SA v. Republic of Uzbekistan, supra* note 16 paras. 192–208 (referring to the *Salini* test but finally opting for a plain meaning approach); Laura Halonen,

CASE

Salini Costruttori SPA and Italstrade SPA v. the Kingdom of Morocco[17]

The Salini group of companies won a bid to construct and maintain a highway in Morocco. Having completed their work several months late, Salini sent its request for payment to the government.

Among Morocco's objections to jurisdiction was a claim that the highway project was not an 'investment'. The tribunal, adopting the double-keyhole approach, recognized the need to address both the BIT's definition and the scope of the ICSID Convention. Given the absence of a definition in the ICSID Convention and a paucity of prior tribunal attention to the matter, the *Salini* arbitrators had to justify their position with an extensive discussion of the term.

50. ICSID jurisdiction is determined by Article 25 of the Washington Convention which stipulates that:

'The jurisdiction of the Centre shall extend to any legal dispute arising directly out of relation to an investment, between a Contracting State (or any constituent subdivision or agency of a Contracting State designated to the Centre by that State) and a national of another Contracting State, which the Parties to the dispute consent in writing to submit to the Centre.'

51. No definition of investment is given by the Convention. The two Parties recalled that such a definition had seemed unnecessary to the representatives of the States that negotiated it. Indeed, as indicated in the Report of the Executive Directors on the Convention:

'No attempt was made to define the term 'investment' given the essential requirement of consent by the parties, and the mechanism through which Contracting States can make known in advance, if they so desire, the classes of disputes which they would or would not consider submitting to the Centre (art. 25(4)).'

52. The Tribunal notes that there have been almost no cases where the notion of investment within the meaning of Article 25 of the Convention was raised.

Bridging the Gap in the Notion of 'Investment' between ICSID and UNCITRAL Arbitrations: Note on an Award Rendered under the Bilateral Investment Treaty between Switzerland and Uzbekistan (Romak SA v. Uzbekistan), 29(2) ASA Bulletin 312 (2011).

17 *Salini Costruttori SPA and Italstrade SPA v. the Kingdom of Morocco,* ICSID Case No. ARB/00/4, Decision on Jurisdiction (July 23, 2001), 42 ILM 609 (2003) [unofficial English translation of French original].

However, it would be inaccurate to consider that the requirement that a dispute be '*in direct relation to an investment*' is diluted by the consent of the Contracting Parties. To the contrary, ICSID case law and legal authors agree that the investment requirement must be respected as an objective condition of the jurisdiction of the Centre [. . .].

The criteria to be used for the definition of an investment pursuant to the Convention would be easier to define if there were awards denying the Centre's jurisdiction on the basis of the transaction giving rise to the dispute. With the exception of a decision of the Secretary General of ICSID refusing to register a request for arbitration dealing with a dispute arising out of a simple sale [. . .], the awards at hand only very rarely turned on the notion of investment. Notably, the first decision only came in 1997 [. . .]. The criteria for characterization are, therefore, derived from cases in which the transaction giving rise to the dispute was considered to be an investment without there ever being a real discussion of the issue in almost all the cases.

The doctrine generally considers that investment infers: contributions, a certain duration of performance of the contract and a participation in the risks of the transaction [. . .]. In reading the Convention's preamble, one may add the contribution to the economic development of the host State of the investment as an additional condition.

In reality, these various elements may be interdependent. Thus, the risks of the transaction may depend on the contributions and the duration of performance of the contract. As a result, these various criteria should be assessed globally even if, for the sake of reasoning, the Tribunal considers them individually here.

53. The contributions made by the Italian companies are set out and assessed in their written submissions. It is not disputed that they used their know-how, that they provided the necessary equipment and qualified personnel for the accomplishment of the works, that they set up the production tool on the building site, that they obtained loans enabling them to finance the purchases necessary to carry out the works and to pay the salaries of the workforce, and finally that they agreed to the issuing of bank guarantees, in the form of a provisional guarantee fixed at 1.5% of the total sum of the tender, then, at the end of the tender process, in the form of a definite guarantee fixed at 3% of the value of the contract in dispute. The Italian companies, therefore, made contributions in money, in kind, and in industry.

54. Although the total duration for the performance of the contract, in accordance with the CCAP, was fixed at 32 months, this was extended to 36 months. The transaction, therefore, complies with the minimal length of time upheld by the doctrine, which is from 2 to 5 years [. . .].

55. With regard to the risks incurred by the Italian companies, these flow from the nature of the contract at issue. The Claimants, in their reply memorial on jurisdiction, gave an exhaustive list of the risks taken in the performance of the said

contract. Notably, among others, the risk associated with the prerogatives of the Owner permitting him to prematurely put an end to the contract, to impose variations within certain limits without changing the manner of fixing prices; the risk consisting of the potential increase in the cost of labour in case of modification of Moroccan law; any accident or damage caused to property during the performance of the works; those risks relating to problems of co-ordination possibly arising from the simultaneous performance of other projects; any unforeseeable incident that could not be considered as *force majeure* and which, therefore, would not give rise to a right to compensation; and finally those risks related to the absence of any compensation in case of increase or decrease in volume of the work load not exceeding 20% of the total contract price.

56. It does not matter in this respect that these risks were freely taken. It also does not matter that the remuneration of the Contractor was not linked to the exploitation of the completed work. A construction that stretches out over many years, for which the total cost cannot be established with certainty in advance, creates an obvious risk for the Contractor.

57. Lastly, the contribution of the contract to the economic development of the Moroccan State cannot seriously be questioned. In most countries, the construction of infrastructure falls under the tasks to be carried out by the State or by other public authorities. It cannot be seriously contested that the highway in question shall serve the public interest. Finally, the Italian companies were also able to provide the host State of the investment with know-how in relation to the work to be accomplished.

58. Consequently, the Tribunal considers that the contract concluded between ADM and the Italian companies constitutes an investment pursuant to Articles 1 and 8 of the Bilateral Treaty concluded between the Kingdom of Morocco and Italy on July 18, 1990 as well as Article 25 of the Washington Convention.

The *Salini* tribunal's four elements, corresponding largely to the economic view of what an investment is, have themselves been extensively discussed by subsequent tribunals and commentators. Each element is addressed separately below.

Contribution of an asset

The contribution of an asset in the host is a factor that characterizes an investment. While the absolute size of the contribution is not determinative of whether a contribution exists,[18] some amount of financial outlay, material shipment, technical transfer, or personnel involvement by the investor within

---

18 An early draft provision of the ICSID Convention included a requirement that an investment be of at least $100 000 to have access to the Centre. The provision was rejected, and the current Convention contains no such minimum. *See* World Bank staff's initial proposal on 'The Jurisdiction of the Center', Section 1(1).

the framework of the investor-host relationship is necessary. The mere ownership of property that could be considered an investment will not be an 'investment' if it had been acquired as a gift, free of charge, or at a price which is significantly under-valued.[19]

At the same time, if an investor has not contributed resources prior to the host's violation of the project, the tribunal may still find an investment. The *Malicorp Ltd v. Egypt* tribunal addressed this issue in dicta:

> 108. [. . .] [The BIT's] definition [of investment] does not so much stress the contributions made by the party acting, as the rights and assets that such contributions have generated for it. In reality, the wording of other provisions of the Agreement clearly presupposes that there have been contributions, in particular Article 2(1), which makes it an obligation for each Party (to the Agreement) to '[*encourage*] *and create favourable conditions for nationals or companies of the other Contracting Party to invest capital in its territory* [. . .].' The definition given by Article 1 seems directly related to the measures a State can take to jeopardise them, in particular by expropriation.
>
> 109. b) *Article 25 of the ICSID Convention*, on the other hand, contains no definition of the notion. The drafters intentionally refrained from doing so in order to leave the maximum freedom for its application in practice [. . .].
>
> 110. At first blush, the two definitions do not overlap since they come from *different perspectives*. In the opinion of the Arbitral Tribunal these two aspects are in reality complementary. Indeed, the notion of investment must be understood from the perspective of the objectives sought by the Agreement and the ICSID Convention. They are there to '*promote*' investments, that is to say, to create the conditions that will encourage foreign nationals to make contributions and provide services in the host country, but also, and to that end, to '*protect*' the fruits of such contributions and services [. . .]. There must be '*active*' economic contributions, as is confirmed by the etymology of the word '*invest*', but such contributions must '*passively*' have generated the economic assets the instruments are designed to protect. Both aspects are reflected in the two underlying texts, but in a complementary manner. Clearly Article 1(a) of the Agreement emphasises the fruits and assets resulting from the investment, which must be protected, whereas the definitions generally used in relation to Article 25 of the ICSID Convention lay stress on the contributions that have created such fruits and assets. It can be inferred from this that assets cannot be protected unless they result from contributions, and contribu-

---

19 For more on this topic, see the discussion note explaining the connection between determining whether a shareholder will be considered as controlling an investment for purposes of lending nationality to the investor. *See infra* Discussion note.

tions will not be protected unless they have actually produced the assets of which the investor claims to have been deprived.

111. *In the present case*, both aspects exist, but in differing proportions:

- It is not disputed that under the Contract the Claimant benefited from a long-term concession that could have generated significant returns, just as it is undisputed that the Grantor prematurely ended that Contract, thereby depriving the Claimant of the revenues it could have made. . . . For the Claimant, the loss allegedly represented tens or even hundreds of millions of dollars.

- It is also not disputed that the relations of the Parties ended very rapidly without the Concessionaire having actually made any significant contributions. Undoubtedly it incurred expenses in preparing its bid and negotiating the Contract; [. . .]. [T]here is nothing *per se* to prevent the view that the long-term contractual commitment of a party to thereafter perform services fulfilling traditional criteria also amounts to a contribution. It was envisaged that the construction alone would entail costs in excess of 200 million dollars, that the work and most of all the operation of the airport would continue for several years, that the investor would reap profits from it that it estimates in these proceedings at several hundred million dollars, that the project involved risk and that by its nature and size it would contribute to the development of the region's tourism and economy.

In other words, if proved, the expropriation concerns the expectations from a contract which, although signed, had not yet been performed in any way but which contained a basic commitment.

[. . .]

113. [. . .]In the case of a contract, it has been rightly held that the costs incurred during negotiations with a view to concluding a contract do not constitute an investment if in the end the State finally refuses to sign it [. . .] The situation in the present case is different since the Contract was indeed signed. [. . .] It is true that Malicorp does not appear to have performed many services in connection with it. Nonetheless, the fact of being bound by that Contract implied an obligation to make major contributions in the future. That commitment constitutes the investment; it entails the promise to make contributions in the future for the performance of which that party is henceforth contractually bound. In other words, the protection here extends to deprivation of the revenue the investor had a right to expect in consideration for contributions that it had not yet made, but which it had contractually committed to make subsequently.[20]

---

20 *Malicorp Limited v. Egypt, supra* note 12, at paras. 108–13.

Duration

The length of the claimant's relationship with the host is another flexible element of the *Salini* test. Duration was typically taken into account to bar single sales transactions from investment protection. In the ICSID Convention negotiations, there was a suggestion of placing a minimum of five years on projects deemed an 'investment'.[21] Current practice is more generous with the duration. As one tribunal noted, 'one cannot place the bar very high' given that contracts are often extended and financial liabilities maintained beyond the active phase of relations.[22] While no tribunals have set a clear minimum period of time for an activity to qualify as an investment, a two-year time-span is generally considered sufficient.[23] Moreover, tribunals have recognized the possibility that a government could abuse a rule that would make the actual length of the investor's activities in the host the standard. Thus, the expected duration may be considered the more relevant figure than the actual duration.[24]

Risk

Along with the contribution of an asset, the idea that an undertaking must face more than normal business risks to be considered an investment is widely regarded as fundamental. Historically, it was the claimant's acceptance of the extra risk of putting resources into a foreign sovereign's territory that necessitated the particular protections for aliens. Today, the risk faced by foreign investors is often qualitatively less due to the foreignness of the investor than to either the quality of the host's governance or the 'inherent risk in long-term contracts'.[25] Given that, it is surprising that the risk element is one that 'has [. . .] turned out to be of limited value' regarding the qualification of an activity as an investment.[26] Surprising or not, however, few claimants will

---

21 *See* Christoph H. Schreuer, Loretta Malintoppi, August Reinisch, and Anthony Sinclair, The ICSID Convention: A Commentary 115 (second edn, 2009) (recounting the text of draft ICSID Convention Article 30).

22 *Bayindir v. Pakistan, supra* note 15, at para. 133 (citing *LESI v. Algeria*).

23 *See*, e.g. *Malaysian Historical Salvors Sdn Bhd v. the Government of Malaysia*, ICSID Case No. ARB/05/10, Decision on Jurisdiction, para. 110 (May 17, 2007). Available at: http://italaw.com/documents/MHS-jurisdiction.pdf; *Jan de Nul NV Dredging International NV v. Arab Republic of Egypt*, ICSID Case No. ARB/04/13, Decision on Jurisdiction, para. 93 (June 16, 2006). Available at: http://www.italaw.com/sites/default/files/case-documents/ita0439.pdf; *Salini v. Morocco, supra* note 17.

24 *Bayindir v. Pakistan, supra* note 15, para. 136.

25 *See* Christoph H. Schreuer, Loretta Malintoppi, August Reinisch, and Anthony Sinclair, The ICSID Convention: A Commentary 115 (second edn, 2009) (recounting the text of draft ICSID Convention Article 30).

26 *KT Asia Investment Group B.V. v. Republic of Kazakhstan*, ICSID Case No. ARB/09/8, Award, para. 209 (Oct. 17, 2013); *Deutsche Bank AG v. Socialist Republic of Sri Lanka*, ICSID Case No. ARB/09/02, Award, para. 304 (Oct. 31, 2012). *See also* Dolzer and Schreuer, *supra* note 1, at 75.

fail to convince a tribunal of the investment characteristics of their activities on the basis of a lack of risk alone.

Contribution to economic development
The most controversial element of the *Salini* test is that of an investment's contribution to the economic development of the host state. To what extent should the definition of a project as an investment depend on the benefits the project brings to the host? From one point-of-view, hosts accept the restrictions of protecting foreign property in exchange for the promise of greater economic development. Thus, if no developmental effects can be cited, they should not be under an obligation to protect the activity:

> The notion of a quid pro quo between a foreign investor and the host state is the cornerstone for the system of investment treaty arbitration. In exchange for contributing to the flow of capital into the economy of the host contracting state, the nationals of the other contracting state [. . .] are given the right to bring international arbitration proceedings against the host contracting state and to invoke the international minimum standards of treatment contained in the applicable investment treaty. [. . .]
>
> Given that the stated objective of investment treaties is to stimulate flows of private capital into the economies of the contracting states, the claimant must have contributed to this objective in order to attain the rights created by the investment treaty.[27]

This view is supported by the preambular language of the ICSID Convention and indeed, the institution's placement within the World Bank Group.

A different view, however, denies that a 'contribution to economic development' is relevant to the host's duty to protect the property of the foreign national. This perspective can be based on alternative grounds. One set of authors reason that any activity 'lawfully admitted and implemented' in the host territory should be deemed to be contributing to the host's development.[28] Others argue on a more practical basis: arbitral tribunals will have

---

27 Zachary Douglas, The International Law of Investment Claims 161–2 (2009).

28 Rudolf Dolzer and Christoph Schreuer, Principles of International Investment Law (2008) (first edition), at 69. Schreuer's view of the relevance of economic development, however, is differentiated. In his 2001 Commentary, Schreuer notes that the intention that an investment will contribute to economic development is found in the first sentence of the ICSID Convention's Preamble. This, he continues, is 'the only possible indication of an objective meaning' of investment, concluding from that that the object and purpose of the treaty would require an investment to make some contribution to the host's economic development to fall within the scope of the agreement's protections. Christoph H. Schreuer, The ICSID Convention: A Commentary 124 (Cambridge: Cambridge University Press, 2001). The 2011 edition modifies this position slightly, warning

a difficult time figuring out what activities foster development and which do not, and therefore should not be required to make a host's duties of protection turn on such a determination.[29] In *Phoenix Action Ltd. v. the Czech Republic*, the tribunal faced the question of whether a corporation allegedly without any economic activities in the host's territory could be considered an 'investment'. Accepting the criteria approach, the tribunal addressed the contribution to economic development element with the following words:

> It is the Tribunal's view that the contribution of an international investment to the *development* of the host State is impossible to ascertain—the more so as there are highly diverging views on what constitutes 'development'. A less ambitious approach should therefore be adopted, centered on the contribution of an international investment to the *economy* of the host State, which is indeed normally *inherent in the mere concept of investment as shaped by the elements of contribution/duration/risk*, and should therefore in principle be presumed. This analysis can also be found in the arbitral award in *Sedelmayer v. Russian Federation*, where the tribunal stated:
>
> > 'It must be presupposed, however, that investments are made within the frame of a commercial activity and that investments are, in principle, aiming at creating a further economic value.'[30]

Applying the elements

When using an objective approach to defining 'investment', the tribunal must not only decide which elements it feels are appropriate, it must also determine whether the absence of one will cause the claimant to fail the test. The *Salini* tribunal required the existence of all elements to conclude that an investment existed. The *Phoenix* tribunal, too, saw each element as essential, even while noting that the analysis of each does not have to be rigorous, as

---

that while the wording of the Preamble might mean that an activity that does lead to the host's economic development should enjoy a presumption of being an investment, 'it does not follow that an activity that does not obviously contribute to economic development must be excluded from the Convention's protection'. Christoph H. Schreuer et al. eds., The ICSID Convention: A Commentary 134 (second edn, 2011). *See also* Dolzer and Schreuer, *supra* notes 1 and 5, at 75–6.

29 For example, *Victor Pey Casado et Fondation 'Presidente Allende' v. Republique du Chili*, ICSID Case No. ARB/98/2, Award, para. 232 (May 8, 2008). Available at: http://italaw.com/documents/Peyaward.pdf. But see *Mr. Patrick Mitchell v. The Democratic Republic of Congo*, ICSID Case No. ARB/99/7, Decision on the Application for Annulment of the Award, para. 33 (Nov. 1, 2006). Available at: http://italaw.com/documents/mitchellannulment.pdf ('of course, ICSID tribunals do not have to evaluate the real contribution of the operation in question. It suffices for the operation to contribute in one way or another to the economic development of the host State, and this concept of economic development is, in any event, extremely broad but also variable depending on the case').

30 *Phoenix Action Ltd. v. the Czech Republic*, ICSID Case No. ARB/06/5, Award, para. 85 (Apr. 15, 2009). Available at: http://italaw.com/documents/PhoenixAward.pdf.

'they are most often fulfilled on their face, 'overlapping' or implicitly contained in others, and that they have to be analysed with due consideration of all circumstances.'[31]

The *Jan de Nul* award emphasized that rather than using the indicators of 'investment' as a checklist, 'these elements may be closely interrelated, should be examined in their totality and will normally depend on the circumstances of each case.'[32] This 'flexible and pragmatic approach'[33] allows each element to be examined, weighed, and evaluated within the context of the overall relationship with the host. The absence of one, then, can be relativized by a strong influence of another; while the ambiguity of the existence of one can be tested through the examination of the others.

A good illustration of the differing views on the economic contribution issue, the *Malaysian Historical Salvors* dispute also demonstrates how arbitrators use the individual elements of the objective test differently. The initial award, written by sole arbitrator Hwang, is an example of a differentiated use of the *Salini*-based criteria as a modified checklist for defining 'investment'.

 CASE

Malaysian Historical Salvors Sdn Bhd v. the Government of Malaysia[34]

The Claimant, Malaysian Historical Salvors Sdn Bhd (MHS) is a ship salvaging company that locates and recovers sunken vessels. In 1991, MHS contracted with the Malaysian Government to find and bring up a British vessel that sank off the Malaysian coast in 1817. They agreed on a scaled division of any profits from the sale of the recovered treasure, with MHS entitled to 70 percent if the aggregate worth was less than $10 million.

After MHS salvaged the ship and handed over the contents, Malaysia auctioned off a portion of the recovered treasure for approximately US$3 million and retained several pieces allegedly worth over $400 000. Receiving only 40 percent of the proceeds from the auction, MHS claimed that it had been unfairly treated by its host.

---

31 Id. para. 115.
32 *Jan de Nul v. Egypt, supra* note 23.
33 *Biwater Gauff (Tanzania) Ltd. v. United Republic of Tanzania*, ICSID Case No. ARB/05/22, Award, para. 316 (July 24, 2008). Available at: http://italaw.com/documents/Biwateraward.pdf.
34 *Malaysian Historical Salvors v. Egypt, supra* note 23.

In 2004, MHS filed a request for arbitration at the International Centre for the Settlement of Investment Disputes (ICSID). The Malaysian Government made jurisdictional objections based, *inter alia*, on an alleged lack of investment. The arbitrator set forth an extensive discussion of this issue.

43. For jurisdiction to be established, the Claimant must show that the Contract falls within the definition of 'investment' as found under Article 25(1) of the [ICSID] Convention ('Article 25(1)'), as well as the definition of 'investment' as contained in the BIT. This two-stage approach is recognized in the [ICSID] jurisprudence cited by the Parties in this case.

44. Professor Christoph Schreuer in his book *The ICSID Convention: A Commentary* (2001) ('*Schreuer*') notes that it would not be realistic to attempt a definition of 'investment' but he identifies the following as features of 'investment' under the ICSID Convention:

> But it seems possible to identify certain features that are typical to most of the operations in question: the first such feature is that the projects have a certain *duration*. Even though some break down at an early stage, the expectation of a longer term relationship is clearly there. The second feature is a certain *regularity of profit and return*. A one-time lump sum agreement, while not impossible, would be untypical. Even where no profits are ever made, the expectation of return is present. The third feature is the assumption of *risk* usually by both sides. Risk is in part a function of duration and expectation of profit. The fourth typical feature is that the commitment is *substantial*. This aspect was very much on the drafters' mind although it did not find entry into the Convention . . . .
> The fifth feature is the operation's significance for the host State's development. This is not necessarily characteristic of investments in general. But the wording of the Preamble and the Executive Directors' Report . . . suggest that development is part of the Convention's object and purpose. These features should not necessarily be understood as jurisdictional requirements but merely as typical characteristics of investments under the Convention.

45. As elaborated below [. . .], this is one of two possible ways ICSID jurisprudence may be taken to have approached the issue of determining whether there is an 'investment' within the meaning of Article 25(1).

[. . .]

(aa) Lack of Regularity of Profit and Returns is Immaterial in Relation to the Present Facts

108. The Tribunal first considers a hallmark of 'investment' cited in *Joy Mining*, which is that there must be regularity of profits and returns. This particular hallmark did not feature in the so-called *Salini* test, although it is mentioned in *Schreuer*. There is no regularity of profits and returns on the present facts. However,

[. . .] the Tribunal agrees that this criterion is not always critical. Further, this has not been held to be an essential characteristic or criterion in any other case cited in this Award, and its presence or otherwise may therefore not be determinative of the question of 'investment'. [. . .] Accordingly, [. . .] the Tribunal concludes that the absence of this hallmark is immaterial. [. . .]

(bb) Contributions

109. It is not in dispute that the Claimant has expended its own funds, whether in the form of equipment, know-how or personnel, or in the performance of the Contract in its entirety, without any cash payment or other financial assistance from the Respondent. Accordingly, the Tribunal finds that the Claimant has, like the claimants in *Salini*, made contributions in money, in kind and in industry although, as the Respondent has pointed out in its submissions of December 14 2006, the size of the contributions were in no way comparable to those found in *Salini*, *Bayindir* and *Jan de Nul* or even in *Joy Mining*. Furthermore, the nature of the Claimant's contributions are largely similar to those which might have been made under a commercial salvage contract (albeit with additional obligations in assisting in the ultimate sale of the salvaged articles).

(cc) Duration of the Contract

110. The Contract took almost four years to complete. Accordingly, it complies with the minimum length of time of two to five years, as discussed in *Salini*. However, owing to the nature of the Contract, the Claimant only managed to satisfy this factor in a quantitative sense. The original stipulated duration of the Contract was only for 18 months, which was extended by mutual consent. One might well argue that the Contract was only able to meet the minimum length of time of two years because of the element of fortuity. [. . .] The nature of the project meant that the Claimant could have completed it within a shorter period than two years and was in fact contractually required to do so within 18 months.

111. The ICSID tribunals in *L.E.S.I.-DIPENTA* and *Bayindir* considered that, in the context of construction contracts, one could take into consideration the time extensions that would often be required in determining whether a contract was an 'investment' within the meaning of Article 25(1). In the Tribunal's view, the key reason for allowing time extensions to be considered was motivated by the fact that, in *L.E.S.I.-DIPENTA*, the tribunal suggested that an assessment of the criterion of duration was linked to whether the contract was for an operation that promoted the economy and the development of the host State. Presumably, the longer the duration, the greater the economic commitment. Where the underlying contract does not promote the economy and development of the host State, there may be less justification to factor in the extensions granted under the Contract.

The Tribunal, therefore, considers that:

a)   since the duration of the Contract was dependent, in part, on the element of fortuity, and

b)   for the reasons stated at Paragraphs 113–45 below, this Contract does not appear to be a contract that would promote the economy and development of the host State as the criterion of duration is not satisfied in the qualitative sense envisaged by ICSID jurisprudence.

Thus, the Tribunal concludes that, although the Claimant satisfies the duration characteristic or criterion in the quantitative sense, it fails to do so in the qualitative sense. However, such failure does not, by itself, mean that the project was not an 'investment' within the meaning of Article 25(1) since a holistic assessment of all the hallmarks still needs to be made.

(dd) Risks Assumed Under the Contract

112. It is not in dispute that all the risks of the Contract were borne by the Claimant. The fact that these risks were not in any way borne by the Respondent would appear to afford a stronger reason to hold that the activity is an 'investment' within the meaning of Article 25(1) as compared to an investment where the risks were shared. However, it has been conceded by counsel for the Claimant that salvage contracts are often on a 'no-finds-no-pay' basis. [. . .] The nature of a salvage contract would mean that the assumption of risk by the salvor would be inherent in the transaction, rather than a special feature of the Contract which affected the salvor's decision to undertake the project in question. [This] is evidence that the risks assumed under the Contract were no more than ordinary commercial risks assumed by many salvors in a salvage contract. [. . .] It is clear under ICSID practice and jurisprudence that an ordinary commercial contract cannot be considered as an 'investment'. While the Claimant may have satisfied the risk characteristic or criterion in a quantitative sense (*i.e.*, that there was inherent risk assumed under the Contract), the quality of the assumed risk was not something which established ICSID practice and jurisprudence would recognize. Accordingly, since the Claimant can only superficially satisfy the so-called classical *Salini* features of investment, in the qualitative sense envisaged under established ICSID practice and jurisprudence, consideration of the remaining hallmarks of 'investment' will assume greater significance on the particular facts of the case.

(ee) Economic Development of Host State

113. Finally, the Tribunal has to consider whether the Contract contributed to the economic development of Malaysia. There appears to be a difference in ICSID

jurisprudence as to whether there is a need for a contract to make a significant contribution to the economic development of the host State. The tribunal in *Salini* considered that there should be a contribution to such economic development without stressing that it must be 'significant.' However, on the facts of that case, it was likely that the tribunal would have formed the view that the contribution was significant. The tribunal in *L.E.S.I.-DIPENTA* took the view that this requirement need not even be considered, because it was implicitly covered in the previous three characteristics of an 'investment'.

114. On the other hand, the tribunal in *Joy Mining* took the view that, to qualify as an 'investment', the contribution to the economic development of the host State must be 'significant'.

115. The *Bayindir* tribunal cited *Joy Mining* in saying that an 'investment' should be significant to the host State's development. The tribunal in *Bayindir* then cited *L.E.S.I.-DIPENTA* to assert that this condition was often already included in the other three criteria of 'investment'. On the facts, the *Bayindir* tribunal considered that the respondent did not dispute that a road infrastructure project would be important to the development of the country. The *Bayindir* tribunal's interpretation of *L.E.S.I.-DIPENTA* suggests that it considered the possibility that, while this hallmark would usually be subsumed within the previous three hallmarks of 'investment', there might be situations where it would not be so subsumed. It also endorsed the general view that a contribution had to be significant to the host State's development.

116. The tribunal in *Jan de Nul*, citing *Salini*, *Bayindir* and *L.E.S.I.-DIPENTA*, stated that a contribution to the host State's development would be indicative of an 'investment' within the meaning of Article 25(1). The tribunal took the view that, on the facts, the contract was of '*paramount significance*' to the host State's economy and development. [. . .].

117. In *CSOB*, the tribunal also made a finding that the contract made a significant contribution to the economic development of the host State.

118. In *Patrick Mitchell*, the *ad hoc* Committee departed from *L.E.S.I.-DIPENTA*, and considered this hallmark of 'investment' as '*an essential – although not sufficient – characteristic or unquestionable criterion*' of 'investment.' [. . .]. However, the *ad hoc* Committee added that this '*does not mean that this contribution must always be sizable or successful . . .*'. The *ad hoc* Committee also stated that it '*suffices for the operation to contribute in one way or another to the economic development of the host State, and this concept of economic development is, in any event, extremely broad but also variable depending on the case.*'

119. In contrast, the tribunal in *PSEG* [. . .] did not appear, at first blush, to consider it important for an 'investment' to contribute significantly to the economy of the host State . . . In this Tribunal's view, the main reason why the *PSEG* tribunal did not discuss the *Salini* criteria was because the investment in question was a 'readily recognizable investment.' The concept of 'readily recognizable investment'

was cited in Schreuer and credited to Dr. Aron Broches who, during the debate over the draft of the Executive Directors' Report, *recalled that none of the suggested definitions for the word "investment" had proved acceptable . . . [W]hile it might be difficult to define the term, an investment was in fact readily recognizable.*

[. . .]

123. The Tribunal considers that the weight of the authorities cited above swings in favour of requiring a significant contribution to be made to the host State's economy. Were there not the requirement of significance, any contract which enhances the Gross Domestic Product of an economy by any amount, however small, would qualify as an 'investment'. It also bears noting that in *Joy Mining*, the value of the bank guarantee had a value of GBP 9.6 million and yet did not qualify as a contribution to the economy of Egypt. Taking into account the entire factual matrix of the case, this feature may be of considerable, even decisive, importance. This is due in part to the Tribunal's findings that the other features of 'investment', such as risk and duration of contract, only appear to be superficially satisfied on the facts of this case, and not in the qualitative sense envisaged under ICSID practice and jurisprudence. The Tribunal is therefore left only with the contributions made by the Claimant, and has to determine whether these contributions would represent a significant contribution to the host State's economic development.

124. In unusual situations such as the present case, where many of the typical hallmarks of 'investment' are not decisive or appear to be only superficially satisfied, the analysis of the remaining relevant hallmarks of 'investment' will assume considerable importance. The Tribunal therefore considers that, on the present facts, for it to constitute an 'investment' under the ICSID Convention, the Contract must have made a significant contribution to the economic development of the Respondent.

(ff) Whether There Was Economic Contribution to Malaysia's Economic Development Under the Contract

125. Any contract would have made some economic contribution to the place where it is performed. However, that does not automatically make a contract an 'investment' within the meaning of Article 25(1). As stated by *Schreuer*, there must be positive impact on a host State's development. *Schreuer* cites *CSOB* in concluding that an 'investment' must have a positive impact on a host State and, in *CSOB*, the tribunal stated that there must be significant contributions to the host State's economic development.

126. The approach of *Schreuer* and *CSOB* can be contrasted with the decision of the *ad hoc* Committee in *Patrick Mitchell*, which endorsed a broader approach, simply requiring some form of contribution to the economy of the host State in one way or another.

[. . .]

129. In the present case, the Contract is not a 'readily recognizable' 'investment'. This is also the first time a marine salvage claim has been brought before the Centre.

[. . .]

131. Unlike the Construction Contract in *Salini* which, when completed, constituted an infrastructure that would benefit the Moroccan economy and serve the Moroccan public interest, the Tribunal finds that the Contract did not benefit the Malaysian public interest in a material way or serve to benefit the Malaysian economy in the sense developed by ICSID jurisprudence, namely that the contributions were significant.

132. In the oral proceedings, the Claimant attempted to show that the Contract did provide some form of benefit to the Malaysian economy, when it was indicated . . . that local residents were employed by the Claimant to '*wash, pack, inventorise and photograph the porcelains*' [. . .] salvaged from the DIANA. To the extent that the Claimant had provided gainful employment to these Malaysians, the Tribunal accepts that the Contract did benefit the Malaysian public interest and economy to some extent. However, this benefit is not of the same quality or quantity envisaged in previous ICSID jurisprudence. The benefits which the Contract brought to the Respondent are largely cultural and historical. These benefits, and any other direct financial benefits to the Respondent, have not been shown to have led to significant contributions to the Respondent's economy in the sense envisaged in ICSID jurisprudence.

133. The oral submissions were subsequently elaborated upon . . . where the Claimant submitted, *inter alia*, that it had employed over 40 people in Malaysia, as well as a village of local residents, imparted valuable know-how and knowledge on the science and process of historical marine salvage, which would ultimately benefit Malaysian museums, and its performance under the Contract had raised Malaysia's international profile and drew welcome attention to Malaysia as a favourable and attractive location or destination for history, treasure, archaeology and revenue-generating tourism. The Claimant also argued that the Contract had contributed over US$1 million in cash to the Malaysian treasury.

134. The Claimant also elaborated on the Contract's 'contribution' to the development of the host State. . . . The Claimant submits that, while its contributions may be small compared to the contributions of electrical utilities, oil exploration companies or highway builders, the contribution from the Contract was the largest within the salvage industry (at least US$3.8 million), and it is in that particular frame of reference within which its contributions and commitments must be measured.

135. The Tribunal cannot accept the Claimant's submission. . . . The frame of reference for the purposes of determining whether the Contract is an 'investment' under the ICSID Convention cannot depend on whether the Contract is the largest ever made within its particular industry. To determine whether the Contract

is an 'investment', the litmus test must be its overall contribution to the economy of the host State, Malaysia.

[. . .]

138. Not every contract entered into with a sovereign state will have a positive impact on the economic development of the host State in the sense envisaged under the ICSID Convention. Although the Contract was directly entered into by the Claimant with the Respondent, that does not *ipso facto* make the Contract an 'investment' within the ICSID Convention. The economic impact of the benefits of the Contract must be assessed to determine whether there was an 'investment'. Accordingly, the Tribunal must reject any perceived political or cultural benefits arising from the Contract in assessing whether it constituted an 'investment' except where such benefits would have had a significant impact on the Respondent's economic development. Stripped of all political and cultural benefits arising from the Contract, the Tribunal must assess whether the benefits arising from the Contract were simply a commercial benefit arising from the Contract or whether the Contract provided a significant contribution to the Respondent's economy.

139. It should not be thought that investments of relatively small cash sums can never amount to an 'investment'. Investments can be valued in ways other than pure cash, *e.g.* as human capital or intellectual property rights. So long as the putative investor has committed to making a contribution which results in some form of positive economic development, this *Salini* hallmark can be fulfilled. . . .

140. The Tribunal now turns to examine previous ICSID jurisprudence to determine what kind of contributions have been held by ICSID tribunals to constitute a significant contribution to the economy of the host State.

[. . .]

143. The Tribunal finds that [. . .] the Contract did not make any significant contributions to the economic development of Malaysia. [. . .]

144. [. . .] The benefits flowing from the Contract were no different from the benefits flowing to the place of the performance of any normal service contract. The benefit was not lasting, in the sense envisaged in the public infrastructure or banking infrastructure projects. The submission that historical marine salvage contracts could lead to a thriving tourism industry appears speculative. [. . .]

(dd) Conclusion

146. Accordingly, the Tribunal concludes that the Contract is not an 'investment' within the meaning of Article 25(1) of the ICSID Convention. The Claimant's claim therefore fails *in limine* and must be dismissed for want of jurisdiction.

Dissatisfied with the arbitrator's dismissal of its claims, MHS applied for an annulment of the award. The annulment tribunal had a distinctly different view on the application of the investment criteria (as well as denying the need for contributing to the host's economic development) than did Arbitrator Hwang.

 CASE

Malaysian Historical Salvors Sdn Bhd v. the Government of Malaysia, Annulment Decision[35]

56. This case concerns the interpretation of treaties. [. . .]

57. The 'ordinary meaning' of the term 'investment' is the commitment of money or other assets for the purpose of providing a return. In its context and in accordance with the object and purpose of the treaty—which is to promote the flow of private investment to contracting countries by provision of a mechanism which, by enabling international settlement of disputes, conduces to the security of such investment—the term 'investment' is unqualified. The purpose of the ICSID Convention was described in a draft of the Convention conveyed by the Bank's General Counsel to the Executive Directors of the Bank in these terms: '[t]he purpose of this Convention is to promote the resolution of disputes arising between the Contracting States and nationals of other Contracting States by encouraging and facilitating recourse to international conciliation and arbitration.' The meaning of the term 'investment' may however be regarded as 'ambiguous or obscure' under Article 32 of the Vienna Convention and hence justifying resort to the preparatory work of the Convention 'to determine the meaning'. As the pleadings in the instant case illustrate, there certainly have been marked differences among ICSID tribunals and among commentators on the meaning of 'investment' as that term appears in Article 25(1) of the Convention. Thus the provision may be regarded as ambiguous. [. . .]

[. . .]

63. What of the intentions of the Parties in concluding the Washington Convention? The term 'investment' was deliberately left undefined. [. . .] Mr. Broches [. . .] explained that:

> since the jurisdiction of the Center is limited by the overriding condition of consent, the exclusions desired by the one or the other delegation could be achieved by a refusal of consent in those cases in which in their view there was no proper case for use of the facilities of the Center. Refusal of consent would be an adequate safeguard for host States. . . . The purpose of Section 1 is not to define the circumstances in which recourse to the facilities of the Center would in fact occur, but rather to indicate the outer limits within which the Center would have

---

35 *Malaysian Historical Salvors v. Malaysia*, ICSID Case No. ARB/05/10, Decision on the Application for Annulment (April 16, 2009); footnotes omitted.

jurisdiction provided the parties' consent had been attained. Beyond these outer limits no use could be made of the facilities of the Center even with such consent.

[...]

69. However it is important to note that the *travaux préparatoires* do not support the imposition of 'outer limits' such as those imposed by the Sole Arbitrator in this case. [...]

[...]

79. The [...*Biwater v. Tanzania*] Award [...] is, in the view of this Committee, the most persuasive. Its pertinent passages read:

> In the Tribunal's view, there is no basis for a rote, or overly strict, application of the [...] *Salini* criteria in every case. These criteria are not fixed or mandatory as a matter of law. They do not appear in the ICSID Convention. On the contrary, it is clear from the *travaux préparatoires* of the Convention that several attempts to incorporate a definition of 'investment' were made, but ultimately did not succeed. In the end, the term was left intentionally undefined, with the expectation (*inter alia*) that a definition could be the subject of agreement as between Contracting States. [...]
>
> Further, the *Salini Test* itself is problematic if, as some tribunals have found, the 'typical characteristics' of an investment as identified in that decision are elevated into a fixed and inflexible test, and if transactions are to be presumed excluded from the ICSID Convention unless each of the [...] criteria are satisfied. This risks the arbitrary exclusion of certain types of transaction from the scope of the Convention. It also leads to a definition that may contradict individual agreements (as here), as well as a developing consensus in parts of the world as to the meaning of 'investment' (as expressed, e.g., in bilateral investment treaties). If very substantial numbers of BITs across the world express the definition of 'investment' more broadly than the *Salini Test*, and if this constitutes any type of international consensus, it is difficult to see why the ICSID Convention ought to be read more narrowly.
>
> [...]
>
> The Arbitral Tribunal therefore considers that a more flexible and pragmatic approach to the meaning of 'investment' is appropriate, which takes into account the features identified in *Salini*, but along with all the circumstances of the case, including the nature of the instrument containing the relevant consent to ICSID.
>
> [...]

F. Decision

83. For the foregoing reasons, the Committee DECIDES,

(1) that the Award on Jurisdiction of 17 May 2007 of the Sole Arbitrator in *Malaysian Historical Salvors v. The Government of Malaysia* is annulled; [...].

? **DISCUSSION NOTES**

1 The *Salini* criteria are similar to the economic definition of investment, but omit the element of regularity of profit. Why? Would adding such an element significantly limit the investments eligible for ICSID protection? How should tribunals approach pre-investment activities when it comes to looking at whether a project qualifies as an 'investment'? Should, for example, the money and time it takes to negotiate a contract which becomes the basis of the investment be counted toward the assets contributed and duration criteria? In *Deutsche Bank v. Sri Lanka*, the majority noted that the hedging contract which was the alleged investment foresaw a 12-month lifespan, but it had been negotiated for two years. Thus, there was adequate 'duration' to be considered an investment. See *Deutsche Bank AG v. Democratic Socialist Republic of Sri Lanka*, ICSID Case No. ARB/09/02, Award, para. 304 (31 October 2012).

The dissent, however, argued that the negotiation efforts were 'irrelevant' to the characterization of the claimant's activities. He wrote,

'61. [. . .] I am of the view that to determine whether a particular financial instrument—in this case the Hedging Agreement—entails a substantial contribution or commitment, it is the financial instrument itself, which must be evaluated. Any activity—in this case negotiations, correspondence and meetings between the Claimant and [the host]—preceding the execution of the financial instrument is irrelevant for this purpose.

62. In view of the above, it is difficult to see how the Hedging Agreement involved any contribution or commitment let alone any *substantial* contribution or commitment for the purpose of economic development in Sri Lanka [. . .]'

Deutsche Bank AG v. Democratic Socialist Republic of Sri Lanka, ICSID Case No. ARB/09/02, Dissenting Opinion of Makhdoom Ali Khan (23 October 2012).

2 What impact would a 'contribution to economic development' element have on investments placed in industrialized countries? With a growing number of investment claims against industrialized governments' actions, the question of whether a factor of economic development should be a prerequisite for investment protections could become an issue.

On the one hand, IIAs have a single set of preambular goals and the substantive passages do not differentiate between the treaty parties' obligations. This would indicate that the definition of 'investment' should also be the same—including the economic development portion. On the

> other hand, if a country is already industrialized, holding it responsible only for violating that foreign property which further contributes to its development would severely reduce the scope of protection.

b.ii   Conceptual ('outer limits') approach

Not all tribunals find the 'criteria check-list' approach to the definitional question of investment helpful. Given the differing views on which criteria are required, investors are left unsure about whether their activities will be considered 'investments' for purposes of investment protection. The alternative to such uncertainty is to look at 'investment' as a concept with an inherent meaning. In the words of the *Romak* tribunal, the concept of 'investment' forms the 'outer limits' of what can be considered an investment.

 CASE

Pantechniki SA Contractors and Engineers v. the Republic of Albania[36]

Pantechniki SA Contractors and Engineers (Pantechniki) is a Greek corporation that was in possession of contracts to build roads in Albania. In 1997, severe civil disturbances spread throughout Albania. Pantechniki's site was overrun by rioters who destroyed and stole equipment. Pantechniki sought to have the General Road Directorate cover its losses as per contract clauses that provided for the government's acceptance of the risk of loss. While the Directorate accepted the liability, it did not have funds to pay the over $4.8 million claimed and the Ministry of Finance refused to take on the costs.

Consequently, Pantechniki submitted a request for arbitration. Albania responded that no investment existed.

> 35. The Claimant appears easily to qualify under the explicit terms of Article 1(1) of the Treaty. The difficulty arises under Article 25(1) of the ICSID Convention:
>
> > 'The jurisdiction of the Centre shall extend to any legal dispute arising directly out of an investment, between a Contracting State . . . and a national of another Contracting State, which the parties to the dispute consent in writing to submit to the Centre'.

---

36 *Pantechniki SA Contractors and Engineers (Greece) v. the Republic of Albania*, ICSID Case No. ARB/07/21, Award (July 30, 2009). Available at: http://italaw.com/documents/PantechnikiAward.pdf; footnotes omitted.

36. What does 'an investment' mean here? Other ICSID tribunals have hesitated. A number of tribunals have struggled with what has become known as the 'Salini Test' (by reference to the award in *Salini v. Morocco*). This appears to be a misnomer. It is not so much a test as a list of characteristics of investments. The *Salini* award identified five elements as 'typical' of investment but made clear that the absence of one could be compensated by a stronger presence of another. The resulting wide margin of appreciation is unfortunate for the reason articulated succinctly by Douglas:

> 'If the fundamental objective of an investment treaty is to attract foreign capital, then the concept of an investment cannot be one in search of meaning in the pleadings submitted to an investment treaty tribunal that is established years, perhaps decades, after the decision to commit capital to the host state was made'.

Douglas proposes a formulation ('Rule 23' in his Diceyan propositional mode) which excludes two of the *Salini* elements as unacceptably subjective: 'a certain duration' and 'contribution to the host state's development'. Recent cases and commentary suggest that Douglas's Rule 23 may well encapsulate an emerging synthesis. It reads: 'The economic materialisation of an investment requires the commitment of resources to the economy of the host state by the claimant entailing the assumption of risk in expectation of a commercial return'. My own analysis is at any rate as follows.

37. Numerous states have concluded BITs which define investments capaciously. Many of these BITs purport to give access to arbitration under the ICSID Convention. The question that has vexed a number of tribunals is whether the ICSID Convention itself contains an autonomous and more restrictive definition which closes the door irrespective of such BITs.

38. Paragraph 25 of the Report to the Executive Director of the World Bank reflects the problem:

> 'consent alone will not suffice to bring a dispute within [ICSID] jurisdiction. In keeping with the purpose of the Convention, the jurisdiction of the Centre is further limited by reference to the nature of the dispute and the parties thereto'.

39. Does this mean that the word 'investment' as used in Article 25(1) of the Convention requires objective features that cannot be varied by agreement? Textually the answer need not be affirmative. Article 25(1) defines two other types of limitations which suffice to show that 'consent alone will not suffice'. The first is that the dispute must be *legal*. The second is that it must involve a Contracting State and a national of another Contracting State. Both of these limitations are conscious institutional boundaries established by the founders of ICSID. It stands to reason that these constitutive limitations cannot be ignored by those who would intrude into a system not designed for them or for their problems.

40. This observation satisfies the notion that 'consent alone will not suffice'. There appears to be no explicit requirement that the absence of an investment (in some meaning specifically developed for the purposes of the ICSID Convention) should also defeat purported consent.

41. Indeed in the context of BITs the notion of an autonomous investment requirement would be of a different nature than the 'legal dispute' and 'Contracting States' requirement. It would deny Contracting States the right to refer legal disputes to ICSID if they have defined investments too broadly. One may wonder about the purpose of such a denial. If the words of the Convention nevertheless said so that would of course be decisive. But there is no such express limitation. The drafters of the Convention decided not to define 'investments'. Does this mean that the matter is left to the determination of states?

42. For ICSID arbitral tribunals to reject an express definition desired by two States-party to a treaty seems a step not to be taken without the certainty that the Convention compels it.

43. It comes down to this: does the word 'investment' in Article 25(1) carry some inherent meaning which is so clear that it must be deemed to invalidate more extensive definitions of the word 'investment' in other treaties? *Salini* made a respectable attempt to describe the characteristics of investments. Yet broadly acceptable descriptions cannot be elevated to jurisdictional requirements unless that is their explicit function. They may introduce elements of subjective judgment on the part of arbitral tribunals (such as 'sufficient' duration or magnitude or contribution to economic development) which (a) transform arbitrators into policy-makers and above all (b) increase unpredictability about the availability of ICSID to settle given disputes.

44. It may be objected that some types of economic transactions simply cannot be called 'investments' no matter what a BIT may say; one cannot *deem* a person to be 10 feet tall. The typical example given is that of a 'pure' sales contract. There is force in the argument. Yet it may quickly lose traction in the reality of economic life. It is admittedly hard to accept that the free-on-board sale of a single tractor in country A could be considered an 'investment' in country B. But what if there are many tractors and payments are substantially deferred to allow cash-poor buyers time to generate income? Or what if the first tractor is a prototype developed at great expense for the specificities of country B on the evident premise of amortisation? Why should States not be allowed to consider such transactions as investments to be encouraged by the promise of access to ICSID?

45. The monetary magnitude of investments cannot be accepted as a general restriction. It was considered but rejected in the course of preparing the ICSID Convention. Any State might of course adopt a policy of never giving its consent to ICSID arbitration with respect to investments below a certain magnitude. (The expense of ICSID arbitration at any rate constitutes an important practical obstacle to small claims; there need be no fear of crashing floodgates.) But other States

may precisely want to benefit from the aggregate investment flows of attracting the small- to middle-sized businesses which have contributed so notably to the development of economies such as those of Germany and Italy. This is *their* policy choice; not that of ICSID arbitrators.

46. In the end the best outcome might be a consensus to the effect that the word 'investment' has an inherent common meaning. This would avoid unintended conflicts among treaties. Such an inconsistency would be striking in the case of BITs which give the investor a choice between arbitrations under the ICSID Convention and other rules. A special paradox could arise under treaties which allow UNCITRAL arbitration only until the States-party become members of ICSID. That would mean that investors' protection may suddenly narrow as a result of an uncertain future event. This is not a fanciful hypothesis; the Treaty in this very case envisages such an abandonment of the UNCITRAL option once the States-party have acceded to the ICSID Convention.

47. Douglas's Rule 23 proposes an inherent common meaning. It would perhaps lead to useful and proper distinctions. An example might be the contrast between residences and rental properties. But it is not my task to make general pronouncements about an emerging synthesis intended to resolve all controversies. My only duty is to determine whether in this case there was an investment that satisfied both the Treaty and the ICSID Convention.

48. To conclude: it is conceivable that a particular transaction is so simple and instantaneous that it cannot possibly be called an 'investment' without doing violence to the word. It is not my role to construct a line of demarcation with the presumption that it would be appropriate for all cases. But I have no hesitation in rejecting this jurisdictional objection in the present case. Albania does not come close to being able to deny the presence of an investment. Albania cannot and does not dispute that the Claimant committed resources and equipment to carry out the works under the Contracts. Its own officials have accepted that material committed to infrastructural development was brought by the Claimant to Albania and lost there.

49. The Claimant's Project Manager (Ms Pinelopi Dourou) testified vividly about the shortage of material and skilled personnel in Albania at the time. She said that everything from cement to guardrails had to be imported from Greece. She easily countered Albania's attempt to minimize the Claimant's work as mere repairs rather than true construction by describing the work required to rehabilitate roads built during the Italian presence in Albania in the 1940s. There is no need to use one's imagination to list the possible risks associated with the Contracts; one need only consider what actually happened. The Contracts envisaged aggregate remuneration to the Claimant of some US$7 million. The expectation of a commercial return is self-evident. The objection is unsustainable.

DISCUSSION NOTES

1 Is an arbitral award itself an 'investment' for which an investor can claim protection? The *GEA Aktiengesellschaft v. Ukraine* tribunal said no, calling an award 'a legal instrument, which provides for the disposition of rights and obligations'.[37] The trend among tribunals, however, seems to be one of permitting investors to claim protection for rights contained in arbitral awards as a part of their original 'investment'. See *White Industries v. India*,[38] paras. 7.6.1–7.6.10 (referring also to *Saipem*,[39] *Mondev*,[40] *Chevron*,[41] and *Frontier Petroleum Services*[42]). In *White Industries v. India*, the complainant had received an award from a commercial arbitration proceeding in the ICC, but was not paid by India. In the Australia–India BIT, 'investment' included a 'right to money or to any performance having a financial value' (Article 1(c)(iii)). The tribunal noted that an award arising from an investment are not investments themselves, but rather are 'part of the original investment'. Given that, the host had the obligation to protect the rights from the award.[43] It therefore contradicted the GEA approach, noting:

'The Tribunal considers that the conclusion expressed by the GEA Tribunal represents an incorrect departure from the developing jurisprudence on the treatment of arbitral awards to the effect that awards made by tribunals arising out of disputes concerning 'investments' made by 'investors' under BITs represent a continuation or transformation of the original investment'.

---

37 *GEA Group Aktiengesellschaft v. Ukraine*, ICSID Case No. ARB/08/16, Award, para. 161 (Mar. 31, 2011). Available at: http://www.italaw.com/cases/documents/479.

38 *White Industries, supra* note 16, at para. 7.6.8.

39 *Saipem SpA v. the People's Republic of Bangladesh*, ICSID Case No. ARB/05/07, Decision on Jurisdiction and Recommendation on Provisional Measures, para. 127 (Mar. 21, 2007). Available at: http://icsid.worldbank.org/ICSID/FrontServlet?requestType=CasesRH&actionVal=showDoc&docId=DC529._En&caseId=C52. 28 *Mondev International Ltd. v. United States of America*, NAFTA Arbitration, ICSID Case No. ARB(AF)/99/2, Final Award, paras. 88–91 (Oct. 11, 2002), 6 ICSID Rep. 192 (2004).

40 *Mondev International Ltd. v. United States of America*, NAFTA Arbitration, ICSID Case No. ARB(AF)/99/2, Final Award, paras. 88–91 (Oct. 11, 2002), 6 ICSID Rep. 192 (2004).

41 *Chevron Corporation (USA) and Texaco Petroleum Company (USA) v. The Republic of Ecuador*, UNCITRAL, PCA Case No. 34877, Interim Award, paras. 180 and 189 (Dec. 1, 2008). Available at http://www.italaw.com/documents/Chevron-TexacovEcuadorInterimAward.pdf.

42 *Frontier Petroleum Services v. Czech Republic*, PCA Award IIC 465 (Nov. 12, 2010). Available at: http://www.italaw.com/documents/FrontierPetroleumv.CzechRepublicAward.pdf.

43 Id., 111.

> **?** **DISCUSSION NOTES**

2 Another possible approach to defining 'investment' is a mixed one. The *Fakes v. Turkey*[44] arbitrators, for example, made a strong argument for adapting the *Salini* test factors into core requirements:

> 108. [. . .] The Tribunal believes that an objective definition of the notion of investment was contemplated within the framework of the ICSID Convention, since certain terms of Article 25 would otherwise be devoid of any meaning. 109. In this respect, the Tribunal agrees with the Tribunal in the *Joy Mining v. Egypt* case, which emphasized that the 'Convention itself, in resorting to the concept of investment in connection with jurisdiction, establishes a framework to this effect: jurisdiction cannot be based on something different or entirely unrelated . . . The parties to the dispute cannot by contract or treaty define as investment, for the purposes of ICSID jurisdiction, something which does not satisfy the objective requirements of Article 25 of the Convention.' [footnote omitted] 110. Second, the present Tribunal considers that the criteria of (i) a contribution, (ii) a certain duration, and (iii) an element of risk, are both necessary and sufficient to define an investment within the framework of the ICSID Convention. In the Tribunal's opinion, this approach reflects an objective definition of 'investment' that embodies specific criteria corresponding to the ordinary meaning of the term 'investment', without doing violence either to the text or the object and purpose of the ICSID Convention. *These three criteria derive from the ordinary meaning of the word 'investment,'* be it in the context of a complex international transaction or that of the education of one's child: in both instances, *one is required to contribute a certain amount of funds or know-how, one cannot harvest the benefits of such contribution instantaneously, and one runs the risk that no benefits would be reaped at all,* as a project might never be completed or a child might not be up to his parents' hopes or expectations.[45]

See also *RSM Production Corporation v. Grenada*, ICSID case No. ARB/05/14, Award, para. 235 (Mar. 13, 2009), http://italaw.com/documents/RSMvGrenadaAward.pdf ('[t]here are certain objective elements to an investment which must be present and it is the duty of this Tribunal to ensure that they are present, lest its assertion of jurisdiction be false and amount to an abuse of power'); *Malaysian Historical Salvors, SDN, BHD v. Malaysia*, ICSID Case No. ARB/05/10, Decision on the Application for Annulment: Dissenting Opinion of Judge

---

44 *Mr Saba Fakes v. Republic of Turkey*, ICSID Case No. ARB/07/20, Award (July 14, 2010). Available at: http://italaw.com/documents/Fakes_v_Turkey_Award.pdf.

45 *Id. at paras.*, 108–10.

Mohamed Shahabuddeen (Feb. 19, 2009), http://italaw.com/sites/default/files/case-documents/ita0498.pdf:

> 3. [. . .] The Applicant accepts that international investment plays a role in the economic development of the host State but makes it clear that the playing of that role is not a condition of an ICSID investment. That may suggest that the Applicant is trying to have it both ways. In my opinion, the Applicant is to be acquitted of endeavouring to do so. The difference between the two propositions is small but definite. According to the Applicant (as I understand its case), the non-playing of a role in the economic development of the host State does not break a condition of an ICSID investment and so does not disentitle the investment to the protection of ICSID. And so the question remains whether a contribution to the economic development of the host State is a condition of an ICSID 'investment'.
>
> 4. My main reasons for holding that economic development of the host State is a condition of an ICSID investment are these: (a). However wide is the competence of parties to determine the terms of an investment, that competence is subject to some outer limits outside of their will, if only to measure the width of their competence within those limits. (b). The outer limits in this case included a requirement that an investment must contribute to the economic development of the host State. (c). The Tribunal was correct in finding that the contribution to the economic development of the host State had to be substantial or significant. (d). The Tribunal was also correct in finding that the Applicant's outlay did not promote the economic development of Malaysia in a substantial or significant manner. (e). It is a reversal of the logical process to begin the inquiry with a consideration of what is an investment under the 1981 Agreement between the Government of the United Kingdom of Great Britain and Northern Ireland and the Government of Malaysia for the Promotion and Protection of Investments (the 'BIT') [. . .].

c   *The* Salini *Test Today*

There are signs that reliance on the full *Salini test* is waning.[46] In particular, the debate over whether economic development should be included as an

---

46 The Tribunal in *Philip Morris v. Uruguay* was explicit in its opinions of the *Salini* test, noting, 'Whether the so-called *Salini* test relied upon by the Respondent has any relevance in the interpretation of the concept of 'investment' under Article 25(1) of the ICSID Convention is very doubtful.' *Philip Morris Brands SÀRL, Philip Morris Products SA v. Oriental Republic of Uruguay*, ICSID Case No. ARB/10/7, Decision on Jurisdiction, para. 204 (July 2, 2013). *See also Hassan Awdi, Enterprise Business Consultants, Inc. and Alfa El Corporation v. Romania*, ICSID Case No. ARB/10/13, Award, para. 197 ('The *Salini* criteria may be useful to describe typical characteristics of an investment, but they cannot, as a rule, override the will of the parties, given the undefined and somewhat flexible term used by the drafters of the ICSID Convention.')

element in the objective test for an 'investment' has lessened considerably since the mid-2000s. One tribunal even went so far as to proclaim:

> 306. [. . .] [T]he criterion of contribution to economic development has been discredited and has not been adopted recently by any tribunal. It is generally considered that this criterion is unworkable owing to its subjective nature. [. . .] Moreover, some transactions may undoubtedly be qualified as investments, even though they do not result in a significant contribution to economic development in a post hoc evaluation of the claimant's activities. [. . .]
>
> 307. What is important is the commitment of the investor and not whether he positively contributed to the economic and social development of the host State. [. . .].[47]

While not all tribunals reject the theoretical importance of a project's contributions to the host's development,[48] there seems to be agreement that economic development is 'an expected consequence, not a separate requirement, of the investment projects carried out by a number of investors in the aggregate'.[49]

Recent awards indicate tribunals are instead focusing mainly on contribution, duration, and risk. Moreover, as the *Nova Scotia Power v. Venezuela* award emphasized, examining this 'triad' of characteristics is not one involving the application of a checklist, but rather of looking at interrelated elements. As the tribunal explained, 'the type of alleged contribution will often affect the measurement of risk, as does duration (e.g. the longer the duration potentially the greater the risk); duration and risk can only be measured by the term of any contribution that has been made; and so on'.[50]

An interesting evolution in the drafting of investment treaties is the explicit narrowing of the definition of 'investment'. For states that are looking to reduce their exposure to dispute settlement, there are numerous ways that

---

47 *Deutsche Bank v. Democratic Socialist Republic of Sri Lanka*, ICSID Case No. ARB/09/02, Award, paras. 306–7 (Oct. 31, 2012). *See also Quiborax SA, Non Metallic Minerals SA and Allan Fosk Kaplún v. Plurinational State of Bolivia*, ICSID Case No. ARB/06/2, Decision on Jurisdiction, para. 220 (Sept. 27, 2012).

48 Economic development was discussed or referred to in, e.g. *Ambiente Ufficio SPA and others v. The Argentine Republic*, ICSID Case No. ARB/08/9, Decision on Jurisdiction and Admissibility para. 487 (Feb. 8, 2013); *M. Meerapfel Söhne AG v. Central African Republic*, ICSID Case No. ARB/07/10, paras. 206–9 (May 12, 2011); *Renée Rose Levy de Levi v. The Republic of Peru*, ICSID Case No. ARB/10/17, Award, para. 151 (Feb. 26, 2014); *Antoine Abou Lahoud and Leila Bounafeh-Abou Lahoud v. Democratic Republic of the Congo*, ICSID Case No. ARB/10/4, para. 325 (Feb. 7, 2014).

49 *Saba Fakes v. Turkey, supra* note 44 at para. 111.

50 *Nova Scotia Power, supra* note 14, para. 84.

the scope can be limited. One is to use an enterprise-approach rather than the asset-approach.[51] Another is to exclude certain types of commercial activities from the scope in a manner similar to that by which included assets are listed today.[52] Finally, Parties who continue to apply the asset-based approach could elaborate on the criteria that should be considered in determining whether a project falls within the inherent definition—such as by including a particular duration as a minimum, or expressing the need for the program to have contributed (or be likely to contribute) to the economic development of the host.[53]

 DISCUSSION NOTES

> Would an industry-specific approach to the *Salini* factors make the characterization of economic activities by tribunals easier? Jung Engfeldt argues that in growth industries such as social media-driven entertainment, the *Salini* factors would prevent investment protections from applying to projects that are beneficial to economic development because they are too short or have non-quantifiable risks.[54]

3.2.3 Other jurisdictional issues surrounding the investment

Not only must there be an investment for a claimant to proceed with an arbitration under an IIA, the investment must have been a 'covered' investment. This means it must have been made in the territory of the host and that it was legally undertaken.

---

51 Model India BIT, Art. 1.6.

52 Agreement between Canada and the Republic of Serbia for the Promotion and Protection of Investments, Art. 1 (signed 1 September 2014) (closed-list approach to what projects constitute an investment combined with a list of excluded activities); Agreement between the Government of the State of Israel and the Government of the Republic of the Union of Myanmar for the Reciprocal Promotion and Protection of Investments, Art. 1(a)(6) (signed 5 October 2014); Model India BIT, Art. 1.7 ('For greater clarity, Investment does not include the following assets of an Enterprise: [. . .] (iii) portfolio investments').

53 The Australia–China Free Trade Agreement is less precise than what is suggested, but does make mention of the parties' intended limits on the term: '(d) investment means every kind of asset that an investor owns or controls, directly or indirectly, which has the characteristics of an investment, such as the commitment of capital or other resources, the expectation of gain or profit, or the assumption of risk. Forms that investments may take include'.

Free Trade Agreement between the Government of Australia and the Government of the People's Republic of China, Art. 9.1 (signed 17 June 2015).

54 Helena Jung Engfeldt, *Should ICSID Go Gangnam Style in Light of Non-Traditional Foreign Investments Including Those Spurred on by Social Media? Applying an Industry-Specific Lens to the Salini Test to Determine Article 25 Jurisdiction*, 32 BERKELEY J. INT'L LAW. 44 (2014). Available at: http://scholarship.law.berkeley.edu/bjil/vol32/iss1/2.

a   Was the investment made in the host's territory?

Many investment projects are clearly located in the host's territory. Mines, manufacturing plants, infrastructure—all of these are physical manifestations of the transferred assets. Therefore, when a government acts in a way that affects one of these investments, the territorial link is clear. Yet, while this is generally the case, it is not always so. First, there have been claims made on the basis of a host's actions that had negative impacts on the claimant's activities in the home state. Second, intangible investments leave the question of 'where is it?' open to significant debate. Each of these possibilities is discussed briefly below.

 CASE

Bayview Irrigation District et al. v. Mexico[55]

103. In the opinion of the Tribunal, it is quite plain that NAFTA Chapter Eleven was not intended to provide substantive protections or rights of action to investors whose investments are wholly confined to their own national States, in circumstances where those investments may be affected by measures taken by another NAFTA State Party. The NAFTA should not be interpreted so as to bring about this unintended result.

104. In this case the Tribunal does not consider that the Claimants were 'foreign investors' in Mexico. Rather, they were domestic investors in Texas. The economic dependence of an enterprise upon supplies of goods—in this case, water—from another State is not sufficient to make the dependent enterprise an 'investor' in that other State.

105. Article 1101(1)(b) stipulates that Chapter Eleven applies to 'investments of investors of another Party in the territory of the Party.' It is true that the text of the definition of an 'investor' in Article 1139 does not explicitly require that the person or enterprise seeks to make, is making or has made an investment *in the territory of another NAFTA Party*. But the text of the definition does require that the person make an 'investment'; and although investments can of course be made in the investor's home State such domestic investments are, as was explained above, not within the scope of Chapter Eleven. Chapter Eleven applies to 'investments of investors of another Party in the territory of the Party': Article 1101(1)(b). It is clear that the words 'territory of the Party' in that phrase do not refer to the territory of the Party whom the investors are nationals. It requires investment in the territory of another NAFTA Party—the Party that has adopted or maintained the measures challenged. In short, in order to be an 'investor' under Article 1139 one must make an investment in the territory of another NAFTA State, not in one's own.

---

55 *Bayview Irrigation District et al. v. United Mexican States*, ICSID Case No. ARB(AF)/05/1, NAFTA, Award (June 19, 2007). Available at: http://italaw.com/documents/bayview.pdf.

The question of territorial location becomes particularly difficult when the alleged investment was in the form of a financial instrument that was purchased on the international markets. Because in such cases the investor may be buying such an instrument from a financial intermediary (such as an investment bank) on the international market, the concept of there being a 'location' of the investment is difficult to manage. In *Abaclat v. Argentina*, a group of individuals lodged a claim against Argentina for the government's non-payment of state bonds. The individuals had purchased the bonds from issuing banks, which in turn had received them from Argentina in exchange for making money available to it. When Argentina complained that no investment had been 'made in' Argentina, the tribunal had to address the criterion of territorial linkage. The arbitrators differed strongly on this point, with both the majority and the dissent setting forth their opinions.

 CASE

Abaclat and Others v. The Argentine Republic[56]

374. The Tribunal finds that the determination of the place of the investment firstly depends on the nature of such investment. With regard to an investment of a purely financial nature, the relevant criteria cannot be the same as those applying to an investment consisting of business operations and/or involving manpower and property. With regard to investments of a purely financial nature, the relevant criteria should be where and/or for the benefit of whom the funds are ultimately used, and not the place where the funds were paid out or transferred. Thus, the relevant question is where the invested funds ultimately made available to the Host State and did they support the latter's economic development? This is also the view taken by other arbitral tribunals.

375. A further question is whether it is necessary that investment of purely financial nature be further linked to a specific economic enterprise or operation taking place in the territory of the Host State. Based on the above consideration (see § 355) that in Article 1 BIT Argentina and Italy designated financial instruments as an express kind of investment covered by the BIT and thereby intending to provide such investment with BIT protection, the Tribunal considers that it would be contrary to the BIT's wording and aim to attach a further condition to the protection of financial investment instruments.

376. Respondent makes an additional argument out of the fact that the payment of the purchase price occurred after the payment of the lump sum price by the underwriters, and that only the latter payment can be considered to have been made

---

56 *Abaclat and Others* (case formerly known as *Giovanna A Beccara and Others*) *v. The Argentine Republic*, ICSID Case No. ARB/07/5, Decision on Jurisdiction and Admissibility (Aug. 4, 2011) (footnotes omitted).

available to Argentina. The Tribunal is of the opinion that such argument ignores the reality of the bond issuance process. Indeed, although the payment of the lump sum price for the bonds and the payment of the purchase price by the individual holders of security entitlements happened at different points in time, the latter constitutes the basis for the former. As mentioned above (see § 359), the bonds and the security entitlements are part of one and the same economic operation and they make only sense together: Without the prior insurance to be able to collect sufficient funds from the individual purchasers of security entitlements, the underwriters would never have committed to the payment of the lump sum payment. In other words, the lump sum payment is an advance made by the underwriters to Argentina on the future payments of individual investors.

377. Thus, the funds generated by the purchase of the relevant security entitlements are—for the purpose of establishing where they were made—no different than the lumps sum payment paid by the underwriters for the bonds.

378. There is no doubt that the funds generated through the bonds issuance process were ultimately made available to Argentina, and served to finance Argentina's economic development. Whether the funds were actually used to repay pre-existing debts of Argentina or whether they were used in government spending is irrelevant. In both cases, it was used by Argentina to manage its finances, and as such must be considered to have contributed to Argentina's economic development and thus to have been made in Argentina.

In dissent, arbitrator Georges Abi-Saab countered with a discussion that proceeded from a core concern with host states' reason for offering international investment protections in the first place.

 CASE

Abaclat v. Venezuela, Dissent[57]

The Territorial Link

73. . . . [T]here remains the third, and more problematic question, namely: do these security entitlements satisfy the other, substantive, conditions of the Convention and the BIT, particularly that of a territorial nexus or link with Argentina?

74. A territorial link or nexus is inherent in the concept of 'investment' in article 25 of the ICSID Convention. The whole idea behind the Convention was to encourage the flow of private foreign investment to developing countries by offer-

---

57 *Abaclat and Others* (case formerly known as *Giovanna A Beccara and Others*) v. *The Argentine Republic*, ICSID Case No. ARB/07/5, Decision on Jurisdiction and Admissibility, Dissenting Opinion Georges Abi-Saab (Oct. 28, 2011) (footnotes partially omitted).

ing an international guarantee in the form of an alternative neutral adjudication of disputes arising out of such investment in the territory of the host States, typically subject to its laws and courts.

75. In addition, the Argentina–Italy BIT unambiguously requires a territorial link between the alleged investment and the host country. The Preamble of the Argentina-Italy BIT expresses the State parties' intentions to 'create favourable conditions for investments by nationals and companies of either State *in the territory of the other*'—a standard formulation found in many BITs. The definition of investment in Article 1 refers to 'any contribution or asset invested or reinvested by physical or juridical persons of one Contracting Party *in the territory of the other*', and Article 1/4 carefully delimits the BIT's territorial ambit.

76. The BIT's substantive provisions are also conditioned on a territorial link, including:

> —Article 2 (protection and promotion of investments) calls on each contracting party to 'encourage the making of investments *in its territory* by investors of the other Contracting Party';
> —Article 2/2 (full protection and security) obliges each party to refrain from 'adopting unjustified or discriminatory measures that impair the management, maintenance, enjoyment, transformation, cessation and liquidation of investments made *in its territory* by investors of the other Contracting Party';
> —Article 3 (national and most favoured treatment) likewise contains the qualifier 'within its own territory';
> —Article 4 (compensation for damage or loss) refers to 'the Contracting Party in whose territory the investment was made'.

77. This requisite territorial link is clearly absent in the present case. The alleged investment, the security entitlements, are not located in Argentina by applying either the legal or the material criteria for determining such location.

78. 1) *The legal criteria*: the financial securities instruments that constitute the alleged investment, i.e. the security entitlements in Argentinean bonds, have been sold in international financial markets, outside Argentina, with choice of law and forum selection clauses subjecting them to laws and fora foreign to Argentina. In fact, they were intentionally situated outside Argentina and out of reach of its laws and tribunals. There is no way then to say (and no legal basis for saying) that they are legally located in Argentina.

79. The majority award contests this clear conclusion on two grounds: a) The first is that the above conclusion 'would mean that forum selection clauses determine the place where contractual performance is supposed to take place', whilst they are merely 'of a procedural nature aiming to determine the place of settlement of a dispute relating to contractual performance', but 'have nothing to do with the place where a party is supposed to perform its obligations' (para. 379).

80. The majority award appears thus to suggest that the determinative factor is the place of performance. If this criterion is applied, there can be no doubt that the place of performance under the securities instruments at issue is invariably outside Argentina, given the use of fiscal agents, paying agents, depositories and places of payment all situated outside Argentina. Factors other than the place of performance also point to the location of the securities in question outside Argentina.

81. Among these other factors, I consider a clause selecting courts external to the host State, as a prominent one in determining where the security instruments, and the underlying right to repayment of the debt, are located [citing Bayview].

82. To answer the question whether the securities in question are located in Argentinean territory, this Tribunal needs to determine the *situs* of the debt—i.e. the alleged investment—using a systematic approach consistent with well-founded and established precedents and drawing on private international law rules. The foreign governing law and foreign forum, while not determinative by themselves, are important factors in determining *situs*. Other factors include the currency of payment, the place of payment and the residence of the intermediaries. On any of these criteria, the transactions at issue here were deliberately structured so as to have their *situs* outside Argentina.

83. b) The other argument by which the majority award tries to counter the obvious conclusion that the alleged investment is legally located outside Argentina, is that forum selection clauses (ignoring the other numerous connecting factors and criteria mentioned above) are contractual stipulations and as such they are irrelevant for locating the 'investment' for the purposes of a 'treaty claim', which is based on other rights and obligations derived from the BIT (para. 379).

84. But this facile escape route (*échappatoire*) is to no avail in the instant case. A treaty claim is necessarily based on a right that has been allegedly violated; here, the debt that was not repaid. If this right is created by contract, it is the contract that governs its legal existence and the modalities of this existence, including the location of this right (and its reciprocal obligation). And the right in the present case has been purposefully located outside Argentina.

85. The treaty claim cannot by-pass or circumvent this right, or change its modalities of existence, including its *situs* according to its legal title—the contract and the applicable law under which it exists—as this right, in its fixed legal configuration, serves as the legal basis underlying the treaty claim.

86. A treaty claim cannot allege a violation of a right, while ignoring the specific legal configuration of this right. The treaty may define the kinds of violation, but the underlying right subject to these violations, is defined only by its legal title, and the applicable law that governs its existence.

87. In conclusion, the alleged investment, i.e. the financial securities and their underlying debt, by all legally recognized connecting factors and criteria, have their *situs* outside Argentina; a treaty claim based on the nonpayment of this debt, or other violations of the right it represents, cannot change the legal configuration of

this right, including its *situs* outside Argentina. In consequence, the alleged investment does not constitute an 'investment in the territory of Argentina', and thus falls outside the ambit of jurisdiction of the Tribunal *ratione materiae*.

88. 2) *The material criteria for determining the situs of the 'investment'*: As was just explained, the majority award discards the contractual clauses and arrangements stipulated in the securities instruments as relevant factors for the location of the *situs* of the investment under the BIT and the ICSID Convention, whilst proposing other material or economic criteria. It is noteworthy in this respect that the section under which this question is addressed in the majority award is entitled 'Made in Argentina' (i.e. investment 'made in Argentina') and not 'Made in *the territory* of Argentina', following the language of article 1/1 of the BIT, an omission symptomatic of the result-oriented style of the whole award.

89. The majority award starts by an affirmation that 'the determination of the place of the investment . . . depends on the nature of such investment' (para. 374); to reach the conclusion that an 'investment of purely financial nature' need not be 'linked to a specific economic enterprise or operation taking place in the territory of the host State' (para. 375), basing itself on arguments it draws from a) Article 1/1/c of the BIT, and b) the nature of the investment. These arguments are examined in what follows.

90. a) Arguments drawn from article 1/1/c of the BIT: The majority award states that:

i.   Article 1/1/c 'designates financial instruments as an express kind of investment covered by the BIT', i.e. as a covered investment *per se*, or as such; in consequence,

ii.   'it would be contrary to the BIT's wording and aim to attach a further condition to the protection of financial investment instruments' (para. 375)

91. First of all, it is necessary to explain what the qualification '*per se*' (frequently used by the award) exactly means in this context. As was already explained [. . .], financial instruments, because of the intrinsic characteristics that appear to be incompatible with the type of investment envisaged in article 25 of the ICSID Convention, suffered from a kind of informal presumption that they are disqualified *per se* (or as such) from constituting a covered investment under the ICSID Convention [. . .]. But once a BIT includes these financial instruments in its enumeration of investments covered by the treaty, this presumption is obviously rebutted. However, if these financial instruments are not excluded *per se* (or automatically) that does not mean that they are included *per se*, in the sense of being automatically considered as legally self-sufficient to constitute a protected investment. We have here to recall the distinction (dating back to Roman law) between the *instrumentum* and the *negotium*, the instrument that registers and vehicles a legal act or transaction and the legal transaction itself. Article 1/1/c recognizes the financial securities *per se* as valid *instrumenta* for investment. But the investment

itself, as a legal act or transaction that is attested and vehicled by these instruments, has to satisfy the substantive requirements for investment, in article 25 of the ICSID Convention as well as in the BIT, if any.

92. Leaving aside the requirements of article 25 of the Convention discussed above [. . .], does the BIT impose any other substantive conditions? And is linking the investment 'to a specific economic enterprise or operation taking place in the territory of the host State' one of them? This distinction between the *instrumentum* and the *negotium* was clearly on the mind of the drafters of Article 1/1 of the BIT. Thus, in their enumeration, where they considered that confusion between the two may arise, they expressly made the distinction e.g., under (a) 'including, *to the extent they may be used as investments*, security interests on the property of third party; under (d) 'credits *directly related to an investment . . .*' (emphasis added).

93. Here, the majority award interjects its second argument drawn from article 1/1/c, namely that, given the designation, in this provision, of financial instruments as covered investments, 'it would be contrary to the BIT's wording and aim to attach a further condition to the protection of financial investment instruments' (para. 375).

94. This argument disregards a major fact. Of course, one cannot introduce a 'further condition' into the Treaty. However, two such conditions are already writ large therein. It is true that they do not figure in Article 1/1/c itself. But all one has to do is to raise his sight a few lines above this provision to the chapeau of Article 1/1, which applies to all the types and vehicles of investment enumerated under it, including (c), and which defines investment *inter alia* as that made by nationals 'of one Contracting Party *in the territory of the other [Party]*, in accordance with the laws and regulations of the latter' (emphasis added).

95. The ordinary meaning of the emphasized words could not be clearer. And how can the fact that the investment has been made or realized in the territory of the host country be proved or demonstrated, except by tracing it to a specific project, enterprise or activity in that territory that corresponds to the economic meaning of investment in article 25 of the ICSID Convention (i.e. that it contributes to the expansion of the country's productive capacity)?

96. b) Arguments drawn from the nature of the investment: Against this clear 'territorial imperative' of the Convention and the BIT, the majority award develops a second line of argument or defense, consisting of four mutually supporting affirmations, namely:

i. 'The determination of the place of investment depends . . . on the nature of such investment'; and for 'an investment of a purely financial nature, the relevant criteria cannot be the same as those applying to an investment consisting of business operations and/or involving manpower and property';

ii. For 'investments of a purely financial nature the relevant criteria should be where and/or for the benefit of whom the funds are ultimately used, and not the place where the funds were paid out or transferred';

iii. 'This is also the view taken by other arbitral tribunals';

iv. 'Thus, the relevant question is where the invested funds ultimately made available to the Host State [*sic*], and did they support the latter's economic development' (para. 374).

97. None of these affirmations withstands scrutiny.

i. There is absolutely no basis in the ICSID Convention for drawing such a distinction between 'investments of a purely financial nature' and other types of investment in this or other respects. Investment under ICSID is a unified category corresponding to the economic meaning of investment. The question that is raised about financial instruments under ICSID concern their high velocity of circulation which distends their link, as well as that of their last holders, with the ultimate economic enterprise or activity that materializes the investment in the economic, i.e. ICSID, sense of the term, within the territory of the host State. The question is not about the necessity of locating this enterprise or activity in the territory of the host State.

98. Indeed, the most persuasive legal justification for admitting financial instruments as protected investments, in spite of their stark contrast to the ideal type of investment under ICSID, the direct foreign investment [. . .], is that these investments finance, be it at several removes, specific economic projects, enterprises or activities which, had they been undertaken directly by these foreign financial investors, would have constituted foreign direct investment; which of course can only take place within the territory of the host State.

99. ii. The governing texts, particularly article 1/1 of the BIT, are clear as to the relevant criterion for locating the *situs* of the investment. It is 'where' the investment is made or realized, and not 'for the benefit of whom'.

100. It is ironic that the majority award cites the *SGS v. Republic of the Philippines* decision in support of its position; an award enunciating that: 'In accordance with normal principles of treaty interpretation, investments made outside the territory of the Respondent State, however beneficial to it, would not be covered by the BIT'; a dictum repudiating in no uncertain terms the criterion of 'for the benefit of whom' proffered by the majority award.

101. iii. Indeed, the cases cited by the majority award do not lend it as much support as it contends and are all quite distinguishable from the present case. The majority opinion cites three awards [footnote citing *Fedax, SGS v. Pakistan*[58] and *SGS v. Philippines*].[59] Only one of them involves financial instruments, namely *Fedax v.*

---

58 *SGS Société Générale de Surveillance SA v. Islamic Republic of Pakistan*, ICSID Case No. ARB/01/13, Decision of the Tribunal on Objections to Jurisdiction (Aug. 6, 2003).

59 *SGS Société Générale de Surveillance SA v. Republic of the Philippines*, ICSID Case No. ARB/02/6, Decision

Venezuela. And it is the only one of the three (as well, to my knowledge, of all other ICSID arbitral decisions) that carries a dictum suggesting the over-loose, ultimate beneficiary test which is followed by the majority award in the present case (but *Fedax* is distinguishable from the present case on facts as explained below).

102. The *Fedax* decision was widely criticized both by other tribunals and in the literature, including by Professor Dolzer, one of the leading legal experts of the Claimants in the present case, who commented in an article that 'the *Fedax* decision is not without ambiguity in its construction of "investment"; and in relation to the 'territorial dimension of foreign investments', that: 'the *Fedax* decision (paragraph 41) . . . assumed that the absence of a physical transfer of funds will not stand in the way of the existence of an 'investment'. Without explaining the rationale for this view in any detail, the *Fedax* tribunal considered apparently that it is sufficient that the funds made available by the investor are utilized by the host country as the beneficiary of the transaction so as to finance its various governmental needs'.[60]

103. Similarly, the *SGS v. The Republic of the Philippines* decision—that the majority award cites in support of its position! [A]part from its flat repudiation of the *Fedax* test in the dictum reproduced above [. . .] spared no effort to distance itself from that case, not only by distinguishing it, but also by pointing to certain factors that severely limit its general relevance (if any). Thus, after noting that '[t]he Tribunal in the *Fedax* case gave a very broad definition of territoriality', it observes in a footnote to that sentence that:

> 'The territorial requirement in the BIT [Venezuela–Netherlands] was . . . less categorical. It referred to the protection in its territory of investments of nationals of the other Contracting Part . . . and this only in a clause dealing with entry, not in a general clause defining the scope of the Treaty as a whole'.

104. Just after the general remark about the 'very broad definition of territoriality', the Tribunal proceeds to distinguish *Fedax*:

> 'but the focus of the decision was whether the endorsee of a promissory note issued with respect to an investment had itself made an investment, and whether the dispute over non-payment of the note arise 'directly' out of an investment within the meaning of Article 25(1) of the ICSID Convention'.

105. *Fedax* is an isolated case. It is an outlier. But I need not expand further on whether it was correctly decided or not, as it is clearly distinguishable in this respect (of territorial link) from the present case on facts; primarily by two

---

of the Tribunal on Objections to Jurisdiction (Jan. 29, 2004) at para. 99. Available at http://www.italaw.com/cases/documents/1019.

60 *SGS Société Générale de Surveillance SA v. Islamic Republic of Pakistan*, ICSID Case No. ARB/01/13, Decision of the Tribunal on Objections to Jurisdiction (Aug. 6, 2003). Available at: http://www.italaw.com/documents/SGSvPakistan-decision_000.pdf.

significant facts. The promissory notes at issue in *Fedax* were governed by the host State's law. They were not free-standing or unhinged from any specific project or economic activity in the host country, as they were initially given in exchange for the provision of specific services in Venezuela. The issue in that case was whether an endorsement of six promissory notes outside Venezuela severed their link with the underlying transaction, and not about the necessity of the existence of such underlying transaction.

106. The other two cases cited by the majority award, *SGS v. Pakistan* and *SGS v. the Republic of the Philippines*, have nothing to support the majority award's position, either in their reasoning and dicta or in their facts. Indeed, one can say the opposite as far as *SGS v. the Republic of the Philippines*, given its critical and distant position *vis à vis Fedax*, as exposed above. In both *SGS* cases the issue was whether services provided by SGS and attendant expenses largely undertaken outside the territory of the host State, could be considered as an investment 'in the territory' of the host State. And in both cases the Tribunals found that a reasonable part of the service and the expenses, though perhaps not the major part, took place in the territory of the host State; and that the service was not constituted of two operations: one outside and the other inside the territory of the host State, but one overall service straddling the frontier of that State, and as such well anchored in its territory.

107. In none of these cases, including *Fedax*, or others in which the question of territoriality was raised, was the need to trace the alleged investment to an underlying specific project or activity within the territory of the host State, questioned. The issue in all these cases was whether what takes place outside the territory of the host State, such as the payment of funds or the endorsement of the promissory notes, distends this link to the point of legally severing it.

108. The situation in the present case is totally different. The security entitlements in question are free-standing, and totally unhinged. They do not form part of an economic project, operation or activity in Argentina. Nor are they issued in support of a public project or a commercial undertaking there. In other words, they have no specific economic anchorage in Argentina, allowing them to be seen and considered as an investment 'in the territory of Argentina'.

109. The inescapable conclusion of this rapid survey of cases invoked by the majority award in support of its position, is that, unlike these cases, there is a missing link in the present case that prevents the alleged investment from being recognized as covered or protected investment under the BIT and article 25 of the Convention, namely the traceability of the alleged investment (or its link, be it tenuous) to an underlying specific economic project or operation taking place in the territory of Argentina.

110. iv. In order to surmount this tough obstacle, the majority award resorts to an astounding exercise of logical gymnastics, operating a double logical somersault

that ends up standing the sequence of legal reasoning on its head, by way of two unverifiable (and for one totally untenable) assumptions.

111. a) As concerns the first of these assumptions, the majority award asserts that: '*There is no doubt that the funds* generated through the bonds issuance process were *ultimately made available to Argentina* [and here comes the first logical jump dissimulated by the first assumption] and *served to finance Argentina's economic development*' (para. 378, emphasis added). Thus, according to the majority award, any loan or funds made available to a government (and regardless of the way it uses them, which is 'irrelevant') must be deemed, by virtue of an unrebuttable presumption, to be contributing to the development of the country of that government, and thus corresponding to the economic concept of investment of article 25 of the ICSID Convention (i.e. contributing to the expansion of the productive capacities of the country).

112. But this presumption is rebuttable on two grounds. First, not every loan can constitute an investment in the sense of the Convention. A simple loan in itself is merely an 'ordinary commercial transaction'. For it to become an investment, it has to fulfil the conditions discussed above. This is why, for example, in the enumeration of the various types of protected investment in article 1/1 of the BIT, under (d), 'credits', which are a species of loans, are qualified by the clause 'which are directly linked to an investment'.

113. The other ground on which this first presumption is rebuttable is the mere fact that not all funds made available to governments are necessarily used as 'investment' in projects or activities contributing to the expansion of the productive capacities of the country. Such funds can be used to finance wars, even wars of aggression, or oppressive measures against restive populations, or even be diverted through corruption to private ends. This is why, for such loans to constitute investments under the ICSID Convention, they have to be concretely traced, even at several removes, to a particular productive project or activity in the territory of the host country; and not merely by postulating a stop-gap abstract assumption that does not hold its ground.

114. b) The second assumption is even more remarkable than the first, and totally dependent on it. In fact, it is undetachable from it; thus one has to formulate them together, in something like the following: Because the funds were made available to Argentina and used by it (whatever the use which is 'irrelevant' and which is not traceable or proven, but assumed), these funds 'as such, must be considered to have contributed to Argentina's economic development [first assumption] *and thus* [and here comes the second assumption dissimulating the second logical jump] to have been made in Argentina' (para. 378, emphasis added). Put in straight forward language, without the ellipsis, the proposition would be: As the funds made available to Argentina *must be considered* (i.e. assumed) to have contributed to Argentina's economic development, they also, and as a necessary consequence, *must be considered* (or assumed) to have been made in Argentina.

115. Thus, by assuming a contribution to the economic development of Argentina, one necessarily assumes also its location in Argentina, without having to demonstrate or prove either. The falsity of such reasoning is too evident to need further elaboration.

116. Moreover, the presumed logical necessity of drawing or deducing the second presumption from the first is also false. It suffices to recall in this regard the dictum of *SGS v. the Republic of the Philippines* that 'investment made outside the territory of the Respondent State, however beneficial to it, would not be covered by the BIT', and the example it gives of 'the construction of an embassy in a third State or the provision of security services to such an embassy' which 'would not involve investments in the territory of the State whose embassy it was, and would not be protected by the BIT'.

117. Here again, the logical legal sequence is stood on its head. Rather than demonstrating the contribution by tracing the alleged investment to (or proving its link with) a productive project or activity in the territory of the host State, the majority award deduces a *situs* from a presumed contribution hanging in the air.

118. *In conclusion*, the present case is, to my knowledge, the first one to come before an ICSID tribunal in which the alleged investment is totally free-standing and unhinged, without any anchorage, however remote, into an underlying economic project, enterprise or activity in the territory of the host State. None of the logical short-cuts put forward by the majority award to palliate this absence, holds water.

119. As both the ICSID Convention and the BIT require that the investment be made in the territory of the host State for the investment to be covered by the treaty and fall within the jurisdictional ambit of ICSID, and as this territorial link is lacking in the present case, I conclude that in the absence of a 'protected investment', the case has to be dismissed, as falling outside the jurisdiction *ratione materiae* of the Tribunal.

? DISCUSSION NOTES

1 If an alleged investor is not present in the host state, but has contractual rights that the host infringes, can it be said there was an investment 'in the territory' of the host? The tribunal in *Nova Scotia Power v. Venezuela* commented: 'A contractual right by its very nature has no fixed abode in the physical sense, for it is intangible. However, a lack of physical presence is not *per se* fatal to meeting the territoriality requirement'.[61] What do you think of this assessment?

2 How should tribunals treat a claim of an investment when the investor

---

61 Rudolf Dolzer, 'The Notion of Investment in Recent Practice', in Charnovitz et al. eds., *Law in the Service of Human Dignity: Essays in Honour of Florentino Feliciano* (CUP, 2005), at pp. 261, 269, 272.

> has developed products in the home country with the intent to distribute them in the host once they exist, but is prevented from distributing them by the host's refusal to authorize their sale?[62]

b   Was the investment legal?

The legality of an investment can become an issue in one of two ways. The first is through terms limiting the scope of a BIT to investments 'made in accordance with [the host's] laws and regulations'.[63] A second method by which the legality of an investment can limit the protection offered is by limiting the term 'investment' itself. While the ICSID definition of investment contains no explicit language in this respect,[64] many IIAs do. The India/Morocco BIT, for example, specifies:

> The term 'investments' shall mean any kind of asset invested by investors on one Contracting Party in the territory of the other Contracting Party, in conformity with the laws and regulations of the latter.[65]

While either phrase could be interpreted to relate to the processes for admitting the investment as well as to the investment's compliance with the laws of the host during its operations, investment tribunals are hesitant to deny jurisdiction to investments that were made legally. This is true even where they were later operated illegally. The impact of the illegality, say these arbitrators, is an issue that can be examined in the merits phase. Other tribunals, however, consider that international public policy dictates that investments tainted with illegality should not be able to avail themselves of treaty protections.

The main question facing tribunals is therefore which violations of national laws should affect whether the economic activities of the claimant are protected.

---

62 *SGS v. Philippines, supra* note 59.

63 *See,* e.g. Agreement between the Swiss Confederation and the Republic of India for the Promotion and Protection of Investments of 4 April 1997, art. 2 (entered into force on Feb. 16, 2000).

64 Not all tribunals agree that illegality should be determinative of the characterization of an activity as an investment for purposes of ICSID. *See Saba Fakes v. Turkey, supra* note 44, para. 112 ('[L]egality cannot be incorporated into the definition of Article 25(1) of the ICSID Convention without doing violence to the language of the ICSID Convention: an investment might be "legal" or "illegal," made in "good faith" or not, it nonetheless remains an investment. The expressions "legal investment" or "investment made in good faith" are not pleonasms, and the expressions "illegal investment" or "investment made in bad faith" are not oxymorons').

65 Agreement between the Government of the Republic of India and the Government of the Kingdom of Morocco for the Promotion and Protection of Investments of 13 February 1999, art. 1(1) (entered into force on Feb. 22, 2001).

CASE

Gustav F W Hamester GmbH and Co KG v. Republic of Ghana[66]

Mr Hamester is a German businessman who contracted with the Ghanaian government to modernize a cocoa processing plant. The joint venture ended with Hamester's withdrawal from the indebted company and Hamester's allegations of government violations of his investment through the actions of the state-owned cocoa supplier in relation to the plant. Ghana rejected this version of the facts, claiming that illegality had tainted the entire investment relationship.

c. the tribunal's position on the first jurisdictional objection: fraud
123. The Tribunal considers, as was stated for example in *Phoenix v. Czech Republic*, that:

'States cannot be deemed to offer access to the ICSID dispute settlement mechanism to investments not made in good faith'.

An investment will not be protected if it has been created in violation of national or international principles of good faith; by way of corruption, fraud, or deceitful conduct; or if its creation itself constitutes a misuse of the system of international investment protection under the ICSID Convention. It will also not be protected if it is made in violation of the host State's law (as elaborated, *e.g.* by the tribunal in *Phoenix*).

124. These are general principles that exist independently of specific language to this effect in the Treaty.

125. In addition, however, it is clear that States may specifically and expressly condition access of investors to a chosen dispute settlement mechanism, or the availability of substantive protection. One such common condition is an express requirement that the investment comply with the internal legislation of the host State. This condition will typically appear in the BIT where this is the instrument that contains the State's consent to ICSID arbitration. The precise effect of any such express condition will obviously depend upon the wording used.

126. In this case, Article 10 of the BIT contains an express requirement for compliance with the host State's legislation. It states that:

---

66 *Gustav F W Hamester GmbH and Co KG v. Republic of Ghana*, ICSID Case No. ARB/07/24, Award (June 18, 2010). Available at: http://italaw.com/documents/Hamesterv.GhanaAward.pdf; footnotes omitted.

'[t]his Treaty shall also apply to investments made prior to [the Treaty's] entry into force by nationals or companies of either Contracting Party in the territory of the other Contracting Party consistent with the latter's legislation'. (Emphasis added)

127. The Tribunal considers that a distinction has to be drawn between (1) legality as at the *initiation* of the investment ('made') and (2) legality *during the performance* of the investment. Article 10 legislates for the scope of application of the BIT, but conditions this only by reference to legality at the initiation of the investment. Hence, only this issue bears upon this Tribunal's jurisdiction. Legality in the subsequent life or performance of the investment is not addressed in Article 10. It follows that this does not bear upon the scope of application of the BIT (and hence this Tribunal's jurisdiction)—albeit that it may well be relevant in the context of the substantive merits of a claim brought under the BIT. Thus, on the wording of this BIT, the legality of the creation of the investment is a jurisdictional issue; the legality of the investor's conduct during the life of the investment is a merits issue. In the Tribunal's view, the broader principle of international law identified in paragraphs 123–4 above does not change this analysis of Article 10, and in particular its distinction between legality at different stages of the investment.

128. It may be noted that the award in *Fraport v. Philippines* was particularly clear on this distinction. Although the question was not raised by the facts of that case, the respondent State had contended that in principle 'an investment, in order to maintain jurisdictional standing under the BIT, must not only be 'in accordance' with relevant domestic law at the time of commencement of the investment but must continuously remain in compliance with domestic law, such that a departure from some laws or regulations in the course of the operation of the BIT would deprive a tribunal under the BIT of jurisdiction.' The tribunal considered it appropriate to clarify this point of law, and presented the following analysis, with which this Tribunal is in full agreement:

> 'Although this contention is not relevant to the analysis of the problem which the Tribunal has before it, namely the *entry* of the investment and not the way it was subsequently conducted, the Tribunal would note that this part of the Respondent's interpretation appears to be a forced construction of the pertinent provisions in the context of the entire Treaty . . . the effective operation of the BIT regime would appear to require that jurisdictional compliance be limited to the initiation of the investment. If, at the time of the initiation of the investment, there has been compliance with the law of the host state, allegations by the host state of violations of its law in the course of the investment, as a justification for state action with respect to the investment, might be a defense to claimed *substantive* violations of the BIT, but could not deprive a tribunal acting under the authority of the BIT of its jurisdiction.'
> (*Emphasis in the original*)

129. Therefore, in this first step of the analysis of the case relating to jurisdiction, the Tribunal is only concerned with allegations of fraud in the initiation of the investment, and not with the multiple allegations of fraudulent conduct during the life of the investment: violations of the fiduciary duties owed to its partner in a joint-venture; violations of the Ghanaian criminal law and so on, allegedly committed by the Claimant in the performance of the JVA, during the years of its existence. In order to ascertain jurisdiction, the only question here is whether Hamester perpetrated a fraud, and thereby procured the signing of the JVA (as was the case, for example, in *Inceysa v. El Salvador*, where the contract was procured through fraudulent misrepresentation). *If the JVA was obtained on the basis of fraud*, it is an illegal investment that does not benefit from the protection of the ICSID/BIT mechanism. However, the question whether fraudulent behaviour has been committed *during the performance of the joint-venture* is a different issue that has to be taken into account when judging the merits of the dispute.

130. The main contention of the Respondent concerning the illegality of the initial investment is that:

[. . .]

'The very core of Hamester's so-called investment activities in Ghana—[. . .] was [. . .] from the outset planned and executed fraudulently. That is fatal to Hamester's case in this arbitration, since investments not made in accordance with Ghanaian law fall outside the GGBIT by virtue of Article 10. Fraudulent investments are in any event repugnant to the fundamental principle of good faith under international law.'

131. The Tribunal must thus examine whether the investment was illegal from its very inception, because of the foreign investor's alleged fraudulent behaviour in manipulating the invoices for the machinery to be transferred to Wamco under the JVA.

[. . .]

136. Absent further information as to the Claimant's alleged behaviour [. . .] there is insufficient basis for the Tribunal to conclude that there was an overall scheme of deceit orchestrated by the Claimant in the initiation of its investment.

137. In any event, and more importantly, even if the alleged scheme to inflate invoices was fully proven—with details in respect of invoices for all deliveries of machinery or services—the Tribunal would still not be prepared to analyse these practices as amounting to a fraud such as to deprive the Tribunal of its jurisdiction in the present case. According to the Respondent, this would make 'the present case indistinguishable from *Inceysa v. El Salvador*', where the Tribunal declined jurisdiction because the contractor had caused the Government of El Salvador to award it a contract by misrepresenting its finances and qualifications. The Tribunal does not agree. As noted above, it was not established by the Respondent that Cocobod would not have entered into the JVA if it had known that Hamester was making a pre-profit on its contribution. The Tribunal accepts the Claimant's statement that:

> '(t)here is not a single witness from Ghana attesting to the alleged fraudulent action having induced the JVA as was the case with the misrepresentations in the *Inceysa* and *Klockner* cases.'
>
> 138. Hamester's practices might not be in line with what could be called '*l'éthique des affaires*', but, in the Tribunal's view, they did not amount, in the circumstances of the case, to a fraud that would affect the Tribunal's jurisdiction. The Tribunal sees the over-statement of invoices as an issue bearing upon the balance of equities between the two parties, rather than the existence itself of the contract or the investment. Such elements would have been taken into consideration by the Tribunal when discussing the merits, if it had found that any compensation was due to Hamester.
>
> 139. In conclusion, the Tribunal does not consider that the dispute concerning Hamester's investment in Ghana is outside its jurisdiction because the initial investment was fraudulent, as argued by the Respondent.

Even if the illegality of the activity was clearly one that impacted upon the establishment of the activity, there is a question of what to do with investments that are 'slightly illegal'.

 CASE

Mr. Saba Fakes v. Republic of Turkey[67]

Claimant Fakes became the majority owner of Telsim, a large mobile telecommunications provider in Turkey, on 3 July 2003. According to Fakes, the government of Turkey expropriated his investment in Telsim when the authorities arrested his shares of Telsim in that same month and later sold some of the company's assets. The government of Turkey defended its actions as a partial response to the criminal activities of the Uzan family, the previous owners of Telsim and a multitude of other enterprises. Given findings of fraud against the Uzans, the government argued that Fakes could hold no protected 'investment' for purposes of the BIT protections.

> 115. Article 2(2) of the Netherlands–Turkey BIT provides that: '[t]he present Agreement shall apply to investments owned or controlled by investors of one Contracting Party in the territory of the other Contracting Party which are established in accordance with the laws and regulations in force in the latter Contracting Party's territory at the time the investment was made'. This provision plainly states that the BIT protection shall not apply to investments which have not been established in conformity with the Respondent's laws and regulations, the term

---

67 *Saba Fakes v. Turkey, supra* note 44.

'investment' having been defined in Article 1(b) of the BIT. If this condition is not satisfied, the BIT does not apply. [. . .]

116. That said, the Tribunal must interpret the exact scope of the legality requirement of Article 2(2) of the Netherlands-Turkey BIT. The Parties are in disagreement as to whether all or only certain laws and regulations are covered by this provision, and whether there exists a threshold below which a violation would not be considered as relevant for the purposes of the BIT's application.

117. As a general proposition, the Respondent submits that if an investment is made in breach of any of the host State's laws in any way, such breach would 'taint' the investment and deprive it of the protection under the BIT and the ICSID Convention. According to this proposition, a violation of any law or regulation should trigger the application of the legality provision, depriving an investment of the protection offered by the BIT.

118. The Claimant disagrees with the Respondent's interpretation of Article 2(2) of the Netherlands–Turkey BIT and submits that a 'certain level of violation' is required to trigger this provision. According to the Claimant, an investment should be considered 'illegal' only if made in violation of a fundamental legal principle.

119. The Tribunal is not convinced by the Respondent's position that any violation of any of the host State's laws would result in the illegality of the investment within the meaning of the BIT and preclude such investment from benefiting from the substantive protection offered by the BIT. As to the nature of the rules contemplated in Article 2(2) of the Netherlands–Turkey BIT, it is the Tribunal's view that the legality requirement contained therein concerns the question of the compliance with the host State's domestic laws governing the admission of investments in the host State. This is made clear by the plain language of the BIT, which applies to 'investments . . . established in accordance with the laws and regulations . . .'.

The Tribunal also considers that it would run counter to the object and purpose of investment protection treaties to deny substantive protection to those investments that would violate domestic laws that are unrelated to the very nature of investment regulation. In the event that an investor breaches a requirement of domestic law, a host State can take appropriate action against such investor within the framework of its domestic legislation. However, unless specifically stated in the investment treaty under consideration, a host State should not be in a position to rely on its domestic legislation beyond the sphere of investment regime to escape its international undertakings vis-à-vis investments made in its territory.

Where legality is regarded as an issue of jurisdiction, a finding of illegality is determinative. It is not waivable by the respondent. Nor is it, according to the following tribunal, a limit that can be excused by the claimant's ignorance of the illegality.

CASE

Alasdair Ross Anderson et al. v. the Republic of Costa Rica[68]

Costa Rican brothers Luis Enrique and Osvaldo Villalobos Camacho owned and operated a currency exchange licensed by and under the supervision of the Costa Rican central bank. Prior to 1996, the brothers began an additional business of taking deposits of individual investors and paying very high returns (36–40 per cent per year). By making a cash or cheque deposit with Enrique personally, the depositor received a non-cashable cheque allowing for him/her to make monthly withdrawals of interest, but limited withdrawals of several months' worth of interest as well as of principal. In return for the deposit, depositors received non-cashable cheques.

In 2002, Canadian Justice Department made a request for an investigation of Villalobos' activities, which they suspected were being used by a Canadian criminal organization for money laundering. One month later, Costa Rican officials raided the offices and closed down the Mall location. Consequently, a new office was opened in the same mall.

Costa Rican investigation led to charges of a fraudulent financial scheme, a 'Ponzi scheme', where no real investments were being made; rather interest was paid through new deposits.

In 2004 several clients submitted a request for arbitration to the International Centre for the Settlement of Investment Disputes against Costa Rica for 'actions or omissions of the government' to protect their investment. The respondent objected to the tribunal's jurisdiction, alleging that there were no 'investments'.

> 46. Article I(g) of the Canada-Costa Rica BIT states: '"investment" means any kind of asset owned or controlled either directly, or indirectly through an enterprise or natural person of a third State, by an investor of one Contracting Party in the territory of the other Contracting Party in accordance with the latter's laws . . .'.
> [. . .]
> 47. [. . .] Thus, in order to find that the Claimants' deposits and resulting relationships with the Villalobos brothers constituted an investment, the Tribunal at the

---

68 *Alasdair Ross Anderson et al. v. the Republic of Costa Rica*, ICSID Case No. ARB(AF)/07/3, Award (May 19, 2010). Available at: http://italaw.com/documents/AndersonvCostaRicaAward19May2010.pdf; footnotes omitted.

outset must answer two basic questions in the affirmative: A) Did the Claimants' deposits and resulting legal relationships with one or both of the Villalobos brothers constitute 'assets' within the meaning of the BIT?; and B) If so, did the Claimants own or control those assets 'in accordance with the laws of...' Costa Rica?

[...]

51. Under the BIT, not only must the Claimants demonstrate that they own the assets which they assert constitutes an investment, but they must also demonstrate that they own or control those assets in accordance with the laws of Costa Rica.

[...]

52. In interpreting the phrases 'owned or controlled' and 'in accordance with the [...] laws [...],' it should first be emphasized that the BIT states this requirement in objective and categorical terms. Each Claimant must meet this requirement, regardless of his or her knowledge of the law or his or her intention to follow the law. Thus, the Claimants' statements that they intended to follow the law or that they did not know the law are irrelevant to a determination of whether they actually owned or controlled their investments in accordance with the laws of Costa Rica.

53. Not all BITs contain a requirement that investments subject to treaty protection be 'made' or 'owned' in accordance with the law of the host country. The fact that the Contracting Parties to the Canada–Costa Rica BIT specifically included such a provision is a clear indication of the importance that they attached to the legality of investments made by investors of the other Party and their intention that their laws with respect to investments be strictly followed. The assurance of legality with respect to investment has important, indeed crucial, consequences for the public welfare and economic well-being of any country.

54. In order to prevent economic hardship to individual citizens and reduce the risk of financial crises, governments ordinarily seek to protect the savings of the public from fraud and other harms that can do significant injury not only to individuals but to the economy as a whole. They therefore seek to achieve this objective by regulating the actions of individuals and companies who would raise capital from the public or otherwise seek to serve as financial intermediaries. One means employed by Costa Rica to protect the public savings is the Organic Law of the Central Bank of Costa Rica, one of whose objectives, according to Article 2(d), is 'to promote a stable, efficient, and competitive system of financial intermediation'. Toward this end, Article 116 of the Law provides that the only entities that may engage in financial intermediation in the country are those that are expressly authorized to do so by law. Furthermore, Article 157 makes it a crime to engage in financial intermediation without authorization.

55. By actively seeking and accepting deposits from the Claimants and several thousand other persons, the Villalobos brothers were engaged in financial intermediation without authorization by the Central Bank or any other government

body as required by law. The courts of Costa Rica after a lengthy and extensive legal process determined that Osvaldo Villalobos, because of his involvement in the scheme, committed aggravated fraud and illegal financial intermediation. In securing investments from the Claimants, the Villalobos brothers were thus clearly not acting in accordance with the laws of Costa Rica. The entire transaction between the Villalobos brothers and each Claimant was illegal because it violated the Organic Law of the Central Bank. If the transaction by which the Villalobos acquired the deposit was illegal, it follows that the acquisition by each Claimant of the asset resulting from that transaction was also not in accordance with the law of Costa Rica. Although the Claimants may not have committed a crime by entering into a transaction with the Villalobos, the fact that they gained ownership of the asset in violation of the Organic Law of the Central Bank means that their owner- ship was not in accordance with the laws of Costa Rica and that therefore each of their deposits and resulting relationships with Villalobos did not constitute an 'investment' under the BIT.

[. . .]

58. The Tribunal's interpretation of the words 'owned in accordance with the laws' of Costa Rica reflects both sound public policy and sound investment practice. Costa Rica, indeed any country, has a fundamental interest in securing respect for its law. . . . At the same time, prudent investment practice requires that any investor exercise due diligence before committing funds to any particular investment pro- posal. An important element of such due diligence is for investors to assure them- selves that their investments comply with the law. Such due diligence obligation is neither overly onerous nor unreasonable. Based on the evidence presented to the Tribunal, it is clear that the Claimants did not exercise the kind of due diligence that reasonable investors would have undertaken to assure themselves that their deposits with the Villalobos scheme were in accordance with the laws of Costa Rica.

DISCUSSION NOTES

1   The questions surrounding what tribunals should do when investments are revealed to have been entered into based on illegal actions of either the claimant or the respondent are gaining in significance. Should a contract gained by bribing government officials be protected if the host (often a new administration) refuses to honour its obligations under that contract? What role should the norm of unjust enrichment play in a tribunal's consideration of whether to afford the claimant compen- sation for an illegally entered relationship? Should the legal analysis depend on whether the bribe was solicited or offered? For more on this, see Ursula Kriebaum, *Illegal Investments, in* Austrian Yearbook

on International Arbitration 307, 307–35 (2010); Hilmar Raeschke-Kessler and Dorothee Gottwald, *Corruption, in* The Oxford Handbook of International Investment Law 584, 584–616 (Peter Muchlinski, Federico Ortino, and Christoph Schreuer eds., 2008).

2 What should a tribunal do if an activity is not illegal, but also not undertaken in a legally recognized form of business? In *Grand River Enterprises*, an UNCITRAL tribunal had to interpret NAFTA's requirements for an 'investment'. Under NAFTA Article 1139, an investment includes an interest in 'an enterprise' undertaking economic activities. NAFTA Article 201 defines 'enterprise' to be 'any entity constituted or organized under applicable law, whether or not for profit, and whether privately-owned or governmentally-owned, including any corporation, trust, partnership, sole proprietorship, joint venture or other association [. . .]'.

The claimants in *Grand River* were engaged in cigarette sales with First Nation tribes. Rather than establishing companies to market their cigarettes, however, they claimed to have used 'cooperative efforts' in an 'undocumented manner customary among indigenous peoples' (para. 91). The tribunal found such informal customs insufficient to fulfil the 'enterprise' requirement for the definition of 'investment' in NAFTA Article 1139. 'These Articles', it reasoned, 'refer to some form of business association with its own juridical personality constituted or organized under applicable law, rather than mere mutually beneficial business, contractual, or culturally-rooted relations' (para. 92).

When the claimants asserted that their activities were legal under the laws of the relevant First Nation peoples, the tribunal clarified its position:

> The Tribunal is respectful of the cultural patterns that inform business relations among First Nations peoples, to which the Claimants repeatedly referred in their written submissions and during the hearing. It is likewise respectful of Seneca law and custom, and does not question that the written or unwritten customary laws of indigenous peoples could be the basis for establishing an enterprise for the purposes of NAFTA. But there is nothing to show that the culturally-based or other business understandings that the Claimants describe are sufficient under Seneca law and thereby under NAFTA.[69]

---

69 *Grand River Enterprises Six Nations, Ltd., et al. v. United States of America*, UNCITRAL (NAFTA), Award, para. 103 (Jan. 12, 2011). Available at: http://www.state.gov/documents/organization/156820.pdf.

3.3 Who is 'an investor' in international investment law?

An 'investor' is a person who has made an investment. Having determined the existence of an investment, however, is only the first step in determining the availability of arbitration-based enforcement of the investor's rights to protection. The investor must fulfil certain conditions as well.

3.3.1 Types of investors

a Under the IIA

Most IIAs will have a definition of 'investor' to which the treaty protections apply. The definition will generally include both natural persons and legal persons and other entities (such as companies or formal organizations which may not be incorporated). The India–Greece BIT is typical:

> 'Investor' means with regard to either Contracting Party:
>
> (a) natural persons having the nationality of that Contracting Party in accordance with its law;
> (b) legal persons or other entities, including companies, corporations, business associations and partnerships, which are constituted or otherwise duly organised under the laws of that Contracting Party and have their substantive business activities in the territory of that same Contracting Party.[70]

b Under the ICSID

The ICSID Convention does not use the term 'investor'. Instead, Article 25 (which sets out the relevant rules on who may invoke the Convention rules) refers to persons who are *nationals* of the home state:

> (1) The jurisdiction of the Centre shall extend to any legal dispute arising directly out of an investment, between a Contracting State [. . .] and a national of another Contracting State [. . .].
> (2) 'National of another Contracting State' means:
>
>> (a) any natural person who had the nationality of a Contracting State other than the State party to the dispute on the date on which the parties consented to submit such dispute to conciliation or arbitration

---

70 Agreement Between the Government of the Hellenic Republic and The Government of the Republic of India on the Promotion and Reciprocal Protection of Investments, Article 1(3) (effective as of 10 April 2008).

as well as on the date on which the request was registered . . ., but does not include any person who on either date also had the nationality of the Contracting State party to the dispute; and

(b) any juridical person which had the nationality of a Contracting State other than the State party to the dispute on the date on which the parties consented to submit such dispute to conciliation or arbitration and any juridical person which had the nationality of the Contracting State party to the dispute on that date and which, because of foreign control, the parties have agreed should be treated as a national of another Contracting State for the purposes of this Convention.

Thus, under ICSID, an investor can be either a natural person or a legal person, just as in most IIAs. As a result, the legal discussions surrounding who is an 'investor' are not the ones regarding how the IIA and the ICSID Convention relate to each other as it so often is with those of 'investment'. Still, there is no lack of questions that can arise. A particularly prominent one in arbitration is whether the investor had the requisite nationality to bring a claim. In the following, each of the two types of investors will be considered in relation to the issue of nationality.

c   *Nationality of investors*

In order to be able to call upon the protection of international investment law, the investor must demonstrate that (s)he/it is a *foreign* investor. That means that the individual has the nationality of the home state on the date(s) relevant to the dispute procedures.[71] For ICSID arbitration, the investor must also demonstrate that (s)he/it did not have the nationality of the host state. These 'positive and negative nationality requirements' are cumulative, so the lack of either can lead to a failure of the claim.

In non-ICSID arbitration, only the IIA rules will apply. That means that often there are no negative nationality requirements. The positive requirements remain the same, as they are regulated by the IIA itself.

---

71 The relevant dates for purposes of ICSID jurisdiction are set forth in Article 25(2) as 'the date on which the parties consented to submit such dispute to . . . arbitration as well as on the date on which the request was registered'. For a critical comment on the choice of these dates, *see Waguih Elie George Siag and Clorinda Vecchi v. Arab Republic of Egypt*, ICSID Case No. ARB/05/15, Decision on Jurisdiction and Partial Dissenting Opinion, at 63–5 (Apr. 11, 2007) (Partial Dissent in Opinion of Professor Francisco Orrego Vicuña). Available at: http://italaw.com/sites/default/files/case-documents/ita0785.pdf.

c.i Nationality of individuals

Determining the nationality of individuals for the purpose of investment protection is not always a simple matter. For one thing, nationality *is not* the same as *residency*—foreign nationals living in the host state may still be 'investors', even if they enjoy the status of permanent resident.[72] Another complication in nationality is that nationality depends on the national laws of the country whose nationality is claimed. Given the variety of bases of nationality, determining the applicable rules in a particular case can be difficult. Finally, the relationship between the concept of 'citizenship' and that of 'nationality' is not always clear. Investors, moreover, may have a particular interest in acquiring multiple nationalities. The following cases demonstrate some of the complexities of determining the nationality of an investor.

 CASE

Hussein Nuaman Soufraki v. United Arab Emirates[73]

Mr Soufraki was born in Italian-ruled Libya to Italian parents. His Italian nationality continued until 1991, when he moved to Canada and acquired Canadian citizenship.

An active businessman, Soufraki signed a 30-year concession agreement with Dubai to develop, manage, and operate a port in Dubai. Having signed the agreement as a Canadian citizen, Soufraki claimed Italian nationality when he began ICSID proceedings against Dubai for allegedly failing to comply with the concession agreement based on the Italy–UAE BIT.

Some facts facing the tribunal were clear: under Italian nationality law, the acceptance of a second citizenship automatically extinguishes Italian citizenship. Thus, Soufraki lost his Italian citizenship in 1991. The question was whether he regained it subsequently. While much of the tribunal's discussion was based on applying the facts of the case to the law, the arbitrators also set out the legal tenets of their decision clearly.

47. The Tribunal must decide:

72 *Marvin Feldman v. Mexico, NAFTA Arbitration*, ICSID Case No. ARB(AF)/99/1, Award (Dec. 16, 2002). Available at: http://italaw.com/sites/de fault/files/case-documents/ita0319.pdf.
73 *Hussein Nuaman Soufraki v. United Arab Emirates*, ICSID Case No. ARB/02/7, Award (July 7, 2004). Available at: http://italaw.com/sites/default/files/case-documents/ita0799.pdf; footnotes omitted.

[. . .]

(3) whether Claimant reacquired automatically his Italian nationality according to Italian law after 1992;

(4) whether questions of Italian nationality are within the exclusive and dispositive competence of Italy or whether the Tribunal is entitled to look behind the passports, identity cards, certificates and assurances issued by Italian authorities certifying the Italian nationality of Mr. Soufraki.

[. . .]

53. The first contentious question to be decided is whether, as Claimant maintains, the Certificates of Nationality issued by Italian authorities characterizing Mr. Soufraki as an Italian national, and his Italian passports, identity cards and the letter of the Italian Ministry of Foreign Affairs so stating, constitute conclusive proof that Mr. Soufraki reacquired his Italian nationality after 1992 and that he was an Italian national on the date on which the parties to this dispute consented to submit it to arbitration as well as on the date on which the request to ICSID was registered by it.

54. Claimant contends that it is for the Italian authorities to interpret Italian nationality law, and that this Tribunal should apply their conclusions. He emphasizes that Article 1(3) of the BIT specifies that the nationality of a natural person shall be determined according to the law of the Contracting State in question.

55. It is accepted in international law that nationality is within the domestic jurisdiction of the State, which settles, by its own legislation, the rules relating to the acquisition (and loss) of its nationality. Article 1(3) of the BIT reflects this rule. But it is no less accepted that when, in international arbitral or judicial proceedings, the nationality of a person is challenged, the international tribunal is competent to pass upon that challenge. It will accord great weight to the nationality law of the State in question and to the interpretation and application of that law by its authorities. But it will in the end decide for itself whether, on the facts and law before it, the person whose nationality is at issue was or was not a national of the State in question and when, and what follows from that finding. Where, as in the instant case, the jurisdiction of an international tribunal turns on an issue of nationality, the international tribunal is empowered, indeed bound, to decide that issue.

56. While the Claimant does not dispute the foregoing authority of this Tribunal, it submits that it should exercise it so as to override official Italian affirmations of the Italian nationality of Mr. Soufraki only in response to allegations and proof of fraud.

57. While the Respondent did not in terms maintain that evidence in support of Mr. Soufraki's acquisition or reacquisition of Italian nationality was fraudulent, counsel of the Respondent when cross-examining Mr. Soufraki did characterize the evidence that he submitted in support of his claim that he was resident in Italy for more than a year 1993–94 as 'bogus'. Nevertheless, the Tribunal wishes to make clear that, in its view, issues of alleged fraud need not be addressed.

58. The question rather comes to this. Mr. Soufraki asserts as a fact that he was resident in Italy for business purposes for more than one year in 1993–94. In accordance with accepted international (and general national) practice, a party bears the burden of proof in establishing the facts that he asserts. Claimant accordingly bears the burden of proving to the satisfaction of the Tribunal that he was resident in Italy for more than one year in 1993–94 and accordingly that he was an Italian national on the relevant dates and that, as a result, he belongs to the class of investors in respect of whom the Respondent has consented to ICSID jurisdiction.

59. The Tribunal agrees with Claimant that, as an international Tribunal, it is not bound by rules of evidence in Italian civil procedure.

60. The 'substantial' evidence rule, while it may well be required in an Italian court, has no application in the present proceedings.

61. What weight is given to oral or documentary evidence in an ICSID arbitration is dictated solely by Rule 34(1) of the ICSID Arbitration Rules . . . .

62. In the present instance, it is thus for this Tribunal to consider and analyse the totality of the evidence and determine whether it leads to the conclusion that Claimant has discharged his burden of proof.

63. The Tribunal will, of course, accept Claimant's Certificates of Nationality as 'prima facie' evidence. We agree with Professor Schreuer that:

> . . . A certificate of nationality will be treated as part of the 'documents or other evidence' to be examined by the tribunal in accordance with Art. 43 [of the Convention]. Such a certificate will be given its appropriate weight but does not preclude a decision at variance with its contents.

64. It is common ground between the Parties that, if Claimant reacquired his Italian citizenship after 1992, it is as a result of having established his residence in Italy for one year after that date.

65. Consequently, it is evident that Mr. Soufraki's Certificate of Nationality issued in 1988 cannot inform the Tribunal's decision.

[. . .]

69. The Tribunal must now examine the other evidence in the record which, Claimant maintains, demonstrates that Mr. Soufraki resided in Italy for one year after the enactment of Italian Law No. 91.

70. The concept of 'residence' as used in Article 13(1)(d) of Italian Law No. 91 is factual. It is different from the concept of 'legal residence'.

71. Consequently, actual residence for one year is a sufficient requisite for the reacquisition of Italian citizenship.

72. Residence does not imply continuous presence and does not disallow travel. However, the Tribunal agrees with Respondent that proof of some continuity of residence during that year is required.

73. The Tribunal will consider whether the evidence discloses that Mr. Soufraki,

during the relevant period, had his 'habitual abode' in Italy and that he manifested his 'intention to fix in Italy the center of [his] own business and affairs'.

[...]

81. Having considered and weighed the totality of the evidence adduced by Mr. Soufraki, the Tribunal, unanimously, comes to the conclusion that Claimant has failed to discharge his burden of proof. He has not demonstrated to the satisfaction of the Tribunal that he established and maintained his residence in Italy during the period from March 1993 until April 1994.

82. In the circumstances, Claimant cannot rely today on Article 13(1)(d) of Italian law No. 91 of 1992.

83. The Tribunal recognizes that it is difficult for Mr. Soufraki, whose business interests span continents and who constantly travels the world, to reconstruct his actual residence during a twelve or thirteen-month period more than ten years earlier. It recognizes that Mr. Soufraki, had he been properly advised at the time, easily could have reacquired Italian nationality by a timely application. It further appreciates that, had Mr. Soufraki contracted with the United Arab Emirates through a corporate vehicle incorporated in Italy, rather than contracting in his personal capacity, no problem of jurisdiction would now arise. But the Tribunal can only take the facts as they are and as it has found them to be.

84. Since, as found by the Tribunal, Claimant was not an Italian national under the laws of Italy at the two relevant times, namely on 16 May 2002 (the date of the parties' consent to ICSID arbitration) and on 18 June 2002 (the date the Claimant's Request for Arbitration was registered with ICSID), this Tribunal does not have jurisdiction to hear this dispute.

The tribunal's reliance on the claimed state of nationality's law is also applicable for determinations on the negative nationality criteria. Here again, however, the tribunal is careful to approach the documents of citizenship and nationality as evidence rather than proof of the nationality claims.

 CASE

Waguih Elie George Siag and Clorinda Vecchi v. the Arab Republic of Egypt[74]

Mr Siag was born an Egyptian national in 1962. In 1989, Egypt sold property to an Egyptian joint stock company, 'Siag', of which Mr. Siag was the principal investor, to allow Siag to build a tourist resort.

---

74 *Waguih Elie George Siag and Clorinda Vecchi v. The Arab Republic of Egypt,* ICSID Case No. ARB/05/15, Decision on Jurisdiction and Partial Dissenting Opinion of Professor Francisco Orrego Vicuna (April 11, 2007); available at www.italaw.com/cases/1022; footnotes omitted.

On 15 December 1989, Mr. Siag received a nationality certificate from Lebanon. On 19 December 1989, Mr. Siag requested Egypt's permission to take on Lebanese nationality, combined with a request to retain his Egyptian nationality (as pursuant to Article 10.3 of the Nationality Law).

On 5 March 1990, Egypt issued an acknowledgement of Siag's Lebanese nationality and granted him permission to retain Egyptian nationality. A couple of days later, Egypt exempted Siag from performing military service because of his dual nationality. In June of that year, Siag received his Lebanese passport.

In 1993, Mr Siag received Italian nationality by decree as a result of his 1992 marriage to an Italian citizen. In 1995, Siag received an Italian passport.

Between 1991 and 1997, Egypt issued certificates of nationality to Mr Siag. Siag relied on these statements to develop Siag Taba, a limited partnership, as there were governmental incentive programs to encourage Egyptian nationals to promote business activities.

In 1996, however, Egypt confiscated Siag Taba's property. Siag took Egypt to court, but the government refused to pay him the compensation ordered by the court. In 2004, Siag filed a claim for investment arbitration, revealing his Italian nationality in order to rely on the Italy–Egypt BIT.

The Egyptian government objected to the tribunal's jurisdiction, claiming that, as Siag was an Egyptian national, he was barred from bringing the case to an international forum. The tribunal's approach to the nationality claims reflects the typical attitude of investment tribunals in these matters:

> 142. It is common ground between the parties that under Article 25(2)(a) of the ICSID Convention there is a positive and negative nationality requirement. It is important to stress that the Claimants' assertion that they held Italian nationality at the relevant times so as to satisfy the positive nationality under Article 25 of the Convention has not been contested by the Respondent. Rather, the Respondent's *ratione personae* objections to jurisdiction focus on the negative requirement. That is, were the Claimants, at the relevant times under Article 25, nationals of the Host State, Egypt, and so barred from bringing their claim before ICSID under the ICSID Convention?
>
> 143. It is well established that the domestic laws of each Contracting State determine nationality. This has been accepted in ICSID practice. Both parties accepted and followed this general principle of international law in their submissions and at the hearing. Thus, Egypt's Memorial on Jurisdiction at paragraph

21 describes it as 'indisputable'. Claimants' Counter Memorial refers to Articles 1 and 2 of the 1930 Hague Convention ('the Hague Convention') and the 1997 European Convention on Nationality, Article 3(1) as examples of international conventions reflecting the international law principles. Although it never became effective, the Hague Convention is often referred to as reflecting the current international law principles on nationality of individuals. Article 1 states:

> It is for each State to determine under its laws who are its nationals. This law shall be recognised by other States in so far as it is consistent with international conventions, international custom, and the principles of law generally recognized with regard to nationality.

144. Article 1 identifies that international law sets limits on the power of a state to confer nationality. The relevance of international law to the state's determination of nationality under its municipal law as recognised in Article 1 of the Hague Convention is described in Oppenheim's International Law as follows:

> This permits some control of exorbitant attributions by states of their nationality, by depriving them of much of their international effect. Such control is needed since, although the grant of nationality is for each state to decide for itself in accordance with its own laws, the consequences as against other states of this unilateral act occur on the international plane and are to be determined by international law.

145. In the context of the settlement of investment disputes under the terms of the ICSID Convention, Professor Schreuer comments:

> Whether a person is a nation [sic, ed] of a particular State is determined, in the first place, by the law of the State whose nationality is claimed [. . .]. But an international tribunal is not bound by the national law in question under all circumstances. Situations where nationality provisions of national law may be disregarded include cases of ineffective nationality lacking a genuine link between the State and the individual. Other instances where national rules need not be followed are certain situations of involuntary acquisition of nationality in violation of international law or cases of withdrawal of nationality that are contrary to international law.

146. The international law rule that the municipal law of the state determines nationality is also reflected in the BIT. Article 1(3) of the BIT provides: 'The term "natural person" shall mean, with respect to either Contracting State, a natural person holding the nationality of that State *in accordance with its laws*' (underlining added).

147. The Parties in their written and oral submissions both placed primary emphasis on the interpretation of the Egyptian nationality law to determine whether the Claimants were Egyptian nationals at the relevant time and so did not satisfy the

negative nationality test. However, in its Reply the Respondent made reference to the question of effective nationality but this was in response to the opinion of Professor Reisman that since the Claimants were not dual nationals by operation of the Nationality Law, questions of effectiveness of nationality did not arise. The Claimants acknowledged that there was scope for the Tribunal to take into account international law on nationality. The applicability of the concept of effective or dominant nationality is discussed further below.

Documents of Egyptian Nationality *Prima Facie* Evidence Only

148. In its written and oral submissions the Respondent referred to several official documents from the Egyptian Interior Ministry as reflecting that Mr Siag had in fact retained his Egyptian nationality after 1990 and through to the present date. These documents included letters from the Ministry, as well as passport, and company documents relating to the investment in Taba.

149. Claimants asserted that as a matter of Egyptian law the determination of Egyptian nationality was a matter of public order. Article 6 of the Egyptian Constitution of 1971 states that 'the Egyptian nationality is regulated by the law.' As such, it could only be determined by application of the Nationality Law. [. . .]

150. This has also been the practice of other ICSID Tribunals. [. . .]

[. . .]

152. In this case, the Respondent urged the Tribunal to take into account the cumulative effect of the number of documents evidencing the Egyptian nationality of the Claimants that were in existence throughout the 1990s and up until the Request for Arbitration was filed in 2005. However, the Respondent did not present any arguments to counter the expert opinion of Professor Riad and the decisions of Egyptian courts that under Egyptian law such documents were *prima facie* evidence of nationality only and should be disregarded if they were inconsistent with the applicable law.

153. The Tribunal must determine the nationality of the Claimants. Application of international law principles requires an application of the Egyptian nationality laws with reference to international law as may be appropriate in the circumstances. Both Egyptian law and the practice of international tribunals is that the documents referred to by the Respondent evidencing the nationality of the Claimants are *prima facie* evidence only. While such documents are relevant they do not alleviate the requirement on the Tribunal to apply the Egyptian nationality law, which is the only means of determining Egyptian nationality. [. . .]

Egyptian Nationality Law

Applicability of Article 10 of the Nationality Law – voluntary/involuntary acquisition of foreign nationality – acquisition prior to seeking permission

Article 10 of the Nationality Law

An Egyptian may not gain a foreign nationality except after being permitted by virtue of a decree from the Minister of Interior; otherwise such person shall still be considered an Egyptian in every respect and under all circumstances, unless the Cabinet decides to withdraw his nationality under the provision of Article 16 of this Law.

In the event an Egyptian is permitted to gain a foreign nationality, then this shall lead to the withdrawal of the Egyptian nationality. However, permission to acquire a foreign nationality may allow the person for whom such permission is given, his wife and minor children to retain the Egyptian nationality, provided he notifies his wish to take advantage of such benefit within a period not exceeding one year from the date of gaining the foreign nationality, and in such case they may retain the Egyptian nationality despite having gained a foreign nationality.

[. . .]

156. The Respondent contended that since Mr Siag acquired his Lebanese nationality prior to seeking permission under Article 10 of the Nationality Law, Article 10 was, in fact, not applicable to Mr Siag. In this respect Respondent made detailed submissions devoted to the issue of the accuracy of the documentation that Mr Siag submitted to the Egyptian Interior Ministry and to the categorization of Mr Siag's Lebanese nationality as either voluntary in the sense that it was acquired through naturalization or involuntarily in that it was acquired at birth through application of *jus sanguinis.*

157. The Tribunal finds that it is unnecessary for the purpose of this ruling on jurisdiction to determine whether Mr Siag acquired his Lebanese nationality voluntarily or involuntarily. The Tribunal accepts the evidence of Professor Riad that the Nationality Law does not differentiate between involuntary and voluntary acquisition of a foreign nationality in the application of Article 10. [. . .]

158. At the time Mr Siag applied for permission to acquire Lebanese nationality in December 1989 he already possessed Lebanese nationality. [. . .]

159. The Tribunal adopts the opinions of Professor Riad that Article 10 addresses the recognition of foreign nationality in the 'eyes of Egypt'. The view of Professor Riad was that the prior acquisition of a foreign nationality under the law of a foreign state made no difference to the permission sought under Article 10. Article 10 was 'blind' to the operation of the foreign law. [. . .]

[. . .]

161. The Tribunal holds that Article 10 may be used to seek permission for an already acquired foreign nationality. In that case, though, the determining date for the commencement of the one-year period under the third paragraph of Article 10 would not be the date of the acquisition of the foreign nationality. As Professor Riad stated:

> In terms of applying Article 10, the date that should be considered for purposes of the third paragraph of Article 10 is the first date on which there was a *formal expression* of Mr Siag's foreign nationality after the issuance of the

Minister's authorization to acquire the foreign nationality, for it is only at that point in time that Egyptian law acknowledged Mr Siag's acquisition of the foreign nationality.

[...]

Article 10(3) – The One-Year Period

163. Under Article 10(3), an applicant seeking permission to obtain a foreign nationality may at the same time seek permission to retain his or her Egyptian nationality. If permission to retain Egyptian nationality is granted, Article 10(3) states the applicant may retain his or her Egyptian nationality 'provided he notifies his wish to take advantage of such benefit within a period not exceeding one year from the date of acquiring the foreign nationality'.

[...]

165. The Tribunal also agrees with the view of Professor Riad that:

> The existence of this two-step requirement has never been challenged in Egyptian legal doctrine. Egyptian scholars are unanimous in considering that the Minister's authorization alone merely constitutes a permission to acquire the foreign nationality and a license for the applicant to formally declare his wish to retain the Egyptian nationality. Indeed, the two-step requirement contained in article 10 has been deemed by certain authors as rather excessive.

[...]

172. The Tribunal finds that it is settled under Egyptian law that under Article 10(3) an applicant must make a formal declaration within one year of permission being granted in order to retain his or her Egyptian nationality. Whether the relevant date was 5 March 1990 or 14 June 1990, Mr Siag made no such declaration within the one-year period and so lost his Egyptian nationality by operation of Egyptian law in 1991. The only way for him to regain that nationality was through Egyptian law. This has not taken place.

173. For all of the reasons set out above the Tribunal finds that, at all relevant times for the purposes of the ICSID Convention, Mr Siag was an Italian national and did not have Egyptian nationality.

 DISCUSSION NOTES

In *Soufraki*, the Respondent put forth an argument that the tribunal should investigate dual-national's nationality claims on the basis of the investor's 'effective or dominant' nationality (para. 42). The tribunal did not do so, as it found the claimant did not have the requisite nationality at all (para. 46). The *Siag* tribunal, also facing such an argument refused to apply such a test:

> 198. The Tribunal concurs with the finding of the ICSID Tribunal in the *Champion Trading* case that the regime established under Article 25 of the

ICSID Tribunal does not leave room for a test of dominant or effective nationality. [. . .] While it may be asserted that if this were a diplomatic protection case it could be argued differently, the parties have consented to have their dispute resolved under the ICSID Convention and it sets out a particular regime for the determination of jurisdiction. [. . .] Developments in international law concerning nationality of individuals in the field of diplomatic protection including, for example, greater flexibility in the requirement for the link of nationality, while of interest, must give way to the specific regime under the ICSID Convention and the terms of the BIT.

199. This is not a situation where a claimant is seeking to assert a particular nationality in order to bring a claim and that nationality is claimed to be ineffective. Nor is it a case where the consequence of a determination of the nationality of an individual by one state as against other states fails to be determined. This case concerns a state, through operation of its domestic law, ceasing to regard individuals as its nationals. In this case the Claimants contend that they lost their Egyptian nationality through operation of Egyptian domestic law so that they were not dual-nationals at all. In the *Champion Trading* case the claimants asserted that the test of effective nationality should be applied as an alternative argument based on a finding that under the operation of Egypt's nationality law they had acquired Egyptian nationality involuntarily and so were dual-nationals. It is the Tribunal's view that in this case it does not even have to consider that possibility since it has found as a matter of Egyptian law that the Claimants did not possess Egyptian nationality at the relevant times under the ICSID Convention. [. . .]

201. The Tribunal finds that this case does not present a situation where there is scope for international law principles to override the operation of Egyptian domestic law as to nationality. To do so would in effect involve the illegitimate revision of the terms of the BIT and the Nationality Law by the Tribunal.

The Partial Dissenting Opinion by Arbitrator Francisco Orrego Vicuña in *Siag*, however, made a strong plea for the use of an effectiveness test in determining nationality claims. Given the jurisdictional, even *'jus cogens'*-like, character of nationality in investment arbitration, the opportunities given investors to 'shop' for nationality that stems from a refusal to examine real connections between the investor and the named home state are unjustifiable. Orrego Vicuña concludes:

In the end, I believe that the whole question of having acquired Lebanese nationality is in essence artificial as far as the investment is concerned. The investment was made by an Egyptian citizen, a fact which is not disputed by the parties, who has effectively kept all his links with that country, who wishes to remain Egyptian, who then alleges to have become Lebanese and to have lost his Egyptian nationality, but who does not claim under the existing BIT between Egypt and Lebanon, but under a BIT with Italy, a country with which he has at best remote connections.

This is not what international law or the ICSID Convention could have possibly intended. Neither is it what the expression of consent of Egypt could have possibly meant or what the Egypt's Nationality Law could be taken to say.[75]

c.ii Nationality of corporations

Although nationality rules for natural persons can be complex for purposes of investor protection, by far the majority of investors relying on IIAs are actually corporations. These legal persons must also have 'nationality' of the home and not of the host state.

Determining the nationality of a corporation is often more difficult than for an individual. This is because there are numerous grounds upon which the nationality can be based. Because there is no customary rule of international law on corporate nationality, the relevant criteria for this task are generally determined by treaty terms. In IIAs, the following, singularly or in combination, are regularly included as bases for nationality claims:

- place of incorporation or legal establishment;
- place of the principal seat of business;
- place of real economic activity, showing a bond between investor and host;
- place of company's preponderant interest.

The Switzerland–India BIT, for example, defines 'investors' to include 'companies, . . . constituted in accordance with the law of that Contracting Party and engaged in substantive business operations in the territory of the same Contracting Party'[76]—a double requirement of incorporation and economic bond. The Switzerland–Chile BIT is more restrictive, requiring a triple test of legal establishment, seat, and economic bond.[77]

---

75 Id. (Partial Dissenting Opinion of Professor Francisco Orrego Vicuna).

76 *See*, e.g. Agreement between the Swiss Confederation and the Republic of India for the Promotion and Protection of Investments of 4 April 1997, art. 1(1)(b) (entered into force on Feb. 16, 2000).

77 Agreement between the Swiss Confederation and the Republic of Chile on the Promotion and Reciprocal Protection of Investments of 24 September 1999, arts. 1(1)(b) and 1(1)(c) (entered into force on 2 May, 2002).

Moreover, the same IIA may use different definitions of nationality for the different parties.[78] When a respondent challenges the jurisdiction of a tribunal on the basis of the claimant's nationality, the legal issues are the same as for a challenge to the nationality of the investor—is the company a national of the home state and is the company not a national of the host state? Yet, the law upon which the decision is made is generally going to be that of the relevant investment agreement rather than national laws.

 CASE

Alps Finance and Trade AG v. The Slovak Republic[79]

Switzerland and the Slovak Republic have a BIT that entered into force on 7 August 1991. When the Slovak Republic split from Czechoslovakia on 1 January 1993, it became the successor to the BIT.

AFT (Alps Finance and Trade) is a company incorporated in Switzerland. It was in the position of being the assignor for money paid by a debtor which had been declared bankrupt. When the Regional Court of Bratislava issued a decision in September 2007 declaring the credits unenforceable, AFT sued the Slovak Republic under the Swiss–Slovak BIT for violations of the protections of the treaty.

The Slovak Republic responded with a jurisdictional objection that AFT lacked Swiss nationality, and therefore could not be considered an 'investor' for purposes of the BIT.

> 213. In order to qualify as an investor under Article 1(1)(b) and (c) of the BIT, a Swiss claimant must establish that (i) it is 'constituted or otherwise duly organized under the laws of Switzerland'; (ii) that it has its 'seat' in Switzerland; and (iii) that it performs 'real economic activities' in Switzerland. Whether [Claimant] satisfies the second and third requirement has been the subject matter of a long debate [. . .].

---

78 *See*, e.g. Agreement between the Government of the Republic of Korea and the Government of the Swiss Confederation Concerning the Encouragement and Reciprocal Protection of Investments of 7 April 1971, art. 7(b).

79 *Alps Finance and Trade AG v. The Slovak Republic*, UNCITRAL (Switzerland/Slovak Republic BIT), Preliminary redacted version Award (Mar. 5, 2011). Available at: http://italaw.com/documents/AFTvSlovakRepublic_5Mar2011_Part2.pdf; footnotes omitted.

(i) Constitution or other organization under the laws of Switzerland

214. The Claimant provided an excerpt from the [. . .] Commercial Registry, confirming that [Claimant] is a corporation duly constituted and organized under Swiss law with registered office in [. . .], Switzerland. The Respondent does not contest that the Claimant meets this requirement.

(ii) The Swiss seat

215. All that the Claimant has offered to prove that it has a Swiss 'seat' is the following: (i) the fact that it has been incorporated under the laws of Switzerland, as shown by an excerpt from the [. . .] Commercial Registry; (ii) its domicile in [. . .], where it has its 'headquarters'; (iii) the assertion that the company books are kept in Switzerland; (iv) a UBS price-list of the costs of handling a bank account; (v) a tax declaration relating to the fiscal year January to December 2007 showing the company's turnover, profit and/or loss; (vi) the assertion that it has a daughter company active in Slovakia; and (vii) the definition of company 'seat' pursuant to the Slovak commercial code.

216. The Tribunal must agree with the Respondent that the above *indicia* are insufficient to establish the existence of a Swiss seat in the meaning of international business law. At the most, it is established that [Claimant is] domiciled in Switzerland, under the laws of which it is incorporated. The fact that Article 1(1)(b) of the BIT requires a Swiss 'seat' as a distinct element in addition to 'constitution and organization under Swiss law' demonstrates that the mere incorporation in Switzerland is insufficient to constitute a 'seat' in the terms of the BIT.

217. Proof of a 'business seat', in the meaning of an effective center of administration of the business operations, requires additional elements, such as the proof that: the place where the company board of directors regularly meets or the shareholders' meetings are held is in Swiss territory; there is a management at the top of the company sitting in Switzerland; the company has a certain number of employees working at the seat; and address with phone and fax numbers are offered to third parties entering in contact with the company; certain general expenses or overhead costs are incurred for the maintenance of the physical location of the seat and related services, which would be a clear indication that a business entity is effectively organized at a given Swiss place.

218. However, none of these requirements were satisfied by the Claimant. The Respondent requested the Claimant to provide its Swiss phone number, and the reply was that there was none. The Claimant was also requested to disclose the office rental agreement, and the reply was that there is just an 'oral' rental agreement, the parties and terms of which remained unknown. Even the existence of a bank account opened in the name of [the Claimant] is doubtful: the UBS list of

prices is a standard document created for the clients, but . . . has failed to prove that it is one of them.

(iii) Real economic activities

219. Similar conclusions must be drawn in respect of the 'real economic activities' of [Claimant] in Switzerland. The 2007 tax return indicates a quite modest turnover and nothing has been exhibited for the outstanding years. The Claimant was unable to establish number and type of its clients, type of its operations, kind of contracts it enters into, quantity and type of personnel, nature and composition of its managing bodies. It even admitted that it has no employee.
[. . .]
223. [Claimant's] affirmation that [it] holds accounts in Swiss banks is immaterial: to substantiate 'real economic activities' he should have attached the bank account documents relating to the time of the events giving rise to the dispute, i.e. relating to the time when the receivables were acquired in Slovakia and the acquisition was followed by the bankruptcy proceedings. These or other similar documents would have established that, at that time, [Claimant] was actually conducting real economic activities in Switzerland. Even the telephone and fax numbers presented on the letterhead . . . are not those . . . in its comments dated October 29, 2010, the Respondent proved that they belong to . . . a tax advisory service, a fact which was not denied by the Claimant in further correspondence.
224. Under the foregoing circumstances, the Claimant is far from meeting the standard imposed under the BIT. The Tribunal sides with the Respondent in that the BIT requires more than the mere incorporation in one of the contracting parties, and that Article 1(1) is a special (and rather uncommon) clause by which the two contracting States intended to exclude from treaty-protection 'mailbox' or 'paper' companies.
225. The Tribunal is persuaded that the above interpretation coincides with the authentic expression of the intention of the Parties to the BIT. It must therefore give effect to such an intention. Pursuant to Article 31 of the Vienna Convention on the Law of Treaties, any treaty clause must be interpreted '*in good faith and in accordance with the ordinary meaning to be given to the terms of the treaty in their context and in the light of its objective and purpose*' (Article 31(1)). Article 31(2) specifies that the context and purpose comprise the treaty '*preamble*'.
226. Now, the good faith ordinary meaning of the word 'real' cannot but be 'actual', or 'effective', or 'genuine', or 'verifiable', or 'visible', or 'tangible', or 'objective'. The BIT preamble underlines that the purpose pursued by the two Contracting States was intensifying the economic cooperation to the mutual benefit of both States and fostering their economic prosperity. It is illogic [sic] to assume that the above goals could be achieved by giving treaty protection or by attracting into the host country 'shell' companies which are unable to establish

> the kind and level of activities that they conduct in their own State. No State is anxious to promise special guarantees, privileges and protections to investors which bring no benefit to its economy.
>
> 227. Concluding on this matter, the Tribunal is of the view that [Claimant] is not an 'investor' in the meaning of Article 1(1) of the BIT. This is *per se* sufficient to oblige the Tribunal to decline jurisdiction over the Claimant's claims.

The determination of nationality of a corporation may be clouded by the invocation of arguments relating to the nationality of who actually controls the company. Where incorporation is the sole factor listed in the treaty's definition of 'investor', however, the tribunal may ignore such arguments in favour of a strictly textual interpretation of the treaty provisions.

 CASE

Tokios Tokelés v. Ukraine[80]

Tokios Tokelés (TT) is a publishing company that was registered in Lithuania as a joint-stock company in 1991. In 1994, TT established 'Taki', a wholly owned subsidiary in the Ukraine. Taki was also a printing and publishing company. Like TT, which had business in Lithuania and abroad, Taki was active within Ukraine and outside the country. At the beginning of 2002, one of Taki's published books shed advantageous light on Julia Tymoshenko, a politician opposed to the ruling party. Following the book's appearance, the Ukrainian government began investigating Taki for tax violations and illegal financial activities.

Hindered in its ability to operate, TT initiated investment arbitration under the Lithuania–Ukraine BIT. Ukraine argued that TT is not a national of Lithuania. It emphasized that although TT is incorporated in Lithuania, it is not a 'genuine entity' of Lithuania that can rely on the BIT. Rather, Ukraine said, TT is Ukrainian. Owned 99% by Ukrainians, headquartered in the Ukraine, having a seat in the Ukraine and having insubstantial business activities in Lithuania, TT is, according to the respondent, 'in terms of economic substance, a Ukrainian investor in Lithuania, not a Lithuanian investor in Ukraine' (para. 21).

The Ukraine therefore requested the tribunal to 'pierce the corporate veil' that is, to look behind the technical detail of TT's place of incorporation and attribute the nationality of those who control TT to the company. The

---

80 *Tokios Tokelés v. Ukraine*, ICSID Case No. ARB/02/18, Decision on Jurisdiction (Apr. 29, 2004). Available at: http://italaw.com/documents/Tokios-Jurisdiction.pdf; footnotes omitted.

tribunal looked to both the ICSID requirements on investor nationality and those of the BIT for its analysis.

2. Nationality of Juridical entities under article 25 of the ICSID convention

24. Article 25 of the Convention requires that, in order for the Centre to have jurisdiction, a dispute must be between 'a Contracting State . . . and *a national of another Contracting State . . .*'. Article 25(2)(b) defines 'national of another Contracting State,' to include 'any juridical person which had the nationality of a Contracting State other than the State party to the dispute . . .'. The Convention does not define the method for determining the nationality of juridical entities, leaving this task to the reasonable discretion of the Contracting Parties. Thus, we begin our analysis of this jurisdictional requirement by underscoring the deference this Tribunal owes to the definition of corporate nationality contained in the agreement between the Contracting Parties, in this case, the Ukraine–Lithuania BIT. As Mr. Broches explained, the purpose of Article 25(2)(b) is not to define corporate nationality but to:

> . . . indicate the outer limits within which disputes may be submitted to conciliation or arbitration under the auspices of the Centre with the consent of the parties thereto. Therefore *the parties should be given the widest possible latitude to agree on the meaning of 'nationality' and any stipulation of nationality made in connection with a conciliation or arbitration clause which is based on a reasonable criterion.*

[. . .]

26. In the specific context of BITs, Professor Schreuer notes that the Contracting Parties enjoy broad discretion to define corporate nationality: '[d]efinitions of corporate nationality in national legislation or in treaties providing for ICSID's jurisdiction will be controlling for the determination of whether the nationality requirements of Article 25(2)(b) have been met.' He adds, '[a]ny reasonable determination of the nationality of juridical persons contained in national legislation or in a treaty should be accepted by an ICSID commission or tribunal.'

3. Definition of 'Investor' in article 1(2) of the BIT

27. As have other tribunals, we interpret the ICSID Convention and the Treaty between the Contracting Parties according to the rules set forth in the Vienna Convention on the Law of Treaties. . . .

28. Article 1(2)(b) of the Ukraine-Lithuania BIT defines the term 'investor,' with respect to Lithuania, as 'any entity established in the territory of the Republic of Lithuania in conformity with its laws and regulations.' The ordinary meaning of 'entity' is '[a] thing that has a real existence.' The meaning of 'establish' is to '[s]et

up on a permanent or secure basis; bring into being, found (a . . . business)'. Thus, according to the ordinary meaning of the terms of the Treaty, the Claimant is an 'investor' of Lithuania if it is a thing of real legal existence that was founded on a secure basis in the territory of Lithuania in conformity with its laws and regulations. The Treaty contains no additional requirements for an entity to qualify as an 'investor' of Lithuania.

29. The Claimant was founded as a cooperative in 1989 and was registered by the municipal government of Vilnius, Lithuania on August 9 of that year. In 1991, the founders of Tokios Tokelés agreed to reorganize the cooperative into a closed joint-stock company, which the municipal government of Vilnius, Lithuania registered on May 2, 1991. According to the Certificate of Enterprise, the address of Tokios Tokelés is Vilnius, vul. Seskines, 13-3. On August 11, 2000, the Ministry of the Economy of the Republic of Lithuania re-registered the Claimant as an enterprise and re-registered the Claimant's governing statute, both of which note the company's location as Sheshkines, 13-3 (or d. 13 kv. 3), Vilnius. The Claimant, therefore, is a thing of real legal existence that was founded on a secure basis in the territory of Lithuania. The registration of Tokios Tokelés by the Lithuanian Government indicates that it was founded in conformity with the laws and regulations of that country. According to the ordinary meaning of Article 1(2)(b), therefore, the Claimant is an investor of Lithuania.

30. Article 1(2)(c) of the Ukraine—Lithuania BIT, which defines 'investor' with respect to entities not established in Ukraine or Lithuania, provides relevant context for the interpretation of Article 1(2)(a) and (b). Article 1(2)(c) extends the scope of the Treaty to entities incorporated in third countries using other criteria to determine nationality—namely, the nationality of the individuals who control the enterprise and the *siège social* of the entity controlling the enterprise. The Respondent argues that the existence of these alternative methods of defining corporate nationality to *extend* the benefits of the BIT in Article 1(2)(c) should also allow these methods to be used to *deny* the benefits of the BIT under Article 1(2)(b). If the Contracting Parties had intended these alternative methods to apply to entities legally established in Ukraine or Lithuania, however, the parties would have included them in Article 1(2)(a) or (b) respectively as they did in Article 1(2)(c). However, the purpose of Article 1(2)(c) is only to extend the definition of 'investor' to entities established under the law of a third State provided certain conditions are met. Under the well established presumption *expressio unius est exclusio alterius*, the state of incorporation, not the nationality of the controlling shareholders or *siège social*, thus defines 'investors' of Lithuania under Article 1(2)(b) of the BIT.

31. The object and purpose of the Treaty likewise confirm that the control-test should not be used to restrict the scope of 'investors' in Article 1(2)(b). The preamble expresses the Contracting Parties' intent to 'intensify economic cooperation to the mutual benefit of both States' and 'create and maintain favourable

conditions for investment of investors of one State in the territory of the other State.'

[. . .]

33. The Respondent also argues that jurisdiction should be denied because, in its view, the Claimant does not maintain 'substantial business activity' in Lithuania. The Respondent correctly notes that a number of investment treaties allow a party to deny the benefits of the treaty to entities of the other party that are controlled by foreign nationals and that do not engage in substantial business activity in the territory of the other party.

[. . .]

36. These investment agreements confirm that state parties are capable of excluding from the scope of the agreement entities of the other party that are controlled by nationals of third countries or by nationals of the host country. The Ukraine–Lithuania BIT, by contrast, includes no such 'denial of benefits' provision with respect to entities controlled by third-country nationals or by nationals of the denying party. We regard the absence of such a provision as a deliberate choice of the Contracting Parties. In our view, it is not for tribunals to impose limits on the scope of BITs not found in the text, much less limits nowhere evident from the negotiating history. An international tribunal of defined jurisdiction should not reach out to exercise a jurisdiction beyond the borders of the definition. But equally an international tribunal should exercise, and indeed is bound to exercise, the measure of jurisdiction with which it is endowed.

37. We note that the Claimant has provided the Tribunal with significant information regarding its activities in Lithuania, including financial statements, employment information, and a catalogue of materials produced during the period of 1991 to 1994. While these activities would appear to constitute 'substantial business activity,' we need not affirmatively decide that they do, as it is not relevant to our determination of jurisdiction.

38. Rather, under the terms of the Ukraine–Lithuania BIT, interpreted according to their ordinary meaning, in their context, and in light of the object and purpose of the Treaty, the only relevant consideration is whether the Claimant is established under the laws of Lithuania. We find that it is. Thus, the Claimant is an investor of Lithuania under Article 1(2)(b) of the BIT.

39. We reach this conclusion based on the consent of the Contracting Parties, as expressed in the Ukraine–Lithuania BIT. We emphasize here that Contracting Parties are free to define their consent to jurisdiction in terms that are broad or narrow; they may employ a control-test or reserve the right to deny treaty protection to claimants who otherwise would have recourse under the BIT. Once that consent is defined, however, tribunals should give effect to it, unless doing so would allow the Convention to be used for purposes for which it clearly was not intended.

40. This Tribunal, by respecting the definition of corporate nationality in the

Ukraine–Lithuania BIT, fulfills the parties' expectations, increases the predictability of dispute settlement procedures, and enables investors to structure their investments to enjoy the legal protections afforded under the Treaty. We decline to look beyond (or through) the Claimant to its shareholders or other juridical entities that may have an interest in the claim. [. . .]

[. . .]

4. Consistency of article 1(2) of the BIT with the ICSID convention

42. In our view, the definition of corporate nationality in the Ukraine–Lithuania BIT, on its face and as applied to the present case, is consistent with the Convention and supports our analysis under it. Although Article 25(2)(b) of the Convention does not set forth a required method for determining corporate nationality, the generally accepted (albeit implicit) rule is that the nationality of a corporation is determined on the basis of its *siège social* or place of incorporation. Indeed, 'ICSID tribunals have uniformly adopted the test of incorporation or seat rather than control when determining the nationality of a juridical person', Moreover, '[t]he overwhelming weight of the authority . . . points towards the traditional criteria of incorporation or seat for the determination of corporate nationality under Art. 25(2)(b)'. As Professor Schreuer notes, '[a] systematic interpretation of Article 25(2)(b) would militate against the use of the control test for a corporation's nationality'.

[. . .]

5. Equitable doctrine of 'Veil Piercing'

53. Finally, we consider whether the equitable doctrine of 'veil piercing', to the extent recognized in customary international law, should override the terms of the agreement between the Contracting Parties and cause the Tribunal to deny jurisdiction in this case.

54. The seminal case, in this regard, is *Barcelona Traction*. In that case, the International Court of Justice ('ICJ') stated, 'the process of lifting the veil, being an exceptional one admitted by municipal law in respect of an institution of its own making, is equally admissible to play a similar role in international law'. In particular, the Court noted, '[t]he wealth of practice already accumulated on the subject in municipal law indicates that the veil is lifted, for instance, *to prevent the misuse of the privileges of legal personality*, as in certain cases of *fraud* or *malfeasance*, to *protect third persons* such as a creditor or purchaser, or to *prevent the evasion of legal requirements or of obligations*'.

55. The Respondent has not made a *prima facie* case, much less demonstrated, that the Claimant has engaged in any of the types of conduct described in *Barcelona Traction* that might support a piercing of the Claimant's corporate veil. The Respondent has not shown or even suggested that the Claimant has used its status as a juridical entity

of Lithuania to perpetrate fraud or engage in malfeasance. The Respondent has made no claim that the Claimant's veil must be pierced and jurisdiction denied in order to protect third persons, nor has the Respondent shown that the Claimant used its corporate nationality to evade applicable legal requirements or obligations.

56. The ICJ did not attempt to define in *Barcelona Traction* the precise scope of conduct that might prompt a tribunal to pierce the corporate veil. We are satisfied, however, that none of the Claimant's conduct with respect to its status as an entity of Lithuania constitutes an abuse of legal personality. The Claimant made no attempt whatever to conceal its national identity from the Respondent. To the contrary, the Claimant's status as a juridical entity of Lithuania is well established under the laws of both Lithuania and Ukraine and well known by the Respondent. The Claimant manifestly did not create Tokios Tokelés for the purpose of gaining access to ICSID arbitration under the BIT against Ukraine, as the enterprise was founded six years before the BIT between Ukraine and Lithuania entered into force. Indeed, there is no evidence in the record that the Claimant used its formal legal nationality for any improper purpose.

?   **DISCUSSION NOTES**

1 Given that Mr Siag was held to have given up his Egyptian nationality even when he had benefited from his Egyptian passport in building his investment, perhaps investment tribunals should consider the principles of effective or dominant nationality more extensively. What elements could be used to make a determination on such a basis? *See* Engela C. Schlemmer, *Investment, Investor, Nationality, and Shareholders*, in The Oxford Handbook of International Investment Law 49, 72–4 (Peter Muchlinski, Federico Ortino, and Christoph Schreuer eds., 2008).

2 While treaty-shopping via incorporation is allowed, when the investor is relying on its 'home' purely for tax or BIT reasons, homes and hosts may not like it. Some BITs therefore restrict such practices by including a denial of benefits clause. Article 17(1) of the ECT, for instance, provides for a denial of benefits clause:

> Each Contracting Party reserves the right to deny the advantages of this Part to: (1) a legal entity if citizens or nationals of a third state own or control such entity and if that entity has no substantial business activities in the Area of the Contracting Party in which it is organized.

The use of multiple grounds to prove nationality may be a substitute for a denial of benefits clause. The 'economic activities' element, in particular, is functionally equivalent to a denial of benefits provision. The 2009 BIT between Switzerland and China, for instance, requires the following elements:

> The term 'investor' refers with regard to either contracting Party to: . . . (b) legal entities, including companies, corporations, business associations and other organisations, which are constituted or otherwise duly organised under the law of that Contracting Party and have their seat, together with real economic activities, in the territory of the same Contracting Party.[81]

3.3.2 Shareholder protection

Combining the aspects of the definitional queries into 'investment' and 'investor', a major question facing tribunals has been whether to protect the interests of shareholders through international investment law, and if so, under what conditions. The questions extend from the most basic one of whether the shareholder has made an 'investment' by purchase of the shares to the more complicated one of whether a shareholder's status as an investor depends on if (s)he/it is a majority (or controlling) shareholder and whether claims for 'reflective loss' should be rejected due to concerns about double recovery and legal uncertainty.[82]

The role of the shareholder in international investment law brings together several elements of the investor/investment discussions set forth above and can become quite complex. For purposes of this book, only the most basic concepts need to be grasped.

Under customary international law, shareholding is not a basis for diplomatic protection. The ICJ's opinion in *Barcelona Traction* denied that the state of which a majority shareholder is a national could exercise diplomatic protection over a corporation established in another state.[83]

Yet, the *Barcelona Traction* decision did not prohibit the international protection of shareholder rights. It merely denied any customary obligation to extend such protection. Indeed, the Court underlined shareholders' rights to seek protection under national laws for any losses directly incurred (such

---

81 Switzerland–China BIT (signed 27 January 2009, entered into force 13 April 2009), Art. 2(2)(b). Available at: https://www.admin.ch/opc/fr/classified-compilation/20092659/index.html.

82 There are multiple in-depth discussions of shareholder claims in international law. *See*, e.g. Stanisimir A. Alexandrov, The 'Baby Boom' of Treaty-based Arbitrations and the Jurisdiction of ICSID Tribunals: Shareholders as Investors and Jurisdiction Ratione Temporis, 4 L. & Prac. Int'l Courts & Tribunals 19 (2005); David Gaukrodger, Investment Treaties as Corporate Law: Shareholder Claims and Issues of Consistency, a Preliminary Framework for Policy Analysis, OECD Working Papers on International Investment, No. 2013/3 (November 2013).

83 *Barcelona Traction, Light and Power Company, Limited (Belg. v. Spain)*, Judgment, 1970 ICJ 3 (Feb. 5).

as the right to a dividend or a part of the assets in case of dissolution of the company) and recognized states' rights to offer such protection by means of treaty provisions.[84] As one tribunal wrote, it 'is precisely this kind of arrangement that has come to prevail under international law, particularly in respect of foreign investments, the paramount example being that of the 1965 Convention'.[85]

Thus, while shareholders were traditionally left unprotected under investment law, the broad definitions of 'investment' found in most IIAs (which include provisions such as 'shares, stock, and other forms of equity participation in an enterprise') have made it common for tribunals to grant shareholders the status of 'investor' when these are pursuing arbitration for destruction of (or damage to) their holdings. Today, it is well accepted that shareholders can make claims against a host for damages to an entity incorporated in that territory. Indeed, a recent tribunal noted, that 'some two-dozen previous investor-State tribunals have confirmed that the ICSID Convention, in concert with the definition of 'investment' offered by numerous BITs, allows shareholders to bring claims for harms to their investments in locally incorporated companies'.[86]

Numerous similar provisions have been conclusively determined to offer shareholders the same protection as other investors would receive.[87]

---

84 Id. para. 47.

85 *CMS Gas Transmission Company v. Argentine Republic*, ICSID Case No. ARB/01/8, Decision on Objections to Jurisdiction, para. 45 (July 17, 2003), 42 ILM 788 (2003). Available at: http://italaw.com/documents/cms-argentina_000.pdf). The tribunal found this to be evidence of the fact that 'Diplomatic protection itself has been dwindling in current international law, as the State of nationality is no longer considered to be protecting its own interest in the claim but that of the individual affected. To some extent, diplomatic protection is intervening as a residual mechanism to be resorted to in the absence of other arrangements recognizing the direct right of action by individuals.'

86 *Daimler Financial Services AG v Argentine Republic*, ICSID Case No. ARB/05/1, Award, para. 91 (Aug. 22, 2012). Available at: http://italaw.com/sites/default/files/case-documents/ita1082.pdf (footnote omitted).

87 For example, *Azurix Corp. v. The Argentine Republic*, ICSID Case No. ARB/01/12, Decision on Jurisdiction, para. 65 (Dec. 8, 2003). Available at: http://italaw.com/documents/Azurix-Jurisdiction_000. pdf; *Enron Corporation and Ponderosa Assets, LP v. The Argentine Republic*, ICSID Case No. ARB/01/3, Decision on Jurisdiction (Ancillary Claim), paras. 29–31 (Aug. 2, 2004). Available at: http://italaw.com/documents/Enron-DecisiononJurisdiction-FINAL-English.pdf; *Siemens AG v. The Argentine Republic*, ICSID Case No. ARB/02/8, Decision on Jurisdiction, paras. 137–44 (Aug. 3, 2004). Available at: http://italaw.com/documents/SiemensJurisdiction-English-3August2004.pdf; Suez, Sociedad General de Aguas de Barcelona SA, and InterAguas Servicios *Integrales del Agua SA v. The Argentine Republic*, ICSID Case No. ARB/03/17, Decision on Jurisdiction, para. 51 (May 16, 2006). Available at: http://italaw.com/documents/Suez-Jurisdiction.pdf http://italaw.com/documents/Suez-Jurisdiction.pdf;; *RosInvestCo UK Ltd. v. The Russian Federation*, SCC Case No. Arb. V079/2005, Final Award, para. 608 (Sept. 12, 2010). Available at: http://italaw.com/documents/RosInvestCoAward.pdf.

Recalling that tribunals generally find that the size of the investment does not itself pose a jurisdictional hurdle to arbitration,[88] one might still ask if this holds true for shareholding. While majority shareholders clearly have access to treaty protections, what about minority shareholders? And what about indirect shareholders?

A related shareholder question which can arise in investment disputes goes to the concept of 'reflective loss'—the reduction in value of a shareholder's stocks due to the host's actions against the company behind the stocks. Most national corporate law systems deny shareholders the right to claim for such loss (reserving that right to the corporation itself) on the basis of policy concerns such as fairness and efficiency.[89] Tribunals, however, have found reflective losses to be a basis for investor protection of the shareholder.

Both the widely accepted rule for granting IIA protections to non-controlling and indirect shareholders and the reflective loss issue are set out in the tribunal's decision below.

 CASE

CMS Gas Transmission Co. v. Argentina[90]

In 1992, as part of an overall reorganization of the economy that had begun three years earlier, Argentina passed legislation allowing for the privatization of its gas industry. At this time, an Argentine corporation, Tranportadora de Gas del Norte (TGN), received a license to transport gas. Under the privatization legislation, prices for gas would be in US dollars, adjusted every half year to accord with the United States Producer Price Index. At billing, the current prices would then be converted to pesos at the existing exchange rate.

In 1995, CMS, a US company, purchased 25 percent of TGN as well as other governmentally owned shares. By 1999, Argentina was severely affected by an economic, financial, and ultimately social, crisis. Devaluation

---

88 Engela C. Schlemmer, *Investment, Investor, Nationality, and Shareholders, in* The Oxford Handbook of International Investment Law 49, 83 (Peter Muchlinski, Federico Ortino and Christoph Schreuer eds., 2008). *CMS Gas Transmission Co. v. Argentina, supra* note 85, footnotes omitted.

89 David Gaukrodger, Investment Treaties as Corporate Law: Shareholder Claims and Issues of Consistency, a Preliminary Framework for Policy Analysis, OECD Working Papers on International Investment, No. 2013/3, 15–24 (November 2013).

90 *CMS Gas Transmission Co. v. Argentina, supra* note 85, footnotes omitted.

of the peso and new administrative measures were enacted in an attempt to offset the effects of the crisis, but to little avail. Then, in 2001, the government enacted a 'pesification' regime to peg the peso to the dollar, and implemented numerous other measures, including putting an end to the gas industry's right to price adjustments based on the US producer price index. As a result of the government's financial measures, TGN's profits were substantially reduced.

CMS brought a claim against Argentina to the ICSID based on the US–Argentina BIT, alleging that Argentina had expropriated its investment. Respondent Argentina objected to the tribunal's jurisdiction on the basis of CMS' lack of standing. CMS, it argued, was a minority shareholder of an Argentine legal entity and therefore not an 'investor' for purposes of the ICSID. The tribunal addressed these issues by analysing the relevant legal provisions and the trends in investment arbitration.

Shareholder rights under general international law

[...]

46. The Republic of Argentina has advanced the argument that, when shareholders have been protected separately from the affected corporation, this occurred in cases where the shareholders were majority or controlling, not minority shareholders as in the instant case. This fact may be true, but it is equally true, as argued by the Claimant, a question of controlling majorities; rather they were concerned with the possibility of protecting shareholders independently from the affected corporation, that is, solely with the issue of the corporate legal personality and its limits.

47. State practice further supports the meaning of this changing scenario. Besides accepting the protection of shareholders and other forms of participation in corporations and partnerships, the concept of limiting it to majority or controlling participations has given way to a lower threshold in this respect. Minority and non-controlling participations have thus been included in the protection granted or have been admitted to claim in their own right. Contemporary practice relating to lump-sum agreements, the decisions of the Iran–United States Tribunal and the rules and decisions of the United Nations Compensation Commission, among other examples, evidence increasing flexibility in the handling of international claims.

48. The Tribunal therefore finds no bar in current international law to the concept of allowing claims by shareholders independently from those of the corporation concerned, not even if those shareholders are minority or non-controlling shareholders. Although it is true, as argued by the Republic of Argentina, that this is mostly the result of *lex specialis* and specific treaty arrangements that have so allowed, the fact is that *lex specialis* in this respect is so prevalent that it can now

be considered the general rule, certainly in respect of foreign investments and increasingly in respect of other matters. To the extent that customary international law or generally the traditional law of international claims might have followed a different approach—a proposition that is open to debate—then that approach can be considered the exception.

Shareholder rights under the ICSID convention

49. As mentioned above, the 1965 Convention is the paramount example of the approach now prevailing in international law in respect of claims arising from foreign investments.

50. [. . .] It should be recalled that the ownership of shares was one of the specific examples of investment given during the negotiations of the Convention as pertinent for parties to agree in the context of their expressions of consent to jurisdiction. The definition of investment in the Argentina–United States BIT will be considered further below.

51. Precisely because the Convention does not define 'investment', it does not purport to define the requirements that an investment should meet to qualify for ICSID jurisdiction. There is indeed no requirement that an investment, in order to qualify, must necessarily be made by shareholders controlling a company or owning the majority of its shares. It is well known incidentally that, depending on how shares are distributed, controlling shareholders can in fact own less than the majority of shares. [. . .]

52. Article 25(1) of the Convention is also relevant in another respect. In the *Fedax* case, Venezuela had objected to ICSID's jurisdiction on the ground that the dispute transaction was not a 'direct foreign investment.' [. . .]

53. With this background in mind, it is then possible for this Tribunal to examine the meaning of a number of decisions of ICSID tribunals that have dealt with the protection of shareholders. The parties have a different reading of these ICSID cases, with particular reference to *AAPL v. Sri Lanka, AMT v. Zaire, Antoine Goetz et consorts v. Republique du Burundi, Maffezini v. Spain, Lanco v. Argentina, Genin v. Estonia, the Aguas* or *Vivendi* Award and Annulment and *CME v. Czech Republic*. For the Republic of Argentina, all these cases deal with shareholder rights, underlying arrangements and factual situations different from those given in the instant case, and hence do not support jurisdiction in this case. CMS, for its part, believes that, to the contrary, in all those cases the right of shareholders, including minority shareholders, to claim independently from the corporate entity affect has been upheld.

54. There can be no doubt that the factual setting of each case is different and that some may lend themselves more than others to illustrate points of relevance. In some cases, there has been majority shareholding or control by the investor, in others not; in some cases there has been expropriation affecting specifically the

shares, in others not; in some cases, there has been no objection to jurisdiction, in others there has been.

55. However, there can be no doubt that most, if not all, such cases are immersed in the same trend discussed above in the context of international law and the meaning of the 1965 Convention. In the present case, the Claimant has convincingly explained that notwithstanding the variety of situations in ICSID's jurisprudence noted by the Republic of Argentina, the tribunals have in all such cases been concerned not with the question of majority or control but rather whether shareholders can claim independently from the corporate entity. [. . .]

56. The Tribunal can therefore conclude that there is no bar to the exercise of jurisdiction in light of the 1965 Convention and its interpretation as reflected in its drafting history, the opinion of distinguished legal writers and the jurisprudence of ICSID tribunals.

Shareholder rights under the Argentina–United States Bilateral Investment Treaty

57. The Tribunal turns next to the examination of the definition of 'investment' in the Argentina–United States BIT. Article I(1) of this Treaty provides as pertinent:

'(a)   "investment" means every kind of investment in the territory of one Party owned or controlled directly or indirectly by nationals or companies of the other Party, such as equity, debt, and service and investment contracts; and includes without limitation:
(. . .)

(ii)   a company or shares of stock or other interests in a company or interests in the assets thereof . . .'

58. Here again the parties have a different reading of that Article. [. . .]

59. The Republic of Argentina has also asserted that [. . . the Treaty] would only allow claims for measures affecting the shares as such, for example, expropriation of the shares or interference with the political and economic rights tied to those shares. Such interpretation would not allow, however, for claims connected to damage suffered by the corporate entity. If a claim for indirect damage has been allowed, it is further argued, this would have been stated expressly in the Treaty, as has been in other bilateral investment treaties, including some signed by Argentina, or in the context of trade arrangements such as the North American Free Trade Agreement or other instruments. Silence on this point the Respondent argues, cannot be construed as an expression of consent to such type of claims.

60. CMS's understanding is different. In its view, the plain language of the provisions and their legal context can only mean that investment in shares is a protected investment and that the investor has, under the Treaty, the right for its investment

independently from any claims that the company in which it has invested might have. Again here, it is a question of seeking to identify the real economic interests between such transactions. It is argued, in addition, that it was Argentina that required the licensees of the privatization of the gas industry to be local companies. The protection granted by investment treaties was expressly mentioned in these invitations. If shareholders were not left out of such substantive protection, it is further explained, this would render the treaties meaningless.

61. The parties have debated the meaning of the decisions of other ICSID tribunals on this question. Again, it is evident that the factual and legal background of each such decision is different. Counsel for the Republic of Argentina have rightly explained that, in some cases, there has been a treaty authorizing indirect claims by the investor, in others there has been an expropriation of a license of the claimant or of the shares held by it, while in yet other cases claimants have been controlling or majority shareholders and thus their claim becomes a direct one.

62. Counsel for CMS have also explained that while in some cases there have been controlling shareholders and in others not, the relevant fact is that, in all cases, jurisdiction has been accepted on the basis that shareholders have a protected right of their own arising from their investment. None of these cases, it is further stated, has ever reasoned in terms of requiring control of the corporate entity for the protection of such rights.

63. The task of this Tribunal is rendered easier in light of the *Lanco* case, where the same Argentina–United States BIT and the same definition of investment were interpreted. That tribunal examined jurisdiction under two separate headings, one under the Treaty and the other under the concession agreement, concluding that, while jurisdiction could be founded on either heading, the fact that the investor also had specific rights and obligations under the concession agreement, held to be equivalent to an investment agreement, made the conclusion still more evident. The tribunal held in this respect:

> The Tribunal finds that the definition of this term in the ARGENTINA–U.S. Treaty is very broad and allows for many meanings. For example, as regards shareholder equity, the ARGENTINA–U.S. Treaty says nothing indicating that the investor in the capital stock has to have control over the administration of the company, or a majority share; thus the fact that LANCO holds an equity share of 18.3% in the capital stock of the Grantee allows one to conclude that it is an investor in the meaning of Article 1 of the ARGENTINA–U.S. Treaty. Nonetheless, the question is more complex considering that LANCO is not only the owner of an equity share in the capital stock of the grantee company, but also that the definition of 'investment' set forth in the ARGENTINA–U.S. Treaty allows one to conclude that LANCO has certain rights and obligations as a foreign investor under the Concession Agreement with the Government of the Argentine Republic.

64. A similar approach was taken by the Committee on Annulment in the *Compañía de Aguas del Aconquija* or *Vivendi* case, when holding under a different but comparable bilateral investment treaty:

> 'Moreover it cannot be argued that CGE did not have an "investment" in CAA from the date of the conclusion of the Concession Contract, or that it was not an "investor" in respect of its own shareholding, whether or not it had overall control of CAA. Whatever the extent of its investment may have been, it was entitled to invoke the BIT in respect of conduct alleged to constitute a breach of Articles 3 or 5.'

65. In light of the above considerations, the Tribunal concludes that jurisdiction can be established under the terms of the specific provisions of the BIT. Whether the protected investor is in addition a party to a concession agreement or a license agreement with the host State is immaterial for the purpose of finding jurisdiction under those treaty provisions, since there is a direct right of action of shareholders. It follows that the Claimant has *jus standi* before this Tribunal under international law, the 1965 Convention and the Argentina–United States Bilateral Investment Treaty.

? DISCUSSION NOTES

1   Unless the treaty provision specifically limits the protection to majority shareholders, tribunals will find that even minority shareholders can avail themselves of the agreement's protection.

   Granting minority shareholders rights to pursue arbitration certainly fosters the expansion of investment protection. But should each minority shareholder have this right? What would happen if multiple shareholders of a company pursued arbitration? See Rudolf Dolzer and Christoph Schreuer, *Principles of International Investment Law* 60 (second edn, 2012):

   > This generous extension of rights to shareholders can lead to some novel issues. For instance practical problems can arise where claims are pursued in parallel, especially by different shareholders or groups of shareholders. In addition, the affected company itself may pursue certain remedies while a group of its shareholders may pursue different ones. The situation becomes even more complex where indirect shareholding through intermediaries is combined with minority shareholding. In such a case, shareholders and companies at different levels may pursue conflicting or competing litigation strategies that may be difficult to reconcile and coordinate.

2   Can permitting a minority shareholder claim lead to an abuse of process? As Dolzer and Schreuer warned, allowing for minority shareholders to

bring investor-State disputes to arbitration has the potential to complicate litigation strategizing. While this is a difficulty faced by claimants, the burden on the respondent should not be ignored either—if every shareholder is a potential claimant, the potential litigation costs for the state could be crippling. In most cases, however, the practice of keeping the procedural costs on the claimant will prevent such a scenario.

If such costs are lifted—either by shifting the costs at the conclusion of the procedures to the losing party or by permitting third persons to fund the claimants—this inherent 'safety' mechanism breaks down. The issue then becomes one of preventing abusive uses of the system.

The tribunal examining the claims of several of Yukos' minority shareholders was neither influenced by the respondent's warnings that there might be a large number of similar claims waiting to be filed nor the fact that the minority shareholders' individual claims were worth less than they cost to litigate, and so might be seen as harassment.

In an arbitration before the Arbitration Institute of the Stockholm Chamber of Commerce, a third party financed an investor-State arbitration against the Russian state in the name of a group of minority shareholders. See *Quasar de Valores v. Russia*.[91] In its arguments on the merits, Russia pointed out that the costs of arbitration exceeded the value of the shareholders' claimed interests, and suggested that the claimants had other reasons for pursuing arbitration than merely receiving compensation for economic losses. The logical conclusion, Russia argued, was that the shareholders were engaging in an abuse of process and their claims should be denied.

The tribunal dismissed Russia's claims of abuse of process:

> 31. As seen in Paragraphs 11 and 12 above, the Respondent has sought to discredit the Claimants by suggesting that they are not the true parties in interest, and that the entire arbitration is an abuse of process. At its core, this argument is a reaction to the Claimants' disclosure that their costs of prosecuting this case are borne entirely by another party, namely Menatep, in part in order to establish that portfolio investors in Yukos are able to recover under BITs to which the Russian Federation is a party. A multitude of such potential claimants are, so it seems, waiting in the wings [. . .]. In other words, so the Respondent contends, the Claimants have no stake in this claim, and are not *domini litis* in terms of choosing counsel, experts, or other strategic alternatives in the prosecution of these derivate claims.

---

91 *Quasar de Valores SICAV SA et al. v. The Russian Federation*, Arbitration Institute of the Stockholm Chamber of Commerce, Award (July 20, 2012). Available at: http://italaw.com/sites/default/files/case-documents/ita1075.pdf.

32. This objection is unpersuasive. The Claimants purchased shares in Yukos (or, in the case of ALOS 34, stand in the shoes of such a purchaser) and complain about the destruction of their value. They have mandated [a private law firm] to prosecute their claim. They will be the beneficiaries of any award in their favour. [Claimants' attorney] has represented that this claim has been brought to safeguard the specific interests of the immediate Claimants [. . .], and that the Claimants have no legal obligation to share the proceeds with Menatep, and nothing more than a moral debt of gratitude to consider whether they will voluntarily pass on a proportion of any proceeds in recognition of the costs incurred by Menatep [. . .].

33. The Tribunal does not see any element of abuse in this respect. The Claimants held very small stakes of Yukos which would scarcely have warranted the commitment of substantial resources to bring international proceedings against the Russian Federation. But there is no reason of principle why they were not entitled to pursue rights available to them under the BIT, and to accept the assistance of a third party, whose motives are irrelevant as between the disputants in this case. Ultimately, the Respondent's complaint, in the event its liability is established, can hardly be raised against the Good Samaritan, but rather against its own officials who acted in such a way as to give rise to that liability.[92]

a   Control by foreign nationals: Article 25(2)(b) ICSID Convention

In the ICSID Agreement, parties can agree that controlling shareholders can lend their nationality to a corporate investor for purposes of arbitration jurisdiction.

Due to requirements in many states that active investments be incorporated under local laws, the drafters of the ICSID realized that the requirement of 'foreignness' would preclude many enterprises from protection. Thus, the ICSID convention permits its parties to grant nationality to corporations that are incorporated in the host but controlled by home state nationals. Article 25(2)(b) states:

> National of another Contracting State means . . . any juridical person which had the nationality of the contracting state party to the dispute on that date and which, because of foreign control, the parties have agreed should be treated as a national of another contracting state for the purposes of this Convention.

---

92 Id. at paras. 31–3; (citations omitted).

To access Article 25(2)(b)'s protections, there must be an agreement between the host and the investor company. Such an agreement may be found as an explicit clause in a concession contract, through a treaty clause setting out the host's acceptance of ICSID jurisdiction, or it may be implicit by virtue of a reference to ICSID dispute settlement in a BIT.

The terms of ICSID, however, do not conclusively define what is meant by 'control'. This issue was discussed fully by the *Aguas del Tunari* tribunal and the tribunal's dissenting opinion.

 CASE

Aguas del Tunari, SA v. Republic of Bolivia[93]

Aguas del Tunari (AdT) was a company incorporated in Bolivia. In September 1999, AdT received a concession for the right to provide water and sewage services to Cochabamba. Facing massive public resistance to the concession contract, the city rescinded its concession in April 2000. AdT brings an ICSID claim based on the Netherlands–Bolivia BIT.

One of the main issues was whether Aguas del Tunari could access the BIT protection. The BIT provision provided for investors as including corporations incorporated in Bolivia 'controlled directly or indirectly by nationals' of the Netherlands. While clearly AdT was 'controlled' by some foreign person, the parties differed on whether that person was Dutch or American. To resolve the issue, the tribunal had to address the opposing views of 'control':

> 214. Claimant seeks arbitration before the ICSID on the basis of Article 9(6) of the Netherlands–Bolivia BIT.
>
> 215. The Parties do not dispute that the Claimant, AdT, is a national of Bolivia. The issue before the Tribunal is whether AdT is—for the purposes of the BIT and in accordance with the terms of the BIT—to be regarded also as a 'national' of the Netherlands.
>
> 216. The Netherlands–Bolivia BIT, like the ICSID Convention and the majority of BITs, recognizes that the investor of one of the State Parties may incorporate an entity in the other State Party as a vehicle for its investment activity. Indeed, it is by no means uncommon practice that foreign investors may be required to incorporate locally by the host state.

---

93 *Aguas del Tunari, SA v. Republic of Bolivia*, ICSID Case No. ARB/02/3, Decision on Respondent's Objections to Jurisdiction (Oct. 21, 2005). Available at: http://italaw.com/documents/AguasdelTunari-jurisdiction-eng_000.pdf; (footnotes omitted).

217. To address this possible local incorporation of the investor, the Netherlands–Bolivia BIT follows the pattern of many BITs and provides that a 'national' of the Netherlands as defined by Articles 1(b) includes not only:

(i) natural persons having the nationality of that Contracting Party in accordance with its law; (ii) without prejudice to the provisions of (iii) hereafter, legal persons constituted in accordance with the law of that Contracting Party;

but also:

(iii) legal persons controlled directly or indirectly, by nationals of that Contracting Party, but constituted in accordance with the law of the other Contracting Party.

218. It will be recalled that AdT's ownership since December 22, 1999, as depicted in the figure below [Figure 3.1], is as follows:

219. With this ownership structure in mind, it is helpful to recognize what this objection is *not* about.

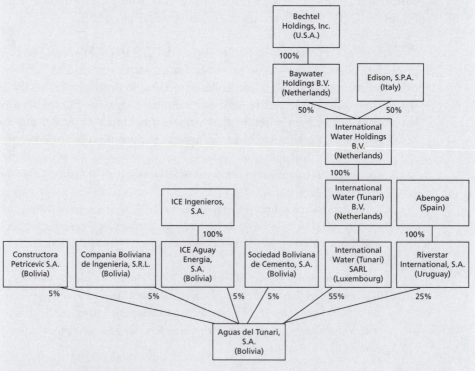

Source: Request for Arbitration, Exhibit 15, November 12, 2001.

Figure 3.1 AdT's ownership structure after December 22, 1999 (referred to as 'figure 2' in the Decision)

First, there does not appear to be any argument that AdT is foreign controlled, rather the disagreement is as to the location of that foreign control.

Second, there does not appear to be any argument that the Dutch upstream ownership [. . .] are all 'legal persons constituted in accordance with the law of' the Netherlands as required by Article 1(b)(ii). Respondent's first objection argued that the act of bringing the Dutch entities into the chain of AdT ownership was a violation of the Concession or representations made to the Respondent. Respondent does not argue, however, that the Dutch corporations are not properly constituted in accordance with Dutch law. Although the requirement of control raised by the second objection is not relevant to these Dutch entities, these entities were not named as claimants in this proceeding. Rather, in this proceeding, it is the Bolivian entity, AdT, that is named as claimant and it is that choice that makes Article 1(b)(iii) the basis for this objection.

220. Moreover, it is noteworthy that no suggestion is made that there is yet some other entity, beyond all those mentioned in Figure 2 [Figure 3.1], which controls AdT. Whatever entity (or entities) controls AdT, it (or they) is (or are) depicted in Figure 2 [Figure 3.1]. Claimant asserts that both IWT B.V. and IWH B.V. qualify as Dutch entities controlling AdT for the purposes of the BIT. Respondent argues that the true controller of AdT at all times was Bechtel, a U.S. corporation.

221. Recognizing what this objection does not concern, the Tribunal identifies two questions raised by the application of Article 1(b)(iii) to this case.

First, Article 1(b)(iii) requires that AdT, the Claimant and a Bolivian corporation, be 'controlled directly or indirectly' by either IWT B.V. or IWH B.V. This question has been argued extensively by the Parties and is primarily a question as to the interpretation and application of the phrase 'controlled directly or indirectly' found in Article 1 of the BIT.

Second, as can be seen in Figure 2 [Figure 3.1], between AdT and the various Dutch companies is IW S.a.r.l., a Luxembourg corporation. IW S.a.r.l. is 100 percent owned by the various Dutch entities. It, however, owns only 55 percent of AdT. For AdT to be 'controlled directly or indirectly', it must be the case that IW S.a.r.l. controls AdT. This question was not argued by the Parties in their written filings, but was raised as a part of the Hearing.

222. The Parties disagree on the legal test governing the question of whether AdT is 'controlled directly or indirectly' by either IWT B.V. or IWH B.V. For the Claimant, 100 percent ownership necessarily equals control and majority share-holding itself is sufficiently determinative of control. For the Respondent, the word 'control' means there must be *more* than 'ownership'. For the Respondent, control means the exercise of powers or direction, not merely the legal potential to do so. Thus Respondent uses terms as 'real control' in its submissions to ask for

'something more' to determine the 'reality of the corporate personality'. Claimant argues that 100 percent ownership entails the legal potential to control and that Respondent's use of modifiers for 'control', such as effective or actual, is unwarranted. Respondent contends that control is a factual question particularly relevant to situations where the company alleged to control another company in fact has little, if any, capacity to exercise such control.

223. Thus the crucial point of disagreement is that Claimant, on the one hand, interprets the phrase 'controlled directly or indirectly' as requiring only the legal potential to control the Claimant and that the phrase thus potentially encompasses not only the ultimate parent of AdT, but also the subsidiaries of the parent above the Claimant. The Respondent, on the other hand, interprets the phrase 'controlled directly or indirectly' as requiring 'ultimate' control of AdT or, if the phrase is not limited to the ultimate controller, then 'effective', 'actual' control of AdT. Thus the difference in view between the Parties is not between 'control' and 'ownership', but rather between 'control' as requiring the legal potential to control and 'control' as requiring the actual exercise of control.

224. Finally, it is important to observe that the framing of the issue before the Tribunal is rendered necessary by Claimant's reliance on its documentary evidence of IWT B.V.'s and IWH B.V.'s legal ownership interest in, and resultant potential control of, AdT as sufficient proof to establish jurisdiction under the BIT. As noted above, Respondent has requested the production of documents from Claimant bearing on the control in fact of AdT by IWT B.V. or IWH B.V. Claimant opposes such a production request arguing that such documents legally are immaterial and that such a broad discovery order as a practical matter would be burdensome. In addition, as discussed in paragraph 246, *infra*, Respondent does not make clear what evidence would be sufficient to establish the exercise of control argued by Respondent to be required by the BIT. The issue as framed by Claimant might be mooted if the Tribunal ordered the production of documents and such documents established not only the legal potential to control, but also the exercise of control. But, given that Respondent has not indicated what evidence would establish effective control, there is not a basis to make an appropriately tailored order for production of documents. Moreover, it is Claimant's prerogative to structure its claim and in doing so it runs the risk of the Tribunal denying jurisdiction in this matter.

The Meaning of the Phrase: 'controlled directly or indirectly'

The Ordinary Meaning of the Phrase: 'controlled directly or indirectly'

225. Article 1(b)(iii) provides that a national of a Contracting Party includes 'legal persons controlled directly or indirectly, by nationals of that Contracting Party, but constituted in accordance with the law of the other Contracting Party'.

226. Article 31(2) of the Vienna Convention requires that the interpreter as one part of his task look to the 'ordinary meaning' of a word or phrase unless a 'special meaning' was intended by the parties. The phrase requiring interpretation is 'controlled directly or indirectly' where 'controlled' is the past participle of the transitive verb 'control.' As anticipated by the Vienna Convention itself in requiring the interpreter to look not only to the ordinary meaning of a phrase, but also to the context in which it is found and in light of the object and purpose of the document, the ordinary meaning of 'controlled directly or indirectly', although clearly an essential element of the task of interpretation, is not determinative in this instance.

227. To find the 'ordinary meaning' of the word 'controlled', the Tribunal sought guidance from standard desk dictionaries. One standard American English dictionary defined the transitive verb 'control' as 'to exercise restraining or directing influence over . . . to have power over'. According to another desk dictionary, the verb control can be defined as to 'manage: to exercise power or authority over something such as a business or a nation'. Similarly, a standard British English dictionary defines 'control' as both 'the fact of controlling' and 'the function or power of directing and regulating; domination, command, sway'. On the one hand, the use of the word 'manage' in the second quotation seems to conform to the Respondent's view that control involves actual exercise of powers or direction. On the other hand, the words 'power' and 'authority' point in the opposite direction. 'Authority' is defined simply as 'the right or power to enforce rules or give orders' and 'power' as either 'the ability, skill, or capacity to do something' or 'the authority to act or do something according to a law or rule.' Thus while some definitions suggest the actual exercise of influence, others emphasize the possession of power over an object. Thus, the ordinary meaning of 'control' would seemingly encompass both actual exercise of powers or direction and the rights arising from the ownership of shares.

[. . .]

231. The legal definition for the verb 'control' provides several meanings for control. [. . .] The first definition of control suggests the actual exercise of control with emphasis on the right to exercise control over an object but does not suggest ownership of the object. The second definition similarly points to a right to control but not ownership of that which is controlled. The third definition of control ties control to ownership interest providing that a 'controlling interest' is understood as a 'legal share in something . . . sufficient ownership of stock in a company to control policy and management; especially a greater-than-50% ownership interest in an enterprise.'

232. The legal definitions of 'controlled' are particularly instructive as they cut directly against the significance to the adjectival past participle usage suggested by Respondent. The phrase 'controlled group (controlled corporate groups)' is defined as 'two or more corporations whose stock is substantially held by five or fewer persons. 'Controlled corporation (controlled company)' is defined as a

'corporation in which the majority of the stock is held by one individual or firm.' And 'controlled foreign corporation' is defined as 'a foreign corporation in which more than 50% of the stock is owned by U.S. citizens who each own 10% or more of the voting stock.' All three of these definitions refer solely to the power to control and not its actual exercise.

233. The Tribunal thus concludes that the word 'controlled', like the word 'control', is not determinative. [. . .] On the one hand, 'controlled' may mean that an entity was subject to the actual control of another. On the other, 'controlled' may mean that an entity was subject to the controlling capacity of another.

234. The Tribunal observes that there is no indication from any of the dictionaries consulted that 'control' necessarily entails a degree of active exercise of powers or direction. If the parties had intended this result, a better choice of word for the BIT would have been 'managed' rather than 'controlled'. In addition, although the contracting states would have eliminated uncertainty by utilizing phrasing such as 'under direct or indirect control of' or 'subject to the direct or indirect control of', rather than 'controlled directly or indirectly' by another company, the ambiguous meaning of 'controlled' leads the Tribunal to find the difference in phrasing to be not determinative.

235. Respondent argues that in light of the lack of a specific definition for 'control' in the BIT, the Tribunal should look to the concept of 'control' as it has been used in defining corporate nationality under international law. Bolivia states that there are four traditional tests for determining corporate nationality of an entity. Both the corporate seat test and the incorporating jurisdiction test 'focus on objective factors for the purposes of simplicity, and ignore the possibility that the assigned nationality may not reflect the reality of the company's activities.' The other two tests focus respectively on control and on predominant interest in the company and, Bolivia argues, states select the 'control' test because it is 'designed to focus on the reality behind the corporate personality . . . [and is] often used "to avoid inequitable results."' There is, however, no indication in the record that the contracting parties had such a particular special meaning for control in mind. Nor should such intent be assumed since the Tribunal finds the contexts of foreign investment protection and the regulation of corporate activity to be sufficiently distinct.

236. [. . .]

[. . .]

The Phrase in its Context and in Light of the Object and Purpose of the BIT

241. It is in the consideration of the context in which the phrase 'controlled directly or indirectly' is found, and in light of the object and purpose of the BIT, that the Tribunal finds the basis for the interpretation of the phrase.

242. As to the object and purpose of the BIT, the Tribunal notes that the Preamble to the BIT provides:

The Government of the Netherlands and the Government of the Republic of Bolivia, desiring to strengthen the traditional ties of friendship between their countries, to extend and intensify the economic relations between them particularly with respect to investments by the nationals of one Contracting Party in the territory of the other Contracting Party.

Recognizing that agreement upon the treatment to be accorded to such investment will stimulate the flow of capital and technology and the economic development of the Contracting Parties and that fair and equitable treatment of investment is desirable [. . .].

Thus the object and purpose of the treaty is to 'stimulate the flow of capital and technology' and the Contracting Parties explicitly recognize that such stimulation will result from 'agreement upon the treatment to be accorded to . . . investments' by 'the national of one Contracting Party in the territory of the other Contracting Party.'

243. As to the context in which the phrase 'controlled directly or indirectly' is found, the Tribunal notes that Article 1 in defining the concept of 'national' not only defines the scope of persons and entities that are to be regarded as the beneficiaries of the substantive rights of the BIT but also defines those persons and entities to whom the offer of arbitration is directed and who thus are potential claimants. Given the context of defining the scope of eligible claimants, the word 'controlled' is not intended as an alternative to ownership since control without an ownership interest would define a group of entities not necessarily possessing an interest which could be the subject of a claim. In this sense, 'controlled' indicates a quality of the ownership interest.

244. The question therefore is how the term 'controlled' in Article 1(b)(iii) is meant to qualify 'ownership.' Claimant argues that 'control' is a capacity that the ownership interest possesses. If one entity owns 100% of another entity, then the first entity, in Claimant's view, possesses the capacity to control the other entity and that entity is a 'controlled' entity. For the Claimant, the word 'control', rather than simply 'ownership', is employed in the BIT to address the situation where a minority shareholder through, for example, voting rights possesses the capacity to control the other entity. Respondent argues that 'control' is a capacity that the ownership interest must exercise. Moreover, Respondent appears to argue that that exercise of control must be done by the owning entity itself.

245. The Tribunal does not find Respondent's view to be persuasive for three reasons.

246. First, Claimant's view that 'control' is a quality that accompanies ownership finds support generally in the law. An entity that owns 100% of the shares of another entity necessarily possesses the power to control the second entity. The first entity may decline to exercise its control, but that is its choice. Moreover, the first entity may be held responsible under various corporate law doctrines for

the actions of its subsidiary, whether or not it actually exercised control over that subsidiary's actions. Respondent contends that IWT B.V. and IWH B.V. are mere 'shells' which cannot even decline to exercise its possible control. Holding companies (if that is all IWT B.V. and IWH B.V. are in this case) owning substantial assets (here the rights under the Concession) are, however, both a common and legal device for corporate organization and face the same legal obligations of corporations generally. The Tribunal acknowledges that the corporate form may be abused and that form may be set aside for fraud or on other grounds. As outlined in paragraph 331, *infra*, the Tribunal finds no such extraordinary grounds to be present on the evidence.

247. Second, Respondent's argument that 'control' can be satisfied by only a certain level of actual control has not been defined by the Respondent with sufficient particularity. Rather, the concept is sufficiently vague as to be unmanageable. Respondent asserts that the phrase 'controlled directly or indirectly' referred to the 'ultimate controller' provides a defined standard, but as stated in paragraph 237, the Tribunal rejects this interpretation as inconsistent with the language 'directly or indirectly'. Once one admits of the possibility of several controllers, then the definition of what constitutes sufficient 'actual' control for any particular controller, particularly when an entity may delegate such actual control, becomes problematic. This becomes apparent with Respondent's difficulty in offering the Tribunal the details of its 'actual' control test. In response to a question of the Tribunal as to the details of an actual control test, counsel for Respondent stated that '[c]ontrol is not a – an objective – there is not an objective bright-line test for control in a corporate organization control sense. You have to know details.' Indeed, Respondent's argument that 'control' can be satisfied by only a certain level of actual control by one entity over another entity ignores the reality that such exercise of control may be delegated to a subsidiary or even to an independent subcontractor. Moreover, the many dimensions of actual control of a corporate entity range from day to day operations up to strategic decision-making. Would the minutes of one Board of Directors meeting delegating to a consulting firm the management of a majority owned company be evidence of actual control of that company? Would the minutes of one Board of Directors meeting delegating to a parent or subsidiary company management of a majority owned company be evidence of actual control of the company? Would the day to day direction by one company of the operations of a majority owned company not be sufficient evidence of actual control if a parent company dictated which business opportunities would be taken up by the majority owned company and which would not?

The difficulty in articulating a test in the Tribunal's view reflects not only the fact that the Respondent did not provide such a test, but also the possibility that it is not practicable to do so and that, as discussed in the next paragraph, the resultant uncertainty would directly frustrate the object and purpose of the BIT.

248. Third, the uncertainty inherent in Respondent's call for a test based on an uncertain level of actual control would not be consistent with the object and purpose of the BIT. The BIT is intended to stimulate investment by the provision of an agreement on how investments will be treated, that treatment including the possibility of arbitration before ICSID. If an investor cannot ascertain whether their ownership of a locally incorporated vehicle for the investment will qualify for protection, then the effort of the BIT to stimulate investment will be frustrated.

[. . .]

Conclusion as to the Meaning of 'controlled directly or indirectly'

264. The Tribunal, by majority, concludes that the phrase 'controlled directly or indirectly' means that one entity may be said to control another entity (either directly, that is without an intermediary entity, or indirectly) if that entity possesses the legal capacity to control the other entity. Subject to evidence of particular restrictions on the exercise of voting rights, such legal capacity is to be ascertained with reference to the percentage of shares held. In the case of a minority shareholder, the legal capacity to control an entity may exist by reason of the percentage of shares held, legal rights conveyed in instruments or agreements such as the articles of incorporation or shareholders' agreements, or a combination of these. In the Tribunal's view, the BIT does not require actual day-to-day or ultimate control as part of the 'controlled directly or indirectly' requirement contained in Article 1(b)(iii). The Tribunal observes that it is not charged with determining all forms which control might take. It is the Tribunal's conclusion, by majority, that, in the circumstances of this case, where an entity has both majority shareholdings and ownership of a majority of the voting rights, control as embodied in the operative phrase 'controlled directly or indirectly' exists.

265. The Declaration of José Luis Alberro-Semerena dissents to the Tribunal's decision as to the interpretation given to the phrase 'controlled directly or indirectly.' The difference between the majority and the dissent as to Respondent's request for production for documents follows directly from their difference in the interpretation of that phrase.

Confirming the Interpretation of 'controlled directly or indirectly'

266. The Tribunal turns to an Article 32 analysis to confirm its interpretation of the phrase 'controlled directly or indirectly'. In doing so, the Tribunal looks to:

a.   The Negotiating History of the BIT

b.   The Jurisprudence regarding Article 25(2) of the ICSID Convention

c. The Holdings of Other Arbitral Awards Concerning 'Control'
d. The BIT Practice Generally of Both Nations [. . .]

The Negotiating History of the BIT

[. . .]

274. This sparse negotiating history thus offers little additional insight into the meaning of the aspects of the BIT at issue, neither particularly confirming nor contradicting the Tribunal's interpretation.

The Jurisprudence Regarding Article 25(2) of the ICSID Convention

275. The jurisdictional aspect of the ICSID Convention relevant to the present proceeding is Article 25(2)(b). It provides in relevant part:

> (2) 'National of another Contracting State' means:
> [. . .]
> (b) any juridical person [. . .] which, *because of foreign control*, the parties have agreed should be treated as a national of another Contracting State for purposes of this Convention. (*Emphasis added.*)

276. The parties both make reference to various tribunal awards, scholarly commentary, and the drafting history regarding the use of the word 'foreign control' in the ICSID Convention at Article 25(2)(b) in order to illuminate the meaning of 'controlled directly or indirectly' in the BIT.

277. Understanding how the ICSID Convention is relevant to an arbitration initiated under a BIT, illuminates why the interpretation of the term control in Article 25(2)(b) may or may not bear on the interpretation of the term 'controlled' in the BIT.

278. The Netherlands–Bolivia BIT contains an offer by Bolivia and by the Netherlands to defined nationals of the other party to arbitrate specified disputes before ICSID. A claimant accepts this offer through its filing of a request for arbitration. This Tribunal is established pursuant to the ICSID Convention and its jurisdiction is limited by the ICSID Convention, as defined in Article 25. This Tribunal must therefore evaluate whether the dispute presented to it under the BIT passes through the jurisdictional keyhole defined by Article 25 of the ICSID Convention. The state parties to the BIT can seek to encompass all manner of disputes. But in attempting to place disputes under their BIT before ICSID, an institution regulated by a separate instrument, the scope of the disputes which may be submitted is necessarily limited to those disputes that pass through the jurisdictional keyhole defined by Article 25.

279. The image of Article 25 of the ICSID Convention as a jurisdictional keyhole makes clear that the jurisprudence concerning the phrase 'foreign

control' in Article 25(2)(b) is of quite limited relevance to the interpretation of
the BIT.

280. Article 1(b)(iii) is an agreement of Bolivia and the Netherlands to treat a
judicial person of one of them as a national of the other if that judicial person is
'controlled directly or indirectly' by nationals of the other. The question is whether
this definition of control in the BIT is such that disputes under the BIT pass
through the jurisdictional keyhole of Article 25. In this light, it is not at all surprising that the drafting history, commentary and arbitral awards concerning that
phrase 'foreign control' in Article 25 all point to 'foreign control' being 'flexible' so
that reasonable definitions in referring instruments may pass through the jurisdictional keyhole.

281. Thus Professor Schreuer notes that national and treaty-based definitions
should be deferred to, so long as they are reasonable:

> Definitions of corporate nationality in national legislation or in treaties provid-
> ing for ICSID's jurisdiction will be controlling for the determination of whether
> the nationality requirements of Art. 25(2)(b) have been met. They are part of
> the legal framework for the host State's submission to the Centre. Upon accept-
> ance in writing by the investor, they become part of the agreement on consent
> between the parties. Therefore, any *reasonable determination* of the nationality
> of juridical persons contained in national legislation or in a treaty should be
> accepted by an ICSID commission or tribunal.

282. Respondent appears to argue that 'the definition of control' under the
Bilateral Investment Treaty would be coextensive with the definition under the
ICSID Convention with an emphasis on control as an 'objective element that
must be determined by the Tribunal.' Claimant argues that Article 25(2)(b)
and the definition of control in the BIT are not co-extensive and that parties
had the flexibility and 'latitude to define "control" in the BIT for the purpose
of Article 25(2)(b) of the ICSID Convention' as long as the agreement was
reasonable.

283. The drafting history of Article 25 as well as arbitral awards and scholarly
commentary indicate, however, that the drafters intended a flexible definition of
control in Article 25 not because they regarded 'control' as requiring a wide ranging
inquiry, but rather—recognizing the keyhole function that would be played by
Article 25—to accommodate a wide range of agreements between parties as to the
meaning of 'foreign control'.

284. Aron Broches, chairman of the consultative meetings for the negotiation of
the ICSID Convention and General Counsel of the World Bank and subsequently
ICSID's first Secretary-General, writes that during the drafting the attempt to
provide an exacting definition of foreign control was 'abandoned' and that instead
it was decided that 'an attempt should be made . . . to give the greatest possible

latitude to the parties to decide under what circumstances a company could be treated as a 'national of another Contracting State'.

285. There is no issue in the Tribunal's view that Article 1 of the BIT under either the Claimant's or Respondent's interpretation would be an agreement as to 'foreign control' that satisfies the flexible and deferential requirement of Article 25(2).

286. For the foregoing reasons, the Tribunal does not find the jurisprudence concerning the phrase 'foreign control' in Article 25(2)(b) to assist the Tribunal in interpreting Article 1(b)(iii) of the BIT.

[...]

Applying the Interpretation: Is AdT 'controlled directly or indirectly' by IWH B.V. or IWT B.V.?

315. It remains for the Tribunal to decide whether AdT is 'controlled directly or indirectly' by either IWT B.V. or IWH B.V., as that phrase has been interpreted by the Tribunal.

316. The first tier of ownership above AdT is as follows [shown in Figure 3.2 below].

[...]

318. The upstream ownership of AdT specifically is that set forth in [Figure 3.3 on page 179].

[...]

321. On the basis of the evidence available, IWH B.V. is not simply a corporate shell set up to obtain ICSID jurisdiction over the present dispute. Rather, IWH B.V. is a joint venture 50% owned by Baywater and 50% owned by Edison S.p.A., an Italian corporation. IWH B.V. is structured so that neither Baywater nor Edison exclusively control IWH B.V., to the exclusion of the other, but rather the two entities must work together in order to direct IWH B.V.

[...]

323. The Tribunal thus concludes that both IWT B.V. and IWH B.V. indirectly controlled AdT in accordance with the Tribunal's interpretation of the phrase 'controlled directly or indirectly' found in Article 1(b)(iii) of the BIT.

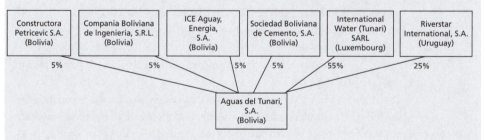

Source: Request for Arbitration, Exhibit 15, November 12, 2001.

Figure 3.2 The first tier of ownership of AdT after December 22, 1999

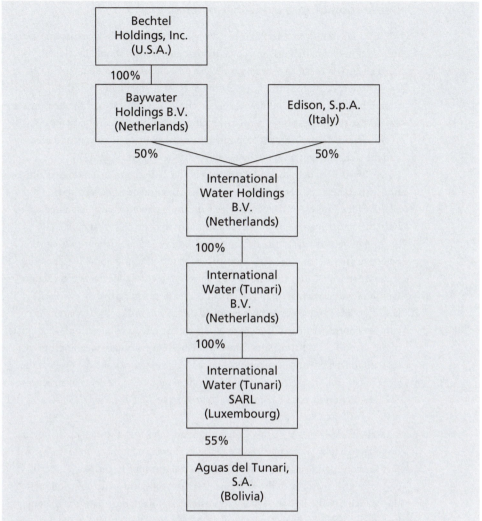

Source: Request for Arbitration, Exhibit 15, November 12, 2001.

Figure 3.3 AdT's ownership structure through the Netherlands after December 22, 1999

[...]

The AdT majority's view of control was not accepted by one of the tribunal members. Arbitrator Alberro-Semerena voiced his dissatisfaction with the majority's refusal to look into the actual influence of the claimant shareholder on the alleged investment:

Declaration of José Luis Alberro-Semerena:[94]

22. [. . .] I dissent from the Tribunal's decision regarding Bolivia's objection to the jurisdiction of the Tribunal and consider that jurisdiction should be denied.

23. The answer to the question is in the use of the term 'controlled'.

24. With respect to the ordinary meaning of control, the majority of the Tribunal found that 'while some definitions suggest the actual exercise of influence, others emphasize the possession of power over an object. Thus, the ordinary meaning of 'control' would seemingly encompass both actual exercise of powers or direction and the rights arising from the ownership of shares.' (Paragraph 227).

25. As for its legal definition, the majority of the Tribunal relies on three definitions: 'to exercise power or influence over; . . . to regulate or govern and . . . to have a controlling interest in.' Hence, the legal meaning of control also encompasses both the actual exercise of control and the right to control. (Paragraph 231).

26. In Article 1(b)(iii) of the BIT, the word 'controlled' is a passive participial adjective formed from the verb 'control' which modifies the noun 'legal persons'. Passive participial adjectives describe nouns that receive the effects of an action. Grammar indicates that for 'legal persons' constituted in accordance with the law of a contracting party to be 'controlled directly or indirectly' by nationals of another contracting party, they have to receive the effects of an action by nationals of the second contracting party. Thus, while both the ordinary meaning and the legal definition of control encompass the actual exercise of control as well as the right to control, the passive participial adjective requires the effects of an action. For jurisdiction to exist, Claimant has to prove that AdT received the effect of actions by Dutch companies.

27. Article 31(4) of the Vienna Convention indicates that a special meaning shall be given to a term, if the parties so intended. There is no indication in the record that the contracting parties intended any special meaning to the word 'control'. I agree with the majority of the Tribunal that the negotiators who contributed to the language of the BIT were likely sophisticated foreign negotiators with some knowledge of business and law. (Paragraph 230). Article 1(b)(iii) of the BIT, however, does not use 'control' but 'controlled'. The parties could have used the expression 'in direct or indirect control of' or 'under direct or indirect control of' or 'because of foreign control' as in the ICSID Convention which was public knowledge before the BIT was negotiated and would have incorporated existing case law and scholarly commentary. In contradistinction, they chose to use the passive participial adjective 'controlled', which requires the effects of an action.

28. It is in the consideration of the context in which we find the phrase 'controlled directly or indirectly', and in the light of the object and purpose of the treaty that we find the basis for its interpretation. (Paragraph 240).

---

94 Id.

29. The object and purpose of the BIT is to stimulate the flow of capital and technology: Indeed, the Contracting Parties explicitly recognize that such stimulation will result from 'agreement upon the treatment to be accorded to . . . investments' by 'the national of one Contracting Party in the territory of the other Contracting Party.' (Paragraph 240). Article 1 of the BIT determines the circle of beneficiaries, which is a subset of all existing persons.

30. Article 1(b)(i) and Article 1(b)(ii) empower all natural persons having the nationality of a Contracting Party and all legal persons constituted in accordance with the law of a Contracting Party.

31. Article 1(b)(iii) extends the protection of the BIT to legal persons against the actions of their own government but limits those benefits to legal persons having the special attribute of being 'controlled' by nationals of the other signatory. Assuming without conceding that an entity that owns 100% of the shares and voting rights of another entity possesses the power to control the second entity, there is no reason to posit that it is more reasonable to extend the privileges concomitant to Article 1(b)(iii) to companies potentially under the control of nationals of the other signatory, as opposed to companies actually receiving the effects of an action from nationals of the other signatory. The opposite is sounder: the access mechanism to the privileges concomitant to Article 1(b)(iii) should be an actual event, an action (controlled) and not a possibility.

32. It is incorrect to equate 'controlled' and 'control'. One should be 'aware of the general principle of interpretation whereby a text ought to be interpreted in the manner that gives it effect—*ut magis valeat quam pereat*. However, this principle of interpretation should not lead to confer, *at posteriori*, to a provision deprived of its object and purpose a result that goes against its clear and explicit terms'. To substitute 'controlled' with the term 'control' is to go against the text's clear and explicit terms. The fundamental issues of foreseeability, transparency and stability accepted by parties to a BIT cannot be resolved by limiting 'control' to majority ownership and voting rights when the Treaty explicitly uses the expression 'controlled directly or indirectly'.

33. Neither the jurisprudence concerning the phrase 'foreign control' in Article 25(2)(b) of the ICSID Convention, nor other Arbitral Awards concerning 'control', nor the BIT practices of the Netherlands and Bolivia can be of assistance in interpreting Article 1(b)(iii) of the BIT.

34. Since the BIT does not provide a definition of 'directly or indirectly controlled' and, unlike the case of the ICSID convention, there is little or no history or commentary on the BIT, it is the Tribunal's responsibility to interpret the meaning of the expression. Many cases underline the importance of the Tribunal's authority to interpret access provisions past formal interpretations to actual relationships. [. . .]

35. This elucidation of the meaning of 'controlled' is strengthened by the fact that the identification of corporate nationality has been difficult from the point of view of international law for almost a century, as wars have shaped the meaning assigned

to it by sovereign powers. Different criteria have been put forward but none has prevailed: neither place of incorporation; nor seat of the company; nor ownership and voting rights. To resort to a mechanistic interpretation of control would be to go against the historical development of the concept. An interpretation that favors an action is in keeping with the search for a functional definition.

36. [. . .]

38. Commentary on the drafting of the ICSID convention makes it clear that share ownership at a level greater than 50% might not be controlling: 'Thus, where nationals of a Contracting State hold 35 percent of the shares of a corporation and nationals of a non-Contracting State hold 55 percent of the shares, an agreement that the corporation has the nationality of the Contracting State may well be upheld by a tribunal'. 'In the course of the drafting of the Convention, it was said . . . even that 51% of the shares might not be controlling.'

39. Previous tribunal awards have established that an investor with minority share ownership can control a company, thereby providing counterexamples to the assertion that majority share ownership and majority voting rights are sufficient to establish control. Even in the case of 100% ownership, Tribunals have examined 'effective control': 'This control is not only a result of the fact that [the claimant's] capital stock was 100% owned by French nationals [. . .], it also results from what appears to be effective control by French nationals; effective control in the sense that, apart from French shareholdings, French nationals dominated the company decision-making structure.' [quotation from *LETCO v. Liberia*[95]]

40. Thus the interpretation of control advanced by Claimant is logically inconsistent. Majority shareholding and majority voting rights do not *per se* constitute control.

41. Given that [. . .] there is no evidence in the filings that AdT received the effects of actions of control and thus no proof that it was 'controlled directly or indirectly' by Dutch nationals, the Tribunal should have requested the production of evidence to substantiate the claim that AdT was directly or indirectly controlled by IWH B.V. or IWT B.V. The tribunal in *Aucoven*, for example, listed criteria, different from share ownership, that could have been used to test control: nationality of the Board members, frequency of visits of board members of the direct shareholder, frequency of 'monitoring' of *Aucoven's* activities, and financial support.

42. In order to specifically evaluate actions of control of AdT, the Tribunal should have requested Claimant to produce, *inter alia*, the following information for the period December 22, 1999—when a Dutch company acquired International Water (Tunari) S.a.r.l. that used to be called IW Ltd of the Cayman Islands—to November 12, 2001—when AdT submitted its Request for Arbitration: (I) all documents reflecting or constituting communications between AdT and

---

95 *Liberian Eastern Timber Corp [LETCO] v Republic of Liberia*, Award of March 31, 1986 and Rectification of June 17, 1986, reprinted as 26 ILM 647 (1987), 2 ICSID Rep 346 (1994).

(a) International Water (Tunari) S.a.r.l, (b) International Water (Tunari) B.V., (c) International Water Holdings B.V. and (d) Baywater Holdings B.V.; (II) all documents reflecting or constituting communications relating to AdT between or among any of the following (a) International Water (Tunari) S.a.r.l, (b) International Water (Tunari) B.V., (c) International Water Holdings B.V. and (d) Baywater Holdings B.V.; and, finally, (III) all board of director minutes and share-holder meeting minutes for (a) AdT, (b) International Water (Tunari) S.a.r.l, (c) International Water (Tunari) B.V., (d) International Water Holdings B.V. and (e) Baywater Holdings B.V. If AdT was indeed controlled directly or indirectly by International Water (Tunari) B.V. and International Water Holdings B.V., those documents would provide evidence of such actions of control.

43. The majority of the Tribunal denied Respondent's request for the production of evidence because it had no object given its interpretation.

44. By resting its case on jurisdiction on majority stock ownership with voting rights and not offering evidence that AdT received the effects of actions of control by Dutch companies, Claimant failed to prove that this dispute is within the juris-dictional reach of the BIT.

It is for the above reasons that I disagree with the Majority's decision in favor of jurisdiction and conclude that Claimant is not entitled to invoke ICSID jurisdic-tion under the BIT between Bolivia and the Netherlands. I wholeheartedly join in the Tribunal's commitment to its duty to protect the integrity of ICSID jurisdiction during the merits phase, as the parties submit their full memorials and supporting evidence.

 DISCUSSION NOTES

1 In *Caratube v. Kazakhstan,* U.S. citizen Devincci Hourani owned 92 percent of the shares of the locally-incorporated claimant. Relying on AdT, Caratube argued that the BIT's provision allowing for ICSID Article 25(2)(b) nationality should apply. The tribunal disagreed:

406. As a witness, Devincci Hourani admitted that he did not participate in a day to day running of [Caratube] in times when he was not a director [. . .]. His evidence of control is based on a reference to [the company's] Charter and Incorporation Agreement, which give him certain competences. However, no evidence was shown that such competences and control were actually exercised by him.

407. Thus, there is not sufficient evidence of exercise of actual control over [Caratube] by Devincci Hourani. In view of the above considerations, the Tribunal concludes that Claimant has not provided sufficient proof for control as required by Art. 25(2)(b) of the ICSID Convention. The Tribunal is not

satisfied that a legal capacity to control a company, without evidence of an actual control, is enough [. . .].

See *Caratube International Oil Company LLP v. Republic of Kazakhstan*, ICSID Case No. ARB/08/12, Award (5 June 2012).

2 In *Champion Trading v. Egypt*, incorporation and control were required for nationality. In this case, Champion Trading was incorporated in the US, but control of the company was held by Egypt–US dual citizens. Faced with Egypt's argument that the Egyptian nationality of the controlling shareholders defeated jurisdiction, the tribunal distinguished between dual citizens as investors and dual citizens as shareholders of a legal person. The former, it noted, makes jurisdiction under ICSID impossible. It considered, however, that because there was nothing to exclude duals from being controllers, the jurisdictional challenge would fail. See *Champion Trading Company, Ameritrade International, Inc., James T. Wahba, John B. Wahba, Timothy T. Wahba v. Arab Republic of Egypt*, ICSID Case No. ARB/02/9, Decision on Jurisdiction, at pp. 9–17 (21 Oct. 2003), *accessed at* http:// italaw.com/documents/ champion-decision.pdf.

This reasoning was implicitly rejected by the more recent *Burimi SRL and Eagle Games v. Albania* dispute.[96] In this case, claimant Eagle Games was a company incorporated in Albania but controlled by a shareholder who possessed both Italian and Albanian nationality. Having found that ICSID Convention Article 25(2)(b) would be applicable, the arbitrators then had to determine whether the controlling shareholder's Albanian nationality posed a bar to the claim. The tribunal found that it did, noting:

> [. . .] it strikes the Tribunal as anomalous that the principle against use of dual nationality in 25(2)(a) would not transfer to the potential use of dual nationality in 25(2)(b). Otherwise, any dual national who is a national of the Contracting State to a dispute could circumvent the bar on claims in Article 25(2)(a) by establishing a company in that state and asserting foreign control of that company by virtue of his second (foreign) nationality. Accordingly, the Tribunal finds that for the purposes of considering whether Eagle Games could be treated as a national of another Contracting State (i.e., Italy) because of 'foreign control', Mr. Ilir Burimi cannot invoke his Italian nationality to establish 'foreign control' of Eagle Games'.

See *Burimi SRL and Eagle Games SH.A v. Republic of Albania*, ICSID Case No. ARB/11/18, Award, para. 121 (29 May 2013).

---

96 The *Burimi* tribunal made no reference to the Champion Trading award.

3 In *Tokios Tokelés,* one of the Respondent's arguments was that ICSID
   Convention Art. 25(2)(b)'s control test to grant jurisdiction supported
   its position that control by host state nationals should defeat jurisdiction of a company incorporated in the other party's territory.
   The tribunal refused to accept this argument, basing its decision not to
   do so on the purpose of the provision:

> 44. The second clause of Article 25(2)(b) provides that parties can, by agree-
> ment, depart from the general rule that a corporate entity has the nationality of
> its state of incorporation. It extends jurisdiction to 'any juridical person which
> had the nationality of the Contracting State party to the dispute on [the date
> on which the parties consented to submit the dispute to arbitration] and which,
> *because of foreign control*, the parties have agreed should be treated as a national
> of another Contracting State . . .'. This exception to the general rule applies
> only in the context of an agreement between the parties . . .
> [. . .]
> 46. . . . [A]s explained by Mr. Broches, the purpose of the control-test in the
> second portion of Article 25(2)(b) is to *expand* the jurisdiction of the Centre:

>> [t]here was a compelling reason for this last provision. It is quite usual for
>> host States to require that foreign investors carry on their business within
>> their territories through a company organized under the laws of the host
>> country. If we admit, as the Convention does implicitly, that this makes the
>> company technically a national of the host country, it becomes readily appar-
>> ent that there is need for an exception to the general principle that that the
>> Centre will not have jurisdiction over disputes between a Contracting State
>> and its own nationals.
>> *If no exception were made for foreign-owned but locally incorporated companies,
>> a large and important sector of foreign investment would be outside the scope of
>> the Convention.*

> 47. ICSID tribunals likewise have interpreted the second clause of Article
> 25(2) to expand, not restrict, jurisdiction. In *Wena Hotels Ltd. v. Egypt*, the
> respondent argued that Wena, though incorporated in the United Kingdom,
> should be treated as an Egyptian company because it was owned by an Egyptian
> national. Egypt relied on Article 8.1 of the U.K.–Egypt BIT provision, which
> states:

>> [s]uch a company of one Contracting Party in which before such dispute
>> arises a majority of shares are owned by nationals or companies of the
>> other Contracting Party shall in accordance with Article 25(2)(b) of the

Convention be treated for the purposes of the Convention as a company of the other Contracting Party.

48. Egypt argued that this provision could be used to deny jurisdiction over disputes involving companies of the non-disputing Contracting Party that are owned by nationals or companies of the Contracting Party to the dispute. Wena, on the other hand, argued that this provision could be used only to extend jurisdiction over disputes involving companies of the Contracting Party to the dispute that are owned by nationals or companies of the non-disputing Contracting Party. Although the tribunal found that both interpretations of the BIT provision were plausible, it decided to adopt Wena's interpretation as the more consistent with Article 25(2)(b) of the Convention.

49. As the *Wena* tribunal stated, '[t]he literature rather convincingly demonstrates that Article 25(2)(b) of the ICSID Convention—and provisions like Article 8 of the United Kingdom's model bilateral investment treaty—are meant to expand ICSID jurisdiction.' The tribunal in *Autopista v. Venezuela* reached a similar result, concluding that the object and purpose of Article 25(2)(b) is not to limit jurisdiction, but to set its 'outer limits.'

50. ICSID jurisprudence also confirms that the second clause of Article 25(2)(b) should not be used to determine the nationality of juridical entities in the absence of an agreement between the parties. In *CMS v. Argentina*, the tribunal states, '[t]he reference that Article 25(2)(b) makes to foreign control in terms of treating a company of the nationality of the Contracting State party as a national of another Contracting State *is precisely meant to facilitate agreement between the parties . . .*'. In the present case, there was no agreement between the Contracting Parties to treat the Claimant as anything other than a national of its state of incorporation, *i.e.*, Lithuania.

51. The second clause of Article 25(2)(b) does not mandatorily constrict ICSID jurisdiction for disputes arising in the inverse context from the one envisaged by this provision: a dispute between a Contracting Party and an entity of another Contracting Party that is controlled by nationals of the respondent Contracting Party.[97]

4 The AdT majority's willingness to accept 100% shareholding as de facto control for purposes of ICSID Article 25(2)(b) was based on its determination that the Dutch claimants were not 'mere shells'. Where the claimant is determined to be a shell company (i.e., a legal vehicle established solely to pass finances from one source to another), the question of control for purposes of determining whether the claimant is an 'investor' can collapse into an investigation of whether the claimant made

---

97 *Tokios Tokelés v. Ukraine, supra* note 80 paras. 44–51.

any 'contribution of assets' for purposes of determining if there was an 'investment'. In *Alapli Eletrik v. Turkey*, arbitrator Parks based his denial of jurisdiction under the Energy Charter Treaty and the Netherlands– Turkey BIT on the fact that the claimant, despite nominally owning 100% of the shares of the project, had neither contributed any of its own assets nor incurred any risk in the creation of the investment project.[98] Similarly, in *KT v. Kazakhstan*, the tribunal noted, '[. . .] KT Asia has made no contribution with respect to its alleged investment, nor is there any evidence on record that it had the intention or the ability to do so in the future. As a consequence, the Claimant has not demonstrated the existence of an investment under Article 25(1) of the ICSID'.[99]

---

98 *Alapli Elektrik BV v. Turkey*, ICSID Case No. ARB/08/13, Award, para. 389 (July 16, 2012).

99 *KT Asia Investment Group BV v. Republic of Kazakhstan*, ICSID Case No. ARB/09/8, Award, para. 206 (Oct. 17, 2013).

Question to an expert: Julien Fouret

Julien Fouret is partner at *betto seraglini* (Paris). Julien specializes exclusively in international arbitration, focusing on investment arbitration. He possesses vast experience both as counsel and as an arbitrator. He is also the author of two books and numerous articles as well as a lecturer in investment arbitration both in France and abroad.

Why stop at allowing dual nationals access non-ICSID international investment arbitration—why not any investor?

The first point concerns the fact that we are dealing with, without saying marginal or residual, a minority of cases where the Claimant or the Claimants are individuals, private foreign investors (notwithstanding the recent Micula brothers, Joseph Lemire or Waguih Siag to name a few).

Indeed, the question of dual-nationality only arises with private individuals, not with corporations.

The second point concerns the answer to this question which can be two-fold:

(i) are we talking here about dual-nationals, the second nationality not being a nationality of one of the State party to the applicable conventional instrument? or,

(ii) are we only talking about the dual-nationals that possess the nationality of the Host State who are potentially suing them? Indeed the problematic is not the same, and the difference with ICSID arbitration is not the same either.

If you are thinking of the first part of the alternative, then it does not matter whether you are before an ICSID tribunal or not because this is not envisaged or limited by Article 25 in the Convention. The issue here can fall back on either what the BIT might say or on general principles or customary principles of international law, i.e. effective and dominant nationality. I believe that Tribunals would be mindful of the risk of treaty shopping and as to whether or not a dual-national has claimed one nationality over another one to invest or not. No tribunal has properly addressed this issue but rather left it to the party to choose which BITs they wished to rely on, unless it clearly appeared to be fraudulent in which case a Tribunal might intervene. But this has not been the case (e.g., even if in ICSID context, the analysis is applicable inside and outside Washington Convention, *Saba Fakes v. Turkey*).

For the second part of the alternative, many BITs address this issue in their first article when defining the investor by indicating that bi-nationals of the nationality of both parties shall be considered as citizens from the given country where they are physically situated (see, for example, the very «traditional» Canada–Lebanon BIT at Article 1(e)(ii), *i.e.* Lebanese in Lebanon and Canadian in Canada). So the question does not really exist in

QUESTION TO AN EXPERT: JULIEN FOURET *(continued)*

that type of situation as the applicable conventional instrument deals with it and generally excludes the possibility for a dual national to attack one of the countries of their nationality.

However, you have rather sophisticated instruments such as the Draft CETA (Comprehensive Economic and Trade Agreement) between Canada and the EU that use concepts strictly deriving from public international law. The problem here is that you are not dealing with a two-country treaty but with an FTA between a country and the EU which is comprised of many countries. In Article X.3 (definitions) this draft FTA considers the fact that dual nationals shall be submitted to the «effective nationality» test to determine which nationality they can rely on («*A natural person who is a citizen of Canada and has the nationality of one of the Member States of the EU shall be deemed to be exclusively a natural person of the Party of his or her dominant and effective nationality*»).

Thus, Canadians that also have the nationality of one of the EU Member States could eventually bring a claim against one of their States of nationality, depending if the nationality they want to rely on is their effective nationality, using the principle derived from the famous ICJ *Nottebohm* Case. Again, this will only be possible outside the ICSID scheme as this is clearly in opposition to Article 25 of the ICSID Convention. However, this may pave the way for a new type of investment claim, dual-nationals actually acting against their own State under the nationality umbrella of another State.

I am not fully certain that this is exactly what was aimed to be achieved when drafting such provision but this promises, if it stays the same when ratified, to raise numerous complicated issues in the future.

4

Expropriation

4.1 Direct expropriation

4.1.1 Introduction

In this chapter, we begin to look at the substantive set of rules surrounding the host's obligations to the foreign investor. We take the most basic rules first: those surrounding the expropriation of a foreign investor's property.

Why start with expropriation? For one thing, expropriation is—apart from violence toward the person of the investor—the most serious infringement of an investor's rights that a state can accomplish, so the rules governing such actions are correspondingly important. Moreover, expropriations are occurring more frequently than had been the case from the 1970s through 2000. Although there are still few expropriations in absolute numbers, when expropriations do occur, the signals sent to the international community are of heightened importance precisely because of the infrequency of such actions. Determining the legal characterization of expropriations is therefore important for understanding the reactions of the stakeholders.

There is also a didactic reason to start our study of host state obligations toward the investor with expropriation: expropriation occupies the most prominent position in the history of investment law and the legal framework has consequently been given sustained attention by courts, tribunals, and scholars. The rules of international investment were largely constructed to ensure that foreign investors' property could not be taken away without compensation. Appearing by the seventeenth century in bilateral commercial treaties, legal consideration of expropriatory actions is highly developed and relatively straightforward. It is therefore a good basis upon which to proceed to the less developed areas of investor protection.

This chapter will first examine the nature of the customary law rule on expropriation, including the elements necessary to characterize an expropriation as 'legal'. It will then turn to treaty-based protections against regulatory, or indirect, expropriations. The latter provisions are the focus of many recent investment disputes and are often a touchstone of legal controversy.

4.1.2 Expropriation: the definitions

a *What is an expropriation?*

The term 'expropriation' refers to a state's taking property—something of value—away from its owner. As modern international investment law protects both an investor's legal title to its investment and the investor's rights to use and profit from its investment, government actions that take away any of these may constitute an expropriation.[1] While there are different terms for the taking of title (direct expropriation) and the taking of value or control (indirect expropriation), both are expropriations and are governed by the same legal framework. The term 'nationalization' currently refers to the expropriation of an entire industrial sector. Not all authors differentiate between nationalizations and expropriations (because all nationalizations are expropriations), but during the New International Economic Order (NIEO) movement, the terminology had political significance: developing nations described their governmental takings of foreign properties as 'nationalizations' to underscore their sovereign authority to take measures to regulate the economy; industrialized nations, whose investors were the main target of these acts, referred to the takings as 'expropriations' or 'confiscations', emphasizing the investor's loss of property. In this book, the term nationalization will be used neutrally to distinguish government takings of individual investments from those whose scope includes an entire economic sector.

While expropriations can be of anyone's property, it is only when the owner is foreign that an expropriation of property becomes the subject of international economic law.[2] International investment law is particularly concerned with the expropriation of foreign investments—with what constitutes an expropriation and the conditions under which expropriations may take place. Let's look, then, first at this general framework.

---

1 *Grand River Enterprises Six Nations, Ltd., et al., v. United States of America, NAFTA;* UNCITRAL Arbitration, Award, paras. 146–55 (Jan. 12, 2011). Available at: http://italaw.com/documents/GrandRiverEnterprises_v_US_Award_12Jan2011.pdf.

2 There is a large constitutional law literature on national protections against uncompensated government takings. *See*, e.g. Borzu Sabahi and Nicholas J. Birch, *Comparative Compensation for Expropriation, in* International Investment Law and Comparative Public Law 778, 778–84 (Stephan W. Schill ed., 2010) (comparative analysis of the US, German, and French systems).

b Legal expropriation

In customary international law, a state has the *right* to expropriate alien property. As a customary rule, this right applies to all states unless explicitly rejected. Nevertheless, the right to expropriate is repeated in numerous international law instruments,[3] including almost all IIAs.

Legal rights, however, are not always absolute. The interests of other actors often require rights to be limited. In the case of expropriation, the state's right to expropriate is circumscribed by conditions surrounding the expropriation's object for which and the process by which it is carried out. The four commonly accepted elements of a legal expropriation are:

● the expropriation must be undertaken for a *public purpose*;
● the expropriation must be carried out in accordance with the principles of *due process*;[4]
● the expropriation must be *non-discriminatory*; and
● the investor must receive *compensation*.

While not all IIAs refer to these conditions in list form,[5] most do contain a reference to each of these elements in their expropriation provisions. The Canada–Cameroon BIT, for instance, states:

> Neither Party shall nationalize or expropriate a covered investment either directly, or indirectly through measures having an effect equivalent to nationalization

---

3 *See*, e.g. GA Res. 1803 (XVII), paras. 1–5, UN Doc. A/RES/1803 (XVII) (Dec. 14, 1962) (Permanent Sovereignty over Natural Resources); GA Res. 3171 (XXVIII), paras. 1 and 3, UN Doc. A/RES/3171 (XXVIII) (Dec. 17, 1973) (Permanent Sovereignty over Natural Resources); Charter of Economic Rights and Duties of States, GA Res. 3281 (XXIX), art. 2(2)(c), UN Doc. A/RES/29/3281 (Dec. 12, 1974); Protocol 1 to the European Convention for the Protection of Human Rights and Fundamental Freedoms of 20 March 1952, art. 1, ETS No. 9.

4 Rudolf Dolzer and Christoph Schreuer, Principles of International Investment Law 100 (second edn, 2012) posit that the due process requirement may not be an independent obligation of expropriation but BITs often refer to it. Tribunals applying BIT provisions, therefore, will consider an expropriation illegal if the host did not afford due process. *See*, e.g. *Ioannis Kardassopoulos and Ron Fuchs v. The Republic of Georgia*, ICSID Case Nos. ARB/05/18 and ARB/07/15, Award, para. 408 (Mar. 3, 2010). Available at: http://italaw.com/documents/KardassopoulosAward.pdf (where the tribunal, in what it labelled 'a classic case of direct expropriation' (para. 387), held the expropriation illegal for lack of due process).

5 The recent BIT between Japan and Myanmar lists the factors explicitly. *See*, Agreement between the Government of Japan and the Government of the Republic of the Union of Myanmar for the Liberalisation, Promotion and Protection of Investment, Art. 13.1 (in effect as of 7 August 2014):
Neither Contracting Party shall expropriate [. . .] except:
  (a) for a public purpose;
  (b) in a non-discriminatory manner;
  (c) upon payment of prompt, adequate and effective compensation [. . .]; and

or expropriation ('expropriation'), except for a public purpose, in accordance with due process of law, in a non-discriminatory manner and on payment of compensation [. . .].[6]

Each of these terms has been further defined. The following highlights some of the difficulties in determining their precise contours.

c   Conditions for legal expropriation

c.i   Public purpose

For a state to legally exercise its right to take ownership of a foreign investor's property, it must be acting in the interest of the general public. This 'public purpose' requirement for legal expropriations is based on a utilitarian view of governance: the individual's right to property can only be violated by an overriding interest of the greater public in the transfer.[7]

The simple logic behind the public purpose requirement masks its difficult application. This element is difficult to adjudicate effectively because it can generally be assumed that the state is better placed to determine what is in

---

(d) in accordance with due process of law [. . .].

See also, The United States-Rwanda Bilateral Investment Agreement of Feb. 19, 2008, art. 6.1; Agreement between the Government of the United Mexican States and the Government of the People's Republic of China on the Promotion and Reciprocal Protection of Investments, art. 7.1.

Agreement Between Canada and the Republic of Cameroon for the Promotion and Protection of Investments, Art. 10.1 (signed 3 March 2014). *See also* Accordo Tra il Governo della Republicca Italiana ed il Governo della Repubblica del Paraguay sulla promozione e protezione degli Investimenti, art. 6.2 (30 June 2013) ('Gli investimenti degli investitori di una delle Parti Contraenti non saranno [. . .] espropriati [. . .] se non per fini pubblici, interesse sociale, o per motivi di interesse nazionale, contro giusto, adeguato, immediato ed opportuno risarcimento ed a condizione che tali misure siano prese su base non discriminatoria ed in conformità a tutte le disposizioni e procedure di legge'); Accord entre l'Union économique belgo-luxembourgeoise et la Gouvernement de la Règublique de Corée concernant l'encouragement et la protection réciproques des investissements, Art. 5.1 (27 March 2011) ('Les investissements des investisseurs de chacune des Parties contractantes ne seront ni nationalisés, ni expropriés, [. . .] sur le territoire de l'autre Partie contractante, si ce n'est dans l'intérêt public et moyennant le paiement sans délai d'une indemnité adéquate et effective. Les expropriations seront réalisées sur une base non discriminatoire et selon une procédure légale.').

6 Agreement between Canada and the Republic of Cameroon for the Promotion and Protection of Investments, Article 10.1 (signed 3 March 2014).

7 Muthucumaraswamy Sornarajah, The International Law on Foreign Investment (third edn, 2011) refers to this as the distinction between 'confiscation' and 'expropriation'. Other commentators have said that a state's reasons don't matter or that they are not the business of others to judge. *See* Peter T. Muchlinski, Multinational Enterprises and the Law 599–600 (second edn, 2007) (discussing the wide discretion states have regarding the determination of a public purpose). *See also Goetz and Others v. Republic of Burundi*, ICSID Case No. ARB/95/3, Decision on Liability, para. 126 (Sept. 2, 1998), 15 ICSID Rev.–FILJ 169 (2000) (the arbitral tribunal was reluctant to substitute the government of Burundi's assessment that there was a public purpose by its own opinion).

the public purpose than is an international tribunal. Yet, an arbitral tribunal must determine precisely when this is not the case.

Arguments for some limitations on states' legitimate authority to take over private properties for the benefit of the local ruler have existed since Grotius' time. It is controversial, however, how to characterize a government's decision to intervene in the economy when the decision results in some commercial benefits accruing to the state and some commercial harm to a foreign investor. The broad extent of modern states' regulation of their economies makes the potential scope of what could legitimately be considered a 'public purpose' extremely far reaching. Should only cases of egregious self-serving behaviour on the part of the government fail the public purpose test? Surely, many tribunals will give government claims of interest significant deference. Thus, it would only be where investors could show that the government took their property in retaliation or for the personal enrichment of the host's leaders that there would be finding of a violation of the public interest element.[8]

The nationalization of natural resource exploitation in the wake of governmental change, however, brought up a different issue: a state's taking control of productive assets for purely financial motives be considered a 'public interest' for purposes of expropriation? The following case demonstrates the considerations surrounding such claims.

 CASE

Amoco International Finance Corp. v. Iran[9]

Amoco International Finance Corp. is a US corporation. Respondent Iran represented the positions of the wholly owned government companies, the National Petroleum Company (NPC) and the National Iranian Oil Company (NIOC), the parent of NPC.

In 1958, NIOC and Amoco's affiliate, Panintoil, entered into a Joint Structure Agreement to permit Panintoil to explore offshore oil fields and develop their production. The pumping of crude oil in these fields led to the extraction of a large amount of natural gas, so in 1966 Amoco and NPC made a series of

---

8 *See* Muchlinski, *supra* note 7, at 599. Muchlinski also suggests that expropriatory actions accompanying violations of human rights would violate the public purpose element. Id. at 600.

9 *Amoco International Finance Corporation v. The Government of the Islamic Republic of Iran*, National Iranian Oil Company, National Petrochemical Company and Kharg Chemical Company Limited, Iran–US Claims Tribunal, 15 Iran–US CTR 189, Partial Award (July 14, 1987), 27 ILM 1314 (1988); footnotes omitted.

agreements for processing this gas and selling the chemicals extracted from it through a jointly owned, jointly managed company, Khemco. In 1970, Khemco began its operations.

By 1978, civil unrest in Iran began to impact on Khemco's operations. Strikes stopped production at times, and by late December, anti-American feelings were running so high that Amoco's personnel left the country. These persons continued to work for Khemco from Dubai.

In early January 1980, Iran's Revolutionary Council passed the Single Article Act Concerning the Nationalization of the Oil Industry of Iran. This annulled all oil and gas industry contracts that included foreign participants.

On 11 August 1980, Amoco filed for arbitration, arguing that the steps taken by Iran were a wrongful expropriation of Amoco's rights under Article IV(2) of the US–Iran Treaty of Amity from 1957:

> Property of nationals and companies of either High Contracting Party, including interests in property, shall receive the most constant protection and security within the territories of the other High Contracting Party, in no case less than that required by international law. Such property shall not be taken except for a public purpose, nor shall it be taken without the prompt payment of just compensation. Such compensation shall be in an effectively realizable form and shall represent the full equivalent of the property taken; and adequate provision shall have been made at or prior to the time of taking for the determination and payment thereof.[10]

Iran did not dispute that an expropriation had taken place, but claimed that it had acted legally in taking the property. The tribunal considered this argument.

> 112. As a *lex specialis* in the relations between the two countries, the Treaty supersedes the *lex generalis*, namely customary international law. This does not mean, however, that the latter is irrelevant in the instant Case. On the contrary, the rules of customary law may be useful in order to fill in possible *lacunae* of the Treaty, to ascertain the meaning of undefined terms in its text or, more generally, to aid interpretation and implementation of its provisions.
>
> 113. It is worthwhile, in this context, to compare the provisions of Article IV, paragraph 2 of the Treaty with the customary rules of international law in the field of expropriation. [. . .] As reflected in judgment of the Permanent Court of

---

10 Treaty of Amity, Economic Relations, and Consular Rights, US–Iran, Aug. 15, 1955, 284 UNTS 9 (entered into force 16 June, 1957).

International Justice in the *Case Concerning Certain German Interests in Polish Upper Silesia* [. . .], the principles of international law generally accepted some sixty years ago in regard to the treatment of foreigners recognized very few exceptions to the principle of respect for vested rights. The Court listed among such exceptions only 'expropriation for reasons of public utility, judicial liquidation and similar measures'. A very important evolution in the law has taken place since then, with the progressive recognition of the right of States to nationalize foreign property for a public purpose. This right is today unanimously accepted, even by States which reject the principle of permanent sovereignty over natural resources, considered by a majority of States as the legal foundation of such a right.

114. The importance of this evolution derives from the fact that nationalization is generally defined as the transfer of an economic activity from private ownership to the public sector. It is realized through expropriation of the assets of an enterprise or of its capital stock, with a view to maintaining such enterprise as a going concern under State control. Modern nationalization often brings into State ownership a number of enterprises of the same kind and may even be applied to all enterprises in a particular industry. It may result, therefore, in a taking of private property of much greater magnitude than the traditional expropriation for reasons of public utility, and is also of a very different nature, since it is always linked to determined political choices. For these reasons, and because it applies to going concerns, taken as such, modern nationalization raises specific legal problems, notably in relation to the issue of compensation.

115. The provisions of Article IV, paragraph 2 of the Treaty must be read against this background, since the negotiation of the Treaty must be presumed to have taken place in this legal context. Although the provisions are phrased in a negative form and emphasize the principle of the respect due to foreign property, they nevertheless amount to a clear recognition of the right to nationalize. In stating that '[s]uch a property shall not be taken except for a public purpose', the Treaty implies that an expropriation which is justified by a public purpose may be lawful, which is precisely the rule of customary international law.

[. . .]

(V) Lack of public purpose

144. [. . .] Claimant's counsel suggested, during the Hearing, that 'a principal motive and perhaps the principal motive' for the expropriation of Khemco was simply to free NPC from the obligations created by the Khemco Agreement and, particularly, from the obligation to share the profits of the venture. The Claimant asserted that such a motive certainly is not legitimate. Counsel added that 'only the ventures where all the money had been put up were expropriated, not the others'. This last remark, indeed, suggests a differentiation for financial reasons rather than discrimination on the basis of nationality.

145. A precise definition of the 'public purpose' view for which an expropriation may be lawfully decided has neither been agreed upon in international law nor even suggested. It is clear that, as a result of the modern acceptance of the right to nationalize, this term is broadly interpreted, and that States, in practice, are granted extensive discretion. An expropriation, the only purpose of which would have been to avoid contractual obligations of the state or of an entity controlled by it, could not, nevertheless, be considered as lawful under international law. [. . .] Such an expropriation, indeed, would be contrary to principle of good faith and to accept it was lawful would run counter to the well-settled rule that a State has the right to commit itself by contract to foreign corporations. [. . .] It is also generally accepted that a State has no right to expropriate only for financial purpose. It must, however, be observed that, in recent practice and mostly in the oil industry, States have admitted expressly, in a certain number of cases, that they were nationalizing foreign properties primarily in order to obtain a greater share, or even the totality, of the revenues drawn from the exploitation of a national natural resource, which, according to them, should accrue to the development of the country. Such a purpose has not generally been denounced as unlawful and illegitimate.

146. The Tribunal need not determine the delicate legal issues raised in the preceding paragraph. It cannot be doubted that the Single Article Act was adopted for a clear public purpose, namely to complete the nationalization of the oil industry in Iran initiated by the 1951 Nationalization of the Iranian Oil Industry Act, with a view to implementing one of the main economic and political objectives of the new Islamic Government. The decision of the Special Commission relative to Khemco was taken in apparent conformity with the Single Article Act. Even if financial considerations were considered in the adoption of such a decision—which would have been only natural, but which has not been evidenced—this fact would not be sufficient, in the opinion of the Tribunal, to prove that this decision was not taken for a public purpose.

147. In conclusion the Tribunal finds that the Claimant's arguments so far considered do not sustain the contention that the expropriation of Khemco was unlawful. [. . .]

Taking over a single investor's investment is different from the nationalization of an economic sector. The host's financial profit incentives may be more critically assessed if the expropriation appears to be purely a commercial action.

CASE

ADC Affiliate Limited and ADC and ADMC Management Limited v. Hungary[11]

ADC is a Canadian construction company. In 1995, ADC signed a Build, Operate and Transfer (BOT) contract with Hungary to renovate and expand the Budapest International Airport. The contract included a 12-year operation clause for ADC's Hungarian subsidiary.

In 1998, the company finished its work and began operating the terminal. At the same time, Hungary's Airport Administration agency was privatized as a joint-stock company. This new entity sent a letter to ADC on 20 December 2001 saying it was taking over the operation of the airport as of 1 January 2002.

In 2003 ADC initiated arbitral proceedings under the Agreement between the Government of the Hungarian People's Republic and the Government of the Republic of Cyprus on Mutual Promotion and Protection of Investment ('BIT'), which entered into force on 24 May 1989. One of ADC's arguments was that the taking was illegal because the government had no public purpose in taking their investment (ADC also argued on the basis of a lack of due process, discrimination, and the absence of compensation).

Among the responses by the host was that even if ADC had been expropriated (a position that Hungary disputed), the expropriation was legal. As to the public purpose requirement, Hungary pointed to their efforts to harmonize their law with that of the European Union. The changes, moreover, were 'in the strategic interests of the state'.

The tribunal analysed these claims:

State's right to regulate

423. The Tribunal cannot accept the Respondent's position that the actions taken by it against the Claimants were merely an exercise of its rights under international law to regulate its domestic economic and legal affairs. It is the Tribunal's understanding of the basic international law principles that while a sovereign State possesses the inherent right to regulate its domestic affairs, the exercise of such

---

11 *ADC Affiliate Limited and ADC and ADMC Management Limited v. The Republic of Hungary*, ICSID Case No. ARB/03/16, Award (Oct. 2, 2006). Available at: http://italaw.com/documents/ADCvHungaryAward. pdf; footnotes omitted.

right is not unlimited and must have its boundaries. As rightly pointed out by the Claimants, the rule of law, which includes treaty obligations, provides such boundaries. Therefore, when a State enters into a bilateral investment treaty like the one in this case, it becomes bound by it and the investment-protection obligations it undertook therein must be honoured rather than be ignored by a later argument of the State's right to regulate.

[. . .]

Public Interest

429. The Tribunal can see no public interest being served by the Respondent's depriving actions of the Claimants' investments in the Airport Project.

430. Although the Respondent repeatedly attempted to persuade the Tribunal that the Amending Act, the Decree and the actions taken in reliance thereon were necessary and important for the harmonization of the Hungarian Government's transport strategy, laws and regulations with the EU law, it failed to substantiate such a claim with convincing facts or legal reasoning.

431. The reference to the wording *'the strategic interest of the State'* as used in the Amendment Motion [. . .] does not assist the Respondent's position either. While the Tribunal has always been curious about what interest actually stood behind these words, the Respondent never furnished it with a substantive answer.

432. In the Tribunal's opinion, a treaty requirement for *'public interest'* requires some genuine interest of the public. If mere reference to *'public interest'* can magically put such interest into existence and therefore satisfy this requirement, then this requirement would be rendered meaningless since the Tribunal can imagine no situation where this requirement would not have been met.

433. With the claimed *'public interest'* unproved and the Tribunal's curiosity thereon unsatisfied, the Tribunal must reject the arguments made by the Respondent in this regard. In any event, as the Tribunal has already remarked, the subsequent privatization and the agreement with BAA renders this whole debate somewhat unnecessary.

Subsequent tribunals have adopted the ADC decision's more sceptical approach to government claims of public purpose that are left unexplained. The scepticism may lead to looking into further issues, such as the necessity of the public interest behind the particular expropriation as opposed to only asking whether a nationalization program fulfilled the public purpose requirement. In the following case, the tribunal had to determine whether the acquisition of a bank's financial rights to money from a telecommunications company needed to be in the public interest, or whether the admittedly public purpose of nationalizing the telecommunications sector was sufficient to make the expropriation legal.

British Caribbean Bank England v. Belize[12]

The claimant was a bank incorporated in the British overseas territory of Turks and Caicos. When the government of Belize nationalized the telecommunications industry, among the companies acquired was Telemedia, with whom the British Caribbean Bank England (BCB) had certain financing contracts (called facility agreements) that gave BCB a right to payments as mortgagee. With the takeover of the companies, the government declared that it also took over any contractual or proprietary rights held by BCB in relation to the telecommunications companies.

BCB took its dispute to the Permanent Court of Arbitration on claiming a violation of the UK–Belize BIT. It alleged that Belize had illegally expropriated BCB.

The government defended itself by noting that the cancellation of the contractual rights was an integral part of the broader program of ensuring a stable and affordable telecommunications network, and therefore, clearly an act to further a public purpose. The tribunal thus had to decide whether, even if the nationalization itself had a legitimate public purpose, the acquisition of this claimant's interests was necessary to that purpose.

> 234. There is no dispute that the Respondent has directly acquired the Claimant's interest in the [contractual rights]. It is also not in dispute that these acquisitions were against the wishes of the Claimant [. . .].
>
> 235. Furthermore, [the expropriation occurred according to] the 2009 Order, which provided that the public purpose behind the acquisition was 'the stabilisation and improvement of the telecommunications industry and the provision of reliable telecommunication services to the public at affordable prices in a harmonious and non-contentious environment'. The remaining Loan and Security Agreements were acquired by the 2009 Amendment Order 'to give effect to the public purpose' of the earlier order. The stated public purpose of the two acquisitions was thus the same. In the course of these proceedings, the Respondent has explained the need to expropriate the [Claimant's rights] entirely to 'give effect to', or to 'protect' the acquisition of Telemedia. In the Respondent's own words:
>
> to protect the expropriation of Telemedia, it was necessary to expropriate the [. . .]

---

12 *British Caribbean Bank Limited (Turks and Caicos) v. The Government of Belize*, PCA Case No. 2010-18, Award (Dec. 19, 2014) (footnotes omitted). In recent developments the Belizean government has signaled that it will comply with the award and pay BCB, USD 48 million in compensation and legal fees.

agreements. Otherwise, BCB would have been able to declare a default and take financial control of all assets and some shares of Telemedia.

236. In the Tribunal's view, this justification falls close to a statement that the public purpose for the acquisition [. . .] was to avoid or delay the repayment to which the Claimant was contractually entitled. While the Tribunal accepts that a State is entitled to broad latitude to devise its public policy as it sees fit, it does not accept that the mere avoidance of payment, without more, can serve as a legitimate public policy objective for the expropriation of property. This is particularly the case when expropriation under the Treaty requires the provision of just and equitable compensation.

237. While the Respondent has sought to present its actions in terms of the risk that British Caribbean Bank would seek to wind up or seize control of Telemedia in the course of collecting on the Loan and Security Agreements, the Tribunal does not see that this changes matters. [. . .]

238. The Tribunal also observes certain statements made by the Prime Minister of Belize [. . .] on the adoption of the 2009 Act as follows:

> There will thus be no more Telemedia awards against us; no more Telemedia court battles; no more debilitating waste of governments' energies and resources; and there will be no more suffering of this one man's campaign to subjugate an entire nation to his will.

239. Following the adoption of the 2009 Amendment Order, [. . .] the Prime Minister stated further as follows:

> [. . .] if [the Government] had fairly acquired Telemedia but leaving the assets exposed to our enemies it would have rendered the entire taking nugatory. [. . .]
>
> This is the people of Belize against the Ashcroft interests and I will never relent in the same way as he is indicating he will never relent.

240. To the Tribunal, these words suggest that the motivation for the 2009 Orders included a personal animus to Lord Michael Ashcroft that—whether justifiable or not—bears no identifiable relation to the ostensible public purposes of stabilizing and improving the telecommunications industry of Belize, or of providing reliable telecommunications services to the public.

241. The Tribunal considers that, for the purposes of Article 5 of the Treaty with which it is concerned, a defence that an expropriation was undertaken 'for a public purpose related to the internal needs of [the] Party' requires—at least—that the Respondent set out the public purpose for which the expropriation was undertaken and offer a *prima facie* explanation of how the acquisition of the particular property was reasonably related to the fulfilment of that purpose. The Tribunal is of the view that the Respondent has not convincingly shown that the 2009 acquisition of the Loan and Security Agreements was undertaken for a public purpose. [. . .]

The prevailing view on public purpose seems to be one where tribunals will continue to give state claims of what is in their interest substantial deference, but they will subject such claims to some scrutiny. The *OI v. Venezuela* tribunal, for instance, examined each of the Respondent's three proclaimed public purposes and rejected two for lack of supporting evidence.[13] Still, just because tribunals are more willing to question governments' true motivations for taking expropriatory measures, they are unlikely to accuse hosts of making a 'mere reference' to the public interest except in clear cases.

? DISCUSSION NOTES

1 Compare the *Amoco* decision with that of *ADC*. What are the key features distinguishing the two cases?
2 Some tribunals balance high levels of deference and critical scrutiny by taking a holistic approach. The *Kardassopoulos v. Georgia* decision, for example, was careful to base its finding of public interest on a totality-of-the-circumstances view:

> Beginning with the first criterion, the Tribunal finds that, on all the evidence, it is arguable that the expropriation of Mr. Kardassopoulos' rights was in the Georgian public interest. As the Claimants acknowledge, the Respondent is entitled to a measure of deference in this regard. The Tribunal heard both fact and expert industry witnesses who asserted that the development of Georgia's oil pipeline infrastructure was of crucial national importance to the country's political independence in the region and its economic development. The Tribunal finds this evidence compelling in light of all the circumstances prevailing in Georgia and the wider region during the relevant period. [. . .]
>
> 392. [. . .] There was a broader context to the expropriation of GTI's rights, namely the need to find someone who could deliver a pipeline solution on a scale required to satisfy the prevailing geopolitical and economic concerns of Georgia during the mid-1990s. Considered in this light, Georgia's decision to pursue an arrangement with AIOC, even at the expense of the Claimants, may be understood as a decision taken in the public interest, even though, as shall be seen below, the manner in which it was carried out cannot be reconciled with Georgia's treaty obligations. Therefore, the Tribunal is accordingly not convinced that the Respondent breached the 'public interest' requirement in the ECT's expropriation provision.[14]

---

13 *OI European Group BV v. Bolivarian Republic of Venezuela*, ICSID Case No. ARB/11/25, Award, paras. 368–84 (March 10, 2015) (finding Venezuela was acting to promote endogenous development, but that its claims of protecting food security and ensuring free competition in the relevant market were unsupported by the evidence).
14 *Kardassopoulos v. Georgia*, paras. 391–2.

3 Tribunals are particularly likely to find an expropriation illegal for lack of public purpose if the taking was done for revenge. The British Caribbean Bank tribunal's explicitly noted that it was the detected 'personal animosity' between the investor and the government that influenced their finding of illegality. *British Caribbean Bank v. Belize, supra* note 12, at para. 240. This parallels earlier awards. See, e.g. *British Petroleum Exploration Company Ltd. v. The Government of the Libyan Arab Republic,* 10 October 1973, 53 ILR 297 (1979); *Banco Nacional de Cuba v. Sabbatino,* 376 U.S. 398 (1964).

c.ii   *Due process*

Due process is a legal concept well developed in Anglo-American law, where it has both procedural and substantive law content.[15] In international investment law, due process is a frequent but by no means universally apparent condition of a legal expropriation. Its status as customary law is questionable (see discussion notes below). Thus, in the absence of treaty language requiring due process for expropriatory actions, respondents may make a legitimate claim that there was no obligation of this sort at all.[16]

Where the treaty refers to due process, it has been viewed as a requirement of procedural fairness, protecting the investor's rights to the rule of law throughout the expropriation period. This includes requiring the host to notify the investor of impending expropriation, to offer transparency in administrative proceedings before and during the expropriation, and perhaps of giving the expropriated investor an opportunity to request a reconsideration of the decision through a hearing and to receive written reasons for the government's decision should the expropriation plans be continued. Given this content, administrative actions are often the focus of due process claims by expropriated investors.

In *Guaracachi America and Rurelec v. Bolivia,* the dissenting arbitrator considered expropriations to be 'administrative act[s] infringing on the rights of the individual', and therefore subject to the legal norms of due process.[17] He

---

15 For a concise introduction to due process *see* Richard Clayton and Hugh Tomlinson eds., 1 The Law of Human Rights 708–10 (2d edn 2009). *See also* Timothy Sandefur, *In Defense of Substantive Due Process, or the Promise of Lawful Rule,* 35 Harv. J.L. & Pub. Pol'y 283, 286–93 (2012) (setting out the historical background and current legal theory of the concept of due process).

16 *See, Guaracachi America and Rurelec v. Bolivia,* PCA Case No. 2011-17, Award, para. 439.

17 *Id.* Dissent Opinion of Manuel Conthe, para. 5.

elaborates by naming three basic elements that the host must fulfil in order to minimally satisfy the requirement of due process:

'(i) [The host's action] *must be reasoned*—i.e. accompanied by a justification of its key features [. . .].

(ii) Both the act and its reasons *must be formally communicated* to the individual.

(iii) The legal procedure in question should *allow the individual,* after being notified of such reasons, *to be heard* before the State adopts its final decision (i.e. sets the final fair value)'.[18]

Other tribunals have also demanded reasoned, communicated decision-making from host states and an investor's right to challenge a decision. In *ADC v. Hungary* (discussed above), for example, the ICSID tribunal found that Hungary had not adhered to due process because the host failed to offer such procedural safeguards. The arbitrators' analysis illustrates how the standard elements of due process can be applied to the facts of a particular dispute:

 CASE

ADC v. Hungary

Due Process of Law

434. The Tribunal concludes that the taking was not under due process of law as required by Article 4 of the BIT.

435. The Tribunal agrees with the Claimants that '*due process of law*', in the expropriation context, demands an actual and substantive legal procedure for a foreign investor to raise its claims against the depriving actions already taken or about to be taken against it. Some basic legal mechanisms, such as reasonable advance notice, a fair hearing and an unbiased and impartial adjudicator to assess the actions in dispute, are expected to be readily available and accessible to the investor to make such legal procedure meaningful. In general, the legal procedure must be of a nature to grant an affected investor a reasonable chance within a reasonable time to claim its legitimate rights and have its claims heard. If no legal procedure of such nature exists at all, the argument that '*the actions are taken under due process of law*' rings hollow. And that is exactly what the Tribunal finds in the present case.

436. One of the Respondent's defences in this regard is that the Claimants were aware of the depriving actions well before the legislative changes were adopted in December 2001. The Tribunal finds this assertion groundless. To recall, Dr. Kiss testified at the hearing that it was not until January 2002 that he first heard that the Project Company would be displaced and its operations taken over. Similarly, Mr. Gansperger denied

---

18 Id. (emphasis added).

at the hearing that he had any knowledge that the legislative changes were contemplated prior to the date they were adopted. Assuming these statements are true and correct, which the Tribunal does not accept, they would contradict the logic in the Respondent's argument. For if persons at the very centre of the decision making body had no prior knowledge of the contemplated legislative changes, how could it be expected and argued that a foreign investor should have had such knowledge well in advance? Setting this evidence aside, the accepted evidence of Mr. Somogyi-Tóth indicates that the discussions of the takeover stayed well within governmental circles. The Tribunal therefore does not believe, as the Respondent has suggested, that Mr. Huang and his colleagues should have known the content of such discussions before the legislative changes were adopted on December 18, 2001.

437. The Respondent also failed to establish a connection between the '*need to transform the ATAA*' and the deprivation of the Claimants' investments in the Airport Project.

438. As to Respondent's argument that Hungarian law does provide methods for the Claimants to review the expropriation, the Tribunal fails to see how such claim was substantiated and in any event cannot agree in the light of the facts established in this case that there were in place any methods to satisfy the requirement of '*due process of law*' in the context of this case.[19]

? DISCUSSION NOTES

1 Is the requirement of 'due process' in expropriations customary international law? This issue is disputed. Dolzer and Schreuer, for example, question whether due process is a standard element of legal expropriations.[20] Reinisch, too, is cautious about claims that due process in investment law has customary law status:

> General conclusions on the 'due process' requirement must remain tentative. As opposed to the public purpose and the non-discrimination prerequisite, the due process requirement seems to be less certainly established in customary international law. It is, however very widely used in IIAs where it appears in different forms. Sometimes, the due process condition is phrased as a mere legality requirement according to which the expropriation has to be effectuated in conformity with national law and procedure, whereas in a number of IIAs due process expressly requires a right to have the expropriation and, in particular, the compensation decision reviewed. The limited case law suggests that a fair procedure offering the possibility of judicial review is crucial.[21]

---

19 *ADC v. Hungary, supra* note 11, paras. 434–40.
20 *Dolzer and Schreuer, supra* note 4, at 100.
21 August Reinisch, *Legality of Expropriations, in* Standards of Investment Protection 193 (August Reinisch ed., 2008).

2 Some commentators[22] and a few tribunals[23] have asked whether the standard of due process set forth in IIAs is one of local due process or international due process. This query, however, presumes that there is an international standard of due process to evaluate—something that is not obvious. William Brennan, Jr., writing in 1962, suggested that states bind themselves to a treaty to ensure due process throughout the world.[24] Such a treaty never came to be, and although Charles Kotuby writes of an '*emerging notion* of international due process by which local legal processes are judged beyond their own sovereign borders',[25] there is little positive international law to bind states to judicial or administrative procedural minimum standards.

Regionally, the outlook is somewhat different than it is internationally. Building on the right to fair trial found in a number of human rights instruments, Article 41 of the European Charter of Fundamental Rights establishes a right to good administration for European Union citizens. This is furthered by the European Commission's European Code of Good Administrative Behaviour[26] and the European Ombudsman's set of principles based on the Code. The Ombudsman's principles include lawfulness (Art. 4), proportionality (Art. 6), objectivity (Art. 9), and fairness (Art. 11), but also legitimate expectations and consistency (Art. 10) and—interestingly—courtesy (Art. 12). See http://www.ombuds man.europa.eu/en/resources/code.faces#/page/1. Recall these principles when reading about Fair and Equitable Treatment in Chapter 5.

3 One interesting issue that arises with the heavily procedural aspect of due process implied by its inclusion in the expropriation provision of IIAs is that of whether it is an obligation of conduct or result. The question is particularly significant for cases in which the host has violated local procedural rules when expropriating a foreign investor, as Newcombe and Paradell elaborate:

> It is unclear whether due process of law imports an obligation of conduct, rather than result. If it is an obligation of conduct, any defect in process, even if reviewable or correctable, amounts to a breach of due process. For example, if a state fails to provide an investor notice of an expropriation, the state's conduct would

---

22 *See* Ursula Kriebaum, Expropriation, in: Marc Bungenberg, Jörn Griebel, Stephan Hobe, and August Reinisch, eds., International Investment Law 959–1030, 1028 (Beck/Hart/Nomos, 2015); Andrew Newcomb and Lluís Paradell, Law and Practice of Investment Treaties 376 (Kluwer Law International, 2009).

23 *Amoco v. Iran, supra* note 9, para. 283; *Kardassopoulos v. Georgia, supra* note 4, para. 394.

24 William J. Brennan, Jr., International Due Process and the Law, 48:7 Va. L. Rev. 1258 (1962).

25 Charles T. Kotuby, General Principles of Law, International Due Process, and the Modern Role of Private International Law, 23 Duke J. Comp. & Int'l L. 411–12 (2013) (emphasis added).

26 OJ L 267, 20.10.2000.

breach due process, even if the investor found out through other means. In the Middle East, the tribunal held that the seizure and auction of a ship was not in accordance with due process of law because there was a failure to provide direct notification of the seizure and auction to the investor.

In contrast, if due process is an obligation of result, a state accords due process provided local remedies are available to correct defects in process. Some support for this position might be garnered from the Feldman award. In considering the requirement in Article 1110(1)(c), NAFTA, that the expropriation be 'in accordance with due process of law' and Article 1105(1), a minimum standards provision, the tribunal appeared to equate a denial of due process with a denial of justice. The tribunal noted that since the courts and administrative procedures were available to the claimant there was no denial of due process or denial of justice that would rise to the level of a violation of international law. The better view is that due process is properly viewed as an obligation of conduct. Due process requires, first and foremost, compliance with local law. Breaches of local procedural laws are *prima facie* breaches of due process. Second, the international standard of due process may be breached by serious procedural irregularities, even if these are later corrected. However, if the basis of the entire expropriation claim is purely due process violations, it is an open question as to what, if any, compensation is payable.

A due process requirement in an IIA could be viewed as having two components. On the one hand, due process of law could mean nothing more than adherence to the principles of natural justice. If this is the case, the executive branch of state can expropriate without legislative fiat provided an opportunity to be heard as given before an impartial body. On the other hand, due process of law could be interpreted as requiring a procedure established by law. In this situation, the executive branch can only expropriate if the property is earmarked for expropriation by legislative fiat which also lays down the procedure for expropriation. On balance, it seems that due process imports a requirement that an expropriation be in accordance with the law of the host state as well as an international minimum standard of due process, including notice, a fair hearing and non-arbitrariness.[27]

c.iii *Non-discrimination*

The rule of non-discrimination in international investment law prohibits a host from treating certain investors unfavourably in comparison to other investors. As a general rule of international economic law, the

---

27 Andrew Newcombe and Lluís Paradell, Law and Practice of Investment Treaties: Standards of Treatment 375–6 (2009).

non-discrimination rule prohibits governments from distinguishing the treatment of economic resources or actors on the basis of national origin in order to ensure the competitive equality between comparable economic actors. In investment law, the rule similarly obligates the host to offer foreign investors both national treatment and most favoured nation treatment.[28] In the context of expropriations, these rules stipulate that a host that only expropriates the property of foreigners or only the property of one group of foreigners is acting illegally. In *ADC*, for instance, the tribunal determined that Hungary had acted discriminatorily in expropriating the only foreign company while not affecting the competing national firm.

As an element characterizing a legal expropriation, however, the non-discrimination obligation goes further than the national treatment and most-favored nation treatment standards. It means that a host must also disregard the investor's personal characteristics when expropriating properties. This is in accordance with the rule of non-discrimination as a general principle of international law. Non-discrimination in that context prohibits states from treating individuals disadvantageously on the basis of 'race, colour, sex, language, religion, political or other opinion, national or social origin, property, birth or other status'.[29]

The prohibition on discrimination is particularly strong in international law.[30] Thus, in investment law, too, discrimination of foreign investors on the basis of their race, religion, or national origin is prohibited. It is no surprise, then, that the expropriation of Jewish property by the Nazi regime was found to be illegal,[31] as were Idi Amin's takings of the property of Indian Ugandans.[32]

There is one outlier from this general rule against discriminatory expropriations. The divergent view is based on the economic reality of some governments' need to forcibly redistribute productive assets to traditionally

---

28 *See* Chapter 5 of this textbook.

29 This language is shared by the Universal Declaration of Human Rights (Art. 2), the UN Covenant on Civil and Political Rights (Art. 2), and the UN Covenant on Economic, Social and Cultural Rights (Art. 2). *See* Charter of Economic Rights and Duties of States, GA Res. 3281 (XXIX), UN Doc. A/RES/29/3281 (Dec. 12, 1974).

30 *Barcelona Traction, Light and Power Company, Limited (Belgium v. Spain)*, Judgment, 1970 ICJ 3, para. 34 (Feb. 5); Alexander Orakhelashvili, Peremptory Norms in International Law 54 (2006).

31 *See*, e.g. Didi Herman, *'I do not Attach Great Significance to it': Taking Note of 'The Holocaust' in English Case Law*, 17(4) Social Legal Studies 437 (2008).

32 Idi Amin's 1972 expulsion of 80 000 Asians from Uganda has been considered ethnic cleansing, making the subsequent expropriation of their properties illegal. In 1982, the Ugandan government enacted the Expropriated Properties Act (Act No. 9 of 1982) to permit expropriated Asians to apply for repossession of their property.

disadvantaged groups in order to achieve effective equality within a structurally divided society. Arising out of the experiences of the newly independent states of Africa and Asia post-World War II, a discussion arose that questioned whether the non-discrimination rule for expropriations should apply when the host took productive property solely from the former ruling race.[33]

The 1960s logic of treating post-colonial expropriations differently was explained at the time by Hans Baade: 'Independence would seem an empty gesture or even a cruel hoax to many a new country if it were prevented from singling out the key investments of the former colonial power for nationalization'.[34] What many legal experts did not agree upon was why such expropriations ought to be permitted. Baade himself seemed to reject the relevance of discrimination on the legality of expropriations, but this seems an anomalous view. Others argued that such takings were legal because the objects of differential treatment were not the same, and thus, the act was not discriminatory. Still others found the differential treatment justified, again leading to the conclusion that there was no discrimination. Most recently, an arbitral tribunal assessed whether the counter-colonial expropriation was perhaps legal despite being discriminatory: on the basis that a remedial taking might form an exception to the rule against discriminatory expropriations.

In the case of *Campbell v. Zimbabwe*, the tribunal had to assess whether the government's dispossession of white farmers was illegal on the basis of racial discrimination.

 CASE

Mike Campbell (Pvt) Ltd., William Michael Campbell and others v. The Republic of Zimbabwe[35]

The Campbells were Dutch citizens owning farmland in Zimbabwe. In 2005, Zimbabwe's Constitution was amended to provide for the 'acquisition' of agricultural land for resettlement and other purposes and its subsequent transfer with full title to the state. The amendments included a clause stipulating that no compensation would be payable for the land itself and that no

---

33 *See* Sornarajah, *supra* note 7, at 409.

34 Hans W. Baade, Permanent Sovereignty over Natural Resource Wealth and Resources, in: Richard S. Miller and Roland J. Stanger, eds., Essays on Expropriation 24 (Ohio State Univ. Press, 1967).

35 *Mike Campbell (Pvt) Ltd., William Michael Campbell and others v. The Republic of Zimbabwe*, in the Southern African Development Community (SADC), Tribunal Windhoek, Namibia, SADC (T) Case No. 2/2007, Judgment (Nov. 28, 1008) pp. 41–54. Available at: http://www.saflii.org/sa/cases/SADCT/2008/2.pdf; footnotes omitted.

court could review the acquisition, although a former owner could challenge the amount of compensation offered for the improvements to the land.

Following the government's taking of their farm, the Campbells brought an arbitration under the Treaty of the Southern African Development Community (SADC), arguing that the government's actions were illegal as a racially discriminatory taking. The tribunal analysed the highly politicized situation by extensively discussing the sources and content of the nondiscrimination obligation and applying it to Zimbabwe's actions:

VI. Racial discrimination

The other issue raised by the Applicants is that of racial discrimination. They contended that the land reform programme is based on racial discrimination in that it targets white Zimbabwean farmers only. The Applicants further argue that Amendment 17 was intended to facilitate or implement the land reform policy of the Government of Zimbabwe based on racial discrimination. This issue is captured in the Applicants' Heads of Arguments, paragraph 175, in the following terms:

> 'That the actions of the Government of Zimbabwe in expropriating land for resettlement purposes has been based solely or primarily on consideration of race and ethnic origin . . . It is being directed at white farmer. . . . In reality it was aimed at persons who owned land because they were white. It mattered not whether they acquired the land during the colonial period or after independence'.

The Applicants further argued at paragraph 128 of the Heads of Argument that:

> 'The evidence presented to this Tribunal shows as a fact that the decision as to whether or not agricultural raw land in Zimbabwe is to be expropriated is determined by the race or country of origin of the registered owner. In terms of a policy designed to redress the ownership of land created during the colonial period, the GoZ has determined that no person of white colour or European origin was to retain ownership of a farm, and all such farms were to be expropriated. The fact that this could not be done through the normal procedures between 2000 and 2005 led to the enactment of Amendment 17, which was the ultimate legislative tool used by the GoZ to seize all the white owned farms'.

The Applicants went on to argue that, even if Amendment 17 made no reference to the race and colour of the owners of the land acquired, that does not mean that the legislative aim is not based on considerations of race or colour since only white owned farms were targeted by the Amendment. There is a clear legislative intent directed only at white farmers. According to the Applicants, the Amendment strikes at white farmers only and no other rational categorization is apparent therein. The Applicants further contended that the targeted farms were expropriated and given to certain beneficiaries whom they referred to as 'chefs' or a class of politically connected beneficiaries. These were, in the words of the Applicants, *'senior political or judicial, or senior members of the armed services'.*

It is on the basis of those arguments that the Applicants, therefore, submitted in conclusion that the Respondent is in breach of Article 6(2) of the Treaty, prohibiting discrimination, by enacting and implementing Amendment 17.

The Respondent, for its part, refuted the allegations by the Applicants that the land reform programme is targeted at white farmers only. It argued instead that the programme is for the benefit of people who were disadvantaged under colonialism and it is within this context that the Applicants' farms were identified for acquisition by the Respondent. The farms acquired are suitable for agricultural purposes and happen to be largely owned by the white Zimbabweans. In implementing the land reform programme, therefore, it was inevitable that the people who were likely to be affected would be white farmers. Such expropriation of land under the Programme cannot be attributed to racism but circumstances brought about by colonial history. In any case, according to the Respondent, not only lands belonging to white Zimbabweans have been targeted for expropriation but also those of the few black Zimbabweans who possessed large tracts of land. Moreover, some white farmers have been issued with offer letters and 99-year leases in respect of agricultural lands. The Respondent has, therefore, not discriminated against white Zimbabwean farmers and has not acted in breach of Article 6(2) of the Treaty.

The Tribunal has to determine whether or not Amendment 17 discriminates against the Applicants and as such violates the obligation that the Respondent has undertaken under the Treaty to prohibit discrimination.

It should first be noted that discrimination of whatever nature is outlawed or prohibited in international law. There are several international instruments and treaties which prohibit discrimination based on race, the most important one being the United Nations Charter, which provides in Article 1(3) that one of its purposes is:

> *'To achieve international corporation in solving international problems of an economic, social, cultural or humanitarian character, and in promoting and encouraging respect for human rights* and fundamental freedoms for all without distinction as to* **race**, *sex, language or religion'.* (emphasis added).

There is also the Universal Declaration of Human Rights which provides in Article 2 as follows:

> *'Everyone is entitled to all the rights and freedoms set forth in this Declaration without distinction of any kind, such as* **race**, *colour, sex, language, religion, political or other opinion, national or social origin, property, birth or other status'.* (emphasis added).

Moreover, Article 2(1) of the International Covenant on Civil and Political Rights and Article 2(2) of the International Covenant on Economic, Social and Cultural Rights prohibit racial discrimination, respectively, as follows:

> 'Each State party to the present Covenant undertakes to respect and ensure to all individuals within its territory without distinction of any kind such as **race**, colour, sex, language, religion, political or other opinion, national or social origin, property, birth or other status'. (emphasis added).
>
> 'The States parties to the present Covenant undertake to guarantee that the rights enunciated in the present Covenant will be exercised without discrimination of any kind as to **race**, colour, sex, language, religious, political or other opinion, national or social origin, property, birth or other status'. (emphasis added).

The above provisions are similar to Article 2 of the African Charter on Human and Peoples' Rights (African Charter) and Article 14 of the European Convention on Human Rights.

Discrimination on the basis of race is also outlawed by the Convention On the Elimination of All Forms of Racial Discrimination (the Convention). It is worth noting that the Respondent has acceded to both Covenants, the African Charter and the Convention and, by doing so, is under an obligation to respect, protect and promote the principle of non-discrimination and must, therefore, prohibit and outlaw any discrimination based on the ground of race in its laws, policies and practices.

Apart from all the international human rights instruments and treaties, the Treaty also prohibits discrimination. Article 6(2) states as follows:

> 'SADC and Member States shall not discriminate against any person on grounds of gender, religion, political views, **race**, ethnic origin, culture, ill health, disability or such other ground as may be determined by the Summit'. (emphasis added).

This Article, therefore, enjoins SADC and Member States, including the Respondent, not to discriminate against any person on the stated grounds, one of which is race.

The question then is, what is racial discrimination? It is to be noted that the Treaty does not define racial discrimination or offer any guidelines to that effect. Article 1 of the Convention is as follows:

> 'Any distinction, exclusion, restriction or preference based on race, colour, descent, or natural or ethnic origin which <u>has the purpose or effect of nullifying or impairing the recognition, enjoyment or exercise on an equal footing, of human rights </u>and fundamental freedoms in the political, economic, social, cultural or any other field of public life'. (emphasis added).

Moreover, the Human Rights Committee in its General Comment No. 18 on non-discrimination has, in paragraph 7, defined discrimination as used in the Covenant on Civil and Political Rights as implying:

> <u>'Any distinction, exclusion, restriction or preference which is based on any ground such as race,</u> colour, sex, language, religion, political or other opinion, national or

social origin, property, birth or other status, and which has the purpose or effect of nullifying or impairing the recognition, enjoyment or exercise by all persons, on an equal footing, of all rights and freedoms'. (emphasis added).

The Committee on Economic, Social and Cultural Rights, for its part, in its General Comment No. 16 on the equal right of men and women to the equality of all economic, social and cultural rights underlined at paragraph 13 that *'guarantees of non-discrimination and equality in international human rights treaties mandate both de facto and de jure equality. De jure (or formal) equality and de facto (or substantive) equality are different but interconnected concepts'.*

The Committee further pointed out that formal equality assumes that equality is achieved if a law or policy treats everyone equal in a neutral manner. Substantive equality is concerned, in addition, with the effects of laws, policies and practices in order to ensure that they do not discriminate against any individual or group of individuals. The Committee went on to state at paragraphs 12 and 13 respectively that:

> *'Direct discrimination occurs when a difference in treatment relies directly and explicitly on distinctions based exclusively on sex and characteristics of men or women, which cannot be justified objectively'.*
> *'Indirect discrimination occurs when a law, policy or programme does not appear to be discriminatory but has a discriminatory effect when implemented'.* (emphasis added).

It is to be noted that what the Committee is stating about direct and indirect discrimination in the context of sex applies equally in the case of any other prohibited ground under the Covenant such as race.

The question that arises is whether Amendment 17 subjects the Applicants to any racial discrimination, as defined above. It is clear that the Amendment affected all agricultural lands or farms occupied and owned by the Applicants and all the Applicants are white farmers. Can it then be said that, because all the farms affected by the Amendment belong to white farmers, the Amendment and the land reform programme are racially discriminatory?

We note here that there is no explicit mention of race, ethnicity or people of a particular origin in Amendment 17 as to make it racially discriminatory. If any such reference were made, that would make the provision expressly discriminatory against a particular race or ethnic group. The effect of such reference would be that the Respondent would be in breach of its obligations under the Article 6(2) of the Treaty.

The question is whether, in the absence of the explicit mention of the word 'race' in Amendment 17, that would be the end of the matter. It should be recalled that the Applicants argued that, even if Amendment could be held not to be racially discriminatory in itself, its effects make it discriminatory because the targeted agricultural lands are all owned by white farmers and that the purpose of Amendment 17 was to make it apply to white farmers only, regardless of any other factors such as the proper use of their lands, their citizenship, their length of residence in Zimbabwe or any other factor other than the colour of their skin.

Since the effects of the implementation of Amendment 17 will be felt by the Zimbabwean white farmers only, we consider it, although Amendment 17 does not explicitly refer to white farmers, as we have indicated above, its implementation affects white farmers only and consequently constitutes indirect discrimination or *de facto* or substantive inequality.

In examining the effects of Amendment 17 on the applicants, it is clear to us that those effects have had an unjustifiable and disproportionate impact upon a group of individuals distinguished by race such as the Applicants. We consider that the differentiation of treatment meted out to the Applicants also constitutes discrimination as the criteria for such differentiation are not reasonable and objective but arbitrary and are based primarily on considerations of race. The aim of the Respondent in adopting and implementing a land reform programme might be legitimate if and when all lands under the programme were indeed distributed to poor, landless and other disadvantaged and marginalized individuals or groups. We, therefore, hold that, implementing Amendment 17, the Respondent has discriminated against the Applicants on the basis of race and thereby violated its obligation under Article 6(2) of the Treaty.

We wish to observe here that if: (a) the criteria adopted by the Respondent in relation to the land reform programme had not been arbitrary but reasonable and objective; (b) fair compensation was paid in respect of the expropriated lands, and the lands expropriated were indeed distributed to poor, landless and other disadvantaged and marginalized individuals or groups, rendering the purpose of the programme legitimate, the differential treatment afforded to the Applicants would not constitute racial discrimination.

We can do no better than quote in this regard what the Supreme Court of Zimbabwe stated in *Commercial Farmers Union v. Minister of Lands* 2001 (2) SA 925 (ZSC) at paragraph 9 where it dealt with the history of land injustice in Zimbabwe and the need for a land reform programme under the rule of law:

> 'We are not entirely convinced that the expropriation of white farmers, if it is done lawfully and fair compensation is paid, can be said to be discriminatory. But there can be no doubt that it is unfair discrimination . . . to award the spoils of expropriation primarily to ruling party adherents'.

DISCUSSION NOTES

1 The international law prohibition on discrimination does not mean that states can never treat individuals differently. It means they may not do so without adequate grounds. Likewise, hosts are not always required to expropriate either everyone or no one. The tribunal in *Amoco v. Iran* explained its finding of non-discrimination in that case, where Iran had

nationalized the oil sector, but had made an exception for one of Amoco's Japanese competitors:

139. In support of its contention that the expropriation was discriminatory, the Claimant relies on the fact that, in another of NPC's joint ventures, the Japanese share of a consortium, the Iran–Japan Petrochemical Company (IJPC) was not expropriated. In contrast, all American interests in petrochemical joint ventures with NPC were expropriated. The Claimant thus argues that the expropriation of Amoco's interest in Khemco was based on discrimination against American interests and was unlawful for this reason.

140. Discrimination is widely held as prohibited by customary international law in the field of expropriation. Although Article IV, paragraph 2 does not expressly prohibit a discriminatory expropriation, paragraph 1 of the same article obliges each party to 'refrain from applying unreasonable or discriminatory measures that would impair (the) legally acquired rights and interests' of the nationals and companies of the other party. This wording is so broad that it certainly applies to expropriations. In any event, the Respondents recognize that a discriminatory expropriation is wrongful, but deny that the expropriation was discriminatory in the instant Case.

141. The Respondents assert that the Single Article Act applied to the entire oil industry, irrespective of the nationality of the foreign companies involved in this industry. In the event, it was applied to non-United States corporations as well as United States corporations. Therefore, it cannot be held to be discriminatory. That the Special Commission did not include the contract with IJPC among those which were nullified, the Respondents submit, was an exception due to specific circumstances. They mention specifically the fact that the operation of the IJPC joint venture was not closely linked with other contracts relating to the exploitation of oil fields, whereas the operation of the Khemco plant was linked to the supply of gas from the oil fields operated jointly by Amoco and NIOC pursuant to the JSA. Furthermore, the Respondents emphasize that IJPC was not yet an operational concern at the relevant time, a point that was confirmed by the Claimant.

142. The Tribunal finds it difficult, in the absence of any other evidence, to draw the conclusion that the expropriation of a concern was discriminatory only from the fact that another concern in the same economic branch was not expropriated. Reasons specific to the non-expropriated enterprise, or to the expropriated one, or to both, may justify such a difference of treatment. Furthermore, as observed by the arbitral tribunal in Kuwait and American Independent Oil Company (AMINOIL), (Reuter, Sultan and Fitzmaurice arbs, Award of 24 March 1982), reprinted in Int'l Legal Mat'ls 976, 1019, a coherent policy of nationalization can reasonably be operated gradually in successive stages. In the present Case, the peculiarities discussed by the Parties can

explain why IJPC was not treated in the same manner as Khemco. The Tribunal declines to find that Khemco's expropriation was discriminatory.[36]

> **2** When considering a post-colonial land redistribution exception to the nondiscrimination requirement of a legal expropriation, how strictly should a tribunal regard the host's efforts to ensure the truly disadvantaged receive the assets? What if the most disadvantaged segments of society are less likely to be able to maintain the productive capacity of the property? See, for example, Luke E. Peterson and Ross Garland, *Bilateral Investment Treaties and Land Reform in Southern Africa*, Rights and Democracy (June 2010); Evangelista Mudzonga and Tendai Chigwada, *Agriculture: Future Scenarios for Southern Africa–A Case Study of Zimbabwe's Food Security* (International Institute for Sustainable Development 2009).

c.iv Compensation

The fourth element of a host's duties when exercising its right to expropriate is that it compensates the investor. For the average investor, the right to compensation[37] is the most critical element of the expropriation.

Not contentious in itself, the compensation element of expropriation is heavily litigated mainly because of the arguments over the level of payment the host owes the investor in the particular expropriation situation. In any expropriation claim, three fundamental questions arise regarding compensation: (1) was the expropriation legal? (2) if so, what is the measure of compensation for a legal expropriation? and (3) what is the value of the particular expropriated investment? We will look at the second question now, leaving the first and third for separate discussions below.

Customary law on compensation for legal expropriations?
Regardless of the precise formulation of the provision, a non-discriminatory expropriation undertaken with a public purpose and with due process is a legal act under most IIAs. It will still require compensation, however. The level of compensation owed to the investor in such cases will depend on the

---

36 *Amoco International Finance Corp. v. Iran, supra* note 9, paras. 139–42.

37 I use the term 'compensation' to refer to any payment from the host to the investor as a result of an expropriation, whether legal or illegal. While 'compensation' is a more general term than 'damages', the former is widely used to refer to payments made for either lawful conduct or treaty violations. *See* Thomas W. Wälde and Corzu Sabahi, *Compensation, Damages, and Valuation, in* Oxford Handbook of International Investment Law 1049, 1052–3 (Peter Muchlinski, Federico Ortino and Christoph Schreuer eds., 2008).

terms of the treaty, on the customary law of expropriations, or on both (if the treaty provision is open to interpretation).

Although the necessity of compensating investors has long been recognized by all states, governments disagree as to whether there is an international norm on the level of compensation owed to an investor. The issue was one of significant disagreement in the post-World War I years, and is still not resolved today. The main protagonists of the conflicting views were hosts and home states, all too often corresponding to industrialized and developing states, respectively.

In the context of the nationalization of oil companies undertaken by Mexico during the interwar period, the positions taken by the United States and Mexico typified the characteristic stances. In 1938, US Secretary of State Cordell Hull sent a message protesting Mexico's expropriation of US oil companies, claiming that there was a recognized rule of international investor protection that called for full compensation for the expropriations. The measure of 'full compensation', claimed the United States, was clear:

> The Government of the United States merely adverts to a self-evident fact when it notes that the applicable precedents and recognized authorities on international law support its declaration that, under every rule of law and equity, no government is entitled to expropriate private property, for whatever purpose, without provision for prompt, adequate and effective payment therefore. [. . .][38]

The 'Hull Formula', as it became known, contained the three key elements of payment important to the investor.

- Prompt: the temporal element; an investor should not need to wait years for payment for its lost investment;
- Adequate: the quantum element; an investor should receive the proper value for its loss, one which reflects the value of the assets put in and the expected profits that would have resulted from the investment had it not been taken; and
- Effective: the functional element; the investor should receive compensation in a form that benefits the former owner; this generally means that the compensation needs to be paid in a readily convertible currency to allow the money to be able to flow back out of the country.

---

38 Green Hackworth, 3 Digest of International Law 658–9 (1942) reprinting the statement of Cordell Hull addressed to the Government of Mexico on 22 August, 1938.

Most of the debate over the customary status of expropriation compensation centred on the quantum element of the payment (that is, the 'adequacy' standard). The 'prompt' and 'effective' standards were much less disputed in theory, although they were often ignored in practice. Today, compensation is generally paid in convertible, freely transferable currency.[39] Ensuring the promptness of the payment, however, remains a challenge.[40]

Hull's 'adequacy' element, however, was provocative to begin with and became even more contentious during the early post-World War II years of decolonialization. Under the New International Economic Order (NIEO) movement, newly independent states began challenging the US/European view of how much compensation hosts owed investors. Supporters of NIEO were not only the host governments of most foreign direct investment at the time, they were also economically developing and often low-income countries who could ill afford to pay the full market value for the assets taken. Facing a situation in which foreign investors owned many of the most profitable assets in the country, the hosts were unable to finance the expropriations at the full market value. Compensation, they argued, should consequently be 'appropriate' to the situation of post-colonial governments, not 'adequate' as defined by the investor-driven economic context.

While remaining vocally opposed to the Hull Rule's 'adequate' standard in the international political arena, by the second half of the 1980s adherents of the NIEO nevertheless began to conduct themselves differently in bilateral treaty negotiations. Hoping to attract foreign investment, developing country governments began to sign IIAs in increasing numbers despite the inclusion of obligations to compensate investors 'fully' or 'adequately'.[41] These actions, one could argue, point to the existence of a customary norm of adequate compensation. Alternatively, however, the continued opposition to such a measure could indi-

---

39 *See* for further information Borzu Sabahi, Compensation and Restitution in Investor-State Arbitration 153–6 (2011). According to Sabahi, in investor-state arbitration, the arbitral tribunals have commonly awarded the amount of compensation in the claimant's home state's currency. This and other possibilities would seem to have as primary goal the protection of the investor from currency devaluation. *See also Compañia de Aguas del Aconquija SA and Vivendi Universal SA v. Argentine Republic,* ICSID Case No. ARB/97/3, Award, para. 8.4.5 (Aug. 20, 2007). Available at: http://italaw.com/documents/VivendiAwardEnglish.pdf.

40 The Russian Federation's refusal to pay German investor Franz Sedelmayer has become the most notorious recent case of a host's non-payment of an expropriation award. Having expropriated Sedelmayer's properties in St. Petersburg, an arbitral tribunal ordered compensation in a 1998 decision. Russia refused to pay the award, leading to over 15 years of litigation in Germany and Sweden. In Fall 2014, Sedelmeyer became the first investor to be paid by the Russian government. Available at: http://italaw.com/cases/982; Anna Kempter, Enteignung: Franz Sedelmayer gegen Russland, ZeitMagazin 47/2014 (Nov. 14, 2014). Available at: http://www.zeit.de/zeit-magazin/2014/47/enteignung-entschaedigung-franz-sedelmayer-russland.

41 For a description of the 'BIT Generation's' emergence, *see* Santiago Montt, State Liability in Investment Treaty Arbitration: Global Constitutional and Administrative Law in the BIT Generation 83–123 (2009).

cate that treaty provisions calling for adequate compensation are necessary precisely because no such customary rule exists. The fact that the existence of customary international law requires both state practice and *opinio juris necessitatis* makes claims of an international standard of compensation difficult to justify.

As contemporary investment law is heavily dominated by treaty law, the provisions of which can trump customary rules, the confusion over the customary law status of the Hull Rule may not seem, in the end, to be of much significance to today's investor. Oscar Schachter's commented that '[T]he Hull formula, admittedly rejected by a great many states, has become largely political rhetoric, perceived on both sides as symbolic in the confrontation between North and South. It is very doubtful that the "prompt, adequate and effective" formula has much of a role, beyond preliminary incantation, in a serious negotiation on compensation. [. . .] To present it as an effective element of investor protection is, at best, an exaggeration, if not an illusion.'[42]

This is even more true today than it was when Schachter wrote it, as an increasing number of IIAs exist with explicit language on the level of compensation expected. Still, where treaty language is not clear, the customary norm on compensation—and the question of whether it exists—remains relevant to interpretation.

Compensation in IIAs

Whether or not the Hull Rule's 'adequate' standard is customary law, it is often reflected in the investment treaty provisions specifying the level of compensation owed expropriated investors, and it is these that are of the most significance today. As *lex specialis*, treaty provisions can differ from customary international law rules and tribunals will be obliged to apply the provisions to the parties.[43] Such provisions vary, with a few calling for 'appropriate compensation', but most calling 'full', 'just', 'adequate', or simply for 'compensation' in the case of expropriation. These latter terms, in turn, are frequently defined explicitly to mean the market value of the investment.[44]

The equivalence of 'compensation' to paying the 'market value' of the expropriated property has long been pushed by industrialized home states in treaty

---

42 Oscar Schachter, *Compensation for Expropriation*, 78(1) AJIL 121, 125–6 (1984).

43 *ADC v. Hungary, supra* note 11, para. 481 ('There is general authority for the view that a BIT can be considered as a *lex specialis* whose provisions will prevail over rules of customary international law').

44 *See*, e.g. Model BIT of the United States 2004, art. 6.1(c) (prompt, adequate, and effective compensation) and art. 6.2(b) (fair market value); Model BIT of Germany 2008, art. 4.2 (compensation equivalent to the value of the investment); Model BIT of India 2003, art. 5.1 (requiring fair and equitable compensation as equivalent to the 'genuine value' of the investment).

negotiations. Given the strong support for the standard by the World Bank,[45] it is not surprising that this rule has been widely accepted by their capital-importing treaty partners as well. What is striking, though, is the frequency with which 'South-South' BITs incorporate the fair market value standard.[46] This may be explained by the emerging economies' new role as home states, but it is also a signal of the broad acceptance of the investor-friendly attitude of investment law.

Even where a legal expropriation takes place, a tribunal will often have to determine the quantum of compensation the host must pay the claimant. The *Amoco v. Iran* tribunal also addressed this point:

 CASE

Amoco International Finance Corp. v. Iran[47]

182. For the reasons set forth above, the Tribunal finds that Amoco's rights and interests under the Khemco Agreement, including its shares in Khemco, were lawfully expropriated by Iran, through a process starting in April 1979 and completed by the decision of the Special Commission, notified by telex on 24 December 1980. The next issue, therefore, relates to the rules to be applied in determining the compensation to be paid in such a circumstance.
[...]
207. The standard of 'just compensation' for a lawful expropriation referred to in Article IV, paragraph 2, of the Treaty is more precisely defined in the last sentence of the paragraph, which provides that 'such compensation shall be in an effectively realizable form and shall represent the full equivalent of the property taken.'
208. As previously noted, by the phrase 'just compensation' the parties to the Treaty chose one of the various ways of describing the compensation due in case

---

45 As the World Bank Guidelines on the Treatment of Foreign Direct Investment note:

Compensation will be deemed 'adequate' if it is based on the fair market value of the taken asset as such value is determined immediately before the time at which the taking occurred or the decision to take the asset became publicly known.

World Bank Guidelines on the Treatment of Foreign Direct Investment, in World Bank, *Legal Framework for the Treatment of Foreign Investment* (Washington, DC: The World Bank, 1992). The Guidelines are *reprinted in* 31 ILM 1379. Available at: http://italaw.co m/documents/WorldBank.pdf. *Amoco International Finance Corp. v. Iran*, *supra* note 9; footnotes omitted.
46 For example, Agreement Between the Government of the Republic of India and the Government of the People's Republic of Bangladesh for the Promotion and Protection of Investments, Article 5 (in effect as of 7 July 2011); *Convenio entre la Republica de Bolivia y la República del Ecuador para la promotion y protección reciproca de inversiones*, Article IV.1 (in effect 15 August 1997); Agreement Between the Government of the Republic of Indonesia and the Government of the Lao People's Democratic Republic Concerning the Promotion and Protection of Investments, Article IV(c) (in effect as of 14 October 1995).
47 *Amoco Interntional Finance Corp. v. Iran, supra* note 9; footnotes omitted.

of nationalization. It is therefore apparent that the wording chosen in Article IV, paragraph 2, has as a first purpose and effect to exclude consideration of factors foreign to the value of the expropriated assets, such as excessive past profits or the rate of return on the initial investment, which have been invoked in a few cases of nationalization in order to reduce the compensation due to an amount less than the full value of these assets. Although counsel for the Respondents made some references to the rate of return on Amoco's initial investment, the Respondents do not appear to suggest that this factor should enter into the calculation of the compensation due, and no other factor of this kind was invoked.

209. 'Just compensation' has generally been understood as a compensation equal to the full value of the expropriated assets. This is confirmed in the wording of Article IV, paragraph 2, which refers to 'the full equivalent of the property taken.' The Tribunal does not see any material difference between this phrase and the usual term of 'just compensation.' [. . .].

A finding that 'just compensation' is equal to full value leaves open the precise answer the difficult question of the proper method to be used in order to determine what the 'full value' or 'full equivalent' of the property taken means in figures. This question of method goes beyond the issue of the standard of compensation, because several methods are available and the choice between them depends on the particular circumstances of each case. This will be dealt with in the following section.

? DISCUSSION NOTES

1 The NIEO movement's views of investment law were set forth in several United Nations General Assembly (UNGA) Resolutions. The most prominent of these was UNGA Resolution 1803 which promised 'permanent sovereignty over natural resources' to each government and required appropriate, rather than adequate, compensation. Moreover, the host's national courts should make the determination of how much compensation would be appropriate in any given expropriation situation.

General assembly resolution 1803 (XVII) of 14 December 1962, 'Permanent sovereignty over natural resources'

The General Assembly, [. . .]
Bearing in mind its resolution 1314 (XIII) of 12 December 1958, by which it established the Commission on Permanent Sovereignty over Natural Resources and instructed it to conduct a full survey of the status of permanent sovereignty over natural wealth and resources as a basic constituent of the right

to self-determination, with recommendations, where necessary, for its strengthening, and decided further that, in the conduct of the full survey of the status of the permanent sovereignty of peoples and nations over their natural wealth and resources, due regard should be paid to the rights and duties of States under international law and to the importance of encouraging international cooperation in the economic development of developing countries,

Bearing in mind its resolution 1515 (XV) of 15 December 1960, in which it recommended that the sovereign right of every State to dispose of its wealth and its natural resources should be respected,

Considering that any measure in this respect must be based on the recognition of the inalienable right of all States freely to dispose of their natural wealth and resources in accordance with their national interests, and on respect for the economic independence of States,

Considering that nothing in paragraph 4 below in any way prejudices the position of any Member State on any aspect of the question of the rights and obligations of successor States and Governments in respect of property acquired before the accession to complete sovereignty of countries formerly under colonial rule,

[...]

Attaching particular importance to the question of promoting the economic development of developing countries and securing their economic independence,

Noting that the creation and strengthening of the inalienable sovereignty of States over their natural wealth and resources reinforces their economic independence,

Desiring that there should be further consideration by the United Nations of the subject of permanent sovereignty over natural resources in the spirit of international co-operation in the field of economic development, particularly that of the developing countries,

Declares that:

1. The right of peoples and nations to permanent sovereignty over their natural wealth and resources must be exercised in the interest of their national development and of the well-being of the people of the State concerned.

2. The exploration, development and disposition of such resources, as well as the import of the foreign capital required for these purposes, should be in conformity with the rules and conditions which the peoples and nations freely consider to be necessary or desirable with regard to the authorization, restriction or prohibition of such activities.

3. In cases where authorization is granted, the capital imported and the earnings on that capital shall be governed by the terms thereof, by the national legislation in force, and by international law. The profits derived must be shared in the proportions freely agreed upon, in each case, between the

investors and the recipient State, due care being taken to ensure that there is no impairment, for any reason, of that State's sovereignty over its natural wealth and resources.

4. Nationalization, expropriation or requisitioning shall be based on grounds or reasons of public utility, security or the national interest which are recognized as overriding purely individual or private interests, both domestic and foreign. In such cases the owner shall be paid appropriate compensation, in accordance with the rules in force in the State taking such measures in the exercise of its sovereignty and in accordance with international law. In any case where the question of compensation gives rise to a controversy, the national jurisdiction of the State taking such measures shall be exhausted. However, upon agreement by sovereign States and other parties concerned, settlement of the dispute should be made through arbitration or international adjudication.

[...]

8. Foreign investment agreements freely entered into by or between sovereign States shall be observed in good faith; States and international organizations shall strictly and conscientiously respect the sovereignty of peoples and nations over their natural wealth and resources in accordance with the Charter and the principles set forth in the present resolution.

In 1974, the Charter of Economic Rights and Duties of States reinforced this direction with an explicit purpose of establishing an NIEO. Article 2(c) of the Charter sets out the rights of states to control foreign investment:

To nationalize, expropriate or transfer ownership of foreign property, in which case appropriate compensation should be paid by the State adopting such measures, taking into account its relevant laws and regulations and all circumstances that the State considers pertinent. In any case where the question of compensation gives rise to a controversy, it shall be settled under the domestic law of the nationalizing State and by its tribunals, unless it is freely and mutually agreed by all States concerned that other peaceful means be sought on the basis of the sovereign equality of States and in accordance with the principle of free choice of means.[48]

2 One problem with assessing the fair market value of an investment is that as soon as property is expropriated (or said to be under threat of expropriation), its market value sinks. As a result the 'true' price no longer exists. This problem can be resolved by treaty language

---

48 *See* Charter of Economic Rights and Duties of States, GA Res. 3281 (XXIX), UN Doc. A/RES/29/3281 (Dec. 12, 1974).

specifying at what date the value is to be calculated. Many IIA parties opt to include language such that the 'fair market value 'is equal to the value of the property on the day before the expropriation became known.

3 The proposed Indian Model BIT from 2015 is pointedly host-friendly.[49] The expropriation provision, however, provides for 'payment of adequate compensation' in Article 5.1. Why? In fact, the standard is less conventional than it would appear. The term 'adequate compensation' is modified by Articles 5.6 and 5.7, which are integral to the provision:

> 5.6 Compensation provided under this Article shall be adequate and reflect the fair market value of the expropriated Investment, as reduced after application of relevant Mitigating Factors. The amount of compensation shall not vary based on whether an expropriation has complied with the criteria of Article 5.1.
> 5.7 Mitigating Factors under Article 5.6 include: (a) current and past use of the Investment, including the history of its acquisition and purpose; (b) the duration of the Investment and previous profits made by the Investment; (c) compensation or insurance payouts received by the Investor or Investment from other sources; (d) the value of property that remains subject to the Investor or Investment's disposition or control; (e) options available to the Investor or Investment to mitigate its losses, including reasonable efforts made by the Investor or Investment towards such mitigation, if any; (f) conduct of the Investor that contributed to its damage; (g) any obligation the Investor or its Investment is relieved of due to the expropriation; (h) liabilities owed in the Host State to the government as a result of the Investment's activities; (i) any harm or damage that the Investor or its Investment has caused to the environment or local community that have not been remedied by the Investor or the Investment; and (j) any other relevant considerations regarding the need to balance the public interest and the interests of the Investment.

4 What is the difference between this definition of 'adequate' and the notion of appropriateness?

---

49 Model Text for the Indian Bilateral Investment Treaty, Art. 5 (2015). Available at: https://mygov.in/sites/default/files/master_image/Model%20Text%20for%20the%20Indian%20Bilateral%20Investment%20Treaty.pdf.

4.1.3 Illegal expropriations

a *What constitutes an illegal expropriation*

As stressed above, states have the right to expropriate the property of foreign investors. The expropriation, however, must adhere to the conditions set out in the treaty, usually: for public purpose, in accordance with due process, non-discriminatorily, and against compensation.

If a host expropriates in a way that does not conform to the conditions, it acts wrongfully, and the expropriation is illegal. The main consequence of this illegality is that the measure for damages is different than it would be for a legal expropriation.

b *Level of compensation for an illegal expropriation*

Most IIA provisions on expropriation set forth the conditions applying to a legal taking. The level of compensation stated in the treaty, then, applies solely to the duties of the host for its legal actions. When a state has acted illegally, the treaty norms setting out the level of compensation for legal takings will no longer apply. Instead, general international law rules on reparations become the measure of the state's obligations toward the investor.

c *The basic measure of compensation for wrongful acts of states*

The basic measure of a state's duty to compensate wronged individuals is widely recognized as customary law. The classic statement on this basic rule issued from the Permanent Court of International Justice, in the 1928 *Factory at Chorzów* case.

 CASE

The Factory at Chorzów (Germany v. Poland)[50]

Following World War I, the Treaty of Versailles provided for the transfer of German territories to Poland. The Convention gave the new authorities the right to take the land owned by the German government and use the value as a credit toward Germany's war reparations owed that government.

---

50 *The Factory at Chorzów* (Germany v. Poland), Claim for Indemnity/The Merits, 1928 PCIJ (ser. A) No. 17 (Sept. 13). Available at: http://www.worldcourts.com/pcij/eng/decisions/1928.09.13_chorzow1.htm; footnotes omitted.

Once Poland took control of the town of Chorzów, a Polish court declared that land belonging to a German company, the Oberschlesische Stickstoffwerke, was to be turned over to Poland. The company's owners complained that it was a private enterprise, and not a part of the German state, and thus, that the seizure of it was contrary to law.

The PCIJ concluded that the land was privately owned, and that Poland's actions had therefore been an illegal expropriation. The key issue facing the Court then was to decide what the responsibility of a state that had violated international law should be. The PCIJ distinguished the level of payment owed in a legal expropriation with that owed in an illegal expropriation (which it calls a 'seizure of property, rights and interests').

III.

The existence of a damage to be made good being recognized by the respondent party as regards the Bayerische, and the objections raised by the same Party against the existence of any damage that would justify compensation to the Oberschlesische being set aside, the Court must now lay down the guiding principles according to which the amount of compensation due may be determined. The action of Poland which the Court has judged to be contrary to the Geneva Convention is not an expropriation—to render which lawful only the payment of fair compensation would have been wanting; it is a seizure of property, rights and interests which could not be expropriated even against compensation, save under the exceptional conditions fixed by Article 7 of the said Convention. As the Court has expressly declared in Judgment No. 8, reparation is in this case the consequence not of the application of Articles 6 to 22 of the Geneva Convention, but of acts contrary to those articles.

It follows that the compensation due to the German Government is not necessarily limited to the value of the undertaking at the moment of dispossession, plus interest to the day of payment. This limitation would only be admissible if the Polish Government had had the right to expropriate, and if its wrongful act consisted merely in not having paid to the two Companies the just price of what was expropriated; in the present case, such a limitation might result in placing Germany and the interests protected by the Geneva Convention, on behalf of which interests the German Government is acting, in a situation more unfavourable than that in which Germany and these interests would have been if Poland had respected the said Convention. Such a consequence would not only be unjust, but also and above all incompatible with the aim of Article 6 and following articles of the Convention— that is to say, the prohibition, in principle, of the liquidation of the property, rights and interests of German nationals and of companies controlled by German nationals in Upper Silesia—since it would be tantamount to rendering lawful liquidation and unlawful dispossession indistinguishable in so far as their financial results are concerned. The essential principle contained in the actual notion of an illegal act—a principle which seems to be established by international practice and in particular by the decisions of arbitral tribunals—is that reparation must, as far as possible, wipe-out all the consequences of the illegal act and re-establish the situation which would, in all probability, have existed if that act had not been committed. Restitution in kind, or, if this is not possible, payment of a sum corresponding to the value which a restitution in kind would bear; the award, if need be, of damages for loss sustained which would not be covered by restitution in kind or payment in place of it—such are the principles which should serve to determine the amount of compensation due for an act contrary to international law.

[. . .] The impossibility, on which the Parties are agreed, of restoring the Chorzów factory could therefore have no other effect but that of substituting payment of the value of the undertaking for restitution; it would not be in conformity either with the principles of law or with the wish of the Parties to infer from that agreement that the question of compensation must henceforth be dealt with as though an expropriation properly so called was involved.

Responsibility of States for Internationally Wrongful Acts

The ILC Articles on Responsibility of States for Internationally Wrongful Acts
The principle set out in the *Factory at Chorzów* case has now been codified by the International Law Commission (ILC) in the Articles on Responsibility of States for Internationally Wrongful Acts ('Articles on State Responsibility').[51] Articles 34–37 set out the measures of reparation for wrongful actions.

Article 34 forms of reparation

Full reparation for the injury caused by the internationally wrongful act shall take the form of restitution, compensation and satisfaction, either singly or in combination, in accordance with the provisions of this chapter.

Article 35 restitution

A State responsible for an internationally wrongful act is under an obligation to make restitution, that is, to re-establish the situation which existed before the wrongful act was committed, provided and to the extent that restitution:

(a)   is not materially impossible;
(b)   does not involve a burden out of all proportion to the benefit deriving from restitution instead of compensation.

---

51 Responsibility of States for Internationally Wrongful Acts, (2001). Available at: http:// untreaty.un.org/ ilc/texts/instruments/english/draft%20articles/9_6_2001.pdf.

Article 36 compensation

1. The State responsible for an internationally wrongful act is under an obligation to compensate for the damage caused thereby, insofar as such damage is not made good by restitution.
2. The compensation shall cover any financially assessable damage including loss of profits insofar as it is established.

Article 37 satisfaction

1. The State responsible for an internationally wrongful act is under an obligation to give satisfaction for the injury caused by that act insofar as it cannot be made good by restitution or compensation.
2. Satisfaction may consist in an acknowledgement of the breach, an expression of regret, a formal apology or another appropriate modality.
3. Satisfaction shall not be out of proportion to the injury and may not take a form humiliating to the responsible State.

These provisions refer to the measures of reparation for a state's 'wrongful acts'. In investment law, the 'wrongfulness' of the act of expropriation is termed 'illegality'. Thus, if a state expropriates discriminatorily, without due process, in the absence of a public interest in the expropriation, or without compensating the investor, it acquires an obligation to offer reparations to the investor: theoretically to give back the property, or if that is impossible, to financially compensate the investor so as to wipe out the effects of the illegality and/or to offer satisfaction. Investment tribunals have rarely questioned the ASR provisions. One, however, suggested that a tribunal does not have the competence to order the state to give the actual property back to the investor. In *Sistem Muhendislik v. Kyrgyz Republic*,[52] the award quoted from *Chorzów Factory* and immediately noted:

> 'It is questionable whether an arbitral tribunal has the power to order a State to restore expropriated property to its original owner. In any event, restoration of expropriated property is plainly no longer the primary judicial remedy in cases of expropriation, if it ever was. Monetary compensation is the normal remedy, and its role is precisely 'to take the place of restitution'.[53]

What implications does the finding of illegality have on the actual sum the investor should receive from the host? Viewing the ILC rules on reparations,

---

52 *Sistem Mühendislik Insaat Sanayi ve Ticaret A.S. v. Kyrgyz Republic*, ICSID Case No. ARB(AF)/06/1 (Sept. 9, 2009).
53 Id. at para. 158.

most authors and arbitral tribunals admit that the compensation granted the wrongfully expropriated investor will be higher than the compensation given the legally expropriated investor.[54] The difference in amount is not based on a punitive rationale, but rather because the reparation amount includes expected future profits and any consequential damages as well as the current value of the investment. The tribunal in *Siemens AG v. Argentina* summarized:

> The key difference between compensation under the Draft Articles and the *Factory at Chorzów* case formula, and Article 4(2) of the Treaty is that under the former, compensation must take into account 'all financially assessable damage' or 'wipe out all the consequences of the illegal act' as opposed to compensation 'equivalent to the value of the expropriated investment' under the Treaty. Under customary international law, Siemens is entitled not just to the value of its enterprise as of May 18, 2001, the date of expropriation, but also to any greater value that enterprise has gained up to the date of this Award, plus any consequential damages.[55]

The decision in *Funnekotter v. Zimbabwe*[56] clarified the different results of applying the customary international law standard for wrongful acts and the BIT standard for legal expropriations. In this case, similar to that of Mike Campbell (discussed above), Zimbabwe expropriated the claimant's farm and denied him compensation. Having found that Zimbabwe had expropriated discriminatorily, the tribunal continued to address the amount the government owed:

> 108. It remains for the Tribunal to fix the damages due to the Claimants. In this respect Zimbabwe submits that the damages must be calculated as specified in Article 6(c). For their part, the Claimants contend that the standard of compensation provided for in Article 6(c) is the standard applicable in case of lawful expropriation. By contrast, compensation due in case of unlawful expropriation must be calculated according to customary international law as decided by the Permanent Court of International Justice in the *Chorzów Factory* case.
>
> 109. In that case, the Permanent Court made a distinction between lawful and unlawful expropriation. It held that, in case of lawful expropriation, the damages suffered must be repaired through the 'payment of fair compensation' or 'the just price of what was expropriated' at the time of the expropriation. By contrast, it decided that, in case of unlawful expropriation, international law provides for

---

54 *See* Reinisch, *supra* note 21, at 199–203; Sabahi, *supra* notes 2 39 41, at 100–102; *ADC v. Hungary, supra* note 11, paras. 480–99.

55 *Siemens AG v. Argentine Republic*, ICSID Case No. ARB/02/8, Award, para. 352 (Feb. 6, 2007). Available at: http://italaw.com/documents/Siemens-Argentina-Award.pdf.

56 *Bernardus Henricus Funnekotter and others v. Republic of Zimbabwe*, ICSID Case No. ARB/05/6, Award (Apr. 22, 2009). Available at: http://italaw.com/documents/ZimbabweAward.pdf.

restitutio in integrum or, if impossible, its monetary equivalent at the time of the judgment.

110. In recent years, there has been some debate on that distinction. The Iran–United States Claims Tribunal in the *Amoco* case observed in 1987 that, in spite of the fact that the *Chorzow Factory* case 'is nearly sixty years old, this judgment is widely regarded as the most authoritative exposé of the principles applicable in this field and is still valid to day [*sic*].' More recently an ICSID Tribunal similarly held that the BIT's standards of compensation apply only to lawful expropriations and that those standards 'cannot be used to determine the issue of damages payable in the case of an unlawful expropriation.' However, the contrary opinion has also been advanced and case law is not perfectly clear in this respect in particular in case of lack of compensation.

111. As the Iran–United States Claims Tribunal rightly observed in the Amoco case, 'Obviously, the value of an expropriated enterprise does not vary according to the lawfulness or the unlawfulness of the taking . . . . The difference is that, if the taking is lawful the value of the undertaking at the time of the dispossession is the measure and the limit of the compensation, while if it is unlawful, this value is or may be, only a part of the reparation to be paid.' In general, as the same Tribunal stated in the *Phillips Petroleum* case, 'the lawful/unlawful taking distinction . . . is relevant only to two possible issues: whether restitution of the property can be awarded and whether compensation can be awarded for increase of the value of the property between the date of the taking and the date of the judicial or arbitral decision awarding compensation.'

112. In the present case, both Parties finally exclude restitution of the farms expropriated. Moreover, it is not alleged that there was some increase of the value of those farms between the date of the taking and the date of the present award. Therefore, the major points of difference that distinguish computation of damages for lawful expropriation from computation of damages for unlawful expropriation are not here in issue.[57]

The result of the rule of 'making the investor whole' is that the level of compensation for an illegal expropriation is usually higher than what the host would have to pay if the expropriation had been a legal one. This is because, first, consequential losses can be included in the calculations. Second, the date on which the valuation is assessed differs: for a legal expropriation, the value of the asset is taken as of the date of the expropriation; for an illegal expropriation, the date is generally the value on the date of the award. This permits the illegally expropriated investor the benefit of any appreciation of

---

57 Id. at paras. 108–12.

the investment's value post-taking. Where the increase in value is significant, the difference can therefore be substantial.

The tribunal in *ADC v. Hungary* reviewed tribunals' traditional approach to this issue:

> 496. The present case is almost unique among decided cases concerning the expropriation by States of foreign owned property, since the value of the investment after the date of expropriation (1 January 2002) has risen very considerably while other arbitrations that apply the *Chorzów Factory* standard all invariably involve scenarios where there has been a decline in the value of the investment after regulatory interference. It is for this reason that application of the restitution standard by various arbitration tribunals has led to use of the date of the expropriation as the date for the valuation of damages.
>
> 497. However, in the present, *sui generis*, type of case the application of the *Chorzów Factory* standard requires that the date of valuation should be the date of the Award and not the date of expropriation, since this is what is necessary to put the Claimants in the same position as if the expropriation had not been committed. This kind of approach is not without support. The PCIJ in the *Chorzów Factory* case stated that damages are '*not necessarily limited to the value of the undertaking at the moment of dispossession*' [. . .]. It is noteworthy that the European Court of Human Rights has applied *Chorzów Factory* in circumstances comparable to the instant case to compensate the expropriated party the higher value the property enjoyed at the moment of the Court's judgment rather than the considerably lesser value it had had at the earlier date of dispossession. In *Papamichalopoulos and Others v. Greece* ((1966) E.H.R.R. 439) [. . .] the Greek Government in 1967 had expropriated unimproved real estate for the purpose of building housing for Greek Navy personnel, and in 1993 the Court had ruled that '*the applicants de facto . . . have been expropriated in a manner incompatible with their right to the peaceful enjoyment of their possession*'. [. . .] In the remedies stage the Court ruled [. . .]:

> > '*The unlawfulness of such a dispossession inevitably affects the criteria to be used for determining the reparation owed by the respondent State, since the pecuniary consequences of a lawful expropriation cannot be assimilated to those of an unlawful dispossession.*'

> Then, citing the oft-quoted passage from *Chorzów Factory* [. . .], the Court concluded [. . .]:

> > '*In the present case the compensation to be awarded to the applicants is not limited to the value of their properties at the date [1967] on which the Navy occupied them . . . For that reason [the Court had] requested the experts [appointed by the Court] to estimate also the current value of the land in issue.*'

The Court ordered restitution of the land, including all of the buildings and other improvements made over the intervening years by the Greek Navy, [. . .].

498. Moreover, Sole Arbitrator Dupuy in *Texaco Overseas Petroleum Company v. Government of the Libyan Arab Republic* 53 ILR p. 389 cited a number of authorities on the contours of the principle of *restitutio in integrum* as set out in the *Chorzów Factory* case. Dupuy cited in particular the view of former ICJ President Jiménez de Aréchaga, writing extra-judicially, who stated:

> 'The fact that indemnity presupposes, as the PCIJ stated, the 'payment sum corresponding to the value which a restitution in kind would bear ', has important effects on its extent. As a consequence of the depreciation of currencies and of delays involved in the administration of justice, the value of a confiscated property may be higher at the time of the judicial decision than at the time of the unlawful act. Since monetary compensation must, as far as possible, resemble restitution, the value at the date when indemnity is paid must be the criterion.'

499. Based on the foregoing reasons, the Tribunal concludes that it must assess the compensation to be paid by the Respondent to the Claimants in accordance with the *Chorzów Factory* standard, i.e., the Claimants should be compensated the market value of the expropriated investments as at the date of this Award, which the Tribunal takes as of September 30, 2006.

The *Kardassopoulos v. Georgia* tribunal affirmed the reasoning of giving the investor the benefit of any increases in the property's value, but underscored that offering compensation in place of restitution to 'make the investor whole' must not lead to overcompensation even in the context of an illegal expropriation. The dispute in that case was lodged by early investors in Georgia's energy sector. As the sector grew, the government began to rely on providers other than the claimants to secure the economic and strategic position in the region. As a consequence, the investment was expropriated, but in a manner that violated the due process. The discussion is informative:

> 512. In the present case, it is clear that restitution is no longer possible. The Tribunal must therefore determine the amount of compensation owing to Mr. Kardassopoulos.
>
> 513. As may be seen from the cases above in which a higher recovery has been permitted under the customary international law standard of compensation, there must be a factual basis on which to award such higher recovery. Any such recovery must, furthermore, measure the damage sustained and not impose punitive damages on the Respondent State.
>
> 514. In certain circumstances full reparation for an unlawful expropriation will require damages to be awarded as of the date of the arbitral Award. It may be appropriate to compensate for value gained between the date of the expropriation and

the date of the award in cases where it is demonstrated that the Claimants would, but for the taking, have retained their investment. For the reasons set out herein, however, this is not the case on the facts of these arbitrations.

515. The evidence on the record indicates that the Claimants would likely have sold their shares in GTI to AIOC (or a member of AIOC) in 1995 had Georgia affirmed the Claimants' rights. The Claimants appear to concede this proposition, although they argue that it is a conservative scenario [. . .]. This is precisely the outcome they sought, however, in entering into negotiations with Velt Energie and United Perlite. While the Claimants may have preferred to remain in the game in some capacity, the record confirms that selling their shares in the GTI project would have been an entirely acceptable outcome, assuming a fair price for those shares could be obtained.

516. Moreover, regardless of the Claimants' preference to retain some interest in the Gachiani–Supsa pipeline, the oral evidence of Mr. Adams suggests that AIOC's shareholders would have viewed their presence as an irritant, being a very small company on the scale of the consortium and not having any technical expertise, and sought to negotiate the purchase of their shares in the pipeline rather than work together [. . .]. This is confirmed by both industry experts, Mr. Beazley [. . .] and Mr. Effimoff [. . .], who expressed the view that had the Georgian Government confirmed GTI's rights AIOC would likely have sought to negotiate with Tramex and purchase its interest in GTI outright.

517. The Tribunal therefore finds that the appropriate standard of compensation from which to approach the calculation of the damage sustained by Mr. Kardassopoulos is the FMV of the early oil rights (including export rights) as of 10 November 1995. Whilst this pre-dates the expropriation effected by Decree No. 178, the Tribunal considers that the circumstances of this case require it to value Mr. Kardassopoulos' investment as of the day before passage of Decree No. 477 precisely to ensure full reparation and to avoid any diminution of value attributable to the State's conduct leading up to the expropriation. This compensation is, in effect, the amount that Mr. Kardassopoulos should have been paid as a result of the compensation process which the Respondent was obliged to put in place promptly after the taking of the Claimants' investment.[58]

If the value of the investment declines between the time of expropriation and the time of the award, however, the tribunal may decide to award the higher value.

---

58 See Kardassopoulos, *supra* note 14, paras. 512–17.

1 The reparation provisions of the Articles of State Responsibility are widely recognized as customary rules, applying to all states. They can, however, be overridden by specific treaty language. Thus, should the parties so choose, the terms of an IIA can limit the amount of compensation due the investor even in the case of a wrongful expropriation.

2 What should happen to the level of compensation if the value of the investment increases following a *legal* expropriation? Should the investor receive the value of the investment as of the expropriation or as of the date of the tribunal's decision?

3 While the law regarding state expropriations of foreign property is central to the study of international investment protection, given its long history, the law on expropriation is also well developed in general international law (as a matter of treatment of foreigners) and in human rights law (as an issue of the right to property). The above focused on the protection as an investment issue, but the reader is encouraged to delve further into the other aspects to notice how they interact with each other and with international economic law. See, for example, Borzu Sabahi and Nicholas J. Birch, *Comparative Compensation for Expropriation*, *in* International Investment Law and Comparative Public Law 755 (Stephan W. Schill ed., 2010); Jeff Waincymer, *Balancing Property Rights and Human Rights in Expropriation*, *in* Human Rights in International Investment Law and Arbitration 275 (Pierre-Marie Dupuy, Francesco Francioni, and Ernst-Ulrich Petersmann eds., 2009).

4.2 Indirect expropriation

4.2.1 Introduction

Although they still occur, outright expropriations of foreign property have become rare events. This is not surprising, for a full nationalization process or even a single major expropriation is likely to damage the reputation of a country as a host state too much for it to be worth the attempt.

A 'compulsory transfer of property rights', as the Amoco tribunal defined 'expropriation', needs not be a transfer of ownership, however. Since any right that has a commercial value can be diminished or eliminated, any governmental measure which affects such rights can be problematic for the investor. There are, for instance, many situations in which an investor loses expected profits through state actions–even if those actions are not directed at that investor. Consider the following hypothetical:

An Egyptian textile manufacturer sets up a factory in India, producing thousands of white T-shirts for export; but the owner gives some political contributions to the opposition candidate for state parliament, so the incumbent sees to it that a law is passed that limits the number of export licences granted to that company to 150 per year. Is there a direct expropriation? No, the government does not touch the ownership of the company. Is there a loss of expected profits? Yes.

Would the answers be different if that same company, which employs 300 people at 50 rupees per hour, dumping its dyes and bleaches into a river that runs along the edge of the property, is faced with a new law regarding sustainable business practices that requires a minimum wage of 500 rupees per hour and prohibits the untreated disposal of industrial waste? No. The reaction to the claim, however, may be different.

How do international investment tribunals deal with steps that a government takes that reduce the value of a company without taking it over? Or those that reduce the investor's control over the management of the investment? This is the subject matter of the study of indirect expropriations.

Courts have long realized that governments can effectively damage an investor's profit expectations through measures that have no direct impact on the ownership of the property. The label for actions that restrict use, management, or the profitability of the company is *indirect expropriation*. This term includes: *material expropriation, measures similar/tantamount/having equivalent effect to expropriation.*

The US Model BIT, for example, states:

> Neither Party may expropriate or nationalize a covered investment either directly or indirectly through *measures equivalent to expropriation or nationalization* ('expropriation')[59]

The German BIT, similarly, provides:

> Investments . . . may not directly or indirectly be expropriated, nationalized or subjected to any *other measure the effects of which would be tantamount to expropriation or nationalization.*[60]

---

59 US Model BIT 2012, art. 6.1 (emphasis added).
60 Germany Model BIT 2008, art. 4.2 (emphasis added).

The China-Côte d'Ivoire BIT, is only slightly different:

> Neither Contracting Party shall expropriate, nationalize or take *other similar measures* (hereinafter referred to as 'expropriation').[61]

The differences in wording among indirect expropriation provisions are largely irrelevant. The legal problem facing decision-makers instead is to determine when a governmental measure that negatively affects a property right is to be classified as an indirect expropriation and when it is 'merely' governmental regulation. This classification process is of the utmost importance because a regulation is *not compensable*, whereas an indirect expropriation implies the same international responsibility as does a direct expropriation. An 'indirect' expropriation, in other words, *is* an expropriation. A government must, therefore, adhere to the same standards in indirectly expropriating property as in directly expropriating it. It must be able to demonstrate that:

- there was a public purpose for the expropriation;
- the expropriation was non-discriminatory;
- the investor enjoyed due process; and
- that compensation was offered.[62]

4.2.2 Factors indicating an indirect expropriation

The difference between a direct expropriation and an indirect expropriation rests with the type of property right affected: while direct expropriations take the right of ownership or possession away from the investor, indirect expropriation takes away other property rights, either tangible or intangible— including claims to payment and rights to participate in a project, possibly the expectations of profit, and arguably good-will.[63]

---

61 Agreement between the Government of the People's Republic of China and the Government of the Republic of Côte d'Ivoire on the Promotion and Protection of Investments of 30 September 2002, art. 4.1 (emphasis added).

62 Whether the lack of compensation for a regulatory act that is categorized as an expropriation makes the expropriation illegal is debatable. Dolzer and Schreuer, *supra* note 4, at 100 claim that any non-compensated expropriation is illegal and requires the payment of restitution. Sornarajah, *supra* note 7, at 410, on the other hand, hints that for otherwise legal acts that are not accompanied by compensation, then the compensation due the investor is merely that set out in the treaty terms. Regulatory takings, which Sornarajah, *supra* note 7, at 411 distinguishes from 'compensatory takings', would require no compensation in his view.

63 *See Tidewater Inc. and Others v. Bolivarian Republic of Venezuela*, ICSID Case No. ARB/10/5, Award, para. 118 (March 13, 2015) (asserting that the BIT's reference to good will as a type of investment indicated that it could be expropriated).

More significant, however, is the difference between an expropriatory act and a non-expropriatory act that affects a property right. The difference between an indirect expropriation and a (non-compensable) regulation does not lie in the nature of the governmental measure. A newly promulgated restriction on cigarette packaging designs, for example, can reasonably be seen as either an indirect expropriation of the investor's intellectual property right or as a general health-promoting regulation by the government. Thus, tribunals determining whether a particular governmental act is expropriatory or not have to use other markers to distinguish the two.

There are numerous possible factors a tribunal could take into account in making a decision on whether a particular governmental measure is an indirect expropriation. Four of these criteria that have been set out in various tribunal attempts to define indirect expropriation are:

- Did the governmental measure result in an interference in the investor's enjoyment of its investment?
- Was the effect of the loss (*of value, management, use, or control*) *substantial?*
- Was the loss *permanent* or long-lasting?
- Was the measure taken for the *general welfare of the public?*

a   *Type of interference with the investor*

The significance of extending investment protection to include host measures that do not interfere with the ownership of a property characterizes the concept of requiring compensation for 'indirect' expropriations and measures 'having effects similar to' or 'tantamount to' expropriations. An interference with the owner's use, enjoyment, or management of the property might be considered unreasonable if it is of an intensity and duration such as to be considered 'unreasonable'.

Tribunals have differed over the types of interference they will require. While some arbitrators weigh losses to profitability heavily, most will focus on whether the investor maintains control over the investment and will deny relief if such control exists even if the investment's profitability is dramatically reduced. Many tribunals discuss a combination of factors, and, taking a totality-of-the-circumstances approach, determine if the complained-of measure or program interfered with the investor's enjoyment of its investment.

Taxation measures are generally considered non-expropriatory. In extreme cases, however, they can be 'takings'. Moreover, their application might be problematic under other standards of treatment required by the relevant IIA (see Chapter 5).

b   Severity of the interference

Not every interference with an investor's enjoyment of its property is worthy of the label 'expropriation'.[64] It is undisputed that state regulations may impact on an investor's property rights without incurring responsibility, but the limit of when the impact becomes compensable as an expropriation has been the subject of varying opinions. At one extreme, one US–Iran Claims Tribunal decision determined that the failure of the host's appointed manager for the investor's property to communicate with the investor was an expropriation because the 'deprivation [was] not merely ephemeral'.[65] An early case, the *Tippetts* opinion is admittedly very lenient for investor claims. At the other extreme was the *LG&E* tribunal that would have required a 'severe deprivation of LG&E's rights with regard to its investment, or almost complete deprivation of the value of LG&E's investment'.[66]

While terms such as 'significant' may also qualify the 'deprivation' referred to as the criterion for interference,[67] the more widely accepted standard of severity is to consider 'substantial deprivations' to be compensable.[68]

c   Duration

To be equivalent to a direct expropriation (which removes ownership of the investment from the investor), a measure would need to divest the inves-

---

64 *See Azurix Corp. v. The Argentine Republic*, ICSID Case No. ARB/01/12, Award, paras. 306–22 (July 14, 2006). Available at: http://italaw.com/documents/AzurixAwardJuly2006.pdf; *CMS Gas Transmission Company v. The Argentine Republic*, ICSID Case No. ARB/01/8, Award, paras. 260–64 (May 12, 2005). Available at: http://italaw.com/documents/CMS_FinalAward.pdf; LG&E Energy Corp., LG&E Capital Corp. and *LG&E International Inc. v. Argentine Republic*, ICSID Case No. ARB/02/1, Decision on Liability, paras. 185–200 (Oct. 3, 2006). Available at: http://italaw.com/documents/ARB021_LGE-Decision-on-Liability-en.pdf.

65 *Tippetts, Abbett, McCarthy, Stratton v. TAMS-AFFA Consulting Engineers of Iran*, Award No. 141-7-2, 6 Iran-US CTR 219, 225 (June 29, 1984).

66 *LG&E v. Argentina, supra* note 64, para. 200.

67 *See*, e.g. *Metalclad Corporation v. United Mexican States*, ICSID Case No. ARB(AF)/97/1, NAFTA Arbitration, Award, para. 103 (Aug. 30, 2000). Available at: http://italaw.com/documents/MetacladAwardEnglish_000.pdf. *Marvin Feldman v. Mexico*, ICSID Case No. ARB(AF)/99/1, NAFTA Arbitration, Award, paras. 100, 152 (Dec. 16, 2002). Available at: http://italaw.com/documents/feldman_mexico-award-english.pdf (e.g. was not relying explicitly on the substantial deprivation test).

68 *Pope and Talbot Inc. v. The Government of Canada*, UNCITRAL (NAFTA), Interim Award, paras. 96, 102 (June 26, 2000). Available at: http://italaw.com/documents/InterimAward.pdf; *Occidental Exploration and Production Company v. Republic of Ecuador*, LCIA Case No. UN 3467, Final Award, para. 89 (July 1, 2004). Available at: http://italaw.com/documents/Oxy-EcuadorFinalAward_001.pdf; *CMS Gas Transmission Company v. Argentine Republic, supra* note 64, paras. 262–3; Suez, *Sociedad General de Aguas de Barcelona SA, and InterAgua Servicios Integrales del Agua SA v. The Argentine Republic*, ICSID Case No. ARB/03/17, Decision on Liability, paras. 123, 129, 134, 145 (July 30, 2010). Available at: http://italaw.com/documents/SuezInterAguaDecisiononLiability.pdf.

tor of its control, use, or enjoyment of the property permanently. Tribunals, however, have been less strict, permitting regulations that deprive investors of the benefits even temporarily. Exactly how temporary a measure can be and still be considered an indirect expropriation is an open question. While one tribunal denied a claim based on a regulation in place for 18 months,[69] a different tribunal was satisfied with the claimant's complaint based on a one-year denial of its enjoyment of its investment.[70]

d Regulation for the general welfare of the public

If a state takes measures of general application that are designed to promote public welfare, most tribunals will not hold the state responsible for compensating the investor. The *Suez* tribunal expressed this deference succinctly:

> [. . .] in evaluating a claim of expropriation it is important to recognize a State's legitimate right to regulate and to exercise its police power in the interests of public welfare and not to confuse measures of that nature with expropriation. . . .[71]

Tax laws, for example, are widely held to be measures that will not generally be found to be expropriatory.[72]

---

69 S.D. *Myers, Inc. v. Government of Canada*, UNCITRAL (NAFTA), First Partial Award, paras. 284–8 (Nov. 13, 2000). Available at: http://italaw.com/documents/PartialAward_Myers.pdf (the arbitral tribunal considered the temporary closure of the border that postponed market access for about 18 months as not amounting to indirect expropriation).

70 *Wena Hotels Ltd. v. Arab Republic of Egypt*, ICSID Case No. ARB/98/4, Award, para. 99 (Dec. 8, 2000), 41 ILM 881 (2002); *Wena Hotels Ltd. v. Arab Republic of Egypt*, ICSID Case No. ARB/98/4, Decision on Application for Interpretation of Award, paras. 119–23 (Oct. 31, 2005). Available at: http://italaw.com/documents/ WenaInterpretationDecision.pdf.

71 *Suez v. Argentina, supra* note 68 at para. 139.

72 But even tribunals that place significant value on the state's regulatory role will examine whether the measure is in fact taken under the state's 'police powers' and that they are non-discriminatory in fact as well as in law. This attention to the implementation of the regulation was a particularly important issue in the *RosInvest v. Russia* dispute. According to the claimant, the government used an aggressive enforcement of its tax code to harass and ultimately dispossess the investor of its property. While the government argued that it was merely enforcing its laws, the tribunal disagreed on the facts. It stressed the need to attend to the realities of the context of the investor-host relationship: 'It is undisputed, and in the present case confirmed by Article 11(3) of the Denmark–Russia BIT, that the normal application of domestic tax law in the host state cannot be seen as an expropriatory act. On the other hand, it is generally accepted that the mere fact that measures by a host state are taken in the form of application and enforcement of its tax law, does not prevent a tribunal from examining whether this conduct of the host state must be considered, under the applicable BIT or other international treaties on investment protection, as an abuse of tax law to in fact enact an expropriation.' See *RosInvestCo UK Ltd. v. Russian Federation*, SCC Case No. Arb. V079/2005, Final Award, para. 628 (Sept. 12, 2010), http:// italaw.com/documents/RosInvestCoAward.pdf.

Host state claims that environmental and health-promoting regulations are for the public welfare, on the other hand, have not always been granted exemption from the requirement of compensation. One tribunal stated emphatically:

> While an expropriation or taking for environmental reasons may be classified as a taking for a public purpose, and thus may be legitimate, the fact that the Property was taken for this reason does not affect either the nature or the measure of the compensation to be paid for the taking. That is, the purpose of protecting the environment for which the Property was taken does not alter the legal character of the taking for which adequate compensation must be paid.
>
> The international source of the obligation to protect the environment makes no difference.[73]

 DISCUSSION NOTES

1 What should a tribunal decide if a host bans the distribution of profits to investors, but the measure is successfully challenged in local courts? Should the intent to permanently deprive an investor of property override the fact that the actual deprivation was temporary for purposes of determining if an indirect expropriation has taken place? The *Achmea v. Slovakia* tribunal said no:

> 288. [. . .] While some measures that interfere with the enjoyment by an investor of its rights of ownership of an investment may be so severe as to amount in law to [. . .] a deprivation, not all measures of interference are capable of doing so. In the present case the ban on profits, if maintained, would have violated [the BIT provision on expropriation]. But the ban was declared unconstitutional by the Constitutional Court of the Slovak Republic.
>
> 289. This might be argued to amount to a 'temporary expropriation'; but this controversial label is particularly unhelpful in this case. There is an important distinction between (i) a 'deprivation' for what is from the outset intended to be a limited (and relatively short) period, and (ii) a 'deprivation' that is intended at the time of its adoption to be permanent but which, in the event, is in fact reversed after a relatively short period of time. Deprivations of the former kind would not ordinarily amount to an expropriation, although they may amount to interferences with the property-owner's rights that violate other protections under a treaty [. . .].
>
> 290. In the present case, however, the 'deprivation' was temporary because

---

73 *Compañía del Desarrollo de Santa Elena SA v. The Republic of Costa Rica*, ICSID Case No. ARB/96/1, Final Award, para. 71 (Feb. 17, 2000), 15 ICSID Rev.–FILJ 169 (2000).

of a reversal of a policy that had been enshrined in law and was intended to operate indefinitely. The imposition of the ban on profits was reversed by the Constitutional Court [. . .] in the wake of internal Governmental memoranda that questioned the legality of the ban on profits.

291. Had this present BIT case been decided before the decision of the Constitutional Court and the declaration that the ban on profits was unconstitutional, it is likely that this Tribunal would have held that there was a 'permanent' deprivation that could amount to an expropriation in violation of [. . .] the Treaty. The question is, therefore, whether such a temporary deprivation should be treated differently now that the Constitutional Court has given its decision.

292. In the view of the Tribunal, the facts must be taken as they exist at the time of the hearing. The declaration of unconstitutionality by the Constitutional Court cannot be ignored. While there is no duty to exhaust local remedies under the Treaty, there is no reason to ignore such remedies as have in fact been obtained. Although the episode did constitute a temporary interference with the investment and cause injury to the investor, it is not to be regarded as having resulted in a permanent deprivation of the investor of its investment. It was a wrong corrected by the proper operation of checks and balances within the Slovak legal system. This analysis is consistent with the approach adopted by other tribunals to the question of the necessary characteristics of an expropriation and the significance of the permanence of interference with property rights.

See *Achmea BV v. Slovak Republic*, UNCITRAL, PCA Case No. 2008-13, Award (7 December 2012).

4.2.3 Leading approaches to determining an indirect expropriation

Any tribunal faced with a claim of indirect expropriation should look at each of the above-mentioned factors in the context of the particular case. Even then, however, each tribunal will have to decide for itself where to place the emphasis for its decision on where to draw the line between regulation and expropriation. This will rely less on a rigorous theoretical analysis than on the tribunal's philosophy on the limits of state interference.

There are several main approaches to distinguishing indirect expropriation from regulation that tribunals have employed.

a   *Sole effect doctrine*

According to the Sole Effect Doctrine only the effects on the investor's control over or profits from its investment matter and not the intentions of the state in regulating. This approach is used by many tribunals.[74] The *AES v. Hungary* tribunal, for instance, captured this approach in its brief examination of AES's claim of indirect expropriation based on Hungary's adjustment of its electricity pricing regulations:

> 14.3.1 It is evident that many state's acts or measures can affect investments and a modification to an existing law or regulation is probably one of the most common of such acts or measures. Nevertheless, a state's act that has a negative effect on an investment cannot automatically be considered an expropriation. For an expropriation to occur, it is necessary for the investor to be deprived, in whole or significant part, of the property in or effective control of its investment: or for its investment to be deprived, in whole or significant part, of its value.
>
> 14.3.2 But, in this case, the amendment of the 2001 Electricity Act and the issuance of the Price Decrees did not interfere with the ownership or use of Claimants' property. Claimants retained at all times the control of the AES Tisza II plant, thus there was no deprivation of Claimants' ownership or control of their investment.
>
> 14.3.3 Moreover, Claimants continued to receive substantial revenues from their investments during 2006 and 2007, which proves that the value of their investment was not substantially diminished and that they were not deprived of the whole or a significant part of the value of their investments.
>
> 14.3.4 In these circumstances, the Tribunal concludes that the effects of the reintroduction of the Price Decrees do not amount to an expropriation of Claimants' investment(s).[75]

Tribunals applying a sole effects test for indirect expropriation will deny the relevance of the host's intentions in regulating. Values such as environmental protection or social justice, then, are seen as laudable, but not excuses to avoid the requirement of compensating the investor deprived of its investment. According to Reinisch, the US–Iran Claims Tribunals offer the starkest examples of awards that recognize the existence of significant public interests in the

---

74 *See*, e.g. *Starrett Housing Corp. v. Islamic Republic of Iran*, Interlocutory Award, 4 Iran-U.S. CTR 122, at 154 (Dec. 19, 1983); *Compañia de Aguas del Aconquija SA and Vivendi Universal v. Argentina*, *supra* note 39, paras. 7.5.20–7.5.21; *Saipem SpA v. The People's Republic of Bangladesh*, ICSID Case No. ARB/05/7, Award, paras. 133–4 (June 30, 2009). Available at: http://italaw.com/documents/SaipemBangladeshAwardJune3009_000.pdf. *See also* Ursula Kriebaum, *Regulatory Takings: Balancing the Interests of the Investor and the State*, 8 The Journal of World Investment & Trade 717, 724–5 (2007).

75 *AES Summit Generation Limited and AES-Tisza Erömü Kft v. The Republic of Hungary*, ICSID Case No. ARB/07/22, ECT Arbitration, Award, paras. 14.3.1–14.3.4 (Sept. 23, 2010). Available at: http://italaw.com/documents/AESvHungaryAward.pdf.

host measures at issue, but refuse to see that as a justification for not paying the investor for its losses.[76] The *Phelps Dodge* tribunal, for instance, reasoned:

> The Tribunal fully understands the reasons why the Respondent felt compelled to protect its interests through this transfer of management, and the Tribunal understands the financial, economic and social concerns that inspired the law pursuant to which it acted, but those reasons and concerns cannot relieve the Respondent of the obligation to compensate Phelps Dodge for its losses.[77]

b   *Effects and state interest*

Some tribunals look at allegedly expropriatory regulatory measures by placing most of the weight on the measure's effects on the investor, but then balancing the host's interests in regulating as it did. While the *Tecmed* tribunal adopted a traditional effects doctrine to determine the existence of an indirect expropriation, it continued its analysis by undertaking an extensive consideration of Mexico's proffered reasons for its actions, in what it termed an examination of the measure's 'characteristics'. If the measure could display sufficient public policy reasons for its implementation, the tribunal could consider it a regulation rather than a measure tantamount to expropriation.

 CASE

Técnicas Medioambientales Tecmed SA v. The United Mexican States[78]

Técnicas Medioambientales Tecmed was incorporated in Spain. In 1996, Tecmed's Mexican subsidiary Cytrar bought property, buildings, facilities, and other assets for a controlled landfill for hazardous industrial waste. The site, located 8 kilometres from the town of Hermosillo, had been previously authorized as a landfill despite the existence of laws requiring a minimum of 25 kilometres between landfills and large towns.

The operation of the landfill required a licence from the government. The Federal Government of Mexico issued Tecmed with a renewable annual licence in place of the indefinite licence earlier held by the landfill.

---

76 August Reinisch, *Expropriation, in* The Oxford Handbook of International Investment Law 407, 444–5 (Peter Muchlinski, Frederico Ortino and Christoph Schreuer eds., 2008).

77 Id. at 445 (quoting *Phelps Dodge Corp. v. Iran*, 10 US–Iran CTR 121, 139 (1986-I).

78 *Técnicas Medioambientales Tecmed SA v. The United Mexican States*, ICSID Case No. ARB (AF)/00/2, Award (May 29, 2003). Available at: http://italaw.com/documents/Tecnicas_001.pdf (unofficial English translation); footnotes omitted.

In the summer of 1997, a new Mayor of Hermosillo was elected. The new municipal administration was hostile to the landfill project, and allegedly supported the local opponents of the landfill in their actions to protest its operations.

In the following year, the federal government refused to renew Tecmed's operating license, citing breaches in the operational aspects of the landfill.

Tecmed, convinced that the new local government's ideologies, rather than legal issues, were the cause of the withdrawal of the licence, brought a claim to arbitration based on the NAFTA's provision for compensation for indirect expropriations and measures 'tantamount to nationalization or expropriation' (Article 1110). The local population, it claimed, had been incited to protest against the landfill and to close it down.

> 95. The Claimant alleges that, when the INE [National Ecology Institute of Mexico] did not renew the permit to operate the Las Víboras Landfill (the 'Landfill') through its resolution dated November 25, 1998 (hereinafter the 'Resolution'), it expropriated the Claimant's investment and that such expropriation has caused damage to the Claimant. The Claimant relates the expropriation [. . .] to the prior actions of a number of organizations and entities at the federal, state and municipal levels, and also states that those actions are attributable to the Respondent and that they are adverse to the Claimant's rights under the Agreement and to the protection awarded to its investment thereunder. The Claimant further alleges that those actions objectively facilitated or prepared the subsequent expropriatory action carried out by INE.
> 96. The Claimant alleges that the Agreement protects foreign investors and their investments from direct and indirect expropriation; i.e. not only expropriation aimed at real or tangible personal property whereby the owner thereof is deprived of interests over such property, but also actions consisting of measures tantamount to an expropriation with respect to such property and also to intangible property. The Claimant states that, as the resolution deprived Cytrar of its rights to use and enjoy the real and personal property forming the Landfill in accordance with its sole intended purpose, the Resolution put an end to the operation of the Landfill as an on going [sic] business exclusively engaged in the landfill of hazardous waste, an activity that is only feasible under a permit, the renewal of which was denied. Therefore, Cytrar alleges that it was deprived of the benefits and economic use of its investment. The Claimant highlights that without such permit the personal and real property had no individual or aggregate market value and that the existence of the Landfill as an on going business, as well as its value as such, were completely destroyed due to such Resolution which, in addition, ordered the closing of the Landfill.

97. The Respondent alleges that INE had the discretionary powers required to grant and deny permits, and that such issues, except in special cases, are exclusively governed by domestic and not international law. On the other hand, the Respondent states that there was no progressive taking of the rights related to the permit to operate the Las Víboras landfill by means of a legislative change that could have destroyed the *status quo*, and that the Resolution was neither arbitrary nor discriminatory. It also states that the Resolution was a regulatory measure issued in compliance with the State's police power within the highly regulated and extremely sensitive framework of environmental protection and public health. In those circumstances, the Respondent alleges that the Resolution is a legitimate action of the State that does not amount to an expropriation under international law.

[. . .]

99. The Resolution refuses renewal of the Permit on the following grounds: (i) the Landfill was only authorized to receive waste from agrochemicals or pesticides or containers and materials contaminated with such elements; (ii) PROFEPA's delegates in Sonora had informed, in the official communication dated November 11, 1998, that the waste confined far exceeded the landfill limits established for one of the Landfill's active cells, cell No. 2; (iii) the Landfill temporarily stored hazardous waste destined for a place outside the Landfill, acting as a 'transfer center', an activity for which the Landfill did not have the required authorization; Cytrar was requested on October 16, 1997 to file reports in connection with this activity, but to date the relevant authorization had not been issued; and (iv) liquid and biological-infectious waste was received at the Landfill, an activity that was prohibited and that amounted to a breach of the obligation to notify in advance any change or modification in the scope of the Permit, and to unauthorized storage at the Landfill of liquid and biological-infectious waste. [. . .]

100. The Claimant challenges those statements because, among other things, the excess of the authorized landfill levels of cell no. 2 was the subject matter of an investigation and an audit by PROFEPA, as a result of which a fine was imposed on Cytrar by means of an official communication dated December 16, 1999. That fine was a minor penalty, substantially smaller than the maximum fine established by law. The Claimant also highlights that the official communication issued by PROFEPA to impose the fine stated that the infringement did not have a 'significant effect on public health or generate an ecological imbalance'. The Claimant also stated that in another similar official communication issued by PROFEPA,

> [. . .] PROFEPA expressly stated that . . . the infringements committed by the company involved are not sufficient to immediately cancel, suspend or revoke the permit for carrying out hazardous material and/or waste management activities, nor do they have an impact on public health or generate an ecological imbalance.

[. . .]

106. [. . .] Reportedly, in deciding to refuse to renew the Permit, INE took into account the fact that the location of the site did not comply with the regulations as well as the resulting community pressure.

[. . .]

113. The Agreement does not define the term 'expropriation', nor does it establish the measures, actions or behaviors that would be equivalent to an expropriation or that would have similar characteristics. Although formally an expropriation means a forcible taking by the Government of tangible or intangible property owned by private persons by means of administrative or legislative action to that effect, the term also covers a number of situations defined as *de facto* expropriation, where such actions or laws transfer assets to third parties different from the expropriating State or where such laws or actions deprive persons of their ownership over such assets, without allocating such assets to third parties or to the Government.

114. Generally, it is understood that the term '. . . equivalent to expropriation . . .' or 'tantamount to expropriation' included in the Agreement and in other international treaties related to the protection of foreign investors refers to the so-called 'indirect expropriation' or 'creeping expropriation', as well as to the above-mentioned *de facto* expropriation. Although these forms of expropriation do not have a clear or unequivocal definition, it is generally understood that they materialize through actions or conduct, which do not explicitly express the purpose of depriving one of rights or assets, but actually have that effect. This type of expropriation . . . may be carried out through a single action, through a series of actions in a short period of time or through simultaneous actions. [. . .]

115. To establish whether the Resolution is a measure equivalent to an expropriation under the terms of section 5(1) of the Agreement, it must be first determined if the Claimant, due to the Resolution, was radically deprived of the economical use and enjoyment of its investments, as if the rights related thereto—such as the income or benefits related to the Landfill or to its exploitation—had ceased to exist. In other words, if due to the actions of the Respondent, the assets involved have lost their value or economic use for their holder and the extent of the loss. This determination is important because it is one of the main elements to distinguish, from the point of view of an international tribunal, between a regulatory measure, which is an ordinary expression of the exercise of the state's police power that entails a decrease in assets or rights, and a *de facto* expropriation that deprives those assets and rights of any real substance. Upon determining the degree to which the investor is deprived of its goods or rights, whether such deprivation should be compensated and whether it amounts or not to a *de facto* expropriation is also determined. Thus, the effects of the actions or behavior under analysis are not irrelevant to determine whether the action or behavior is an expropriation. Section 5(1) of the Agreement confirms the above, as it covers expropriations, nationalizations or . . . any other measure with similar characteristics or *effects* . . .

The following has been stated in that respect:

> In determining whether a taking constitutes an 'indirect expropriation', it is particularly important to examine the effect that such taking may have had on the investor's rights. Where the effect is similar to what might have occurred under an outright expropriation, the investor could in all likelihood be covered under most BIT provisions.

116. In addition to the provisions of the Agreement, the Arbitral Tribunal has to resolve any dispute submitted to it by applying international law provisions (. . .), for which purpose the Arbitral Tribunal understands that disputes are to be resolved by resorting to the sources described in Article 38 of the Statute of the International Court of Justice considered, also in the case of customary international law, not as frozen in time, but in their evolution. Therefore, it is understood that the measures adopted by a State, whether regulatory or not, are an indirect *de facto* expropriation if they are irreversible and permanent and if the assets or rights subject to such measure have been affected in such a way that '. . . any form of exploitation thereof . . .' has disappeared; i.e. the economic value of the use, enjoyment or disposition of the assets or rights affected by the administrative action or decision have been neutralized or destroyed. Under international law, the owner is also deprived of property where the use or enjoyment of benefits related thereto is exacted or interfered with to a similar extent, even where legal ownership over the assets in question is not affected, and so long as the deprivation is not temporary. The government's intention is less important than the effects of the measures on the owner of the assets or on the benefits arising from such assets affected by the measures; and the form of the deprivation measure is less important than its actual effects. To determine whether such an expropriation has taken place, the Arbitral Tribunal should not . . . restrict itself to evaluating whether a formal dispossession or expropriation took place, but should look beyond mere appearances and establish the real situation behind the situation that was denounced.

117. The Resolution meets the characteristics mentioned above: undoubtedly it has provided for the non-renewal of the Permit and the closing of the Landfill permanently and irrevocably, not only due to the imperative, affirmative and irrevocable terms under which the INE's decision included in the Resolution is formulated, which constitutes an action—and not a mere omission—attributable to the Respondent, with negative effects on the Claimant's investment and its rights to obtain the benefits arising therefrom, but also because after the non-renewal of the Permit, the Mexican regulations issued by INE become fully applicable. Such regulations prevent the use of the site where the Landfill is located to confine hazardous waste due to the proximity to the urban center of Hermosillo. Since it has been proved in this case that one of the essential causes for which the renewal of the Permit was denied was its proximity and the community pressure related

thereto, there is no doubt that in the future the Landfill may not be used for the activity for which it has been used in the past and that Cytrar's economic and commercial operations in the Landfill after such denial have been fully and irrevocably destroyed, just as the benefits and profits expected or projected by the Claimant as a result of the operation of the Landfill. Moreover, the Landfill could not be used for a different purpose since hazardous waste has accumulated and been confined there for ten years. Undoubtedly, this reason would rule out any possible sale of the premises in the real estate market. Finally, the destruction of the economic value of the site should be assessed from the investor's point of view at the time it made such an investment. In consideration of the activities carried out, of its corporate purpose and of the terms and conditions under which assets related to the Landfill were acquired from Promotora, the Claimant, through Tecmed and Cytrar, invested in such assets only to engage in hazardous waste landfill activities and to profit from such activities. When the Resolution put an end to such operations and activities at the Las Víboras site, the economic or commercial value directly or indirectly associated with those operations and activities and with the assets earmarked for such operations and activities was irremediably destroyed. [. . .]

118. However, the Arbitral Tribunal deems it appropriate to examine, in light of Article 5(1) of the Agreement, whether the Resolution, due to its characteristics and considering not only its effects, is an expropriatory decision.

119. The principle that the State's exercise of its sovereign powers within the framework of its police power may cause economic damage to those subject to its powers as administrator without entitling them to any compensation whatsoever is undisputable. Another undisputed issue is that within the framework or from the viewpoint of the domestic laws of the State, it is only in accordance with domestic laws and before the courts of the State that the determination of whether the exercise of such power is legitimate may take place. And such determination includes that of the limits which, if infringed, would give rise to the obligation to compensate an owner for the violation of its property rights.

120. However, the perspective of this Arbitral Tribunal is different. Its function is to examine whether the Resolution violates the Agreement in light of its provisions and of international law. The Arbitral Tribunal will not review the grounds or motives of the Resolution in order to determine whether it could be or was legally issued. However, it must consider such matters to determine if the Agreement was violated. That the actions of the Respondent are legitimate or lawful or in compliance with the law from the standpoint of the Respondent's domestic laws does not mean that they conform to the Agreement or to international law:

> An Act of State must be characterized as internationally wrongful if it constitutes a breach of an international obligation, even if the act does not contravene the State's internal law—even if under that law, the State was actually bound to act that way.

121. After reading Article 5(1) of the Agreement and interpreting its terms according to the ordinary meaning to be given to them (Article 31(1) of the Vienna Convention), we find no principle stating that regulatory administrative actions are *per se* excluded from the scope of the Agreement, even if they are beneficial to society as a whole—such as environmental protection—, particularly if the negative economic impact of such actions on the financial position of the investor is sufficient to neutralize in full the value, or economic or commercial use of its investment without receiving any compensation whatsoever. It has been stated that:

> Expropriatory environmental measures—no matter how laudable and beneficial to society as a whole—are, in this respect, similar to any other expropriatory measures that a state may take in order to implement its policies: where property is expropriated, even for environmental purposes, whether domestic or international, the state's obligation to pay compensation remains.

122. After establishing that regulatory actions and measures will not be initially excluded from the definition of expropriatory acts, in addition to the negative financial impact of such actions or measures, the Arbitral Tribunal will consider, in order to determine if they are to be characterized as expropriatory, whether such actions or measures are proportional to the public interest presumably protected thereby and to the protection legally granted to investments, taking into account that the significance of such impact has a key role upon deciding the proportionality. Although the analysis starts at the due deference owing to the State when defining the issues that affect its public policy or the interests of society as a whole, as well as the actions that will be implemented to protect such values, such situation does not prevent the Arbitral Tribunal, without thereby questioning such due deference, from examining the actions of the State in light of Article 5(1) of the Agreement to determine whether such measures are reasonable with respect to their goals, the deprivation of economic rights and the legitimate expectations of who suffered such deprivation. There must be a reasonable relationship of proportionality between the charge or weight imposed to the foreign investor and the aim sought to be realized by any expropriatory measure. To value such charge or weight, it is very important to measure the size of the ownership deprivation caused by the actions of the state and whether such deprivation was compensated or not. On the basis of a number of legal and practical factors, it should be also considered that the foreign investor has a reduced or nil participation in the taking of the decisions that affect it, partly because the investors are not entitled to exercise political rights reserved to the nationals of the State, such as voting for the authorities that will issue the decisions that affect such investors.

[. . .]

124. This Arbitral Tribunal considers that the violations to the Permit mentioned in the Resolution, to the extent they have been verified by PROFEPA or INE under

the applicable Mexican law, are issues that the Tribunal does not need to review. However, the Arbitral Tribunal points out that such Resolution does not suggest that the violations compromise public health, impair ecological balance or protection of the environment, or that they may be the reason for a genuine social crisis. [...]

127. [...] it is irrefutable that there were factors other than compliance or noncompliance by Cytrar with the Permit's conditions or the Mexican environmental protection laws and that such factors had a decisive effect in the decision to deny the Permit's renewal. These factors included 'political circumstances'. [...]

[...]

129. These socio-political circumstances are the reason why INE has considered the renewal of the Permit as an 'exceptional case'. As a consequence, INE, instead of deciding by itself—as it was empowered by law—as to the Permit's renewal on the basis of considerations exclusively related to INE's specific function linked to the protection of the environment, ecological balance and public health, it consulted with the mayor of the Municipality of Hermosillo and the Governor of the State of Sonora as to Cytrar's requests related to the expansion of cell Nº 2 and the construction of cell Nº 3 in the Landfill. The only conclusion possible is that such consultation or inquiries were driven by INE's socio-political concerns, [...].

[...]

133. There is no doubt as to the existence of community or political pressure [...] against the Landfill. However, a substantial portion of the community opposition is based on objective situations that are beyond Cytrar or Tecmed's control or even beyond the Claimant's control. On the other hand, the Arbitral Tribunal should consider whether community pressure and its consequences, which presumably gave rise to the government action qualified as expropriatory by the Claimant, were so great as to lead to a serious emergency situation, social crisis or public unrest, in addition to the economic impact of such a government action, which in this case deprived the foreign investor of its investment with no compensation whatsoever. These factors must be weighed when trying to assess the proportionality of the action adopted with respect to the purpose pursued by such measure.

[...]

144. Finally, the Respondent has not presented any evidence that community opposition to the Landfill—however intense, aggressive and sustained—was in any way massive or went any further than the positions assumed by some individuals or the members of some groups that were opposed to the Landfill. Even after having gained substantial momentum, community opposition, although it had been sustained by its advocates through an insistent, active and continuous public campaign in the mass media, could gather on two occasions a crowd of only two hundred people the first time and of four hundred people, the second time out of a community with a population of almost one million inhabitants, '... which makes it the city with the highest population in the state of Sonora'. Additionally,

the 'blockage' of the Landfill was carried out by small groups of no more than forty people. The absence of any evidence that the operation of the Landfill was a real or potential threat to the environment or to the public health, coupled with the absence of massive opposition, limits 'community pressure' to a series of events, which, although they amount to significant pressure on the Mexican authorities, do not constitute a real crisis or disaster of great proportions, triggered by acts or omissions committed by the foreign investor or its affiliates.

[. . .]

151. Based on the above; [. . .] the Arbitral Tribunal finds and resolves that the Resolution and its effects amount to an expropriation in violation of Article 5 of the Agreement and international law.

c   Legitimate expectations of investor

Yet another approach taken by tribunals focusses on the investor's expectations of profit and control when it established its investment. The qualification of investor expectations as 'legitimate' means that the approach relies upon a finding of the host's explicit or implicit assurances to the investor.

Faced with a claim of indirect expropriation, the *Methanex v. United States* tribunal applied the legitimate expectations approach, stressing the objective nature of protectable expectations:

7.[. . .] [A]s a matter of general international law, a non-discriminatory regulation for a public purpose, which is enacted in accordance with due process and, which affects, inter alios, a foreign investor or investment is not deemed expropriatory and compensable unless specific commitments had been given by the regulating government to the then putative foreign investor contemplating investment that the government would refrain from such regulation.

8. As the arbitration tribunal decided in *Revere Copper and Brass, Inc. v. OPIC*:

'*We regard these principles as particularly applicable where the question is, as here, whether actions taken by a government contrary to and damaging to the economic interests of aliens are in conflict with undertakings and assurances given in good faith to such aliens as an inducement to their making the investments affected by the action.*'

And in *Waste Management v. Mexico*, the tribunal stated, with respect to the 'minimum standard of fair and equitable treatment', that 'in applying this standard it is relevant that the treatment is in breach of *representations made by the host State which were reasonably relied upon by the claimant*'.

9. No such commitments were given to Methanex. [. . .][79]

---

79 *Methanex Corporation v. United States of America*, UNCITRAL (NAFTA), Final Award, Part IV, Chapter D, paras. 7–9 (Aug. 3, 2005). Available at: http://italaw.com/documents/MethanexFinalAward.pdf.

CASE

Grand River Enterprises Six Nations, Ltd., et al., v. the United States of America[80]

The claimant Grand River Enterprises Six Nations was a Canadian corporation and the three individuals that owned it, all members of the Six Nations of the Iroquois Confederacy. In the business of cigarette sales and distribution in Canada, the United States, and First Nation territories, the one claimant over whom the tribunal had jurisdiction alleged that the rigorous enforcement of United States laws related to tobacco sales was an expropriation of his investment. To examine this claim, the tribunal had to determine if the claimant had a legitimate expectation that his investment would not be subject to US legal enforcement actions.

1. Reasonable expectations: First nations status

128. Arthur Montour stressed his status as a member of one of the First Nations in North America and the nature of his business activities, which he described as involving trade among sovereign indigenous peoples. On this basis, he maintained that he had a legitimate expectation not to be subjected to MSA-related regulatory actions by the states of the United States in respect of his tobacco-related activities. Citing the opinions of the Claimants' experts, Professors Clinton and Fletcher, Mr. Montour urged that he was 'entitled to expect that none of [his] business activities would even be subjected to the Escrow Statutes, the Allocable Share Amendments, the Contraband laws or any Equity Assessment legislation.'

129. Mr. Montour emphasized that he is a member of the Haudenosaunee, the Iroquois Confederation, which was never defeated militarily and was assured the right to pursue parallel and independent political and economic life by the Seventeenth-Century Two Row Wampum Treaty and subsequent treaties . . . . He placed particular emphasis on his understanding of Article 3 of the 1794 Jay Treaty and the Treaty of Ghent, which ended the War of 1812 between the United States and the United Kingdom and reaffirmed the relevant Jay Treaty provisions. Article 3 of the Jay Treaty provides:

> It is agreed that it shall at all Times be free to His Majesty's Subjects, and to the Citizens of the United States, and also to the Indians dwelling on either side of the said Boundary Line freely to pass and repass by Land, or Inland Navigation, into the respective Territories and Countries of the Two Parties on the Continent of America (the Country within the Limits of the Hudson's

---

80 *Grand River Enterprises Six Nations, Ltd., et al., v. the United States of America, supra* note 1; footnotes omitted.

Bay Company only excepted) and to navigate all the Lakes, Rivers, and waters thereof, and freely to carry on trade and commerce with each other. . . .

No Duty of Entry shall ever be levied by either Party on Peltries brought by Land, or Inland Navigation into the said Territories respectively, nor shall the Indians passing or repassing with their own proper Goods and Effects of whatever nature, pay for the same any Impost or Duty whatever. But Goods in Bales, or other large Packages unusual among Indians shall not be considered as Goods belonging bona fide to Indians.

130. Mr. Montour also urged that under U.S. domestic law, individual states of the United States do not have jurisdiction to regulate commerce among Native Americans, especially when it involves transactions outside of the states' geographic boundaries or within 'Indian country,' including reservation lands. In this regard, his tobacco distribution businesses . . . purchased large quantities of cigarettes F.O.B. from Grand River at its plant in Canada and imported them into the United States. Many were sold at wholesale to Native American purchasers on the reservation lands within the Seneca Nations Territory in northern New York, who then offered them for sale, either at retail outlets on the Seneca reservation or to customers across the United States, often via the Internet. Such wholesale sales to customers on the Seneca reservation accounted for much of NWS' business, constituting about 68% of NWS' total sales in 2007.

131. The state of New York has not applied its MSA-related legislation to Mr. Montour's companies on the Seneca reservation. . . . However, NWS also sold substantial quantities of Grand River's cigarettes to Native American wholesalers and retailers operating on reservation lands in other states of the United States . . . Authorities in several of these other states have sought to apply their complementary legislation with respect to the Claimants' on-reservation and other Indian country sales.

132. As viewed by the Claimants' experts, Professors Clinton and Fletcher, under the provision of the Commerce Clause of the U.S. Constitution related to 'Indians' and the related body of domestic law generally referred to as 'federal Indian law,' the power to regulate commerce among Native Americans is reserved solely to the U.S. federal government, such that, with limited exceptions, states cannot regulate their activities, especially within their recognized lands, absent a delegation from the U.S. Congress. . . . The Claimants' experts provide elaborate and highly technical arguments to this effect, citing an array of judicial precedents and stressing the factual nexus between the Claimants' business activities, their status as First Nations investors, and the location of the transactions.

133. The Respondent disputed the Claimants' characterizations of the Jay Treaty and applicable U.S. domestic law, and denied that Arthur Montour could reasonably expect that his activities would be wholly immune from state regulation.

134. With respect to the Jay Treaty, the United States asserted that the Claimants

had no reasonable expectation that the Treaty would shield their business from governmental regulation. In the Respondent's view, the treaty assures rights for individual Native Americans to cross the U.S.–Canadian border, as well as limited rights for their peltries and personal goods. It does not insulate an international and interstate tobacco business involving billions of cigarettes from regulation.
[. . .]

135. As to U.S. domestic law, the Respondent relied on expert reports . . . and contended that the Claimants . . . had no reasonable expectation of immunity from state regulation arising from U.S. federal Indian law. It urged . . . that U.S. states can regulate activities involving Native Americans outside of Indian country as well as activities occurring partially inside and partially outside.
[. . .]

137. The Tribunal believes that both Parties advanced positions regarding the state of U.S. federal Indian law that were unjustifiably categorical. . . . In the Tribunal's understanding, U.S. federal Indian law is a complex and not altogether consistent mixture of constitutional provisions, federal statutes, and judicial decisions by the U.S. Supreme Court and other courts. Determining the contents of that law, and its likely impact on particular types of state regulation, often calls for necessarily uncertain predictions of how future courts will apply past decisions involving different settings and different types of state regulation.

138. What is clear from the Parties' submissions and their experts' reports is that U.S. domestic law is currently far from conclusive about the question raised here of the extent of permissible state regulation.
[. . .]

139. Both parties apparently would have the Tribunal resolve this highly contested question of U.S. domestic law, which the Tribunal declines to do. In determining, within the framework of this NAFTA proceeding, whether Arthur Montour could have reasonably harbored an expectation that his tobacco distribution activities would not face state regulation, it is not for this Tribunal to decide whether or not he is correct on the underlying domestic legal proposition of immunity from the state regulation. Even if the Tribunal ultimately were to agree with him on the question of U.S. domestic law, that would not settle the matter of what regulatory response he could reasonably expect when he and his company embarked on their business ventures involving sales in the United States.

140. The Tribunal understands the concept of reasonable or legitimate expectations in the NAFTA context to correspond with those expectations upon which an investor is entitled to rely as a result of representations or conduct by a state party. As the tribunal in *Thunderbird Gaming* explained, the 'concept of "legitimate expectations" relates . . . to a situation where a Contracting Party's conduct creates reasonable and justifiable expectations on the part of an investor (or investment) to act in reliance on said conduct, such that a failure by the NAFTA Party to honour those expectations could cause the investor (or investment) to suffer damages.' The

question of reasonable expectations, therefore, is not equivalent to whether or not an investor is ultimately right on a contested legal proposition that would favor the investor.

141. The 'conduct' of the United States pointed to by the Claimants as giving rise to reasonable expectations of immunity from MSA measures is U.S. federal Indian law and the Jay Treaty. Ordinarily, reasonable or legitimate expectations of the kind protected by NAFTA are those that arise through targeted representations or assurances made explicitly or implicitly by a state party. Even accepting that cited U.S. federal Indian law and the Jay Treaty might serve as sources of reasonable or legitimate expectations for the purposes of a NAFTA claim, the Tribunal finds that they do not in this case.

142. As to U.S. domestic law, given its unsettled nature in relevant respects, it is implausible to find that Mr. Montour could have reasonably expected, and reason-ably relied on such an expectation as a prudent investor, that states would refrain from applying the MSA measures to him as they have done. . . . U.S. states had at least a colorable argument under domestic law for valid application of the MSA measures to his activities. . . . The point is that the relative strength of this argu-ment and the range of relevant domestic judicial precedents were such that Mr. Montour was not in a position to reasonably harbor an expectation, upon which he would be entitled to rely under NAFTA, that he would be free from application of the MSA measures. The Tribunal believes, however, that Mr. Montour did have a reasonable expectation that he could pursue his challenge to the application of the MSA measures to his activities on the basis of U.S. domestic law in U.S. domestic courts, and the Tribunal understands that he in fact has done so.

143. Similarly, the Tribunal declines to resolve the opposing interpretations of the Jay treaty. . . . What is readily apparent . . . are the ambiguities in the meaning of the text in respect of the far-reaching claimed immunity, especially in light of the understandings and practice of the contemporary treaty parties, Canada and the United States, which are contrary to the Claimants' interpretation and which must be taken into account. Professor Clinton offers a novel, detailed argument and historical narrative in support of the Claimants' interpretation. However persuasive his argument may be, it does not establish that interpretation as having the degree of certainty that might reasonably ground in the Claimant—for the purposes of his NAFTA claim—a reasonable expectation that he could avoid state application of the MSA measures.

144. The Tribunal also notes that trade in tobacco products has historically been the subject of close and extensive regulation by U.S. states, a circumstance that should have been known to the Claimant from his extensive past experience in the tobacco business. An investor entering an area traditionally subject to extensive regulation must do so with awareness of the regulatory situation.

145. Given the circumstances—including the unresolved questions involving the Jay Treaty and U.S. domestic law, and the practice of heavy state regulation of sales

of tobacco products—the Tribunal holds that Arthur Montour could not reasonably have developed and relied on an expectation, the non-fulfillment of which would infringe NAFTA, that he could carry on a large-scale tobacco distribution business, involving the transportation of large quantities of cigarettes across state lines and into many states of the United States, without encountering state regulation.[. . .]

? **DISCUSSION NOTES**

1 Although there is generally no 'legitimacy' in an expectation that laws will not change, intransparent procedures or unreasonable application of laws might lead a tribunal to judge a measure to be expropriatory. The arbitral tribunal in *RosInvest v. Russia*, for instance, regarded the cumulative effect of various tax measures as amounting to expropriation:

> 621. In **conclusion** therefore, the Tribunal considers that the totality of Respondent's measures were structured in such a way to remove Yukos' assets from the control of the company and the individuals associated with Yukos. They must be seen as elements in the cumulative treatment of Yukos for what seems to have been the intended purpose. The Tribunal, in reviewing the various alleged breaches of the IPPA,[81] even if the justification of a certain individual measure might be arguable as an admissible application of the relevant law, considers that this cumulative effect of those various measures taken by Respondent in respect of Yukos is relevant to its decision under the IPPA. An illustration is, as Claimant has pointed out, that despite having used nearly identical tax structures, no other Russian oil company was subjected to the same relentless and inflexible attacks as Yukos. In the view of the Tribunal, they can only be understood as steps under a common denominator in a pattern to destroy Yukos and gain control over its assets.
>
> [. . .]
>
> 624. [. . .] The Tribunal shares Respondent's view that the term '*measures having effect equivalent to nationalisation or expropriation*' covers indirect expropriation, but without dispensing with the requirement of a substantial or total deprivation of (i) the economic value of an investment (as Claimant articulated the standard at the hearing), (ii) fundamental ownership rights, in particular, control of an ongoing business, or (iii) deprivation of legitimate investment-backed expectations. However, in that regard Claimant's argument is indeed relevant that, in determining whether a measure (or set of measures) is 'equiva-

---

81 Note from author: IPPA stands for Agreement between the Government of the United Kingdom and the Government of the USSR for the Promotion and Reciprocal Protection of Investments, signed in London on April 6, 1989.

lent to' expropriation, the Tribunal should evaluate whether the 'net effect' of the measure (or set of measures) is the same as an outright expropriation, *i.e.*, a substantial or total deprivation of the economic value of an asset [. . .].

[. . .]

626. Therefore, it needs no further explanation that a taking took place.

627. The only question is whether this taking was justified and thus there is no breach of Article 5.

628. It is undisputed, and in the present case confirmed by Article 11(3) of the Denmark-Russia BIT, that the normal application of domestic tax law in the host state cannot be seen as an expropriatory act. On the other hand, it is generally accepted that the mere fact that measures by a host state are taken in the form of application and enforcement of its tax law, does not prevent a tribunal from examining whether this conduct of the host state must be considered, under the applicable BIT or other international treaties on investment protection, as an abuse of tax law to in fact enact an expropriation.

[. . .]

630. As seen above in the consideration of Respondent's measures, these measures in their totality, including but going beyond application of tax law, can only be understood to have had the aim to deprive Yukos from its assets. Such a taking would only be admissible under Article 5 if the conditions of that provision are fulfilled.

631. The first of these conditions according to Article 5(1) is that the taking must be *for a purpose which is in the public interest*. Even if it could be argued that, in the judgment of the Russian Government, it was indeed in the public interest to take Yukos' assets, the Tribunal notes that this has never been claimed or shown by Respondent in these proceedings as it does not concede that there was indeed an expropriation.

632. And even if this were so, according to Article 5 IPPA the taking would have to be '*not discriminatory and against the payment, without delay, of adequate and effective compensation*'. From the above considerations in this award it can be seen that these conditions were not fulfilled. Even if one interprets the term 'discriminatory' only as dealing with discrimination between nationals and foreigners and not as dealing with discrimination between various domestic companies as here between Yukos and its competitors in Russia, it is clear that Respondent did not offer or pay any compensation to Claimant for the taking.

633. Therefore, the Tribunal concludes that Respondent's measures, seen in their cumulative effect towards Yukos, were an unlawful expropriation under Article 5 IPPA.[82]

---

82 *RosInvestCo v. Russia, supra* note 72, paras. 621, 624, 626–8, 630–33.

A judicial decision may also be considered expropriatory if it interferes significantly with an investor's property rights. The tribunal in *Saipem v. Bangladesh*, relying on jurisprudence from the European Court of Human Rights, set forth the key position that 'there is no reason why a judicial act could not result in an expropriation'. *Saipem SpA v. The People's Republic of Bangladesh*, ICSID Case No. ARB/05/07, Decision on Jurisdiction and Recommendation on Provisional Measures, para. 132 (21 Mar., 2007), http://italaw.com/sites/default/files/case-documents/ita0733.pdf (referring in para. 130 to *Stran Greek Refineries and Stratis Andreadis v. Greece*—13427/87 [1994] ECHR 48 (9 Dec., 1994), paras. 59–62). This is because the host's courts' actions are attributable to the host and because property rights can be extinguished by court order. In *Sistem Muhendisklik v. Kyrgyz Republic*, for example, the tribunal's review of the Kyrgyz Supreme Court's decision to invalidate a share purchase agreement led to a decision that that action was an indirect expropriation because '[t]he Court decision deprived the Claimant of its property rights in the hotel just as surely as if the State had expropriated it by decree' (para. 118). Moreover, the measure can be considered an expropriation even where a court decision does not transfer the investor's right to the host: 'If the Claimant has been deprived of its property rights by an act of the State, it is irrelevant whether the State itself took possession of those rights or otherwise benefited from the taking' (id., citing *CME Czech Republic B.V. (The Netherlands) v. The Czech Republic* (UNCITRAL Arb. Proc.), Partial Award, paras. 591–609 (13 Sept., 2001)).

Other tribunals have clarified, however, that to be an expropriation, the judicial action must amount to a denial of justice or an illegal act as well as an interference in the investor's property rights.

Thus, the judiciary cannot be said to have expropriated an investor only by virtue of finding the investor in breach of a contract. Rather, the court must have engaged in wrongful conduct before its decision will be held to the level of an expropriation. See e.g., *Saipem v. Bangladesh* at para. 181 ('expropriation by the courts presupposes that the courts' intervention was illegal'); *Swisslion DOO Skopje v. The Former Yugoslav Republic of Macedonia*, ICSID Case No. ARB/09/16, Award, para. 314 (6 July 2012) ('The internationally lawful termination of a contract between a State entity and an investor cannot be equated to an expropriation of contractual rights simply because the investor's rights have been terminated; otherwise, a State could not exercise the ordinary right of a contractual party to allege that its counterparty breached the contract without the State's being found to be in breach of its international obligations. Since there was no illegality on the part of the courts, the first element of the Claimant's expropriation claim is not established'); *Franck Charles Arif v. Republic of Moldova*, ICSID Case No. ARB/11/23, Award, para. 417 (8 April 2013) ('[. . .] this Tribunal is not persuaded that there can be deprivation of invalid rights. The invalidity of these agreements (and hence of the rights [. . .] recognised under these agreements, [. . .] resulting from the application of Moldovan law by the Moldovan courts as a result of lawsuits filed by private competitors cannot be interpreted as an expropriation [. . .]. No wrongful taking results from the legitimate application of Moldova's legal system [. . .]').

Under this view if an investor challenges a local court decision which has denied that the investor had property rights at all, the claim of expropriation will only succeed if the local decision was wrongful as a matter of international law. *Linman Caspian Oil BV and NCL Dutch Investment BV v. Republic of Kazakhstan*, ICSID Case No. ARB/07/14, Award, paras. 430–32 (22 June 2010) ('The mere fact that decisions of the Kazakh courts declared that Claimants did not prevail and were not holders of rights they claimed to have, therefore, is not sufficient to find an expropriatory measure [. . . T]he [. . .] Kazakh court decisions were not arbitrary, grossly unfair, unjust, idiosyncratic, discriminatory or lacking due process, even if they might have been incorrect as a matter of Kazakh law, and that correspondingly they have to be accepted from the perspective of international law [. . .] For these reasons, it cannot be concluded that the transfer was wrongfully annulled [. . .]'). But see *Eli Lilly and Company v. Government of Canada*, UNCITRAL/NAFTA Case No. UNCT/14/2, Claimant's Memorial para. 179 (29 September 2014) ('In other words, no special rules attach to claims of expropriation based on judicial measures. It is not necessary, for example, that the claimant establish a 'denial of justice' or otherwise demonstrate any deficiency in the process afforded by the national courts. What *is* necessary is to show that the judicial measure (i) resulted in a 'substantial deprivation' and; (ii) qualifies as a compensable taking as opposed to a 'non-compensable exercise of state authority').

4.2.4 Incremental steps/creeping expropriation

The devaluation of an investor's interests does not always happen from one moment to the next or by means of a single regulation or policy. Rather, a combination of governmental actions can lead to a dwindling of control or use of property that at some point becomes an expropriation. The term describing such a process or series of steps that may have a *cumulative effect* of expropriation is 'creeping', or incremental, expropriation. Tribunals can find creeping expropriation even if each of the host's individual measures was not itself either expropriatory or illegal.[83]

The legal difficulty arising from creeping expropriations is in determining the 'moment of expropriation'. This is particularly relevant for determining the compensation owed the investor.

4.2.5 Compensation of indirect expropriation

In most respects, a finding that an indirect expropriation exists results in the application of all of the conditions for determining its legality. (IIA provisions on expropriation generally include both direct and indirect expropriations within the same article.) Where the host's regulatory action is the basis for the finding of expropriation, however, tribunals have differed as to whether the failure to compensate the investor will result in the expropriation being deemed 'illegal'.

The issue is an important one because of the possible difference in measurement of compensation due for a legal versus an illegal expropriation. For the indirectly expropriated investor, who by definition is in a position equivalent to a directly expropriated investor, the preferred answer is that compensation must be forthcoming in either case. For the host, however, the difference in directly taking property and indirectly infringing on its value is significant—particularly when it comes to compensation. Assuming the government was acting in good faith, it may have had no reason to believe that its regulation would be considered an expropriation. Thus, it may have quite legitimately not considered it necessary to compensate the investor.

? DISCUSSION NOTES

1 Should an investor's behaviour during the expropriation affect the level of compensation awarded? In the *Yukos v. Russia* arbitration, there were a number of actions over several years that the claimant alleged to be expropriatory. Among these were the government's extreme measures taken allegedly in response to the company's abuse of the tax regime. When faced with determining the compensation due for those acts which the tribunal determined to be clearly expropriatory, it faced an argument by the Russian government to reduce the fair market value to reflect the investor's contributory fault.

---

83 *Siemens AG v. Argentina, supra* note 55, para. 263.

4.2.6 Critiques of investor-oriented indirect expropriation jurisprudence

The legal difficulties of determining whether a governmental measure is an indirect expropriation or regulation are certainly not minimal. As a result, there is no cohesive body of jurisprudence that has emerged from the tribunals' differing perspectives. This leaves the investor, the host, and the arbitrator with elements to consider, but no clear expectations on what the outcome of a particular case will be.

The reason for these difficulties, one can well imagine, stems from the inherent policy dilemma that underlies the line-drawing: the need to ensure the state sufficient regulatory flexibility to protect its citizens while not allowing it to unreasonably burden foreign investors with the costs of such regulation. Balancing these competing interests can only be done within a specific context. Hence, the case-by-case approach to indirect expropriation law is both understandable and justifiable.

Yet, there are numerous commentators who fear that the uncertainty of the law itself poses a threat to the protection of public interests. The 'chilling effect' argument goes like this: given that governments can be held financially accountable to foreign investors if they substantially interfere with their investments by means of regulations (even if such regulations pursue public purpose), and given that governments cannot know in advance whether a particular regulation will be considered a substantial interference with a foreign investment, governments will tend not to regulate as extensively as they may feel would be appropriate to safeguard the public's interest. As a result, foreign investors benefit from the uncertainty while the public at large suffers from it.[84]

Discussing this issue, Marc Poirier points to the 'split nomos' problem inherent in provisions protecting investors from indirect expropriations. His ideas, written in the context of the NAFTA investment protections, apply more generally to investment protection. This provides an interesting perspective

---

84 *See* Alberto R. Salazar V., *NAFTA Chapter 11, Regulatory Expropriation, and Domestic Counter-Advertising Law*, 27(1) Ariz. J. Int'l & Comp. L. 31 (2010). Salazar suggests institutional and governance solutions for the problem of regulatory chill:

'To mitigate the above problems associated with the regulatory chill, it is desirable not only to correct the loop-holes and inconsistencies of NAFTA Chapter 11 jurisprudence, but also to encourage consumer-citizenship' activism in order to both counter-balance a possible corporate influence in the regulatory process and help legitimize, legally and politically, bona fide, non-discriminatory regulatory measures for pressing public purposes.'

on the interplay between international and local interests that are, in Poirier's view, unavoidably at odds:

LITERATURE

Marc E. Poirier, The NAFTA Chapter 11 Expropriation Debate through the Eyes of a Property Theorist[85]

[. . .] Developments under NAFTA Chapter 11 have unleashed a torrent of commentary. Much of it recognizes that proper interpretation of NAFTA Article 1110 calls for an appropriate balance between respect for the stability of property expectations and legitimate needs for environmental regulation. In other words, NAFTA Article 1110 is not to be understood as just a guarantee against direct, full-blown expropriations. It is functioning as a regulatory takings doctrine. That is, it promises investors compensation in at least some circumstances for losses from regulation that 'goes too far'. Investors are therefore entitled to compensation at least some of the time for their losses from regulation.

Once this fact is acknowledged, commentators typically fall into one or more of several problematic discussions. What ought the rule of transnational regulatory takings be, for example? This is no more easily resolvable in the transnational context than it is in the domestic U.S. context, where vagueness seems endemic. Another line of argument asks whether it is even necessary to have a separate treaty provision on regulatory takings. Another article of Chapter 11 already provides for national treatment, thus guaranteeing foreign investors access to whatever regulatory takings protection would be available in domestic courts for property owned by nationals. A third inquiry explores what role international law ought to play in shaping regulatory takings doctrine, given the different approaches to regulatory takings reflected in the domestic laws of various countries

[. . .]

III. The Fundamental theoretical distinction between 'direct expropriation' and 'Indirect expropriation' or 'measures tantamount to expropriation'

[. . .]

[. . . B]ona fide regulatory takings disputes implicate an ongoing societal dialogue about the proper scope of the police power and of private property protections. It is not obvious that the property owner always deserves compensation. It is not obvious that the property owner never deserves compensation. What is clear is that societal dialogue over the formalities of property law and compensation needs

---

85 Marc E. Poirier, *The NAFTA Chapter 11 Expropriation Debate through the Eyes of a Property Theorist*, 33(4) Envtl. L. 851 (2003); partially reprinted hereinafter; footnotes omitted.

to occur within a broader context of social practices in order to be informed by it and maintain its legitimacy. Articulation of the rationale for specific determinations of boundaries between private property protection and police power based regulation through the resolution of specific disputes in turn reinforces and shapes social practices and reasonable property expectations. Consequently, the broader public must be involved in the resolution of regulatory takings disputes, in order to achieve the appropriate societal dialogue about, and balance concerning, the public and private sides of property.

[. . .]

IV. Consequences of the distinction between 'expropriation' and 'indirect expropriation' or 'measures tantamount to expropriation' for conceptualization of NAFTA article 1110 Issues

A. The split nomos problem

The problem presented by disputes between foreign investors and government regulation under NAFTA Chapter 11 can be seen, in this new light, as especially difficult for several related reasons. First, typically, let us posit that societal dialogue over the contours of property and regulation occurs within a 'nomos', to use Robert Cover's term. A nomos represents both a community of like-minded individuals sharing a way of life, and the world view that facilitates and expresses that way of life. One could find an analogy in a Burkean account of the social practices in which property is grounded. That is, property norms reflect shared social custom, which is not static but evolves slowly over time. Within this conceptual framework, the regulatory takings doctrine can be understood as putting the question whether the law as a tool of property practice has diverged too far from those practices. As Daniel Hulsebosch puts it, 'Understood functionally, when the Court holds that a regulation effects a taking, it is signaling that the legislature has tried to accelerate change faster than the Justices believe fair or wise'. The effect of the regulatory law is measured against the legitimate expectation.

In the context of international investment, however, not one but two nomoi are involved. The community within which any resource- and regulation-based dispute occurs is different from the community of foreign investors. Take the latter first. Like the medieval merchants who developed the law merchant and the law of insurance to facilitate commercial relationships inter sese, foreign investors have an interest in developing a property rule around regulatory takings that is 1) clear, 2) portable to different cultures worldwide, and 3) protective of their investments to the maximum extent possible. In contrast, local, regional, and often national level conflicts between private property rights and bona fide regulatory adjustments involve particular resource use conflicts that may well be local, especially in their locally felt adverse environmental effects. Government regulators typically seek to balance private property guarantees and community-protective actions, as do tribunals faced with claims of regulatory taking. This dialogic conception of the property-regulatory takings interface is pragmatic and evolutionary, not based on clear or universal property rules. In contrast to what the international merchant and finance nomos would like, property practices on the ground in communities where environmental effects will be felt are expected often to be contextual standards, rather than clear and portable rules. Moreover, the resolution of these conflicts seeks to accommodate all interests in a resource, not just the interest of the property owner.

[. . .]

B. Split nomos and territoriality problems in the context of globalization

[. . .]

The tension between the two approaches is made more salient by the fact that foreign investors are not physically part of the locality where the effects of their actions will be felt. Michael Walzer may have had a basis for writing, in 1983, that 'autonomous corporations will always be adjuncts, and probably parasitic adjuncts, of territorial states . . .' But in an era of globalization, he is wrong. As Richard Falk opines, 'the states system as the self-sufficient organizing framework for political life on a global level is essentially over . . .' Robert Wai describes the international business community nowadays as a 'semi-autonomous social field'. Many transnational corporations are larger than all but the largest national economies. Capital flows freely in and out of many countries, so that it may dictate national policy rather than vice-versa. Many analysts suggest that autonomous corporations seem to be well along the way to detaching themselves from particular territorial states. Similarly, in some arenas, including importantly trade and environment matters, decision making has been increasingly removed from national arenas and even from state-to-state negotiations. The WTO's compulsory dispute settlement process is a prime example. Negotiation and administration of intellectual property treaties away from fora where those interested in access could more easily witness and perhaps influence the principles being developed is another example. Unease about the globalization of property processes is evident in the tensions involved when world trade leaders meet in a populated locale where they are vulnerable to protest; as is the move, in reaction to protests, to hold such meetings in publicly inaccessible locations like the Arabian peninsula (Doha). In short, the territorial and locality-based politics of the tension between globalization on the one hand and environmental, labor, and human rights concerns on the other is unmistakable. It forms the inescapable backdrop to the NAFTA Chapter 11 controversy.

The property process theory of regulatory takings exposes the NAFTA Chapter 11 litigation as, plausibly, another front in what Doug Kendall and Charlie Lord have called the 'takings project,' a deliberate attempt to use a rhetoric of property rights to undermine the regulatory state. At stake is no less than the extent to which locally harmful activities pursuant to transnational investments can be regulated by a host country. This indeed could be described as potentially a new set of corporate private property rights.

The description of NAFTA Chapter 11 as an attempt to reframe certain property rights is especially plausible when it is understood that the NAFTA model for investment protection is likely to be incorporated, with some changes, into forthcoming, broader multilateral free trade agreements. One could also link the charge of a domestic 'takings project' to charges of 'predatory globalization,' which includes a tendency to disable regulatory restrictions on foreign capital's use of land and extraction of resources. Globalization is arguably accompanied by a neo-liberal mind set that is 'deeply opposed to social public sector expenditures devoted to welfare, job creation, environmental protection, health care, education, and even the alleviation of poverty.'

[. . .]

V. Consequences for interpretation and restructuring of NAFTA Chapter 11 and Article 1110

The question of how practically to respond to 'indirect expropriation' and 'tantamount to expropriation' claims from foreign investors has two aspects: 1) how to articulate and apply the substantive law, such as it is, addressing regulatory actions that result in the loss of property value; and 2) what forum(s) and procedures should be made available to do so. [. . .]

The substantive and procedural questions are not altogether separate inquiries, however. Where there is a tradition of societal dialogue within a nomos, a vague balancing test can serve all the necessary substantive purposes (though it must be expected that clear rules will develop wherever there is enough social consensus to do so). At the margin, in the difficult cases of arguably harsh regulatory effects on property, the rule can only continue to be a vague one. Such a vague promise of negotiation towards a fair result works best to reconstitute community around property and regulation issues when those who feel they have been, or could be, injured are willing to trust in the promise of negotiation. In the context of international investment, it is much dicier to presume that there will be a common background for societal dialogue, grounded in mutual trust, between foreign investors and a regulating governmental entity, let alone the locals who may be affected by any particular resolution of the dispute. This is the split nomos problem. Strangers to the community, who do not trust its processes, will want clear rules and a territorial fora to protect their property. Foreign investors concerned about the security of their investments are likely to be strangers in this sense. Careful design of the adjudication process can partially address this issue of trust. A reassuring process might help to balance out the distrust generated by a vague substantive standard. Here, both the split nomos problem and issues of territoriality and place are important considerations.

A. A substantive Norm for 'Indirect Expropriation' and 'Measures Tantamount to Expropriation'

1. A Vague Substantive Standard

International law on regulatory takings, such as it is, provides a clear obligation to compensate for direct expropriations. It also provides an obligation to compensate for 'indirect expropriations' or 'measures tantamount to expropriation.' But there is no obligation to compensate for losses due to bona fide regulations uniformly applied.

There is some agreement at this very general level about international law on expropriations in the form of regulatory takings. The problem is how to apply this standard. [. . .]

The problem cannot be escaped by giving up on current international law and setting out to draft a clearer treaty provision. 'Attempts to restate regulatory takings doctrine in clearer form—whether of the distillation or 'start over' variety—sooner or later almost always rely on terms or procedures that reinsert vagueness into the formulation.' [. . .]

[. . .]

[. . .] What ought an international regulatory takings doctrine say? As Frank Michelman has pointed out, general statements about property and regulation are likely to be unhelpful. They are too general to get at the complicated factors that ought to be considered, and, if made specific, are too inflexible over time. The simplest positions are easy to state, but unacceptable. They do not address balance properly. Thus, the strong property rights protection adumbrated in some of the NAFTA Chapter 11 arbitrations is wrong, for it would impair traditional police power regulation in novel and harmful ways. Abolishing the regulatory takings principle altogether is wrong, for it would fail to account for occasional gross unfairness and would not symbolically represent the importance of stability of property. That leaves us in an in-between territory, needing to determine the difficult conflicts case by case, on an all-things-considered basis.

In other words, I come out right where international law currently stands. Setting aside the issue of direct appropriations, which should be dealt with separately, international regulatory takings doctrine cannot sensibly be anything other than a Penn Central-like gesture towards a vague balancing test. Surveying international precedent, Martin Wagner concluded that it would involve examining the reasonableness of the regulation, the severity of the impact on the property owner, the duration of the regulation, and the reasonableness of the owner's expectations. This sounds about right . . . .

2. The Role of National Variation, Given Vagueness in the Substantive Standard

[...]

To the extent that any particular society adopts private property as a basic framework for that particular society, I do not see how it can do so without some form of a domestic regulatory takings doctrine. The tension between stability and change in property relations as conditions shift is unavoidable, and the mediating function of regulatory takings doctrine serves an important purpose. Whether such a principle has to be constitutionalized, or can survive on a strong preference for respect to property still ultimately subject to the legislature, is another question. These matters go beyond the scope of this article.

I do not wish to imply, however, that there should be a single substantive standard of international law protecting property that must be applied by all nations. All that ought to be required, given the issue of nomos and the function of regulatory takings doctrine, is that some type of balancing and negotiation will take place under the aegis of a regulatory takings doctrine. The international standard should be that a regulatory takings balancing rule must be formally in place, that it must be understood to be real, and that it must be carried out in practice. The content of the test, however, will inevitably be vague in some regards, and I mean to leave it vague. [. . .]

? DISCUSSION NOTES

1 One concern that underlies much of the criticism on the use of the various tests to define actions as indirect expropriation is that it is left to tribunals to determine the analytical framework in any particular case. Not all observers worry about this, however. One author, himself a prominent arbitrator, finds that the 'arbitrators participating in these cases are highly competent . . ., with experience and expertise in the relevant areas of law exceeding that of the vast majority of the domestic judiciary . . . . The quality of the decisions being rendered in these cases is high and there is every indication that the tribunals are properly balancing the legitimate interests' of the disputing parties. See Charles N. Brower and Lee A. Steven, *Who Then Should Judge? Developing the International Rule of Law Under NAFTA Chapter 11*, 2 Chi. J. Int'l L. 193, 200–201 (2001).

2 One response to the fears of arbitration awards that grant compensation for governmental regulation for the public's welfare is an attempt to draft expropriation provisions to limit tribunals' discretion in deciding how to characterize governmental measures. According to the UNCTAD's research, there are three main approaches to limiting arbitral discretion apparent so far: explicitly setting out the criteria for a finding of an indirect expropriation; setting out criteria that would

result in a finding of no indirect expropriation; and only obliging Parties to compensation for direct expropriations.[86]

The first approach is found, for instance in the Canada–China BIT. The drafters were among the first to specify more closely when an indirect expropriation has occurred. The language of Annex B.10 leaves no doubt that the parties intended tribunals to take a multifactor approach to expropriation determinations:

> The Contracting Parties confirm their understanding that:
>
> 1. Indirect expropriation results from a measure or series of measures of a Contracting Party that has an effect equivalent to direct expropriation without formal transfer of title or outright seizure.
> 2. The determination of whether a measure or series of measures of a Contracting Party constitutes an indirect expropriation requires a case-by-case, fact-based inquiry that considers, among other factors:
>
>   (a) the economic impact of the measure or series of measures, although the sole fact that a measure or series of measures of a Contracting Party has an adverse effect on the economic value of an investment does not establish that an indirect expropriation has occurred;
>
>   (b) the extent to which the measure or series of measures interferes with distinct, reasonable, investment-backed expectations;
>
>   (c) and the character of the measure or series of measures. [...][87]

Since then, numerous other expropriation provisions have appeared with similar clarifications. The investment chapters of the Canada–European Union Trade Agreement, of the Transatlantic Trade and Investment Partnership (TTIP), and of the TPP all include this type of explanatory annex on what the parties understand the scope of indirect expropriation to be.

The second approach (which is often combined with the first) is illustrated by the ASEAN Comprehensive Investment Agreement, which has an explanation of indirect expropriations in its Annex 2. Paragraph 4 provides: '4. Non-discriminatory measures of a Member State that are designed and applied to protect legitimate public welfare objectives, such as public health, safety and the environment, do not constitute an

---

86 UNCTAD, Policy Options for IIA Reform: Treaty Examples and Data (Supplementary Material to World Investment Report 2015) (version 24 June 2015).

87 Agreement between the Government of Canada and the Government of the People's Republic of China for the Promotion and Reciprocal Protection of Investments Annex B.10 (in effect as of 1 October 2014).

[indirect] expropriation.' Other IIAs specify that the issuance of compulsory licenses in accordance with the World Trade Organization rules are not to be considered indirect expropriation[88] or both limitations.[89] The third approach is typified by Brazil's recent treaties, but has existed since at least the late 1990s.[90] These provisions simply limit the parties' compensation obligation to direct expropriation. The expropriation provision in the Brazil-Malawi BIT, for example, reads: 'Subject to its laws and regulations, a Party shall not directly nationalize or expropriate covered investments by this Agreement, except [. . .].' 'Investment Cooperation and Facilitation Agreement between the Federative Republic of Brazil and the Republic of Malawi, Art. 8.2 (signed 25 June 2015). The Brazil–Mexico agreement is similarly limited: 'Las Partes no podrán nacionalizar ni expropiar las inversions cubiertas por el presente Acuerdo, solvo que sea: [. . .]'. Acuerdo de Cooperación y de Faciiltación de las inversiones entre la República Federativa del Brasil y los Estados Unidos Mexicanos, Art. 6.1.1 (signed 26 May 2015).

4.2.7 Current approach to indirect expropriation jurisprudence

The above review of the different approaches to indirect expropriation shows that it is not just the difference in treaty language that determines whether a particular governmental action will be considered indirect expropriation or regulation. While each award is specific to the facts and the applicable treaty, there are also simply a variety of perspectives that tribunals have as to how the disputes should be decided. It is therefore questionable whether drafting new provisions will actually achieve what the treaty negotiators hope to do.

Arbitrators' normative perspectives are not static, however. As the different views get discussed within the legal community and among the public, arbitrator attitudes sometimes evolve. Indeed, the new treaty language may be as much a result of new ways of thinking about the proper role of international

88 For example, Agreement between Japan and the Oriental Republic of Uruguay for the Liberalization, Promotion and Protection of Investment, Art. 16.4 (signed 26 January 2015).

89 For example, ASEAN Comprehensive Investment Agreement, Art. 14.5 and Annex 2.4; Free Trade Agreement between Republic of Korea and Columbia, Art. 8.7(5) and Annex 8-B(b) (signed 21 February 2013); Canada-Cote d'Ivoire, Art. 10(5) and Annex B.10(3).

90 *See* Agreement Between the Government of the Republic of Macedonia and the Government of Malaysia for the Promotion and Reciprocal Protection of Investments, Art. 5.1 (March 17, 1999). *See also*, Agreement Between the Republic of Serbia and the Kingdom of Morocco on the Reciprocal Promotion and Protection of Investments, Art. 4.1 (signed 6 June 2013); Agreement Between the Government of the Hashemite Kingdom of Jordan and the Government of the Republic of Lebanon for the Encouragement and Protection of Investments, Art. 4 (Aug. 30, 2003).

investment law in the local property law regime that have appeared in awards already handed down as a way of remedying this thinking in the future.

Indeed, several recent awards on indirect expropriation have demonstrated a movement away from viewing only the investor's interests and there seems to be a broader acceptance of the host states' need for policy space. The Mamidoil tribunal's discussion of what an indirect expropriation is—and what it is not—reviews a number of the newer cases on indirect expropriation and applies the general analytical framework they contain to the facts at hand.

 CASE

Mamidoil v. Albania

Facts: Claimant was a Greek company engaged in the storage and trade of petroleum products. With long-standing commercial activities in Albania, Claimant responded quickly to Albania's 1993 liberalization of investment opportunities. In the mid- to late 1990s, Claimant proposed an investment project in the port of Durres, the largest port in Albania. The project was to consist in the renovation of a tank farm and the port's infrastructure to allow for vessels to access the tanks, as well as the establishment of a network of gas stations. In 1998, the Claimant requested a lease on the land upon which the storage tank was to be constructed and in 1999, a 20-year lease was granted to the Claimant's joint venture company.

In 2000, the Albanian government entered into a loan agreement with international development institutions. As a result of suggestions made by the funders of this agreement, the government approved a plan to relocate its oil storage facilities to less densely populated areas.

During early 2000, Claimant began construction and by 2001, was able to begin filling the tanks from vessels at the port. During this period, Albanian authorities reportedly warned Mamidoil that construction should not proceed, and in July 2000, the government banned all construction projects in the port. The ban was lifted in December 2000, when the Greek government intervened on behalf of several Greek companies. The Claimants then received an exceptional 10-year trading permit which allowed them to operate until 2011. In 2009, the government closed the port to ships, ending the claimant's vessel trade. In 2011, not having applied for an extension of their trade permit, claimants were unable to continue operating.

Bringing a complaint under the Greece–Albania BIT, Mamidoil alleged an indirect expropriation among other violations.

> 558. [. . . T]he Tribunal must determine whether any or a combination of the following amount to an expropriation of Claimant's investment:
>
>> – the enactment of the new zoning plan for the port of Durres in June 2000, which had been announced to Claimant as imminent at the latest in November 1999;
>> – the order of a temporary suspension of construction works in July 2000 which was lifted in December 2000 by an authorization to complete the construction and to start operations;
>> – the issuance of a wholesale trading license in February 2001, valid until it expired in February 2011, after Claimant had chosen not to apply for its renewal; and/or
>> – the prohibition to land and discharge petroleum products from vessels in the port of Durres, decreed in July 2007 and effective from July 2009.
>
> 559. Two preliminary remarks are appropriate. Claimant asserts that the measures destroyed the *'necessary stable legal framework for further investment'* as well as the initial expectation that it could operate the tank farm profitably until the expiration of the term of the lease. Claimant further contends that it does not matter that the measures have not directly taken any of its property rights because they have deprived them of all value because *'without the possibility to discharge tankers in the port the operation of the tank farm was completely uneconomical'.*
>
> 560. Firstly, the Tribunal emphasizes that there are distinct standards of protection, with distinct requirements, under the BIT [. . .]. Damage caused by a violation of legitimate expectations, or by arbitrary measures, or by a destabilization of the legal framework, or by a lack of regulation and distortions of the fuel market may give rise to claims under either of the standards of fair and equitable treatment, or the prohibition of discriminatory measures, or the most constant protection and security. However, they are not at the same time *per se* indicative of an illegal expropriation.
>
> 561. In order to be capable of being considered expropriatory – even indirectly – the consequences for the property must be substantiated in accordance with the specificities of the claim for expropriation. The simple allegation that (the lack of) policy measures *'made it impossible to earn any profits which could be distributed to Claimant'* does not suffice to elevate the description of conduct into the sphere of a loss of the investment. This is all the more so when, as here, Claimant did earn profit before the port of Durres was closed, i.e. before the last of the alleged measures in the line of the alleged creeping expropriation was taken. The allegation that the lack of regulation and the distortion of the fuel market *'made it impossible to earn any profits'* is not supported by the evidence provided by Claimant.

Secondly, and more importantly under the circumstances of the present dispute, the BIT and the ECT expressly provide that not only the direct taking of property rights may cause expropriation but also measures tantamount to or having the effect equivalent to an expropriation. In the Tribunal's view, this language encompasses indirect expropriation, which can be the consequence of one measure or compound measures. The Parties do not contest this principle.

563. That being said, the Tribunal has to determine whether the effect of the compounded measures amounted to an expropriation. The term 'expropriation' is specific and not a synonym for damages that can be sought for the breach of other standards such as 'fair and equitable treatment', which require distinct conditions for a breach to be established.

564. In its affirmative presentation of the legal standard, Claimant relies on a number of awards, [. . .] where international arbitral tribunals held that measures that deprive an investor completely or in part of its property, or of its economic enjoyment, must be qualified as an expropriation. The termination of a free zone certificate, the revocation of a license, and unreasonable regulatory regimes are quoted as examples.

565. The Tribunal has read the cited awards carefully. Although not bound by them since binding precedent is alien to international investment arbitration, the Tribunal certainly respects and seeks guidance from legal opinions and interpretation expressed by learned colleagues.

566. The Tribunal holds that the decisive criterion for most tribunals that find expropriation is not the fact of having incurred a damage and/or the loss of value as such, but the finding – as stated in *Santa Elena v. Costa Rica* – '*that the owner has truly lost all the attributes of ownership*'. [citing *Compañia del Desarrollo de Santa Elena S.A. v. Republic of Costa Rica*, ICSID Case No. ARB/96/1, Award, para. 76 (17 February 2000).] As the tribunal in *El Paso v. Argentina* expressed in its award, [. . .] '*at least one of the essential components of the property rights must have disappeared for an expropriation to have occurred*'. [citing *El Paso Energy International Company v. Argentine Republic*, ICSID Case No. ARB/03/15, Award, para. 245 (31 October 2011).]

567. The concept is clearly applied in *AES v. Hungary*. Claimant correctly quotes the tribunal in that case as stating that '*it is necessary for the investor to be deprived, in whole of significant part, of the property in or effective control of its investment: or for its investment to be deprived, in whole or significant part, of its value*'. [citing *AES Summit Generation Limited and AES-Tisza Erömü Kft. v. Hungary*, ICSID Case No. ARB/07/22, Award, para. 14.3.1 (23 September 2010).] However, the tribunal goes on to state that '*the amendment of the 2001 Electricity Act and the issuance of the Price Decrees did not interfere with the ownership or use of Claimant's property. Claimant retained at all times the control of the AES Tisza II plant, thus there was no deprivation of Claimant's ownership or control of their investment*'. On this basis, the tribunal held that no expropriation had taken place.

568. The same rationale is found in the careful analysis of *Tecmed, Goetz and Middle East Cement* carried out by the tribunal in *El Paso v. Argentina*. It appears that in all of these awards, emphasis was laid not only on the fact that the investment lost value and the investor was deprived of benefits, but also that these effects resulted from a loss of one or several attributes of ownership.

569. The Tribunal concurs with this opinion. In its literal translation, expropriation describes a specific effect on property itself and not a damage inflicted to property. The effect can be a direct taking as it can be an indirect deprivation of one or several of its essential characteristics. These are traditionally defined by its use and enjoyment, control and possession, and disposal and alienation. If one of these attributes is affected, the resulting loss of value and/or benefit may lead to a claim for expropriation.

570. The definition of expropriation has developed over time and gone beyond the formalistic concentration on title. It encompasses the substance of property and protects the property even if title is not taken. However, a further extension into the sphere of damages, loss of value and profitability, without regard to the substance and attributes of property, would deprive the claim of its distinct nature and amalgamate it with other claims. Thus, a mere loss of value or a loss of benefits that is connected to and caused by the dissolution of at least one attribute of property, does not constitute indirect expropriation. The contrary approach would not only contradict the literal meaning of the term 'expropriation', but would also be inconsistent with the clear intention of State parties when they entered into the [IIA] and provided for separate standards of protection.

571. In sum, illegal conduct will not give rise to a claim for expropriation (though it may ground a different claim) if the substance and attributes of property are left intact. Conversely, legal conduct may be expropriatory if the essence of property is touched, as set out above, and no compensation is paid.

572. The Tribunal agrees therefore with the tribunal in *El Paso v. Argentina* when it held:

> Regulations that reduce the profitability of an investment but do not shut it down completely and leave the investor in control will generally not qualify as indirect expropriations even though they might give rise to liability of other standards of treatment, such as national treatment or fair and equitable treatment.
>
> In conclusion, the Tribunal, consistently with mainstream case-law, finds for an expropriation to exist, the investor should be substantially deprived not only of the benefits, but also of the use of its investment. A mere loss of value, which is not the result of an interference with the control or use of the investment, is not an indirect expropriation.

573. In applying these findings to the circumstances of the dispute, the Tribunal finds that Respondent has not expropriated Claimant's investment.

574. With the first incriminated measure – the enactment in June 2000 of the new

Land Use Plan for the port of Durres – Respondent has executed part of an overall transport sector policy, which had been carefully prepared, with international professional and financial assistance, to modernize the country's infrastructure and to enforce environmental, social and economic policy goals. Claimant was aware of this when it started to construct the tank farm.

575. With the second incriminated measure – the order to suspend the construction a month after the enactment of the new Land Use Plan and the ensuing authorization to complete it as well as the issuance of the trading permit – Respondent has accommodated Claimant's request and laid the basis for a profitable operation under the circumstances, which Claimant pursued until after the closure of the port for petroleum vessels.

576. The operation was so successful that Claimant decided to buy out the minority shareholder in 2006 for a price of 1 Million USD and prepare its listing at the Alternative Investment Market (AIM) in London. When Claimant first suspended and later abandoned its plans [. . .], this decision was not motivated by the incriminated measures but *'in light of the unorthodox formation of the local market in Albania, contrary to our initial estimate, as well as the uncertain investment environment that this creates'*. This statement documents that at the time and until the closure of the port of Durres, Claimant was far from thinking that the regulatory environment made it impossible to earn any profit. It recognized difficulties, which led it to change its strategy. This is different from a loss of any of the attributes of property.

577. Therefore, the Tribunal does not qualify these first measures as part of a process of creeping expropriation but as an appropriate enactment of public policy and a subsequent accommodation of Claimant's interests. This view seems to be shared by Claimant's contemporaneous appreciation.

578. The third incriminated measure – the closure of the port for petroleum vessels – led, indeed, to a loss of value of Claimant's investment and a dramatic loss of benefits. It was, however, not the *'straw that broke the camel's back '*but part of the implementation of Respondent's public policy'. [. . .]

579. The result of the measure was not Claimant's loss of any of the attributes of its property over the investment. Claimant remained entitled to continue to use, possess, control, and dispose of the property. It is not the Tribunal's task to evaluate business opportunities but to determine whether the dramatic losses of benefit are caused by the loss of one or all elements which constitute the essence of property. The Tribunal holds that this is not the case and that Respondent neither directly nor indirectly expropriated Claimant's investment.

580. The Tribunal therefore rejects the claim for expropriation.

? DISCUSSION NOTES

1 The *Mamidoil* decision indicates a possible future direction of indirect expropriation jurisprudence. It would be too soon to stop consider-

ing investor-focused approaches altogether, however. The *Yukos v. Russia* case—significant mainly for the size of its award—demonstrates a continuing allegiance to the importance of the investor's legitimate expectations in examinations of indirect expropriation claims. See *Yukos Universal Limited (Isle of Man) v. The Russian Federation*, PCA Case No. AA 227, Award (18 July 2014). The tribunal reviewed Russia's attempts to enforce tax laws that the Claimant was avoiding and determined that an indirect taking had occurred. In its concise analysis, the tribunal stressed Yukos' inability to expect the extremity of the government's measures:

> 1578. In the view of the Tribunal, the expectations of Claimants may have been, and certainly should have been, that Yukos' tax avoidance operations risked adverse reaction from Russian authorities. It is common ground [. . .] that Yukos and its competitors viewed positions taken by the tax authorities on issues of tax liability to be exigent, erratic and unpredictable. The Tribunal however is unable to accept that the expectations of Yukos should have included the extremity of the actions which in the event were imposed upon it. Not only did Mikhail Khodorkovsky not appear to expect to be arrested [. . .], he and his colleagues surely could not have been expected to anticipate the rationale and immensity of the tax assessments and fines. They could not have been expected to anticipate that their legal counsel would labor under the disabilities imposed upon them. They could not have been expected to anticipate the sale of [their investment] for so low a price under such questionable circumstances. They could not have been expected to anticipate that more than thirteen billion dollars in unpaid taxes and fines would be imposed on Yukos for unpaid VAT on oil exports when that oil had in fact been exported. They could not have been expected to anticipate that they risked the evisceration of their investments and the destruction of Yukos. Id. at para. 1578.

Was the violation of Yukos' legitimate expectations really the motivation for the tribunal's finding that an indirect expropriation had taken place? This question arises because in the following paragraph, it looked mainly at Russia's motivations:

> 1579. The Tribunal has earlier concluded that 'the primary objective of the Russian Federation was not to collect taxes but rather to bankrupt Yukos and appropriate its valuable assets' [. . .] if the true objective were no more than tax collection, Yukos, its officers and employees, and its properties and facilities, would not have been treated, and mistreated, as in fact they were. Among the many incidents in this train of mistreatment that are within the remit of this Tribunal, two stand out: finding Yukos liable for the payment of more than 13 billion dollars in VAT in respect of oil that had been exported [. . .]; and the auction of [part of

the company] at a price that was far less than its value. But for these actions, [. . .] Yukos would have been able to pay the tax claims of the Russian Federation justified or not; it would not have been bankrupted and liquidated [. . .].

1580. Respondent has not explicitly expropriated Yukos or the holdings of its shareholders, but the measures that Respondent has taken [. . .] have had an effect 'equivalent to nationalization or expropriation [. . .]'. Paras. 1578–80 (citations omitted).

What role do you think the malicious intent imputed to the government play in the tribunal's finding? Could the emphasis on bad faith/malicious intent be considered an aspect of the test for indirect expropriation that focuses on the government's right to regulate?

4.3 Valuation

4.3.1 Quantification of value

International investment agreements require that an expropriated investor receive some amount of compensation. In calculating the level of financial compensation, hosts and tribunals will need to place a value on the investment, as the amount received by the investor should have some relationship to the value of the property or rights lost, whether the applicable treaty standard is 'adequate', 'full', 'appropriate', or left open. Even when tribunals are assessing compensation for an illegal expropriation, the value of the interests taken are the starting point for the compensation calculations.

In a competitive market, value is based on the price at which a buyer is willing to give the seller and the amount the seller is willing to accept (the point at which the demand curve intersects with the supply curve). The market 'value' of an investment, then, can be seen as the price a buyer would pay for that investment, the 'willingness to pay'.

Despite the apparent simplicity in applying the willingness to pay test, investment arbitration tribunals do not use it very often. This is because the willingness to pay method of valuation depends on there being (1) a market and (2) a willing buyer. In the case of expropriated property, either or both of these elements may be missing. A potential lack of a market could be the result of restrictions on competition in the sector of investment, whether regulatory or 'natural'. Public monopolies such as water supply services or postal services; infrastructure-heavy industries such as mining; or highly regulated businesses such as banking reduce the number of potential entrants to an extent that makes discussions of a market for the service illusory. Expropriations, moreover, destroy the 'market value' of an investment by eliminating the willingness of any buyer to pay for the assets. Knowing that the state will take ownership of the property, no buyer would willingly pay a price reflective of the investment's profit-making potential. Many treaties circumvent this problem by including language that values the investment as of the day before the expropriation became known. Nevertheless, the highly hypothetical nature of such an analysis lessens its attractiveness to tribunals in many cases.

Thus, in conducting a valuation, tribunals are often left without much guidance beyond the parties' arguments. While IIAs frequently require compensation at the level of the investment's 'fair market value', they rarely specify the method by which the tribunal should determine this value. Tribunals must, then, decide for themselves (or use expert advice) how to value the expropriated property or interest.

Valuation is not a traditionally legal activity. Called by one prominent scholar 'a secondary issue' in comparison to the standard to be applied in determining compensation,[91] it is nevertheless an issue in which investors and hosts have a very strong interest and to which many pages of claims, responses, and explanatory decision-making are devoted. The following will therefore set out the general aspects of the basic approaches to valuation used by arbitral tribunals. A decision setting out the considerations of the tribunal in choosing among the possible methods will then illustrate how the choice can influence the award.

a   *Book value*

Perhaps the simplest method of valuation is to look at either the book value of the investment or the tax value. The book value is the difference between the investment's assets and liabilities as recorded in its financial records. An accounting figure, this closely reflects the actual present value of a company. It does not include any possible future profits or losses, making it a satisfactory method for calculating the amount of compensation owed to a legally expropriated investor for the physical assets of an active and profitable business.[92]

---

91 Sornarajah, *supra* note 7, at 450.

92 *See* Sornarajah, *supra* note 7, at 451 (who further notes that book value was used by many of the Iran–US Claims tribunals); *Amoco International Finance Corp. v. Iran, supra* note 9, para. 251.

The *LIAMCO v. Libya*[93] award applied a book value analysis to determine the 'just and equitable' compensation sum for the expropriated oil wells, oil in tankers, office supplies, and other equipment. Very computational, the tribunal sets forth the value of each of the current assets individually, reduces the face value of the fixed assets by 'depreciation, depletion and amortization', and then adds these totals.

> The total value of both current and fixed assets equals $16 148 768. It has to be reduced by current liabilities for income tax, surtax and supplemental payment amounting to $2 266 091, so as to make the net value of all physical assets $13 882 677.
>
> The above evaluations represent the market value of LIAMCO's 25.5 per cent interest in said assets. That value is based on the original cost of only seventy wells as shown on the Company's books and records, adjusted for variations in construction costs by application of the appropriate international Middle East construction index.[94]

b Net investment/costs

Valuing an investment on the basis of net investment requires calculating how much the investor spent in setting up its investment rather than in looking at the present or future profit-making probabilities. Because it is based on past expenditures, the claimant can prove the level of compensation with relative certainty, independent of current market conditions or projections of future changes. It is therefore a highly objective method for tribunals to apply.

If an investment is losing money, moreover, the investor is likely to base her claim on the net investment rather than on the willingness to pay, book value, or discounted cash flow method. Whereas each of the others would yield a result of no payment, as long as the investor did contribute financially to the investment (which is a tautology given the definition of an investment), she would be entitled to recapture these payments.

---

93 *Libyan American Oil Company (LIAMCO) v. Government of the Libyan Arab Republic*, Award (Apr. 12, 1977), 20 ILM 1 (1981).
94 Id. at 78.

CASE

Metalclad Corporation v. United Mexican States[95]

Metalclad, a US corporation, purchased Coterin, a Mexican company, through its wholly owned subsidiaries in September 1993. At that time, Coterin owned a landfill 70 kilometres from Guadalcazar, a city in the state of San Luis Potosi. As the Mexican government had granted Coterin construction permits for a hazardous waste transfer station and a landfill, as well as an operating permit for the transfer station, Metalclad invested in Coterin with the purpose of developing, managing, and operating both at the site.

Although the state government granted Coterin a landfill construction permit in May 1993, this permit was conditioned on certain technical adaptations of the plans and approval of such changes by the requisite authorities. Relying on the governor's support for the project and the federal government's assertions of competence in the issuing of the operation licences, Metalclad purchased the company.

Thereafter began a complex process of negotiations to attain the necessary permits for construction and operation of the landfill from federal, state, and local authorities. While federal construction permits were forthcoming and acted upon by Metalclad, the city denied the operating permit application in December 1995. Following Metalclad's unsuccessful attempts to obtain redress through Mexican administrative courts, the company initiated arbitration under NAFTA's Chapter 11. Nine months later, the governor of San Luis Potosí declared the site a nature reserve, permanently ending any use Metalclad could make of the land.

The tribunal had little difficulty finding that Mexico had indirectly expropriated Metalclad without compensation. The issue of how to calculate the fair market value of the barely operational enterprise, however, was less straightforward.

a. Basic Elements of Valuation

[...]

114. Metalclad has proposed two alternative methods for calculating damages: the first is to use a discounted cash flow analysis of future profits to establish the fair

---

95 *Metalclad Corporation v. United Mexican States, supra* note 67; footnotes omitted.

market value of the investment (approximately $90 million); the second is to value Metalclad's actual investment in the landfill (approximately $20–25 million).

[. . .]

116. Mexico asserts that a discounted cash flow analysis is inappropriate where the expropriated entity is not a going concern. Mexico offers an alternative calculation of fair market value based on COTERIN's 'market capitalization'. Mexico's 'market capitalization' calculations show a loss to Metalclad of $13–15 million.

117. Mexico also suggests a direct investment value approach to damages. Mexico estimates Metalclad's direct investment value, or loss, to be approximately $3–4 million.

118. NAFTA, Article 1135(1)(a), provides for the award of monetary damages and applicable interest where a Party is found to have violated a Chapter Eleven provision. With respect to expropriation, NAFTA, Article 1110(2), specifically requires compensation to be equivalent to the fair market value of the expropriated investment immediately before the expropriation took place. This paragraph further states that 'the valuation criteria shall include going concern value, asset value including declared tax value of tangible property, and other criteria, as appropriate, to determine fair market value'.

119. Normally, the fair market value of a going concern which has a history of profitable operation may be based on an estimate of future profits subject to a discounted cash flow analysis. . . .

120. However, where the enterprise has not operated for a sufficiently long time to establish a performance record or where it has failed to make a profit, future profits cannot be used to determine going concern or fair market value. In *Sola Tiles, Inc. v. Iran (1987)*, the Iran–U.S. Claims Tribunal pointed to the importance in relation to a company's value of 'its business reputation and the relationship it has established with its suppliers and customers'. Similarly, in *Asian Agricultural Products v. Sri Lanka*, another ICSID Tribunal observed, in dealing with the comparable problem of the assessment of the value of good will, that its ascertainment 'requires the prior presence on the market for at least two or three years, which is the minimum period needed in order to establish continuing business connections'.

121. The Tribunal agrees with Mexico that a discounted cash flow analysis is inappropriate in the present case because the landfill was never operative and any award based on future profits would be wholly speculative.

122. Rather, the Tribunal agrees with the parties that fair market value is best arrived at in this case by reference to Metalclad's actual investment in the project. Thus, in *Phelps Dodge Corp. v. Iran*, the Iran–U.S. Claims Tribunal concluded that the value of the expropriated property was the value of claimant's investment in that property. In reaching this conclusion, the Tribunal considered that the property's future profits were so dependent on as yet unobtained preferential treatment from the government that any prediction of them would be entirely

speculative. Similarly, in the *Biloune* case [. . .], the Tribunal concluded that the value of the expropriated property was the value of the claimant's investment in that property. While the Tribunal recognized the validity of the principle that lost profits should be considered in the valuation of expropriated property, the Tribunal did not award lost profits because the claimants could not provide any realistic estimate of them. In that case, as in the present one, the expropriation occurred when the project was not yet in operation and had yet to generate revenue. The award to Metalclad of the cost of its investment in the landfill is consistent with the principles set forth in *Chorzów Factory*, namely, that where the state has acted contrary to its obligations, any award to the claimant should, as far as is possible, wipe out all the consequences of the illegal act and re-establish the situation which would in all probability have existed if that act had not been committed (the *status quo ante*).

123. Metalclad asserts that it invested $20 474 528.00 in the landfill project, basing its value on its United States Federal Income Tax Returns and Auditors' Workpapers of Capitalized Costs for the Landfill . . . . The calculations include landfill costs Metalclad claims to have incurred from 1991 through 1996 for expenses categorized as the COTERIN acquisition, personnel, insurance, travel and living, telephone, accounting and legal, consulting, interest, office, property, plant and equipment, including $328 167.00 for 'other'.

124. Mexico challenges the correctness of these calculations on several grounds, of which one is the lack of supporting documentation for each expense item claimed. However, the Tribunal finds that the tax filings of Metalclad, together with the independent audit documents supporting those tax filings, are to be accorded substantial evidential weight and that difficulties in verifying expense items due to incomplete files do not necessarily render the expenses claimed fundamentally erroneous.

125. The Tribunal agrees, however, with Mexico's position that costs incurred prior to the year in which Metalclad purchased COTERIN are too far removed from the investment for which damages are claimed. The Tribunal will reduce the Award by the amount of the costs claimed for 1991 and 1992.

[. . . .]

131. For the reasons stated above, the Tribunal hereby decides that, reflecting the amount of Metalclad's investment in the project, less the disallowance of expenses claimed for 1991 and 1992, ..., the Respondent shall, within 45 days from the date on which this Award is rendered, pay to Metalclad the amount of $16 685 000.00. Following such period, interest shall accrue on the unpaid award or any unpaid part thereof at the rate of 6% compounded monthly.

c   Discounted cash flow

The method of discounted cash flow (DCF) value assessment takes into account an investment's probable future profit-making. The investor's costs associated with increasing its future profits will be subtracted from the tribunal's determination of the value that would be derived in the future from such further investments to arrive at a discounted payment sum that the host is to pay the investor immediately. The method thus closely resembles the measure of willingness to pay, having the additional advantage of avoiding the need to have a free market or willing buyer to be applied. Popular with tribunals, the DCF valuation of a profitable investment will generally exceed its book value and the net investment value.

 CASE

Amoco International Finance Corp. v. Iran[96]

224. Any investment depends on the free decision of the investor and, in any case, such a future oriented decision requires the acceptance of a certain measure of risks. Any investment, therefore, includes a speculative element. Moreover, an investment can be motivated by extraneous factors, like the financial and commercial strategy of the investor.

225. It may be convenient, at this juncture, to recall that a nationalization cannot be equated to a normal business investment or to a transaction in a free market. This is so not only because the expropriated owner is usually not a willing seller, as already noted, but also because the expropriating State acts for a public purpose. Commercial motivations are rarely paramount in decisions to nationalize, and may even be lacking altogether. Political considerations and considerations of economic policy or general national interest are usually more decisive. It goes without saying that the Tribunal is not in the position of a prospective investor. Rather the Tribunal must determine, ex post facto, the most equitable compensation required by the applicable law for a compulsory taking, excluding any speculative factor. Its first duty is to avoid any unjust enrichment or deprivation of either Party.

226. This conclusion is fully in conformity with the practice of international arbitral tribunals, which, in considering lawful expropriation, have consistently tried to determine according to the law, by all the available means, often using several methods, the appropriate compensation to be paid in the circumstances of each case, even when the parties have submitted elaborate calculations made with the help of the DCF method. [. . .]

---

96 *Amoco International Finance Corp. v. Iran, supra* note 9; footnotes are omitted.

b) The DCF Method

227. As previously noted by the Tribunal, the DCF method was specifically proposed by the Claimant as a method that would 'place the foreign investor in as good an economic position as he was before the expropriation'. Such a statement is equivalent to the words of the Permanent Court of International Justice in the Chorzów Factory case: 'as far as possible, [to] wipe out all the consequences of the illegal act and re-establish the situation which would, in all probability, have existed if this act had not been committed.' As discussed above, however, such a restitutio in integrum was contemplated by the Court only in the case of an unlawful expropriation. Since the Tribunal in the instant Case, has found the expropriation to be lawful, the DCF method *prima facie* seems not fitted to the present issue. [. . .]

228. As used by the Claimant in the present Case, however, the DCF method goes even further: it amounts to a complete departure from, and a reversal of, the approach traditionally adopted in international practice, notably, by international tribunals. Under the traditional approach, in case of expropriation of an enterprise the compensation to be paid is calculated according to the net value of the transferred – that is, expropriated – assets. As we have seen this can extend to physical properties, movable and immovable, as well as to intangibles, including profitability in the case of an ongoing enterprise: the 'going concern' value. To this element of damnum emergens, a complementary one is added where the expropriation is unlawful: the value of the revenues that the owner would have earned if the expropriation had not occurred, i.e., lucrum cessans.

229. The Claimant's calculation completely leaves aside the net value of the expropriated assets; this value has no place whatsoever in the Claimant's reasoning. Exit damnum emergens. The Claimant's method is instead a projection into the future to assess the amount of the revenues which would possibly be earned by the undertaking, year after year, up to eighteen years later in this Case. These forecasted revenues are actualized at the time by way of a discounting calculation, and capitalized as the measure of the compensation to be paid, as well as the alleged market value of the enterprise. With such a method, lucrum cessans becomes the sole element of compensation.

230. Such a substitution has been justified as reflecting a better understanding of economics and of the usual practice in the business world. The Tribunal has already recognized that the DCF method is probably extremely helpful when an investor has to decide whether to make a large investment: his first concern, obviously, relates to the time necessary to recoup his money and to the likely level of return. The Tribunal can also perceive the advantages of such a method for a claimant seeking substantial compensation. The calculation of the revenues expected to accrue over a long period of time in the future, which opens a large field of speculation due to the uncertainty inherent in any such projection, will probably yield higher results than any other method. For this reason, however, such a method

cannot easily be accepted by a tribunal, and the reluctance of all tribunals and claims commissions, including domestic fora, even in the United States, to make use of it is easy to understand.

231. In the case of a going concern, as the AMINOIL tribunal aptly put it, the value of the enterprise as a whole is higher than the sum of the discrete elements which constitute it [. . .], but it remains related to these elements. With the DCF method, as used in this Case, the alleged value of the undertaking has no relation whatsoever to the value of these elements—and therefore to the investment made in order to create the concern and to maintain its profitability. The replacement value, that is the investment necessary to create a similar undertaking, is no more taken into consideration. The capitalization of the future earnings will probably amount to a much higher figure, which could lead to unjust enrichment for the beneficiary of such compensation, since he could, hypothetically, establish a similar enterprise with comparable earnings, spending only a portion of the compensation received, and earn additional revenues with the remaining part. If the enterprise were less profitable, the Claimant would probably refer to another method, as the claimant did in the Chorzów Factory case. It is one thing to recognize, as this Tribunal and many other international tribunals and courts before it have done, that the profitability of a going concern is one of the elements to be considered in the valuation of such a concern; it is another thing to substitute a capitalization of hypothetical future earnings for all other elements of valuation.

232. These initial remarks do not necessarily lead to an absolute rejection of the DCF method for any purpose in this Case. For the reasons already set forth, one element of valuation of a going concern, as was Khemco, is its profitability. This element is not easy to translate into figures, and the DCF method could provide the Tribunal with useful information pertaining to profitability, if the method is correctly applied. Accordingly, it will be appropriate to consider how this method has been used in the present Case and to determine to what extent the results arrived at are reliable.

c) The DCF Calculations

233. Apart from a general rejection by the Respondents of the DCF method in the instant case, almost all of the assertions brought forward by the Claimant in supporting the use of this method have been severely criticized by the Respondents. The Tribunal does not intend to take sides in the debate between the experienced and distinguished experts of both Parties. Nevertheless, without entering into the technical aspects of the matter, some assumptions relied upon by one Party or the other call for a few general comments, especially from a legal point of view.

234. The projection of the cash flow into the future, as made by the Claimant's experts, was subject to a sharp and highly technical dispute about the availability of sufficient quantities of gas for processing during the relevant period of time.

Without entering into the details of the dispute, it is sufficient to note that the disagreement between the Parties relates less to the quantity of the existing reserves than to their availability for processing by Khemco, in view of possible fluctuations in oil production levels and possible diversions to other uses of the gas produced. These objections, therefore, are dependent on factors which are relevant to the most important issue—the forecasts of the cost of gas available to Khemco for processing and of the likely sales price of Khemco products—and will be considered in relation with those factors.

235. The price of gas produced from the JSA fields operated by NIOC and Amoco was set by the Gas Purchase Agreement and was very low ($.02 per thousand cubic feet for fifteen years, until 1985, with a prescribed formula for determining maximum price increases thereafter). The same price was applicable to gas that NIOC agreed to provide from other sources. The Claimant's expert assumed that the agreed formula would be strictly applied during the whole life of the Khemco Agreement. This assumption inevitably is correct from a legal point of view. However, in view of the past experience in the oil industry, especially among oil producing countries surrounding the Persian Gulf, it could not be excluded that, at some point in time, this price would be renegotiated in order to take into consideration the evolution of the market. In such a case the gas price could be modified without a breach of the contract. It is not possible, however, to evaluate the probability and the consequences of such a renegotiation, since the experts of the Parties did not fully brief this issue. Furthermore, the fact that the JSA itself was nullified by application of the Single Article Act introduces additional uncertainty.

236. Significantly, the Claimant's expert projected gas prices as well as Khemco product prices over 18 years, from 1979 onward to 1997, i.e., until the end of the Khemco Agreement. The sales price projections for LPG and NGL products were made by reference to the expected changes in oil prices, since the Khemco NGL production was sold at a per-barrel price determined by reference to the price for crude oil from the JSA Darius field, and LPG production sold at prices closely related to the price of crude oil. For the purpose of these projections, the Claimant's expert used what he described as the most conservative and reasonable product-price forecasts prepared by well-known econometric and forecasting firms. To use his own terms, 'these forecasts are an indispensable part of such evaluations.' They 'are based on available data and expert judgment at the time of the valuation.'

237. As conceded by the same expert, in the case of a gas processing plant earnings are a direct function of product prices that vary from year to year, so that past earnings cannot provide a reliable measure of the value of such a plant. Actually, it is well known that oil prices have demonstrated a great instability. Independently of the fluctuations of the free market, decisions relating to fixed prices or to the volume of production, taken in the past by the big oil companies, or more recently by OPEC or other producing countries, have been responsible for these price variations. The difficulties and risks of error inherent in every price forecast are there-

fore considerably aggravated. A clear illustration of this situation is provided by the discrepancies which can be observed between the oil price forecasts used in the Claimant's expert study and the actual evolution of prices from 1979 to 1987.

238. As a projection into the future, any cash flow projection has an element of speculation associated with it, as recognized by the Claimant. For this very reason it is disputable whether a tribunal can use it at all for the valuation of compensation. One of the best settled rules of the law of international responsibility of States is that no reparation for speculative or uncertain damage can be awarded. This holds true for the existence of the damage and of its effect as well. Such a rule, therefore, applies in the case of unlawful expropriation. A fortiori, the reasoning on which it rests must also apply in the case of compensation for a lawful expropriation. It does not permit the use of a method which yields uncertain figures for the valuation of damages, even if the existence of damages is certain.

239. The element of speculation in a short-term projection is rather limited, although unexpected events can make it turn out to be wrong. The speculative element rapidly increases with the number of years to which a projection relates. It is well known, and certainly taken into account by investors, that if it applies to a rather distant future a projection is almost purely speculative, even if it is done by the most serious and experienced forecasting firms, especially if it relates to such a volatile factor as oil prices. Such projections can be useful indications for a prospective investor, who understands how far it can rely on them and accepts the risks associated with them; they certainly cannot be used by a tribunal as the measure of a fair compensation.

240. The projection of the future earnings of Khemco over 18 years was made by the Claimant in order to take into account the totality of the return which could be derived from the Khemco Agreement for the remaining time of its life. Clearly, this is a consequence of the Claimant's misconception that the measure of the compensation is restitutio in integrum. A case of expropriation of an undertaking with no contractual time limit would, under this reasoning, require a projection into the future ad infinitum, or, to be more precise, up to the time when the application of the discount rate would result in a return amounting to nil. The Tribunal need not express an opinion upon the admissibility of such a projection when the reparation must wipe out all the consequences of an illegal taking, but it certainly cannot accept it for the compensation due in case of a lawful expropriation.

241. The second stage of the DCF method is the calculation of the proper discount rate. It starts with the determination of a reference or 'benchmark' discount rate, based on market data allowing comparisons within a certain industry or type of investment. The Claimant's expert chose as a reference nine large oil companies with substantial international operations and concluded from their relevant market data that the reference discount rate would be 3.5 percent. This figure was disputed by the Respondents. The Claimant's expert admitted that some differences existed between the operations of these companies and those of Khemco but gave the

assurance that they were duly taken into consideration. The Tribunal is unable to test the veracity or the importance of the adjustments made for this purpose. A certain degree of uncertainty, therefore, is to be borne in mind in taking cognizance of the results of this part of the study.

242. As a second step in the calculation of the proper discount rate, an adjustment must be made specifically to account for the relative risk characteristics of Khemco's future net cash flow. Three series of risks were considered: tax and currency risk, business risk, and force majeure risk. The risk of uncompensated breach or expropriation, on the contrary, was disregarded as irrelevant upon counsel's instruction. The Claimant's expert concluded that tax risk and force majeure risk were higher than the average for Khemco, but that currency risk and business risk were lower. On the whole, these risks were weighted to an upward adjustment of 3 percent. The total discount to be used in evaluating Khemco rights would, therefore, be 6.5 percent.

243. No precise information was provided by the Claimant on the technique used in order to translate into figures the general qualitative considerations presented in the expert's report on each specific risk. These considerations, indeed, were relatively succinct and not very elaborated. Furthermore, the mere mention that a risk was higher or lower than the average is too vague to furnish a valuable indication and to assist the Tribunal to assess the validity of the adjustment of 3 percent.

244. In the words of the Claimant's expert, 'there necessarily will be room for some variations in detail and the exercise of expert judgment in applying the [DCF] analysis in a specific instance.' It appears that 'the exercise of expert judgment' is at a peak for the determination of the adjustment of the reference discount rate. With all respect for the undoubted experience of such a distinguished expert, it remains true that expert judgment means subjective judgment, and that the reasons on which it rests in relation to this specific issue have not been fully disclosed.

245. In addition, some comment is appropriate concerning the Claimant's general approach to evaluation of specific risks. Not all of these risks relate only to economics and, in the words of one of the Claimant's experts, the assessment of some of them was given by him 'just as a common-sense layman.' In certain instances, these risks seem to have been underestimated, as subsequent events have demonstrated, even if unforeseeable risks are disregarded.

246. Such is the case for currency risk and force majeure risk. At the time, although the Revolution in Iran was successful in establishing a new government, the political turmoil was still very high and the situation far from a return to the normal, with all the uncertainties and economic consequences inherent in such a hectic environment. In spite of the provisions of the Khemco Agreement to this effect, free convertibility was not certain (exchange controls not necessarily being a breach of contract in the circumstances). Civil disorder and labor strife could last for an unlimited time and, in spite of its geographic location, Khemco was not immune from these disorders. Furthermore, while it was impossible to forecast the

war with Iraq as it actually developed, no one acquainted with the history of relations between the two countries could, in the circumstances prevailing at the time,
discard entirely the risk of military actions, which would directly concern Kharg
Island. In any event, there was a clear risk that Iran's relations with the outside
world could be profoundly disturbed for an unpredictable period of time, with
evident consequences for the operation of an undertaking like Khemco.

247. The exclusion of uncompensated expropriation is still more troubling.
According to the Claimant, such an exclusion was imposed as a matter of law,
since the Respondents cannot take advantage of their unlawful acts. The legal
principle on which the Claimant relies is undoubtedly correct, but should more
accurately be expressed as forbidding the taking into account of the consequences
of an unlawful expropriation in the calculation of the compensation to be paid.
Conversely, lawful expropriation should not be excluded. The risk of such an
expropriation, to be sure, would have constituted a deterrent for any prospective
investor, especially if such a taking might occur in the near future. Furthermore, as
noted before, compensation in such case of lawful expropriation does not mean
restitutio in integrum, as reducing the risk to zero presupposes. In fact, expropriated oil companies have often found it to be in their best interest to accept settlements at net book value of the expropriated asset. Even if such a concession was
usually made in the framework of a broader, positive commercial arrangement, this
cannot be construed as nullifying the risk of expropriation. The instruction given
to the expert by the Claimant assumed that any compensation would re-establish
things, at least financially, as they would have been if the expropriation did not take
place. In other words, it was grounded on the contention that compensation for a
lawful expropriation and damages for an unlawful one are one and the same thing,
which the Tribunal has rejected.

248. Even if limited to lawful expropriation, the inclusion of this risk would have
considerably changed the results of the study. Taking into consideration actual
threats of expropriation, according to the Claimant's expert, would have resulted
in valuing a lawsuit rather than the value of a particular facility. In fact, the dispute
between the two Parties about this particular risk takes on a surrealistic character
given the fact that the risk actually was realized. It is another illustration of the arti-
ficiality, in such circumstances, of an exercise devoted to the determination of the
price that would result from a free transaction between a hypothetical willing buyer
and a hypothetical willing seller negotiating at arms length. Expropriation cannot
be construed as a mere risk when it has actually taken place. On the other hand, it
has always been recognized that the effects of the prospect of expropriation on the
market price of expropriated assets must be eliminated for the purpose of evaluating the compensation to be paid, since they are artificial and unrelated to the real
value of such assets.

When calculating the FMV of an investment with the DCF method, tribunals add up not only the assets and future profits of the project, but they also must subtract the foregone costs involved with running the enterprise over time. Operating costs, of course, are included, but so are the costs of capital investment, depreciation, any special contributions required, royalties, and taxes.

Once the net cash flow is set, the next critical element in determining DCF compensation is calculating the applicable discount rate. The discount rate, remember, is used to reduce the value of the capital assets, in order to estimate what the hypothetical willing buyer would have paid for the opportunity to profit in the future. While this is mainly an assessment to be made by economists, there are also legal questions that arise. In the following case, the tribunal had to consider whether a particular aspect of country risk known as the 'confiscation risk'—the reflection of the likelihood that a particular host will expropriate an investment—should be included in the discount rate of a project which *has been* expropriated.

 CASE

Venezuela Holdings v. Bolivarian Republic of Venezuela[97]

Venezuela is one of the world's largest oil suppliers and its economy is heavily reliant on the profits from the oil industry's revenues. Like many similar economies, Venezuela's oil sector had been nationalized, but was opened to foreign participation in the 1990s. Claimant Mobil began exploring the Venezuelan market in 1991, just as liberalization was beginning, and by 1997 had secured authorization from the Venezuelan Congress to establish a joint venture investment with the host. The conditions of the series of agreements provided for advantages over the rest of the oil sector.

When Hugo Chavez became President, his political program led to a return to nationalized oil. Tax advantages were revoked and several years later, following unsuccessful negotiations over the price for the claimants' shares, the Claimants' participation in state joint ventures was cancelled.

---

97 *Venezuela Holdings, Mobil Cerro Negro Holdings, Mobil Venezolana de Petróleos Holdings, Mobil Cerro Negro, and Mobil Venezolana de Petróleos v. The Bolivarian Republic of Venezuela*, ICSID Case No. ARB/07/27, Award (Oct. 9, 2014) (footnotes omitted).

The tribunal found an illegal expropriation had taken place. The next step was to determine the value of the taking.

364. The Tribunal observes that the basic divergence between the Parties concerns the question of what they refer to as the 'confiscation risk', or more specifically, whether the risk of confiscation should be taken into account when calculating the discount rate applicable to the compensation due for an expropriation. The Claimants submit that under Article 6(c) of the BIT, 'a valuation of the expropriated property that complies with the Treaty cannot include the risk that the property might be expropriated later without the compensation required by the Treaty'. In their opinion, the discount rate can take into consideration country risks such as those resulting from a volatile economy or civil disorder, but not the confiscation risk. The Respondent does not share that interpretation of article 6(c) and contends that elements such as the risk of taxation, regulation and expropriation are essential to the country risk and must be taken into consideration in the determination of the discount rate.

365. Article 6(c) of the BIT requires that the compensation due in case of expropriation represent 'the market value of the investments affected before the measures are taken or the impending measures became public knowledge, whichever is earlier'. This means that the compensation must correspond to the amount that a willing buyer would have been ready to pay to a willing seller in order to acquire his interests but for the expropriation, that is, at a time before the expropriation had occurred or before it had become public that it would occur. The Tribunal finds that, it is precisely at the time before an expropriation (or the public knowledge of an impending expropriation) that the risk of a potential expropriation would exist, and this hypothetical buyer would take it into account when determining the amount he would be willing to pay in that moment. The Tribunal considers that the confiscation risk remains part of the country risk and must be taken into account in the determination of the discount rate. Accordingly, the Tribunal is unable to adopt the approach used by the Claimants' expert, which does not take this risk into account.

366. The Tribunal observes that the Respondent's experts have used different methods to calculate the discount rate, which take into account the confiscation risk and a number of other relevant elements. On these bases they arrive to discount rates ranging from 18.5% to 23.9%.

367. Other arbitral tribunals have adopted discount rates in circumstances comparable to the present case. In those cases, they have used rates ranging from 18.5% to 21%. The Tribunal in the ICC Award applied a discount rate of 18%.

368. In the Tribunal's view, that 18% discount rate appropriately reflects the existing risks in the present case. Accordingly, the Tribunal has decided to adopt it, and arrived to a discounted net cash flow of US$ 1411.7 million [. . .].

d Other methods

d.i 'All relevant circumstances'

While the valuation methods mentioned above are frequently applied, there are other valuation methods that tribunals can use. One of those was applied by the tribunal in the following case. There the arbitrators spoke of examining 'all relevant circumstances' to calculate the compensation due the claimant.

 CASE

Compañía del Desarrollo de Santa Elena SA v. Costa Rica[98]

United States citizens owned a majority of the share of Compañía del Desarrollo de Santa Elena, SA (CDSE), a building developer that purchased property on Costa Rica's northwest coastline to establish a tourist resort and residential properties. Comprising over 15 000 square kilometres of biodiversity-rich land, the Santa Elena property cost CDSE $395 000 in 1970.

In May 1978, the Costa Rican government decreed that Santa Elena would be expropriated to ensure the sustainability of its plant and animal wealth, as well as to afford further research, tourism, and recreational activities. The government offered CDSE approximately $1.9 million in compensation, a figure it took from an April 1978 assessment of the property's value.

Although CDSE had not completed its development plans, it agreed to the expropriation. It objected strongly, however, to the amount of compensation offered. The investment, it argued, was worth over $6 million in February 1978. CDSE brought Costa Rica to arbitration on the issue of compensation.

K. Valuation

75. On the question of valuation, as noted earlier, the views of the parties are widely divergent. The Tribunal considers it useful to summarise the parties' positions here:

- Claimant states that the fair market value of the Santa Elena Property, based on its highest and best use in the market place, is equivalent to its present day value, undiminished by any expropriatory actions of the Government and, in particular, by any environmental statutes or regulations enacted after 1978.
- Respondent contends that the relevant date at which the fair market value of

---

98 *Compañía del Desarrollo de Santa Elena SA v. Costa Rica, supra* note 76; footnotes omitted.

the Property is to be assessed is the date of the expropriation decree, i.e., 5 May 1978.

[. . .]

2) Value of the Santa Elena Property as of 5 May 1978

85. As noted earlier, Claimant purchased the Santa Elena Property in 1970 with the intention of developing it partly as a tourist resort.

86. It is interesting to note that Respondent's own 1978 Appraisal recognizes that the Property, at that time, had a certain potential for tourism development. In that appraisal, the Tribunal finds expressions such as:

> a beach with good potential for tourism';
> 'it is thought that the coast could be developed for tourism projects, giving it a special value';
> 'beaches and the lands around them where certain tourist projects may be feasible'.

87. Similarly, the 1993 Appraisal conducted for Costa Rica contained descriptions of portions of the property such as the following:

> 'could be exploited for tourism';
> 'excellent prospects for tourism';
> 'the Potrero Grande beach is the largest and has the greatest potential for tourism';
> 'well suited for the construction of tourism infrastructure';
> 'Santa Elena is a rural property that combines ingredients of agriculture, ecology and tourism amidst great unexploited beauty'.

88. The great difficulty in this case is that, apart from Costa Rica's unilateral appraisal of 14 April 1978 and CDSE's February 1978 valuation, there is no other evidence of what the Property was actually worth as at the date of expropriation.

89. We agree with the parties that the Tribunal cannot go back in time to 1978 to perform its own appraisal of the Property, but that we can, and must, '. . . make some assessment of the two [1978] appraisals that the parties have provided'.

90. In determining the fair market value of the Property as of the date of expropriation, 5 May 1978, the Tribunal has proceeded by means of a process of approximation based on the appraisals effected by the parties in 1978 and submitted to the Tribunal in the context of these proceedings, as has been done in several international arbitrations, as discussed below

91. As regards the type of conclusions that may be drawn from this sort of evidence, we refer to the reasoning of the Iran–U.S. Claims Tribunal in the *AIG* case, where it is stated:

> 'From what has been stated above, it might be possible to draw some conclusions regarding the higher and the lower limits of the range within which the value of the company could reasonably be assumed to lie. But the limits are widely apart.

In order to determine the value within those limits, to which value the compensation should be related, the Tribunal will therefore have to make an approximation of that value, taking into account all relevant circumstances in the case.'

92. In the *Philips Petroleum* case, the same Tribunal found that, in deciding the price that a purchaser could be expected to have been willing to pay for the asset in question at the date the asset was taken, the Tribunal was required to exercise its own judgment, taking into account all relevant circumstances, including equitable considerations:

'The Tribunal recognizes that the determination of the fair market value of any assets inevitably requires the consideration of all relevant factors and the exercise of judgment.'
[. . .]
'In Starrett, . . . the Tribunal made various adjustments to the conclusions [of the Tribunal-appointed outside expert] and the resulting amounts. The need for such adjustments is understandable, as the determination of value by a tribunal must take into account all relevant circumstances, including equitable considerations.'

93. As discussed above, Costa Rica's valuation of Santa Elena in 1978 was approximately U.S. $1 900 000. Claimant's 1978 valuation was approximately U.S. $6 400 000.

94. The Tribunal will, consequently, take as a starting point these appraisals. It can safely be assumed that the actual and true fair market value of the Property was not higher than the price asked by the owners and not lower than the sum offered by the Government, i.e., that it was somewhere between these two figures. It can also safely be assumed that both of these appraisals took account of, and included, the 'potential for tourism development' of the Property, discussed above.

95. In the circumstances of this case, making the assessment that we have been invited to make and having considered the evidence submitted by the parties and the factors relevant to the value of the Santa Elena Property in 1978, the Tribunal has determined that the sum of U.S. $4 150 000 constitutes a reasonable and fair approximation of the value of the Property at the date of its taking.

d.ii   *Replacement value/comparable sales*

Yet another possible method of valuing the loss of the investment is to determine the amount necessary to replace the expropriated property. If claimant or host can prove what similar assets or equipment would have cost at the time of expropriation, it can submit a claim for calculating the fair market value based on these replacement or substitution costs.

The *Amoco International Finance* tribunal addressed the advantages and disadvantages of this method briefly:

> 257. In the same vein, another way of valuing an expropriated property is to use the replacement cost, which in the instant case was calculated by the Claimant as being about $110 million for the Khemco plant, and, therefore, $55 million for Amoco's share. The Claimant considered that such a method was inappropriate, since it is without relation to the earning power of the asset. For their part, the Respondents did not dispute the figure advanced by the other Party, but denied that replacement cost was relevant in the instant Case, since there is no question of the assets being reacquired. Such an objection manifestly confuses two issues. The intentions of the expropriated owner relating to the reinvestment of the amount it will receive as compensation for the expropriation of its asset is immaterial to the determination of the measure of the loss sustained.[99]

If a tribunal decides to consider such a method, its main effort will necessarily be in evaluating the relative strength of the parties' experts' submissions. The SEDCO arbitrators remarked candidly, '. . . the Tribunal cannot easily evaluate the substance of property appraisals, but it can evaluate the legal and factual sufficiency of the assumptions underlying appraisals'.[100]

e   *The truth about FMV?*

The various methods of valuation, as mentioned above, are legal instruments to perform what is not legal analysis. It is, in that way, unsatisfying. One tribunal's reflections on the usefulness of calculating the 'fair market value' (FMV) of an expropriated investment aptly captures this underlying frustration.

 CASE

Sistem Muhendislik v. Kyrgyz Republic[101]

> 154. The Tribunal is conscious of the desirability for conceptual clarity in valuing assets for the purposes of calculating compensation payable; and it is conscious of the criticism of 'triangulation' methods, which select a figure that lies somewhere in the middle ground of estimates put forward by the parties.
> 155. The Tribunal is also aware of the fact that all valuations in the absence of an

---

99 *Amoco v. Iran, supra* note 9.
100 *SEDCO, Inc. v. National Iranian Oil Co.*, Award No. 59-129-3, 10 Iran-U.S. Claims Tribunal Report 180, para. 74 (March 27, 1986).
101 *Sistema Muhendislik v. Kyrgyz Republic*, ICSID Case No. ARB(AF)/06/1, Award, paras. 154–6 (Sept. 9, 2009).

actual sale are estimates, and is mindful of the fact that the Tribunal has a legal duty to render an award under a process which the Respondent has freely agreed to establish and the Claimant has freely chosen to pursue, and to do so on the basis of the material that the parties have decided to put before it. That is, necessarily, an exercise in the art of the possible; and the Tribunal has sought to arrive at a rational and fair estimate, in accordance with the BIT, of the loss sustained by the Claimant rather than to engage in a search for the chimera of a sum that is a uniquely and indisputably correct determination of the value of what the Claimant lost. The Tribunal derives some comfort from Immanuel Kant's observation that 'Out of the crooked timber of humanity no straight thing was ever made.'

156. The Tribunal is obliged by the BIT to determine the 'real value of the expropriated investment. 'It has approached this task by asking first, which valuation method most closely corresponds to that standard of compensation, and second, whether there is adequate evidence to generate a valuation according to that method. If there is not adequate evidence to support a valuation based on the appropriate method, the Tribunal will have to proceed to a third stage and ask what rational and reasonable valuations can be derived from the available evidence.

 DISCUSSION NOTES

1 Customary law on compensation payments for wrongful acts requires interest to be paid on any awarded moneys (ASR Article 38). Most IIAs also specify that interest is to be paid on compensation for expropriations falling within the framework of the agreement (that is, legal expropriations) from the date of the expropriation until the date of payment. See, for example, Energy Charter Treaty, Article 13.1; NAFTA, Article 1110(4) and (5); German Model BIT, Article 5. If the host does not immediately pay the compensation, the interest payments can become significant. Sedelmayer's award of just over $8 million, for instance, is subject to 10% interest rates. Given that Russia's refusal to pay stems from its expropriations over 15 years ago, the interest is a substantial portion of its current debt to the investor.

2 Should a claimant's own contribution to the losses sustained through an illegal expropriation be taken into account in the damages valuation? The tribunal in *RosInvestCo v. Russia* addressed this issue as follows:

666. By Claimant's own admission, it is a company which specialises in 'purchasing shares at such moments of market distress, judging that the market has overreacted to transient events and has undervalued a company's underlying assets.' (para.6 C-I) The Tribunal finds it can accept Claimant's assertion that it made an investment at such a point in time when the market had in fact overreacted to transient events and the price of the shares was unjustifiably low, but that it cannot simply accept

Claimant's alleged optimistic expectations regarding the future development of the value of the investment.

667. While it is difficult to make an assessment of the 'true value' at the time of purchase, Respondent's contention that the market price of the shares reflected the likelihood of Yukos ceasing to exist as a viable company is plausible. Respondent has established, and Claimant's evidence supports that view, that the information available to the public and investors regarding the likely outcome of the bankruptcy proceedings, court proceedings and YNG auction was that Yukos would cease to exist as a viable company – irrespective of the legality or other aspects of those proceedings. Indeed, before Claimant's first and second purchases of shares, Yukos had itself announced it would likely enter bankruptcy before the end of 2004.

668. Claimant made a speculative investment in Yukos shares. The Tribunal must take this into account when awarding damages (if any).

669. Although the Tribunal might steer into dangerous territory by attempting to enter its own economic valuation into the findings of the respective economic experts' opinions contained in the Dow Reports and LECG Reports, nevertheless, the Tribunal finds that these Reports are detailed and clear enough to enable it to come to conclusions regarding the disputed valuation. The Tribunal finds Respondent's submissions regarding compensation to be more persuasive. The approach in the LECG Report (termed the 'but-for' approach in that report) does not sufficiently take into account the nature of Claimant's investment and that Claimant made a speculative investment consistent with the modus operandi of Claimant and Elliott Group.

670. Claimant admits that 'some of [its] investments turn out to be profitable, and some do not, and the investor may be presumed to understand the market risks when it makes the investment.' (para. 6 C-I) Having regard to this underlying nature of the investment, the Tribunal finds that any award of damages that rewards the speculation by Claimant with an amount based on an ex-post analysis would be unjust. The Tribunal cannot apply the most optimistic assessment of an investment and its return. Claimant is asking the Tribunal not only to realise and implement the Elliott Group's 'buy low and sell high' strategy, but to go further and apply a best-case approximation of today's value. The Tribunal considers the Dow Report correctly identifies that at the point in time at which Claimant purchased the legal title to the shares, the market had already taken into account the effect of the Russian Federation's measures and any possibility Yukos would (profitably) endure beyond the enforcement of those measures.[102]

---

102 *RosInvestCo v. Russia, supra* note 72.

3 How should tribunals determine the 'fair market value 'of a property for which there really is no market? Far from being restricted to transactions which used to take place in what were known as 'non-market economies ', there are many commercial activities that take place without a free exchange among numerous buyers and sellers. The *Amoco v. Iran*[103] tribunal highlighted the difficulties arising in their decision-making:

> For the purpose of valuing the compensation due in case of the lawful expropriation of an asset, market value, apparently, is the most commendable standard, since it is also the most objective and the most easily ascertained when a market exists for identical or similar assets, i.e., when such assets are the object of a continuous flow of free transactions. [. . .]
>
> Market value, on the other hand, is an ambiguous concept, to say the least (it might be more accurate to term it misleading), when an open market does not exist for the expropriated asset or for goods identical or comparable to it. A situation of this kind can be observed in the case of transactions of such a magnitude that they are relatively rare, always individualized, and prompted by special circumstances and motives, like transactions relating to large corporations the shares of which are not traded on stock exchanges. In such circumstances, referring to market value for the purpose of determining compensation in case of expropriation inevitably leads to a pyramid of hypotheses, since it is necessary to conjecture as to the price on which a hypothetical willing buyer and a hypothetical willing seller negotiating at arms length would eventually agree. Such a conjecture is more especially artificial as the owner of the expropriated asset usually is not a willing seller.
>
> The truth is that the absence of a market giving rise to the fixing of an objective market value compels recourse to alternative methods of valuation [. . .]. Their proponents inevitably contend that these methods permit a determination of 'full value,' the just price, an adequate or equitable value, and so on. None of these values can, however, legitimately be labelled 'market value.' Such a label is used as a magic word intended to encourage the belief that the value determined by a specific method is the value which must be accepted as the scientifically true one. Obviously, however, it is impossible to verify that had a free transaction taken place the price would have corresponded to this value. At the most, it is a question of probability, but it is hard to say, when one takes note of all the subjective conjectures incorporated into most of these methodologies, what is the degree of probability attained. The Tribunal is therefore of the view that the phrase 'market value' is of no help in the absence of regular transactions in a free market and can too easily be misleading. The choice between all the

---

103 Id. at, paras. 666–70.

available methods must rather be made in view of the purpose to be attained, in order to avoid arbitrary results and to arrive at an equitable compensation in conformity with the applicable legal standards. The use of several methods, when possible, is also commendable.

f   Timing

f.i   Legal expropriation

When establishing the value of an investor's property, the question of when the investment was expropriated is of great significance. For legal expropriation, the FMV calculation is generally taken as of the date of the expropriation. This is a common treaty specification to protect the investor against losses of value that might occur as a result of the change in ownership. If the treaty provisions usually also direct the tribunal to determine the value of the investment at the moment immediately preceding publication of the expropriation decision.

The calculations become more difficult, however, where the expropriation was 'creeping', or where several discrete governmental actions were taken over a period of time that had the final effect of depriving the investor of ownership. In such cases, the date of expropriation must be determined as part of the valuation process. The *Santa Elena v Costa Rica* tribunal addressed this issue.

 CASE

Compañía del Desarrollo de Santa Elena SA v. Costa Rica[104]

1) The Date as at Which the Property Must be Valued

76. As is well known, there is a wide spectrum of measures that a state may take in asserting control over property, extending from limited regulation of its use to a complete and formal deprivation of the owner's legal title. Likewise, the period of time involved in the process may vary – from an immediate and comprehensive taking to one that only gradually and by small steps reaches a condition in which it can be said that the owner has truly lost all the attributes of ownership. It is clear, however, that a measure or series of measures can still eventually amount to a taking, though the individual steps in the process do not formally purport to amount to a taking or to a transfer of title. What has to be identified is the extent

---

104 *Compañía del Desarrollo de Santa Elena SA v. Costa Rica*, *supra* note 98 (footnotes omitted).

to which the measures taken have deprived the owner of the normal control of his property. A decree which heralds a process of administrative and judicial consideration of the issue in a manner that effectively freezes or blights the possibility for the owner reasonably to exploit the economic potential of the property, can, if the process thus triggered is not carried out within a reasonable time, properly be identified as the actual act of taking.

77. There is ample authority for the proposition that a property has been expropriated when the effect of the measures taken by the state has been to deprive the owner of title, possession or access to the benefit and economic use of his property:

> '*A deprivation or taking of property may occur under international law through interference by a state in the use of that property or with the enjoyment of its benefits, even where legal title to the property is not affected.*
>
> *While assumption of control over property by a government does not automatically and immediately justify a conclusion that the property has been taken by the government, thus requiring compensation under international law, such a conclusion is warranted <u>whenever events demonstrate that the owner was</u> <u>deprived of</u> <u>fundamental rights of ownership and it appears that this deprivation is not merely</u> <u>ephemeral.</u> The intent of the government is less important than the effects of the measures on the owner, and the form of the measures of control or interference is less important than the reality of their impact.*' [Emphasis added.]

78. Stated differently, international law does not lay down any precise or automatic criterion, such as the date of the transfer of ownership or the date on which the expropriation has been 'consummated' by agreed or judicial determination of the amount of compensation or by payment of compensation. The expropriated property is to be evaluated as of the date on which the governmental 'interference' has deprived the owner of his rights or has made those rights practically useless. This is a matter of fact for the Tribunal to assess in the light of the circumstances of the case.

79. Claimant does not really contest this approach. The determination of the relevant date, so Claimant writes, '. . . may vary under different circumstances, thereby affecting the determination of the actual date of expropriation.'

80. Although the expropriation by the decree of 5 May 1978 was only the first step in a process of transferring the Property to the Government, it cannot reasonably be maintained, as Claimant seeks to do, that this Decree expressed no more than an 'intention' to expropriate or that, in 1978, the Government merely 'sought to expropriate'. In the circumstances of this case, the taking of the Property occurred as of 5 May 1978, the date of the 1978 Decree.

81. As of that date, the practical and economic use of the Property by the Claimant was irretrievably lost, notwithstanding that CDSE remained in possession of the Property. As of 5 May 1978, Claimant's ownership of Santa Elena was effectively blighted or sterilised because the Property could not, thereafter,

be used for the development purposes for which it was originally acquired (and which, at that time, were not excluded) nor did it possess any significant resale value.

82. As noted in the U.S. Senate Staff Report entitled 'Confiscated Property of American Citizens Overseas: Cases in Honduras, Costa Rica and Nicaragua':

> 'This odd situation has caused the owners of the land to lose a great deal of money because they are not allowed to develop the property as a profit-making, eco-tourism project, yet they are required to pay for the maintenance of the property . . .'

83. Since the Tribunal is of the view that the taking of the Property occurred on 5 May 1978, it is as of that date that the Property must be valued. There is no evidence that its value at that date was adversely affected by any prior belief or knowledge that it was about to be expropriated. Consequently, for the purpose of retrospectively attributing a value to the Property in 1978, the Tribunal has not had to consider later appraisals, such as the Government's 1993 Appraisal or those submitted by the parties in these proceedings.

84. The significance of identifying the date of taking lies in its bearing on the factors that may properly be taken into account in assessing the 'fair market value' of the Property—a value which, as noted, both sides are agreed must be the basis of the present Award. If the relevant date were the date of this Award, then the Tribunal would have to pay regard to the factors that would today be present to the mind of a potential purchaser. Of these, the most important would no doubt be the knowledge that the Government has adopted an environmental policy which would very likely exclude the kind of tourist, hotel and commercial development that the Claimant contemplated when it first acquired the Property. If, on the other hand, the relevant date is 5 May 1978, factors that arose thereafter—though not necessarily subsequent statements regarding facts that existed as of that date—must be disregarded.

f.ii   Illegal expropriation

Where the expropriation is illegal, the valuation date is most often calculated as of the date of the award.[105] If, however, the value of the company has declined between expropriation and award, this practice would not put the Claimant back into the position in which she would have been, had the illegal act never taken place. Thus, the *Yukos* tribunal declared that the wronged Claimant should be permitted to choose either of the two dates on which to base the compensation calculations. The arbitrators explained:

---

105 *ConocoPhilips Petrozuata v. Bolivarian Republic of Venezuela*, ICSID Case No. ARB/07/30, Decision on Jurisdiction and Merits, para. 343 (Sept. 3, 2013).

1765. Neither the text of Article 13 of the [Energy Charter Treaty as the applicable IIA] nor its *travaux* provide a definitive answer to the question of whether damages should be assessed as of the date of expropriation or the date of the award. The text of Article 13, after specifying the four conditions that must be met to render an expropriation lawful, provides that for such an expropriation, that is, for a lawful expropriation, damages shall be calculated as of the date of the taking. *A contrario*, the text of Article 13 may be read to import that damages for an unlawful taking need not be calculated as of the date of taking. It follows that this Tribunal is not required by the terms of the ECT to assess damages as of the time of the expropriation. Moreover, conflating the measure of damages for a lawful taking with the measure of damages for an unlawful taking is, on its face, an unconvincing option.

1766. In the view of the Tribunal, and in exercise of the latitude that the terms of Article 13 of the ECT afford it in this regard, the question of whether an expropriated investor is entitled to choose between a valuation as of the expropriation date and the date of an award is one best answered by considering which party should bear the risk and enjoy the benefits of unanticipated events leading to a change in the value of the expropriated asset between the time of the expropriatory actions and the rendering of an award. The Tribunal finds that the principles on the reparation for injury as expressed in the ILC Articles on State Responsibility are relevant in this regard. According to Article 35 of the ILC Articles, a State responsible for an illegal expropriation is in the first place obliged to make restitution by putting the injured party into the position that it would be in if the wrongful act had not taken place. This obligation of restitution applies as of the date when a decision is rendered. Only to the extent where it is not possible to make good the damage caused by restitution is the State under an obligation to compensate pursuant to Article 36 of the ILC Articles on State Responsibility.

1767. The consequences of the application of these principles (restitution as of the date of the decision, compensation for any damage not made good by restitution) for the calculation of damages in the event of illegal expropriation are twofold. First, investors must enjoy the benefits of unanticipated events that increase the value of an expropriated asset up to the date of the decision, because they have a right to compensation in lieu of their right to restitution of the expropriated asset *as of that date*. If the value of the asset increases, this also increases the value of the right to restitution and, accordingly, the right to compensation where restitution is not possible.

1768. Second, investors do not bear the risk of unanticipated events decreasing the value of an expropriated asset over that time period. While such events decrease the value of the right to restitution (and accordingly the right to compensation in lieu of restitution), they do not affect an investor's entitlement to compensation of the damage 'not made good by restitution' within the meaning of Article 36(1) of the ILC Articles on State Responsibility. If the asset could be returned to the investor on the date where a decision is rendered, but its value had decreased since the expropriation, the investor would be entitled to the difference in value, the reason being that in the absence of the expropriation the investor could have sold the asset at an earlier date at its previous higher value. The same analysis must also apply where the asset cannot be returned, allowing the investor to claim compensation in the amount of the asset's higher value.

1769. It follows for the several reasons stated above that in the event of an illegal expropriation an investor is entitled to choose between a valuation as of the expropriation date and as of the date of the award. The Tribunal finds support for this conclusion in the fact that this approach has been adopted by tribunals in a number of recent decisions dealing with illegal expropriation. [. . .].[106]

Note, however, that if the Claimant does choose the earlier point in time for calculating the value of the investment, it must be consistent with its further payment requests, such as those on interest rates. As the *Guarachi America and Rurelec* tribunal commented:

The illegality of the expropriation could, according to the authorities cited by Rurelec, justify shifting the effective date of valuation back to a date later than the actual date of the expropriation as a means to restore the Parties to the positions they would have held but for the unlawful expropriation. However, Rurelec has opted not to argue for the application of this principle in this case, presumably because its application would actually work to [its] disadvantage. Yet, at the same time Rurelec asks the Tribunal to use [the cost of capital] as at May 2010 as the applicable interest rate to compensate it as if it had remained invested in Bolivia throughout the pre-award period. Rurelec cannot shield itself from any negative changes to the fundamentals that make up the [cost of capital] during the post-May 2010 period and simultaneously introduce the May 2010 [figure] through the backdoor as the most appropriate interest rate.[107]

4.3.2 A closer look at the issue of causation

In any legal analysis of compensation, establishing the link between the action and the damage is critical to the plaintiff's claim for damages. Causation is an integral element of an investor's claims for compensation for an expropriation as well. The issue is rarely discussed explicitly because, in the typical expropriation case, causation is clear.

---

106 *Yukos Universal Limited (Isle of Man) v. The Russian Federation*, UNCITRAL, PCA Case No. AA 227, Final Award (July 18, 2014).

107 *Guaracachi America and Rurelec PLC v. The Plurinational State of Bolivia*, UNCITRAL, PCA Case No. 2011–17, Award, para. 614 (Jan. 31, 2014).

The *Biwater Gauff* tribunal, however, had a specific set of facts before it: by the time the state wrongfully expropriated the investment, the investor was already facing imminent bankruptcy. The majority of the tribunal determined that the expropriation of an investment that would have been disbanded could not have caused the claimant any financial harm. One arbitrator disagreed, however, pointing to the finding of the expropriation's illegality. He considered that the wrongfulness of the state's acts was in itself a cause of harm, but that the level, or 'quantum', of damages for such harm was zero. The exchange between the majority and the dissent highlights an interesting, but little commented-upon, issue of investment compensation.

 CASE

Biwater Gauff (Tanzania) Ltd. v. United Republic of Tanzania[108]

In 2003 Tanzania received international funding to repair the Dar es Salaam water and sewer system which had degenerated into an 'advanced stage of disrepair' and was a threat to the health of the city's population.[109] One condition of the grant of funds was that the government had to have a private operator manage and operate the system and to perform some of the repairs.[110]

After a series of procurement tender processes, the government awarded the project to Biwater International and Gauff, the only bidders, in 2002. Together the British and German entities formed a Tanzanian company named City Water. City Water concluded a set of contracts with DAWASA, the Tanzanian state company that had previously operated the water and sewage systems: a lease contract; a supply and installation contract; and a procurement contract. Under the terms of the lease contract, City Water was to perform Dawasa's job for ten years, providing its services at a set tariff. It was also to make some improvements to the infrastructure in addition to paying DAWASA rent. In return, DAWASA was obliged to let City Water have exclusive and uninterrupted access to the assets, not to allow other companies to provide water or sewage services, and to permit City Water to operate without interference. The supply and installation contract required City Water to make and install equipment such as pumps in the area of operation, while the procurement contract

---

108 *Biwater Gauff (Tanzania) Ltd. v. United Republic of Tanzania*, ICSID Case No. ARB/05/22, Award (July 24, 2008). Available at: http://italaw.com/documents/Biwaterreward.pdf; footnotes omitted.

109 Id. at 28, para. 106.

110 A second condition was for the operator to incorporate in Tanzania and ensure that a minority shareholder be a Tanzanian person.

stipulated that City Water would supply potable water meters. City Water also received a Certificate of Initiative which exempted them from VAT requirements.

From the beginning of its operations, City Water performed poorly. A consequence of numerous factors, the poorly prepared bid combined with inexperienced management and staff, lack of governance, and a client base that was unwilling to pay the mandated tariffs, the financial failure of City Water was foreseeable within the first two years.

The government of Tanzania and the people of Dar es Salaam were dissatisfied with City Water's failures, and, with elections coming up, the government capitalized on City Waters failure and announced the impending expropriation at a public rally. The government then withdrew the VAT exemption on City Water's purchases, occupied the facilities, and took over control of the company; then it deported City Water's staff.

City Water started arbitration for illegal expropriation and requested compensation for 'fair market value'. The tribunal made the following findings:

> 779. *Causation*: Compensation for any violation of the BIT, whether in the context of unlawful expropriation or the breach of any other treaty standard, will only be due if there is a sufficient causal link between the actual breach of the BIT and the loss sustained by BGT.
>
> 780. The requirement of causation is commonly considered in the context of compensation for non-expropriatory breaches of treaty, on the basis (i) that the measure of damages for expropriation is usually the subject of detailed regulation in the treaty itself, such that the application of any wider principles of international law is not needed, or (ii) that the element of causation is implicit in the initial determination that an expropriation has taken place.
>
> 781. As explained . . . above, the Arbitral Tribunal considers that an expropriation may take place by reason of a substantial interference with rights, even if no *economic* loss is caused thereby, or can be quantified. In such cases, non-pecuniary remedies (e.g. injunctive, declaratory or restitutionary relief) may still be appropriate. Whether any economic loss has in fact been caused by the 'taking' in question is a matter to be considered in the context of a claim for compensation, rather than being a necessary ingredient in the cause of action of unlawful expropriation itself.
>
> 782. It follows that the requirement of causation needs to be considered here with respect to each of BGT's claims for compensation, both for expropriation and non-expropriatory breaches of the treaty.
>
> 783. Article 31(2) of the ILC Articles defines 'injury' (for which a State is obliged to make reparation) as including:

'. . . any damage, whether material or moral, caused by the internationally wrongful act of a State.'

784. There is little guidance as a matter of international law on the precise test of causation to be applied (there being a number of different possible formulations). Accordingly, many international tribunals have had recourse to private law analyses in their application of this requirement, and a number of commentators have recommended this approach.

785. The requirement of causation comprises a number of different elements, including (*inter alia*) (a) a sufficient link between the wrongful act and the damage in question, and (b) a threshold beyond which damage, albeit linked to the wrongful act, is considered too indirect or remote. In his commentary on Article 31 of the ILC Articles, and drawing from a wide range of international decisions, Professor Crawford describes these elements as follows (with citations omitted):

'. . . Various terms are used to describe the link which must exist between the wrongful act and the injury in order for the obligation of reparation to arise. For example, reference may be made to losses "attributable [to the wrongful act] as a proximate cause", or to damage which is "too indirect, remote, and uncertain to be appraised", or to "any direct loss, damage, including environmental damage and the depletion of natural resources, or injury to foreign Governments, nationals and corporations as a result of" the wrongful act. This causality in fact is a necessary but not a sufficient condition of reparation. There is a further element, associated with the exclusion of injury that is too "remote" or "consequential" to be the subject of reparation. In some cases, the criterion of "directness" may be used, in others "foreseeability" or "proximity". But other factors may also be relevant: for example, whether State organs deliberately caused the harm in question, or whether the harm caused was within the ambit of the rule which was breached, having regard to the purpose of that rule. In other words, the requirement of a causal link is not necessarily the same in relation to every breach of an international obligation. In international as in national law, the question of remoteness of damage "is not a part of the law which can be satisfactorily solved by search for a single verbal formula". The notion of a sufficient causal link which is not too remote is embodied in the general requirement in article 31 that the injury should be in consequence of the wrongful act, but without the addition of any particular qualifying phrase.'

786. The key issue in this case is the factual link between the wrongful acts and the damage in question, as opposed to any issue as to remoteness or indirect loss. The Arbitral Tribunal notes in this regard the approach of the ICJ in the *ELSI* case. In that case, the ICJ held that the primary cause of the claimant's difficulties lay in its own mismanagement over a period of years, and not the act of requisition imposed

by the governmental authorities. In reaching this conclusion, the Court applied an 'underlying' or 'dominant' cause analysis. For example:

> '100. It is important in the consideration of so much detail, not to get the matter out of perspective: given an under-capitalized, consistently loss-making company, crippled by the need to service large loans, which company its stockholders had themselves decided not to finance further but to close and sell off because, as they were anxious to make clear to everybody concerned, the money was running out fast, it cannot be a matter of surprise if, several days after the date at which the management itself had predicted that the money would run out, the company should be considered to have been actually or virtually in a state of insolvency for the purpose of Italian bankruptcy law.
>
> 101. . . . . There were several causes acting together that led to the disaster to ELSI. No doubt the effects of the requisition might have been one of the factors involved. But the underlying cause was ELSI's headlong course towards insolvency; which state of affairs it seems to have attained even prior to the requisition.'

787. The Arbitral Tribunal considers that in order to succeed in its claims for compensation, BGT has to prove that the value of its investment was diminished or eliminated, and that the actions BGT complains of were the actual and proximate cause of such diminution in, or elimination of, value.

788. In applying these principles to this case, it is convenient to summarise the position with respect to BGT's investment (a) as at 12 May 2005, being the date immediately prior to the first act of the Republic which the Arbitral Tribunal has found to be in breach of the BIT, and (b) as at 1 June 2005, being the date on which BGT states its investment was expropriated, and the relevant date for the valuation of its damages claim.

789. *Position as at 12 May 2005*: As set out earlier in this Award, serious problems were encountered in the performance of the Lease Contract from the very start. In particular (and in summary):

(a)   BGT's bid was poorly prepared.

(b)   BGT (and City Water) did not take the benefit of the EMP – notwithstanding the fact that this was an available method for re-calibrating base figures, and thereby addressing many of the data inconsistencies for which complaint was made.

(c)   As a result of the poor bid, coupled with numerous management and implementation difficulties, BGT (and City Water) did not generate the income which had been foreseen, and accordingly the project quickly encountered substantial difficulties.

(d)   The position was soon reached where it was clear that City Water simply could not continue without a fundamental renegotiation of the contract.

(e)   This renegotiation took place, but failed. As had been announced by DAWASA at the beginning of the renegotiation process, this failure, in turn, necessarily implied the termination of the Lease Contract.

790. As noted in the Castalia Report, and as emphasised by the Republic, by 12 May 2005, City Water had shareholders' equity of less than negative USD 8 000 000. It was not paying its bills and was subject to winding up at the instance of any of its creditors. In particular, it was withholding the Lessor Tariff, the FTNDWSC Tariff, and the Rental Fee. As set out earlier, BGT had repeatedly said City Water was not financially viable under the status quo; and joint financial projections showed that City Water would suffer significant operating losses going forward.

791. By the beginning of May 2005, and *before* the events that began on 13 May 2005, the normal contractual termination process was underway, and in the Arbitral Tribunal's view, in all the circumstances, termination of the Lease Contract was inevitable and was going to materialise within a matter of weeks – quite apart from the events that then occurred as of 13 May 2005.

792. *Position as at 1 June 2005*: In the Arbitral Tribunal's view, by 1 June 2005, being the date BGT states its investment was expropriated by the Republic, the said investment was of no economic value. This, indeed, had been the position since well before this date, and well before 13 May 2005.

793. In assessing value for the purposes of a damages claim, the Arbitral Tribunal considers that the appropriate method in the present case is the Discounted Cash Flow method (which is the method used in most BIT cases). Contrary to BGT's case, the Arbitral Tribunal does not consider that the Costs – or Net Investment – method is appropriate.

794. Indeed, the application of the Costs / Net Investment method by Grant Thornton consists of claiming a guaranteed return of 20% or 25% on every conceivable City Water–related expenditure, which has no justification. Further, as a testament to the inappropriateness of the method, the Grant Thornton calculations lead to a conclusion that 51% of City Water was worth US$20 million as of 1 June 2005, the date the expropriation took place. On any view, this is completely inconsistent not only with the relevant evidence, but also with BGT's repeated statements at the time, and City Water's own accounts.

795. In the Arbitral Tribunal's view, the correct approach to valuation here is that set out in the Castalia Report. The resounding conclusion (as summarised by the Respondent) is that City Water had no economic value on 1 June 2005; that as of that date, BGT was not willing to spend another shilling to keep City Water from collapsing and no rational buyer with reasonable knowledge of the relevant facts would have spent a shilling to buy it; that City Water had total liabilities in the

amount of Tsh 9.6 billion more than its total assets, operating losses of Tsh 15.6 billion in two years of operations and projected operating losses averaging Tsh 400 million per month for the next four years.

796. Moreover, City Water's single source of operating profits, the Lease Contract, was about to be terminated.

797. Consequently, the 'fair market value' of City Water at the date of the expropriation, 1 June 2005, was nil.

798. *Causation*: Applying the principles elaborated earlier, the Arbitral Tribunal concludes in all the circumstances that the actual, proximate or direct causes of the loss and damage for which BGT now seeks compensation were acts and omissions that had already occurred by 12 May 2005. In other words, none of the Republic's violations of the BIT between 13 May 2005 and 1 June 2005 in fact caused the loss and damage in question, or broke the chain of causation that was already in place.

799. As at the 1 June 2005, the only 'investment' which was the subject of the Republic's expropriation comprised contractual termination rights, which themselves were of no value. The Republic, in effect, interfered with and accelerated the contractual termination process, but by that stage termination was inevitable in any event, and BGT has not established that, had these acts not taken place, the fair market value of City Water as of 1 June 2005 would have raised above zero. As for the specific violations of the BIT:

(a) *Public announcement on behalf of the Republic of the termination of the Lease Contract on 13 May 2005*: Minister Lowassa's announcement on 13 May 2005 interfered with the contractual termination process, but that process was already underway, and the harm which resulted and for which BGT now seeks compensation was caused by the termination itself, and not by the announcement. The acceleration of the termination did not cause any separate compensable loss, given the absence of any value in the project by that time. Further, as noted earlier, there is no clear evidence of a resultant effect on the customers', suppliers' and employees' of City Water's willingness to, respectively, pay bills, deliver supplies or work effectively. Although it is not unimaginable that such effects could have occurred, there is nothing to indicate that they in fact did.

(b) *The subsequent address to City Water staff on 17 May*: The same points arise with respect to this event. BGT has not shown that any separate economic harm was caused by this event. There is no evidence, for example, that the address had any material effect on City Water's cash receipts or the scale of City Water's operating losses, or produced adverse economic effects that were not already existent or inevitable at that stage.

(c) *The withdrawal of the VAT certificate by the TRA on 24 May*: There is no evidence that the withdrawal of the VAT certificate on 24 May 2005 had any material effect on the value of BGT's 51% shareholding, in particular given that City Water was already incapable of paying its creditors by that stage and was about to go out of business. No other adverse effects (which were not already existent or inevitable) have been shown.

(d) *The seizing of the assets of City Water, the immediate installation of DAWASCO, and the deportation of City Water's management on 1 June 2005*: Had the normal contractual termination mechanism been allowed to take its course, City Water would have been replaced by DAWASCO on about 24 June 2005. By reason of the Republic's actions, this occurred instead on 1 June 2005. However, the investment that was seized early was of no economic value. Indeed, as the Republic pointed out, the economic effect of the Republic's actions was to save City Water from losing approximately Tsh 175 million per week or Tsh 525 million over the three-week period in question.

[...]

801. *The Distinction Between Causation and Quantum*: It has been suggested that the above analysis wrongly elides the issues of 'causation' and 'damages', and that the proper analysis should be as follows:

(a) that the Republic's wrongful acts (e.g. seizure of City Water's business and premises) *caused injury* to City Water (by depriving it prematurely of the use and enjoyment of its property); but that

(b) as a matter of evidence, BGT failed to prove that there was any monetary value associated with the injury that it suffered, or in other words, the monetary value of the injury was zero.

802. On this basis, it is said that BGT's claim fails as a matter of quantum, but not causation.

803. The majority of the Tribunal considers both approaches tenable. One reason for preferring an analysis based on 'causation', however, is the difficulty in concluding that the Republic's wrongful acts in fact 'caused injury' to City Water, as set out in paragraph 798(a) above. In this regard, some meaning must be given to the concept of 'injury'. In particular, 'causing injury' must mean more than simply the wrongful act itself (e.g. an expropriation, or unfair or inequitable treatment), otherwise the element of causation would have to be taken as present in every case, rather than being a separate enquiry.

804. It is therefore insufficient to assert that simply because there has been a 'taking', or unfair or inequitable conduct, there must necessarily have been an 'injury' caused such as to ground a claim for compensation. Whether or not each wrongful act by the Republic 'caused injury' such as to ground a claim for compensation must be analysed in terms of each specific 'injury' for which BGT has in fact claimed damages.

805. As set out earlier, the conclusions on causation reached by the majority of the Tribunal are based on the lack of linkage between each of the wrongful acts of

the Republic, and each of the actual, specific heads of loss and damage for which BGT has articulated a claim for compensation. In other words, the actual loss and damage for which BGT has claimed – however it is quantified – is attributable to other factors.

806. Ultimately, however, this is a difference in analysis, not result. Whichever approach is adopted, the conclusion is the same, namely, that BGT has failed to demonstrate compensable monetary damages or loss in this case.

3. Conclusions

807. Given that none of the Republic's violations of the BIT caused the loss and damage for which BGT now claims compensation, it follows that each of BGT's claims for damages must be dismissed, and that the only appropriate remedies for the Republic's conduct can be declaratory in nature.

808. The Tribunal notes that no claim has ever been made (or quantified) for so-called 'moral' damages, and no argument was advanced on this issue by any party at any stage. Even if any such claim had been advanced, the circumstances of this case, and in particular BGT's own conduct, would render any such award inappropriate.

 CASE

Biwater Gauff (Tanzania) Ltd. v. United Republic of Tanzania[111]

III. Causation and Valuation

15. [. . .] I am also unable to join in the Tribunal's apparent conclusion that BGT is entitled to no financial compensation on grounds of 'causation'. . . . The Tribunal concludes that 'the actual, proximate or direct causes of the loss and damage for which BGT now seeks compensation were acts and omissions that had already occurred by 12 May 2005'. . . . The Tribunal also reasons that 'the Republic, in effect, interfered with and accelerated the contractual termination process, but by that stage [i.e., 1 June 2005] termination was inevitable in any event' . . . Furthermore, the Tribunal concludes that there is a 'lack of linkage between each of the wrongful acts of the Republic and each of the actual, specific heads of loss and damage for which BGT has articulated a claim for compensation'. . . .

16. In my view, this analysis confuses issues of causation, on the one hand, and quantification or quantum of damages, on the other; this analytical confusion is

111 *Biwater Gauff (Tanzania) Ltd. v. United Republic of Tanzania*, ICSID Case No. ARB/05/22, Concurring/ Dissenting Opinion by Gary Born (July 18, 2008). Available at: http://italaw.com/documents/Biwater-concurringanddissentingopinion.pdf; footnotes omitted.

ultimately not decisive to the specific outcome in the present case, but it could well be in future cases and I am therefore unable to join it.

17. Preliminarily, it should be clear that the Republic's expropriatory, unfair and inequitable and other wrongful acts caused injury to BGT. Specifically, it is beyond debate that the Republic wrongfully seized City Water's business, premises and assets at a point in time (I June 2005) at which the Republic had no right . . . to do so. That wrongful seizure clearly caused injury to City Water by depriving it prematurely of the use and enjoyment of its property: whether measured in weeks (to 24 June 2005, as the Tribunal concludes) or months (some longer period which would have obtained in reasonable dealings between contracting parties conducting themselves in good faith) or years (the remaining lease term under the Lease Contract), City Water was wrongfully evicted from its leased premises, and wrongfully denied the use of its assets, its management and its staff, for some ascertainable period of time.

18. In this respect alone, in my view, the Republic's actions clearly caused injury to BGT, by prematurely taking City Water's property and resources from it, and it is mistaken therefore to conclude, as the Tribunal does, that BGT's claims fail on the grounds of causation. Rather, the proper question is what quantum of loss or monetary value to attribute to the injury that the Republic caused to BGT.

19. Despite my disagreement with its analysis, I concur in the Tribunal's conclusions that BGT has failed to demonstrate, on the current record, compensable and quantifiable monetary damages or loss. That is because the evidence fails to show that that there was any monetary value associated with the injury that BGT suffered.

20. BGT's request for relief broadly sought all damages caused by the Republic's wrongful actions:. . . . That request is not limited to specific sums or items of damages, but instead seeks recovery for all injury flowing from the Republic's wrongful actions. In turn, this requires determining the value of City Water's expropriated property (and, in particular, the value of City Water's remaining leasehold under the Lease Contract and other properties associated with its business).

21. The answer to this question appears, on the record in these proceedings, to be that no monetary value can be associated with City Water's remaining leasehold and other properties . . . . Put differently, although the Republic caused BGT injury, including by expropriating its property and prematurely terminating the contractual relations between City Water and DAWASA, the property that the Republic wrongfully seized had no quantifiable monetary value.

22. Specifically, the evidence showed that City Water was persistently losing money under the Lease Contract and that, even with significant contractually-permitted modifications . . ., City Water would continue to lose money both in the short term and over the life of the Lease Contract. Only with a fundamental renegotiation of the Lease Contract, and its economic terms, would it have been possible for City

Water to have become a sustainable and profitable enterprise; nothing entitled City Water to such a fundamental renegotiation. . . .

Accordingly, whatever the remaining term of the Lease Contract (i.e., three weeks or a number of years) the evidence showed that City Water's business simply did not have a quantifiable positive monetary value. Thus, although the Republic wrongfully took City Water's remaining leasehold and the associated assets, thereby causing BGT injury, the monetary value of the commercial injury to BGT was zero.

23. The distinction between causation and quantification of injury is not, as the Tribunal appears to suggest, an academic one. Importantly, had City Water been earning a profit, or had the Lease Contract had a positive value, then BGT would have been entitled to a monetary award of damages. In that case, the fact that the 'termination of the Lease Contract was inevitable and was going to materialise within a matter of weeks' (Award, para. 791) would be irrelevant. Even if one assumed that the Lease Contract would be terminated (and putting aside questions of the lawfulness of termination (see below)), the premature termination of a profitable lease or premature cessation of a profitable business would cause quantifiable monetary damage. Issues would arise in valuing that damage, but these would concern the matter of attributing a value to a prescribed period of time. It is for this reason that it is inaccurate to characterize BGT's claims for monetary damages as failing for lack of causation; rather, BGT's monetary damages claims fail because the injury that was caused to it had no quantifiable monetary value.

24. This analysis is important as a conceptual matter, and also consistent with more general principles of international law. The International Law Commission's Articles on Responsibility of States for Internationally Wrongful Acts (ILC Articles) make clear that a state which commits an internationally wrongful act, such as an expropriation, is under a number of obligations. These include the obligation to cease the wrongful act and the 'obligation to make full reparation for the injury caused by the internationally wrongful act.' In turn, and importantly, Article 31(2) provides that 'injury includes any damage, whether material or moral, caused by the internationally wrongful act of a State', while Article 36(1) provides that a State that commits an internationally wrongful act 'is under an obligation to compensate for the damage caused thereby, insofar as such damage is not made good by restitution.'

25. Commentary to the ILC Articles explains that 'injury' includes any material or moral damage 'and that the formulation is intended as inclusive, covering both material and moral damage broadly understood'. In particular: 'there is no general requirement, over and above any requirements laid down by the relevant primary obligation, that a State should have suffered material harm or damage before it can seek reparation for a breach. The existence of actual damage will be highly relevant

to the form and quantum of reparation. But there is no general requirement of material harm or damage for a State to be entitled to some form of reparation.'

26. The structure of these provisions makes clear that an internationally wrongful act results in an obligation to make reparation for 'injury', which includes, but is not limited to, an obligation to 'compensate for damage'. An injury can very readily include matters not entailing monetary damage, and require relief not limited to monetary compensation for damage. Specifically, a state's expropriation or denial of fair and equitable treatment causes injury to the investor by depriving it of property or procedural or legal rights. The fact that this injury does not entail monetary damage in no way implies that there was no injury; on the contrary, an injury can very readily exist even without monetary damage.

27. Thus, and importantly, the fact that BGT suffered injury that entailed no quantifiable monetary value does not in any way contradict the fact that the Republic's wrongful expropriation caused BGT injury. Rather, as the ILC's Articles and accompanying commentary make clear, injury is distinguishable from the form and quantum of damage. Here, the Republic caused BGT injury through the premature and wrongful expropriation of its property—regardless whether that injury had a quantifiable monetary value. Specifically, as noted above, the Republic's action deprived BGT of the use of its property and leasehold rights for at least some specified period of time, and of its rights to be treated fairly and equitably, regardless of the monetary value of those rights.

28. The Tribunal reasons that 'causing injury must mean more than simply the wrongful act itself' (Award, para. 803). That is correct, but the essential point is that injury need not have a quantifiable monetary value: here, as stated, the injury is the premature taking of BGT's property and the attendant deprivation of the use of that property.

29. The Tribunal also suggests that there is a 'lack of linkage between each of the wrongful acts of the Republic and each of the actual, specific heads of loss and damage for which BGT has articulated a claim for compensation.' (Award, para. 805) That implies that BGT's claim was limited to only specific, precisely-quantified amounts of loss, which is incorrect. Although BGT requested precisely quantified amounts (i.e. 'damages in the range of US$19 059 205 to US$20 158 775' Claimant's Memorial, para. 275(6)(b)) it separately, and naturally, more generally requested compensation for all damages caused by the Republic's actions: again, 'the financial equivalent of full reparation for the unlawful expropriation of BGT's investment' and 'compensation for the expropriation of BGT's investment in accordance with Article 5 of the Treaty.' (. . .). Importantly, the reason that BGT's general request for reparations is to be denied is that the evidence showed that the value of City Water's business and remaining leasehold, however calculated, was zero. That is not an absence of causation of injury but a matter of valuation and quantum of damage.

30. Finally, although the negative long-term value of City Water's business makes it unnecessary to decide the issue in this case, if City Water's business would have been profitable over the life of the Lease Contract, even if unprofitable in the short-term, then the Tribunal would have been required to consider, for the purposes of this arbitration, the contractual entitlement of City Water to continuation of the Lease Contract on either new or different terms. In turn, that would have raised questions regarding the scope of the Tribunal's jurisdiction to consider and decide contractual issues and the relevance (if any) of the UNCITRAL Award made pursuant to the Lease Contract. In this regard, it would not be sufficient to conclude, as the Tribunal does, that 'termination of the Lease Contract was inevitable' (. . .); rather, the decisive consideration would have been whether 'lawful termination of the Lease Contract' would have occurred.

31. Indeed, the conclusion that the Lease Contract would inevitably have been terminated is, taken alone, neither relevant to the proper outcome in this case nor a conclusion, given the issues presented to this Tribunal, that can properly be reached. Rather, the decisive point is that, whether or not it was terminated, the Lease Contract did not provide City Water and its business with a positive financial value.

IV. Costs and related issues

32. Fourth, I am unable to join in the Tribunal's decision only to grant declaratory relief. In circumstances where a State deliberately conducts itself in a manner it knows at the time to be wrongful, disregarding the basic legal rights and protections of private parties, it is at best anomalous for a tribunal to grant no affirmative relief. It is ancient law that there is no right without a remedy (*Ubi jus ibi remedium*) and that adage applies here no less than elsewhere. Whether denominated as moral damages (as some tribunals have done, but which has not been specifically requested here), recognized by way of a costs award (as other tribunals have done), or otherwise, it better advances the objectives of bilateral investment treaties and the ICSID Convention to require a measure of tangible reparations for violation of internationally-protected rights.

33. Here, while BGT did not demonstrate a quantifiable monetary loss, it did demonstrate an unacceptable breach of fundamental international rights and protections. In my view, that breach demands a remedy beyond merely declaring it a violation of the relevant BIT. The Republic's conduct caused moral damages to BGT, as well as the legal costs inevitable, given the Republic's refusal to acknowledge in any fashion the effects and nature of its conduct, in BGT obtaining international recognition of the violation of its rights. In these circumstances, I am unable to join in a decision granting only declaratory relief and would instead make an award of costs in favor of BGT.

V. Conclusion

34. For these reasons, I am unable to join the Award and must with all due respect issue this concurring and dissenting opinion.

Question to an expert: Dimitrios Ioannidis

Dimitrios Ioannidis practices primarily in the areas of international business transactions, civil litigation in both state and federal, trial and appellate courts in Massachusetts. He has worked on various high profile cases providing litigation intelligence gathering, corporate investigations, asset recovery, due diligence and global business intelligence through Boston, New York, London, Turkey, Greece and Cyprus. Mr. Ioannidis has extensive due diligence experience and has completed investigations for large financial institutions; was a consultant to US security firms on projects including the 2004 Olympic Games and a bid with the US State Department; and was an expert on several cases, including a case for the US Attorney's office in Boston and a large UK banking institution.

Would a decision to value the expropriated property as of the date of judgment lead to slower resolution of the dispute?

The decision to value expropriated property is based on an initial finding that an expropriation had indeed taken place. Thus, an arbitrator(s) must find that there was some governmental conduct that amounts to an expropriation, for which damages may be due. In the context of this analysis, a determination must also be made as to the time of the expropriation or the time the vested or other rights of the investor have been taken away, or reduced. It is also possible that an expropriation action may have a time component where the rights or the interests of the investor are affected over a period of time, making the determination of the precise date of expropriation somewhat unsettled. Even in such cases, the damages to the investor generally begin to accrue at the time of the effective date of the expropriation.

Once a finding of expropriation is made, the arbitrator(s) must then proceed to the determination of damages, which is a calculation of various components, such as diminishing property values, profits, future earnings etc. The deprivation of the rights or interests of the investor is, therefore, the basis for calculations and the only fair and just compensation of damages. With respect to property values, the arbitrator(s) must attempt to measure the extent of the damages and utilize most likely, appraisals or other methods or evaluation, so that in the end, the arbitration award is based on principles of fairness and justice. Thus, any measure of damages that does not begin to accrue from the moment of the deprivation of rights or interests fails to address the expectations of the parties as those may be established in the contractual arrangements or governmental policies.

In the context of valuations of property as of the date of judgment, the arbitrator(s) will face several dilemmas in determining a fair measure of damages. Unless there is an express agreement by the parties to use the judgment date, any calculations of damages under this approach will not reconcile the wrongful conduct with the deprivation of rights or interests and subsequent harm. The failure to account for even a small amount of compensatory damages under this approach will render the entire arbitration process subject to question

QUESTION TO AN EXPERT: DIMITRIOS IOANNIDIS *(continued)*

and challenge. Of significance are also possible intervening causes that may be unrelated to the parties and beyond their control, such as economic, social or political. In most cases, the valuation as of the date of judgment will either undervalue or overvalue property since it is not tied to the wrongful conduct that resulted in the deprivation of rights or interests, with an unpredictability factor that has nothing to do with the expectations of the parties at the time they entered into their contractual or business ventures.

The length of the arbitration process is indeed an issue and valuations as of the date of judgment may make it easier for arbitrator(s) to calculate awards since they do not have to go back in time to determine values. Consequently, the valuations may be easier to perform which arguably, could shorten the timetable for completion of the arbitration. However, retrospective valuations are common and reliable and provide a measure of damages that is fair and accurate as it is derived from the deprivation of the rights or interests of the investor. A valuation as of the date of judgment does not accomplish that principle despite any savings of time in the completion of the process.

5

Standards of host state behaviour

In the last chapter we looked at expropriation, both direct and indirect. While protection of the investor from uncompensated expropriations is clearly one of the central aims of investment law, there are a number of other obligations a state has toward the foreign investor. Some of these standards can be considered customary international law, some are treaty-based. The investor can invoke any of them, however, as the basis of a cause of action.

This chapter will examine several of the protection standards found in most IIAs. First, we look at the international minimum standards: non-arbitrariness, non-discrimination, and the full protection and security (FPS) obligation. Second, we then turn to the frequently litigated treaty obligation of fair and equitable treatment (FET).

5.1 Background: the idea of minimum standards

As mentioned in the introductory chapter of this book, from the beginning of the nineteenth century until the second decade of the twentieth century, foreign investors could be reasonably secure in relying on states' national treatment obligations for protection of their property. Constitutional protections of the safety of the individual and of private property were widespread. Combined with national treatment obligations in bilateral treaties, these legal protections sufficed to ensure foreigners rights to compensation for a government's injuries to themselves or for state takings of their property wherever they might be located.

The Bolshevik success in the Russian Revolution ended this universal investor/investment protection security. Refusing to acknowledge the right of its own citizens to property, the Soviet government effectively removed the right of foreigners to property protection as well.[1] National treatment now

---

1 Konstitutsiia RSFSR (1918) [Konst. RSFSR] [RSFSR Constitution] art. I, Chapter 2, para. 3 (abolished all private property in land, and all land was declared to be national property) (art. I, Ch. 2, para. 3).

meant only that: the foreigner would be treated as a national, whether or not the 'treatment' included rights to property.

The issue of treatment standards quickly became contentious. In the 1920s, when the Mexican revolutionary government declared its intention to adhere to a strict view of national treatment, the United States objected. The US government called for the recognition of an international standard of treatment for foreign investors that would ensure a minimum of protection independent of the protections offered to the host state's nationals. While customary international law on minimum standards of treatment of aliens existed to ensure persons certain protections, a claim for minimum standards of treatment of foreign-owned property was a different matter. In the context of expropriations by the Mexican government, the United States pressed for a further development of customary international law to extend minimum standards to all areas of the host state's treatment of investment. In one exchange, US Secretary of State Cordell Hull called on Mexico to honour its international legal obligations: 'when aliens are admitted into a country the country is obligated to accord them that degree of protection of life and property consistent with the standards of justice recognized by the law of nations'.[2]

The wide recognition of basic human rights has defined the existence of minimum standards of protection due foreign individuals.[3] Whether states are under a duty to protect foreigners' property up to some minimum standard independent of their duties under national law, is still questionable. However, the existence of standards of investment protection in international investment agreements makes the 'customary or not' question less relevant than it was in the 1930s: the treaty standards are clearly host state obligations.

Still, while the parties have agreed (via specific references) to the standards of treatment they will afford the investor, the exact level of protection owed often depends on an unspecified content of the standard. Thus, tribunals

---

2 Green Hackworth, 3 Digest of International Law 659–60 (1942).

3 The concept of a 'minimum core obligations' of a state toward individuals within its jurisdiction has been widely discussed in the context of economic, social, and cultural rights. *See* UN Committee on Economic, Social and Cultural Rights (CESCR), *General Comment No. 3: The Nature of States Parties' Obligations (Art. 2, Para. 1, of the Covenant)*, 14 December 1990, E/1991/23. In the context of civil and political rights, Article 4 of the Covenant on Civil and Political Rights makes clear that derogation from the protected rights is at best strictly limited, and for some rights completely prohibited. *See also* UN Committee on Civil and Political Rights (CCPR), *General Comment No. 29: States of Emergency (Article 4)*, 31 August 2001, CCPR/C/21/Rev.1/Add.11.

may have to revert to a determination of what the 'international minimum standard' would require in order to apply a treaty provision.

Currently, there are several standards found so widely in IIAs as well as other areas of international law that one can consider them 'the least' a state must do with regards to its treatment of foreign investments within its jurisdiction. Four of the most widely accepted minimum standards are: non-arbitrariness in regulation; reasonableness in regulatory oversight; non-discriminatory treatment; and the full protection and security of the investment and the investor.

5.2 Non-arbitrariness

An arbitrary action is one that is based on the will of the actor rather than on a rational application of principle to facts.[4] Antithetical to a system pursuing decision-making based on reasoned analysis, the principle of non-arbitrariness is fundamental to all law—international and domestic— independent of the subject matter of the law it covers. The obligation of non-arbitrariness' relevance to investment law, then, derives from its basic character of providing foreign investors with protection against state actions that are outside of the realm of legal acceptability.

As a general principle of international law, rules prohibiting arbitrariness would not need explicit mention in a treaty to be binding. Nevertheless, they appear frequently in provisions on treatment of investments.[5] The legal questions surrounding them centre on how to define the content of arbitrariness and determining in specific cases whether the state acted in an arbitrary fashion.

5.2.1 Content of the arbitrariness standard

While a general definition of arbitrariness highlights its non-rational, or disconnection, between the law and the facts at issue, a more exact notion of what rational state action is must be determined before a tribunal can investigate whether a particular action was non-arbitrary. Is all unlawful action arbitrary? Is bad faith application of laws arbitrary? The International Court

---

4 *See* Black's Law Dictionary 119 (ninth edn, 2009) (defining arbitrary as 'depending on individual discretion' or 'determined by a judge rather than by fixed rules, procedures, or law'); as specifically regarding judicial decisions, *see id.* ('founded on prejudice or preference rather than on reason or fact').

5 Often a single provision will combine the obligations of non-arbitrariness with non-discrimination.

of Justice set out the current majority view of the level of state misconduct that would be necessary for a finding of arbitrariness in the *ELSI* case.

 CASE

Elettronica Sicula SpA (ELSI) (United States of America v. Italy)[6]

Two US companies, Raytheon Company (Raytheon) and the Machlett Laboratories Incorporated (Machlett) established and incorporated Elettronica Sicula SpA (ELSI) in Palermo, Italy. Employing 900 employees, ELSI was a major economic force in the city.

Between 1964 and 1966, ELSI lost money. In 1968, having failed to make ELSI self-sufficient or to find an Italian partner for the company, Raytheon and Machlett decided to close the company.

In response to this news, Italian officials pressed ELSI to continue its production. In April 1968, the Mayor of Palermo issued an immediately effective order that requisitioned ELSI's plant and related assets for six months. Following this order, ELSI filed a bankruptcy petition arguing that the requisition would make it impossible for the corporation to dispose of its liquid funds and that, therefore, it could not make the payments that were due.

In 1987, the US instituted proceedings against Italy before the International Court of Justice based on the 1948 Treaty of Friendship, Commerce and Navigation and its Supplementary Agreement, claiming that the Italian authorities had acted arbitrarily by requisitioning the factory. Article I of the Supplementary Agreement provided:

> The nationals, corporations and associations of either High Contracting Party shall not be subjected to arbitrary or discriminatory measures within the territories of the other High Contracting Party resulting particularly in: *(a)* preventing their effective control and management of enterprises which they have been permitted to establish or acquire therein; or, *(b)* impairing their other legally acquired rights and interests in such enterprises or in the investments which they have made . . .

---

6 Elettronica Sicula SpA (ELSI) (*United States of America v. Italy*), Judgment, 1989 ICJ 15 (July 20) [hereinafter '*ELSI* case'] (quoted at *Asian Agriculture Products Limited v. Democratic Socialist Republic of Sri Lanka*, ICSID Case No. ARB/87/3, Final Award, para. 49 (June 27, 1990), 6 ICSID Rev.–FILJ 526 (1991) [*AAPL v. Sri Lanka*]).

The ICJ analysed the principle of non-arbitrariness as found in that provision. Note the emphasis placed on distinguishing the international concept of arbitrariness with domestic legal concepts of arbitrariness:

123. In order to show that the requisition order was an 'arbitrary' act in the sense of the Supplementary Agreement to the FCN Treaty, the Applicant has relied (*inter alia*) upon the status of that order in Italian law. It contends that the requisition 'was precisely the sort of arbitrary action which was prohibited' by Article I of the Supplementary Agreement, in that 'under both the Treaty and Italian law, the requisition was unreasonable and improperly motivated'; it was 'found to be illegal under Italian domestic law for precisely this reason'. Relying on its own English translation of the decision of the Prefect of Palermo of 22 August 1969, the Applicant concludes that the Prefect found that the order was 'destitute of any juridical cause which may justify it or make it enforceable' . . . .

124. [I]t must be borne in mind that the fact that an act of a public authority may have been unlawful in municipal law does not necessarily mean that that act was unlawful in international law, as a breach of treaty or otherwise. A finding of the local courts that an act was unlawful may well be relevant to an argument that it was also arbitrary; but by itself, and without more, unlawfulness cannot be said to amount to arbitrariness. It would be absurd if measures later quashed by higher authority or a superior court could, for that reason, be said to have been arbitrary in the sense of international law. To identify arbitrariness with mere unlawfulness would be to deprive it of any useful meaning in its own right. Nor does it follow from a finding by a municipal court that an act was unjustified, or unreasonable, or arbitrary, that that act is necessarily to be classed as arbitrary in international law, though the qualification given to the impugned act by a municipal authority may be a valuable indication.

125. The principal passage from the decision of the Prefect which is relevant here has already been quoted (. . .), but it is convenient to set it out again here:

[. . .]

> 'There is no doubt that, even though, from the purely theoretical standpoint, the conditions of grave public necessity and of unforeseen urgency warranting adoption of the measure may be considered to exist in the case in point, the intended purpose of the requisition could not in practice be achieved by the order itself, since in fact there was no resumption of the company's activity following the requisition, nor could there have been such resumption. The order therefore lacks, generically, the juridical cause which might justify it and make it operative.'

126. In support of this conclusion, the Prefect explained that the Mayor had believed that he could deal with the situation by means of a requisition, without appreciating that

'the state of the company as a result of circumstances of a functional-economic and market nature, was such as not to permit of the continuation of its activity'.

He also emphasized the shutdown of the plant and the protest actions of the staff, and the fact that the requisition had not succeeded in preserving public order. Finally the Prefect also observed that the order had been adopted [. . .]

'also under the influence of the pressure created by, and of the remarks made by the local press; therefore we have to hold that the Mayor, also in order to get out of the above and to show the intent of the Public Administration to intervene in one way or another, issued the order of requisition as a measure mainly directed to emphasize his intent to face the problem in some way [or, as quoted in the judgment of the Court of Appeal of Palermo, in the translation supplied by the Applicant: "his intention to tackle the problem just the same"]'.

It was of course understandable that the Mayor, as a public official, should have made his order, in some measure, as a response to local public pressures; and the Chamber does not see, in this passage of the Prefect's decision, any ground on which it might be suggested that the order was therefore arbitrary.

127. In the action brought by the trustee in bankruptcy for damages on account of the requisition, the Court of Palermo and subsequently the Court of Appeal of Palermo had to consider the legal significance of the decision of the Prefect . . . . The analysis of the Prefect's decision as a finding of excess of power, with the result that the order was subject to a defect of lawfulness does not, in the Chamber's view, necessarily and in itself signify any view by the Prefect, or by the Court of Appeal of Palermo, that the Mayor's act was unreasonable or arbitrary.

128. Arbitrariness is not so much something opposed to a rule of law, as something opposed to the rule of law. This idea was expressed by the Court in the *Asylum* case, when it spoke of 'arbitrary action' being 'substituted for the rule of law' (*Asylum, Judgment, I.C.J. Reports 1950*, p. 284). It is a wilful disregard of due process of law, an act which shocks, or at least surprises, a sense of juridical propriety. Nothing in the decision of the Prefect, or in the judgment of the Court of Appeal of Palermo, conveys any indication that the requisition order of the Mayor was to be regarded in that light.

129. The United States argument is not of course based solely on the findings of the Prefect or of the local courts. United States counsel felt able to describe the requisition generally as being an 'unreasonable or capricious exercise of authority'. Yet one must remember the situation in Palermo at the moment of the requisition, with the threatened sudden unemployment of some 800 workers at one factory. It cannot be said to have been unreasonable or merely capricious for the Mayor to seek to use the powers conferred on him by the law in an attempt to do something about a difficult and distressing situation. Moreover, if one looks at the requisition order itself, one finds an instrument which in its terms recites not only the reasons for its being made

but also the provisions of the law on which it is based: one finds that, although later annulled by the Prefect because 'the intended purpose of the requisition could not in practice be achieved by the order itself' (paragraph 125 above), it was nonetheless within the competence of the Mayor of Palermo, according to the very provisions of the law cited in it; one finds the Court of Appeal of Palermo, which did not differ from the conclusion that the requisition was *intra vires*, ruling that it was unlawful as falling into the recognized category of administrative law of acts of '*eccesso di potere*'. Furthermore, here was an act belonging to a category of public acts from which appeal on juridical grounds was provided in law (and indeed in the event used, not without success). Thus, the Mayor's order was consciously made in the context of an operating system of law and of appropriate remedies of appeal, and treated as such by the superior administrative authority and the local courts. These are not at all the marks of an 'arbitrary' act.

130. The Chamber does not, therefore, see in the requisition a measure which could reasonably be said to earn the qualification 'arbitrary', as it is employed in Article I of the Supplementary Agreement. Accordingly, there was no violation of that Article.

The ICJ's approach of looking at arbitrariness has been adopted by numerous investment arbitration tribunals. While some are more permissive than others in judging the reasonability of the host state's action, most arbitrators are looking for a breach of *the* rule of law rather than a breach of *a* rule of law when examining a claim of arbitrary state action.

 CASE

Alex Genin, Eastern Credit Limited, Inc. and A.S. Baltoil v. Republic of Estonia[7]

Claimant Genin was a United States national and owner and director of Eastern Credit Limited, a Texas corporation. Eastern Credit Limited, in turn, was wholly-owned Baltoil, a shareholder of Estonian Innovation Bank (EIB).

In August 1994, the Estonian central bank auctioned off the Koidu branch of an insolvent government bank to EIB, signing a sales agreement the following day. In September 1994, EIB wrote to the government that the balance sheet of the Koidu branch, which had been given to interested buyers prior to the auction, contained mistakes, and that they had suffered losses as a result.

---

7 *Alex Genin, Eastern Credit Limited, Inc. and A.S. Baltoil v. The Republic of Estonia*, ICSID Case No. ARB/99/2, Award (June 25, 2001), 17 ICSID Rev.-FILJ 395 (2002); footnotes omitted.

When the central bank refused to accept liability, EIB successfully sued for damages in the local court in Tallin.

In lieu of payment, the government agreed with EIB to exchange obligations owed to it by third banks for Koidu bank. This was, however, never finalized, so EIB brought suit in Texas against the central bank.

At that point, the central bank required the claimants to apply for holding permits to satisfy the laws on foreign stockholders. Claimants challenged this March 1997 measure, but before a decision could be taken, the central bank Council took a decision to immediately revoke EIB's banking license.

> 370. The Tribunal has [. . .] considered whether the Bank of Estonia's actions con-
> stituted an 'arbitrary' treatment of investment as that term is used in Article II(3)
> (b) of the BIT. In this regard, it is relevant that the Tribunal has found no evidence of
> discriminatory action. In addition, the Tribunal accepts Respondent's explanation
> that it took the decision to annul EIB's license in the course of exercising its statutory
> obligations to regulate the Estonian banking sector. The Tribunal further accepts
> Respondent's explanation that the circumstances of political and economic transi-
> tion prevailing in Estonia at the time justified heightened scrutiny of the banking
> sector. Such regulation by a state reflects a clear and legitimate public purpose.
> 371. It is also relevant that the Tribunal, having regard to the totality of the evi-
> dence, regards the decision by the Bank of Estonia to withdraw the license as justi-
> fied. In light of this conclusion, in order to amount to a violation of the BIT, any
> procedural irregularity that may have been present would have to amount to bad
> faith, a wilful disregard of due process of law or an extreme insufficiency of action.
> None of these are present in the case at hand. In sum, the Tribunal does not regard
> the license withdrawal as an arbitrary act that violates the Tribunal's 'sense of juridi-
> cal propriety'. Accordingly, the Tribunal finds that the Bank of Estonia's actions did
> not violate Article II(3)(b) of the BIT.

The *Genin* tribunal's refusal to find Estonia's measures arbitrary is not unusual. Equating non-arbitrariness with the rule of law (as set forth in the ELSI case), many tribunals are generous in approaching the host's actions and take a sur-prisingly clear 'public law' standpoint on the rule of law issue—a standpoint that, in the words of Jeremy Waldron, conceives 'the rule of law so that it is [. . .] sensitive to the needs of administration'.[8]

---

8 Waldron, Jeremy, *The Rule of Law in Public Law*, p. 9 (September 2015). Printed in The Cambridge Companion to Public Law, Cambridge University Press pp. 56–72. Version used available at: http://ssrn.com/abstract=2480632.

DISCUSSION NOTES

1 Reviewing a number of arbitration tribunals' discussions of the obligation of non-arbitrariness, Christoph Schreuer distils the elements of greatest significance to the authorities into four categories:

> The above authority suggests that the following categories of measures can be described as arbitrary:
>
> - measure that inflicts damage on the investor without serving any apparent legitimate purpose. The decisive criterion for the determination of the unreasonable or arbitrary nature of a measure harming the investor would be whether it can be justified in terms of rational reasons that are related to the facts. Arbitrariness would be absent if the measure is a reasonable and proportionate reaction to objectively verifiable circumstances;
> - measure that is not based on legal standards but on discretion, prejudice, or personal preference;
> - measure taken for reasons that are different from those put forward by the decision-maker. This conclusion applies, in particular, where a public interest is put forward as a pretext to take measures that are designed to harm the investor;
> - measure taken in wilful disregard of due process and proper procedure.[9]

2 Tribunals currently require 'something more' than evidence of a host's violation of its domestic laws to establish an arbitrariness claim. The decisions speak of such 'something mores' as 'unjustified repudiation' of laws (*Gami Investments v. The Government of the United Mexican States*, UNCITRAL/NAFTA Chapter 11, Final Award (15 November 2004)), actions 'motivated by sectoral or local prejudice' (*Waste Management Inc. v. United Mexican States*, ARB(AF)/98/2, Arbitral Award (2 June 2000)), 'manifest lack of reasons' for a law (*Glamis Gold Ltd. v. United States of America*, UNCITRAL/NAFTA Chapter 11, Award (8 June 2009)), and 'unfairly target[ing] a particular investor' (*Cargill v. Poland*, UNCITRAL, Award (1 March 2008)). See Patrick Dumberry, The Prohibition against Arbitrary Conduct and the Fair and Equitable Treatment Standard under NAFTA Article 1105, 15 J. World Investment and Trade 117, 147–50 (2014). This reflects a clear adoption of the ELSI approach of looking at violations of *the* rule of law rather than of *a* rule of law.

---

9 Christoph H. Schreuer, *Protection against Arbitrary or Discriminatory Measures, in* The Future of Investment Arbitration 183, 188 (Catherine A. Rogers and Roger P. Alford eds., 2009).

The *'the'* vs. *'a'* rule of law difference has found further expression in other areas of international law. In developing the human right protection from arbitrary detention, for example, the term 'arbitrary' generated significant debate. While some experts felt that the definition of arbitrary could be limited to unlawfulness, others saw the term more broadly, including a notion of unreasonableness. The distinction between arbitrary as unlawful and arbitrary as unreasonable was decided in favor of the latter, given the potential danger that governments could pass arbitrary laws as well as carry out arbitrary acts. See Laurent Marcoux, Jr., Protection from Arbitrary Arrest and Detention Under International Law, 5:2 B.C. Int'l and Comp. L. Rev. 345 (1982).

3 The concept of arbitrariness is often intermingled with the principle of fair and equitable treatment (FET), which we address later in this chapter. The intermingling is partly a function of the standards' placement within the IIA—generally they are found within a single paragraph. But it is also a conceptual intermingling. Stephan Schill notes that while both standards are related to good faith, arbitrariness is a narrower standard: 'Arbitrary conduct can be seen as a sufficient but not necessary requirement for breach of fair and equitable treatment'. Stephan W. Schill, *Fair and Equitable Treatment, the Rule of Law, and Comparative Public Law, in* International Investment Law and Comparative Public Law 151, 167 (Stephan W. Schill ed., 2010). The tribunal in *Arif v. Moldova* had a different opinion. In that 2013 decision, there was no non-arbitrariness provision in the relevant BIT, but the claimant challenged the host's behaviour as arbitrary and thereby a violation of the fair and equitable treatment provision. The award dismissed this claim:

> '[. . .] Even though non-arbitrariness may be considered as one of the elements of the FET standard a breach of FET does not necessarily imply the existence of arbitrariness. Claimant's general argument that all the acts and omissions alleged to have breached the FET standard also are in breach of Respondent's obligation not to impose unreasonable or arbitrary measures is rejected. Claimant has to successfully prove how the alleged acts and omissions are in breach of Respondent's alleged obligation not to impose arbitrary or unreasonable measures.'

See *Franck Charles Arif v. Republic of Moldova*, ICSID Case No. ARB/11/23, Award, para. 500 (8 April 2013).

4 The Arif tribunal also implied that the lack of a specific non-arbitrariness provision in the BIT meant that there was no obligation on the government to avoid arbitrary conduct. See *id.* at paras. 500 and 503. Does this correspond with general principles of international law?

5.2.2 Reasonableness

Often used in place of non-arbitrary, the obligation for a host state to treat the investment reasonably has been approached in the same way by tribunals. Indeed, in a number of disputes alleging 'arbitrary or unreasonable' host behaviour, tribunals have deemed the terms interchangeable.[10] Moreover, as the relevant IIA text usually contains the conjunction 'or', a breach of either will suffice to establish a violation. Other IIAs (significantly the Energy Charter Treaty's Article 10.1) prohibit 'unreasonable or discriminatory' behaviour. A brief look at reasonableness is therefore warranted.

IIA provisions prohibiting 'unreasonable' measures require the host to treat investments and investors in accordance with the rule of law rather than on the basis of prerogative. Where the treaty refers to 'reasonable treatment', tribunals will often analyse the state's actions by asking if there was a rational relationship between the public goal and the action taken toward the foreign investor.

The following case analyses the reasonableness of a government's imposition of profit limits on utility companies in response to public dissatisfaction with high energy prices.

 CASE

AES Summit Generation Limited and AES–Tisza Erömü Kft. v. Republic of Hungary[11]

The claimants in this case are power companies who had contracted with the Hungarian government to upgrade existing power stations in the wake of the government's energy sector privatization in 1995. The terms under which AES purchased the former public power stations included a pricing schedule and, should the schedule be terminated, a particular formula to be used to calculate the fees the government would pay for the electricity produced. In 2004, Hungary joined the European Union. The original pricing schedule was cancelled, and the new fee formula went into effect.

---

10 For example, *National Grid v. Argentina*, UNCITRAL, Award, para. 197 (Nov. 3, 2008); *Plama Consortium Ltd. v. Bulgaria*, ICSID Case No. ARB/03/24, para. 184 (Aug. 27, 2008); *Siemens v. Argentina*, ICSID Case No. ARB/02/8, Award, para. 319 (Feb. 6, 2007).

11 *AES Summit Generation Limited and AES-TISZA Erömü Kft. v. Republic of Hungary*, ICSID Case No. ARB/07/22, ECT, Award (Sept. 23, 2010). Available at: http://italaw.com/documents/AESvHungaryAward.pdf.

In 2005, nine years after the sales agreement had been signed, a national political debate on the profits of energy generators began. Resistance to what was considered excessive returns led to an administrative pricing scheme that set a fixed price for each generator.

Faced with a legislated price that was 35 percent lower than that agreed to earlier, the claimants filed for arbitration under the Energy Charter Treaty. The new pricing policy, they argued, was an 'impairment of AES' investment by unreasonable and discriminatory measures'.[12] Hungary countered that it had sufficient rational reasons to set maximum profit levels for regulated entities, including the need for electricity to be sold on the free market and concerns about compatibility with EU legal requirements.

10.3 Findings of the Tribunal

10.3.1 Article 10(1) of the ECT provides that 'no Contracting Party shall in any way impair by unreasonable or discriminatory measure their [investment's] management, maintenance, use, enjoyment or disposal.'

10.3.2 Hungary was thus obliged to avoid any impairment of Claimants' investment as a consequence of either: (a) unreasonable or (b) discriminatory measures.

10.3.3 An analysis of the nature of a state's measures, in order to determine if they are unreasonable or discriminatory, is only necessary when an impairment of the investment took place.

10.3.4 It is undisputed that, as a result of the reintroduction of the Price Decrees, Claimants received lower prices than they had been receiving pursuant to the formula set out in the 2001 PPA.

10.3.5 It follows that AES's receipt of a lower payment from MVM, whilst burdened by unchanged costs, had a detrimental impact on Claimants' investment, as it altered – in a negative way – AES Tisza's regular income.

10.3.6 However, for such impairment to amount to a breach of the ECT, it must be the result of an unreasonable or discriminatory measure.

10.3.7 There are two elements that require to be analyzed to determine whether a state's act was unreasonable: the existence of a rational policy; and the reasonableness of the act of the state in relation to the policy.

10.3.8 A rational policy is taken by a state following a logical (good sense) explanation and with the aim of addressing a public interest matter.

10.3.9 Nevertheless, a rational policy is not enough to justify all the measures taken by a state in its name. A challenged measure must also be reasonable. That is, there needs to be an appropriate correlation between the state's public policy

---

12 Para. 5.1(b).

objective and the measure adopted to achieve it. This has to do with the nature of the measure and the way it is implemented.

10.3.10 Hungary has argued that it had three main reasons for introducing the Price Decrees.

10.3.11 First, Hungary was concerned about the failure of generators to agree over several years to any reductions in contracted [power purchase agreement, 'PPA'] capacity, to free up electricity for direct sale to the parallel free market, that had to be developed during the period of transition from the centralized economy to a liberal market.

10.3.12 As to this point, the Tribunal finds that it cannot be considered a reasonable measure for a state to use its governmental powers to force a private party to change or give up its contractual rights. If the state has the conviction that its contractual obligations to its investors should no longer be observed (even if it is a commercial contract, which is the case), the state would have to end such contracts and assume the contractual consequences of such early termination.

10.3.13 This does not mean that the state cannot exercise its governmental powers, including its legislative function, with the consequence that private interests – such as the investor's contractual rights – are affected. But that effect would have to be a consequence of a measure based on public policy that was not aimed only at those contractual rights. Were it to be otherwise, a state could justify the breach of commercial commitments by relying on arguments that such breach was occasioned by an act of the state performed in its public character.

10.3.14 Therefore, the Tribunal cannot consider it to have been reasonable for Hungary to have issued the Price Decrees because of Claimants' failure to agree to, or even to negotiate for, a reduction in the capacity to which it was contractually entitled under the 2001 PPA.

10.3.15 Hungary's second stated reason for the introduction of the Price Decrees was the pressure of the EC Commission's investigations and the foreseeable obligation to correct (recover) state aid that the Commission's decision would impose.

10.3.16 Had Hungary been motivated to reintroduce price regulation with a view to addressing the EC's state aid concerns, there is no doubt that this would have constituted a rational public policy measure. However, the Tribunal notes that as long as the Commission's state aid decision was not issued, Hungary had no legal obligation to act in accordance with what it believed could be the result of the decision and to start a limitation of potential state aid.

10.3.17 During the hearing, it became clear to the Tribunal that SAMO, the Hungarian agency in charge of dealing with state aid issues, had not even been consulted when the government reintroduced regulated pricing in March 2006. Another important fact is that the use of the 7.1% cap on profits had no direct relation with state aid, because state aid occurs when the entity is receiving above-market prices. The elimination of above-market prices is not achieved by a cap on profits. To address such price concerns requires a general market price analysis.

10.3.18 Consequently, the majority concludes that Hungary's decision to reintroduce administrative pricing was not motivated by pressure from the EC Commission.

10.3.19 Arbitrator Stern considers that it was not exclusively so motivated, but that the enquiry and subsequent pressures from the Commission certainly was in the Hungarian authorities' mind when they decided to reintroduce price regulation. In her view, it appears from the record that the high prices were also a serious problem for the Commission and it is quite evident that even before Hungary was under a legal obligation to follow the Commission's decision, it had been made abundantly clear to Hungary that the PPAs raised considerable concerns at the European level, as being in contradiction with the European free market policies. [. . .]

10.3.20 Hungary's third reason for acting had to do with the allegations that the profits enjoyed under the PPAs, in the absence of either competition or regulation, exceeded reasonable rates of return for public utility sales. Hungary does not deny that one of its reasons for acting had to do with these concerns.

[. . .] After a series of unsuccessful attempts at PPA renegotiations, HEO presented the data regarding the generator's returns to the parliament's Energy Subcommittee.

10.3.21In the meantime, the level of the generators' returns became a public issue and something of a political lightning rod in the face of upcoming elections.

10.3.22 However, the fact that an issue becomes a political matter, [. . .] does not mean that the existence of a rational policy is erased.

10.3.23 In fact, it is normal and common that a public policy matter becomes a political issue; that is the arena where such matters are discussed and made public.

10.3.24 Eventually, an amendment to the 2001 Electricity Act and the Price Act, to enable the reintroduction of regulatory pricing, was proposed to parliament [. . .]. The objective of the amendment was that 'the transmission and distribution of electricity, the controlling of the system, the selling of electricity contracted for public utility purposes by generators, trading between the public utility wholesaler and the public utility service provider and the electricity sold to consumers in the public utility sector are subject to the regulatory pricing stipulated under the act on the determination of prices.'

10.3.25 This amendment proposal contained a general explanation in the following terms:

> 'This act shall be enacted by the Parliament to include the generators' price
> of electricity contracted for public utility purposes in the scope of regulatory
> pricing.
> During the privatization of power stations in 1995–96, long-term power
> purchase agreements were concluded [. . .]. By way of the agreements
> stable and foreseeable returns are ensured to those investors who secure
> the availability of electricity generation capacities necessary to meet

domestic demand through the modernization of existing power stations (or the construction of new ones). Price formulas had been identified in the agreements but the application of these formulas was abrogated by regulatory pricing.

In the Government Decree 1074/1995 [. . .] the Horn Cabinet guaranteed an 8% return on capital by way of regulatory pricing during the conclusion of privatization agreements. Pursuant to the above decree an administrative price regulation scheme came into effect for a period of 4 years [. . .].'

In 1997 the generators' average profit was 8.23%, a percentage that steadily increased until 2000 as a result of the efficiency improvement of power stations. By 2000 the average profit of generators was 15.71%.

In 2000 PriceWaterhouseCoopers International consulting company, upon engagement by the Orbán Cabinet, indicated in its report titled 'Energy Market Opening Program' that the long-term agreements are impeding the liberalization of the energy market as the agreements contract nearly all domestic power station capacities until 2010–15 and as such there is no free marketable electricity remaining in the market. Due to the above the international consultant proposed to the Orbán Cabinet to reduce regulatory prices during the new price regulatory period using this as an additional measure to encourage generators to renegotiate the agreements.

Had the Orbán Cabinet given consideration to the proposal presented by the international consultant engaged by it, then the Hungarian Energy Office [. . .] would have been required to propose an administrative price determination that would have repeatedly reduced the generators' profit to 8% in relation to the on-coming 4-year price regulation period to be determined in 2000. On the contrary the administrative price decree [of December 2000] abrogated the regulation concerning the 8% profit margin and introduced new price formulas.

As a result of the decision made by the Minister of Economy on the Orbán Cabinet, the 2001 profit of power stations was 22.83% as opposed to the expected 8%. This price regulation was in effect until the end of 2003 ensuring a steadily high profit level to power station investors. [. . .]

The margins generated by power stations between 1997 and 2004 were as follows:

Table 5.1 Margins generated by power stations, 1997–2004

1997	1998	1999	2000	2001	2002	2003	2004
8.23%	12.73%	12.70%	15.71%	22.83%	21.62%	14.49%	22.36%

This draft legislation includes a proposal for correcting the regulatory error by the Orbán Cabinet and allows for the Government to exercise the measure of administrative pricing in the absence of agreement between the parties, which measure also affects the sale prices stipulated in long-term power purchase agreements providing high profit levels.'

10.3.26 [. . .]

10.3.30 Based on the debates in parliament and outside parliament, the majority of the Tribunal has concluded that Hungary's decision to reintroduce administrative pricing was not based on the EC Commission's investigation. Nor, however, was it made with the intention of affecting Claimants' contractual rights.

10.3.31 Rather, against this factual background, the majority has concluded that Hungary's reintroduction of administrative pricing in 2006 was motivated principally by widespread concerns relating to (and it was aimed directly at reducing) excessive profits earned by generators and the burden on consumers.

10.3.32 This is because virtually all of the debate in parliament at the relevant time was about 'profits'. Indeed, government minister Mr. Tibor Kovács specifically asked the opposition parties if they were prepared to support the proposal, which he said 'gives tools for the government to limit the alleged and so-called luxury profits'.

10.3.33 There is also no reference to be found to EC state aid or negotiations with EC in the official reasons for Act XXXV.

10.3.34 Having concluded that Hungary was principally motivated by the politics surrounding so-called luxury profits, the Tribunal nevertheless is of the view that it is a perfectly valid and rational policy objective for a government to address luxury profits. And while such price regimes may not be seen as desirable in certain quarters, this does not mean that such a policy is irrational. One need only recall recent wide-spread concerns about the profitability level of banks to understand that so-called excessive profits may well give rise to legitimate reasons for governments to regulate or re-regulate.

10.3.35 As to the need for a reasonable correlation between the state's policy objective and the measures adopted to achieve it, the Tribunal notes that before the amendment of the 2001 Electricity Act, Hungary had approached the generators to renegotiate the PPAs. Given that no agreement was reached, and in the absence of a specific commitment to the Claimants that administrative pricing was never going to be reintroduced, the Hungarian parliament voted for the reintroduction of administrative pricing, which parliament considered to be the best option at the moment.

10.3.36 The Tribunal finds that both the 2006 Electricity Act and the implementing Price Decrees were reasonable, proportionate and consistent with the public policy expressed by the parliament.

10.3.37 Having determined that the decision to introduce the Price Decrees was not an arbitrary or unreasonable measure, it is also necessary to determine if, as stated by Hungary, the generators were still going to receive a reasonable return.

10.3.38 [. . .]

10.3.44 Against the factual background which preceded the March 2006 price reregulation, the Tribunal considers that the 7.1% rate of return on assets, which it prescribed, to be comparable to the 8% return on equity target that was in place at the time of the privatization. Consequently, in the Tribunal's view, the prices fixed for AES Tisza pursuant to the Price Decrees were reasonable, taking into account their consistency with the original returns it earned at the time of the Claimants' original investment.

5.3 Non-discrimination

The principle of non-discrimination is fundamental to international law. Found widely in human rights treaties, non-discrimination provisions are also contained in trade and investment agreements.

In international economic law, an obligation of non-discrimination restricts governments from treating a foreign actor (or product or investment) disadvantageously. We have already discussed the non-discrimination principle as an element of a legal expropriation. In the following, we are looking at the principle as a standard for host behaviour in non-expropriation settings.

There are three basic forms of non-discrimination obligation in IIAs: a general statement prohibiting discriminatory treatment; a national treatment obligation; and a most-favoured nation (MFN) treatment obligation. The first requires the host to treat the foreigner no less favourably than it treats its own citizens. The latter requires no less favourable treatment of the foreigner as compared with foreigners of another nationality. Because the general statement provisions are often textually combined with a non-arbitrariness or unreasonableness requirement, most of the attention to non-discrimination focuses on the national treatment and MFN provisions. We will look briefly at how the general provisions are approached before turning to the elements of national treatment and MFN.

5.3.1 General obligation of non-discrimination

Discrimination is the unjustified disadvantageous treatment of one individual or group. As a general principle, non-discrimination is a requirement of equal treatment. Thus, like the prohibition on discriminatory expropriations, a provision in an IIA that says, for example:

> Each Contracting Party [. . .] shall not impair with discriminatory measures the management, maintenance, use, enjoyment, sale or disposition of such investments[13]

---

13 Agreement for the Promotion and Protection of Investments Between the Republic of Columbia and the Republic of India, Art. 3.2 (July 3, 2013).

would prevent a host from subjecting such investment to disadvantages that others did not face on grounds of the investor's race, sex, gender, nationality, or the like unless the different treatment could be justified.

Because IIAs' general non-discrimination requirements are most often found in the general article on 'treatment', however, tribunals have given them little particularized attention and the breadth of grounds for discrimination have therefore not yet been established.[14] One issue that is well-considered is that of whether the intent to discriminate is relevant to a finding of violation.

Intent is generally irrelevant to the non-discrimination analysis. Although customary international law concepts of non-discrimination required the claimant to prove the host's intent to discriminate to succeed, under current investment law, a lack of discriminatory intent is not going to save a discriminatory measure from condemnation by most tribunals.[15]

Some tribunals maintain the view that intent is a necessary element of the discrimination claim, however.[16] The *Methanex* tribunal stated, for instance:

> In order to sustain its claim under Article 1102(3), Methanex must demonstrate, cumulatively, that California intended to favour domestic investors by discriminating against foreign investors and that Methanex and the domestic investor supposedly being favored by California are in like circumstances.[17]

At the same time, demonstrated existence of intent to discriminate will not always result in an automatic finding of violation of non-discrimination. For some arbitrators, government intent to discriminate is a necessary but not sufficient element of the claimant's case if the investor was not, in fact, subjected to less favourable treatment.[18]

---

14 *See* Urusual Kriebaum, Arbitrary/Unreasonable or Discriminatory Measures in: Marc Bungenberg, Jörn Griebel, Stephan Hobe, and August Reinisch, eds., International Investment Law, 790–806, 798 (2015).

15 *Parkerings-Compagniet AS v. The Republic of Lithuania*, ICSID Case No. ARB/05/8, Award, para. 368 (Sept. 11, 2007), http://italaw.com/documents/Pakerings.pdf.

16 *LG&E Energy Corp. et al. v. The Argentine Republic*, ICSID Case No. ARB/02/1, Decision on Liability, para. 146 (Oct. 3, 2006), http://italaw.com/documents/ARB021_LGE-Decision-on-Liability-en.pdf; *Alex Genin, Eastern Credit Limited, Inc. and A.S. Baltoil v. Estonia*, *supra* note 7, para. 369.

17 *Methanex Corporation v. United States of America*, UNCITRAL (NAFTA), Final Award, at Part IV, Chapter B, p. 6 (Aug. 3, 2005). Available at: http://italaw.com/documents/MethanexFinalAward.pdf.

18 *Siemens AG v. The Argentine Republic*, *supra* note 10, at, para. 321 ; S.D. Myers, Inc. v. Canada, UNCITRAL (NAFTA), Partial Award, para. 254 (Nov. 13, 2000). Available at http://italaw.com/sites/default/files/case-documents/ita0747.pdf, para. 254. *See also* Schreuer, *supra* note 9, at 196.

a   National treatment and Most Favoured Nation (MFN) treatment

The general non-discriminatory treatment provision of an IIA is often accompanied by more specific obligations of national treatment and most-favoured nation treatment. Whereas some IIAs have separate provisions for national treatment and MFN, the two are frequently combined in a single provision that ensures that the investor will receive the *better* of the two treatments. Article 4.1 of the BIT between Switzerland and India is typical, providing:

> Each Contracting Party shall in its territory accord to investments of investors of the other Contracting Party treatment not less favourable than that which it accords to investments of its own investors or to investments of investors of any third State, whichever is more favourable. Such treatment shall in particular apply to the operation, management, maintenance, use, enjoyment or disposal of such investments.[19]

b   Scope

The non-discrimination provisions apply to any form of treatment of a foreign investor or investment, whether legislative, administrative, or informal. Many IIAs include specific exceptions to the national treatment and most-favoured nation obligations, however. These exceptions are essentially limitations on the scope of the provision, and where found, tribunals are bound to apply them.

Two limitations are found in nearly all IIAs, and to date neither has raised much controversy. The first is an exception allowing preferential treatment of investors from economic integration area partner territories. Typical wording would be:

> 'If a Contracting Party has accorded special advantages to nationals of any third State by virtue of agreements establishing customs unions, economic unions, monetary unions or similar institutions, or on the basis of interim agreements leading to such unions or institutions, that Contracting Party shall not be obliged to accord such advantages to nationals of the other Contracting Party.'[20]

---

19 Paragraph 2 excludes taxation preferences based on double taxation treaties from the obligation of non-discrimination.

20 Agreement on encouragement and reciprocal protection of investments between the Federal Democratic Republic of Ethiopia and the Kingdom of the Netherlands, Article 3.3 (July 1, 2005).

The second widely used limitation on the scope of non-discrimination provisions secures hosts' ability to give tax preferences to investors or investments from states with which it has bilateral tax treaties. The Ethiopia–Netherlands BIT states:

> 'With respect to taxes, fees, charges and to fiscal deductions and exemptions, each Contracting Party shall accord to nationals of the other Contracting Party who are engaged in any economic activity in its territory, treatment not less favourable than that accorded to its own nationals or to those of any third State who are in the same circumstances, whichever is more favourable to the nationals concerned. For this purpose, however, there shall not be taken into account any special fiscal advantages accorded by that Party:
>
> a) under an agreement for the avoidance of double taxation; or
> b) by virtue of its participation in a customs union, economic union or similar institution; or
> c) on the basis of reciprocity with a third State'.[21]

A third limitation on scope has been one of the most common in the past, but liberalizations of it have begun to spur some heated discussions. This is the limitation on the temporal application of the non-discrimination obligations. Removing this limit means that a host will have the obligation to treat all foreign investors equally and as it does nationals, not only once the investment has been made, but also prior to the investment. The host, in other words, loses the absolute right to choose which investments enter its territory.

Until the mid-1990s, most non-discrimination obligations applied only to the post-establishment phase of the investment. The NAFTA introduced the trend to agree to pre-establishment non-discrimination provisions. Applying to 'the *establishment, acquisition, expansion,* management, conduct, operation, and sale or other disposal of investments', NAFTA's national treatment provision takes a large step away from the traditional host state discretion in choosing what investments may enter the country.[22] Pre-establishment obligations, while still relatively rare, can now be found in BITs and other IIAs of both industrialized and developing countries.[23] Arbitral tribunals will therefore have to decide claims of discrimination based, for instance, on more

---

21 Agreement on encouragement and reciprocal protection of investments between the Federal Democratic Republic of Ethiopia and the Kingdom of the Netherlands, Article 4 (July 1, 2005).

22 NAFTA Article 1102(1) (emphasis added).

23 Most BITs of Canada and of the United States contain pre-establishment national treatment provisions. Other states are also beginning to extend protections to include acquisition. For example, Agreement Between

burdensome rules for foreigners to establish a legal entity than for nationals to do so[24] or based on a host's screening laws.

Given the depth of intrusion on a state's sovereignty that such provisions provide, it is not surprising that in those IIAs with pre-entry national treatment obligations, the parties often make exemptions for sensitive sectors. Sornarajah notes that for both NAFTA and ASEAN, member governments have made extensive use of exemption lists.[25] These lists are to shorten over time, but the parties are not always quick to remove sectors.[26]

5.3.2   The elements of non-discrimination

In analysing any non-discrimination provision, there are several legal elements that must be evaluated on the facts: the comparability of the investors; whether the treatment was less favourable treatment; and the applicability of any justifications. The claimant has the burden of proof on the first four of these, while the respondent state must prove any invoked justification or exception applies.

a   Comparability of investors

One of the most difficult elements of non-discrimination analyses is that of comparability. This is no less true in the investment context than it is in trade law, and much more difficult than in human rights, where all humans are equal in dignity.

In order to compare the treatment of investors, the relevance of the comparison must be proven. To do this, the claimant must show that it is in a like situation or like circumstance as a more favourably treated investor was. Likeness is a very flexible term, however. A broad notion of likeness, that is, requiring 'like' investors or 'like' investments be only moderately similar, would support many findings of 'like investments'. Thus, if investors in similar economic sectors are treated differently, the less favoured investor could state a claim of discrimination. The *Occidental v. Ecuador* award reflects an unusually broad view of likeness.

---

the Government of the Republic of Finland and the Government of the Federal Republic of Nigeria on the Promotion and Protection of Investments, Art. 3 (June 22, 2005).

24 *See, e.g. GEA Group Aktiengesellschaft v. Ukraine*, ICSID Case No. ARB/08/16, Award, para. 344 (Mar. 31, 2011), http://italaw.com/documents/GEA_v_Ukraine_Award_31Mar2011.pdf.

25 Muthucumaraswamy Sornarajah, The International Law on Foreign Investment 337 (third edn, 2011).

26 *Id.*

CASE

Occidental Exploration and Production Company v. Ecuador[27]

Occidental Petroleum Corporation is an internationally active oil and gas producer established in the United States. In 1999, it became a joint venture partner with OEPC, an oil producer in Ecuador. The contract provided for the parties to share the profits of production. Following the signing of the contract, Ecuador imposed a VAT tax (value-added tax) on Occidental's profits. Their requests to refund the VAT being refused, Occidental brought a claim of BIT violation to arbitration. While the tribunal refused to find that an expropriation had taken place, they agreed that the provision requiring non-discriminatory treatment might have been violated.

167. Article II (1) of the Treaty establishes the obligation to treat investments and associated activities 'on a basis no less favorable than that accorded in like situations to investment or associated activities of its own nationals or companies, or of nationals or companies of any third country, whichever is the most favorable . . .'. Exceptions to national treatment and most favored nation treatment can be included in a separate Protocol. Ecuador's exceptions under the Protocol to the Treaty are limited to traditional fishing and the ownership and operation of radio and television stations.

168. The Claimant is of the view that Ecuador has breached this obligation because a number of companies involved in the export of other goods, particularly flowers, mining and seafood products are entitled to receive VAT refund and continuously enjoy the benefit. Lumber, bananas and African palm oil have also been referred to in this context. There is in this situation, the Claimant argues, a violation of the national treatment obligation. The Claimant also asserts that the meaning of 'in like situations' does not refer to those industries or companies involved in the same sector of activity, such as oil producers, but to companies that are engaged in exports even if encompassing different sectors.

169. Moreover, in the Claimant's opinion, there can be no differentiation between producers and manufacturers as this is not allowed for under the legislation of Ecuador, Andean Community law or international standards.

170. The Claimant also has argued that there is a failure of most-favored-nation treatment because under bilateral investment treaties made by Ecuador with Spain and Argentina, respectively, the standard of national treatment is not qualified by

27 *Occidental Exploration and Production Company v. The Republic of Ecuador*, LCIA Case No. UN 3467 (UNCITRAL), Final Award (July 1, 2004). Available at: http://italaw.com/documents/Oxy-EcuadorFinalAward_001. pdf; footnotes are omitted.

the reference to 'in like situations'. OEPC would thus be entitled to this less restrictive treatment under the most-favored-nation clause.

171. The Respondent opposes all such arguments on the basis that 'in like situations' can only mean that all companies in the same sector are to be treated alike and this happens in respect of all oil producers. The comparison, it is argued, cannot be extended to other sectors because the whole purpose of the VAT refund policy is to ensure that the conditions of competition are not changed, a scrutiny that is relevant only in the same sector.

172. The Respondent also explains that the treatment of foreign-owned companies and national companies is not different as Petroecuador is also denied VAT refunds, and that there is nothing in the policy that is intended to discriminate against foreign companies. It is also explained that other foreign producers, such as flower exporters, are granted the VAT refund because the law and the policy so allow. Ecuador also opposes the arguments concerning the most-favored-nation clause as no example is given of a Spanish or Argentine company in the oil sector, or any other sector, receiving a more favorable treatment to which the clause could apply.

173. The Tribunal is of the view that in the context of this particular claim the Claimant is right and its arguments are convincing. In fact, 'in like situations' cannot be interpreted in the narrow sense advanced by Ecuador as the purpose of national treatment is to protect investors as compared to local producers, and this cannot be done by addressing exclusively the sector in which that particular activity is undertaken.

174. The Tribunal is mindful of the discussion of the meaning of 'like products' in respect of national treatment under the GATT/WTO. In that context it has been held that the concept has to be interpreted narrowly and that like products are related to the concept of directly competitive or substitutable products.

175. However, those views are not specifically pertinent to the issue discussed in this case. In fact, the purpose of national treatment in this dispute is the opposite of that under the GATT/WTO, namely it is to avoid exporters being placed at a disadvantage in foreign markets because of the indirect taxes paid in the country of origin, while in GATT/WTO the purpose is to avoid imported products being affected by a distortion of competition with similar domestic products because of taxed and other regulations in the country of destination.

176. In the first situation, no exporter ought to be put in a disadvantageous position as compared to other exporters, while in the second situation the comparison needs to be made with the treatment of the 'like' product and not generally. In any event, the reference to 'in like situations' used in the Treaty seems to be different from that to 'like products' in the GATT/WTO. The 'situation' can relate to all exporters that share such condition, while the 'product' necessarily relates to competitive and substitutable products.

177. In the present dispute the fact is that OEPC has received treatment less favora-

ble than that accorded to national companies. The Tribunal is convinced that this has not been done with the intent of discriminating against foreign-owned companies. The statement of Mrs. De Mena at the hearing evidences that the SRI is a very professional service that did what it thought was its obligation to do under the law. However, the result of the policy enacted and the interpretation followed by the SRI in fact has been a less favorable treatment of OEPC.

178. This finding makes it unnecessary for the Tribunal to examine whether there were in addition most-favored-nation-treatment obligations involved. In view of the fact that the parties have discussed in detail the meaning of *Maffezini* in this context, the Tribunal believes it appropriate to clarify that that case is not really pertinent to the present dispute as it dealt with the most-favored-nation-treatment only insofar as procedural rights of the claimant there were involved, not substantive treatment as is the case here.

179. The Tribunal accordingly holds that the Respondent has breached its obligations under Article II (1) of the Treaty.

A narrower concept of likeness demands a greater showing of similarity between investors or investments before differential host state treatment of them will be found to violate the obligation of non-discrimination. This results in fewer findings of discrimination, as the next case demonstrates.

 CASE

Sergei Paushok et al. v. the Government of Mongolia[28]

The Russian businessman Paushok owned Golden East Mongolia (GEM), an exploration and mining company. GEM operates five gold pits and employs 1470 people, approximately half of them Mongolians.

In 2001, world gold prices were under $362/oz. In 2002, the price started to increase. In 2006, the price was over $720/oz. In response, Mongolia's legislature passed a windfall tax law, requiring that gold sales at prices over $500/oz. would have to pay a 68% tax on the additional value and increasing the charges levied on companies with foreign employees composing more than 10% of their workforce.

The claimants pointed out that the tax treatment of the gold sector was less advantageous than that of the copper sector and of the oil sector. Moreover,

---

28 *Sergei Paushok et al. v. Mongolia*, UNCITRAL, Award on Jurisdiction and Liability, (Apr. 28, 2011). Available at: http://italaw.com/documents/PaushokAward.pdf; footnotes omitted.

a competitor, Boroo Gold, successfully negotiated a stability agreement with Mongolia to protect themselves from the legislative changes.

GEM thus brought a claim based on the Russia-Mongolia BIT's 'non-impairment' provision of Article 3(1) promising investors fair and equitable treatment 'whereby discriminatory measures that impair the maintenance or use of the investments are prohibited' by the host and under the non-discrimination provision of Article 3(2), under which the parties obligated themselves to providing a regulatory regime for the foreign investor that 'will be no less favourable than that afforded the investments and activities of the host's own investors or of investors from third countries'.[29]

309. The discrimination argument takes two forms: (i) the WPT should have equally applied to other sectors than the mining industry; and (ii) the WPT discriminates between gold and copper.

310. As to the first argument, the consolidated statutes of many countries are replete with fiscal legislation which, whether using tax breaks or direct subsidies, treats various industries differently from one another. In the specific case of Mongolia, Mongolian oil production represents a minor sector of the Mongolian economy. Mongolia is a net importer of oil. And there is nothing in the Treaty or in international law which generally prohibits Mongolia from imposing a tax regime on gold mining which would be different from other industries. Under such circumstances, there is nothing permitting to reach the conclusion that the fact that the WPT Law does not apply to such industry constitutes illegal discrimination under the provisions of the Treaty. Many will argue that this is not wise economic policy but this does not mean it would constitute a breach of a BIT, particularly in the area of taxation, in respect of which States jealously guard their sovereign powers.

311. As to the second argument, Claimants allege that, by adopting a different taxation regime for copper, Respondent indulged into discrimination contrary to the Treaty. It is true that different tax regimes were enacted between copper and gold, even though they both attained, percentagewise, very significant tax increases; and it might have been wiser if the Great Khural had adopted similar legislation for both products. But this does not allow the Tribunal to jump to the conclusion that its failure to do so constitutes a breach of the Treaty.

312. In the Tribunal's view, Claimants' reliance on the *Occidental* case in support of its two arguments is inapposite.

313. First of all, the national-treatment clause contained in that case has a different wording than the one found in Article 3(2) of the Treaty in the present case.

---

29 Bilateral Investment Agreement between the Russian Federation and Mongolia of 2005. My thanks to Klaus Arnsperger for the unofficial translation from the original Russian text.

Article II(1) of the U.S.–Ecuador BIT establishes the obligation to treat investments and associated activities 'on a basis no less favorable than that accorded in like situations to investments or associated activities of its own nationals or companies, or of nationals or companies of any third country, whichever is the most favorable'. The tribunal in that case, because of the use of the words 'in like situations', differentiated the interpretation to be given to those words from the words 'like products' used in the WTO/GATT which, the tribunal said, 'necessarily relates to competitive and substitutable products'. The Treaty in the present case contains no reference to either 'like situations' or 'like products', thus leaving the Tribunal to rely on the general provisions of the Vienna Convention.

314. Moreover, the *Occidental* case had to deal with the interpretation of VAT legislation of general application while the WPT Law deals specifically with two minerals: gold and copper.

315. The Tribunal is of the view that, before concluding to discrimination in the present case, the sectors covered should relate to competitive and substitutable products, an expression regularly used in *WTO/GATT* cases. In doing so, the Tribunal is aware of the differences between the Treaty and the one governing the WTO. It merely states that such a requirement is a reasonable one to apply when considering allegations of discrimination. There is nothing in the WPT Law which would lead the Tribunal to conclude that, by referring to such a standard, there is discrimination in the present instance either on the basis of a cross-industry (e.g. the petroleum industry) or a gold-copper comparison. As stated in the *Sempra* case: '(t)here are quite naturally important differences between the various affected sectors, so it is not surprising that different solutions might have been or are being sought for each'. The different treatment given in this case to gold and copper compared to other industries or between gold and copper cannot support a conclusion of discrimination under the Treaty.

316. Moreover, even if the reference to competitive and substitutable products were not retained as a criterion, the different regimes applied to copper and gold would not justify the Tribunal to conclude to discriminatory treatment. Respondent has explained the distinction introduced as relating, for one part, to greater opportunities for tax evasion existing in the gold mining industry and, for another part, to a desire to see the proceeds from copper exports to be used for the building of a copper-processing plant in Mongolia permitting to add value to Mongolian copper production. In addition, as the Parties have pointed out, copper production in Mongolia was essentially in the hands of Erdenet, a company 51% controlled by the State of Mongolia and 49% by Russia. The WPT may have been a poor instrument to achieve the objectives of the Great Khural and the Tribunal has no evidence to the effect that they were in fact achieved. It is not the role of the Tribunal to weigh the wisdom of legislation, but merely to assess whether such legislation breaches the Treaty. Claimants have not succeeded in demonstrating that this was an abusive or irrational decision and that it constituted discriminatory treatment.

317. The discrimination argument has also been raised by Claimants in relation with the stability agreement issued to Boroo Gold in 2000. This matter will be addressed separately below when dealing with that issue.

318. Finally, Claimants argue that the WPT discriminates illegally against them because it disproportionately applies to GEM. Even accepting Claimants' statement that GEM's WPT payments might have represented up to 89–93% of Mongolia's total WPT income, despite the fact that GEM had never made up more than 25% of total gold production in that country, a major factor in that disproportion results from the fact that even if Boroo Gold's production represented in 2006 some 45% of that total, it benefited from a stability agreement which exempted it from the WPT. Apart from this particular stability agreement, no evidence had been adduced by Claimants to the effect that the tax burden imposed upon GEM was different from the one applying to other gold producers in Mongolia under the WPT.

[. . .]

360. In this section, the Tribunal will address the claim concerning the enactment and the application of the 2006 Minerals Law which provided that mining companies employing foreign citizens in excess of a 10% quota must pay a special monthly fee equal to ten times the minimum salary in Mongolia, while, under the previous law on the subject, the payment was only two times the minimum monthly salary.

[. . .]

362. As to its argument under Article 3, Claimants base it on the alleged lack of protection of their legitimate expectations, of transparency, of a stable and predictable regulatory framework, the discriminatory character of the FWF and its unreasonableness.

363. The Tribunal is not convinced by the argument advanced by Claimants to the effect that it is impossible for GEM to limit the employment of foreign workers to 10% of its workforce, Mongolia not having the qualified personnel to meet its particular requirements. They say that, because of this, Claimants' business was negatively impacted in a significant way; according to them, at the end of 2007, the required payment in that respect amounted to about USD 500 000 a month.

364. First of all, it is not unheard of that States impose restrictions on the hiring of foreign workers; such restrictions can take various forms. By themselves, such restrictions, including a total ban on foreign workers, do not automatically constitute a breach of a BIT. The burden is upon the investor to prove that a particular provision of a BIT has been breached.

365. Secondly, in the present case, the particular challenged measure does not appear to be discriminatory or breaching the fair and equal treatment standard under Article 3 of the Treaty, in any of the forms alleged above by Claimants.

366. Claimants argue that it is discriminatory because it is limited to the mining

industry. The Tribunal has already ruled that the WPT Law did not constitute a discriminatory measure simply because it imposed heavier taxation on the gold mining industry compared to copper mining or the whole mining industry and that there were reasonable explanations why a special tax regime could be imposed upon a particular business sector which would enjoy, at a particular time, large windfall gains. This may not be very wise public policy but it does not by itself make it a breach of a particular BIT. It is therefore all of the more the case when a law applies equally, like in this instance, to a whole industry: the mining industry. It may be true that the required qualifications for a truck driver in the mining industry may not be significantly different from those required for the same function in the rest of the economy. But such an issue is not generally the one considered by a State when it enacts specific legislation concerning the import of foreign workers. In the present instance, the mining sector is a strategic sector for Mongolia, representing a large part of its industrial activity and being the one which attracted most foreign workers. In such circumstances, it is quite understandable that the State wished to impose severe restrictions on the use of foreign workers, in order to foster the employment of nationals. GEM seems to have been the company that has suffered the most from the imposition of entry fees but there was nothing in the relevant legislation which implied, even in a minimal way, that it targeted GEM in particular. Moreover, Mongolia has succeeded in demonstrating that several other foreign mining companies, including gold mining ones, managed to achieve a much smaller percentage of foreign workers than GEM without appearing to suffer prejudice in their activities.

367. It does appear from the evidence that GEM preferred to run a large part of its operations with Russian workers, alleging the special nature of placer mining and the lack of qualified Mongolian personnel to fill the required functions. It may well be that some specialists might have been required to operate dredges and other major machinery and that Mongolia did not have enough qualified local workers for those functions but, still, that cannot explain the large percentage of foreign workers (essentially Russian) employed by GEM compared to any other mining company in Mongolia. Mongolia has demonstrated before the Tribunal that its technical schools were producing a large number of graduates trained for the mining industry but Claimants have not shown that GEM made any special effort to increase its contingent of Mongolian employees.

368. The Tribunal has received unchallenged evidence from the Director of Mining of Mongolia, Mr. N. Batbayar, to the effect that Mongolia has five universities from which students graduate in mining and that, each year, hundreds of students graduate with a bachelor's or a master's degree in mining. In addition, vocational schools also teach mining to their students. Mr. Batbayar referred to his own experience as Operational Manager of a gold placer mining company (like GEM) for several years where all of the workers were Mongolian. Mr. Batbayar also referred to other large foreign mining companies, like Ivanhoe and Boroo, which hire up to 95%

Mongolian workers, while the best that could be achieved by GEM in 2007 was a proportion of about 50%.

369. From the evidence submitted to the Tribunal, it would appear that GEM was of the view that the working language for most of the company's activities should be Russian and that this resulted in the rejection of many candidates for employment who did not speak Russian. This may indeed have been GEM's decision but it should not have been surprised that Mongolia would have adopted legislation which would have created a strong incentive for the employment of its own nationals, even though they may not have been fluent in a foreign language. Mr. Batbayar also gave the example of another mining company (Ivanhoe) which did not require the knowledge of a foreign language by candidates before entry but which had courses for its employees to teach them English.

[. . .]

372. As to the argument that the FWF's objective was really to increase fees revenues rather than to foster the employment of Mongolian nationals, the Tribunal fails to see that, if even this was true, it would turn the FWF into a breach of the Treaty. The way for GEM to avoid or reduce those fees was to increase rapidly and significantly the number of its Mongolian employees, which it did, for instance, at two deposit sites, increasing local staff from about 26% in 2006 to 37% in 2008. An alternative to an increase of the fees could have been for Mongolia to simply set a ceiling of 10% to the employment of foreign workers but this would have had even more dramatic consequences for GEM.

[. . .]

475. The validity of the Boroo Gold agreement is not a matter that is coming under the jurisdiction of this Tribunal and therefore will not be addressed here. However, again assuming that the Tribunal would have jurisdiction over disputes concerning events preceding the entry into force of the Treaty, the argument about unfair treatment would be one that could be properly raised, the question being whether Boroo Gold and GEM were in similar situations.

476. As mentioned before, Boroo Gold committed to substantial investment in the future. [. . .]

477. Respondent argues that GEM was not willing to commit to future investments, even to the tune of the minimum USD 2 million required under the law. [. . .]

487. The question then is: Was Mongolia obligated to reach with GEM an agreement on the same terms as the one concluded with Boroo Gold, on May 9, 2000? The Tribunal does not believe that this was the case.

488. First of all, there is a certain element of administrative discretion in the negotiation of such agreements; the concessions granted by a government will very much depend on the size of the investment contemplated. In the case of Boroo Gold, if one ignores previous investments, as argued by Respondent, Boroo Gold committed to investing some USD 24 million, between July 2000 and July 2003 (USD 9

million in cash and USD 15 million in other forms). This is significantly superior to the USD 5 million over five years mentioned in CE-127.

489. Secondly, the arrival of Boroo Gold (it had arrived earlier but its investment represented only about USD 1 million by the time of the 2000 agreement), represented the arrival of a new player in gold mining, a sector considered strategic by Mongolia. In fact, Boroo Gold quickly became the largest gold producer in Mongolia (GEM being the second). It would be understandable that, in such circumstances, there would have been a strong incentive for Mongolia to make exceptional concessions in favor of Boroo Gold in return for a commitment to substantial investment over the following three years.

490. In light of the above, the Tribunal concludes that, even if it had been called upon to rule on the Negotiations, it would, in any event, have decided that the evidence submitted to it is not sufficient for the Tribunal to conclude that the actions of Respondent in that connection were of such a nature as to constitute a breach of customary international law, whether it be because of bad faith, discrimination or on any other ground.

The *Paushok* tribunal's approach to critically comparing even competitors' characteristics was taken even further by the majority in the *Renée Rose Levy de Levi v. Peru* arbitration. In that case, the claimant argued that financial sector competitors were the relevant comparator to her bank. The tribunal disagreed, first emphasizing the need for a fact-specific case-by-case approach to determining likeness (or similarity) of circumstances. It then continued by noting the particularity of the banking sector:

396. In light of the parties' agreement on the need to first identify the domestic entities that were in similar circumstances with [claimant's bank] BNM, the Arbitral Tribunal considers, as noted by other arbitral tribunals, that discrimination only exists between groups or categories of persons who are in a similar situation, after having assessed, on case-by-case basis, the relevant circumstances. The banks cited by the Claimant are in the same sector (banking) and are regulated by a common entity [. . .]. Notwithstanding this common denominator, the Tribunal considers that, as the banking sector is a sensitive area for any country, there are marked differences between the various banks operating in it. For example, there are banks primarily engaged in asset management and investment, others in corporate and consumer banking [. . .]. The market segment in which a bank is primarily engaged shows how different it is from other banks and determines whether or not they are competitors.

397. In order to consider the consequences of a bank's failure, one has to consider the segment and the number of individuals affected, its market share, and other similar factors.

398. Peru introduced into this proceeding several facts that in the Tribunal's

opinion prove that BNM was not in like circumstances with Banco Wiese, BCP, and Banco Latino. BCP was the first and Banco Wiese the second-largest bank in Peru up to November 2000 and together they accounted for 44 percent of the loans in this country and 51 percent of deposits. In contrast, BNM had 4 percent of loans and 2 percent of deposits up to November 2000. [. . .] Peru has also stated that Banco Latino did not differ so much from BNM in terms of size but in terms of its far-reaching network of individual depositors, which was not the case of BNM, whose clientele mainly comprised companies, other banks, and State-owned enterprises. These elements of comparison between these four banks are convincing in the opinion of the Tribunal.[30]

There is substantial space between *Occidental's* 'any-investor-is-comparable' and *Pauschok's* 'only-direct-competitors-are-comparable' approaches, and most tribunals are less extreme. Instead of making conceptual determinations of the extent of likeness, tribunals tend to weigh the facts of the particular dispute heavily. The *Clayton/Bilcon* tribunal's award is illustrative.

 CASE

Clayton et al. v. Canada[31]

The dispute between the mining company Clayton/Bilcon and Canada arose from the government's process of determining whether to grant the company a license to mine a quarry. When a joint federal-provincial review body denied the license due to a negative environmental impact assessment report, the claimant alleged a variety of violations of NAFTA Chapter 11, including discriminatory treatment under Articles 1102 (national treatment) and 1103 (MFN).

In determining the non-discrimination claims, the tribunal had to decide with which other investors Clayton/Bilcon was 'in like circumstances'. Should Canada's treatment of the claimant be compared to its treatment of all investors whose investments have to undergo environmental assessment or only of investors that have both been subjected to a joint review panel and who have stimulated significant opposition in the community?

---

30 *Renee Rose Levy de Levi v. Peru*, ICSID Case No. ARB/10/17, Award (Feb. 26, 2014). But see Dissent by Arbitrator Morales Godoy at paras. 179–88 (arguing that the majority's approach to distinguishing investments on the basis of market share is inappropriate).

31 *William Ralph Clayton, William Richard Clayton, Douglas Clayton, Daniel Clayton and Bilcon of Delaware, Inc. v. Government of Canada*, PCA Case No. 2009-04, Award on Jurisdiction and Liability (March 17, 2015) (footnotes omitted).

687. Bilcon refers to a number of projects involving quarries and marine terminals in ecologically sensitive zones where the project was evaluated on a more favorable basis than Bilcon's. Bilcon emphasizes that the issue is not whether the outcome of the review was different, but rather whether Canada provided less favorable treatment concerning the mode of review (JRP) and the evaluative standard, including the application of the usual *CEAA* standard of likely significant adverse effects after mitigation.

[. . .]

690. Canada suggests that the only projects that should be compared to Bilcon's are those where there was a joint federal Canada-provincial review panel. Canada has also suggested that a comparator is only in 'like circumstances' if the JRP had to deal with significant opposition within a local community.

691. The Tribunal does not agree that it should confine an Article 1102 analysis in this case to such a narrow range of possible comparators.

692. Article 1102 refers to situations where investors or investments find themselves in 'like circumstances'. The language is not restricted as it is in some other trade-liberalizing agreements, such as those that refer to 'like products'. Article 1102 refers to the way in which either the investor or investment is treated, rather than confining concerns over discrimination to comparisons between similar articles of trade. Moreover, the operative word in Article 1102 is 'similar', not 'identical'. In addition to giving the reasonably broad language of Article 1102 its due, a Tribunal must also take into account the objects of NAFTA, which include according to Article 102(1)(c) 'to increase substantially investment opportunities in the territories of the Parties'.

693. The Investors note that in the *Occidental* case, a violation of national treatment was alleged under a bilateral investment treaty that stipulated national treatment for investors in 'like situations' to domestic investors. [. . .] The *Occidental* tribunal [. . .] observed that 'the purpose of national treatment is to protect investors as compared to local producers, and this cannot be done by addressing exclusively the sector in which the particular activity is conducted'. [. . .]

694. Cases of alleged denial of national treatment must be decided in their own factual and regulatory context. In the present case, what is at issue is whether the Investor was treated less favorably for the purpose of an environmental assessment. The federal Canada law in question, the *CEAA*, is one of very general application. It applies the 'likely significant adverse effects after mitigation' standard of assessment as a necessary component of environmental review across a wide range of modes and industries, including any marine terminals or quarries that are assessed under its provisions.

695. The Investors argue that 'the NAFTA Tribunal should consider all enterprises affected by the environmental assessment regulatory process to be in like circumstances with Bilcon'. While that broad proposition might be correct, adopting it would commit this Tribunal to a more abstract and sweeping proposition than

is necessary to decide this case. The Tribunal finds, that on examination of their particular facts, many of the comparison cases brought forward by the Investors qualify as 'sufficiently' similar to sustain an Article 1102 comparison for the purposes of this case.

696. The actual comparison cases brought forward by the Investors in the present case generally involve federal Canada or JRP assessments of mining projects, including oil and gas exploration, accompanied by exports that involve sea routes. A number of them specifically involved quarry and marine terminal export projects that had the potential to affect a local community. At least three of them involved assessments that included the marine terminal component of a project that was connected to a quarry and took place in an ecologically sensitive coastal area. The fact that assessments in these cases were carried out in accordance with the usual 'likely significant adverse effects after mitigation' analysis is sufficient to conclude that they received more favorable treatment than did the Investors in like circumstances. [. . .]'

b   No less favourable treatment

Although not always set out as a separate provision, where an IIA specifies that investors shall receive treatment 'no less favourable than that received by any other investor', the element of comparable treatment becomes important. Thus, a US oil company with an investment in Ecuador cannot be required to forego VAT refunds for their exports if Ecuadoran exporters receive such monies back.[32] The disadvantages can either be *de jure* or *de facto* or, indeed, hypothetical. The arbitrator in *Bogdanov v. Moldova*, for example, faced an investor's claim that the host had subjected his investment to discriminatory treatment by imposing fees on each transaction within the free trade zone in which the investment was located. Although the host denied discrimination on the grounds that any national company would also have been subjected to such fees, the arbitrator nevertheless upheld the claimant's position:

> [Moldova's] argument [. . .] is wholly abstract: *if* other companies in other zones were to conduct activities of the same nature [. . .], *then* they would also be subjected to the same charges. The Republic of Moldova has not, however, pointed to any specific case where another company has in fact been subjected to the fees [. . .]
>
> Failing [. . .] demonstration of any single instance where a company other than [the investor's] has been subjected to the EUR 200 fee per declaration, the Sole

---

32   *See Occidental Exploration and Production Company v. Ecuador, supra* note 27.

Arbitrator is forced to conclude that Mr Bogdanov has not received [. . .] non-discriminatory treatment.[33]

The fact that there need not be any direct competitors to benefit from the host's actions toward the investor does not prevent a claim of non-discrimination from succeeding. With the focus on the harm done to the investor—rather than on upholding general principles of treatment—it is up to the investor to demonstrate that it has suffered as a result of the allegedly discriminatory treatment.[34]

On the other hand, not just any measure that subjects a foreign investor to treatment that affects foreign and domestic investors differently is prohibited by IIA provisions on non-discrimination. The claimant has the burden of proof to show that it has been subject to a disadvantage and is not merely dis-satisfied with its situation in relation to a competitor. Thus, the *Arif* tribunal found that the placement of the claimant's duty-free store in one part of the airport was not discriminatory even though a competing duty-free store was in a different area of the same airport given that the claimant had chosen its position first on the basis of the location's better commercial potential.[35] While the necessity of showing discriminatory intent on the part of the host has been rejected by the majority of tribunals as an explicit test for non-discrimination claims,[36] if the differences in treatment can be shown to have a reasonable basis, even treatment that is not 'the same' can be acceptable.[37]

c   *Justifications*

Many existing BITs do not provide for general exceptions, making it very difficult to avoid the obligations. In case of non-discrimination obligations, however, there is broad recognition among tribunals that there are often strong public interests in differentiating among investors, so justifications can be used to defend differential treatment of investors.[38]

---

33 *See Yury Bogdanov v. Republic of Moldova, SCC Arbitration No. V* (114/2009), Final Arbitral Award, paras. 88–90 (Mar. 30, 2010). Available at: http://italaw.com/documents/Bogdanovv.Moldova2010Award.pdf.

34 Nicholas DiMascio and Joost Pauwelyn, *Nondiscrimination in Trade and Investment Treaties: Worlds Apart or Two Sides of the Same Coin?*, 102(1) AJIL 48, 70 (2008).

35 *Mr. Frank Charles Arif v. Republic of Moldova*, ICSID Case No. ARB/11/23, Award, para. 513 (Apr. 8, 2003). Available at http://www.italaw.com/cases/1846.

36 *S.D. Myers v. Canada, supra* note 18, para. 254; DiMascio and Pauwelyn, *supra* note 34 at 80.

37 *S.D. Myers v. Canada, supra* note 18, para. 254; *Pope and Talbot v. Government of Canada*, UNCITRAL (NAFTA), Award on the Merits of Phase 2, paras. 102–3 (Apr. 10, 2001). Available at: http://italaw.com/documents/ Award_Merits2001_04_10_Pope.pdf.

38 Rudolf Dolzer and Christoph Schreuer, *Principles of International Investment Law* 202–3 (second edn, 2012).

Establishing the absence of justifications for discrimination has become an integral part of the legal analysis of discriminatory treatment for many arbitrators. 'The purpose' of the national treatment provision, wrote the *Total v. Argentina* tribunal, 'is to ascertain whether the protected investments have been treated worse *without any justification*, specifically because of their foreign nationality'.[39]

The analysis of justifications varies from tribunal to tribunal. Some may consider the legitimacy of differential treatment when determining the comparability of the investors. The *S.D. Myers* tribunal did this, noting:

> The Tribunal considers that the interpretation of the phrase 'like circumstances' in Article 1102 must take into account the general principles that emerge from the legal context of the NAFTA, including both its concern with the environment and the need to avoid trade distortions that are not justified by environmental concerns. The assessment of 'like circumstances' must also take into account circumstances that would justify governmental regulations that treat them differently in order to protect the public interest.[40]

The *Paushok* tribunal, too, rejected the claimants' discrimination arguments in large part due to what it found to be Mongolia's legitimate interest in affording special treatment to its economically important gold mining sector.[41] Others will incorporate the justification into the less favorable treatment/discrimination analysis. Unequal treatment is not 'less favorable' if it is intended to address a policy problem that only one competitor causes. The Egypt–Germany BIT states this explicitly in its combined MFN/national treatment provision:

> [. . .] Measures that have to be taken for reasons of public security and order, public health or morality shall not be deemed 'treatment less favourable' within the meaning of this Article.[42]

Finally, there are some IIAs that do contain general exceptions for policies such as the protection of national security, environment, or health and discussions within the investment policy community suggest that an increasing number of governments will be pressing for such exception provisions in

---

39 *Total S.A. v. Argentine Republic*, ICSID Case No. ARB/04/1, Decision on Liability, para. 344 (Dec. 27, 2010); footnotes omitted. *See*, e.g. *Joseph Charles Lemire v. Ukraine*, *infra* note 94.

40 *S.D. Myers v. Canada*, *supra* note 18, para 250.

41 *Paushok v. Mongolia*, *supra* note 28, para. 315.

42 Agreement between the Arab Republic of Egypt and the Federal Republic of Germany concerning the Encouragement and Reciprocal Protection of Investments, Art. 3.2 (Nov. 22, 2009).

the future. Where these provisions are available, the Respondent can invoke them to excuse preferences being afforded domestic investors.

5.3.3 National treatment

One of the two basic forms of the non-discrimination obligation found in IIAs is the duty to treat foreign investors (and their investments) no less favourably than the host treats its national investors (and their investments). While it shares its basic legal elements with the general non-discrimination principle and the most favoured nation treatment obligation, national treatment provisions are theoretically and practically more complex. States, after all, have a primary duty to their citizens. Democratic governments, at least, are to represent the interests of their people—accepting majority decisions to the extent such do not violate the basic rights of the minority. As a result, prohibiting states from offering nationals preferential commercial conditions is exceptional. On the practical level, distinguishing the regulatory rules applying to foreign economic actors from those for domestic actors often has a rational basis from a governance perspective: more effective oversight, administrative efficiency, or the conservation of financial resources.

Nevertheless, national treatment obligations are found in treaties throughout the international economic legal system, including investment law. Their analysis follows the general pattern set out above.

5.3.4 Most favoured nation treatment

The obligation of most favoured nation (MFN) treatment is a second form of non-discrimination obligation contained in many international economic law treaties. It differs from national treatment by looking to the host's treatment of third party investors in comparison with the foreign investor bringing the claim. The most potent advantage of MFN clauses is the moderating effect such clauses have on differences in negotiating power. For the weaker party, an MFN clause ensures that its nationals will nevertheless be eligible for treatment the stronger party has agreed to offer other investment partners. Of course, there is a countervailing effect of MFNs in requiring all negotiators to be more careful in what they agree to insert in a treaty: while a particular concession may be viable for one treaty partner (in a BIT, for example), it may be less suited as a universal offer (as is the result of an MFN clause in its other BITs). As the number of BITs increases, then, so does the significance of MFN clauses. We shall address the basic obligation below, and return to some of the more difficult issues later.

Under MFN, a host may not treat an investor from a BIT party less favourably than it does a foreign investor from another home state. As an illustration,
assume there is a BIT between Egypt and Romania that offers expropriated
investors compensation that is 'equal to the value of the investment at the
time of the expropriation'[43] and a second BIT between Egypt and Italy that
contains both an MFN clause and a provision that offers investors 'adequate
and fair compensation'.[44] If a case arises where an Romanian investor's debt-
ridden electrical production plant is expropriated by Egypt, the investor
could call upon the MFN clause in the Egypt–Romania BIT to ask for the
'adequate and fair' compensation promised in Egypt's BIT with Italy, claiming that such would be better treatment than the standard provided for in its
own BIT (which could be interpreted to mean the current value—a negative
sum). Having been promised the best treatment Egypt offers (by virtue of
the MFN provision), the Romanian investor could thereby profit from this
other measure of compensation.

The issues of comparability, level of treatment, justification, and intent in
MFN analyses are the same as with national treatment: are the investors in
like circumstances? Was the treatment *de jure* or *de facto* disadvantageous to
the investor? And, does the host's lack of intent to discriminate among investors make a difference?

The fact that most investment agreements are bilateral leads to interesting
policy issues specific to the MFN obligation.[45] Recall that BITs are negotiated agreements between sovereigns. Thus, at least in principle, the negotiations proceed on a reciprocal, concessional basis: each party agreeing to
certain provisions in exchange for others. Each party has the possibility of
not agreeing to all the demands of the other party if it feels that such a concession would make the overall exchange uneven. When protections meant
only for investors of Land A come to an investor of Land B through the MFN
clause, then, the negotiated balance of concessions may be upset in a way that
the host did not expect.

Most tribunals will allow investors to access the advantages of substantive
investment provisions through MFN clauses. We will see, however, that

---

43 Agreement between the Socialist Republic of Romania and the Arab Republic of Egypt on the Promotion
and Mutual Guarantee of Capital Investments, art. 3.1 (1978).

44 *See* Agreement for the Promotion and Protection of Investments between the Republic of Italy and the
Arab Republic of Egypt, art. 5.1(ii) (1989).

45 *See* Dolzer and Schreuer, *supra* note 38, at 206–7.

MFN claims become more debatable when jurisdiction is extended beyond the host's expectations.[46]

CASE

Bayindir Insaat Turizm Ticaret Ve Sanayi AŞ v. Islamic Republic of Pakistan[47]

This case concerns a dispute between Bayindir Insaat Turizm Ticaret Ve Sanayi AŞ (Bayindir) an infrastructure construction company incorporated in Turkey and the Islamic Republic of Pakistan (Pakistan).

In 1993, Bayindir and the Pakistani public corporation, the 'National Highway Authority' (NHA), entered into an agreement stipulating that Bayindir would build a motorway between Islamabad and Peshawar and construct ancillary works (M-1 Project). The parties signed a second contract incorporating the terms of the 1993 agreement and stipulating that the laws of Pakistan would be the governing law between the parties.

Starting in 1998, Bayindir's progress fell behind schedule, and in April 2001, the NHA notified Bayindir that it would impose liquidated damages for the late completion of two priority sections of the project. Three days later, the NHA terminated Bayindir's contract and asked the corporation to hand over possession of the site within two weeks. The NHA secured the site with the help of the Pakistani army and evacuated Bayindir's employees.

On 15 April 2002, Bayindir submitted a Request for Arbitration to the ICSID secretariat arguing, *inter alia*, that Pakistan had not afforded it fair and equitable treatment (FET). The 1995 Pakistan–Turkey BIT did not contain a FET clause, however, so the claimant had to rely on the most favoured nation clause in the Treaty (MFN) to refer to FET provisions found in Pakistan's bilateral investment treaty with the United Kingdom.

a. Importation of FET obligation by operation of MFN clause

1. Bayindir's position

[. . .]

149. The Claimant emphasizes that the interpretation of the Treaty's MFN clause

---

46 *Infra* Chapter 6.

47 *Bayindir Insaat Turizm Ticaret Ve Sanayi AŞ v. Islamic Republic of Pakistan*, ICSID Case No. ARB/03/29, Award (Aug. 27, 2009). Available at: http://italaw.com/documents/Bayandiraward.pdf; footnotes omitted.

supports the importation of an FET guarantee in the light of (i) the Treaty's preamble and of its object and purpose, as directed by Article 31 of the VCLT; (ii) Article
II(4) of the Treaty, which deliberately excludes some matters from the scope of
operation of the MFN clause and, a contrario, implies that matters not excluded
such as FET are covered; and (iii) the decisions in *MTD v. Chile* [. . .], *Plama v.
Bulgaria* and *Salini v. Jordan*, which, in Claimant's submission, make it clear that the
specific purpose of an MFN clause in a BIT is to 'allow an investor to benefit from a
more favourable substantive protection of another Treaty' ([. . .]).

2. Pakistan's position

150. The Respondent argues that reliance on the MFN clause of the Treaty to
import an FET clause from another BIT is only possible if it is not excluded by the
intention of the contracting parties at the time of signing the Treaty. In the present
case, the intention had clearly been to exclude the FET standard to the extent
that Turkey and Pakistan deliberately decided not to include an FET clause in the
Treaty 'notwithstanding that the preamble acknowledges the importance of fair
and equitable treatment and clauses requiring such treatment [. . .] were already
common by 1995 when the Pakistan–Turkey BIT was signed' ([. . .]).

151. With respect to the Pakistan–UK BIT to which Claimant makes special reference, the Respondent noted at the hearing that the Claimant's interpretation would
mean that the decision of Pakistan and Turkey not to include an FET guarantee,
while including an MFN clause, would have had no effect at all, given that the
Pakistan–UK BIT was already in force ([. . .]).

152. According to Pakistan, the Claimant's argument would amount to 'precisely
the kind of "treaty shopping" against which the tribunal in cases like *Maffezini*
and *Telenor* warned, albeit in the context of substantive, rather than jurisdictional,
provisions'([. . .]).

3. Tribunal's determination

[. . .]

154. The relevant passage of the preamble reads as follows

> 'Agreeing that fair and equitable treatment of investment is desirable in order to
> maintain a stable framework for investment and maximum effective utilization
> of economic resources.' ([. . .]).

155. In the Tribunal's view, such language is of little assistance as it does not establish any operative obligation. It is true that the reference to FET in the preamble
together with the absence of a FET clause in the Treaty might suggest that Turkey
and Pakistan intended not to include an FET obligation in the Treaty. The Tribunal
is, however, not persuaded that this suggestion rules out the possibility of importing an FET obligation through the MFN clause expressly included in the Treaty.

The fact that the States parties to the Treaty clearly contemplated the importance of the FET rather suggests the contrary. Indeed, even though it does not establish an operative obligation, the preamble is relevant for the interpretation of the MFN clause in its context and in the light of the Treaty's object and purpose pursuant to Article 31(1) of the VCLT.

156. Article II(2) of the Treaty reads in relevant part as follows:

> 'Each Party shall accord to these investments, once established, treatment no less favourable than that accorded in similar situations to investments of its investors or to investments of investors of any third country, whichever is the most favourable.' ([. . .])

This provision is limited by Article II(4) as follows:

> 'The provisions of this Article shall have no effect in relation to following agreements entered into by either of the Parties:
>
> (a) relating to any existing or future customs unions, regional economic organization or similar international agreements,
> (b) relating wholly or mainly to taxation.'
>   ([. . .])

157. The ordinary meaning of the words used in Article II(2) together with the limitations provided in Article II(4) show that the parties to the Treaty did not intend to exclude the importation of a more favourable substantive standard of treatment accorded to investors of third countries. This reading is supported by the preamble's insistence on FET.

158. It is further supported by the decision of the tribunal in *MTD v. Chile* regarding the application of MFN to import an FET obligation:

> 'The Tribunal has concluded that, under the BIT, the fair and equitable standard of treatment has to be interpreted in the manner most conducive to fulfill the objective of the BIT to protect investments and create conditions favorable to investments. The Tribunal considers that to include as part of the protections of the BIT those included in Article 3(1) of the Denmark BIT and Article 3(3) and (4) of the Croatia BIT is in consonance with this purpose. The Tribunal is further convinced of this conclusion by the fact that the exclusions in the MFN clause relate to tax treatment and regional cooperation, matters alien to the BIT but that, because of the general nature of the MFN clause, the Contracting Parties considered it prudent to exclude. *A contrario sensu*, other matters that can be construed to be part of the fair and equitable treatment of investors would be covered by the clause.'

159. The fact that there is no uniform case law on MFN and procedural rights and that certain decisions, including *Maffezini v. Spain* and *Telenor v. Hungary* referred

to by the Respondent, as well as *Plama v. Bulgaria* and *Salini v. Jordan*, have adopted a different view than the one applied here is of little relevance. Indeed, the *ejusdem generis* principle that is sometimes viewed as a bar to the operation of the MFN clause with respect to procedural rights does not come into play here and the words of the Treaty are clear.

160. As noted by the Respondent, the FET provision to which the Claimant more specifically referred, namely Article II(2) of the Pakistan–UK BIT, pre-dates the MFN clause in the Treaty. In and of itself that chronology does not appear to preclude the importation of an FET obligation from another BIT concluded by the Respondent. In any event, the Claimant has also referred to BITs concluded subsequently to the Treaty. The issue is therefore not whether the Claimant can invoke an FET obligation, but rather which one. . . .

 DISCUSSION NOTES

1 For a thorough look at the issue of non-discrimination in investment law, see Christoph H. Schreuer, *Protection against Arbitrary or Discriminatory Measures, in* The Future of Investment Arbitration 183, 183–98 (Catherine A. Rogers and Roger P. Alford eds., 2009).

2 There is a large international economic law literature on the 'likeness' issue, mostly in the area of trade law. Decisions on what constitute 'like products' under the World Trade Organization's General Agreement on Tariffs and Trade (GATT) have relied heavily on the physical characteristics of the products, with consumer tastes and preferences and the end uses also being analysed.

The nature of investment protection, however, is not the same as the nature of trade regulation. Thus, tribunals are right to be wary of adopting trade law analyses of 'like products' and applying them to IIA provisions on non-discrimination. A full discussion of these approaches was entered into by the NAFTA tribunal in the *Methanex v. United States* arbitration. Addressing whether the United States had discriminated against Canadian investor Methanex by prohibiting the addition of methanol to gasoline, that tribunal noted first that '[t]he key question is: who is the proper comparator?'[48] Having found an 'identical comparator' that received identical treatment (and thus the element of less favourable treatment was absent), the tribunal went on to comment that the differing terms of non-discrimination obligations for trade in goods prevent investment arbitrators from using the same test for determining the term 'like circumstances':

---

48 *Methanex v. USA, supra* note 17 at Part IV, Chapter B, p. 8, para. 17.

29. In conclusion, the Tribunal decides that Methanex's claim under Article 1102 fails for a number of reasons, any one of which would suffice to reject its claim. At the very threshold, Methanex encounters the issue of whether the California ban meted out treatment that it accords in like circumstances to domestic investors. As the Tribunal has observed above and in its Partial Award, NAFTA, as a treaty, is to be interpreted in accordance with Articles 31 and 32 of the Vienna Convention on the Law of Treaties, which codifies the customary international rules of treaty interpretation. Hence, the Tribunal begins with an inquiry into the plain and natural meaning of the text of Article 1102. Paragraphs 1, 2, and 3 of Article 1102 enjoin each Party to accord to investors or investments of another Party 'treatment no less favorable than that it accords, in like circumstances, to its investors [or investments] . . . '. These provisions do not use the term of art in international trade law, 'like products', which appears in and plays a critical role in the application of GATT Article III. Indeed, the term 'like products' appears nowhere in NAFTA Chapter 11.

30. The drafting parties of NAFTA were fluent in GATT law and incorporated, in very precise ways, the term 'like goods' and the GATT provisions relating to it when they wished to do so. [. . .] With respect to trade in goods in Part Two, the obligation of 'no less favourable' treatment applies to 'any like, directly competitive or substitutable goods, as the case may be'. These rather precise criteria allow the importing or receiving state relatively little discretionary scope with respect to the goods entitled to national treatment.

[. . .]

33. It is thus apparent from the text that the drafters of NAFTA were careful and precise about the inclusion and the location of the respective terms, 'like goods', 'any like, directly competitive or substitutable goods, as the case may be', and 'like circumstances'. 'Like goods' is never used with respect to the investment regime of Chapter 11 and 'like circumstances', which is all that is used in Article 1102 for investment, is used with respect to standards-related measures that might constitute technical barriers to trade only in relation to services; nowhere in NAFTA is it used in relation to goods.

34. It may also be assumed that if the drafters of NAFTA had wanted to incorporate trade criteria in its investment chapter by engrafting a GATT-type formula, they could have. [. . .][49]

Indeed, the arguments regarding 'likeness' in investment treaties are more similar to those arising under trade agreement provisions requiring non-discrimination of services and service providers. These aspects of non-discrimination are underdeveloped even in trade law. To the

---

49 *Id*. at Part IV, Chapter B, pp. 14–17, paras. 29–30, 33–4.

extent there is jurisprudence on 'like service suppliers', is it helpful in clarifying the likeness of investors? In the World Trade Organization (WTO) case brought against the EC's banana import regime, the decision-making panel determined that all wholesale service activities supplied within the framework of wholesale services for a certain product are 'like services' and 'suppliers of like services' are 'like service suppliers' for purposes of the General Agreement on Trade in Services. See *European Communities – Regime for the Importation, Sale and Distribution of Bananas (Complaint by Ecuador)*, WT/DS27/R/ECU, para. 7.322 (22 May 1997). Rudolf Dolzer, however, comments that 'probably the most significant development' in the investment jurisprudence on national treatment is the tribunals' turn away from relying on WTO analyses of national treatment when interpreting IIAs. See *National Treatment: New Developments* (presentation for the ICSID, OECD, UNCTAD Symposium, Making the Most of International Investment Agreements: A Common Agenda, Paris (12 Dec. 2005), at 4, http://www.oecd.org/investment/internationalinvestmentagreements/35805957.pdf.

3 Does the differentiation need to be nationality-based for a claim of non-discrimination to succeed? This question is disputed. In the case *Lauder v. Czech Republic*,[50] the tribunal took the view that there needs to be a nationality based motivation, as did the *Total v. Argentina* tribunal (para. 344). The *Thunderbird* tribunal,[51] on the other hand, denied the need to show a nationality motive.

4 Is it plausible to argue that old-order BITs would experience a change if a country signs one more favourable BIT with a—in financial terms— less important negotiation partner?

5 One area of particular concern is the effect the national treatment obligation has on particularly disadvantaged populations within the host territory. To what extent are national treatment obligations in IIAs a hindrance to affirmative action programs?

5.4 Full protection and security

Full protection and security (FPS) is a standard that protects the foreign investor against third party interference in an investment. Under FPS, the

---

50 *Ronald S. Lauder v. The Czech Republic*, UNCITRAL Arbitration, Final Award (Sept. 3, 2001). Available at: http:// italaw.com/sites/default/files/case-documents/ita0451.pdf.

51 *International Thunderbird Gaming Corporation v. The United Mexican States*, UNCITRAL Arbitration, Arbitral Award (Jan. 26, 2006). Available at: http://italaw.com/sites/default/files/case-documents/ita0431.pdf.

investor must be protected from interference from both state powers and from third parties. Thus, the state must guard the investor against employee uprisings or civil disturbances as well as refraining from threatening the investor itself.

Some tribunals and commentators would extend the FPS obligation to cover legal security. Such protection would require the host to ensure a stable legal regime and the availability of timely access to court proceedings to the investor.

5.4.1 Physical security

The investor and the investment enjoy a right to protection and security by the host. If the investor is a natural person, he or she may not be bodily injured, harassed, or threatened. Neither may the investment be damaged, either by the host or by individuals or groups within the host territory. In *Wena Hotels*, for example, private actors forcefully took over the claimant's hotels. While the government was not involved in the seizure, its police did not act to stop the individuals from their illegal actions, nor did they pursue such actors legally subsequent to the seizure. The tribunal found, therefore, that Egypt had clearly failed to act according to the standard required in the BIT.[52]

Importantly, however, the obligation of the host to protect the investor and the investment is not unlimited. The FPS standard is one of performance rather than result, so strict liability is not available to investors, should the host attempt to protect but fail. This principle is firmly established in general international law as well as in investment law. Noting the ICJ's opinion in the *ELSI* case, one of the earliest investor-State dispute panels, the tribunal in *AAPL v. Sri Lanka* confirmed that the Court's refusal to find that states must 'warranty that property shall never in any circumstances be occupied or disturbed'[53] applies to investor protection as well. In the tribunal's words:

> . . . both the oldest reported arbitral precedent and the latest I.C.J. ruling confirms that the language imposing on the host State an obligation to provide 'protection and security' or 'full protection and security required by international law' [. . .] could not be construed according to the natural and ordinary sense of the words as creating a 'strict liability'. The rule remains that:

---

52 *Wena Hotels Ltd. v. Arab Republic of Egypt*, ICSID Case No. ARB/98/4, Award, paras. 84–95 (Dec. 8, 2000), 42 ILM 896 (2002).
53 *ELSI* case, *supra* note 6.

'The State into which an alien has entered . . . is not an insurer or a guarantor of his security . . . It does not, and could hardly be asked to, accept an absolute responsibility for all injuries to foreigners (citation omitted).'

This conclusion, arrived at more than three decades ago, still reflects—in the Tribunal's opinion—the present status of International Law Investment Standards as reflected in 'the worldwide BIT network' (citation omitted).[54]

Even without strict liability, however, hosts must do something to protect an investor and her investment. The tribunal in *American Manufacturing and Trading v. Zaire* expressed the accepted view clearly that a full protection and security clause sets forth an 'objective obligation', one that is:

. . . an obligation of vigilance, in the sense that [the host State] shall take all measures necessary to ensure the full enjoyment of protection and security of its [the Claimant's] investments and should not be permitted to invoke its own legislation to detract from any such obligation. [The host State] must show that it has taken all measures of precaution to protect the investment of [the Claimant] in its territory.[55]

The standard to which hosts are held, then, is one of due diligence. Widely accepted, the standard of due diligence has been further elaborated upon so as to define it relative to the host's capacities—financial as well as institutional. The following case highlights these aspects.

 CASE

Pantechniki SA Contractors and Engineers v. The Republic of Albania[56]

The facts of the case at hand have been previously outlined in Chapter 3. With regard to the alleged violation of the full protection and security standard, the sole arbitrator made the following findings:

71. The Claimant alleges that Albania failed to provide full protection and security of its investment in the Republic of Albania in breach of Article 4(1) of the Treaty which provides:

---

54 *Asian Agricultural Products, Ltd. (AAPL) v. Republic of Sri Lanka*, ICSID Case No. ARB/87/3, Award, para. 49 (June 27, 1990). Available at http://www.italaw.com/sites/default/files/case-documents/ita1034.pdf.
55 *American Manufacturing and Trading, Inc. v. Republic of Zaire*, ICSID Case No. ARB/93/1, Award, paras. 6.05–6.06 (Feb. 21, 1997), 36 ILM 1534 (1997).
56 *Pantechniki SA Contractors and Engineers v. The Republic of Albania*, ICSID Case No. ARB/07/21, Award (July 30, 2009). Available at: http://italaw.com/documents/PantechnikiAward.pdf; footnotes omitted.

'Investments by investors of either Contracting Party shall enjoy full protection and security in the other Contracting Party.'

[. . .]

73. The Claimant considers that Article 4(1) of the Treaty embodies an international standard of treatment imposing an obligation on Albania to exercise 'due diligence' in the protection of its investment against both private and public action. It alleges that the March 1997 riots caused damage to its investment and that Albania was under an obligation not only actively to protect the Claimant's investment from the looting but also to take precautionary measures to prevent it from occurring.

74. Albania relies defensively on the following comment by McNair in relation to state responsibility for the consequences of insurrection:

'a state can usually defeat a claim in respect of loss or damage sustained by resident foreigners by showing that they have received the same treatment in the matter of protection or compensation of any as its own nationals'.

75. Albania asserts that the Claimant has been accorded treatment equivalent to that of all other victims of the events of March 1997. Albania also says that the Claimant has failed to demonstrate that the Republic of Albania acted negligently in relation to the riots.

76. This issue recalls a similar problem that arises with respect to claims of denial of justice. Should a state's international responsibility bear some proportion to its resources? Should a poor country be held accountable to a minimum standard which it could attain only at great sacrifice while a rich country would have little difficulty in doing so? No such proportionality factor has been generally accepted with respect to denial of justice. Two reasons appear salient. The first is that international responsibility does not relate to physical infrastructure; states are not liable for denial of justice because they cannot afford to put at the public's disposal spacious buildings or computerised information banks. What matters is rather the human factor of obedience to the rule of law. Foreigners who enter a poor country are not entitled to assume that they will be given things like verbatim transcripts of all judicial proceedings – but they are entitled to decision-making which is neither xenophobic nor arbitrary. The second is that a relativistic standard would be none at all. International courts or tribunals would have to make ad hoc assessments based on their evaluation of the capacity of each state at a given moment of its development. International law would thus provide no incentive for a state to improve. It would in fact operate to the opposite effect: a state which devoted more resources to its judiciary would run the risk of graduating into a more exacting category.

77. To apply the same reasoning with respect to the duty of protection and security would be parlous. There is an important distinction between the two in terms of

the *consciousness* of state behaviour in each case. A legal system and the disposi-
tions it generates are the products of deliberate choices and conduct developed or
neglected over long periods. The minimum requirement is not high in light of the
great value placed on the rule of law. There is warrant for its consistent application.
A failure of protection and security is to the contrary likely to arise in an unpredictable instance of civic disorder which could have been readily controlled by a
powerful state but which overwhelms the limited capacities of one which is poor
and fragile. There is no issue of incentives or disincentives with regard to unforeseen breakdowns of public order; it seems difficult to maintain that a government
incurs international responsibility for failure to plan for unprecedented trouble of
unprecedented magnitude in unprecedented places. The case for an element of
proportionality in applying the international standard is stronger than with respect
to claims of denial of justice.

78. The case of the *Cutler* claim in 1927 is instructive. It arose after the attack by
a mob on a building in Florence. An American citizen sought to bring a claim for
destroyed property. The Italian Government answered that while it accepted the
obligation of 'ordinary vigilance' it did not accept a duty 'to prevent certain occurrences from taking place'. The US government essentially agreed when it instructed
its embassy that 'a claim could only be made if the authorities had knowledge, or
should have had knowledge, of the impending attack, and failed to take precautions
to thwart it'.

79. O'Connell observed that a sensible distinction might be made between the
'general rule' that a state is obliged to maintain adequate governmental functions
'under normal conditions' but that the obligation would exceptionally dissolve
'when the breakdown is temporary and due to exceptional causes and circumstances'. This was the distinction proposed in the Harvard Research Draft on State
Responsibility in 1929. Yet it fails to resolve the issue of different capability. As
O'Connell put it:

> 'Is the State required to conform to an international standard, and responsible
> for its incapacity to attain it? Or is it obliged only to do what can reasonably
> be expected of it? Judge Huber in *Certain British Claims in the Spanish Zone of
> Morocco* adhered to the latter as the only realistic position. On the other hand, in
> taking into account the capacity of the State we cannot depart altogether from
> the notion of an "international standard".'

[. . .]

80. O'Connell continued as follows:

> '. . . it cannot be said with absolute confidence that the State is responsible
> merely because the event could have been averted if sufficient police had
> been present. It must be established that the situation called for more police
> which could have been provided in time and were not. Obviously there will

be disagreement about the judgment that was made, and that might have been made, and the most that can be said is that a prima facie case exists when it is established that the facts were known to the authorities and that the action which they took, if any, proved inadequate.'

81. My review of the cases and literature leads me to follow this reasoning and to adopt the more recent conclusion of Newcombe and Paradell:

'Although the host state is required to exercise an objective minimum standard of due diligence, the standard of due diligence is that of a host state in the circumstances and with the resources of the state in question. This suggests that due diligence is a modified objective standard – the host state must exercise the level of due diligence of a host state in its particular circumstances. In practice, tribunals will likely consider the state's level of development and stability as relevant circumstance in determining whether there has been due diligence. An investor investing in an area with endemic civil strife and poor governance cannot have the same expectation of physical security as one investing in London, New York or Tokyo.'

82. Ms Dourou's testimony was very clear. As Project Manager she was the Claimant's eyes and ears on the ground. She depicted in striking terms an environment of desolation and lawlessness which she and her team encountered upon arrival in 1994. The Claimant cannot say today that it felt entitled to rely on a high standard of police protection. (Indeed an absence of such expectations may well explain the logic and value to the contractor of Clause 11 of the Contracts by which the Employer accepted the risk of loss caused by civil disturbance.) My view may have been different if police were present and turned their back. Ms Dourou's evidence was to the contrary. She testified that the police said they were *unable* to intervene. That is crucially different from a *refusal* to intervene given the scale of the looting. I conclude that the Albanian authorities were powerless in the face of social unrest of this magnitude.

83. The Claimant pushes its argument to say that Albania should be liable because powerful public officials were complicit in the pyramid schemes that had so enraged the populace. The premise of this contention is problematic in principle. May an alleged chain of causation have so many links? This question need not be answered because the claim is simply unsubstantiated. The Claimant has seized on a general perception that Albania's struggling public institutions were disserved by influential and unscrupulous officeholders. But a claim before an international tribunal simply cannot be made good by casual references to general perception. Specific conduct must be alleged and proved. So must its purported effect. It is difficult to resist the impression that this contention was raised more to enlist intuitive sympathy than with a serious belief that it could prevail in this forum.

84. The Claimant also curiously seeks to establish a violation of the duty to provide

full protection and security by reason of Albania's failure to give compensation for the events of March 1997. This argument is put in a number of ways. They all founder for the same simple reason: they confuse breach and the failure to provide remedy. The latter is not a breach in the absence of predicate acts or omissions. If those predicates are extant the breach is consummated without any need to refer to a failure of compensation. The Claimant has not shown that Albania failed to comply with its duty to extend full protection and security in the circumstances that gave rise to this case.

5.4.2 Legal protection

It is uncontested that states owe investors a duty of diligently attempting to protect the physical assets of an investment and the personal safety of the individual investor. The precise extent of IIA 'full protection and security' clauses, however, is an open issue.

Faced with the claim of a violation of the 'most constant protection and security' clause of the Italy–US investment agreement, the International Court of Justice examined not only the alleged damage done to the investor's factory by the workers, but also ELSI's claims of Italy's failure to review its legal appeal to the requisition order in a timely fashion. While the former claim is a classic 'full protection and security' issue, the second pushed the Court to expand the concept of 'protection and security' to include legal as well as physical intrusions within its scope. The *ELSI* decision ultimately dismissed ELSI's claim, but it did so on the facts rather than on the law. Hosts may, according to the ICJ, have treaty obligations to afford the foreign investor a secure legal environment.[57] Several tribunals have adopted the same attitude toward claims of obligations of legal protection and security, basing their findings on an expansive reading of the relevant treaty clauses.[58] One example is the following decision.

---

57 *ELSI* case, *supra* note 6, paras. 111–12.
58 For example, *CME Czech Republic BV v. Czech Republic*, UNCITRAL, Final Award (Mar. 14, 2003). Available at: http://italaw.com/documents/CME-2003-Final_002.pdf; *Lauder v. the Czech Republic, supra* note 50.

CASE

Suez, Sociedad General de Aguas de Barcelona, SA and Vivendi Universal SA v. the Argentine Republic and AWG Group v. The Argentine Republic[59]

In order to overcome its financial crisis of 1989, Argentina launched several legislative initiatives. One of these was the 'Convertibility Law' that fixed the exchange rate of the peso to one dollar. Another was the State Reform Law, by which Argentina hoped to attract foreign investment and improve public services through the privatization of state-owned companies.

Until 1992, municipal water and sewage services in Buenos Aires were provided by the Argentinian state corporation, Obras Sanitarias de la Nación (OSN). At the end of June 1992, the government issued the Water Decree, setting out the regulations for privatizing OSN and the conditions under which the owners were to be granted the service concession.

A tender process was initiated in which the winning bidder would be the company that could offer the best services at the lowest price to consumers. The tariffs charged by the provider were to be the basis of the price to the consumer.

In 1992 the claimants formed a consortium to enter a bid for the water concession, and in 1993, they were awarded a 30-year concession contract by the Argentine government. Under the terms of the contract, the consortium was prescribed quality standards, expansion and investment goals, and a schedule of fees it would be entitled to charge.

Over the next years, the consortium Aguas Argentinas ('Aguas', of which Suez owned the greatest share) took over $700 million in loans from a variety of sources to improve and expand the water services of Buenos Aires.

In 2001, Argentina entered into a period of financial crisis. From early 2001 through 2002, the government enacted a series of laws to meet the economic challenges. Of relevance to this dispute was the Emergency Law of 6 January 2002. That act ended the system of fixed exchange rates, terminated the right

---

59 *Suez, Sociedad General de Aguas de Barcelona, SA and Vivendi Universal SA v. The Argentine Republic* ICSID Case No. ARB/03/19, and *AWG Group v. The Argentine Republic*, Decision on Liability (July 30, 2010). Available at: http://italaw.com/documents/SuezVivendiAWGDecisiononLiability.pdf; footnotes omitted.

to adjust public utility tariffs, and gave the Executive the power to renegotiate public service contracts to take income distribution and consumers' interests into account as well as the profitability of the companies.

Faced with a declining peso and dollar-denominated interest payments, Aguas requested tariff adjustments. Their repeated requests were rejected by the government as were Aguas' attempts to end the concession agreement.

In 2006, alleging improper nitrate levels in the water, Argentina cancelled the concession with Aguas. The investor, claiming a loss of over one billion dollars, brought an arbitration dispute to the ICSID. Argentina, argued Aguas, had failed to offer their investment the security promised to them under the bilateral investment treaty. Specifically, Argentina had not ensured them *legal* security. The tribunal carefully considered the matter.

> 158. The Claimants also allege that Argentina has breached the provisions of the BITs in that they have denied the Claimants protection and security. The specific treaty provisions on which they rely are as follows: Article 5(1) of the Argentina–France BIT states:
>
> > *Investments made by investors of one Contracting Party shall be fully and completely protected and safeguarded in the territory and maritime zone of the other Contracting Party, in accordance with the principle of just and equitable treatment mentioned in article 3 of this Agreement.*
>
> Article III.1 of the Argentina–Spain BIT provides:
>
> > **Article III**
> > PROTECTION
> > *Each Party shall protect within its territory investments made in accordance with its legislation by investors of the other Party and shall not obstruct, by unjustified or discriminatory measures, the management, use, enjoyment, extension, sale and, where appropriate, liquidation of such investments*
>
> And finally, Article 2(2), entitled 'Promotion and Protection of Investment' of the Argentina–United Kingdom BIT states:
>
> > *Investments of Investors of each Contracting Party shall at all times be accorded fair and equitable treatment and shall enjoy protection and constant security in the territory of the other Contracting Party. Neither Contracting Party shall in any way impair by unreasonable or discriminatory measures the management, maintenance, use, enjoyment or disposal of investments in its territory of investors of the other Contracting Party. Each Contracting Party shall observe any obligation it may have entered into with regard to investments of investors of the other Contracting Party.*

159. At the outset, it should be noted that whereas the Claimants' pleadings refer to these treaty provisions as guaranteeing 'full protection and security', a term found in many bilateral investment treaties, that specific phrase appears nowhere in the three BITs applicable to these cases. The Argentina–France BIT promises that investments will be 'fully and completely protected and safeguarded. . .'; the Argentina–Spain BIT promises only that the Contracting Parties 'shall protect' investments; and the Argentina–United Kingdom BIT promises 'protection and constant security'. It remains to be seen whether these three BITs are in effect promising differing levels of protection and whether the level of protection they provide is different from that offered by the many treaties employing the terminology of 'full protection and security'.

B. Analysis and Jurisprudence

160. In seeking to apply these provisions, this Tribunal is confronted initially with two basic questions: Protection from whom? Protection against what? In other words, from whom is a Contracting Party to protect an investor and against what specific actions by such person is a Contracting Party to secure protection? The Claimants argue that in withdrawing certain alleged guarantees made to the Concessionaire and its investors Argentina withdrew '. . . the legal protection and security previously granted to an investment. . .'. Thus, Claimants' interpretation of the above-quoted treaty provisions is that Argentina promised to protect the investments of the other Contracting Party from actions that Argentina itself might take in the exercise of its legal and regulatory authority. The Respondent, on the other hand, takes the position that the provisions on protection and security apply primarily to protection from physical acts against an investor or investment and that only in exceptional circumstances should they be applied to other situations.

161. The origin of the terms 'full protection and security', 'constant protection and security', or simply 'protection and security' appears to lie in the bilateral commercial treaties that countries concluded in the nineteenth and early twentieth centuries, such as the friendship, commerce and navigation (FCN) treaties made by the United States during that period. For example, of twenty-two early commercial treaties concluded by the United States before 1920, fourteen contained reference to 'special protection' and the remaining eight specified 'full and perfect protection' of persons' private property. As an illustration, Article 3 the FCN treaty that the United States concluded with Brunei in 1850 provided that His Highness the Sultan of Borneo '. . . engages that such Citizens of the United States of America shall as far as lies within in his power, within his dominions enjoy *full and complete protection and security* for themselves and for any property which they may acquire. . .' (emphasis added). A number of bilateral treaties of other countries also employed this term.

162. Traditionally, courts and tribunals have interpreted the content of this

standard of treatment as imposing a positive obligation upon a host State to exercise due diligence to protect the investor and his property from physical threats and injuries, not as imposing an obligation to protect covered investments and investors from all injuries from whatever sources. In the *ELSI* case, in which the United States brought a claim against Italy on grounds that the requisition of a U.S. investor's factory by the Mayor of Palermo, Italy, violated Article V(1) of the United States–Italy FCN treaty obligating the Contracting Parties to provide investors 'the most constant protection and security,' the International Court of Justice Chamber stated that: 'The reference in Article V to the provision of "constant protection and security" cannot be construed as the giving of a warranty that property shall never in any circumstances be occupied or disturbed'.

163. With the development of bilateral investment treaties, whose texts were influenced by the language of the earlier of FCN treaties, the drafters of BITs incorporated the term 'full protection and security', or some variation thereof, in this new legal instrument designed to protect and promote foreign investment in a new era. Early interpretations of BIT provisions on full protection and security applied them essentially to protect investors and investments from physical injuries and threats, particularly from actions, usually unauthorized, by a country's army units or individual soldiers, or from disgruntled workers. In each of these cases, the tribunals stressed that the treaty provision was not a guarantee against all injuries that might befall an investment but only required the host country to exercise due diligence. On the meaning of due diligence, tribunals and scholars have often referred to the statement of Professor A.V. Freeman in his lectures at the Hague Academy of International Law: 'The "due diligence" is nothing more nor less than the reasonable measures of prevention which a well-administered government could be expected to exercise under similar circumstances.' The late Professor Ian Brownlie observed that the decisions of tribunals give no definition of 'due diligence', but that 'obviously no very dogmatic definition would be appropriate, since what is involved is a standard which will vary according to the circumstances.'

164. The fact that the 'full protection and security' standard implies only an obligation of due diligence, as opposed to strict liability, has also been widely recognized in more recent arbitral case decisions. On the other hand, there seems to exist no consensus as to the extent to which the full protection and security standard may exceed the State's obligation to provide mere physical security to the investor and his assets.

165. Traditionally, the cases applying full protection and security have dealt with injuries to physical assets of investors committed by third parties where host governments have failed to exercise due diligence in preventing the damage or punishing the perpetrators. In the present case, the Claimants are attempting to apply the protection and security clause to a different type of situation. They do not complain that third parties have injured their physical assets or persons, as in the traditional protection and security case. They are instead asserting that Argentina

denied it protection and security by dint of the actions which Argentina itself took in exercise of its governmental powers against AASA's contractual rights under the Concession Contract and the governing legal framework. This Tribunal must therefore decide whether the treaty provisions apply to the Claimants' situation.

166. In recent years, a few arbitral tribunals have sought to expand the scope and content of the 'full protection and security' clause beyond protection from physical injury, and have interpreted it to apply to unjustified administrative and legal actions taken by a government or its subdivisions that injured an investment's alleged legal rights. It is on these decisions that the Claimants rely, particularly *CME v. the Czech Republic* and *Azurix Corp. v. Argentina*. For example, in *CME*, which Claimants cite in support of their argument, the tribunal stated: 'The host State is obligated to ensure that neither by amendment of its laws nor by actions of its administrative bodies is the agreed and approved security and protection of the foreign investor's investment withdrawn or devalued'.

167. However, the precedential effect of the *CME* case might be reduced by the fact it was not a unanimous decision, and that the tribunal did not conduct a detailed analysis of this particular point. Furthermore, as is well known, the tribunal in the *Lauder* case, which was very closely related to the *CME* case, reached a diametrically different conclusion. With respect to the application of the full protection and security clause in the U.S.–Czech BIT, the tribunal in *Lauder* held that '. . . none of the facts alleged by the Claimants constitutes a violation by the Respondent of the obligation to provide full protection and security under the Treaty.'

168. The *CME* tribunal was interpreting Article 3(2) of the Netherlands–Czech Republic BIT, stipulating that 'each Contracting Party shall provide to such investments full security and protection' (. . .). That treaty formulation is somewhat different from the BIT provisions applicable to the present case. Notably the Argentina–Spain and Argentina–U.K. BITs refer only to 'protection' and to 'protect' without the qualifying word 'full' or 'fully', while the Argentina–France BITs states that investors shall be 'fully protected'. Does the difference in formulation affect the scope of protection afforded by the BITs? The tribunal in *Azurix Corp. v. Argentina* implied that it did, for it justified on that basis a finding that the Argentina–United States BIT providing for 'full protection and security' applied to measures taken by a government and was not limited to physical actions. It stated: 'However when the terms "protection and security" are qualified by full and no other adjective or explanation, they extend, in their ordinary meaning, the content of this standard beyond physical security.' Thus, *Azurix* seemed to suggest that the omission of 'full' or 'fully', as is the case with two of the applicable BITs in the present cases, restricted the scope of protection only to physical security and protection. The tribunal in *Biwater* adhered to the same line of argument and noted that full protection and security 'implies a State's guarantee of stability in a secure environment, both physical, commercial and legal. It would in the Arbitral Tribunal's view be unduly artificial to confine the notion of "full security" only to

one aspect of security, particularly in light of the use of this term in a BIT, directed at the protection of commercial and financial investments.'

169. Other tribunals have given less weight to the precise language used in the treaty when determining the scope of the full protection and security standard. For example, in *Parkerings v. Lithuania* the tribunal found: 'It is generally accepted that the variation of language between the formulation "protection" and "full protection and security" does not make a difference in the level of protection a State is to provide.'

170. With regard to the third treaty in the present cases, the Argentina–France BIT requires that investors are to be '. . . fully and completely protected . . . in accordance with the principle of just and equitable treatment mentioned in Article 3. . .'. The interpretation of this treaty provision raises questions as to the interplay and scope of the two standards of 'full and completely protected' and 'fair and equitable treatment.' If the Tribunal should find that a breach of the fair and equitable treatment standard has taken place, does that mean that a breach of the guarantee of full and complete protection has also taken? Some tribunals in the presence of a formulation like the language employed in Article 3 quoted above have found that both breaches take place simultaneously.

171. The present Tribunal, however, takes the view that under Article 3, quoted above, the concept of full protection and security is included within the concept of fair and equitable treatment, but that the scope of full protection and security is narrower than the fair and equitable treatment. Thus, State action that violates the full protection and security clause would of necessity constitute a violation of fair and equitable treatment under the French BIT. On the other hand, all violations of fair and equitable treatment are not automatically also violations of full protection and security. Under the French BIT, it is possible for Argentina to violate its obligation of fair and equitable treatment toward the Claimants without violating its duty of full protection and security. In short, there are actions that violate fair and equitable treatment that do not violate full protection and security.

172. The fact that the French BIT employs the fair and equitable treatment standard and the full protections and security standard in two distinct articles and refers to them as separate and distinct standards leads to the conclusion that the Contracting Parties must have intended them to mean two different things. Thus, in interpreting these two standards of investor treatment it is desirable to give effect to that intention by giving the two concepts distinct meanings and fields of application.

173. In this respect, this Tribunal is of the view that the stability of the business environment and legal security are more characteristic of the standard of fair and equitable treatment, while the full protection and security standard primarily seeks to protect investment from physical harm. This said, this latter standard may also include an obligation to provide adequate mechanisms and legal remedies for

prosecuting the State organs or private parties responsible for the injury caused to the investor.

174. The *Enron* tribunal discussed the more limited scope of the full protection and security standard by noting that 'there might be cases where a broader interpretation could be justified, but then it becomes difficult to distinguish such situation from one resulting in the breach of fair and equitable treatment, and even from some form of expropriation.' Generally, this Tribunal also believes that an overly extensive interpretation of the full protection and security standard may result in an overlap with the other standards of investment protection, which is neither necessary nor desirable.

175. As far as this Tribunal is concerned, it is inclined to think that the absence of the word 'full' or 'fully' in the full protection and security provisions in the Argentina–Spain and the Argentina–U.K. BITs supports this view of an obligation limited to providing physical protection and legal remedies for the Spanish and U.K. Claimants and their assets.

176. The importance of the precise legal formulation used in a BIT provision is further illustrated in the *Siemens* award. In that case, the investor initiated the arbitration under the German–Argentina BIT, alleging *inter alia* that Argentina breached its obligation to accord full protection and security through the conduct that led to the frustration of the investor's contract. The respondent and the claimant had opposing positions on the scope of the protection under the BIT standard. According to Argentina, 'security' implied only physical security, while the investor attributed to this term a wider meaning, in particular because the Treaty referred to 'legal security'. Thus, the tribunal had to interpret whether 'security' referred merely to physical security or to security in a wider sense. Having noted that the definition of investment included tangible and intangible assets, the tribunal said that 'the obligation to provide full protection and security is wider than "physical" protection and security.' It provided the following reasoning:

> It is difficult to understand how the physical security of an intangible asset would be achieved. In the instant case, 'security' is qualified by 'legal'. In its ordinary meaning 'legal security' has been defined as 'the quality of the legal system which implied certainty in its norms and, consequently, their foreseeable application.' It is clear that in the context of this meaning the Treaty refers to security that it is not physical. In fact, one may question given the qualification of the term 'security', whether the treaty covers physical security at all. Arguably, it could be considered to be included under 'full protection', but that is not an issue in these proceedings. [§303]

Based on this understanding of 'full protection and security', the tribunal concluded that Argentina's initiation of the renegotiation of the contract for the sole purpose of reducing its costs, unsupported by any declaration of public interest, affected the legal security of Siemens' investment, and thus constituted a violation of its obligations under the BIT. In these cases, none of the three BITs concerned refers to 'legal security'. Therefore, this Tribunal is of the opinion that the various formulations of protection and security employed in the present BITs cannot extend to an obligation to maintain a stable and secure legal and commercial environment.

177. While strict textual interpretation of the treaty language would lead this Tribunal to conclude that the applicable BITs in the present cases do not have the expansive scope on which the Claimants are basing their claim, there is another reason for the Tribunal not to follow the interpretation made in, *inter alia*, *CME* and *Azurix*. Neither the *CME* nor *Azurix* awards provide a historical analysis of the concept of full protection and security or give any clear reason as to why it was departing from the historical interpretation traditionally employed by courts and tribunals and expanding that concept to cover non-physical actions and injuries.

178. A few awards since *CME* have maintained the more traditional approach to interpreting the notion of full protection and security. In *Saluka*, the tribunal determined that the Czech Republic did not violate the Czech Republic–Netherlands BIT which promised investors 'full security and protection' when it took measures to stop trading in the claimant's securities. The tribunal stated: 'The practice of arbitral tribunals seems to indicate however that the "full protection and security clause" is not meant to cover just any kind of impairment of an investor's investment but to protect more specifically the physical integrity of an investment against interference by the use of force.' More recently, a similar rationale has been applied by arbitral tribunals in *BG v. Argentina*, *PSEG v. Turkey* and *Rumeli v. Kazakhstan*.

C. The Tribunal's Conclusions

Having considered the specific language of each of the three applicable BITs and the historical development of the 'full protection and security' standard under international law, as well as the recent jurisprudence, this Tribunal is not persuaded that it needs to depart from the traditional interpretation given to this term. Consequently, the Tribunal concludes that under all the applicable BITs, Argentina is obliged to exercise due diligence to protect investors and investments primarily from physical injury, and that in any case Argentina's obligations under the relevant provisions do not extend to encompass the maintenance of a stable legal and commercial environment. As a result, in the instant cases Argentina has not violated its obligations under the respective BIT provisions.

The *Biwater–Gauff*,[60] *CME*,[61] and *Azurix*[62] tribunals also acknowledge the possibility of 'full' protection including host obligations of protecting legal

60 *Biwater Gauff (Tanzania) Ltd. v. United Republic of Tanzania*, ICSID Case No. ARB/05/22, Award (July 24, 2008). Available at http://www.italaw.com/sites/default/files/case-documents/ita0095.pdf.

61 *Supra* note 58.

62 *Azurix Corp. v. The Argentine Republic*, ICSID Case No. ARB/01/12, Award (July 14, 2006). Available at http://www.italaw.com/sites/default/files/case-documents/ita0061.pdf.

security. Thus, when the *OI* tribunal faced a claimant's argument that legal security is implicitly included in the BIT's scope, the decision makers faced a divided field. In the face of the claimant's argument that the inclusion of intangible assets in the definition of 'investment' should suggest that the required protection cannot only be against physical damage, the tribunal had to take a position.[63] Rather than elaborating on the theoretical aspects of the state's duties to protect investors' interests, the arbitrators regarded the Spanish text of the relevant agreement and simply applied a plain text interpretive method. The Dutch-Venezuelan BIT article states that 'each Contracting Party shall accord to [. . .] investments full physical security and protection.'[64] The explicit use of the term 'physical', made it easy for the tribunal to limit the obligation.[65]

? | **DISCUSSION NOTES**

1 Of how much concern should conflicting decisions on the extension of FPS to legal security be? The *BG Group v. Argentina* and *National Grid v. Argentina* cases were brought on the basis of the same BIT and arose from essentially the same governmental measures. Nevertheless, the two tribunals established for the two claims issued contradictory decisions on the legal security issue. The *BG Group* arbitrators took the conservative approach, maintaining the limitation of FPS to physical security; the *National Grid* tribunal finding was that FPS is 'not inherently limited'. This divergence, as an extreme example of the dichotomy of views of FPS, has caused one commentator to remark that contradictory findings on FPS's scope 'may be the source of challenges to arbitrators or applications for annulment or review, and in the longer term, it raises difficult questions about the inherent coherence of the system'. See Jeffery Commission, The Full Protection and Security Standard in Practice, www. kluwerarbitrationblog.com (Apr. 16, 2009).

2 The *Mamidoil v. Albania* award demonstrates a blurring of the FPS standard with that of FET. In *Mamidoil*, the claimant argued that Albania's failure to stop smuggling and tax evasion by criminal organizations was a violation of its right to receive full protection and security of its investment. Rather than focus on the question of whether the smuggling violated a right to legal security, the tribunal engaged in a discussion of why Mamidoil could not have legitimately expected a

---

63 *OI European Group BV v. the Bolivaran Republic of Venezuela*, ICSID Case No. ARB/11/25, Award (Mar. 10, 2015).

64 *See* Agreement on encouragement and reciprocal protection of investments between the Kingdom of the Netherlands and the Republic of Venezuela, Article 3.2 (Nov. 1, 1993; it has since been terminated).

65 *OI v. Venezuela, supra* note 63, para. 576.

business environment where there was no illegal activity in the energy sector. The tribunal ultimately acknowledged Albania's 'due diligence in its general customs policy and in its specific measures' (para. 829), but left the connection between FPS and investor expectations unclear. See *Mamidoil Jetoil Greek Petroleum Products Societe SA v. Republic of Albania*, ICSID Case No. ARB/11/24, Award (30 March 2015).

3 A state's over-commitment to upholding its FPS obligations has the potential to threaten human rights. If a government is too eager to protect an investor's property from local protestors, it may resort to uses of force that would be considered excessive under human rights law. The following report is not based on an arbitrated claim, but it demonstrates the risk of protecting foreign investment at the cost of the rights of local inhabitants.

> The eastern state of Odisha in India is pitting small farmers against international business interests in a battle that threatens the Indian government's idea of development.
>
> 'POSCO go back!' is a common chant among the hundreds of residents from Jagatsingpur district who have been standing guard at the village borders since June 2, to prevent the forcible acquisition of their lands for a steel plant, the country's largest, that South-Korea based Pohang Steel Company (POSCO) wants to set up. Twenty police battalions have been stationed a few kilometers away, awaiting the state government's instructions.
>
> At $12bn, POSCO, partially funded by Warren Buffett, Citibank and JP Morgan Chase, is stated to be the largest Foreign Direct Investment ever to be made in India, according to the Federation of Indian Chambers of Commerce and Industry. The Odisha government claims the mega-project will wipe out poverty from the state. But in six years, the government has not been able to finish acquiring land for the plant.
>
> On July 16, 10 platoons of police marched into Nuagaon village with the district authorities to restart the process of land acquisition. Over 300 village women tried to stop them from felling trees in the forest. The police attacked with batons, injuring eight people, before they were driven out by the villagers. Odisha has a wealth of mineral resources, and in order to attract investments, the government has made concessions for corporations in the form of tax-free Special Economic Zones and mineral-ore at low prices. But across the state, from Niyamgiri where the Dongria tribals are fighting UK-based Vedanta's bauxite mining project, to Kalinganagar where opposition to Tata's proposed steel plant has resulted in the killing of 19 villagers since January 2006, these large projects are being met with resistance from some of the people they purport to benefit. Besides the steel plant, a Memorandum of Understanding (MoU) between the state government and POSCO includes 600 million

tonnes of iron ore to be mined in the hills of Kandadhar, a captive port in
Paradeep, a 1300 mega-watt power plant, special railway lines and diversion of
water from the Mahanadi river, 86km away.

'This project will not only give direct benefits but it will create ancillary investment that will benefit the region's economy', explains Dama Raut, who was the
elected Legislative Assembly representative from the area when the POSCO
project was initiated. 'To gain something, you have to lose something', he said,
when asked about the displacement of local villagers.

The eight villages where POSCO is looking to acquire land have a flourishing
agriculture-based economy cultivating betel-vine, rice and cashews. The protesting villagers see the steel plant as a threat to the agrarian livelihood of 22 000
people, besides adversely affecting the ecology.[66]

5.5   Fair and equitable treatment

Among the most litigated provisions of IIAs are those that embody the
principle of fair and equitable treatment (FET). The provisions setting out
the host's obligation to treat investments 'fairly' or 'justly' are ambiguous
enough to allow claimants to invite tribunals to view the host's actions com-
prehensively rather than on the basis of the more clearly defined elements
elaborated above. Current IIAs usually contain FET provisions of one of
two main types. One equates the FET standard with the customary international minimum standard. Provisions (such as the NAFTA's Article 1105),
which state that Parties are to accord to each other's investments treatment
'in accordance with international law, including fair and equitable treatment'.

An alternative is the autonomous, or *sui generis*, standard. These provisions
do not refer to 'customary international law' or a 'minimum standard of international law'. Instead, they state only that the host is obliged to offer the
investor 'fair and equitable treatment'. Without any reference to international
standards, such provisions may or may not be interpreted in view of the
international law standard of treatment. It is up to the tribunal facing such
provisions to determine how it should analyse the terms of such provisions.

Given the open language of the provisions, there has been a large number
of claims based on FET and a correspondingly large number of arbitration
awards addressing the standard and its application. These awards reveal a

---

66 Faiza Ahmad Khan, *Indian farmers protest massive steel plant, India's largest ever foreign direct investment
project, valued at $12bn, could displace 22 000 people.* Available at: www.aljazeera.com (July 19, 2011, 2:07 PM),
http://english.aljazeera.net/indepth/features/2011/07/201171711310873319.html.

substantial – sometimes fundamental – lack of agreement among arbitrators as to the proper interpretation of FET provisions. Scholarship on the topic has provided little assistance in bridging the diverging positions – perhaps a sign that there is no 'right way' of determining fairness in the abstract. Providing a coherent overview of the FET standard as applied therefore poses a significant challenge to any textbook author. The following makes no claim of exhausting the topic of FET. Rather, it presents the main directions of thought on what may be international investment law's most malleable concept.

5.5.1 Variations in provisions providing for 'fair and equitable' treatment

Plausibly regarded as a catch-all provision for investor protection, FET is a common reference to a standard that is found widely in investment treaties. Setting out the meaning of 'fair' and 'equitable' is difficult enough, but the fact that the standard's precise wording differs from treaty to treaty means that the interpretation of the standard cannot rely on the text alone.[67]

Ideally, whether the host's treatment of the investor is to be 'fair and equitable',[68] 'just and equitable', 'according to international law', or 'in accordance with customary international law', the parties have a more or less common understanding of what obligation they are accepting. The strong preference for one term by some governments and the varying use of terms by others makes the arbitral interpretive process less predictable, however. While German BITs refer to 'fair and equitable treatment'[69] and the United States generally negotiates investor protection to include the term 'fair and equitable treatment' as a modification of 'treatment in accordance to international law', Argentina uses various terms with its different partners, including 'fair and equitable treatment'[70] and 'just and equitable treatment, in accordance with international law'[71] in its BITs. In any of its textual forms, FET is an obligation whose content is wide open to interpretation. Many tribunals

---

67 Montt comments that 'concepts such as 'fair' and 'equitable' are probably two of the more general and abstract ideas found in the human enterprise known as the law. . . . In such a context, no guidance can be expected from dictionaries'. Santiago Montt, State Liability in Investment Treaty Arbitration: Global Constitutional and Administrative Law in the BIT Generation 300 (2009).

68 In non-English BITs, the terms are the same: 'Gerecht und billig', 'juste et equitable', 'justo y equitativo', or 'giusto ed equo'.

69 German Model BIT 2008, art. 2.2. *See also* Germany–Mexico BIT (1998), art. 2.3; Germany–Jordan BIT (2007), art. 2; Germany–Kenya BIT (1996), art. 2.1.

70 Argentina–Spain BIT (1991), art. IV.1; Argentina–UK BIT (1990), art. 2.2.

71 Argentina–France BIT (1991), art. 3.

recognize that plain meaning interpretations do not help,[72] and commentators note that in fact, for all the differences in wording, 'arbitral tribunals have largely refrained from attributing excessive weight to finer textual variations'.[73] Rather, awards mainly differ on the tribunal's basic approach to the concept of FET.

Within the large (and constantly growing) number of perspectives on what constitutes fair and equitable treatment of an investor, tribunals have indicated a number of significant aspects of the host's behaviour around which most of the arguments now revolve: arbitrariness and a denial of justice; failure to afford due process; lack of transparency; bad faith; and, most significantly, violation of the investor's legitimate expectations. While the openness of the term 'fair and equitable' could permit an even wider scope, recent cases appear to indicate that the content of the standard is solidifying around these elements. For simplicity, one can categorize the tribunals' attention to these elements as one of two basic approaches: an emphasis on investor expectations; or an emphasis on the traditional international minimum standard of state conduct. Remember, however, that these approaches are only the starting point for most FET discussions. Although there are awards that utilize 'pure forms' of these approaches, a growing number of tribunals are describing their analysis of the facts in terms that recognize both the investor's legitimate expectations to substantive and procedural fairness on the part of the host and the host's right to regulate in the public interest.

The following section takes a brief look at the beginnings of the FET jurisprudence as a background to the rest of the chapter's development of the two main approaches taken by tribunals since then: those centring on the content of the international standard of host behaviour; and those focusing on protecting the investor's expectations. A short introduction to the relationship between FET and the right to regulate is found at the end of the section.

---

72 *Saluka Investments BV v. The Czech Republic*, UNCITRAL, Partial Award, para. 297 (Mar. 17, 2006).
73 Marc Jacob and Stephan W. Schill, Fair and Equitable Treatment: Content, Practice, Method, in: Marc Bungenberg, Jörn Griebel, Stephan Hobe and August Reinisch eds., *International Investment Law: A Handbook*, 700–63, 705 (2015).

5.5.2 The first FET claim: establishing the significance of investor expectations

Although FET provisions can be found in IIAs from at least 1963,[74] the first FET claim brought to arbitration was made by U.S. investor Metalclad against Mexico, based on NAFTA's investment protection chapter.[75] The dispute arose because Metalclad had entered Mexico with plans to construct and operate a waste disposal landfill with the encouragement of Mexico's federal government. Support of the federal government, however, proved insufficient. When the State and municipal governments refused to issue the relevant building permits, Metalclad was forced to terminate its invest-ment. The investor brought an arbitration case against Mexico with multi-ple claims, one of which was that Mexico failed to abide by its obligations of NAFTA Article 1105. That provision provides: 'each Party shall accord to investments of investors of another Party treatment in accordance with international law, including fair and equitable treatment [. . .]'. Perhaps not recognizing the implications of its initial foray into the development of FET jurisprudence, the tribunal determined that Mexico had violated the obliga-tion by failing to act transparently, predictably, and efficiently, each of which, it wrote, the investor could have expected it to do:

> 99. Mexico failed to ensure a transparent and predictable framework for Metalclad's business planning and investment. The totality of these circumstances demon-strates a lack of orderly process and timely disposition in relation to an investor [. . .] acting in the expectation that it would be treated fairly and justly in accord-ance with the NAFTA.
> 100. Moreover, the acts of the State and the Municipality [. . .] fail to comply with or adhere to the requirements of NAFTA, Article 1105(1) [. . .].
> 101. The Tribunal therefore holds that Metalclad was not treated fairly or equitably under the NAFTA and succeeds on its claim under Article 1105.

While the facts as set forth in the award can easily be found to be 'unfair' from the investor's point of view, the arbitrators failed to elaborate why the inves-tor's expectations should be the measure of the legality of a state's actions. Indeed, given Mexico's arguments that the company's plans threatened the

---

74 The earliest provision found by this author is from the Germany-Cameroon BIT from 1963. Interestingly, in this and other early BITs, the FET obligation was placed in the first or second article. Traité entre la République fédérale d'Allemagne et la République fédérale du Cameroun relative à l'encouragement des inves-tissements de capitaux, Art. 1 (Nov. 21, 1963)([Aucune Partie Contractante] traitera ces investissements [. . .] de façon juste et équitable).

75 *Metalclad Corporation v. The United Mexican States*, ICSID Case No. ARB(AF)/97/1, Award (Aug. 30, 2000).

environment, and that its denial of the permit was required to protect the local community as well as endangered species in the area of the planned disposal site, many observers were of the opinion that whatever the investor's expectations were, the government was right in taking the action it did.

The fact that the tribunal seemed to ignore the NAFTA provision's reference to 'treatment in accordance with international law' was another interesting aspect of the award, and it meant that the *Metalclad* decision left much room for future development of FET analyses. Simultaneously, however, it lay down the two most durable elements of future tribunal's attention – what the investor legitimately expected of the host and a fact-specific determination of whether the host acted fairly. These aspects continue to arise in FET awards regardless of which IIA underlies the dispute.

5.5.3 FET and the international law standard of host behaviour

Following *Metalclad*, further claimants brought cases based on NAFTA's Article 1105. The respondents in these cases, however, defended themselves on the basis of general international law's traditional deference to the sovereignty of states.[76] Recall that the precise wording of Article 1105 obliges hosts to afford investors 'treatment in accordance with international law, including' FET – not simply fair and equitable treatment. Thus, it arguably requires tribunals to first determine the internationally accepted standard of host behaviour toward aliens, and then apply all aspects of that standard – including the 'fair and equitable' aspects – to the facts at hand.

But what exactly is the international law standard of treatment due investors? In investment law discussions of what precisely fair and equitable treatment requires of a host state, a frequently invoked standard is the one set forth by the majority in the 1926 arbitration *Neer v. Mexico*.[77] In the *Neer* arbitration, the United States instituted proceedings against Mexico for that government's denial of justice to the wife and daughter of Paul Neer, a US citizen killed in Mexico in 1924. According to the Neers, the Mexican authorities failed to investigate Mr. Neer's murder rigorously, leaving the crime unsolved and his family with losses of $100 000. The Claims Commission was faced with the question of whether Mexico's actions demonstrated an 'unwarrantable lack

---

76 Sornarajah points out that while Metalclad was complaining about Mexico's treatment, Canada and the United States were respondents in several claims subsequent to that. This explains the firm resistance to jurisprudence which raised the level of investor protection beyond the minimum and resulted in an authoritative interpretation in July 2001. Sornarajah, Foreign Investment, third edn, at 350.

77 *L.F.H. Neer and Pauline Neer (USA) v. United Mexican States*, 4 R.I.A.A. 60, 60–66 (Oct. 15, 1926).

of diligence or an unwarrantable lack of intelligent investigation' so as to make it liable under international law for denial of justice. In a concise three paragraphs, the Claims Commission set out their standard:

> 3. As to lack of diligence, or lack of intelligent investigation, on the part of the Mexican authorities, after the killing of Paul Neer had been brought to their notice, it would seem that . . . these authorities might have acted in a more vigorous and effective way than they did [. . .]. But in the view of the Commission there is a long way between holding that a more active and more efficient course of procedure might have been pursued, on the one hand, and holding that this record presents such lack of diligence and of intelligent investigation as constitutes an international delinquency, on the other hand.
>
> 4. The Commission recognizes the difficulty of devising a general formula for determining the boundary between an international delinquency of this type and an unsatisfactory use of power included in national sovereignty [. . .]. Without attempting to announce a precise formula, it is in the opinion of the Commission [. . .] to hold (first) that the propriety of governmental acts should be put to the test of international standards, and (second) that the treatment of an alien, in order to constitute an international delinquency, should amount to an outrage, to bad faith, to wilful neglect of duty, or to an insufficiency of governmental action so far short of international standards that every reasonable and impartial man would readily recognize its insufficiency. Whether the insufficiency proceeds from deficient execution of an intelligent law or from the fact that the laws of the country do not empower the authorities to measure up to international standards is immaterial.
>
> 5. It is not for an international tribunal such as this Commission to decide, whether another course of procedure taken by the local authorities at Guanacevi might have been more effective. On the contrary, the grounds of liability limit its inquiry to whether there is convincing evidence either (1) that the authorities administering the Mexican law acted in an outrageous way, in bad faith, in wilful neglect of their duties, or in a pronounced degree of improper action, or (2) that Mexican law rendered it impossible for them properly to fulfil their task. No attempt is made to establish the second point. The first point is negatived by the full record of police and judicial authorities produced by the Mexican Agent, though the Commission feels bound to state once more that in its opinion better methods might have been used.[78]

Notice the Commission's emphasis on deference to the host. Even though Mexico had made decisions that the tribunal found unreasonable or

---

78 *Id.* at 61–2.

inefficient and failed to take actions that might have solved the crime, the tribunal found no violation of the international legal standard of required behaviour because Mexico did not act 'in an outrageous way' or purposefully against the interests of the alien.

The *S.D. Myers v. Canada* arbitration (the second investor claim based on NAFTA's FET provision) directly addressed the relevance of the international law standard referred to in the NAFTA text. In that case, the investor was a hazardous waste disposal company affected by Canada's prohibition on the exportation of hazardous wastes to the United States. The arbitrators explained:

> The Tribunal considers that a breach of Article 1105 occurs only when it is shown that an investor has been treated in such an unjust or arbitrary manner that the treatment rises to the level that is unacceptable from the international perspective. That determination must be made in the light of the high measure of deference that international law generally extends to the right of domestic authorities to regulate matters within their own borders. The determination must also take into account any specific rules of international law that are applicable to the case.[79]

Interestingly, Canada was found to have violated that standard despite its high threshold. The alternative approach to FET analysis, though, was now ready to enter the investment law dialogue.

The *Neer* standard of host state behaviour has been discussed and adopted by numerous tribunals—and not just in the NAFTA context. In *Alex Genin v. Estonia*, where the claim was based on the host's revocation of the investor's banking license, the tribunal found procedural failings on the part of the government. Nevertheless, the claimant's behaviour led to a determination that the scepticism displayed by the host was justified. The FET provision of the US–Estonia BIT was therefore not violated. The tribunal's approach was the same as in the *S.D. Myers* case:

> Article II(3)(a) of the BIT requires the signatory governments to treat foreign investment in a 'fair and equitable' way. Under international law, this requirement is generally understood to 'provide a basic and general standard which is detached from the host State's domestic law.' While the exact content of this standard is not clear, the Tribunal understands it to require an 'international minimum standard' that is separate from domestic law, but that is, indeed, a *minimum* standard. Acts

---

79 *S.D. Myers v. Canada, supra* note 18, para. 263.

that would violate this minimum standard would include acts showing a wilful neglect of duty, an insufficiency of action falling far below international standards, or even subjective bad faith. Under the present circumstances—where ample grounds existed for the action taken by the Bank of Estonia—Respondent cannot be held to have violated Article II(3)(a) of the BIT.[80]

Some later tribunals found the *Genin* tribunal's reliance on the international standard misplaced where the applicable BIT had an autonomous FET provision. The arbitrators in the *Inmaris Perestroika v. Ukraine* case,[81] for instance, noted that the difference in treaty makes a difference in the resulting analysis:

There is nothing in the [applicable Germany–Ukraine] BIT that limits [the FET obligation found in] Article 2(1) to the standard required by customary international law. In the absence of such a statement, the Tribunal interprets the language as written, *i.e.*, the government is obligated to accord fair and equitable treatment to foreign investments, and therefore there is no need to establish that the government's actions were in breach of customary international law in order to establish a breach of Article 2(1). Any government act that is unfair or inequitable with respect to a covered investment breaches that obligation. A government act could be unfair or inequitable if it is in breach of specific commitments, if it is undertaken for political reasons or other improper motives, if the investor is not treated in an objective, even-handed, unbiased, and transparent way, or for other reasons.[82]

Frequently, tribunals who adopt the international standard approach to FET will find that the state's behaviour has not been so shocking as to fall below it. The *Minnotte and Lewis v. Poland* tribunal, determining whether the FET obligation of a US–Poland treaty[83] had been violated when Poland failed to supply the claimants with plasma for their blood fractionation operations and deleteriously impacted the company's credit, wrote:

198. [...] While the precise formulations of the fair and equitable treatment standard in [...] awards differ, they all have in common the notion that the State must be shown to have acted delinquently in some way or other if it is to be held to have violated that standard. It is not enough that a claimant should find itself in an unfortunate position as a result of all of its dealings with a respondent.
199. In the present case, the Tribunal can find no evidence that the Respondent

---

80 *Alex Genin v. Estonia, supra* note 7, para. 367 (footnotes omitted).
81 *Inmaris Perestroika Sailing Maritime Services GmbH and Others v. Ukraine*, ICSID Case No. ARB/08/8, Award (Mar. 1, 2012) (only excerpts of award are publicly available).
82 *Id.* at para. 265.
83 Treaty between the United States of America and the Republic of Poland concerning business and economic relations, II.6 (Aug. 6, 1994).

acted unlawfully, or that it exercised its rights for an improper purpose or in an improper manner. The Tribunal notes that there were long delays in responding to letters from [the investor]. While those delays may have been inappropriate, they are not of a nature to amount to a violation of its obligations under the BIT. The Tribunal concludes that the Claimants have not made out their claim that the Respondent acted in a manner that was unfair or inequitable.[84]

5.5.4 Raising the standard of FET

Applying international law's very low standard of host behaviour as the standard of FET is not the only way to regard the host's obligations. The *Pope and Talbot v. Canada* tribunal was of a different opinion than the *S.D. Myers* and *Genin* tribunals as to the appropriate standard of treatment required. The international law standard, it noted, was the *minimum* to which a host must abide. In the context of an IIA, the goal of investor protection must demand a *higher-than-minimum* standard. The *Neer* standard, that is, is a floor, not a ceiling. In their words:

> 116. It is doubtful that the NAFTA parties would want to present to potential investors and investments from other NAFTA countries the possibility that they would have no recourse to protection against anything but egregiously unfair conduct. The aim of NAFTA seems to be quite the opposite, that is, to present to investors the kind of hospitable climate that would insulate them from political risks or incidents of unfair treatment. Yet Canada's reading of Article 1105 would raise just those concerns it would permit a NAFTA Party to take measures against investors and investments from other NAFTA countries that its domestic law would prevent it from taking against its own investors and investments and that BITs would preclude taking against investors and investments from a number of other countries. It is difficult to believe that the drafters of NAFTA consciously intended such a result, and, as noted, Canada, Mexico and the United States have provided no evidence whatsoever that they did.
> 117. In addition to the context, object and purpose of NAFTA, there is a practical reason for adopting the additive interpretation to Article 1105. As noted, the contrary view of that provision would provide to NAFTA investors a more limited right to object to laws, regulation and administration than accorded to host country investors and investments as well as to those from countries that have concluded BITs with a NAFTA party. This state of affairs would surely run afoul of Articles 1102 and 1103, which give every NAFTA investor and investment the right to national and most favoured nation treatment. NAFTA investors and investments

---

84 *David Minnotte and Robert Lewis v. Republic of Poland*, ICSID Case No. ARB(AF)/10/1, Award, paras. 198–99 (May 16, 2014) (footnotes omitted).

that would be denied access to the fairness elements untrammeled by the 'egregious' conduct threshold that Canada would graft onto Article 1105 would simply turn to Articles 1102 and 1103 for relief.

118. The Tribunal is unwilling to attribute to the NAFTA Parties an intention that would lead to such a patently absurd result. Accordingly, the Tribunal interprets Article 1105 to require that covered investors and investments receive the benefits of the fairness elements under ordinary standards applied in the NAFTA countries, without any threshold limitation that the conduct complained of be 'egregious/, 'outrageous' or 'shocking', or otherwise extraordinary.[85]

The *Pope and Talbot* decision caused significant concern among the NAFTA Parties. The United States, Canada, and Mexico therefore called upon the Free Trade Commission of the NAFTA to issue an interpretation of FET. The result clarified that the international law standard is the standard to apply in NAFTA Article 1105 disputes. Binding on NAFTA Chapter 11 tribunals, the Notes of Interpretation of Certain Chapter 11 Provisions clarify that aspect of interpretation – but only that one aspect of FET and only for NAFTA claims. The floor vs. ceiling question remains where BIT language links FET to the international law standard.

5.5.5   Evolution of the international standard?

In any case, a general question may still be asked: does the *Neer* standard still reflect what the international legal community expects of states? The *Mondev*[86] tribunal rejected the continuing validity of *Neer's* 'outrageous' threshold. In the first place, the tribunal pointed out, the *Neer* opinion looked to state obligations to protect alien persons, not to protect foreign property.[87] Moreover, speaking in terms of a 'reasonable evolutionary interpretation' of the FET provision of the NAFTA, the *Mondev* arbitrators pointed out that the content of hosts' obligations to investors under treaties concluded in the second half of the twentieth century can be seen as evidence of increasing protections of individual rights that have come about in the post-world war international system.[88] With more expected of states, '[t]o the modern eye, what is unfair or inequitable need not equate with the outrageous or the egregious'.[89] Given that, the *Mondev* tribunal saw itself obliged to recognize a higher standard for state behaviour toward investors.

85 *Pope and Talbot v. Canada, supra* note 37.

86 *Mondev International Ltd v. United States of America*, ICSID Case No. ARB(AF)/99/2, NAFTA, Award (Oct. 11, 2002). Available at: http://italaw.com/documents/Mondev-Final.pdf.

87 *Id.* para. 115–16.

88 *Id.* para. 123.

89 *Id.* para. 127.

The debate continues over whether the international standard has evolved. The tribunals in *Glamis Gold* and *Gold Reserve* provided differing insights on the answer. Each has provides a good overview of the development of the different approaches to FET interpretation.

 CASE

Gold Reserve Inc. v. Venezuela[90]

Gold Reserve Inc. is a Canadian company active in gold and other mineral mining projects. The owner of Gold Reserve Corporation, Gold Reserve Inc. became the indirect owner of a mining project in Venezuela in the 1990s. The 'Brisas Project' was to consist of two concessions: the Brisas concession would have given Gold Reserve the right to mine the near-surface gold deposits on the Brisas Property while the Unicornio concession would have been for mining the hard rock deposits underneath Brisas' alluvial deposits. Each of the concessions would have entitled the owner to twenty-years of exploitation, with a possible extension of two further ten-year renewals.

In addition to the mining concessions, Gold Reserve had to file for various operational authorizations, including a study on feasibility, environmental impact assessments, and applications to construct the necessary infrastructure. The government granted a construction permit for the Brisas Project in August 2007, and Gold Reserve filed for an extention of the Brisas Concession that autumn. However, in April 2008, Venezuela revoked the construction permit, citing 'reasons of public order' and in August 2008, declared that the Concession had expired in April of that year. Denying the company an extension of the Brisas Concession, Venezuela terminated it and occupied the site while additionally terminating the Unicornios Concession.

Gold Reserve initiated ICSID proceedings in August 2009 under the Additional Facility Rules. Among the questions addressed was the standard to be used in evaluating the claimant's charge of a violation of the Canada–Venezuela FET provision.

> 567. Article II(2) of the BIT refers to the 'principles of international law' in accordance with which fair and equitable treatment is to be bestowed. To determine these principles the Tribunal must consider the present status of development of public international law in the field of investment protection. It is the

90 *Gold Reserve Inc. v. Bolivarian Republic of Venezuela*, ICSID Case No. ARB(AF)/09/1, Award (Sept. 22, 2014); (footnotes omitted).

Tribunal's view that public international law principles have evolved since the *Neer* case and that the standard today is broader than that defined in the *Neer* case on which Respondent relies. As authoritatively held, the *Neer* award 'had nothing to do with the treatment of foreign investors or investments. It did not address what is fair and equitable' [. . .]. As held by the tribunal in *Mondev* when disregarding the *Neer* standard as controlling today, 'both the substantive and procedural rights of the individual in international law have undergone considerable developments.'

568. Rather than conducting an extensive review of the many decisions that have addressed the conditions under which a breach of the FET may be deemed to have arisen, the Tribunal shall examine a few cases whose factual circumstances appear to be closer to the facts of the present case to then draw the principles applicable for deciding the dispute pending before it.

569. [. . .] The [*Saluka*] tribunal held that the State had failed to accord the investor fair and equitable treatment because it failed to consider in an 'unbiased, even-handed, transparent and consistent way' the investor's good faith proposals to resolve the bank crisis, and by 'unreasonably refus[ing] to communicate with IPB and Saluka/Nomura in an adequate manner'.

570. Other tribunals have underscored the central role of an investor's legitimate expectations in the analysis of whether treatment was fair and equitable in the circumstances. Legitimate expectations are created when a State's conduct is such that an investor may reasonably rely on that conduct as being consistent. Fair and equitable treatment also requires that any regulation of an investment be done in a transparent manner, the importance of transparency in this regard [. . .] being reflected in Article XV of the BIT.

571. The investor's legitimate expectations are based on undertakings and representations made explicitly or implicitly by the host State. [. . .]

572. In *Tecmed*, the tribunal explained that '[t]he foreign investor expects the host State to act in a consistent manner, free from ambiguity and totally transparently in its relations with the foreign investor, so that it may know beforehand . . . the goals of the relevant policies and administrative practices or directives, to be able to plan its investment and comply with such regulations . . . . The foreign investor also expects the host State to act consistently, i.e. without arbitrarily revoking any pre-existing decisions or permits issued by the State that were relied upon by the investor to assume its commitments as well as to plan and launch its commercial and business activities. The investor also expects the State to use the legal instruments that govern the actions of the investor or the investment in conformity with the functions usually assigned to such instruments, and not to deprive the investor of its investment without the required compensation. In that case, the relevant State agency's decision not to renew claimant's permit breached the obligation to provide fair and equitable treatment, because the agency failed to provide the investor with advance notice that its permit might not be renewed and did not

provide the investor an opportunity either to justify its actions or to solve any alleged deficiencies [. . .]'.

573. In *Waste Management v. Mexico* the tribunal summarized its position on the FET standard in the following terms:

> 'the minimum standard of treatment of fair and equitable treatment is infringed by conduct attributable to the State and harmful to Claimant if the conduct is arbitrary, grossly unfair, unjust or idiosyncratic, is discriminatory and exposes Claimant to sectional or racial prejudice, or involves a lack of due process leading to an outcome which offends judicial propriety – as might be the case with a manifest failure of natural justice in judicial proceedings or a complete lack of transparency and candour in an administrative process. In applying this standard it is relevant that the treatment is in breach of representations made by the host State which were reasonably relied on by Claimant.'

[. . .]

575. Article 54 of the Arbitration (Additional Facility) Rules directs ICSID tribunals to apply 'such rules of international law as may be applicable' unless otherwise agreed by the parties. This reference may be considered to include the 'general principles of law recognized by civilized nations' referred to in Article 38 of the Statute of the International Court of Justice.

576. With particular regard to the legal sources of one of the standards for respect of the fair and equitable treatment principle, *i.e.* the protection of 'legitimate expectations', these sources are to be found in the comparative analysis of many domestic legal systems. [. . .] Based on converging considerations of good faith and legal security, the concept of legitimate expectations is found in different legal traditions according to which some expectations may be reasonably or legitimately created for a private person by the constant behaviour and/or promises of its legal partner, in particular when this partner is the public administration on which this private person is dependent. In particular, in German law, protection of legitimate expectations is connected with the principle of *Vertraensschutz* [sic] (protection of trust) a notion which deeply influenced the development of European Union Law, pointing to precise and specific assurances given by the administration. The same notion finds equivalents in other European countries such as France in the concept of *confiance légitime*. The substantive (as opposed to procedural) protection of legitimate expectations is now also to be found in English law, although it was not recognized until the last decade. This protection is also found in Latin American countries [. . .] and exists equally in Venezuelan administrative law [. . .].

Applying FET to the present facts

577. The measures that, according to Claimant, violated the FET provision have been set out in the summary of Claimant's position. The Tribunal shall now review

such measures to determine whether they were contrary to the FET, based on the principles outlined above. Before doing so, however, it shall make reference to the change of the State policy regarding mining since in the Tribunal's view such change is of relevance in the present context.

578. For almost twenty years from the granting of the Brisas Concession, the Administration raised no objections to Claimant's mining activities regarding what in the last stage of the relations it alleged to be a failure to respect time-limits fixed by the corresponding Mining Law and the Mining Title, leading to the termination of the various concessions. By the approval of required studies, [. . .] and, subsequently, by the issuance of the Phase I Permit in March 2007, Respondent had impliedly confirmed the content of the many certificates of compliance consistently issued [. . .].

579. Claimant had therefore good reasons to rely on the continuing validity of its mining titles and rights and an expectation that it would obtain the required authorization to start the exploitation of the concessions. [. . .]

580. In the Tribunal's view, the reasons for the termination of the [. . .] Concessions [. . .] are to be found in the change of political priorities of the Administration. [. . .]

[. . .]

582. The change of policy by the Venezuelan Administration cannot be disregarded by the Tribunal. [. . .]

[. . .]

592. The second measure in alleged breach of the FET is described by Claimant as follows:

> 'The Ministry of Environment's peremptory revocation, in a manner that violated fundamental principles of Venezuelan law, without prior notice to Gold Reserve or an opportunity to be heard, of the Construction Permit it had issued one year earlier and on which Gold Reserve relied to invest more than US$ 115 million more in the Project, which revocation was based on purported environmental grounds that were without legal basis and that were not supported by the facts of the Brisas Project, and where the revocation (and all subsequent government acts directed at the Company) were in reality motivated by the political agenda of the Chávez Administration, revealed and confirmed in words and deeds of the government and its officials, including President Chávez, to remove North American investment in the gold sector and replace it with more politically desirable alternatives. [. . .]'

593. As noted above, in the Revocation Order, [Venezuela] declared the 'absolute nullity' of the Construction Permit issued on 27 March 2007 and as a result revoked the same 'for reasons of public order.' The Revocation Order refers initially to the 'fundamental duty of the Venezuelan State to guarantee the protection of the environment and populations confronted with situations that constitute a threat to,

make vulnerable, or risk the people's physical integrity, as well as involve imminent damage to the environment'. It also refers to the public administration ability 'to review and correct its administrative actions, including the revocation of administrative acts'.

594. The Revocation Order sets out the grounds for the revocation of the Construction Permit, essentially referring to the state of emergency declared on 26 June 2006 in the area of the Imataca Forest Reserve 'as the mining activities in Bolivar State had altered the environment [. . .] thus having affected the nearby populations, indigenous communities, and the rest of the collective'. It then refers to the 'serious environmental deterioration of the rivers, soil, flora, fauna and biodiversity in general, caused by the uncontrolled mining activities performed by the large number of miners present in the area'.

595. The Tribunal acknowledges that a State has a responsibility to preserve the environment and protect local populations living in the area where mining activities are conducted. However, this responsibility does not exempt a State from complying with its commitments to international investors by searching ways and means to satisfy in a balanced way both conditions.

596. The Emergency Decree referred to in the Revocation Order was in force when the Construction Permit was issued on 27 March 2007. It is to be assumed that [Venezuela] had verified, prior to issuing the Construction Permit, that the works to be authorized did not conflict with the objective of the Emergency Decree. That this concern was well considered appears to be confirmed by the reference in the text of the Construction Permit to a number of conditions imposed on Claimant for the protection of the 'environment, including, but not limited to, posting a performance bond guaranteeing the use of the required conservation and recovery measures in the event of environmental deterioration.' Almost all of the conditions set out at the end of the Construction Permit relate to the environment. The Emergency Decree had a one-year term, and thus expired on 26 June 2007. There was no warning [. . .] that the situation regarding the environment had significantly deteriorated since the date on which the Construction Permit was issued.

597. The reference in the Revocation Order to 'uncontrolled mining activities' being conducted in the area by a large number of miners is contradicted by the Inspection Report issued [. . .] one month before the date of the Revocation Order. This Report states (at the end) that 'no evidence of (exploration or exploitation) mining activities was found during the walk around.' It is only logical that had 'uncontrolled mining' been conducted in the area, particularly if by a 'large number of miners', MIBAM's Inspection Report would have so indicated. Respondent contends that following the issuance of the Phase I Permit, [the government's] concerns regarding the impacts of the [. . .] Brisas Project on the environment increased and that, as of April 2008, Claimant had not completed a satisfactory EAE or the requested joint study with Crystallex regarding the development of

joint infrastructure plans. The Tribunal does not underestimate [. . .] concerns regarding environmental protection. It notes that none of the above grounds of concern was mentioned in the Revocation Order and, in any case, that the better course of action for addressing any growing concerns would have been to examine with Claimant how best to proceed to alleviate the same.

[. . .]

600. The Tribunal finds that Respondent's conduct did not accord with the obligations required by the FET standard in the BIT. Respondent issued the Revocation Order without allowing Claimant an opportunity to be heard. It is only reasonable to infer that [Venezuela's] conduct was determined by the change of State's policy inaugurated by President Chávez.

[. . .].

 CASE

Glamis Gold, Ltd v. United States of America[91]

Glamis Gold, Ltd (Glamis) is a publicly held Canadian corporation in the mining sector. Throughout the 1980s and the 1990s, Glamis developed and operated open-pit gold mines in California and Nevada through wholly owned subsidiaries.

In 1995, Glamis applied to the US government for a permit to operate a mine at Imperial Site in southern California. There were three mines proposed, two to be backfilled and the third to be left open. The proposal attracted the attention of the public due to the fact that the site of the mine was near the lands of the Native American Quechan tribe and included the tribe's traditional pathways and religiously significant sites. Indeed, due to their cultural significance, the federal land on which Glamis' proposed site was situated had been removed from the list of permitted mining areas.

Following a six-year review of the application, the Clinton Administration rejected it. This was the first time a project proposal had been rejected. Several months later, however, the new Bush Administration reversed the decision and offered Glamis a permit. Then, in April 2003, the State of California promulgated a new law to require backfilling on all open pit mining projects. Alleging both expropriation and a violation of NAFTA's FET provision, Glamis pursued arbitration, demanding $50 million compensation.

91 *Glamis Gold, Ltd v. United States of America*, UNCITRAL (NAFTA), Award (June 8, 2009). Available at: http://italaw.com/documents/Glamis_Award_002.pdf; footnotes omitted.

The tribunal addressed the FET allegations by reassessing the relationship to customary international standards of investor protection.

598. [. . .] Article 1105(1) of the NAFTA provides that '[e]ach party shall accord to investments of investors of another Party treatment in accordance with international law, including fair and equitable treatment and full protection and security.'

599. There is no disagreement among the State Parties to the NAFTA, nor the Parties to this arbitration, that the requirement of fair and equitable treatment in Article 1105 is to be understood by reference to the customary international law minimum standard of treatment of aliens. Indeed, the Free Trade Commission ('FTC') clearly states, in its binding Notes of Interpretation on July 31, 2001, that 'Article 1105(1) prescribes the customary international law minimum standard of treatment of aliens as the minimum standard of treatment to be afforded to investments of investors of another Party.'

600. The question thus becomes: what does this customary international law minimum standard of treatment require of a State Party vis-à-vis investors of another State Party? Is it the same as that established in 1926 in *Neer v. Mexico*? Or has Claimant proven that the standard has 'evolved'? If it has evolved, what evidence of custom has Claimant provided to the Tribunal to determine its current scope?

601. As a threshold issue, the Tribunal notes that it is Claimant's burden to sufficiently answer each of these questions. The State Parties to the NAFTA (at least Canada and Mexico) agree that 'the test in *Neer* does continue to apply', though Mexico 'also agrees that the standard is relative and that conduct which may not have violated international law [in] the 1920s might very well be seen to offend internationally accepted principles today'. If, as Claimant argues, the customary international law minimum standard of treatment has indeed moved to require something less than the 'egregious', 'outrageous', or 'shocking' standard as elucidated in *Neer*, then the burden of establishing what the standard now requires is upon Claimant.

602. The Tribunal acknowledges that it is difficult to establish a change in customary international law. As Respondent explains, establishment of a rule of customary international law requires: (1) 'a concordant practice of a number of States acquiesced in by others', and (2) 'a conception that the practice is required by or consistent with the prevailing law (*opinio juris*)'.

603. The evidence of such 'concordant practice' undertaken out of a sense of legal obligation is exhibited in very few authoritative sources: treaty ratification language, statements of governments, treaty practice (e.g., Model BITs), and sometimes pleadings. Although one can readily identify the practice of States, it is usually very difficult to determine the intent behind those actions. Looking to a claimant to ascertain custom requires it to ascertain such intent, a complicated and particularly difficult task. In the context of arbitration, however, it is necessarily Claimant's place to establish a change in custom.

604. The Tribunal notes that, although an examination of custom is indeed necessary to determine the scope and bounds of current customary international law, this requirement – repeatedly argued by various State Parties – because of the difficulty in proving a change in custom, effectively freezes the protections provided for in this provision at the 1926 conception of egregiousness.

605. Claimant did provide numerous arbitral decisions in support of its conclusion that fair and equitable treatment encompasses a universe of 'fundamental' principles common throughout the world that include 'the duty to act in good faith, due process, transparency and candor, and fairness and protection from arbitrariness'. Arbitral awards, Respondent rightly notes, do not constitute State practice and thus cannot create or prove customary international law. They can, however, serve as illustrations of customary international law if they involve an examination of customary international law, as opposed to a treaty-based, or autonomous, interpretation.

606. This brings the Tribunal to its first task: ascertaining which of the sources argued by Claimant are properly available to instruct the Tribunal on the bounds of 'fair and equitable treatment'. As briefly mentioned above, the Tribunal notes that it finds two categories of arbitral awards that examine a fair and equitable treatment standard: those that look to define customary international law and those that examine the autonomous language and nuances of the underlying treaty language. Fundamental to this divide is the treaty underlying the dispute: those treaties and free trade agreements, like the NAFTA, that are to be understood by reference to the customary international law minimum standard of treatment necessarily lead their tribunals to analyze custom; while those treaties with fair and equitable treatment clauses that expand upon, or move beyond, customary international law, lead their reviewing tribunals into an analysis of the treaty language and its meaning, as guided by Article 31(1) of the Vienna Convention.

607. Ascertaining custom is necessarily a factual inquiry, looking to the actions of States and the motives for and consistency of these actions. By applying an autonomous standard, on the other hand, a tribunal may focus solely on the language and nuances of the treaty language itself and, applying the rules of treaty interpretation, require no party proof of State action or *opinio juris*. This latter practice fails to assist in the ascertainment of custom.

608. As Article 1105's fair and equitable treatment standard is, as Respondent phrases it, simply 'a shorthand reference to customary international law', the Tribunal finds that arbitral decisions that apply an autonomous standard provide no guidance inasmuch as the entire method of reasoning does not bear on an inquiry into custom. The various BITs cited by Claimant may or may not illuminate customary international law; they will prove helpful to this Tribunal's analysis when they seek to provide the same base floor of conduct as the minimum standard of treatment under customary international law; but they will not be of assis-

tance if they include different protections than those provided for in customary international law.

609. Claimant has agreed with this distinction between customary international law and autonomous treaty standards but argues that, with respect to this particular standard, BIT jurisprudence has 'converged with customary international law in this area'. The Tribunal finds this to be an over-statement. Certainly, it is possible that some BITs converge with the requirements established by customary international law; there are, however, numerous BITs that have been interpreted as going beyond customary international law, and thereby requiring more than that to which the NAFTA State Parties have agreed. It is thus necessary to look to the underlying fair and equitable treatment clause of each treaty, and the reviewing tribunal's analysis of that treaty, to determine whether or not they are drafted with an intent to refer to customary international law.

610. Looking, for instance, to Claimant's reliance on *Tecmed v. Mexico* for various of its arguments, the Tribunal finds that Claimant has not proven that this award, based on a BIT between Spain and Mexico, defines anything other than an autonomous standard and thus an award from which this Tribunal will not find guidance. Article 4(1) of the Spain-Mexico BIT involved in the *Tecmed* proceeding provides that each contracting party guarantees just and equitable treatment conforming with 'International Law' to the investments of investors of the other contracting party in its territory. Article 4(2) proceeds to explain that this treatment will not be less favorable than that granted in similar circumstances by each contracting party to the investments in its territory by an investor of a third State. Several interpretations of the requirement espoused in Article 4(2) are indeed possible, but the *Tecmed* tribunal itself states that it 'understands that the scope of the undertaking of fair and equitable treatment under Article 4(1) of the Agreement described . . . is that resulting from *an autonomous interpretation* . . . .' Thus, this Tribunal finds that the language or analysis of the *Tecmed* award is not relevant to the Tribunal's consideration.

611. The Tribunal therefore holds that it may look solely to arbitral awards – including BIT awards – that seek to be understood by reference to the customary international law minimum standard of treatment, as opposed to any autonomous standard. The Tribunal thus turns to its second task: determining the scope of the current customary international law minimum standard of treatment, as proven by Claimant.

612. It appears to this Tribunal that the NAFTA State Parties agree that, at a minimum, the fair and equitable treatment standard is that as articulated in *Neer*: 'the treatment of an alien, in order to constitute an international delinquency, should amount to an outrage, to bad faith, to wilful neglect of duty, or to an insufficiency of governmental action so far short of international standards that every reasonable and impartial man would readily recognize its insufficiency.' Whether this standard has evolved since 1926, however, has not been definitively agreed upon. The Tribunal considers two possible types of evolution: (1) that

what the international community views as 'outrageous' may change over time; and (2) that the minimum standard of treatment has moved beyond what it was in 1926.

613. The Tribunal finds apparent agreement that the fair and equitable treatment standard is subject to the first type of evolution: a change in the international view of what is shocking and outrageous. As the *Mondev* tribunal held:

> *Neer* and like arbitral awards were decided in the 1920s, when the status of the individual in international law, and the international protection of foreign investments, were far less developed than they have since come to be. In particular, both the substantive and procedural rights of the individual in international law have undergone considerable development. In light of these developments it is unconvincing to confine the meaning of 'fair and equitable treatment' and 'full protection and security' of foreign investments to what those terms – had they been current at the time – might have meant in the 1920s when applied to the physical security of an alien. To the modern eye, what is unfair or inequitable need not equate with the outrageous or the egregious. In particular, a State may treat foreign investment unfairly and inequitably without necessarily acting in bad faith.

Similarly, this Tribunal holds that the *Neer* standard, when applied with current sentiments and to modern situations, may find shocking and egregious events not considered to reach this level in the past.

614. As regards the second form of evolution – the proposition that customary international law has moved beyond the minimum standard of treatment of aliens as defined in *Neer* – the Tribunal finds that the evidence provided by Claimant does not establish such evolution. This is evident in the abundant and continued use of adjective modifiers throughout arbitral awards, evidencing a strict standard. *International Thunderbird* used the terms '*gross* denial of justice' and '*manifest* arbitrariness' to describe the acts that it viewed would breach the minimum standard of treatment. *S.D. Myers* would find a breach of Article 1105 when an investor was treated 'in *such an unjust or arbitrary* manner'. The *Mondev* tribunal held: 'The test is not whether a particular result is surprising, but whether the *shock or surprise* occasioned to an impartial tribunal leads, on reflection, to justified concerns as to the judicial propriety of the outcome. . .'.

615. The customary international law minimum standard of treatment is just that, a minimum standard. It is meant to serve as a floor, an absolute bottom, below which conduct is not accepted by the international community. Although the circumstances of the case are of course relevant, the standard is not meant to vary from state to state or investor to investor. The protection afforded by Article 1105 must be distinguished from that provided for in Article 1102 on National Treatment. Article 1102(1) states: 'Each Party shall accord to investors of another Party treatment no less favorable than that it accords, in like circumstances, to its own investors. . .'. The treatment of inves-

tors under Article 1102 is compared to the treatment the State's own investors receive and thus can vary greatly depending on each State and its practices. The fair and equitable treatment promised by Article 1105 is not dynamic; it cannot vary between nations as thus the protection afforded would have no minimum.

616. It therefore appears that, although situations may be more varied and complicated today than in the 1920s, the level of scrutiny is the same. The fundamentals of the *Neer* standard thus still apply today: to violate the customary international law minimum standard of treatment codified in Article 1105 of the NAFTA, an act must be sufficiently egregious and shocking – a gross denial of justice, manifest arbitrariness, blatant unfairness, a complete lack of due process, evident discrimination, or a manifest lack of reasons – so as to fall below accepted international standards and constitute a breach of Article 1105(1). The Tribunal notes that one aspect of evolution from *Neer* that is generally agreed upon is that bad faith is not required to find a violation of the fair and equitable treatment standard, but its presence is conclusive evidence of such. Thus, an act that is egregious or shocking may also evidence bad faith, but such bad faith is not necessary for the finding of a violation. The standard for finding a breach of the customary international law minimum standard of treatment therefore remains as stringent as it was under *Neer*; it is entirely possible, however that, as an international community, we may be shocked by State actions now that did not offend us previously.

617. Respondent argues below that, in reviewing State agency or departmental decisions and actions, international tribunals as well as domestic judiciaries favor deference to the agency so as not to second guess the primary decision-makers or become 'science courts'. The Tribunal disagrees that domestic deference in national court systems is necessarily applicable to international tribunals. In the present case, the Tribunal finds the standard of deference to already be present in the standard as stated, rather than being additive to that standard. The idea of deference is found in the modifiers 'manifest' and 'gross' that make this standard a stringent one; it is found in the idea that a breach requires something greater than mere arbitrariness, something that is surprising, shocking, or exhibits a manifest lack of reasoning.

618. With this thought in mind, the Tribunal turns to the duties that Claimant argues are part of the requirements of a host State per Article 1105: (1) an obligation to protect legitimate expectations through establishment of a transparent and predictable business and legal framework, and (2) an obligation to provide protection from arbitrary measures. As the United States explained in its 1128 submission in *Pope and Talbot*, and as Mexico adopted in its 1128 submission to the *ADF* tribunal: '"fair and equitable treatment" and "full protection and security" are provided as examples of the customary international law standards incorporated into Article 1105(1) . . . . The international law minimum standard [of treatment] is an umbrella concept incorporating a set of rules that has crystallized over the centuries into customary international law in specific contexts.' The Tribunal

therefore finds it appropriate to address, in turn, each of the State obligations Claimant asserts are potential parts of the protection afforded by fair and equitable treatment.

a. Asserted Obligation to Protect Legitimate Expectations through Establishment of a Transparent and Predictable Legal and Business Framework

619. As explained above, the minimum standard of treatment of aliens established by customary international law, and by reference to which the fair and equitable treatment standard of Article 1105(1) is to be understood, is an absolute minimum, a floor below which the international community will not condone conduct. To maintain fair and equitable treatment as an absolute floor, a breach must be based upon objective criteria that apply equally among States and between investors.

620. The Tribunal notes Respondent's argument that even those expectations that manifest in a contract are insufficient to provide a basis for a breach of the minimum standard of treatment. The Tribunal agrees that mere contract breach, without something further such as denial of justice or discrimination, normally will not suffice to establish a breach of Article 1105. Merely not living up to expectations cannot be sufficient to find a breach of Article 1105 of the NAFTA. Instead, Article 1105(1) requires the evaluation of whether the State made any specific assurance or commitment to the investor so as to induce its expectations.

621. The Tribunal therefore agrees with *International Thunderbird* that legitimate expectations relate to an examination under Article 1105(1) in such situations 'where a Contracting Party's conduct creates reasonable and justifiable expectations on the part of an investor (or investment) to act in reliance on said conduct . . . .' In this way, a State may be tied to the objective expectations that it creates *in order to induce* investment.

622. As the Tribunal determines below that no specific assurances were made to induce Claimant's 'reasonable and justifiable expectations', the Tribunal need not determine the level, or characteristics, of state action in contradiction of those expectations that would be necessary to constitute a violation of Article 1105.

b. Asserted Obligation to Provide Protection from Arbitrary Measures

623. With respect to the asserted duty to protect investors from arbitrariness, the Tribunal notes Claimant's citations to several NAFTA arbitrations that have found a violation of Article 1105 in arbitrary state action. Claimant cites to *S.D. Myers* for its holding that 'a breach of Article 1105 occurs only when it is shown that an investor has been treated in such an unjust and arbitrary manner that the treatment rises to the level that is unacceptable from the international perspective'.

Similarly, it quotes *International Thunderbird*'s holding that 'manifest arbitrariness falling below acceptable international standards' is prohibited under Article 1105. 624. The Tribunal also notes, however, Respondent's argument that no Chapter 11 tribunal has found that decision-making that appears arbitrary to some parties is sufficient to constitute an Article 1105 violation. In *Mondev*, for instance, the tribunal held: 'The test is not whether a particular result is surprising, but whether the shock or surprise occasioned to an impartial tribunal leads, on reflection, to justified concerns as to the judicial propriety of the outcome . . . .' Respondent understands this to be the case because tribunals consistently afford administrative decision-making a high level of deference. Respondent quotes *S.D. Myers* to illustrate this deference: 'determination [that Article 1105 has been breached] must be made in light of the high measure of deference that international law generally extends to the right of domestic authorities to regulate matters within their own borders.' This, Respondent argues, leads to the result that merely imperfect legislation or regulation does not give rise to State responsibility under customary international law.

625. The Tribunal finds that, in this situation, both Parties are correct. Previous tribunals have indeed found a certain level of arbitrariness to violate the obligations of a State under the fair and equitable treatment standard. Indeed, arbitrariness that contravenes *the* rule of law, rather than *a* rule of law, would occasion surprise not only from investors, but also from tribunals. This is not a mere appearance of arbitrariness, however – a tribunal's determination that an agency acted in a way with which the tribunal disagrees or that a state passed legislation that the tribunal does not find curative of all of the ills presented; rather, this is a level of arbitrariness that, as *International Thunderbird* put it, amounts to a 'gross denial of justice or manifest arbitrariness falling below acceptable international standards.'

626. The Tribunal therefore holds that there is an obligation of each of the NAFTA State Parties inherent in the fair and equitable treatment standard of Article 1105 that they do not treat investors of another State in a *manifestly* arbitrary manner. The Tribunal thus determines that Claimant has sufficiently substantiated its arguments that a duty to protect investors from arbitrary measures exists in the customary international law minimum standard of treatment of aliens; though Claimant has not sufficiently rebutted Respondent's assertions that a finding of arbitrariness requires a determination of some act far beyond the measure's mere illegality, an act so manifestly arbitrary, so unjust and surprising as to be unacceptable from the international perspective.

4. Final Disposition of the Tribunal with respect to the Scope of the Fair and Equitable Legal Standard

627. The Tribunal holds that Claimant has not met its burden of proving that something other than the fundamentals of the *Neer* standard apply today. The

Tribunal therefore holds that a violation of the customary international law minimum standard of treatment, as codified in Article 1105 of the NAFTA, requires an act that is sufficiently egregious and shocking – a gross denial of justice, manifest arbitrariness, blatant unfairness, a complete lack of due process, evident discrimination, or a manifest lack of reasons – so as to fall below accepted international standards and constitute a breach of Article 1105. Such a breach may be exhibited by a 'gross denial of justice or manifest arbitrariness falling below acceptable international standards;' or the creation by the State of objective expectations *in order to induce* investment and the subsequent repudiation of those expectations. The Tribunal emphasizes that, although bad faith may often be present in such a determination and its presence certainly will be determinative of a violation, a finding of bad faith is not a requirement for a breach of Article 1105(1).

a   FET as the protection of investor expectations

The majority of awards rely upon an analysis of FET that looks at the investors' expectations of treatment. The strength of the investor expectations approach can be witnessed on the one hand by its increasingly sophisticated elaboration in some awards and the brief reference to it in others, reflecting its widely known and accepted basis.

As mentioned above, the very first tribunal to analyse FET emphasized the investor's expectations of what treatment she could expect of the host. The view that tribunals should interpret FET on the basis of investor expectations is clearly not one that can be based solely on the plain language of the relevant treaty. Rather, it must stem from an emphasis on understanding IIAs as instruments to protect investors – a reading that can be supported by the preambular language of many BITs and the context of IIA negotiations.

This 'plain-meaning-plus-context', or 'Vienna Convention Article 31' approach, can be used to interpret any form of FET provision. While it is particularly attractive for tribunals looking at autonomous FET obligations, an obligation tied to the international law standard can lead to a reliance on investor expectations through a floor-rather-than-ceiling approach. The *Lemire v. Ukraine* award describes the process of interpretation which led them to emphasize the investor's expectations in assessing Lemire's FET claim.

CASE

Joseph Charles Lemire v. Ukraine[92]

US businessman Joseph Lemire was a shareholder of radio station Gala in the Ukraine. Having begun operations in the 1990s, when most radio stations were government controlled, Gala became a great success locally. Gala's success spurred others to imitate Lemire's activities and, by the 2000s, national investors started competing for airwaves.

Wanting to expand its geographic reach and begin informational programming in addition to its music program, Gala took part in several tenders for additional frequencies beginning in 2004. Although its efforts to increase its frequencies were substantial, the regulating authorities continuously denied Gala any additional bandwidth. The regulator instead granted the available airwaves, at the command of the President, to the Executive's political allies.

Lemire brought an arbitration claim in 2000 that resulted in a settlement. Unsatisfied with the host's implementation of the settlement agreement, Lemire again challenged the state. In his 2006 arbitration request, Lemire claimed, *inter alia*, that the Ukraine's violations of its own tender procedures breached its obligations of fair and equitable treatment under the US–Ukraine BIT.

243. The purpose of this section is to determine the general scope and meaning of the FET standard defined in the BIT.

Article II.3 (a) and (b) of the BIT reads as follows:

'3.   *(a)*   *Investment shall at all times be accorded fair and equitable treatment, shall enjoy full protection and security and shall in no case be accorded treatment less than that required by international law.*

    (b)   *Neither Party shall in any way impair by arbitrary or discriminatory measures the management, operation, maintenance, use, enjoyment, acquisition, expansion, or disposal of investments. For purposes of dispute resolution under Articles VI and VII, a measure may be arbitrary or discriminatory notwithstanding the fact that a Party has had or has exercised the opportunity to review such measure in the courts or administrative tribunals of a Party'.*

---

92 *Joseph Charles Lemire v. Ukraine*, ICSID Case No. ARB/06/18, Decision on Jurisdiction and Liability (Jan. 14, 2010). Available at: http://italaw.com/documents/Lemirev.Ukraine2010.pdf; footnotes omitted.

[. . .]

246. [. . .] It is a rule of Delphic economy of language, which manages in just three sentences to formulate a series of wide ranging principles: FET standard, protection and security standard, international minimum standard and prohibition of arbitrary or discriminatory measures.

A) Customary International Law Minimum Standard and FET Standard

247. A classic debate in investment arbitration law is whether the FET standard established by bilateral or multilateral investment treaties coincides with or differs from the international minimum standard of protection for aliens imposed by customary international law.

248. The starting point of this debate is the very definition of the international minimum standard – a question which is fraught with difficulties. For claims arising from administrative or legislative acts of Governments – which are the type of claims typically submitted in investment disputes – the historic leading case seems to be *Roberts*, issued by the United States – Mexico General Claims Commission in 1926, which defined the minimum treatment as that required '*in accordance with ordinary standards of civilization*'. [. . .]

249. *Roberts* is understood to stand for the propositions that a certain treatment may give rise to international responsibility notwithstanding that it affects citizens and aliens alike, and that administrative and legislative actions may amount to a violation of the customary minimum treatment even if the State did not act in bad faith or with willful neglect of duty.

250. The relationship between FET and customary minimum standard has been the subject of much debate, especially in NAFTA based arbitrations, and has led the NAFTA Free Trade Commission[93] to issue a binding interpretation on July 31, 2001. [text of the interpretation as set out above]

251. The same proposition, that the FET standard should be reduced to the customary international law minimum standard, was afterwards adopted in the new 2004 US Model BIT. Article 5 of this model provides:

'*Article 5: Minimum Standard of Treatment*

1. *Each Party shall accord to covered investments treatment in accordance with customary international law, including fair and equitable treatment and full protection and security.*

2. *For greater certainty, paragraph 1 prescribes the customary international law*

---

93 NAFTA Free Trade Commission, *Notes of Interpretation of Certain Chapter 11 Provisions*, B1–2 (July 31, 2001). Available at: http://www.sice.oas.org/tpd/nafta/Commission/CH11understanding_e.asp.

minimum standard of treatment of aliens as the minimum standard of treatment to be afforded to covered investments'.

252. Is this principle of assimilation between customary minimum standard and FET standard also applicable to the US–Ukraine BIT?

253. The answer must be in the negative. The BIT was adopted in 1996, and was based on the standard drafting then proposed by the US. The words used are clear, and do not leave room for doubt: *'Investments shall at all times be accorded fair and equitable treatment . . . and shall in no case be accorded treatment less than that required by international law'.* What the US and Ukraine agreed when they executed the BIT, was that the international customary minimum standard should not operate as a ceiling, but rather as a floor. Investments protected by the BIT should in any case be awarded the level of protection offered by customary international law. But this level of protection could and should be transcended if the FET standard provided the investor with a superior set of rights.

254. In view of the drafting of Article II.3 of the BIT, the Tribunal finds that actions or omissions of the Parties may qualify as unfair and inequitable, even if they do not amount to an outrage, to willful neglect of duty, egregious insufficiency of State actions, or even in subjective bad faith.

255. This leads to the next question: what is the exact meaning of the FET standard acknowledged by the BIT?

B) Meaning of Article II.3 of the BIT

256. The words used by the Article II.3. are the following: 'Investments shall at all times be accorded fair and equitable treatment [. . .]. Neither party shall in any way impair by arbitrary or discriminatory measures the management, operation, maintenance, use, enjoyment, acquisition, expansion or disposal of investments'.

257. These general principles require interpretation in order to give them specific content and this interpretation must comply with the requirements of Article 31.1. of the Vienna Convention – it must be done 'in good faith in accordance with the *ordinary meaning* to be given to the terms of the treaty *in their context* and in the light of its *object and purpose'*.

a) Ordinary meaning

258. An inquiry into the *ordinary meaning* of the expression 'fair and equitable treatment' does not clarify the meaning of the concept. 'Fair and equitable treatment' is a term of art, and any effort to decipher the ordinary meaning of the words used only leads to analogous terms of almost equal vagueness.

259. The literal reading of Article II.3 of the BIT is more helpful. In accordance with the words used, Ukraine is assuming a positive and a negative obligation: the positive is to accord FET to the protected foreign investments, and the negative is

to abstain from arbitrary or discriminatory measures affecting such investments. Any arbitrary or discriminatory measure, by definition, fails to be fair and equitable. Thus, any violation of subsection (b) seems *ipso iure* to also constitute a violation of subsection (a). The reverse is not true, though. An action or inaction of a State may fall short of fairness and equity without being discriminatory or arbitrary. The prohibition of arbitrary or discriminatory measures is thus an example of possible violations of the FET standard.

260. The literal interpretation also shows that for a measure to violate the BIT it is sufficient if it is either arbitrary or discriminatory; it need not be both.

261. Discrimination, in the words of pertinent precedents, requires more than different treatment. To amount to discrimination, a case must be treated differently from similar cases without justification; a measure must be "*discriminatory and expose[s] the claimant to sectional or racial prejudice*'; or a measure must '*target[ed] Claimant's investments specifically as foreign investments*'.

[. . .].

263. [T]he underlying notion of arbitrariness is that prejudice, preference or bias is substituted for the rule of law.

b) Context

264. Words used in treaties must be interpreted through their <u>context</u>. The context of Article II.3 is to be found in the Preamble of the BIT, in which the contracting parties state '*that fair and equitable treatment of investment is desirable in order to maintain a stable framework for investment. . .'*. The FET standard is thus closely tied to the notion of legitimate expectations – actions or omissions by Ukraine are contrary to the FET standard if they frustrate legitimate and reasonable expectations on which the investor relied at the time when he made the investment.

Legitimate expectations

265. Which were the legitimate expectations of Claimant at the time he made his investment?

266. It must be recalled that when in 1995 Mr. Lemire made his first investment and acquired a controlling stake in Gala Radio, this was a small company in a nascent industry. Historically, before independence and political change, the radio industry in Ukraine had been in the hands of the State. In the mid-1990s the sector began to be privatized, a first Law on TV and Radio having been approved on December 21, 1993. All these factors had a bearing on Claimant's legitimate expectations.

267. On a general level, Claimant could expect a regulatory system for the broadcasting industry which was to be consistent, transparent, fair, reasonable, and enforced without arbitrary or discriminatory decisions. It is true that Ukraine and

the United States, when accepting the BIT, had reserved their right to make or maintain limited exceptions to the national treatment in the radio sector. Under this exception, Ukraine could e.g., validly require that the founders of broadcasting companies be Ukrainian nationals. But Mr. Lemire could equally expect that, once he had been awarded the necessary administrative authorization to invest in the Ukrainian radio sector, there would be a level playing field, and the administrative measures would not be inequitable, unfair, arbitrary or discriminatory.

268. And on a more specific and personal level, Mr. Lemire undoubtedly had the legitimate expectation that Gala, which at that time was only a local station in Kyiv, would be allowed to expand, in parallel with the growth of the private radio industry in Ukraine.

[. . .]

270. In the Tribunal's opinion, the available evidence shows that what Mr. Lemire had in mind when he bought into Gala Radio in June 1995, was to convert Gala into a national broadcaster and to create a second AM channel. The idea to create a third radio network – called 'Energy' – seems to have been an afterthought. At the time of the acquisition of Gala, Claimant must have approached the National Council, and asked whether a national licence for Gala and an AM licence could be obtained. The National Council reacted in positive terms, as proven by a letter addressed to the State Centre, in which the National Council states that it is '*considering the possibility*' of issuing to Gala licences for a nationwide FM channel and for a second AM Band, and enquires whether the frequencies would be available. There is no reference to a third channel. The State Centre reacted positively.

271. Respondent has insisted that Claimant has not been able to produce a formal business plan. That is true. But the Tribunal does not attach too much weight to this omission. Formal business plans are customary in sizeable investments in settled economic and business environments. None of these characteristics applied to Mr. Lemire's investment in Gala Radio: a small amount was involved and the situation of Ukraine was anything but settled.

c) Object and purpose

272. The *object and purpose* of the BIT – the third interpretive criterion – is defined in its Preamble: the parties '*desir[e] to promote greater economic cooperation between them, with respect to investment by nationals and companies of one Party in the territory of the other Party*' and recognize that the BIT '*will stimulate the flow of private capital and the economic development of the Parties*'. The main purpose of the BIT is thus the stimulation of foreign investment and of the accompanying flow of capital.

273. But this main purpose is not sought in the abstract; it is inserted in a wider context, the economic development for both signatory countries. Economic development is an objective which must benefit all, primarily national citizens and national companies, and secondarily foreign investors. Thus, the object and

purpose of the Treaty is not to protect foreign investments *per se*, but as an aid to the development of the domestic economy. And local development requires that the preferential treatment of foreigners be balanced against the legitimate right of Ukraine to pass legislation and adopt measures for the protection of what as a sovereign it perceives to be its public interest.

[. . .]

284. The FET standard defined in the BIT is an autonomous treaty standard, whose precise meaning must be established on a case-by-case basis. It requires an action or omission by the State which violates a certain threshold of propriety, causing harm to the investor, and with a causal link between action or omission and harm. The threshold must be defined by the Tribunal, on the basis of the wording of Article II.3 of the BIT, and bearing in mind a number of factors, including among others the following:

- whether the State has failed to offer a stable and predictable legal framework;
- whether the State made specific representations to the investor;
- whether due process has been denied to the investor;
- whether there is an absence of transparency in the legal procedure or in the actions of the State;
- whether there has been harassment, coercion, abuse of power or other bad faith conduct by the host State;
- whether any of the actions of the State can be labeled as arbitrary, discriminatory or inconsistent.

285. The evaluation of the State's action cannot be performed in the abstract and only with a view of protecting the investor's rights. The Tribunal must also balance other legally relevant interests, and take into consideration a number of countervailing factors, before it can establish that a violation of the FET standard, which merits compensation, has actually occurred:

- the State's sovereign right to pass legislation and to adopt decisions for the protection of its public interests, especially if they do not provoke a disproportionate impact on foreign investors;
- the legitimate expectations of the investor, at the time he made his investment;
- the investor's duty to perform an investigation before effecting the investment;
- the investor's conduct in the host country.

286. Once the scope and meaning of the FET standard has been defined in the abstract, the Tribunal must establish the facts and decide whether they constitute a violation of such standard. This will be achieved by reviewing the legal procedure created by Ukrainian law for the awarding of licences in the broadcasting sector (VI.3.3), then by analyzing in detail the facts surrounding the allocation of frequencies which affected Gala (VI.3.4).

[The tribunal goes on to find Ukraine's actions violate its obligation of FET.]

When regarding the investor's expectations, tribunals can be more or less demanding. Those that emphasize subjective expectations place very high demands on hosts. In a prominent award with this viewpoint, the *Tecmed v. Mexico* arbitrators required hosts to 'not affect the basic expectations that were taken into account by the foreign investor to make the investment'.[94] They elaborated on just what these 'basic expectations' were in the following, often-cited, passage:

> [. . .] The foreign investor expects the host State to act in a consistent manner, free from ambiguity and totally transparently in its relations with the foreign investor, so that it may know beforehand any and all rules and regulations that will govern its investments, as well as the goals of the relevant policies and administrative practices or directives, to be able to plan its investment and comply with such regulations. Any and all State actions conforming to such criteria should relate not only to the guidelines, directives or requirements issued, or the resolutions approved thereunder, but also to the goals underlying such regulations. The foreign investor also expects the host State to act consistently, i.e. without arbitrarily revoking any preexisting decisions or permits issued by the State that were relied upon by the investor to assume its commitments as well as to plan and launch its commercial and business activities. The investor also expects the State to use the legal instruments that govern the actions of the investor or the investment in conformity with the function usually assigned to such instruments, and not to deprive the investor of its investment without the required compensation. In fact, failure by the host State to comply with such pattern of conduct with respect to the foreign investor or its investments affects the investor's ability to measure the treatment and protection awarded by the host State and to determine whether the actions of the host State conform to the fair and equitable treatment principle. Therefore, compliance by the host State with such pattern of conduct is closely related to the above-mentioned principle, to the actual chances of enforcing such principle, and to excluding the possibility that state action be characterized as arbitrary; i.e. as presenting insufficiencies that would be recognized '. . . by any reasonable and impartial man', or, although not in violation of specific regulations, as being contrary to the law because: '. . . (it) shocks, or at least surprises, a sense of juridical propriety'.[95]

This particularly strong language has been modified somewhat by tribunals who look not just to what the particular investor expected, but what the investor could *legitimately* have expected. Under current views of FET, the

---

94 *Técnicas Medioamientales Tecmed, SA v. United Mexican States*, ICSID Case No. ARB(AF)/00/2, Award, para. 154 (May 29, 2003).
95 *Id.*

legitimacy of expectations is determined by balancing the host's explicit or implicit promises made to the particular investor with its right to regulate. As a result, scrutinizing the legitimacy of the expectations may result (but does not always result) in a finding in favour of the host.

Just how legitimate it is for investors to expect consistent, transparent, reasonable and non-discriminatory policy making in a real-world context of politics and complex balancing of interests makes some arbitrators hesitant to apply the legitimate expectations test too uncritically. A separate (concurring) opinion in the *Micula v. Romania* dispute by arbitrator and international law professor Georges Abi-Saab sheds light on his view of the legitimate expectations analysis for FET.

 CASE

Ioan Micula et al. v. Romania[96]

The dispute arose over Romania's withdrawal of investment incentives in the wake of its accession to the European Union. Having one of the lowest per capita income levels in Europe, Romania has regions where income levels are particularly low due in part to high unemployment. In order to encourage investment in these areas, the government began offering long-term investors customs as well as tax benefits following the collapse of the Soviet Union.

As a related economic development goal, Romania's government also aimed at admission to the EU. In order to do so, however, the European authorities required legislative changes as well as economic growth. Of special concern to the European Commission was the existence of market distorting subsidies. While regional aid was permissible where needed, Romania had to ensure that such aid did not give an unfair competitive advantage to certain investors.

Claimants began establishing a network of beverage (and subsequently food) companies in the disadvantaged regions of Romania in the late 1990s, using the incentive scheme to benefit from low costs of production and largely untaxed profits. By strategically establishing separate entities, their eligibility for the incentive program should have extended through 2009.

In 2004, however, Romania announced the end of its subsidy program. Its EU accession, it reasoned, would not allow the continuation of such competition-harming practices.

---

96 *Ioan Micula, Viorel Micula, SC European Food SA, SC Starmill SRL and SC Multipack SRL v. Romania*, ICSID Case No. ARB/05/20, Separate Opinion of Professor Georges Abi-Saab (Dec. 5, 2013).

Claimants filed for arbitration on the basis of the Romania–Sweden BIT, arguing, *inter alia*, a violation of FET.

The majority of the tribunal agreed. The claimants, it said, had a legitimate expectation of procedurally and substantively fair treatment. The government's policy framework for investment incentives that was the reason for their establishing themselves in those regions to begin with, could therefore not be simply removed.

Co-Arbitrator Abi-Saab disagreed. While he was in accord on the damages issue, he denied that the claimants' expectations were legitimate.

> **1** – Whilst concurring with the outcome of this very thorough and lengthy award, I have difficulty with some interpretations of the law it provides. Without necessarily endorsing unreservedly all the others, I would like to single out one or two such areas.

I Legitimate expectations

> **2** – The Award bases the liability of Romania, mainly on its frustration, by its premature ending of the Tax Incentives Scheme, EGO 24, of the legitimate expectations of the Claimants, in violation of the Fair and equitable treatment standard stipulated in Article 2(3) of the BIT. According to the Award, in its exposition of the grounds, the acts, conduct and representations generating such 'legitimate expectations' need not rise to the level of sources of legal obligations
>
> **3** – For me, however, to deserve the qualifier 'legitimate', the 'expectations' must be based on some kind of legal commitment. Under general international law, responsibility cannot ensue without a prior breach of a legal obligation. The conduct or representation of the government has to bear the makings of an identifiable legal commitment towards the specific investor, before we can speak of a breach (or frustration) of legitimate expectations, calling for a remedy or compensation.
>
> **4** – Such a commitment on the part of a government cannot transpire or be captured or condensed our [sic] of thin air; from general political statements, pep-up talks of encouraging investments, but must bear the makings of real legal assurances and commitments.
>
> **5** – This does not mean that such commitment must necessarily take the form of a formal or an explicit agreement. It can ensue from behaviour or conduct. But such conduct must be sufficiently concrete and specifically directed to the particular investor, to constitute an objective 'representation' of a legal commitment, that can be objectively seen as generating legitimate expectations. Otherwise, any subjective perception (or self-interpretation) on the part of a potential investor or a favorable declaration or stance of a government, would be sufficient to trigger so called 'legitimate expectations', that can be used (or rather abused) as a basis of an allegation of a breach of an obligation that does not exist; or as means of circumventing

the prior essential condition of responsibility, which is the proof of the obligation whose breach gives rise to that responsibility.

6 – *In casu*, the 'Tax Incentives Scheme' (EGO 24) does not constitute by itself (i.e. the legislation as such) a legal commitment by the Romanian Government towards the investors to whom it is addressed in general. However, the issue of a 'Permanent Investor Certificate' (PIC) to an investor under this Scheme, in addition to specifying the other party (the addressee, *le destinataire*), establishes in my view, a synallagmatic or reciprocal relation of exchange of legal considerations by imposing on the investor certain legal obligations if he invests and takes advantage of the incentives – which bear the makings of legal commitments on both sides.

7 – Still, this does not totally dispose of the matter. It remains to be determined the contents and extent of the commitments of the Romanian Government in this regard. For while the Scheme was adopted for 10 years, terminating in 2009, nowhere does it (or the complementary regulations including the PICS) contain the equivalent of a 'stabilization clause' guaranteeing the freezing of its contents in terms of tax concessions throughout this period. In other words, all the PIC does [is] to confer on the investor the right to take advantage of the facilities provided under the Scheme, whatever they may be, at a given moment of time. The content of the Tax Incentives Scheme can change; and this variability of content has been recognized by the beneficiary investors, who did not contest earlier changes, whether in their favour or to their detriment. It can thus legitimately be argued that Romania did not violate any commitment towards PIC holders, as long as the Scheme continued to function until its term, with some incentives included in it; which was indeed the case here, as the 'profits tax exemption' continued to run until the end of the term of the Scheme in 2009.

8 – It could equally be legitimately argued that by reducing radically the contents of the Tax Incentives Scheme EGO 24, and more particularly by abolishing the Raw Materials Facility, four years before its term, the synallagmatic relationship of exchange of legal considerations (fastened by the PIC) becomes extremely skewed. Such severe imbalance cannot be without legal consequences including possibly a measure of liability.

II – Possible remedies including compensation

9 – Such a severe imbalance between the exchanged legal considerations – be it in a commutative or synallagmatic formal contractual relationship, which is not the case here – gives place to a claim for the revision or the termination of the contract, on grounds of what is called in certain civil law jurisdictions 'lesion'. The claim of revision involves the reduction of the obligations of the other party, to eliminate the substantial disparity between the exchanged considerations. It (or more so the termination of the contract) can be accompanied by a measure of compensation, depending on the reasons that led the first party to reduce its initial legal commitments, and the circumstances surrounding this reduction.

10 – *In casu*, the reduction, and particularly the early termination of the Raw Materials Facility, was motivated by the imperious necessity for Romania to join the European Union, which was an overriding national interest. I realize, however, that the Respondent has not invoked 'necessity', as a ground for precluding wrongfulness (Article 25 of the ILC Draft Articles on State Responsibility), as Romania considers that it has acted rationally and reasonably; hence it did not commit a wrongful act at the face of it, that needs to be exonerated by invoking necessity. That with which I agree, in the absence of the equivalent of a stabilization clause guaranteeing the freezing of the contents of the Scheme until its term and provided that Romania reduces proportionally the obligations of the PIC holders, to re-establish a semblance of balance between the exchanged considerations (which it claims it did, by not requiring the implementation of these obligations).

11 – The Award, however, while conceding that Romania acted reasonably, in good faith, and in pursuit of an overriding national interest, does not find this as precluding responsibility for what it considers the frustration of legitimate expectations of the Claimants.

12 – Another potential source of liability identified in the Award is the slackness of Romania in informing beneficiary investors of the inevitability of early termination of the raw materials facility. At the beginning, none of the major actors – the Romanian Government, the EU Commission, the Claimants – realized the absolute incompatibility of the raw materials facility with the EU law (as a 'hole in the tariff wall'). This is because of the initially prevailing opinion that it may be covered by the 'Regional Aid' exception in European law. The incompatibility became increasingly obvious as the negotiations and exchanges advanced. Thus, for a certain span of time starting at some point in 2003 and ending up on 31 August 2004, with the declaration that the raw materials facility would be terminated 90 days later (subsequently extended to 22 February 2005), part of Romanian authorities, particularly the regional ones, continued to reassure investors that the raw materials facility will be safeguarded one way or another; while another part of the Romanian Government, particularly those who were negotiating with the EU Commission (such as Mr. Orban, the Deputy Chief Romanian negotiator at the time, who testified before the Tribunal) became increasingly convinced that there was no way to save the raw materials facility.

13 – Such situations of two parts of government speaking at cross-purposes, as well as hesitation or wavering, are usual occurrences, particularly in times of rapid (and rather disorderly) change. They can happen in the best of governments. I don't think we can speak here of lack of transparency, as does the Award, which considers it as a breach of the fair and equitable treatment standard. This is because there was no intent of dissimulation or hiding (and diplomatic negotiations are, by their very nature, confidential). It is rather a case of failure of communication and lack of synchronization and coordination between different parts of government. This leads to slackness in 'due diligence' (or negligence) on the part of the government, by failing to inform investors as soon as one of its components reached the conclusion that it would not be able to safeguard the raw materials facility to the end of its term, in order to enable them to mitigate at the earliest the detrimental effect of this before-term termination.

14 – The honest admission of Mr. Orban of the failure of communication within the Government and between the Government and PIC holders, in addition to the declarations of the Prime Minister until early 2005 that the government would try to safeguard what it can of the incentives (which it did to no avail), or convert them into Euro-compatible ones, and to negotiate and possibly compensate investors (which it did not), bear recognition of a measure of responsibility.

15 – The measure of responsibility ensuing from this slackness or negligence, accompanying the taking of reasonable and lawful measures in the pursuit of legitimate overriding national interests, is limited. It is limited to actual ascertained loss, but does not include lucrum cessans according to general international law, in my opinion.

16 – However, Counsel for the Respondent considered that compensation as a general rule covers lost profits, though in casu those claimed are highly speculative. But the Award undertook a very tight and thorough calculation dismissing indeed most of the claimed lost profits as speculative, which makes it difficult not to accept the result, particularly in light of the admission of the principle by Counsel of the Respondent.

17 – In sum, I concur with the pecuniary outcome of the Award, but on other legal grounds, briefly explained above.

5.5.6 Concerns about FET and the right to regulate

Raising the requirements for the host state's behaviour toward foreign property holders has serious implications for the regulatory state. Early experience with investor claims brought against NAFTA governments' environmental and health regulations led the United States and Canada to push for a clarification of the NAFTA Article 1105's fair and equitable treatment standard. Using the Free Trade Commission's (FTC) authority to issue interpretations of NAFTA provisions, the parties to the NAFTA agreed to the Commission's limitation of FET to the international minimum standard. The FTC interpretation states:

1. Article 1105(1) prescribes the customary international law minimum standard of treatment of aliens as the minimum standard of treatment to be afforded to investments of investors of another Party.
2. The concepts of 'fair and equitable treatment' and 'full protection and security' do not require treatment in addition to or beyond that which is required by the customary international law minimum standard of treatment of aliens.[97]

---

97 *See Suez v. Argentina, supra* note 59, para. 184.

Subsequent tribunals faced with challenges to NAFTA hosts' regulation of investors that were aimed to further public purposes had to take account of this limitation.

Another way to reduce regulatory chill is to emphasize the effect of the host's right to regulate in light of what the investor can expect. The focus on the investor's legitimate expectations often results in a finding for the claimant. This is particularly so where subjective expectations are accepted as legitimate. Yet, some tribunals have placed objective legitimacy at the core of their investigation and determined that on the facts the investor could not have expected the government to have acted better than it did.

Recently, a number of tribunals have shifted to viewing FET from a more state-centred perspective, emphasizing the host's 'right to regulate'.

The right to regulate and legitimate expectations views are not incompatible. The *Saluka* tribunal demonstrated how they can be combined.

 CASE

Saluka v. Czech Republic

298. The immediate 'context' in which the 'fair and equitable' language of Article 3.1 is used relates to the level of treatment to be accorded by each of the Contracting Parties to the investments of investors of the other Contracting Party. The broader 'context' in which the terms of Article 3.1 must be seen includes the other provisions of the Treaty. In the preamble of the Treaty, the Contracting Parties recognize[d] that agreement upon the treatment to be accorded to such investments will stimulate the flow of capital and technology and the economic development of the Contracting Parties and that fair and equitable treatment is desirable.
The preamble thus links the 'fair and equitable treatment' standard directly to the stimulation of foreign investments and to the economic development of both Contracting Parties.

iii) The Object and Purpose of the Treaty
299. The 'object and purpose' of the Treaty may be discerned from its title and pre-amble. These read:
Agreement on encouragement and reciprocal protection of investments between the Kingdom of the Netherlands and the Czech and Slovak Federal Republic.
[The] Contracting Parties, Desiring to extend and intensify the economic relations between them particularly with respect to investments by the investor of one Contracting Party in the territory of the other Contracting Party, Recognizing

that agreement upon the treatment to be accorded to such investments will stimulate the flow of capital and technology and the economic development of the Contracting Parties and that fair and equitable treatment is desirable.

Taking note of the Final Act of the Conference on Security and Cooperation in Europe, signed on August, 1st 1975 in Helsinki.

300. This is a more subtle and balanced statement of the Treaty's aims than is sometimes appreciated. The protection of foreign investments is not the sole aim of the Treaty, but rather a necessary element alongside the overall aim of encouraging foreign investment and extending and intensifying the parties' economic relations. That in turn calls for a balanced approach to the interpretation of the Treaty's substantive provisions for the protection of investments, since an interpretation which exaggerates the protection to be accorded to foreign investments may serve to dissuade host States from admitting foreign investments and so undermine the overall aim of extending and intensifying the parties' mutual economic relations.

301. Seen in this light, the 'fair and equitable treatment' standard prescribed in the Treaty should therefore be understood to be treatment which, if not proactively stimulating the inflow of foreign investment capital, does at least not deter foreign capital by providing disincentives to foreign investors. An investor's decision to make an investment is based on an assessment of the state of the law and the totality of the business environment at the time of the investment as well as on the investor's expectation that the conduct of the host State subsequent to the investment will be fair and equitable.

302. The standard of 'fair and equitable treatment' is therefore closely tied to the notion of legitimate expectations which is the dominant element of that standard. By virtue of the 'fair and equitable treatment' standard included in Article 3.1 the Czech Republic must therefore be regarded as having assumed an obligation to treat foreign investors so as to avoid the frustration of investors' legitimate and reasonable expectations. As the tribunal in *Tecmed* stated, the obligation to provide 'fair and equitable treatment' means: to provide to international investments treatment that does not affect the *basic expectations* that were taken into account by the foreign investor to make the investment. [. . .]

303. The expectations of foreign investors certainly include the observation by the host State of such well-established fundamental standards as good faith, due process, and nondiscrimination. [. . .]

304. This Tribunal would observe, however, that while it subscribes to the general thrust of these and similar statements, it may be that, if their terms were to be taken too literally, they would impose upon host States' obligations which would be inappropriate and unrealistic. Moreover, the scope of the Treaty's protection of foreign investment against unfair and inequitable treatment cannot exclusively be determined by foreign investors' subjective motivations and considerations. Their expectations, in order for them to be protected, must rise to the level of legitimacy and reasonableness *in light of the circumstances.*

305. No investor may reasonably expect that the circumstances prevailing at the time the investment is made remain totally unchanged. In order to determine whether frustration of the foreign investor's expectations was justified and reasonable, the host State's legitimate right subsequently to regulate domestic matters in the public interest must be taken into consideration as well. As the *S.D. Myers* tribunal has stated, the determination of a breach of the obligation of 'fair and equitable treatment' by the host State must be made in the light of the high measure of deference that international law generally extends to the right of domestic authorities to regulate matters within their own borders.

306. The determination of a breach of Article 3.1 by the Czech Republic therefore requires a weighing of the Claimant's legitimate and reasonable expectations on the one hand and the Respondent's legitimate regulatory interests on the other.

307. A foreign investor protected by the Treaty may in any case properly expect that the Czech Republic implements its policies *bona fide* by conduct that is, as far as it affects the investors' investment, reasonably justifiable by public policies and that such conduct does not manifestly violate the requirements of consistency, transparency, even-handedness and nondiscrimination. In particular, any differential treatment of a foreign investor must not be based on unreasonable distinctions and demands, and must be justified by showing that it bears a reasonable relationship to rational policies not motivated by a preference for other investments over the foreign-owned investment.

308. Finally, it transpires from arbitral practice that, according to the 'fair and equitable treatment' standard, the host State must never disregard the principles of procedural propriety and due process and must grant the investor freedom from coercion or harassment by its own regulatory authorities.

iv) Conclusion

309. The 'fair and equitable treatment' standard in Article 3.1 of the Treaty is an autonomous Treaty standard and must be interpreted, in light of the object and purpose of the Treaty, so as to avoid conduct of the Czech Republic that clearly provides disincentives to foreign investors. The Czech Republic, without undermining its legitimate right to take measures for the protection of the public interest, has therefore assumed an obligation to treat a foreign investor's investment in a way that does not frustrate the investor's underlying legitimate and reasonable expectations. A foreign investor whose interests are protected under the Treaty is entitled to expect that the Czech Republic will not act in a way that is manifestly inconsistent, non-transparent, unreasonable (*i.e.* unrelated to some rational policy), or discriminatory (*i.e.* based on unjustifiable distinctions). In applying this standard, the Tribunal will have due regard to all relevant circumstances.[98]

---

98 *Saluka v. Czech Republic, supra* note 72.

5.5.7 Reactions to FET jurisprudence

The differing views on what FET provisions require have been a cause of major concern to governments and civil society groups. The possibility that tribunals will find a governmental program or particular regulation a violation of the state's obligation to offer fair and equitable treatment allegedly casts a 'chill' on hosts' willingness to regulate in the public interest. Not knowing what framework of analysis any particular tribunal will apply can itself lead to regulatory restraint. This is the case even though some tribunals would give governments more deference in shaping their policies (finding, for example, that investors have no legitimate expectations of regulatory stasis or that governmental behaviour which is reprehensible but not outrageous does not violate the obligation). Merely the potential that the particular tribunal selected is one that will emphasize the investor's right to expect stability can make risk-averse governments refrain from regulation.

Such concerns have led to an intense re-consideration of FET's proper place in the investment protection framework. While there are few calls for a complete discarding of FET obligations, there have been a number of suggestions for limiting them by making FET an aim (but not an obligation), by removing violations of FET from the dispute settlement provisions of the IIA, or by re-drafting the provisions.[99]

The latter efforts are apparent in some recent IIAs and model BITs whose (proposed) language is intended to narrow tribunals' interpretive discretion. They may provide, for example, that 'fair and equitable treatment' means treatment in accordance with the international minimum standard (we shall see that approach is not new, but its growing popularity among governments is significant). Alternatively (or in addition), the text may list specific types of behaviour as examples of FET violations. The most narrowly circumscribed provisions would set forth a FET provision that contains an exclusive list of host state treatments that would violate the obligation. The following are good examples of these different forms.

5.5.8 Australia–Japan Economic Partnership Agreement[100]

Article 14.5 Minimum Standard of Treatment
Each Party shall accord to covered investments treatment in accordance with

---

99 *See particularly* UNCTAD, Investment Policy Framework for Sustainable Development 94–5 (2015) (setting out policy options for ensuring that FET obligations do not lead to a reduction in regulatory options for promoting sustainable development).

100 Agreement between Australia and Japan for an Economic Partnership (Jan. 15, 2015).

customary international law, including fair and equitable treatment and full protection and security.

Note 1: This Article prescribes the customary international law minimum standard of treatment of aliens as the minimum standard of treatment to be afforded by a Party to covered investments. The concepts of 'fair and equitable treatment' and 'full protection and security' do not require treatment in addition to or beyond that which is required by the customary international law minimum standard of treatment of aliens.

Note 2: A determination that there has been a breach of another provision of this Agreement, or of a separate international agreement, does not establish that there has been a breach of this Article.

5.5.9 Trans-Pacific Partnership (TPP), (draft version: 20 January 2015)[101]

Article II.6: Minimum Standard of Treatment

1. Each Party shall accord to covered investments treatment in accordance with applicable customary international law principles, including fair and equitable treatment and full protection and security.

2. For greater certainty, paragraph 1 prescribes the customary international law minimum standard of treatment of aliens as the standard of treatment to be afforded to covered investments. The concepts of 'fair and equitable treatment' and 'full protection and security' do not require treatment in addition to or beyond that which is required by that standard, and do not create additional substantive rights. The obligations in paragraph 1 to provide:

   (a) 'Fair and equitable treatment' includes the obligation not to deny justice in criminal, civil, or administrative adjudicatory proceedings in accordance with the principle of due process embodied in the principal legal systems of the world; [. . .]

3. A determination that there has been a breach of another provision of this Agreement, or of a separate international agreement, does not establish that there has been a breach of this Article.

India Model BIT, Article 3 (2015)[102]

3.1 Each Party shall not subject Investments of Investors of the other Party to Measures which constitute:

---

101 Available at: https://wikileaks.org/tpp-investment/ (footnotes omitted).
102 Model Text for the Indian Bilateral Investment Treaty (footnotes omitted).

(i) Denial of justice under customary international law;

(ii) Un-remedied and egregious violations of due process; or

(iii) Manifestly abusive treatment involving continuous, unjustified and outrageous coercion or harassment.

? DISCUSSION NOTES

1 When interpreting FET provisions, tribunals are creating a basis upon which to review state actions or inactions. This is, according to Montt, an act of creating a standard of review. The interpretive method, then, must be suited to this particular purpose – something a dictionary approach to the words 'fair' and 'equitable' is not. For Montt, who takes the position that FET provisions should be read as controls on arbitrary state action, text-based attempts at definition of such provisions are 'naïve' at best; harmful at worst. He writes:

> International investment law, then, must articulate a new standard of review. But what does this mean? The essence of any standard of review lies in the level of deference . . . that the reviewing body gives to the reviewed entity.
>
> However, as the comparative experience of domestic administrative law demonstrates, establishing a standard of review, in the abstract, is far from sufficient. The complexities and intricacies of the process of judicial review require the establishment of a 'dense' argumentative framework that structures and determines the way in which parties present their claims, and the manner in which the reviewing body reasons and is persuaded.
>
> It is naïve to think that such a goal can be achieved through a literal approach to concepts such as 'fair' and 'equitable', probably two of the more general and abstract ideas found in . . . the law. . . .
>
> Not only is the literalist stance inadequate for developing the FET standard as a test of arbitrariness, but it actually obfuscates this essential challenge of international investment law. . . .

Santiago Montt, State Liability in Investment Treaty Arbitration 300–301 (2009).

2 Should a tribunal consider only the individual acts or the treatment as a whole when deciding whether there has been a violation of the FET standard? The *Glamis* tribunal preferred to combine the two approaches:

> 756. To begin its application of the above-defined standard to the facts presented by the Parties, the Tribunal notes Claimant's request that, in the words of *GAMI*, '[t]he record as a whole – not isolated events – determines whether there has been a breach of international law.' Despite this request, Claimant has

presented its argument with respect to each of the individual governmental actions that make up the whole, arguing why each contravenes Article 1105, and then asserting that, taken as a whole, they violate the customary international law minimum standard of treatment accorded under Article 1105. The Tribunal also notes that Respondent has not objected to this approach and instead adopts Claimant's methodology that focuses on the analysis of each individual action. In addition, with respect to Claimant's assertion that all of the measures should be evaluated as a whole, Respondent neither endorses nor disputes this view.

757. The Tribunal therefore utilizes this approach employed by the Parties, first reviewing each individual action by the federal and state governments and assessing each against the Tribunal's legal standard, and then analyzing the actions together as a collective whole to determine whether, viewed together, the combined acts violate the obligations of the United States pursuant to the customary international law minimum standard of fair and equitable treatment articulated in Article 1105(1).[103]

3 We read about the concept of a 'creeping expropriation' in the last chapter. Should there be a corresponding claim of 'creeping FET violation'? Several tribunals have determined that the host may violate its FET obligations by the sum total of its – individually non-violating – actions or inactions. See *El Paso v. Argentina*, ICSID Case No. ARB/03/15, Award, para. 518 (31 October 2011) ('A *creeping violation of the FET standard* could thus be described as a process extending over time and comprising a succession or an accumulation of measures which, taken separately, would not breach that standard but, when taken together, do lead to such a result'). See also *Swisslion DDO Skopje v. The Former Yugoslav Republic of Macedonia*, ICSID Case No. ARB/09/16, Award, para. 275 (6 July 2012); *Antoine Abou Lahoud and Leila Bounafeh-Abou Lahoud v. Democratic Republic of Congo*, ICSID Case No. ARB/10/4, Award, para. 445 (7 February 2014); *Gold Reserve Inc. v. Bolivarian Republic of Venezuela*, ICSID Case No. ARB(AF)/09/1, Award, para. 566 (22 September 2014). But see the qualification on this approach emphasized by the *Rompetrol* tribunal: '[. . .] this Tribunal can join other recent tribunals in accepting that the cumulative effect of a succession of impugned actions by the State of the investment can together amount to a failure to accord fair and equitable treatment even where the individual actions, taken on their own, would not surmount the threshold for a Treaty breach. *But this would only be so where the actions in question disclosed some link of underlying pattern or*

---

103 *Glamis Gold v. USA, supra* note 91.

purpose between them; a mere scattered collection of disjointed harms would not be enough'. *The Rompetrol Group NV v. Romania*, ICSID Case No. ARB/06/3, Award, para. 271 (6 May 2013) (emphasis added).

4 Although it did not make explicit comments about the equitable nature of its arguments, the tribunal in *Total v. Argentina* approached FET from a perspective in which fairness and equity were highlighted. The *Total* tribunal examined a number of measures taken by Argentina during the financial crisis in determining whether the company's right to fair and equitable treatment had been violated. Focussing heavily on legitimate expectations and mentioning the effects of the measure, the tribunal nevertheless emphasized the good faith of the government and denied the investor's claim with respect to one of its gas contracts:

> 164. [. . .] Unfairness must be evaluated in respect of the measures challenged, both in the light of their objective effects but also in the light of the reasons that led to their adoption (subjective good faith, proportionality to the aims and legitimacy of the latter according to general practice). [. . .] Such changes to general legislation, in the absence of specific stabilization promises to the foreign investor, reflect a legitimate exercise of the host State's governmental powers that are not prevented by a BIT's fair and equitable treatment standard and are not in breach of the same. [. . .]
>
> 165. The general character, the good faith and absence of discrimination by Argentina, as well as the exceptional circumstance that 'forced' Argentina to adopt the measures at issue, viewed objectively, preclude the Tribunal from finding that Argentina breached the fair and equitable obligations of treatment under the BIT with respect to the dollar denomination of the tariff [. . .].[104]

What role does the intent or bad faith play in the realm of the FET standard? Although FET has been described numerous times as containing a good faith requirement, most arbitrators express the opinion that there is no need to prove bad faith on the part of the government in order to win a claim of violation of FET. As noted by the *Glamis* tribunal, a showing of bad faith is, however, sufficient to show a violation of the standard.[105] The *CMS* tribunal refuses to go so far. That decision noted that whether or not the host has violated FET is an issue 'unrelated to whether the

---

104 *Total SA v. Argentine Republic, supra* note 39, paras. 164–5. Dolzer and Schreuer, *supra* note 38, at 133. *See also* Jeswald W. Salacuse, The Law of Investment Treaties 222 (2010); Andrew Newcombe and Lluís Paradell, Law and Practice of Investment Treaties: Standards of Treatment 276–7 (2009). *See*, e.g. *Parkerings-Compagniet AS v. Lithuania, supra* note 15, para. 277 (stating that the broad interpretation of the 'fair and equitable treatment' standard indicates that different terms, such as 'equitable and reasonable' rather than 'fair and equitable' treatment, make no difference to the substance of the obligation).

105 *Glamis Gold v. USA, supra* note 91, para. 627.

Respondent has had any deliberate intention or bad faith in adopting the measures in question'. See *CMS Gas Transmission Company v. Argentine Republic*, ICSID Case No. ARB/01/8, Award, para. 208 (12 May 2005), accessed at http://italaw.com/documents/CMS_FinalAward.pdf.

5 Should the fact that a government's actions are tainted by corruption be relevant to an FET claim? According to the *RSM v. Grenada* tribunal, not necessarily. In that case, the investors bribed government officials to secure a contract under which they could apply for oil drilling licences. When RSM failed to file within the time granted under the contract, they were denied the licences. They brought the government to arbitration, alleging, *inter alia*, a violation of the FET standard due to the government's corruption. The tribunal noted:

> [. . .] even if Grenada was motivated, by bribes, to offer its off-shore exploration rights to Global Petroleum, its reliance on its contractual rights to terminate the Agreement cannot be said to infringe the fair and equitable standard when Grenada had done nothing to induce RSM's failure to file its application within the time limits the parties had agreed.[106]

6 One danger of extending the obligations of hosts beyond the level of non-outrageous treatment through the FET standard is that the openness of the standard can lead to its interpretation as an 'umbrella clause' for the investor's complaints. Arbitrator Jürgen Voss highlighted this problem in his dissent to the *Lemire v. Ukraine* decision.[107]

> The Majority interprets the FET standard broadly with respect to both its scope of protection and the legal consequences of its violation. The standard is liberally construed as an 'umbrella clause' upgrading 'blatant' violations of the host country's tender legislation *ipso iure* to international delicts even absent any specific relation to Claimant, let alone to Claimant as a foreign investor. The standard is moreover developed towards empowering tribunals *ex aequo et bono* to generate international case law superseding municipal laws in point even where they conform to *general principles of law recognized by civilized nations* (Art. 38(1) ICJ Statute).
>
> The Majority ignores particular features of the scenario in this arbitration which suggest judicial self-restraint in delineating the FET standard with a view to reconciling BIT protection with conflicting public interests of the host country.

---

106 *Rachel S. Grynberg, Stephen M. Grynberg, Miriam Z. Grynberg, and RSM Production Corporation v. Grenada*, ICSID Case No. ARB/10/6, Award, para. 7.2.25 (Dec. 10, 2010). Available at: http://italaw.com/documents/ RSMvGrenadaBITAward.pdf.

107 *Joseph Charles Lemire v. Ukraine*, ICSID Case No. ARB/06/18, Dissenting Opinion of Arbitrator Dr. Jürgen Voss, at vi–vii (Mar. 1, 2011). Available at: http://italaw.com/documents/LemirevUkraine_ DissentOfJurgenVoss_1March2011.pdf.

Tender scenario

This arbitration concerns the treatment of Gala in public tenders. In these, Gala, itself a 'corporate citizen' of Ukraine, competes with domestically-owned radio companies for market shares through allocation of frequencies.

In such tenders, a '*level playing field*' is essential where all contenders compete under the same framework conditions. Any preference accorded to some contenders tends to translate into '*reverse discrimination*' of other contenders. It thus undermines fair competition in and effectiveness of the tender process. BIT protection accords protection to beneficiary investors in addition to the protection afforded to domestic investors and foreign investors without BIT protection by the laws of the host country. This is legitimate. However, BIT protection must be reconciled with the rights of contenders to fair competition and the host country's reserved regulatory powers.

This aspect militates against developing a protection level under the FET standard which grants BIT protected investors a competitive advantage over their contenders without such protection. Added protection can distort competition.

Tender applications represent investments in opportunities. Multiple contenders apply – only one can win. The economics of tender applications are determined by the chances of winning relative to the risk of losing the resources invested in the application. Legal protection and recovery rights in particular reduce the risk of loss. Where recovery rights extend to loss of profits, as awarded by the Majority, they even increase the chances of winning – not the award as such but the profits which would have accrued from the award. Such rights tend to enhance the risk-return ratio of tender applications. And if they are granted to selected applicants, e.g., BIT protected applicants, they tend to accord these applicants competitive advantages over their contenders.

Recovery rights of unsuccessful tender applicants imply considerable liability risks for the State. Typically multiple contenders apply so that any irregularity may trigger multiple claims. These can accumulate to incalculable liability avalanches. Municipal laws therefore tend to restrict recovery rights in tenders with a view to containing fiscal exposure to liability. For instance, European law provides only for recovery of the costs incurred in relation to the tender (*damnum emergens*) but not for recovery of loss of profits (*lucrum cessans*) as awarded by the Majority.

Such restrictions must be taken into consideration in applying the FET standard to tenders for two reasons. Disregard of such restrictions may widen the gap between the protection of BIT protected applicants and their contenders with prejudice to fair competition. And such restrictions reflect a – widely accepted – public interest of limiting exposure to liability at taxpayer's expense.

7 Should investment tribunals worry about requiring more favourable treatment of foreign investors than the host's citizens receive? On the one hand, the very core of an 'international minimum standard' rests on the idea that no matter how poorly citizens are treated by their government, foreigners are to be afforded certain protections. The tribunal in the *Roberts* case made clear that equality of treatment is irrelevant when determining international minimal treatment standards. Similarly, recent awards have emphasized that a government's adherence to or neglect of its national legislation is not dispositive of an FET claim. On the other hand, if a host is known to offer its own citizens poor services, such as very slow resolution of legal claims, a tribunal might presume that the foreign investor could place no legitimate expectation in receiving better treatment. As the tribunal in *White Industries* put it, '[q]uite apart from the point that an investor must generally take a host State (including its court system) as it finds it, [. . .] absent an express assurance [. . .] that any award would be enforced in a particular manner or timeframe, it is simply not possible for White, legitimately, to have had the expectation as to the timely enforcement of the Award that it now asserts.'[108]

8 Should the negotiating power of the Parties be a factor in the tribunal's analysis of whether FET was afforded?

a *Denial of justice*

A final claim that is substantively similar to both the arbitrary or unreasonable treatment standard and FPS (if the tribunal entertains a notion of legal FPS), but which is generally made as a claim for violation of FET is that of 'denial of justice'. Related mainly to the judicial process, denial of justice claims are often brought against decisions taken by local courts. An investor who has been refused the opportunity to seek remedies or to challenge administrative findings, or who has been subject to long delays in the court system can claim a violation of the IIA on the basis of a denial of justice. So, too, can the investor who challenges a court decision that it considers wilfully incorrect or even tainted by corruption, or an investor who has been the target of abusive criminal proceedings.

---

108 *White Industries Australia Limited v. The Republic of India*, UNCITRAL Arbitration, Final Award, para. 10.3.15 (Nov. 30, 2011). Available at: http://italaw.com/sites/default/files/case-documents/ita0906.pdf.

Although rarely successful,[109] denial of justice claims deserve notice because they bring out the difficulty in separating IIA treatment standards. As summarized by the *Dan Cake v. Hungary*[110] tribunal:

> Arbitral Tribunals have used, in order to characterize judicial decisions as denials of justice, various expressions which all perfectly fit the [host state's Bankruptcy Court's] decision: 'administer[ing] justice in a seriously inadequate way', [citing *Azinian v. Mexico*[111]] 'clearly improper and discreditable', [citing *Mondev v. US*[112]] '[m]anifest injustice in the sense of a lack of due process leading to an outcome which offends a sense of judicial propriety. . . .' [citing *Loweven v. US*[113]] The International Court of Justice defined denial of justice as 'a willful disregard of due process of law, an act which shocks, or at least surprises, a sense of juridical propriety.'[114] [citing the *ELSI* case].[115]

These terms certainly fit many tribunals' notion of FET, but they would be equally viable as arguments for violations of the protection against arbitrary and unreasonable treatment. Whether, in the end, it really matters which provision is selected seems to be of secondary concern to tribunals who want to ensure the rule of law is upheld.

b *Interaction or overlap? Applying the various investor protection standards*

It is apparent from our look at the standards of investor protection in this chapter and in the discussion on indirect expropriation in the last chapter that there is no way to clearly demarcate the boundaries between many of them. Tribunals who are faced with a complaint about a host's sudden or unjustified breach of a contract may be required to examine it as an expropriation, as a violation of the investor's right to full protection and (legal) security, as a breach of FET, and possibly even as a discriminatory act or denial of justice. Such openness makes fully grasping the intricacies of the standards difficult

---

109 'Tribunal finds Hungarian court's handling of bankruptcy proceedings to be flawed, leading to finding of a denial of justice under intra-EU BIT' IAReporter, Nov. 8, 2015. (Available at: http://www.iareporter.com/articles/tribunal-finds-hungarian-courts-handling-of-bankruptcy-proceedings-to-be-flawed-leading-to-finding-of-a-denial-of-justice-under-intra-eu-bit/.)

110 *Dan Cake (Portugal) SA v. Hungary*, ICSID Case No ARB/12/9, Decision on Jurisdiction and Liability (Aug. 24, 2015).

111 *Robert Azinian et al. v. United States of Mexico*, ICSID Case No ARB(AF)/97/2, Award, para. 102 (Nov. 1, 1999).

112 *Mondev v. USA, supra* note 86, para. 127.

113 *The Loewen Group and Raymond L. Loewen v. United States of America*, ICSID Case No ARB(AF)/98/3, Award, para. 132 (June 26, 2003).

114 *Elsi* case, *supra* note 6, para. 128.

115 *Dan Cake v. Hungary* at para. 146 (subsequently finding the court's decision prevented the claimant from pursuing the establishment of a hearing by creditors was a denial of justice).

even for experts. In the arbitration context, at least, the structure of IIAs can substitute for a fully theorized conception of the various standards. To close this chapter, a helpful summary by the *El Paso v. Argentina* tribunal is set forth explaining how the standards of investor protection relate to each other.

 CASE

El Paso Energy International Co. v. The Republic of Argentina

226. ICSID case-law has developed in a way that generates some confusion and overlap between these different standards of protection found in most BITs. In view of this situation, which is not conducive to security of the legal framework and predictability of its application to foreign investments, the Tribunal will endeavour to clarify as much as possible the scope of the different standards of protection, for it is convinced that they should not be used indifferently one for the other. Before doing so, it thinks it appropriate to give a few examples of the prevailing confusion which, in its view, justifies its approach.

227. There is not always a clear distinction between *indirect expropriation* and *violation of legitimate expectations*, as can be seen from an excerpt of the Claimant's Memorial stating that 'measures that are inconsistent with an investor's legitimate expectations constitute an expropriation' or of the Claimant's Reply, where it is asserted that

> '[s]everal other ICSID cases have held that an indirect expropriation occurs when the State repudiates fundamental commitments in frustration of an investor's legitimate expectations deriving from the rights granted in contracts, law or decrees (which, under the BIT, clearly are "investments" protected against any form of expropriation).'

According to this Tribunal, the violation of a legitimate expectation should rather be protected by the fair and equitable treatment standard.

228. Sometimes, there is also *no distinction between the fair and equitable treatment (FET) and the full protection and security (FPS)* standards. This has been the position adopted by the tribunal in *Azurix*:

> 'The Tribunal is persuaded of the interrelationship of fair and equitable treatment and the obligation to afford the investor full protection and security . . . when the terms "protection and security" are qualified by "full" and no other adjective or explanation, they extend, in their ordinary meaning, the content of this standard beyond physical security. To conclude, the Tribunal, having held that the Respondent failed to provide fair and equitable treatment to the investment, finds that the Respondent also breached the standard of full protection and security under the BIT.'

Another example of this confusion can be found in the so-called VAT arbitration, *Occidental Exploration and Production Company v. Ecuador*, where the tribunal declared that 'treatment that is not fair and equitable automatically entails an absence of full protection and security of the investment.' The Claimant in our case takes the same position and assimilates FET and FPS, alleging that the FPS has been breached because Argentina has adopted laws interfering with the Claimant's investment [. . .].

229. Sometimes there is *no distinction between several standards of treatment*, which are all amalgamated, as was done by the tribunal in *Noble Ventures*, stating that:

> 'Considering the place of the fair and equitable treatment standard at the very beginning of Art.II(2), one can consider this to be a more general standard which finds its specific application in *inter alia* the duty to provide full protection and security, the prohibition of arbitrary and discriminatory measures and the obligation to observe contractual obligations towards the investor.'

230. The distinction seems also often difficult *between arbitrary or discriminatory treatment* and *violation of the FET*. It must of course be emphasised that it is quite non-controversial that an arbitrary or discriminatory treatment is necessarily a violation of the FET as well, as mentioned for example in *CMS*:

> 'The standard of protection against arbitrariness and discrimination is related to that of fair and equitable treatment. Any measure that might involve arbitrariness or discrimination is in itself contrary to fair and equitable treatment.'

This is of course true, but the reverse might not necessarily be, as violations of the fair and equitable treatment standard could result from types of situations other than arbitrariness or discrimination. The difference should be sufficient to prevent an assimilation of the two categories of violations. It is, in fact, the Tribunal's view that FET is designed to guarantee that, in situations where the other more precise standards are not violated, but where there is an unreasonable interference bringing about an unjust result regarding an investor's expectations, that investor can claim a violation of the FET and obtain reparation therefore.

231. In conclusion, it seems to the Tribunal that, in order not to engage in redundant analyses, interferences with a foreign investment should be analysed successively with reference to the different standards of protection in a sequential order, proceeding from expropriation to violation of the FPS. In other words, the Tribunal will examine first whether there is an indirect expropriation, second whether there is arbitrary or discriminatory treatment, third whether there is a violation of the FET, and fourth whether there is a breach of the FPS.[116]

---

116 *El Paso Energy International Company v. The Argentine Republic*, ICSID Case No. ARB/03/15, Award (Oct. 31, 2011); (footnotes omitted).

Question to an expert: Diego Brian Gosis

Diego Brian Gosis is of counsel at the law firm Gomm and Smith (Miami) and special counsel at the law firm Guglielmino and Asociados (Buenos Aires). Mr. Gosis has acted as counsel or arbitrator in over 50 cases under several rules, including as counsel to Argentina, Venezuela and Bolivia in investment arbitration proceedings.

The move by some states to clarify the content of their FET obligations has not resulted in the disappearance of the concept— just its definition. Why not simply eliminate the label and leave the content?

If we trace what FET is and how it came to be in the early to mid-twentieth century, we will find that IIA-sanctioned FET obligations merely provide a conduit through which duties towards investors originating under international customary law may be arbitrated. Thus, the purpose and true—read 'legitimate'—effect of FET is to allow for a certain, discrete portion of the international obligations of States to be submitted to arbitration, as part of the duties agreed upon by such States in the context of IIAs.

As certain other international customary law obligations—and a host of other international public law obligations—will not by necessity qualify under these provisions, and to clarify the proper extent of those customary law obligations which can properly be arbitrated, it is no doubt a useful device to provide a listing or mapping of the type of obligations that will—now, by definition—come to benefit from the possibility of being arbitrated.

If, on the other hand, a listing of specific duties to, or rights vested upon, foreign investor were to be enumerated in the language of a IIA, and the reference to FET were to be eliminated, that would elevate the specific obligation to abide by those duties or rights to the status of treaty obligations, rather than identify the correlating customary law obligation as one which, if breached, could validly constitute a treaty cause of action. There are, in a number of areas, matters where the State parties to an IIA have chosen to depart from a rule of international customary law with respect to the nationals of each other—including through heightening or lowering the protections granted—, and while including those areas as part of the scope of FET under a treaty would ratify their face value enforceability and create their arbitrability, removing the reference to FET and simply transcribing the customary law duty as part of the IIA would most probably substitute the IIA language for the customary law duty as between those two States, leading to potential diverging results.

6

Dispute settlement

6.1 ICSID and the other fora for investor-State arbitration

6.1.1 Overview

The typical investor does not make an investment thinking that the investment will be expropriated, treated unfairly, or be damaged by the state's failure to provide it full protection. Investment law, however, often focuses on the investment experience 'gone bad' and consequently on how to remedy the situation. The dispute settlement mechanism for investment is therefore of particular interest to students and practitioners of investment law, even if investors themselves often only become interested in the topic once a dispute arises.

When a commercial actor—national or foreign—is unsatisfied with the treatment of its financial interests by the government, that actor can challenge the legality of the government's action under national law. Local courts applying local rules have always been the primary fora for investors seeking relief. Even if international treaty law is the basis for a claim, as long as judges are impartial and independent and the legal system functions efficiently, the host's local courts should, arguably, be the preferred fora for investor disputes. Fears that the judges were not impartial and independent and experiences of delayed proceedings, however, led to the search for an international mechanism for resolving disputes—one where the foreignness of the investor and the weakness of local institutions would not be a handicap to investors' accessing justice.

This chapter reviews the basic forms of international dispute settlement available to wronged investors. The focus is placed on understanding the investor-State dispute settlement mechanism of the International Centre for the Settlement of Investment Disputes (ICSID), as it is the most prominent method currently.

a   *The origins of investment dispute settlement*

As we read earlier in the book, foreign direct investment has a long history, and rules protecting foreigners have been a feature of local law since at least the days of Ancient Greece. It was not until the late Renaissance, however, that bilateral commercial treaties began to incorporate the protection of alien property explicitly at the international law level. The development of treaty-based protections for foreign property had clear implications for the settlement of disputes relating to the host's treatment of the property.

Prior to the development of investment protections based on treaty law, the foreign merchant was not entirely without recourse for violations of his right to property. If his property was seized, for example, he could turn to the local courts for relief. There, local judges would apply local laws to determine if the merchant should be reimbursed for his loss.

By the late seventeenth century, however, the European nation-states' growing significance in the international arena spurred the conclusion of treaties to support the international movements of goods that would contribute to national economies. It was those treaty provisions that specifically protected the foreigner's property that most changed the position of the wronged alien within this new global system. Importantly, the exclusively local nature of dispute resolution was replaced by a more international approach. The newly concluded treaties provided a legal mechanism to change a private claim into a sovereign claim: espousal. The term 'espousal' refers to a government's taking on of a citizen's legal claims as its own. Under common understandings of sovereignty in international law, states may only be sued by other states. Offering an investor a promise of protection that could be claimed against the host government through the investor's state espousal transformed the investment dispute resolution process.

b   *Diplomatic protection*

Once espoused, an investor's claims become the home state's. Thus, violations of investment protection promised to a private investor become the object of sovereign disputes. The classic international law method of resolving sovereign disputes is through the use of diplomacy, where discussions between government representatives (often resulting in explanations and apologies or assurances) can resolve conflicts with minimal damage to the governments' mutual interest in maintaining peaceful relations.

The main benefit of diplomatic protection for the wronged investor is that the home state, as a legal equal to the host, is more likely to command the attention of the host in its calls for restoring the property or offering compensation for the wrongs performed than such calls would if stemming from the individual investor himself.

The main drawback to relying on diplomatic protection for investors, however, is that the individual has no right to espousal. The ICJ has determined that espousal lies within the discretion of the state, calling the government itself the 'sole judge' of espousal requests.[1] If, then, a home state fears the political implications of beginning a dispute, if the home government's resources or priorities lie outside of protecting the investor's properties, or if the home state is engaging in similar activities with its own foreign investors, it might refuse to afford its citizen diplomatic protection even where there is a clear violation of the citizen's rights by the host. Further, even if there are no concerns relating to the investor's dispute itself, the state may choose not to espouse a claim under its competence to take into account 'considerations of a political or other nature, unrelated to the particular case'.[2]

A further drawback for the investor is that the claims pursued by the state may not be the same as those the investor would have chosen. Given that the espoused claim becomes the state's own, the tactical decisions—including the substantive propositions put forward, the relief sought, and the decision whether or not to settle the case—are left to the home state.

Perhaps most importantly for the investor, any payment of compensation is due to the state—not the investor. Damages paid do not need to be transferred to the investor once they are collected, although many governments would in fact turn them over.

c   State-to-state dispute resolution

If a host fails to protect foreign investments as stipulated in a treaty, the home state could also bring a direct claim as a party to the agreement.

---

1 Barcelona Traction, Light and Power Company, Limited (*Belgium v. Spain*), Judgment, 1970 ICJ 3, at 44, para. 79 (Feb. 5). *See, e.g. also* John R. Dugard, *First Report on Diplomatic Protection*, UN Doc. A/CN.4/506 (Mar. 7, 2000); Riccardo Pisillo Mazzeschi, *Impact on the Law of Diplomatic Protection, in* The Impact of Human Rights Law on General International Law 211, 211–33 (Menno T. Kamminga and Martin Scheinin eds., 2009).

2 Barcelona Traction, *supra* note 1.

Most BITs provide for dispute resolution by the parties (governments) in a stand-alone article or as a separate paragraph within the dispute settlement article. These provisions will often give the parties a choice of either taking their dispute to the International Court of Justice or to arbitration.

The 2013 BIT between Tanzania and Mauritius, for example, states:

Article 9

SETTLEMENT OF DISPUTES BETWEEN THE CONTRACTING PARTIES

(1) Any dispute between the Contracting Parties concerning the interpretation or application of this Agreement should, if possible, be settled through negotiations between the Governments of the two Contracting Parties.

(2) If the dispute cannot be settled within a period of six months following the date on which such negotiations were requested by either Contracting Party, it may upon the request of either Contracting Party, be submitted to an arbitral tribunal.[3]

Such provisions are not often invoked, with the ICJ having heard only six cases on investment, three of which were refused on jurisdictional grounds. Despite that, of the three cases analysed, two are among the most well-recognized decisions of investment law: *ELSI* and *Barcelona Light and Traction*. Each has become a guide for future tribunals on the issues addressed by the Court, so the relevance of state-to-state dispute resolution should not be overlooked.

State-to-state arbitration may also occur. Paragraphs 3 and 5 of Article 9 of the Tanzania-Mauritius Agreement illustrates one example of how such procedures are provided for:

3. Such an arbitral tribunal shall be constituted for each individual case in the following way: within two months of the receipt of the request for arbitration, each Contracting Party shall appoint one arbitrator for the tribunal. Those two arbitrators shall then select a national of a third State who, upon approval by the two Contracting Parties, shall be appointed Chairperson of the tribunal. [. . .].
[. . .]
5. The arbitral tribunal shall reach its decision by a majority of votes. Such decision shall be binding on both Contracting Parties. [. . .].[4]

---

3 *See* The Investment Promotion and Protection Agreement (United Republic of Tanzania) Regulations 2009, [Mauritius] Government Notice No. 131, 2009 (Mar. 2, 2013).
4 *Id.*

Like state-to-state BIT litigation, sovereign arbitration on investment claims has become less common with the advent of modern BIT dispute resolution procedures, but IIA provisions for them remains common.

d   Use of force

The other traditional method to settle disputes between states is the use of force. Now prohibited by the United Nations Charter, aggressive use of military force is illegal unless authorized by the international community through the Security Council.[5] As the prohibition on aggression is also considered *jus cogens*, even a home state's unilateral attempts to enforce investment protection obligations by threatening to send (let alone use) armed troops could not be considered a legal option for a government to settle an investment claim. Military force's symbolic role in earlier state relations, however, makes it worthy of further comment.

The protection of the rights of investors was a frequent reason for home state governments to militarily intervene in the host state's territory in the past, particularly as the beginnings of industrialization created a national interest in ensuring that a nation's own investors were not disgorged of property or profits when abroad. From the late eighteenth through the mid-twentieth centuries, industrialization and imperialism defined the international economic context. While industrialization in Europe and the United States required a large and reliable supply of resources, imperialism provided—through its ready military capacity—the means of ensuring that the increasingly foreign-located production or extraction sites were unimpeded in their profit-making activities. This helped the home country's local industries expand, creating yet more wealth to be invested abroad.

It thus was not only in the political interest of the home state to espouse its citizens' claims, it was also in its economic interest to ensure the property rights of citizens extraterritorially. Britain, Germany, Italy, and France all used troops or warships to force governments abroad to protect property.

Interestingly, however, as commercial relations became ever more international, business did not always want the protection of their home government. Home government interference tended to upset private contractual arrangements that the large firms had with local hosts and caused more complications than it resolved.

---

5 UN Charter art. 2, para. 4. *See also* UN Charter Ch. VII.

Aversion to military intervention also increased among the capital importing states. Led by the Argentinian scholar Carlos Calvo's ideas, many of the Latin American states in particular began to challenge the legitimacy of home state involvement in investment disputes. Such disputes, stated Calvo, should be resolved solely between the host and the investor and in the host state's courts. While the 'Calvo Doctrine' was never widely adopted outside of Latin America, the disproportionateness of forceful intervention for property protection was internationally recognized.

Thus, in 1907, the Hague Convention II Respecting the Limitations on the Employment of Force for the Recovery of Contract Debts (Drago-Porter Convention) made the use of force illegal for the recovery of state debts unless the host state refused to submit to arbitration. An important step toward solidifying modern notions of peaceful resolution of disputes, the Convention has now been essentially superseded by the UN Charter principle of non-aggression.

e   *Arbitration between the investor and the host state*

While the involvement of the home state in investment dispute settlement has a long history and fits with the traditional state orientation of international law, it is inefficient. A dispute caused by a host's violation of the property rights of a foreign investor involves two parties: the host state and the investor. Bringing in a third party (the home state) would seem to just add to the complexity, cost, and time involved in resolving the dispute. So why do it?

It is just such a question that motivated the move to make international investment law less like other areas of public international law in its dispute settlement possibilities. While diplomatic protection and state-to-state cases are still possible, by far the most frequent method of settling investment disputes today is for the investor to bring a claim against the host directly. The attractiveness of this 'investor-State' dispute settlement option for the investor is clear: she need not petition her government to take up the cause; she can shape her claims, and she can collect the full damages if successful. Indeed, given this option, most dissatisfied investors would probably choose it.

The problem with investor-State claims lies with the second party to the dispute—the host. The host does not always want to be sued by an individual before an international dispute settlement body. An aspect of sovereignty, state immunity from legal actions is held too tightly. For an investor to bring a claim against the state for a governmental action taken in its own sovereign territory is exceptional, and requires ensuring that the host has agreed to be sued on the particular grounds set forth in the complaint before it can be permitted.

The next pages lay out the different mechanisms of investor-State dispute settlement and investigate the treaty-based process in particular.

? **DISCUSSION NOTES**

If a business is incorporated in one state, but its main shareholders are citizens of another state, which of the governments should be approached for espousal? The ICJ's *Barcelona Traction* opinion is mostly known for its statement on the rights of shareholders—an opinion that has been largely surpassed by clear provisions in IIAs to grant shareholders protection. The Court's position on the diplomatic protection issue, however, is also interesting. The majority strongly suggests that the company's home state should be the state to grant diplomatic protection rather than the state of the shareholders. In coming to this conclusion, the Court points to the possibility of multiple home states for multiple shareholders and the balance of risks and benefits assumed by the owners of a company incorporated abroad:

> It should also be observed that the promoters of a company whose operations will be international must take into account the fact that States have, with regard to their nationals, a discretionary power to grant diplomatic protection or to refuse it. When establishing a company in a foreign country, its promoters are normally impelled by particular considerations; it is often a question of tax or other advantages offered by the host State. It does not seem to be in any way inequitable that the advantages thus obtained should be balanced by the risks arising from the fact that the protection of the company and hence of its shareholders is thus entrusted to a State other than the national State of the shareholders.[6]

But what about the state (in this case Belgium) that wants to give diplomatic protection to its citizens as shareholders? Does the ICJ's opinion give enough weight to the shareholder's home state's desire to espouse the claim?

---

6 Barcelona Traction, *supra* note 1 at para. 99.

6.1.2 Dispute settlement between investors and their host states: investor-State arbitration

In the early days of formal investment dispute settlement, foreigners' claims against a state were often settled through ad hoc commissions or arbitral tribunals. These tribunals were often set up to examine claims stemming from a particular event. The first example of such event-specific tribunals was the system of mixed commissions created out of the Jay Treaty at the end of the 18th century.[7] Offering individual investors the possibility to directly claim against a foreign government, the Jay Treaty tribunals were the first modern international investment dispute settlement instances.[8] The mixed tribunals, composed of US and British arbitrators, heard individuals' claims against the United States and Britain for compensation for damages caused to their property by the American Revolutionary War. While the tribunals have been criticized on a number of counts,[9] their basic concept of permitting investors to both gain relief where the formal judicial system failed to do so and to side-track the espousal process when pursuing property claims was highly successful. The model was replicated numerous times during the nineteenth and twentieth centuries in Europe and America, with claims commissions taking the place of national courts and international diplomacy in providing compensation to foreign investors. The post-World War II years' wave of nationalizations led to a corresponding increase in the number of investor-State arbitrations over investment property rights. Up through the 1960s, the main legal basis of such arbitrations was the investment contract between the investor and the host state. These contracts frequently contained a *consent-to-arbitrate clause* which explicitly set out the host state's acceptance of jurisdiction in front of an international tribunal for disputes arising out of the contract. Contract-based investment arbitration was a departure from international law's state-to-state dispute settlement emphasis, but the host's consent to arbitrate remained based on a specific relationship between it and the particular investor.

By the late 1950s investment protection was recognized as a subject for greater attention from the international legal community. In 1959, the Agreement on Protection and Promotion of Investments signed between Pakistan and the Federal Republic of Germany became the first bilateral treaty to solely regu-

---

7 Treaty of Amity, Commerce, and Navigation, between His Britannick Majesty and The United States of America, by Their President, with the advice and consent of Their Senate (proclaimed 29 February 1796) (Articles 6 and 7 provide for the mixed commissions).

8 *See* Richard B. Lillich, *The Jay Treaty Commissions*, 37 St. John's L. Rev. 260–61 (1963).

9 *See*, e.g. Jerald A. Combs, The Jay Treaty—Political Battleground of the Founding Fathers 152–3 (1970).

late states' treatment of investors. That treaty contained a dispute settlement provision based on state-to-state arbitration.

As more and more bilateral investment agreements were signed, investors themselves began seeking greater access to dispute settlement procedures in order to ensure hosts' adherence to their treaty obligations. In the mid-1970s, the dispute settlement provisions of some BITs started to set out a significant new kind of dispute settlement provision—the ISDS dispute settlement mechanism. The UK–Singapore BIT from 1975 contained one of the earliest such provisions. It began:

> Each Contracting Party hereby consents to submit to the International Centre for the Settlement of Investment Disputes [. . .] for settlement by arbitration under the Convention on the Settlement of Investment Disputes between States and Nationals of other States [. . .] any legal dispute arising between that Contracting Party and a national or company of the other Contracting Party concerning an investment of the latter in the territory of the former.[10]

The novelty of ISDS is that the treaty provisions providing for it contain a general consent-to-arbitrate provision binding on the treaty parties. ISDS, that is, moves the host state's consent directly into a treaty with the home state rather than having the consent remain in the contract/concession agreement with the investor. This seemingly modest change triggered a fundamental alteration of the host's liability.

In the first place, consent given in a treaty is open-ended. Called 'arbitration without privity',[11] the BIT provision functions as an offer to arbitrate that can be accepted by the investor through the submission of a request for arbitration. While the existence and scope of consent are questions of law to be determined by the tribunal, such consent is available equally to any investor from the other party to the treaty, not just to those investors and to that degree to which the host agrees.

Second, by giving its consent to be challenged by individual investors in a state treaty, the host becomes liable directly to the investor for a violation of any treaty provision. While the parties can limit their consent to offer arbitration for only certain types of claims (for instance to provide the expropriated

---

10 Agreement between the Government of the United Kingdom of Great Britain and Northern Ireland and the Government of the Republic of Singapore for the Promotion and Protection of Investments, Article 8(1) (July 22, 1975).

11 *See* Jan Paulsson, *Arbitration without Privity*, 10(2) ICSID Review 232 (1995).

investor arbitration regarding the level of compensation received), unless such a limitation is explicit, arbitrators will often allow the investor to call upon any of the treaty provisions to base a claim.

These aspects will be discussed further below. For now, we turn to an institution created specifically to provide a forum for investor-State dispute resolution: the International Centre for the Settlement of Investment Disputes, or 'ICSID'.

a   International Centre for Settlement of Investment Disputes (ICSID)

a.i   History and role of the ICSID

As the post-war global economy began to normalize and investment activity picked up in the 1950s, the capital importing states' nationalization programs became a cause of concern to many industrialized governments. By the late 1950s, investors from Britain and Germany were seeking to convince their governments to begin negotiations on a multilateral agreement on investment protection. In 1960, Germany took up the cause, choosing the Organisation for European Economic Cooperation (today's Organisation for Economic Co-operation and Development, or OECD) as the fora for such negotiations. As the Paris-based organization's membership included the main capital-exporting states, this choice was not unreasonable, and 14 other member governments joined the drafting effort. The resulting draft agreement, the Draft Convention on the Protection of Foreign Property,[12] made the minimum substantive standards of investment protection common in current IIAs (including fair and equitable treatment, non-discrimination, non-arbitrariness, and full protection and security), as well as the payment of just compensation[13] (defined as the 'genuine value' of the property[14]), for expropriations binding on all states. Its dispute settlement procedures for addressing violations of these standards included the possibility of either state-to-state arbitration[15] (or litigation, if mutually agreed upon)[16] or investor-State arbitration.[17] As we already know, however, the efforts to support the draft's completion were destined to fail, largely because even

---

12 *See* OECD, Draft Convention on the Protection of Foreign Property: Text with Notes and Comments (Oct. 12, 1967). Available at: http://www.oecd.org/dataoecd/35/4/39286571.pdf.

13 *Id.*, art. 3(iii).

14 *Id.*, Notes and Comments to art. 3 at 21.

15 *Id.*, art. 7(a).

16 *Id.*, Notes and Comments to art. 7 at 35–6.

17 *Id.*, art. 7(b).

among the limited membership there could be no agreement on the relevant standards.[18]

Sensing the long-term intractability of the problem, the legal counsel to the World Bank, Aron Broches, came up with an idea to focus on procedural norms for investment protection rather than substantive norms. Broches' idea was to establish a politically neutral multilateral forum where investment disputes could be resolved between investor and host state.[19] This forum would have to be independent of the courts of either party and offer internationally unified procedures for resolution to foster predictability.

Broches' idea was embraced and developed quickly. First discussed in 1961, by 1963, a draft convention setting out the organizational basis for such a forum was in negotiation. Sponsored by the World Bank, whose interest in developing industrial capacities corresponded closely with investment protection, the drafting process proceeded quickly, with inputs from legal experts in all Bank regions. The final draft was accepted by the Executive Council of the Bank in 1965, ratifications were sought from member states, and in October 1966, the International Centre for the Settlement of Investment Disputes, 'ICSID', came into being.

a.ii   Structure of ICSID as an organization

Form and purpose
The ICSID is an international institution sitting in Washington, DC as part of the International Bank for Reconstruction and Development (World Bank). As its formative Convention on the Settlement of Investment Disputes between States and Nationals of Other States (ICSID Convention or 'Convention') states, the purpose of the ICSID is 'to provide facilities for conciliation and arbitration of investment disputes between Contracting States and nationals of other Contracting States in accordance with the provisions of this Convention'.[20] Possessing legal personality, ICSID and its staff enjoy the privileges and immunities that accompany this position.

---

18 Peter T. Muchlinski, *The Rise and Fall of the Multilateral Agreement on Investment: Where Now?*, 34 Int'l Law. 1033, 1036 (1999) (attributing the failure to the southern European countries' opposition).

19 Ibrahim F.I. Shihata defined the ICSID as 'a forum for conflict resolution in a framework which carefully balances the interests and requirements of all the parties involved, and attempts in particular to "depoliticize" the settlement of investment disputes'. Ibrahim F.I. Shihata, *Towards a Greater Depoliticization of Investment Disputes: The Roles of ICSID and MIGA*, 1(1) ICSID Rev.–FILJ 1 (1986) (Shihata was the ICSID Secretary General from 1983 to 2000).

20 ICSID Convention art. 1.2.

Membership

Membership of the ICSID is open to states that are either members of the World Bank or parties to the International Court of Justice invited by two-thirds of the other ICSID members to join.[21] Having signed and then ratified the ICSID Convention, the state's membership begins 30 days following its deposit of the ratification instrument with the World Bank.[22] As of June 2016, ICSID has 153 member states (161 signatories), including all industrial countries.[23] There are some significant non-members, however, including Brazil, India, Mexico, Poland, and the Russian Federation (which has signed, but not ratified, the Convention). The significance of the ICSID for the latter cannot be denied, however, as the existence of the so-called ICSID 'Additional Facility' (discussed below) opens the institution and its rules to non-members. Moreover, the prevalence of ICSID arbitration decisions means that they have a strong influence on non-ICSID arbitrations as well.

Organizational structure

ICSID's institutional structure is simple, composed of only two parts: an Administrative Council and the Secretariat.

Administrative Council

The Administrative Council is composed of one representative of each ICSID member and the President of the World Bank acting as non-voting chair. Meeting once a year, Council members are the legislators for the Centre, deciding on administrative and budgetary matters as well as on procedural and substantive rules. Based on a one-member, one-vote, majoritarian decision-making process, the ICSID is more egalitarian than its sister organizations in the World Bank Group.

Secretariat

The ICSID Secretariat manages the daily operational aspects of the institution as a forum for dispute settlement. Led by the Secretary-General, the staff oversees the administration of cases for the parties to the disputes and maintains the panel of arbitrators and conciliators. The Secretariat registers complaints, organizes the tribunals, collects party submissions, organizes the proceedings, and authorizes awards. It also collects information, performs

---

21 ICSID Convention art. 67.

22 *See* Memorandum on Signature and Ratification, Acceptance or Approval of the Convention on the Settlement of Investment Disputes between States and Nationals of Other States. Available at: http://icsid.worldbank.org/.

23 Bolivia withdrew as of 3 November 2007, and Ecuador withdrew as of 17 January 2010, and Venezuela withdrew as of July 25, 2012. *See* ICSID List of Contracting States and Other Signatories of the Convention. Available at: http://www.icsid.worldbank.org.

research, publishes a journal, and organizes conferences on multiple aspects of the law of investment protection.

Panel of arbitrators and panel of conciliators

Because the ICSID is not a court, but rather an administrator of dispute settlement, it calls upon external individuals to hear and decide dispute claims. The members of the tribunals, whether arbitrators or conciliators, may be selected from lists of candidates proposed by members. Each member may appoint up to four persons to be on the two lists. According to the Convention, the persons appointed are to be of 'high moral character and recognized competence in the fields of law, commerce, industry or finance, who may be relied upon to exercise independent judgment'.[24] The provision elaborates that while the members need not appoint lawyers or judges, the arbitrator nominees ought to have knowledge of law.

The persons listed remain on the list for a period of four years, with the possibility of renewal by the member. Their appointment to a tribunal, however, is far from assured. Disputants may—and regularly do—choose non-listed persons as tribunal members. It is only if the ICSID itself composes the tribunal that the listed names are the only ones from which to select.

Growth of the ICSID

Comparing the number of registered cases from the inception of ICSID with those currently pending, one is struck with the large number of 'new' disputes the Secretariat must administer. In their published statistics over the past several years, the ICSID Secretariat has been able to report double-digit annual increases in their caseload.[25] In the face of this large and rapid expansion in the number of cases, the ICSID Secretariat is under pressure to improve its efficiency.

a.iii   *Dispute settlement procedure*

An investment arbitration proceeding under ICSID rules is open to investors of a member state against a host that is a member state. For non-party investors or hosts, the ICSID offers the possibility of requesting arbitration in the framework of the 'Additional Facility'. The Additional Facility was established in 1978 to permit investors from or in non-ICSID states to access the dispute settlement fora of the ICSID, to permit arbitrations on issues that do

---

24 ICSID Convention art. 14.1.

25 *See*, e.g. ICSID, *Annual Report 2014* 5, 21–2. Available at: https://icsid.worldbank.org/apps/icsidweb/resources/pages/ICSID-Annual-Report.aspx.

not arise directly out of an investment, or to perform fact-finding.[26] The procedural rules for arbitrations under the additional facility are similar to those of the ICSID, so the following will focus on the ICSID rules, only pointing out where the Additional Facility rules differ.[27]

Making a claim

If an investor has a dispute with its host, and both the home and the host (or either the home or the host in the case of the Additional Facility) are members of the ICSID, it can choose to request the ICSID to be the forum. The request must be accompanied by a brief description of the claim to permit the Secretary-General to make a preliminary determination of jurisdiction. Unless the Secretary-General finds the claim to be 'manifestly outside the jurisdiction of' the ICSID Convention,[28] the case will be registered on the Centre's docket. If there is clearly no dispute stemming from an investment, or if it is clear that the complaint does not come from a national of the home state, or that the home and host states are not members of the ICSID, or if the host clearly has not consented to arbitration, the Secretary-General will refuse to let the Request for Arbitration proceed.[29] There are very few claims that get rejected at this stage of the proceedings,[30] as the Secretariat will assume as true those facts which are most amenable to the complainant's case.[31] Once a request has been approved, the ICSID will register the case and send the parties the notice of registration.

Selection of the tribunal

Choice of arbitrators

The parties then must decide on the tribunal. While arbitrations with a single arbitrator are permitted, most tribunals are composed of three arbitrators: one appointed by each party, and the third—who will act as president of the tribunal—appointed by agreement of the parties or the parties' arbitrators. If no agreement can be reached, the Chairman of the Administrative Council

---

26 Rules Governing the Additional Facility for the Administration of Proceedings by the Secretariat of the International Centre for Settlement of Investment Disputes (Additional Facility Rules) art. 2. Available at: http://icsid.worldbank.org/ICSID/StaticFiles/facility/AFR_English-final.pdf.

27 *See* ICSID, Rules of Procedure for the Institution of Conciliation and Arbitration Proceedings (April 2006); Rules of Procedure for Arbitration Proceedings (April 2006); Arbitration (Additional Facility) Rules (April 2006).

28 ICSID Convention art. 36.

29 The Secretariat will often ask the claimant for clarifications if the request for arbitration appears faulty. Should the complaint still be lacking, the request will often be withdrawn before it can be rejected. *See Birth of an ICSID Case – Act I, Scene II*, 24(1) Arbitration Int'l 17, 23 (2008).

30 If a complaint is brought on the basis of a treaty, the ICSID Secretariat will look to the jurisdictional requirements of the treaty as well.

31 *See supra* note 29 at 19.

(President of the World Bank) chooses. While the parties can appoint any non-national, only persons on the Panel of Arbitrators are available to the Administrative Council Chairman, should he be making the appointment.

Challenge of arbitrators

Parties can, and increasingly do, challenge arbitrator appointments. Under ICSID Convention Article 57:

> A party may propose to a Commission or Tribunal the disqualification of any of its members on account of any fact indicating a manifest lack of the qualities required by paragraph (1) of Article 14. A party to arbitration proceedings may, in addition, propose the disqualification of an arbitrator on the ground that he was ineligible for appointment to the Tribunal under Section 2 of Chapter IV.

Article 14.1 refers to the arbitrator's required qualities: high moral character, ability to make an independent judgment in the case, and competence in legal analysis. Chapter IV, Section 2 sets forth the procedures for establishing the tribunal, including a requirement that the majority be non-party nationals. Any challenges brought on these bases must be made 'promptly'—soon after either the party realized or should have realized the potential for challenge—or the opportunity will be deemed waived.[32]

Once challenged, the arbitrator may decide to step down. If the arbitrator feels the challenge was inappropriate, the remaining arbitrators will take the decision to sustain or reject the challenge.[33] While no challenges on the grounds of moral character or legal skills are known, the independence of arbitrators has been disputed numerous times. In fact, the attention given to the question of arbitrators' independence is increasing rapidly. It is therefore one of the topics covered in this chapter's section on current concerns (see below at 6.2.7).

---

32 ICSID Arbitration Rule 9.1. 'Promptly' has been interpreted as allowing parties a reasonable opportunity to prepare the challenge. *See* Suez, *Sociedad General de Aguas de Barcelona S.A., and InterAguas Servicios Integrales del Agua S.A. v. The Argentine Republic,* ICSID Case No. ARB/03/17, and, *Suez, Sociedad General de Aguas de Barcelona S.A., and Vivendi Universal S.A. v. The Argentine Republic,* ICSID Case No. ARB/03/19, *AWG Group v. The Argentine Republic, Decision on the Proposal for the Disqualification of a Member of the Arbitral Tribunal,* para. 26 (Oct. 22, 2007). Available at: http://italaw.com/documents/Suez-VivendiChallenge.pdf (reasoning on the basis of the complexity of the information that one or two days would not have been reasonable within which to expect a challenge, but that 53 days was unreasonably long for the challenge to have been submitted).

33 ICSID Convention art. 58. *Compare* SCC Rules of Arbitration art. 15.4 (arbitrator challenges are determined by the Board); ICC Rules of Arbitration art. 14.3 (the Court decides arbitrator challenges); PCA Rules of Procedure art. 12 (appointing authority decides the arbitrator challenge).

Preliminary consultations

Once the tribunal is established, the proceedings may begin. The first meeting of the tribunal and parties, called the preliminary procedural consultation, sets the agenda for the proceedings. The ICSID has a standard organizational meeting agenda which includes the elements for discussion. These include the place of arbitration, the language(s) of the proceedings, the details of document submission, whether or not oral and written proceedings will be held, the division of costs, and how the hearing is to be recorded. A pre-trial conference may be held as well for the parties to agree to stipulate uncontested facts, exchange information, and potentially to settle their differences.

Adversarial proceedings
<u>Written submissions</u>

The two-step adversarial proceedings then begin. The first step is the written stage, which begins with the claimant submitting a memorial with her view of the facts and the legal arguments to support the claims. The respondent's counter-memorial follows. Any jurisdictional objections the respondent has must be presented in the counter-memorial.

If necessary, the claimant can next submit a reply, to which the respondent may hand in a rejoinder. The reply and rejoinder documents may respond to the jurisdictional or merits arguments of the other party.

<u>Oral arguments</u>

A second stage is that of oral arguments. The parties will appear before the tribunal to present their arguments and answer any questions that the tribunal might have. Experts and witnesses may also be presented at this time, and can be questioned by either the tribunal or the other party. It is up to the tribunal, albeit in consultation with the parties, whether or not the oral argument phase is open to observation by non-party representatives. While not yet common, one can expect publicized arguments to become more frequent in the ISDS context as civil society pressure for greater transparency in investment law decision-making increases.

b *Dispute proceedings overview*

See Figure 6.1 and Figure 6.2 on pages 444 and 445.

c *Non-ICSID investor-State arbitration*

Remember that ISDS existed before BITs and before the ICSID. Therefore, it should come as no surprise that there are a number of other possibilities for

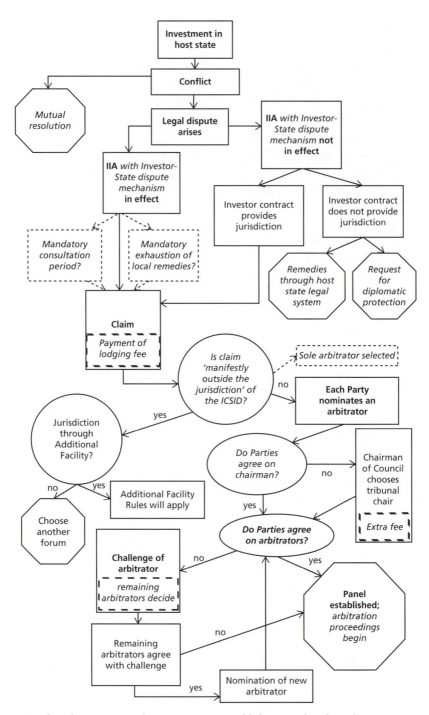

Figure 6.1 When the investment plans sour: steps in establishing an arbitral panel

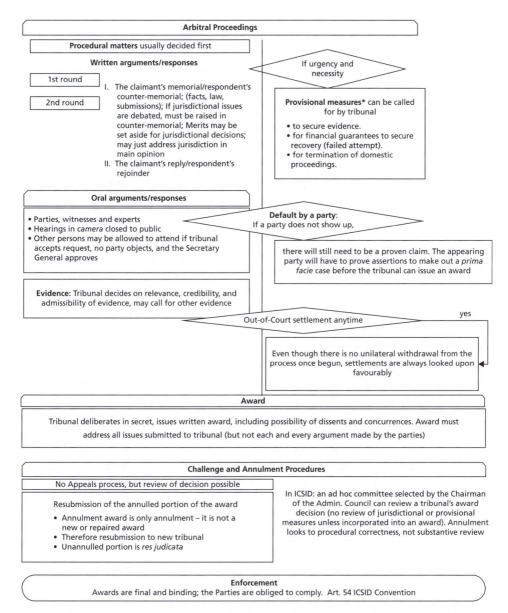

Note: According to Dolzer and Schreuer (*op. cit.*) ICSID Convention Article 47 suggests a non-binding character of provisional measures, but tribunals have held them to be binding.

Figure 6.2 Investor-State dispute proceedings: from panel establishment to enforcement of the award

ISDS beyond the ICSID. Arbitration between an investor and a State can take place in one of a number of institutional fora or through non-institutional 'ad hoc' arbitration. The precise manner may be set forth in the concession contract or the applicable institutional rules in the IIA. The following gives a very brief overview of the dispute settlement fora frequently chosen by disputants.

c.i   *Other investor-State arbitration institutional fora*

International Chamber of Commerce (ICC)

One of the investor-State arbitration fora is the International Chamber of Commerce (ICC) based in Paris. The ICC, established in 1923, handles both public investment arbitrations and international commercial arbitration. It is home to the International Court of Arbitration (ICA), which provides administrative and technical assistance to arbitrating parties. Despite its name, the ICA is not a 'court' itself—it does not give judgments. Dolzer and Schreuer note that the arbitrators write up 'terms of reference' summarizing the issues to be decided upon once the files are submitted by the parties.[34] Then, once the tribunal in the case comes to a decision, the report is given to the ICA for proofreading.

The ICC bills itself as the most international of the investment dispute resolution fora:

> There are no restrictions as to who can use ICC Arbitration or who can act as arbitrators. This is reflected in the increasing number of nationalities represented. Since its inception, the Court has administered more than 19 000 cases involving parties and arbitrators from some 180 countries.[35]

It also is able to adapt to the specific wishes of the parties more flexibly than the ICSID: language choice, place of arbitration, and the law governing the arbitration are all open to the parties.

London Court of International Arbitration (LCIA)

Following the 1892 London Chamber of Arbitration, the LCIA also administers arbitrations for either investments or commercial transactions. The LCIA is a non-profit company with limited guarantee. It has a three-part structure, with the Company (managed by a Board of Directors composed of

---

34 Rudolf Dolzer and Christoph Schreuer, *Principles of International Investment Law* 242 (second edn, 2012).
35 *ICC Arbitration* available at: http://www.iccwbo.org/products-and-services/arbitration-and-adr/arbitration/.

London-based arbitrators), the Secretariat, and the Arbitration Court. The Secretariat helps administer cases, but its involvement varies based on the case/parties' desires. It can act as an appointing authority under the UN Commission on International Trade Law (UNCITRAL) rules, but also has its own set of rules that can be used outside the LCIA forum.

The Arbitration Court is a group of up to 35 members (specialists in commercial arbitration) headed by a president and vice president that appoints tribunals, determines challenges, and controls for costs. It is the president and vice presidents who do most of the business of the court. The court itself appoints arbitrators under the LCIA rules—parties may nominate, but the court may reject the nomination if it finds him/her unsuitable. Unlike the ICSID, in LCIA arbitrations, there is a presumption that a single arbitrator will hear the case. If the parties indicate they want more than that or if the court decides the case requires several decision-makers, three judges can be named.

The LCIA also pursues other methods of alternative dispute resolution (ADR) methods, such as mediation.

Permanent Court of Arbitration (PCA)
Sitting in The Hague, the PCA is another administrator/facilitator of arbitration rather than a court. This organization was established in 1899 as a result of the Hague Peace Conference and was the first global dispute settlement mechanism for states. It may, however, establish tribunals for investor-State arbitration as well.

The PCA is structured similarly to the ICSID, with an Administrative Council composed of representatives of the 111 member states, a secretariat, called the International Bureau, headed by the Secretary-General, and panel members to be put together as tribunals. The PCA also has a specialized list of persons to serve as arbitrators for natural resource-specific cases.

While the Administrative Council shapes the policy of the court, it is the International Bureau that does much of the daily work: keeping documents, giving legal assistance, managing finances, and arranging for the hearings.

Tribunals of the PCA use rules based on the UNCITRAL rules. These rules provide for appointing authority powers for the Secretary-General—that is, the Secretary-General can be requested to find someone or act by choosing a third arbitrator where the parties cannot agree, or to determine a challenge to one of the arbitrators.

Stockholm Chamber of Commerce's Institute of Arbitration
The Stockholm Chamber of Commerce's (SCC) Institute of Arbitration is a fourth arbitration forum available to investors. A division of the SCC, the Institute of Arbitration was established in 1917 and is enjoying growing popularity among investors seeking investor-State arbitration due to its efficiency (decisions are to be awarded within six months and there is the possibility of expedited proceedings, with awards issued in three months), confidentiality, and finality of awards.

The Institute has a two-part organization. The Board of Directors is composed of individuals from around the world who meet once a month to make decisions related to the arbitrators, seat of arbitration, and applicable rules. They also determine jurisdiction questions and arbitrator challenges. The Secretariat carries out the administrative aspects of arbitration and performs research activities.

c.ii   *Ad hoc arbitration*

While many investor-State arbitrations take place within the framework of the ICSID, an unknown number of arbitrations take place 'ad hoc'. Provided for in most IIAs, the ad hoc arbitration option permits parties the freedom to choose either the UNCITRAL rules for their arbitration or their own agreed-upon rules.

LITERATURE

Luke Eric Peterson, All Roads Lead Out of Rome: Divergent Paths of Dispute Settlement in Bilateral Investment Treaties[36]

The World Bank's ICSID has become the most well-known and, based on available information, most commonly invoked *institutional* avenue for dispute settlement. However, treaties often allow recourse to a number of other arbitral options, both institutional and ad hoc . . . .
Neither [ICSID nor the Additional Facility] rules are available in cases where *both* parties to a dispute do not hail from an ICSID signatory country. For this reason,

---

36 Luke Eric Peterson, *All Roads Lead Out of Rome: Divergent Paths of Dispute Settlement in Bilateral Investment Treaties*, International Sustainable and Ethical Investment Rules Project, Nautilus Institute for Security and Sustainable Development (2002). Available at: http://www.iisd.org/pdf/2003/investment_nautilus.pdf (footnotes omitted).

the majority of investment treaties since the 1980s have incorporated references to other (non-ICSID) arbitral avenues . . . .

More often, treaties will supplement the ICSID option, not by reference to other commercial institutions—like the ICC and SCC—but with an *ad hoc* arbitration process, where only a tribunal (but no supervising institution) oversees the conduct of the arbitration. Examples of ad hoc arbitrations include, those under the UN Commission on International Trade Law (UNCITRAL) rules or those arbitrated in a classical ad hoc fashion (i.e. before a panel with no prescribed rules whatsoever, apart from what the treaty explicitly prescribes). This paper explores some of the features of these six arbitral options:

- *Institutional*: International Chamber of Commerce, Stockholm Chamber of Commerce, ICSID, and the so-called ICSID Additional Facility rules;
- *Ad hoc*: UNCITRAL or classical ad hoc.

Attention to the last of these is limited, however, because classical ad hoc arbitration is less often mentioned in treaties. Nor, as shall be seen, does it have any rules which can be helpfully compared with the other sets; as the name implies, arbitrations on these rules are entirely ad hoc, and totally off-the-record—with the parties devising the rules of arbitration themselves.

One important implication of the inclusion of a *menu* of arbitral options in most BITs, is that investors generally enjoy the ability to select their favored arbitral option from all those listed in the treaty's menu. In effect, they may 'rule-shop' for the set of arbitral rules most favorable to their interests. Thus, effective monitoring of emerging investment disputes must not only countenance all of the arbitral options discussed here, but it must also come to appreciate certain important differences between these different rules.Monitoring of investor usage of these treaties—and an assessment of their implications—is hampered by various deficiencies in transparency, legitimacy and accountability. This ought not be surprising, as, with the exception of the ICSID system, these arbitral rules were designed for what one sympathetic textbook characterizes as a system of 'private justice in the service of merchants'. . . .

? DISCUSSION NOTES

1 If a treaty provides for ISDS, may a State still offer the investor diplomatic protection if the investor would prefer it? Some IIAs explicitly prohibit home state interference in the dispute resolution process if ISDS is an alternative. See, e.g. UK–Singapore BIT, Article 8(2):

> (2) Neither Contracting Party shall pursue through diplomatic channels any dispute referred to the Centre unless:
>
> (a) the Secretary-General of the Centre, or 'an arbitral tribunal constituted'

by it, decides that the dispute is not within the jurisdiction of the Centre; or

(b) the other Contracting Party should fail to abide by or to comply with any award rendered by such a tribunal.

Moreover, the ICSID Convention prohibits home states from offering diplomatic protection once a case is filed with its secretariat. Article 27 states:

(1) No Contracting State shall give diplomatic protection, or bring an international claim, in respect of a dispute which one of its nationals and another Contracting State shall have consented to submit or shall have submitted to arbitration under this Convention, unless such other Contracting State shall have failed to abide by and comply with the award rendered in such dispute. (2) Diplomatic protection, for the purposes of paragraph (1), shall not include informal diplomatic exchanges for the sole purpose of facilitating a settlement of the dispute.

What would happen if an investor chose ad hoc arbitration on the basis of a BIT that was silent about diplomatic protection?

2 Arbitration is not only about dispute settlement. For the administrators, arbitration is a competitive business. Each arbitration brings in profits, so each forum wants to attract more arbitration 'clients'. Because the jurisdictions of the fora overlap, they need to compete to attract consumers of their service. There are several possible aspects for competition, including efficiency, location, cost, confidentiality, and the level of party control over the proceedings.

3 International arbitration is a dispute settlement process designed to avoid lengthy and formalistic domestic legal processes. Foreign investors prefer the international context and the commercial benefits of adapting the process to their particular needs. They determine many of the rules to be applied during the arbitration while the party-selected tribunal can provide for a decision on complex legal issues that takes into account the commercial interests behind the disagreement.

Cost-effective and efficient, arbitration is not, however, inexpensive. Besides the costs of legal consultants and advocates, the increasingly formalized procedures of institutional arbitration require additional outlays of money for each party.

The ICSID publishes a Schedule of Fees each year. With the registration of a complaint costing the investor US$25 000, one notices immediately that an investor must have a substantial feeling of unjust treatment to begin an arbitration. While this might prohibit smaller investors from pursuing all violations of their rights to protection and fair treatment, it does help diminish the potential for harassment suits and thereby reduces the burden on the host. See Schedule of Fees of the International Centre for Settlement of Investment Disputes at https://icsid.worldbank.org/apps/ICSIDWEB/icsiddocs/Pages/ICSID-Schedule-of-Fees.aspx.

Other international investment arbitration fora also charge for their services. The precise formula used, however, varies. The International Chamber of Commerce charges a filing fee and sets the costs on the basis of the amount at issue in the arbitration. The advantage, it says, is that this method 'offers predictability for the parties, who can estimate the range of costs as soon as the value of the claims is known'.[37]

The London Court of International Arbitration and the Permanent Court of Arbitration are more similar to the ICSID, charging on the basis of tribunals' time spent on the case.

6.2   ICSID arbitration dispute proceedings

This section will examine the dispute settlement procedures of the International Centre for the Settlement of Investment Disputes (ICSID or the Centre). Set up specifically to address these quasi-public disputes, the ICSID is the main fora for treaty-based investor-State dispute resolution in terms of number of known arbitrations administered.

The ICSID's Convention and its Arbitration Rules apply only to that subset of investment cases that are decided by ICSID tribunals.[38] The decisions of tribunals convened under the ICC, LCIA, PCA, or SCC frameworks, as well as ad hoc tribunals rely on their own institutional rules and on the procedural rules the parties have agreed upon (often the Arbitration Rules of the United Nations Commission on International Trade Law, or 'UNCITRAL') The various sets of institutional and procedural rules are, however, quite similar to each other and to those of the ICSID, and so for simplicity's sake, we will remain with the ICSID.

The following will focus on several of the main legal issues arising in ICSID ISDS arbitration. These are vigorously discussed in the literature and case law of both ICSID and non-ICSID tribunals. While the approach to some of

---

37 *See, Is ICC arbitration confidential?* Available at: http://www.iccwbo.org/FAQs/Frequently-asked-questions-on-ICC- Arbitration/.

38 In fact, the ICSID tribunals can also conduct proceedings under other procedural rules.

the issues can be said to enjoy general acceptance by tribunals, other issues remain divisive. Thus, the reader is encouraged to approach this chapter as only an initial investigation of investor-State arbitral procedures and to use it as a basis for further studies.

6.2.1 Elements of ICSID jurisdiction: Article 25 ICSID Convention

One issue of fundamental significance to the investor-State dispute settlement process is that of whether the arbitral tribunal has the competence to hear a case. This is the question of the tribunal's jurisdiction.

a   Introduction

Jurisdiction is basic to any dispute settlement system: a decision-maker must have the authority to make particular decisions if the results are to be valid. In international law, where there is no global 'highest' authority, the competence of any tribunal to make decisions is based on the powers given to it by the states subject to those decisions. Thus, the rules for ICSID arbitrations are contained in the ICSID Convention, which is a treaty accepted by its member states. The Convention gives the ICSID arbitral tribunal the authority to determine whether members are in compliance with their international obligations relating to investments. In addition, the ICSID Convention gives the tribunal the role of determining its own competence over the particular investor-State dispute it is asked to resolve. This '*Kompetenz-Kompetenz*' is set out in Article 41 of the ICSID Convention:

> (1)   The Tribunal shall be the judge of its own competence.
>
> (2)   Any objection by a party to the dispute that that dispute is not within the jurisdiction of the Centre, or for other reasons is not within the competence of the Tribunal, shall be considered by the Tribunal which shall determine whether to deal with it as a preliminary question or to join it to the merits of the dispute.

Exercising the competence to assess whether jurisdiction exists requires a clear idea of the limits of that power. These limits must be assessed both in general—as a matter of international law—and in particular—in the context of the particular case. In his dissent to the majority's Decision on Jurisdiction and Admissibility in the *Abaclat v. Argentina* case, arbitrator Abi-Saab set forth a clarification of jurisdiction as it applies to ISDS.

CASE

Abaclat v. Argentina[39]

Following the Latin American economic crisis of the 1980s, Argentina began efforts to restructure its economy. One of the programs it embarked upon to increase growth and reduce public debt was the issuing of sovereign bonds to international banks and institutions. These 'intermediaries' re-sold the bonds on capital markets to retail customers. When the financial crisis of the late 1990s hit, Argentina became unable to meet its payment obligations on those bonds. It therefore offered bondholders an option of exchanging the existing instruments for ones of reduced value.

A large group of 180 000 Italian bondholders refused the offer. Instead, under the aegis of a single entity acting on their behalf, they filed for investment arbitration at ICSID based on the Argentina–Italy BIT. The arbitrators' first task was to determine whether jurisdiction existed.

The majority said yes, but one tribunal member disagreed. The question of jurisdiction in international investment law, Professor Georges Abi-Saab wrote, is significantly different from that of jurisdiction in international commercial arbitration, where national law is the ultimate source of tribunal authority.

6 i) This is technically an international *ad hoc* arbitral Tribunal. It is '*ad hoc*' because specially established to hear one specific case [. . .]. It is 'international' because it is rooted in two layers of international treaties: the ICSID Convention and the Bilateral Investment Treaty between Italy and Argentina. As such it functions under, and is governed by international law, and has to be clearly distinguished from 'international' commercial arbitration tribunals, [. . .] which function under national law and ultimate national judicial control. It is necessary to keep this distinction in mind, as [. . .] what is sometimes permissible in municipal law, is not necessarily acceptable in international law.

7 ii) In international law, all tribunals not only arbitral, but even judicial are tribunals of attributed, hence limited jurisdiction (*juridictions d'attribution*). There is no tribunal or system of tribunals of plenary or general jurisdiction (*juridiction de droit commun*) that covers all cases and subjects [. . .]. This is because, in the absence of a centralized power on the international level that exercises the judicial function through a judicial system empowered from above (or rather incarnating the judicial

---

39 *Abaclat and Others v. Argentine Republic*, ICSID Case No. ARB/07/5, Dissenting Opinion to Decision on Jurisdiction and Admissibility (Aug. 4, 2011).

power as part of the centralized power), all international adjudicatory bodies are empowered from below, being based on the consent and agreement of the subjects (i.e. the litigants, *les justiciables*) themselves (with the very limited exception of tribunals created by international organizations in the exercise of their powers under their constitutive treaties [. . .]).

8 iii) This is the reason why, the fundamental principle and basic rule in international adjudication, is that of the consensual basis of jurisdiction. [. . .]

9 iv) Jurisdiction as a concept in international law, partakes of its generic meaning in the general theory of law; but is further specified and particularized in function of the fundamental principle of the consensual basis of international adjudication.

10 The term 'jurisdiction' (from the latin '*jurisdictio*', literally to 'pronounce' or 'enunciate the law', *dire le droit*) [. . .] denotes 'the legal power of an organ to decide cases (in general) or a case (in particular) by application of law'. In other words, it is the empowerment to exercise the judicial function. Thus, jurisdiction refers first and foremost to a *legal power* to exercise a certain type of activity, the judicial function.

11 In English, however, the term 'jurisdiction' is also used to designate the 'ambit' or 'sphere' within or over which this power is exercised, though in other languages, such as French and Spanish, another term is used to designate the 'ambit', which is 'competence'.

Some writers and arbitral decisions seem to be oblivious of the primary and more fundamental meaning of jurisdiction as power, limiting the term to the ambit of this power. Jurisdiction as ambit is defined as a four-dimensional sphere, by its extent and limits in time (*ratione temporis*) and space (*ratione loci*), and over subjects (*ratione personae*) and objects or subjects-matters (*ratione materiae*).

12 v) In international law, because of its consensual basis, jurisdiction as an ambit is analyzed and scrutinized at two different levels, where adjudication is not intended for one case only, but takes place within an institutional setting, either of a standing organ (such as the ICJ) or a framework within which *ad hoc* tribunals are established (such as the PCA and the ICSID):

a) 'general jurisdiction' which defines the objective range and outer limits of the ambit for all cases, according to the constitutive instrument of the organ (e.g. the ICJ Statute), or the framework convention (e.g. the ICSID Convention[]);

b) 'special jurisdiction' which defines the subjective range and limits of the ambit of jurisdiction of the organ in a particular case, according to the specific jurisdictional title bearing the consent of the parties, on the basis of which the case is brought before the organ.

13 The consent of the parties cannot go beyond the objective limits of the general jurisdiction of the organ, but can restrict its jurisdiction further within these objective limits, by the parties subjecting their consent to additional limits, conditions or reservations. These can relate to any of the four dimensions of the ambit. But they can also relate to the powers of the organ as such (the primary meaning of jurisdiction), as long as this does not touch the hard core requirements of the judicial function, for example by excluding from its powers the indication of provisional measures.

14 In case of ICSID arbitration, the jurisdictional title for general jurisdiction is the Convention itself. For 'special jurisdiction', the title is usually two-tiered: the BIT between the two States and the consent in writing of the two parties to the dispute.

15 Thus, for an ICSID *ad hoc* tribunal, a triple-layered consent is usually required. For such a Tribunal to take jurisdiction over a case, it has to ascertain:

a) that the case falls within the jurisdiction of the ICSID as defined by the ICSID Convention and related instruments (Rules of Procedure, etc.);

b) that it falls within the bounds defined by the BIT between the State party to the ICSID arbitration and the national State of the investor (which usually but not necessarily also carries the consent of the two states to arbitrate);

c) and that the case is covered by the specific written consent of the parties to the dispute (which can be for the State party, the BIT or another unilateral act bearing its consent. But it can also be a compromissory clause in a contract between the parties; and for the investor it can be the request of arbitration itself).

The Tribunal has to ascertain the existence and scope of the consent of the parties within the limits prescribed by them in each of the above-mentioned instruments.

16 vii) The requirement to ascertain the existence and scope of consent, while strict and exacting in international law, does not mean the restrictive interpretation of the jurisdictional title (the old theory of interpretation in favour of sovereignty, as far as the State party is concerned). But it does not mean either its extensive interpretation beyond 'the horizon of foreseeability'; i.e. extending jurisdiction to what the party or parties could not have foreseen at the time the treaty was concluded or consent was given. Interpretation is limited here to the establishment of the reality and extent of the consent of the party or parties, at the time it was given.

What specifically must a tribunal find to conclude that it has the authority to decide a dispute? The following will investigate the main elements of ICSID tribunals' jurisdiction as set out in the Convention.

b   *Elements of ICSID jurisdiction*

The relevant article concerning the jurisdiction of the ICSID is Article 25 of the ICSID Convention, in which paragraph 1 reads as follows:

The jurisdiction of the Centre shall extend to any *legal dispute* arising *directly out of an investment*, between a *Contracting State* (or any constituent subdivision or agency of a Contracting State designated to the Centre by that State) and a *national* of another Contracting State, which the parties to the dispute *consent* in writing to submit to the Centre. When the parties have given their consent, no party may withdraw its consent unilaterally. [emphasis added]

The jurisdiction of ICSID is therefore subject to four main elements:

- The dispute is between a contracting state and an investor of another contracting state.
- The parties to the dispute have agreed to submit the dispute to ICSID.
- The dispute is a 'legal dispute'.
- The dispute arises 'directly out of an investment made in the host contracting state'.

We will look at each in turn.

c   *Dispute is between a contracting state and an investor of another contracting state*

In order to access ICSID's institutionalized dispute settlement procedures, both the home state of the investor and the host state of the investment must be members of the Centre. The nationality issue has been discussed in Chapter 3. It is, of course, of critical importance to show that the investor can claim to be a national of an ICSID member state, but also that it is not the national of the host state against which it is bringing the case. The host itself must also be an ICSID member. If ICSID membership does not exist for either the home or the host state (but is not lacking for both), the Additional Facility would be available as a forum.

While nationality itself is important, the temporal aspect of nationality is also important for determining jurisdiction: according to ICSID Convention Article 25(2), the investor must demonstrate that it possessed the home state's nationality (and not the host's nationality) 'on the date on which the parties consented to submit such dispute to conciliation or arbitration as well as on the date on which the request was registered'.[40] As filing a claim against a host suffices to indicate the investor's consent to arbitrate, that date is used as well as the date of registration by the ICSID.

---

40 ICSID Convention art. 25.2(a).

Because investors have the opportunity to change their nationality, the fact that the timing of the requisite nationality is post-investment leaves open the opportunity for nationality-planning. Similar to choosing a nationality for tax purposes, nationality planning for arbitration is logical from a commercial perspective. Indeed, a number of tribunals have looked at the question of forum shopping and the majority approach is supportive of the use of corporate restructuring to ensure investment protections apply. Yet, hosts may see such restructuring as an abuse of the system. This is particularly true where the dispute already exists or is reasonably foreseeable.

The *Phoenix v. Czech Republic* tribunal set out the standard explanation for denying treaty protection to investors who rearrange their nationality in the midst of a dispute with a government:

> The conclusion of the Tribunal is therefore that the Claimant's initiation and pursuit of this arbitration is an abuse of the system of international ICSID investment arbitration. If it were accepted that the Tribunal has jurisdiction to decide Phoenix's claim, then any pre-existing national dispute could be brought to an ICSID tribunal by a transfer of the national economic interests to a foreign company in an attempt to seek protections under a BIT. Such transfer from the domestic arena to the international scene would *ipso facto* constitute a "protected investment"—and the jurisdiction of BIT and ICSID tribunals would be virtually unlimited. It is the duty of the Tribunal not to protect such an abusive manipulation of the system of international investment protection under the ICSID Convention and the BITs.'[41]

Thus, tribunals will generally look to determine whether the restructuring for jurisdictional access took place up to the time that an investment dispute was reasonably foreseeable or actually emerged. If so, it will be considered legitimate. If the dispute already exists, however, nationality changes will be deemed an abuse of process. The *Mobile v. Venezuela* tribunal set forth the majority approach:

> 204. [Claimant's] aim of the restructuring of their investments in Venezuela through a Dutch holding was to protect those investments against breaches of their rights by the Venezuelan authorities by gaining access to ICSID arbitration through the BIT. The Tribunal considers that this was a perfectly legitimate goal as far as it concerned future disputes.
> 205. With respect to pre-existing disputes, the situation is different and the

---

41 *Phoenix Action Ltd. v. The Czech Republic*, ICSID Case No. ARB/06/5, Award, para. 144 (April 15, 2009).

Tribunal considers that to restructure investments only in order to gain jurisdiction under a BIT for such disputes would constitute, to take the words of the Phoenix Tribunal, 'an abusive manipulation of the system of international investment protection under the ICSID Convention and the BITs'.[42]

Among the questions that must be asked to determine whether a nationality change is 'legitimate corporate planning' or an abuse of rights is that of when the 'dispute' arose. This poses particularly interesting questions because a deterioration in the investor-host relationship often happens over a period of months or years. Creeping violations are particularly difficult to assess, as the parties may differ on whether multiple host actions were a series of disputes or a single dispute. Here, 'the critical element [. . .] is whether or not they concern the same subject matter', that is, 'whether or not the facts or considerations that gave rise to the earlier dispute continued to be central to the later dispute'.[43]

Where a claim is based on the failure of a host to act, determining when the inaction began can be particularly complicated. The following case is an example of how the commencement of a dispute can be assessed in a context of multiple actions and inactions.

 CASE

Pac Rim Cayman LLC v. The Republic of El Salvador[44]

Pacific Rim Mining Corporation is a Canadian corporation with several subsidiaries in El Salvador. Located east of the capital, explorations for the El Dorado project began in 2002 by Pac Rim Cayman. The wholly owned subsidiary of Pacific Rim Mining incorporated in the Cayman Islands discovered gold and mineral deposits two years later. Upon these discoveries, the company applied to the government for environmental permits and a licence to exploit these deposits.

Over the course of the next three years, the El Salvadoran government refused to respond to the application. The company reincorporated itself as a US corporation on 13 December 2007, allegedly as a cost-reduction

---

42 *Venezuela Holdings BV et al. v. The Bolivarian Republic of Venezuela*, ICSID Case No. ARB/07/27, Decision on Jurisdiction (June 10, 2010).

43 *Empresas Lucchetti SA and Lucchetti Peru SA v. The Republic of Peru*, ICSID Case No. ARB/03/4, Award, para. 50 (Feb. 7, 2005); *Tidewater Inc., et al. v. The Bolivarian Republic of Venezuela*, ICSID Case No. ARB/10/5, Decision on Jurisdiction, para. 149 (Feb. 8, 2013).

44 *Pac Rim Cayman LLC v. The Republic of El Salvador*, ICSID Case No. ARB/09/12, Decision on the Respondent's Jurisdictional Objections (June 1, 2012). Available at: http://italaw.com/documents/PacRimDecisiononJurisdiction.pdf; footnotes omitted.

measure. Moreover, at the time of this restructuring, the company claimed, it was still optimistic about its chances of succeeding in its application requests.

On 11 March 2008, the president of the country announced publicly that he opposed granting Pac Rim Cayman any mining permits. According to the claimant, it was only then that their dispute arose (although the mistreatment of their investment had begun earlier). They brought a claim in the ICSID under the provisions of the Central American Free Trade Agreement (CAFTA) and under El Salvadoran national law.

El Salvador denied the tribunal's jurisdiction for the CAFTA claim. The dispute with Pac Rim, it argued, began before December 2007. As a result, the investor did not have the requisite nationality at the time the dispute arose. While nationality-planning on its own is acceptable, in this case, using the change to provide for jurisdiction over an existing dispute was an act of abuse of process.

> The Tribunal finds as a relevant fact, based on the Claimant's own evidential materials, that one of the principal purposes of the change in the Claimant's nationality was the access thereby gained to the protection of investment rights under CAFTA and its procedure for international arbitration available against the Respondent. [. . .]
>
> 2.43. That, however, is not a sufficient answer to determine the issue of Abuse of Process in this case. [. . .]
>
> 2.44. At the outset, the Tribunal subscribes to the general approach set out in the decision made in *Mobil v. Venezuela*:
>
>> *'The Tribunal first observes that in all systems of law, whether domestic or international, there are concepts framed in order to avoid misuse of the law. Reference may be made in this respect to "good faith" ("bonne foi"), "détournement de pouvoir" (misuse of power) or "abus de droit" (abuse of right).'*
>
> 2.45. The Claimant's restructuring consisted of its change of nationality on 13 December 2007. To adopt the tribunal's approach in *Mobil v. Venezuela*, '(s)uch restructuring could be "legitimate corporate planning" as contended by the Claimant or an "abuse of right" as submitted by the Respondent. It depends upon the circumstances in which it happened.'
>
> [. . .]
>
> 2.47. The Tribunal does not dispute (nor did the Respondent) that if a corporate restructuring affecting a claimant's nationality was made in good faith before the occurrence of any event or measure giving rise to a later dispute, that restructuring should not be considered as an abuse of process. That is not, however, the issue in the present case [. . .]

[. . .]

2.52. [. . . I]n order to determine whether the Claimant's change of nationality was or was not an abuse of process, the Tribunal must first ascertain whether the relevant measure(s) or practice, which (as the Claimant allege) caused damage to its investments from March 2008 onwards, took place before or after the change in nationality on 13 December 2007. This approach in turn requires the Tribunal to ascertain the legal nature of the relevant measure(s) or practice alleged by the Claimant.

2.53. *The Relevant Measure(s) or Practice:* In order to identify these measures or practice, the Tribunal must necessarily analyse the Claimant's own pleadings. [. . .]

2.54. [. . .] Starting with the Jurisdiction Counter-Memorial, the emphasis is increasingly placed by the Claimant on the alleged de facto ban publicly disclosed in President Saca's speech.

2.55. At this early stage, the Claimant based its pleaded case on the allegation that the Respondent had taken precise *measures* (in the plural) that improperly refused to grant [. . .] an exploitation concession and to deliver [. . .] environmental permits. [. . .]

[. . .]

2.58. [. . .] the Tribunal treats the Claimant's pleaded case as alleging a practice by the Respondent which came to the Claimant's knowledge only with President Saca's reported speech in March 2008, which practice is alleged to consist of either a continuing or composite act in breach of CAFTA and for which the Claimant claims damages only from March 2008 onwards. The Tribunal accepts that a governmental practice, by definition, has necessarily to comprise a multiplicity of pre or co-existing acts or omissions. It is necessary to ascertain the legal nature and timing of such a practice where a claimant's pleaded allegations are directed both at the acts or omissions themselves and to the practice comprising such acts or omissions, which practice only become known to a claimant at a later date.

2.59. What then is the role of President Saca's speech as now alleged and explained by the Claimant in its pleadings? According to the Claimant, it was not by itself a measure, but it is what made public an alleged pre-existing governmental practice:

> 'This is why President Saca's March 2008 public acknowledgment of the ban is so important. Claimant does not contend that the President's statement is by itself the measure at issue. But the President's statement did provide critical information, given the inherent difficulty in discerning the measure at issue, and as such may be seen as the consummation point of the administration's action and inaction constituting the offending measure at issue in this arbitration.'

2.60. From this and other explanations from the Claimant, it follows that, although the President's speech is not alleged to be a measure by itself, it is the point in time when, according to the Claimant, its dispute with the Respondent arose. It would be possible to use other language to describe the emergence of this dispute, as employed by both Parties in this case (e.g. 'born', 'crystallised' etc); but all these terms convey the same concept; and the Tribunal here prefers substance to semantics.

2.61. However, in the Tribunal's view, it is necessary as a matter of international law (being applicable to the Claimant's CAFTA claims) to distinguish between President's Saca's speech as the alleged culminating point of a pre-existing practice and the effective beginning of a practice causing injury to the Claimant and its Enterprises. [. . .].

[. . .]

2.66. The question of identifying precisely when an internationally wrongful act takes place is often a difficult factual question; it has important consequences on the law of international responsibility; and, as far as it concerns investment arbitration under a treaty, it can directly affect (as here) the exercise of jurisdiction by a tribunal.

2.67. In any particular case, three different situations can arise: (i) a measure is a 'one-time act', that is an act completed at a precise moment, such as, for example, a nationalisation decree which is completed at the date of that decree; or (ii) it is a 'continuous' act, which is the same act that continues as long as it is in violation of rules in force, such as a national law in violation of an international obligation of the State; or, (iii) it is a 'composite' act, that is an act composed of other acts from which it is legally different. These important and well-established distinctions under customary international law are considered in the Commentaries of the ILC Articles on State Responsibility.

2.68. *(i) One-Time Act:* As far as a one-time act is concerned, the ILC Commentaries explain both its instant realisation, at a precise moment in time, and the fact that it can have continuous effects:

> *'The critical distinction for the purpose of article 14 is between a breach which is continuing and one which has already been completed. In accordance with paragraph 1, a completed act occurs "at the moment when the act is performed", even though its effects or consequences may continue. . .'*
>
> *'An act does not have a continuing character merely because its consequences extend in time.'*

Based on such a definition, it is relatively easy to determine the moment when a measure takes place as a one-time act.

2.69. *(ii) Continuous Act:* In contrast, a continuous act is the same act extending throughout a period of time, as also explained in the ILC Commentaries:

> *'In accordance with paragraph 2, a continuing wrongful act, on the other hand, occupies the entire period during which the act continues and remains not in conformity with the international obligation, provided that the State is bound by the international obligation during that period.'*

2.70. *(iii) Composite Act:* Finally, a composite act is not the same, single act extending over a period of time, but is composed of a series of different acts that extend over that period; or, in other words, a composite act results from an aggregation of other acts and acquires a different legal characterisation from those other acts, as described in the ILC Commentaries:

> 'Composite acts give rise to continuing breaches, which extend in time from the first of the actions or omissions in the series of acts making up the wrongful conduct. Composite acts covered by article 15 are limited to breaches of obligations which concern some aggregate of conduct and not individual acts as such. In other words, their focus is "a series of acts or omissions defined in aggregate as wrongful."'
>
> 'Only after a series of actions or omissions takes place will the composite act be revealed, not merely as a succession of isolated acts, but as a composite act, i.e. an act defined in aggregate as wrongful.'

2.71. The fact that a composite act is composed of acts that are legally different from the composite act itself means that the composite act can comprise legal acts and still be unlawful or that it can comprise unlawful acts violating certain norms which are different from the legal norm violated by the composite act. For example, several legal acts (of which each by itself is not unlawful) can become unlawful as the composite aggregation of those legal acts; or a series of unlawful acts interfering with an investment (which by themselves are not expropriatory) can by their aggregation result in an unlawful expropriation.

2.72. Was the relevant measure in the present case, as alleged by the Claimant, a continuous act or a composite act? This is important, if the continuous or composite act extends over a critical date, here the Claimant's change of nationality on 13 December 2007.

2.73. As regards a continuing act, the ILC Commentaries state the following:

> 'Thus, conduct which has commenced sometime in the past, and which constituted (or, if the relevant primary rule had been in force for the State at the time, would have constituted) a breach at that time, can continue and give rise to a continuing wrongful act in the present.'

In this situation, the unlawful act only starts when the rule which this act violates is applicable.

2.74. As regards a composite act, the ILC Commentaries state the following:

> 'In cases where the relevant obligation did not exist at the beginning of the course of conduct but came into being thereafter, the "first" of the actions or omissions of the series for the purposes of State responsibility will be the first occurring after the obligation came into existence.
>
> Paragraph 1 of article 15 defines the time at which a composite act "occurs" as the time at which the last action or omission occurs . . .'

In this situation, the unlawful composite act is composed of aggregated acts and takes place at a time when the last of these acts occurs and violates (in aggregate) the applicable rule.

2.75. *Application to this Case:* Having here set out the relevant general principles of international law, the Tribunal turns to the present case, as pleaded by the Claimant and disputed by the Respondent.

2.76. *The Respondent's Submission:* In summary, the Respondent submits that the relevant acts alleged by the Claimant were completed before the change in the Claimant's nationality on 13 December 2007:

[. . .]

2.77. [. . .] The Respondent specifically alleges that: (i) with regard to the environmental permit, [the government] did not meet the time limit established under Salvadoran law to either issue or deny the environmental permit by December 2004 (i.e. three years before the Claimant's change of nationality); and (ii) with regard to the exploitation concession filed with the Bureau of Mines, once the Bureau of Mines sent the two warning letters to the Claimant in October and December 2006 triggering the provisions of Article 38 of the Mining Law, that application was effectively terminated; nothing more could have been done by the Claimant after the expiration of the 30-day extension to revive it; and, therefore, such application should be treated as having been effectively terminated under the laws of the Respondent by January 2007 (i.e. one year before the Claimant's change of nationality).

2.78. *The Claimant's Submission:* In summary, the Claimant alleges that the relevant measure was the de facto mining ban consisting of a practice of withholding mining-related permits and concessions which only became public and known to the Claimant in March 2008 (with President Saca's speech); and which then wiped out the value of its mining investments and nullified its legitimate expectations and other protections under CAFTA, thereby giving rise to its present dispute with the Respondent.

[The tribunal analyses the situation as a one-time act and as a composite act, but finds it was neither.]

[. . .]

2.89. *Continuous Act:* Can the alleged practice be characterised as a continuous act, as also pleaded by the Claimant? If the Tribunal were to determine that there was a continuous act in this case, only that portion of the continuous act taking place after the change of nationality on 13 December 2007 could be considered by the Tribunal for the purpose of engaging possible responsibility by the Respondent

[. . .]

2.90. As regards this question, the Claimant explained that:

> '. . . (w)hile the ban may have come into existence at some earlier point in time, it continued to exist after Pac Rim Cayman acquired its U.S. nationality in December 2007, which is when CAFTA became applicable to measures relating to Pac Rim Cayman.'

2.91. The Tribunal also bears in mind that the Claimant pleads that the alleged unlawful practice by the Respondent is a negative practice not to grant any mining application, i.e. it allegedly comprises omissions to act and not positive acts; and that, consequently, it is difficult to give a precise date for such omissions (compared to a specific positive act). Once an act takes place, it affects the parties' legal position; but, in contrast, an omission to act does not necessarily affect the parties as long as it is not definitive; and an omission can remain non-definitive throughout a period during which it could be cured by a positive act. As determined above by the Tribunal, although there were deadlines fixed under Salvadoran law for the granting of the permits and the concession, the Claimant understood that the Salvadoran authorities themselves did not treat these deadlines as definitive deadlines after which permits or concessions could no longer be granted to the Claimant at all.

2.92. In the Tribunal's view, on the particular facts of this case as pleaded by the Claimant, an omission that extends over a period of time and which, to the reasonable understanding of the relevant party, did not seem definitive should be considered as a continuous act under international law. The legal nature of the omission did not change over time: the permits and the concession remained non-granted. The controversy began with a problem over the non-granting of the permits and concession; and it remained a controversy over a practice of not granting the mining permits and concession.

[. . .]

2.94. Accordingly, the Tribunal determines that the alleged de facto ban should be considered as a continuing act under international law, which: (i) started at a certain moment of time after the Claimant's request for environmental permits and an exploitation concession but before the Claimant's change of nationality in December 2007; and (ii) continued after December 2007, being publicly acknowledged by President's Saca speech in March 2008; or, in other words, that the alleged practice continued after the Claimant's change of nationality on 13 December 2007.

2.95. *Legal Consequences:* What then are the legal consequences of the existence of an alleged continuous act overlapping the Claimant's change of nationality?

[. . .]

2.96. *Abuse of Process:* The Tribunal [. . .] considers the point in time when a change of nationality can become an abuse of process. Several different answers were suggested by the Parties as the crucial dividing-line: (i) where facts at the root of a later dispute have already taken place and that future dispute is foreseen or reasonably foreseeable; (ii) where facts have taken place giving rise to an actual dispute; and (iii) where facts have taken place giving rise to an actual dispute referable under the parties' relevant arbitration agreement.

[. . .]

2.99. [. . .] In the Tribunal's view, the dividing-line occurs when the relevant party can see an actual dispute or can foresee a specific future dispute as a very high probability and not merely as a possible controversy. In the Tribunal's view, before that dividing-line is reached, there will be ordinarily no abuse of process; but after that dividing-line is passed, there ordinarily will be. The answer in each case will, however, depend upon its particular facts and circumstances, as in this case. As already indicated above, the Tribunal is here more concerned with substance than semantics; and it recognises that, as a matter of practical reality, this dividing-line will rarely be a thin red line, but will include a significant grey area.

2.100. To this extent, the Tribunal accepts the Respondent's general submission that: '. . . it is clearly an abuse for an investor to manipulate the nationality of a shell company subsidiary to gain jurisdiction under an international treaty at a time when the investor is aware that events have occurred that negatively affect its investment and may lead to arbitration.' [. . .]

[. . .]

2.107. In the Tribunal's view, the relevant date for deciding upon the Abuse of Process issue must necessarily be earlier in time than the date for deciding the Ratione Temporis issue. Where the alleged practice is a continuous act (as concluded above by the Tribunal), this means that the practice started before the Claimant's change of nationality and continued after such change. This analysis would found the basis of the Tribunal's jurisdiction ratione temporis under CAFTA; but it would preclude the exercise of such jurisdiction on the basis of abuse of process if the Claimant had changed its nationality during that continuous practice knowing of an actual or specific future dispute, thus manipulating the process under CAFTA and the ICSID Convention in bad faith to gain unwarranted access to international arbitration.

[. . .]

2.109. As unequivocally explained at the Hearing on several occasions, the Claimant's alleged measure, the de facto ban forming the legal and factual basis pleaded for its CAFTA claims, must be understood by the Tribunal as a continuous act relevant for the Claimant's claims for compensation from March 2008 onwards (not before); that, as such, it became known to the Claimant only from the public report of President Saca's speech on 11 March 2008; and that, also as such, it was not known to or foreseen by the Claimant before 13 December 2007 as an actual or specific future dispute with the Respondent under CAFTA.

(08) Decisions

2.110. For these reasons, [. . .] the Tribunal determines that the change in the Claimant's nationality on 13 December 2007, on all the evidential materials adduced by the Parties in these proceedings, is not proven to have been an abuse of process precluding the exercise of the Tribunal's jurisdiction to determine such claims under CAFTA and the ICSID Convention; and the Tribunal therefore rejects the Respondent's case on the Abuse of Process issue.

[The tribunal, however, ultimately determines that the denial of benefits clause of the CAFTA precluded Claimants' CAFTA-based claims. The Non-CAFTA claims were allowed to proceed.]

d   Consent to arbitrate

Beyond the legal issues of the temporal aspects of jurisdiction are the questions of whether the host has given its consent to arbitrate.

Unlike a judicial proceeding, where respondents can be required to appear for a hearing, arbitration is based on the willingness of both parties to resolve their differences before a third decision-maker. If one party does not agree to a third party arbitrator, it cannot be made to submit to arbitration. Thus, the requirement of consent is of critical importance: if there is no consent to be involved in an arbitration, the arbitrators have no authority to hear the claims.

d.i   Consent of the investor-complainant

Under the ICSID rules, both parties to a dispute must give written consent to an investor-State arbitration. Garnering consent of the investor generally does not pose legal difficulties: as claimant, the investor's consent is indicated by its filing of a claim with the ICSID Secretariat.

d.ii   Consent of the host state respondent

Ensuring the state's consent is often less straightforward. As sovereigns, states are not generally subjected to judicial procedures without having granted authority to be taken to court to resolve a particular dispute. The practice of international law, however, witnesses states increasingly obliging themselves to submit to the jurisdiction of international decision-making tribunals.

In investment law, too, ICSID's investor-State arbitration mechanism allows for a state to give consent with or without privity[45]—the consent given by the respondent can be made in general as well as specifically to the claimant. Significantly, though, membership in the ICSID alone does not lend consent to arbitration (or conciliation). The state must provide written consent in a separate legal instrument to be within the jurisdiction of the tribunal.

---

45 The phrase 'arbitration without privity' has become a well-known reference to this general giving of consent. *See* Paulsson, *supra* note 9 (describing 'arbitration without privity' as arbitration 'where the claimant need not have a contractual relationship with the defendant and where the tables could not be turned').

Where to find host's consent

There are various ways a state can consent to arbitration. One source of consent to arbitrate is a contract between the parties to the dispute. There can be a consent provision in the investment contract which functions as an agreement to submit any future disputes to arbitration. The ICSID provides a model clause to assist investors and hosts in the drafting of such a provision:

> The [Government]/[*name of constituent subdivision or agency*] of *name of Contracting State* (hereinafter the 'Host State') and *name of investor* (hereinafter the 'Investor') hereby consent to submit to the International Centre for Settlement of Investment Disputes (hereinafter the 'Centre') any dispute arising out of or relating to this agreement for settlement by [conciliation]/[arbitration]/ [conciliation followed, if the dispute remains unresolved within *time limit* of the communication of the report of the Conciliation Commission to the parties, by arbitration] pursuant to the Convention on the Settlement of Investment Disputes between States and Nationals of Other States (hereinafter the 'Convention').[46]

If the investor's activities with the host are contained in several contracts, a compromissory clause in one is likely to be extended to the related contracts as well. Alternatively, the investor and the host could contract a *compromis*, an agreement to submit past disputes to arbitration. There, the provision would give explicit consent to the arbitral tribunal to hear and decide the matter. Again, an ICSID model clause is available:

> The [Government]/[*name of constituent subdivision or agency*] of name of Contracting State (hereinafter the 'Host State') and *name of investor* (hereinafter the 'Investor') hereby consent to submit to the International Centre for Settlement of Investment Disputes (hereinafter the 'Centre') for settlement by [conciliation]/ [arbitration]/[conciliation followed, if the dispute remains unresolved within *time limit* of the communication of the report of the Conciliation Commission to the parties, by arbitration] pursuant to the Convention on the Settlement of Investment Disputes between States and Nationals of Other States, the following dispute arising out of the investment described below:[47]

National legislation is a second source for state consent (functions as an offer) to arbitrate. Investment codes, for example, may specify that claims by investors against the state may be brought to a particular institution or to ad hoc arbitration. It cannot be said that the mention of an arbitral forum in

---

46 *Basic Submission Clauses*, http://icsid.worldbank.org/ICSID/StaticFiles/model-clauses-en/7.htm.
47 *Id.*

itself establishes standing consent, but such an offer may be implicit in the wording of the provision.[48]

Importantly, with legislative consent, the state may unilaterally revoke its offer to consent to arbitration prior to the investor's acceptance of the offer. As the investor accepts the offer to arbitrate by beginning the arbitration, if the host revokes its offer before the investor makes a claim, the consent will need to be found elsewhere if the case is going to proceed.

Very often an IIA provision will function as an offer to arbitrate. The US Model BIT, for example, contains a separate article titled 'Consent of Each Party to Arbitration':

1. Each Party consents to the submission of a claim to arbitration under this Section in accordance with this Treaty.
2. The consent under paragraph 1 and the submission of a claim to arbitration under this Section shall satisfy the requirements of:
    a. Chapter II of the ICSID Convention[49]

While consent is not offered by virtue of the BIT merely mentioning the possibility of investor-State arbitration (language such as 'shall consider submitting to the jurisdiction of the Centre' is not an offer of consent), as is the case with national legislation, explicit or implicit offers of consent may be found in the content of the dispute settlement provisions.

Not all consent provisions give unlimited consent, either. A state can offer consent to arbitrate only certain issues arising under the agreement (China, for example, limits its standing consent to issues regarding expropriation com-

---

48 The Venezuelan national law on foreign investment contains a dispute settlement provision that is ambiguous as to consent to ICSID jurisdiction. Article 22 states: 'Las controversias que surjan entre un inversionista internacional, cuyo país de origen tenga vigente con Venezuela un tratado o acuerdo sobre promoción y protección de inversiones, o las controversias respecto de las cuales sean aplicables las disposiciones del Convenio Constitutivo del Organismo Multilateral de Garantía de Inversiones (OMGI-MIGA) o del Convenio sobre Arreglo de Diferencias Relativas a Inversiones entre Estados y Nacionales de Otros Estados (CIADI), serán sometidas al arbitraje internacional en los términos del respectivo tratado o acuerdo, si así éste lo establece, sin perjuicio de la posibilidad de hacer uso, cuando proceda, de las vías contenciosas contempladas en la legislación venezolana vigente'. While the claimant bases its claim on the jurisdiction provided through this provision, the Venezuelan government denies the law gives consent. *See Tidewater et al. v. The Bolivarian Republic of Venezuela*, ICSID Case No. ARB/10/5, Procedural Order No. 1 on Production of Documents, http://italaw. com/sites/default/files/case-documents/ita0861.pdf (tribunal requests more information from Venezuela regarding the legislative intent of Article 22).

49 US Model BIT (2004), art. 25. *See also* US–Uruguay BIT, art. 25 (same language); US–Rwanda BIT, art. 25 (same language).

pensation[50]), include only or exclude certain classes of investments from its consent,[51] or require the prior exhaustion of local remedies before consent will be deemed given (Israel, for example, will only consider giving consent once the investor has attempted to get relief from local courts or administrative authorities[52]). Limitations on consent can be placed in the IIA dispute settlement provision, in an annex to the IIA, or in a notification to the ICSID Convention.

As with legislative consent, the investor can accept a BIT-granted offer of consent by filing a claim. Withdrawal of consent, however, requires a basis in the treaty.

Determining if consent exists

By giving its consent to enter into arbitration with an investor, a host state sacrifices a part of its sovereignty. Given that sovereignty is generally not sacrificed for the interest of private individuals, tribunals have maintained a position of not lightly assuming that consent has been offered.[53] Consent to arbitrate needs to be clearly expressed. The China–Switzerland BIT is a good example of a provision that clearly sets out the parties' consent to submit to arbitration:

(1) For the purpose of solving disputes with respect to investments between a Contracting Party and an investor of the other Contracting Party and without prejudice to Article 12 of this Agreement . . ., consultations will take place between the parties concerned.

(2) If these consultations do not result in a solution within six months . . . the investor may submit the dispute either to the courts . . . or to international arbitration. In the latter event the investor has the choice between either of the following:

    a. the [ICSID] . . .;

    b. or an ad hoc-arbitral tribunal . . .

---

50 *See* ICSID Notification under art. 25(4), 7 January 1993 ('[P]ursuant to Article 25(4) of the Convention, the Chinese Government would only consider submitting to [ICSID] . . . jurisdiction of . . . disputes over compensation resulting from expropriation and nationalization').

51 For example, Papua New Guinea has notified the ICSID that 'it will only consider submitting those disputes to the Centre which are fundamental to the investment itself'. ICSID, Notifications Concerning a Class or Classes of Disputes Which the Contracting State Would or Would Not Consider Submitting to the Jurisdiction of the Centre (Article 25(4)) 14 September 1978.

52 *See* ICSID, Notifications Concerning the Exhaustion of Local Remedies as a Condition of the Contracting State's Consent to Arbitration Under the Convention (Article 26) 22 June 1983.

53 *See*, e.g. *Société Ouest Africaine des Bétons Industriels v. Senegal*, ICSID Case No. ARB/82/1, Award, paras. 4.09–4.56 (Feb. 25, 1988), 6 ICSID Rev.–FILJ 125 (1991).

(3) Each Contracting Party hereby consents to the submission of an investment dispute to international arbitration.
[...].[54]

The United Kingdom–Mexico BIT even has a separate provision on consent.[55] Whereas Article 11 provides the investor with an offer to submit a dispute to arbitration, Article 12 states the following:

Contracting Party Consent

1. Each Contracting Party hereby gives its unconditional consent to the submission of a dispute to international arbitration.
2. The consent under paragraph 1 above and the submission of a claim to arbitration by the disputing investor shall satisfy the requirements of:

   (a) Chapter II of the ICSID Convention (Jurisdiction of the Centre) and the ICSID Additional Facility Rules for written consent of the disputing parties; and
   (b) Article II of the United Nations Convention on the Recognition and the Enforcement of Foreign Arbitral Awards ('New York Convention') for an 'agreement in writing'.

Not all grants of consent to arbitrate are explicit. Some are implicit but still clear. For example, the Germany–Botswana BIT says, '[i]f the divergency cannot be settled within six months . . ., it shall, at the request of the national or company of the other Contracting State, be submitted for arbitration'.[56]

The wording of other provisions, can leave it unclear whether the consent to the specific forum (ICSID, for example) has been definitively given or if the consent was simply to arbitrate. In the latter case, an ICSID tribunal could not claim jurisdiction absent further agreement by the host.

If a claimant argues that implied consent exists and the host disputes this claim, the tribunal must determine whether a particular clause that mentions investor-state arbitration is truly a granting of consent or whether it is merely a mention of a possibility that could be offered in the future. Various cases

---

54 Agreement between the Swiss Federal Council and the Government of the People's Republic of China on the Promotion and Reciprocal Protection of Investments (done 27 January 2009), art. 11.

55 Agreement between the Government of the United Kingdom of Great Britain and Northern Ireland and the Government of the United Mexican States for the Promotion and Reciprocal Protection of Investments (25 July 2007).

56 Treaty between the Federal Republic of Germany and the Republic of Botswana Concerning the Encouragement and Reciprocal Protection of Investments (done 23 May 2000), art. 11.2.

have stated this principle, but its application relies completely on the specific wording of the relevant law. In *SPP v. Egypt*[57] the tribunal found that the following compromissory clause didn't need any 'further ad hoc manifestation of consent to the Centre's jurisdiction and was an offer to arbitrate before the ICSID'.[58]

> Investment disputes in respect of the implementation of the provisions of this Law shall be settled in a manner to be agreed upon with the investor, or within the framework of the agreements in force between the Arab Republic of Egypt and the investor's home country, or within the framework of the Convention for the Settlement of Investment Disputes between the State and the nationals of the other countries to which Egypt has adhered by virtue of Law No. 90 of 1971, where such Convention applies.[59]

In several of the numerous cases against Venezuela, on the other hand, the tribunals have found that the national investment legislation provision on arbitration does not grant consent to ICSID, despite the mention of that institution in the text. The English translation of Venezuela's Foreign Investment Law, Article 22 provides:

> Disputes arising between an international investor whose country of origin has in effect with Venezuela a treaty or agreement on the promotion and protection of investments, or disputes to which are applicable the provision of the Convention Establishing the Multilateral Investment Guarantee Agency [. . .] or [ICSID], shall be submitted to international arbitration according to the terms of the respective treaty or agreement, if it so provides, without prejudice to the possibility of making use, when appropriate, of the dispute resolution means provided for under the Venezuelan legislation in effect.

Interpreting this language using the Vienna Convention Article 31 principles has led arbitrators to determine that the ambiguous wording and the government's reluctance at the time of drafting to bind themselves to international arbitration procedures meant that no consent could be imputed.[60]

---

57 *Southern Pacific Properties (Middle East) Ltd. v. Arab Republic of Egypt*, ICSID Case No. ARB/84/3, Decision on Jurisdiction I (Nov. 27, 1985), 3 ICSID Reports 112 (1995) [hereinafter '*SPP v. Egypt*'].
58 *Id.*, paras. 89–101.
59 *Id.*, para. 70.
60 *See*, e.g. *Mobile Corp., et al. v. The Bolivarian Republic of Venezuela*, ICSID Case No. ARB/07/27, Decision on Jurisdiction, paras. 97–141 (June 10, 2010); *Cemex Caracas Investments BV and Cemex Caracas II Investments BV v. Bolivarian Republic of Venezuela*, ICSID Case No. ARB/08/15, Decision on Jurisdiction, para. 90–138 (Jan. 10, 2010).

Limits on consent

As mentioned above, when a state gives consent to arbitrate, it has the possibility of limiting the extent of its grant. Limited consent can be in the form of offering consent only for particular provisions of the IIA or of explicitly excluding arbitration on certain classes of claims. A government may, for example, offer ISDS only for disputes about compensation for expropriations. The China-Bahrain BIT illustrates such a limitation:

> The dispute on the amount of compensation resulting from nationalization and expropriation, if unable to be settled within five months [. . .], shall be submitted at the request of either party to: (a) [ICSID]; or (b) an ad hoc arbitral tribunal.[61]

Consultation periods

Investor-State dispute settlement aims to resolve disputes. Thus, many IIAs will explicitly support non-adversarial attempts at resolution of differences. Having the disputants sit down and talk with one another is often all it takes to resolve the problem. Thus, mandatory consultations are a frequent feature of IIAs.

Consent provisions may therefore contain a requirement of consultations taking place for a minimum number of months prior to beginning arbitration. The following is an example from the Finland–South Africa BIT:

> (1) Disputes between an investor of one Contracting Party and the host Party relating to an investment by an investor of the former Contracting Party in the territory of the host Party should be settled amicably.
>
> (2) If such a dispute cannot thus be settled within a period of six months from the date at which either party to the dispute requested amicable settlement, the investor may submit the case [to ICSID or to an ad hoc tribunal].[62]

Despite the clear and mandatory text of such provisions, their legal nature has spurred the discussion among commentators and arbitrators. Several tribunals contend that minimal waiting times are procedural rules that can be waived by the tribunal at its discretion.[63] Others view waiting

---

61 Agreement between the Government of the People's Republic of China the Government of the State of Bahrain Concerning the Encouragement and Reciprocal Protection of Investment, Article 9.3 (June 17, 1999).
62 The Government of the Republic of Finland and the Government of the Republic of South Africa on the Promotion and Reciprocal Protection of Investments, Article 8 (Oct. 3, 1999).
63 For example, *Ronald S. Lauder v. Czech Republic*, UNCITRAL Arbitration, Final Award, para. 187 (Sept. 3, 2001), http://italaw.com/documents/LauderAward.pdf ('Arbitral Tribunal considers that this requirement of a six-month waiting period of Article VI(3)(a) of the Treaty is not a jurisdictional provision, i.e. a limit set to the authority of the Arbitral Tribunal to decide on the merits of the dispute, but a procedural rule that must be satisfied by the Claimant'); *SGS Société Générale de Surveillance S.A. v. Islamic Republic of Pakistan*, ICSID

periods as conditions of jurisdiction *ratione materiae*: if a claimant has not waited the minimum time stated in the treaty provision, the tribunal has no competence to hear the case.[64] The following tribunal gives a good analysis of the significance of each of the positions and modifies the 'merely procedural' attitude of some earlier awards. It ultimately finds that compliance with consultation provisions is necessary to establish a tribunal's jurisdiction.

 CASE

Murphy Exploration and Production Co. International v. Republic of Ecuador[65]

140. Murphy international contends that '. . . the failure to comply with a waiting period is not a bar to jurisdiction.' It further claims that '[t]he majority of ICSID tribunals addressing this issue have taken the position that waiting periods constitute procedural, rather than jurisdictional requirements.'

141. Claimant seems to assert that the requirements prescribed in certain rules (the 'jurisdictional') are of a category such that its non-compliance leads to the lack of competence of the tribunal hearing the dispute. Instead, the 'procedural requirements,' can be breached without having any consequence whatsoever. The Tribunal does not share this view.

142. The Tribunal also does not accept the consequences Claimant seeks to derive between 'procedural' and 'jurisdictional' requirements. According to Murphy International, 'procedural requirements' are of an inferior category than the 'jurisdictional requirements' and, consequently, its non-compliance has no legal consequences. It is evident that in legal practice this does not occur, and that noncompliance with a purely procedural requirement, such as, for example, the time to appeal a judgment, can have serious consequences for the defaulting party.

Case No. ARB/01/13, Award on Jurisdiction, para. 184 (Aug. 6, 2003), http://italaw.com/documents/ SGSvPakistan-decision_000.pdf ('Tribunals have generally tended to treat consultation periods as directory and procedural rather than as mandatory and jurisdictional in nature. Compliance with such a requirement is, accordingly, not seen as amounting to a condition precedent for the vesting of jurisdiction').

64 *Enron Corporation and Ponderosa Assets, LP v. Argentine Republic*, ICSID Case No. ARB/01/3, Decision on Jurisdiction, para. 88 (Jan. 14, 2004), http://italaw.com/documents/Enron-Jurisdiction_000.pdf ('the six month negotiation . . . is in the view of the Tribunal very much a jurisdictional one. A failure to comply with that requirement would result in a determination of lack of jurisdiction'). *See also* Muthucumaraswamy Sornarajah, The International Law on Foreign Investment 320 (third edn, 2011) (referring to 'negotiations' in his section on jurisdiction *ratione materiae*).

65 *Murphy Exploration and Production Co. International v. Republic of Ecuador*, ICSID Case No. ARB/08/4, Award on Jurisdiction (Dec. 15, 2010). Available at: http://italaw.com/documents/MurphyExplorationand ProductionCompanyJurisdiction.pdf; footnotes omitted.

143. Article 31 of the Vienna Convention on the Law of Treaties, which contains the general rules of interpretation, provides as follows in paragraph 1:

'A treaty shall be interpreted in good faith in accordance with the ordinary meaning to be given to the terms of the treaty in their context and in the light of its object and purpose.'

144. In accordance with that text, it is not possible to ignore the existence of the norms contained in Article VI of the BIT, regarding the obligation of the parties to attempt negotiations in order to resolve their disputes and the impossibility to resort to ICSID before the six-month term has elapsed.

145. Claimant's interpretation of Article VI of the BIT simply ignores the existence of provisions mandating the parties to have consultations and negotiations to resolve their disputes (paragraph 2) and preventing them from resorting to ICSID before six months have elapsed from the date on which the dispute arose (paragraph 3).

146. The Tribunal's interpretation of paragraph 3 of Article VI is that in order for the investor ('the company or national concerned') to request that its claim be resolved by an ICSID arbitral tribunal, the following two circumstances shall be present:

a) that it has not submitted the dispute to the courts or to any dispute resolution proceeding; and

b) that 'six months have elapsed from the date on which the dispute arose', during which the concerned party sought to resolve it through consultation and negotiation.

147. The tribunal in the *Lauder* case concluded that the six-month waiting period '. . . is not a jurisdictional provision, *i.e.* a limit set to the authority of the Arbitral Tribunal to decide on the merits of the dispute, but rather a procedural rule that must be satisfied by the Claimant. . . .' That tribunal however, does not decide what happens if claimant does not comply with such obligation. It is contrary to the fundamental rules of interpretation to state that while it constitutes a 'procedural rule that must be satisfied by the claimant', non-compliance does not have any consequence whatsoever. Such a way of interpreting the obligation simply ignores the 'object and the purpose' of the rule, which is contrary to Article 31(1) of the aforementioned Vienna Convention.

148. Similarly, the *SGS v. Pakistan* tribunal held that '. . . Tribunals have generally tended to treat consultation periods as directory and procedural rather than as mandatory and jurisdictional in nature.' This Tribunal cannot agree with that statement which implies that, even though there is an explicit treaty requirement, the investor may decide whether or not to comply with it as it deems fit.

149. This Tribunal finds the requirement that the parties should seek to resolve their dispute through consultation and negotiation for a six-month period does not constitute, as Claimant and some arbitral tribunals have stated, 'a procedural

rule' or a 'directory and procedural' rule which can or cannot be satisfied by the concerned party. To the contrary, it constitutes a fundamental requirement that Claimant must comply with, compulsorily, before submitting a request for arbitration under the ICSID rules.

150. This was recognized by the tribunal which resolved the jurisdictional issues in the arbitration brought by Burlington Resources Inc., which held that:

'. . . by imposing upon investors an obligation to voice their disagreement at least six months prior to the submission of an investment dispute to arbitration, the Treaty effectively accords host States the right to be informed about the dispute at least six months before it is submitted to arbitration. The purpose of this right is to grant the host State an *opportunity* to redress the problem before the investor submits the dispute to arbitration. In this case, Claimant has deprived the host State of that opportunity. That suffices to defeat jurisdiction.'

151. With the goal to '. . . promote greater economic cooperation' and stimulate 'the flow of private capital and the economic development', as stated in the preamble of the BIT, as well as to create a harmonious relationship between the investors and States, the Governments who signed that Treaty and those signing similar ones, enshrined the six-month negotiation period requirement. The purpose of such requirement is that during this 'cooling-off period', the parties should attempt to resolve their disputes amicably, without resorting to arbitration or litigation, which generally makes future business relationships difficult. It is not an inconsequential procedural requirement but rather a key component of the legal framework established in the BIT and in many other similar treaties, which aims for the parties to attempt to amicably settle the disputes that might arise resulting of the investment made by a person or company of the Contracting Party in the territory of the another State.

152. In its Memorial on Objections to Jurisdiction, Ecuador makes reference to the *Enron v. Argentina* case in which, although the Tribunal found that the waiting period provision in the US–Argentina BIT (which is practically identical to the one contained in the US–Ecuador BIT) had been complied with, it held that:

'. . . the Tribunal wishes to note in this matter, however, that the conclusion reached is not because the six-month negotiation could be a procedural and not a jurisdictional requirement as has been argued by the Claimants and affirmed by other tribunals. Such requirement is in the view of the Tribunal very much a jurisdictional one. A failure to comply with that requirement would result in a determination of lack of jurisdiction.'

153. Claimant minimizes the importance of the *Enron* tribunal's findings and considers it as *obiter dicta*. This Tribunal does not share that view and finds that,

contrary to Murphy International's opinion, the *Enron* tribunal wanted to include that statement in its Decision precisely because of the importance it attributed to the issue, even though the waiting period having been complied with in that case, it was not essential to resolve the issue on jurisdiction.

154. The tribunal in *SGS v. Pakistan* held that '. . . it does not appear consistent with the need for orderly and cost-effective procedure to halt this arbitration at this juncture and require the Claimant first to consult with the Respondent before re-submitting the Claimant's BIT claims to this Tribunal'. Claimant raises this same argument in its letter dated April 30, 2010, which has already been cited. This Tribunal finds that rationale totally unacceptable: it is not about a mere formality, which allows for the submission of a request for arbitration although the six-month waiting period requirement has not been met, and if the other party objects to it, withdraws and resubmits it. It amounts to something much more serious: an essential mechanism enshrined in many bilateral investment treaties, which compels the parties to make a genuine effort to engage in good faith negotiations before resorting to arbitration.

155. Of course, this Tribunal does not ignore the fact that if both parties cling obstinately to their positions, the possibilities for having a successful negotiation become null. However, there have been many cases in which parties with seemingly irreconcilable points of view at first, manage to reach amicable solutions. To find out if it is possible, they must first try it. Evidently, the way in which Murphy International proceeded in this case prevented Ecuador and Murphy itself from even commencing the negotiations required by the BIT.

156. For the above reasons, the Tribunal rejects Claimant's argument that the six-month waiting period required by Article VI(3)(a) does not constitute a jurisdictional requirement.

157. Based on the statements above, the Tribunal concludes that Murphy International did not comply with the requirements of Article VI of the Bilateral Investment Treaties entered into by the Republic of Ecuador and the United States of America; that such omission constitutes a grave noncompliance, and that because of such noncompliance, this Tribunal lacks competence to hear this case.

Exhaustion of local remedies

Traditional international law requires complainants to go through a domestic court system before pursuing their claims on the international law level. A norm of customary international law of diplomatic protection, the rule ensures that a state has the opportunity to remedy its wrongful actions before being ordered to do so by an international tribunal. Thus, '[b]efore resort may be had to an international court in such a situation, it has been considered necessary that the State where the violation occurred should have an opportunity to redress it by its own means, within the framework of its own domestic legal system'.[66] Failure to exhaust local remedies may be excused only in limited circumstances, such as when resort to the remedy would have no possibility of giving the investor relief.[67]

For investment law, the exhaustion rule would mean that the investor must be able to show that the state courts have refused to remedy its violations of the BIT or contract before it brought the claim to arbitration. Prior to the rise of IIAs, during what Montt calls 'the denial of justice age', a foreign investor could only rely on the protections of state responsibility after national courts had examined the investor's claims of the host's wrongful treatment.[68] The international tribunal's assessment, then, was essentially a review of the host's domestic justice system: 'international law was essentially concerned with the proper administration of justice and adequate maintenance of the *ordre publique . . .* '.[69]

The status of the local exhaustion principle in the current law of investment protection is much less clear. Not only has the status of exhaustion as a custom in investment law been questioned,[70] but investors' reliance on customary law has waned with the growth of IIAs.

Modern BITs often preclude the need for exhaustion of local remedies, permitting an investor to bring its claim directly to international dispute settlement. Clearly, an explicit treaty provision obviating the need for exhaustion can override the customary rule that requires it. But even a general arbitration clause in an IIA, besides offering standing consent, may be interpreted as doing away with the requirement of exhaustion. There is disagreement among commentators and arbitrators on this latter point, however. If the BIT does not explicitly exclude or explicitly require exhaustion, must an investor engage in local court proceedings before it brings its claims to investor-State arbitration? The answer to this question remains open.

---

66 Interhandel Case (*Switzerland v. USA*), Judgment, 1959 ICJ 6, at 27 (Mar. 21).

67 *See* Elettronica Sicula S.p.A. (ELSI) (*United States of America v. Italy*), Judgment, 1989 ICJ 15, at 94 (July 20) (Dissenting Opinion of Judge Schwebel) ('It has . . . long been of the essence of the rule of exhaustion of local remedies that local remedies need not be exhausted where there are no effective remedies to exhaust').

68 Santiago Montt, State Liability in Investment Treaty Arbitration: Global Constitutional and Administrative Law in the BIT Generation 17 (2009).

69 *Id.* at 18.

70 Chittharanjan Felix Amerasinghe, Local Remedies in International Law 7 (second edn, 2004). 75.

In the ICJ's *ELSI* case,[71] a majority found (in the context of Friendship, Commerce and Navigation (FCN) Treaty) that exhaustion is a rule of international law, and without explicit rejection, the requirement remains in place for foreign investors:

> The Chamber has no doubt that the parties to a treaty can therein either agree that the local remedies rule shall not apply to claims based on alleged breaches of that treaty; or confirm that it shall apply. Yet the Chamber finds itself unable to accept that an important principle of customary international law should be held to have been tacitly dispensed with, in the absence of any words making clear an intention to do so.[72]

Whether the general customary rule holds for investment law, however, is a matter upon which arbitrators and scholars disagree.

The ICSID Convention Article 26 states '. . . A Contracting State may require the exhaustion of local administrative or judicial remedies as a condition of its consent to arbitration under this Convention'. Thus, it could be that—at least for ICSID arbitration—investment law forms an exception to the general rule. Several prominent scholars[73] are of the opinion that the exhaustion of local remedies is not necessary if it is not explicitly required by a BIT. Others just as prominent, however, consider the exhaustion of local remedies as necessary if the treaty does not explicitly exclude the requirement in its text.[74]

Note that exhaustion of local remedies provisions do not always require 'exhaustion' in the sense of getting a final decision by the highest court available. Provisions mandating complainants to bring their claims to local courts

---

71 Elettronica Sicula S.p.A. (ELSI) (*U.S. v. It.*), Judgment, 1989 ICJ 15, at 15 (July 20).

72 *Id.* at 42, para. 50. Although in dissent on other issues, Judge Schwebel's opinion emphasizes the majority's position that not every issue must have been pursued locally, but rather that the claimant's exhaustion of the general substance of the claim is sufficient. *See* Elettronica Sicula S.p.A., *supra* n. 71 (Dissenting Opinion of Judge Schwebel) ('where the substance of the issues of a case has been definitively litigated in the courts of a State, the rule does not require that those issues also have been litigated by the presentation of every relevant legal argument which any municipal forum might have been able to pass upon, however unlikely in practice the possibilities of reaching another result were').

73 James Crawford, Treaty and Contract in Investment Arbitration, 24(3) Arb. Int'l 351, 352 (2008) ('. . . there is no requirement of exhaustion of local remedies prior to commencing investment arbitration, unless, exceptionally, that requirement has been expressly maintained'); Rudolf Dolzer and Christoph Schreuer, Principles of International Investment Law, 264-7 (2d edn 2012).

74 Amerasinghe, *supra* note 70, at 6; Jeswald W. Salacuse, The Law of Investment Treaties 386 (2010); Sornarajah, *supra* note 64 at 220. Sornarajah clarifies his position as being limited to arbitration claims alleging the host's violation of an investor's contract; *supra* note 64, at 221. For treaty-based claims, he asserts, there is such an 'established . . . arbitration practice' denying the need for exhaustion 'that it is too late to be contested'. *Id.*

for a minimum period of time are also common in IIAs. The fact that the highest local court may not have issued a decision will not be a bar to the arbitration if the minimum time period has run. The *Wintershall v. Argentina* arbitration explained:

> The plea that Argentina has not conditioned its acceptance of the Centre's jurisdiction and the Tribunal's competence 'upon the prior *exhaustion* of local remedies' may be correct only if the emphasis be on the word '*exhaustion*'. However even that phrase ('exhaustion of local remedies') in the context of BITs is now treated (in UN practice) as including pursuit of time—stipulated remedies in local courts as well. [. . .][75]

Is there a futility exception?
The approach any particular tribunal takes on minimum consultation and local exhaustion obligations is often the same—seeing either each as a jurisdictional issue or each as a question of procedure. Even if a tribunal finds them to be jurisdictional, however, does not mean it will refuse the claimant's claim. This is because the international law on diplomatic protection arguably provides room for a 'futility exception' to the general requirement of local exhaustion.[76]

The *Ambiente Ufficio v. Argentina* tribunal found no reason to declare the relevant BIT's pre-requisites to consent either jurisdictional issues or questions of admissibility.[77] Instead, it focused on whether the failures to adhere to the prerequisites were justified. Finding an absence of a 'realistic chance for meaningful consultations because they have become futile or deadlocked'[78] and a similarly lacking 'reasonable possibility to obtain effective redress from the local courts',[79] the tribunal found that the claimants were justified in proceeding directly to arbitration.

The third tribunal in the series of claims brought by Italian bondholders against Argentina took a further look at the question of whether a claimant who admitted to having filed for arbitration too early could have its claim

---

75 *Wintershall Aktiengesellschaft v. Argentine Republic*, ICSID Case No. ARB/04/14, Award, para. 124 (Dec. 8, 2008). Available at: http://italaw.com/documents/Wintershall.pdf.

76 *See* Julian Davis Mortenson, The Futility Exception to the Exhaustion Requirement: *Apotex v. United States*, Kluwer Arbitration Blog, 25 August 2014 (http://kluwerarbitrationblog.com/2014/08/25/the-futility-exception-to-the-exhaustion-requirement-apotex-v-united-states/).

77 *See Ambiente Ufficio S.P.A. and Others v. The Argentine Republic*, ICSID Case No. ARB/08/9, Decision on Jurisdiction and Admissibility, para. 599 (Feb. 8, 2013).

78 *Id.*, para. 582.

79 *Id.*, para. 603.

heard on the basis of the hopelessness of any pre-arbitration settlement attempts. Rather than focus on the characterization of consultation and local litigation periods as simply jurisdictional or procedural/admissibility questions, the *Alemanni v. Argentina* tribunal emphasized the underlying goal of such provisions: allowing the claimant a local remedy.

 CASE

Giovanni Alemanni et al. v. Argentina[80]

As in the *Abaclat* and *Ambiente* arbitrations, the *Alemanni* case was brought by a number of foreign purchasers of Argentinian sovereign bonds. Argentina again objected to the tribunal's jurisdiction by pointing out that the claimants had not engaged in pre-arbitration dispute resolution for the BIT's prescribed 18 months. The claimant argued that not only did earlier contact with the government forebode failure of negotiations, but that new legislation allegedly forbade the government from engaging in negotiations and a recent Supreme Court decision would prevent lower courts from finding in his favour.

The tribunal, accepting that Argentina's consent was limited, saw this as a limitation on jurisdiction. Nevertheless, it found space to ask whether there was a futility exception to this limitation such that if a complainant could prove consultations would not lead to a mutually acceptable result, such consultations could be foregone.

> 301. The standing Argentine offer to arbitrate is contained in Article 8(3) of the BIT, but is preceded by two paragraphs bearing on the settlement of disputes between an investor and the host State of the investment: under paragraph (1) any dispute shall be resolved through amicable consultations 'insofar as possible'; under paragraph (2) if these consultations do not lead to a resolution, the dispute 'may be submitted' to a competent administrative or judicial process of the host State. This leads on to paragraph (3), under the first part of which 'If a dispute still exists between investors and a Contracting Party, after a period of 18 months has elapsed since notification of the commencement of the proceeding before the national jurisdictions indicated in paragraph (2), the dispute may be submitted to international arbitration', which is then completed by the second part of the paragraph under which each Contracting Party gives 'its advance and irrevocable consent' to arbitration. On its face therefore Article 8 sets up three prior steps

---

80 *Giovanni Alemanni and Others v. Argentine Republic*, ICSID Case No. ARB/07/08, Decision on Jurisdiction and Admissibility (Nov. 17, 2014) (footnotes omitted).

before opening the way to arbitration: amicable consultations—then domestic proceedings—then 18 months.

[. . .]

311. [. . .] On the one hand, it cannot be supposed that two sophisticated governments could have intended that foreign investors be required to begin an action before the local courts or administrative authorities just for show. The underlying assumption must logically have been that the local courts or administrative authorities would be in a position to pronounce a definitive and binding solution to the dispute; that much is evident from the opening words of Article 8(3) with their obvious implication that, within the specified time period, the dispute might have ceased to 'exist'. On the other hand, the specification of the time period itself shows unambiguously, to the mind of the Tribunal, that the Contracting States had in view as the intervening step a process that would be potentially effective to settle the issue in dispute.

312. It remains, therefore, for the Tribunal to consider whether the evidence before it shows (as has been held on similar facts by the *Abaclat* and *Ambiente Ufficio* tribunals) that neither prior course of proceeding held out any realistic likelihood of a settlement of the dispute.

313. The Tribunal begins by noting that it is the Claimants who are advancing a justifying excuse for their admitted failure to pursue literally the course of action foreseen in Article 8, paragraphs (1)–(3), of the BIT. It follows on standard principles that the Claimants carry the burden of establishing to the Tribunal's satisfaction the facts on which they base their justification [. . .].

314. The Claimants' argument is, firstly, that there was no realistic prospect of settling the dispute by amicable consultations in the light of the policies espoused by the Argentine government and (post-2005) of the legal effect of the [law requiring legislative consent for negotiated settlements with bondholders, the '*Ley Cerrojo*' or '*Law 26 017*']; secondly, that there was no realistic prospect of securing an effective remedy from the Argentine courts in light of the judicial decisions that had been handed down by those courts before the present arbitration was initiated. They base the first limb of this argument essentially on the assertion that the 2005 [Public Offer of Exchange, 'POE'] (like the revised POE of 2010) was presented on a take-it-or-leave it basis, with a very short time period for acceptance, and involved a sacrifice of alternative legal remedies, and was very soon set in stone by the *Ley Cerrojo*. They accept that there had been discussions with bondholder interests in various formations before the POE was made, but point out that the POE was not the outcome of agreement with bondholder representatives, and involved only certain limited concessions to the interests that had been advanced on the part of bondholders. They base the second limb of the argument squarely on the judgment of the Argentine Supreme Court in the *Galli* case, [. . .] in which the Supreme Court declared that the restructuring of the national debt lay within the purview of the political power, to which the judicial power had to defer so long

as the actions of the political power were reasonable and non-discriminatory, and held moreover that failure by a bondholder to accept the POE was a voluntary act which therefore entailed as a consequence that the entitlement to raise a claim in Argentina had been forfeited. The Respondent's answer depends on drawing a distinction of principle between contract claims (under the bond instruments themselves) and treaty claims (e.g. under the BIT). It maintains that Law 26 017 only affects contractual claims under the bond instruments but has 'no impact on any negotiation that may be conducted in connection with such treaty claims' [. . .].

315. Faced with similar, or indeed identical arguments, the *Abaclat* and *Ambiente Ufficio* tribunals dealt with the matter as follows. The *Abaclat* tribunal treated the discussions that had taken place prior to 2005 between the Argentine authorities and Task Force Argentina ('TFA') as in effect covering the interests of all Italian bondholders, whether or not the particular claimants in the arbitration were party to the TFA's formal mandate. On that basis, it held that Argentina was precluded from raising any failure of the claimants before it to pursue consultations under Article 8(1). As to the requirement for local litigation under Article 8(2), [. . .] the tribunal reached the conclusion that actions before the courts of Argentina were doomed to fail in the light of the terms of the Emergency Legislation. The *Ambiente Ufficio* tribunal, on the other hand, found as a finding of fact that 'at least since the adoption of [Law 26 017] it was clear that no realistic possibility of meaningful consultations to settle the dispute with the Argentine Government existed,' and found equally that that result was not affected by the fact that the Argentine Congress could have at any time suspended or eliminated the ban on consultations and negotiations and that it actually did so in 2010 [. . .]. It found the crucial consideration to be that the potential negotiating partner was not in a position so to act while the law was in force (i.e. from 2005 onwards), and that the very reason for the non-availability of meaningful consultations was above all the Argentine Congress's adoption of Law No. 26 017. As to the question of prior recourse to the local courts, the tribunal cites the Draft Articles of the International Law Commission (ILC) on Diplomatic Protection 2006 as evidence of a general rule that requirements of this kind are treated in international law as being subject to a futility exception. The tribunal finds a strong structural parallel between the typical clause found in the dispute settlement provisions of investment treaties and provisions for the exhaustion of local remedies, in that both are designed to allow the domestic legal system to correct a potential breach before the international legal responsibility of the State becomes engaged; the significant difference between the two is the existence in the former case of a time limit, where in the latter case there typically is none, but the tribunal concludes that the time limit only serves to reinforce the argument for applying a common futility exception. Putting this together with the facts of the case, and relying once again on the test enunciated by the ILC, the tribunal declines to apply as a criterion either the trouble and expense a claimant would be put to, or the actual likelihood that judgment would be reached within the 18 months stipulated in Article 8(3), but focuses

its attention on the main issue of substance, i.e. whether recourse to the Argentine courts would have offered the claimants a reasonable prospect of effective redress. Its conclusion that there would not in the circumstances have been such a prospect is based on the decision in the *Galli* case coupled with the further holding by the Supreme Court [. . .] that international responsibility is precluded in international law where a State suspends or modifies payment of the external debt for reasons of financial necessity.

317. For the reasons given above, therefore, the Tribunal concludes that the Claimants have met the burden on them to show that no substantial purpose would have been served by attempting either to engage the Argentine authorities in amicable consultations or in bringing an action before the Argentine courts. The Tribunal therefore decides that the Claimants' admitted failure to do so does not act as a jurisdictional bar to their commencing ICSID arbitration. [. . .]

The *Guarachi America v. Bolivia* case, on the other hand, refused to admit of a futility exception. A tribunal for a PCA-administered dispute rather than an ICSID tribunal, the *Guarachi* arbitrators looked at the same issue of limited consent as their colleagues:

386. The Tribunal is mindful that the particular circumstances of the present case might allow one to surmise that applying the general 'cooling off' period envisaged in the BIT to the so-called 'New Claims' would be a waste of time. Indeed, the fact that Bolivia has expropriated Rurelec investment leads the Tribunal to believe that the practical effects sought to be achieved by the cooling off theory and rule would in the end have been non-existent. Nevertheless, [the claimant] was fully aware of the rule at play here and it would not have been difficult to comply with the cooling off period, which did not in fact occur. The Tribunal has no mandate to 'rewrite' the BIT.

[. . .]

388. The explicit wording requiring a written notification and the expiry of a period of six months from that notification leads the Tribunal to consider that the 'cooling off period' narrows the consent given by the Contracting Parties to international arbitration.

389. It is not up to the Tribunal to evaluate the importance or effect of such a condition, but simply to acknowledge that it was agreed by the two Contracting Parties as a condition precedent to the availability of an arbitral forum which is, and must be, based on consent.

The fact is that the Contracting Parties only gave their consent to arbitration subject to the existence of a *written notification of a claim* and subject to the passing of six months' time between such notification and any request of arbitration.

390. The Tribunal thus concludes that, at least in this case, the 'cooling off period' is a jurisdictional barrier conditioning the jurisdiction of the Tribunal *rationae*

voluntatis, since it is not up to a claimant to decide whether and when to notify the host State of the dispute, just as it is not up to such claimant to decide how long they must wait before submitting the request for arbitration.

[. . .]

392. It is irrelevant for the issue at hand whether it could be anticipated [. . .] that nothing would happen during said six-month period and that the Respondent would not react to the notification and take advantage of the chance to negotiate a resolution. The 'cooling off period' clause imposes an obligation of means and not an obligation of result. All clauses of the BIT must be given equal effect and, if the Contracting Parties gave their consent subject to those conditions, Rurelec could only accept the offer of arbitration as it was presented and not as it would have liked to receive it. The Tribunal thus feels no need to elaborate any further on what it believes the Respondent's behaviour would have been if it had been properly notified.[81]

Fork in the road provisions

A so-called 'fork in the road' provision is a clause that requires an investor to choose a single forum for dispute resolution: either the host's national court (or administrative decision-making) system or international arbitration. If the investor begins proceedings in one, then a fork in the road provision will require that no other proceedings be initiated.

Complications in the application of such provisions arise because not every dispute related to a particular investment will fall within the fork in the road provision's scope. The general rule is that only 'the same dispute involving the same cause of action between the same parties'[82] will trigger such a clause. This 'triple identity' test is difficult to pass. Perhaps, posits one tribunal, the test is too difficult to pass: if 'sameness' is regarded strictly by tribunals, the intention may be undercut by the impossibility of proving identity.

Chevron Corporation and Texaco Petroleum Company v. Republic of Ecuador[83]

4.74 In the Tribunal's view, 'the dispute' in this context must mean 'the same dispute': it is not suggested that the submission of a different dispute between the

---

81 *Guaracachi America, Inc. and Rurelec PLC v. the Plurinational State of Bolivia*, UNCITRAL, PCA Case No. 2011-17 (Jan. 31, 2014).

82 Dolzer and Schreuer, *supra* note 34, at 267.

83 *Chevron Corporation and Texaco Petroleum Company v. Republic of Ecuador*, PCA Case No. 200923, Third Interim Award on Jurisdiction and Admissibility (Feb. 27, 2012). Available at: http://italaw.com/sites/default/files/case-documents/ita0175.pdf.

Claimants and the Respondent could trigger the fork in the road provision in relation to the Parties' dispute before this Tribunal. Plainly, what is literally one and the same dispute cannot be before two tribunals simultaneously. 'Sameness' must refer to material identity or sameness determined in the context of a fork in the road provision. The question is therefore: what is required to establish this particular 'sameness'?

4.75 Tribunals in earlier investment cases have applied a 'triple identity' test, requiring that in the dispute before the domestic courts and the dispute before the arbitration tribunal there should be identity of the parties, of the object, and of the cause of action. In the present case, there is no identity of parties, of object or of cause of action between the *Lago Agrio* litigation or, indeed, in the *Aguinda* litigation in the New York Courts.

4.76 It is unlikely that the triple identity test will be satisfied in many cases where a dispute before a tribunal against a State under a BIT and based upon an alleged breach of the BIT is compared with a dispute in a national court. National legal systems do not commonly provide for the State to be sued in respect of a breach of treaty as such, even though actions for breach of a national law giving effect to a treaty might be possible. A strict application of the triple identity test would deprive the fork in the road provision of all or most of its practical effect.

4.77 The triple identity test was developed to address questions of res judicata and to identify specific issues that have already been determined by a competent tribunal. It has also been applied to similar questions arising in the broadly comparable context of lis pendens. It is not clear that the triple identity test should be applied here in order to determine if it is the same 'dispute' that is being submitted to national courts and to the arbitration tribunal . . . .

[The tribunal then determines that, in this case, one of the claimants is not party to the case in front of the national courts, and so finds no identity of the parties.]

Extending consent through MFN
This issue of whether a host has given consent to arbitrate with foreign investors is particularly touchy when the MFN clause is used to give an investor access to investor-State dispute settlement procedures. If a host grants consent to investors of treaty partner A and not to those of treaty partner B, but has an MFN clause in the treaty with B, some tribunals will permit the investor from B to access the consent provision from the treaty with A.

Parties can, of course, make explicit exclusions from the MFN obligation. As a result, some tribunals find that a plain language approach to interpretation demands MFN treatment for all treaty provisions unless there are words indicating that the MFN was intended only for particular treaty benefits. The

Maffezini tribunal, for instance, allowed an MFN clause in an Argentina–Spain BIT (which had an 18-month consultation period) to access consent to an instant arbitration clause in a Chile–Spain BIT based on this reasoning. That tribunal looked at the history of MFN in trade treaties and found the situation of investors to be similar. It reasoned, therefore, that '[n]otwithstanding the fact that the basic treaty containing the clause does not refer expressly to dispute settlement as covered by the most favoured nation clause, the Tribunal considers that there are good reasons to conclude that today dispute settlement arrangements are inextricably related to the protection of foreign investors' and that therefore, a general obligation of MFN treatment ought to extend to dispute settlement provisions as well as to substantive treatment standards.[84] The tribunal then compared many of the Spanish BITs' MFN provisions with that found in the treaty with Argentina, and concluded that the claimant was justified in relying on the more favourable treatment set out in Spain's treaty with Chile.[85]

In *Plama v. Bulgaria* the tribunal took a different approach. In an award-winning[86] decision, the *Plama* tribunal thoroughly analyses the consent-through-MFN issue.

 CASE

Plama Consortium Limited v. Republic of Bulgaria[87]

In 1998, Trammel Investment Ltd. purchased the shares of Plama, a privatized Bulgarian company. Over the course of the next four years, Plama alleged, Bulgaria (the respondent) treated it unfairly, discriminated against it, and failed to protect it, with the overall result of lowering the value of Plama's investments. In 2002, Plama filed a claim with ICSID, alleging violations of the BIT and the Energy Charter Treaty. Bulgaria objected to the tribunal's jurisdiction, as the Bulgaria–Cyprus BIT has an arbitration clause

---

84 *Emilio Agustín Maffezini v. The Kingdom of Spain*, ICSID Case No. ARB/97/7, Decision on Objections to Jurisdiction, paras. 38–64 (Jan. 25, 2000), 5 ICSID Rep. 396 (2002). Note, however, that the tribunal did mention that there could be public policy reasons for denying MFN-based extensions of consent, including if there is a requirement of exhaustion of local remedies or if there is a fork in the road provision. *Id.* paras. 62–3.

85 *See id.* at paras. 58–9.

86 Jonathon Hamilton, *Plama Consortium Limited v. Republic of Bulgaria—the Best and Most Surprising Award of 2008*, kluwer arbitration blog (Feb. 11, 2009). Available at: http://kluwerarbitrationblog.com/blog/2009/02/11/ plama-consortium-limited-v-republic-of-bulgaria-the-best-and-most-surprising-award-of-2008/.

87 *Plama Consortium Limited v. Republic of Bulgaria*, ICSID Case No. ARB/03/24, Decision on Jurisdiction (Feb. 8, 2005). Available at: http://italaw.com/sites/default/files/case-documents/ita0669.pdf; footnotes omitted.

that applies only to compensation issues for expropriations. Article 4 of the agreement set forth:

> 4.1 The legality of the expropriation shall be checked at the request of the concerned investor through the regular administrative and legal procedure of the contracting party that had taken the expropriation steps. In cases of dispute with regard to the amount of the compensation, which disputes were not settled in an administrative order, the concerned investor and the legal representatives of the other Contracting Party shall hold consultations for fixing this value. If within 3 months after the beginning of the consultations no agreement is reached, the amount of the compensation at the request of the concerned investor shall be checked either in a legal regular procedure of the Contracting Party which had taken the measure on expropriation or by an international 'Ad hoc' Arbitration Court.

The BIT, however, also has an MFN clause, and Bulgaria has a BIT with Finland that offers broad consent to arbitration. Plama argued that the Cyprus–Bulgaria BIT's MFN provision should permit the incorporation of the more favourable arbitration consent offer of the Bulgaria–Finland BIT, and thereby give the tribunal jurisdiction over its non-expropriation claims.

c. Jurisdiction of the arbitral tribunal under the Bulgaria–Cyprus BIT

183. The Claimant contends that [. . .] Bulgaria consented to ICSID arbitration of the present dispute in the 1987 Bulgaria–Cyprus BIT through the MFN provision contained therein. The mechanism for arriving at that conclusion is, according to the Claimant, the following: (a) the Claimant qualifies as an investor under the Bulgaria–Cyprus BIT; (b) the Bulgaria–Cyprus BIT contains an MFN provision; (c) the MFN provision in the Bulgaria–Cyprus BIT applies to all aspects of 'treatment;' and (d) 'treatment' covers settlement of disputes provisions in other BITs to which Bulgaria is a Contracting Party. In that connection, the Claimant relies, *inter alia*, on the Bulgaria–Finland BIT. The Respondent contests the Claimant's contention on grounds that will be considered below.

The Tribunal concludes that the MFN provision of the Bulgaria–Cyprus BIT cannot be interpreted as providing consent to submit a dispute under the Bulgaria–Cyprus BIT to ICSID arbitration for the reasons set forth hereafter.
[. . .]

186. The Claimant's position appears to be prompted by the limited dispute settlement provisions in the Bulgaria–Cyprus BIT [. . .]. [. . .] A dispute '*with regard to the amount of compensation . . . shall be checked either in a legal regular*

*procedure of the Contracting Party which has taken the measure on expropriation or by
an international "Ad Hoc" Arbitration Court'* [. . .].

187. The MFN provision set forth in Article 3 of the Bulgaria-Cyprus BIT reads as
follows:

1. *Each Contracting Party shall apply to the investments in its territory by investors
   of the other Contracting Party a treatment which is not less favourable than that
   accorded to investments by investors of third states.*
2. *This treatment shall not be applied to the privileges which either Contracting Party
   accords to investors from third countries in virtue of their participation in economic
   communities and unions, a customs union or a free trade area.*

[. . .]

189. It is not clear whether the ordinary meaning of the term 'treatment' in the
MFN provision of the BIT includes or excludes dispute settlement provisions contained in other BITs to which Bulgaria is a Contracting Party. Inclusion or exclusion may or may not satisfy the *ejusdem generis* principle (i.e., when a general word
or phrase follows a list of specifics, the general word or phrase will be interpreted
to include only items of the same type as those listed), but . . . it is not relevant to
address that question.

[. . .]

191. The second paragraph of Article 3 of the Bulgaria–Cyprus BIT contains an
exception to MFN treatment relating to economic communities and unions, a
customs union or a free trade area. This may be considered as supporting the view
that all other matters, including dispute settlement, fall under the MFN provision
of the first paragraph of Article 3 (on the basis of the principle *expressio unius est
exclusio alterius*). However, the fact that the second paragraph refers to 'privileges'
may be viewed as indicating that MFN treatment should be understood as relating
to substantive protection. Hence, it can be argued with equal force that the second
paragraph demonstrates that the first paragraph is solely concerned with provisions
relating to substantive protection to the exclusion of the procedural provisions
relating to dispute settlement.

192. The 'context' may support the Claimant's interpretation since the MFN provision is set forth amongst the Treaty's provisions relating to substantive investment
protection. However, the context alone, in light of the other elements of interpretation considered herein, does not persuade the Tribunal that the parties intended
such an interpretation. And the Tribunal has no evidence before it of the negotiating history of the BIT to convince it otherwise.

193. The object and purpose of the Bulgaria–Cyprus BIT are: '*the creation of
favourable conditions for investments by investors of one Contracting Party in the
territory of the other Contracting Party.*' (Preamble, see also title which refers to
'mutual encouragement and protection of investments'). The Claimant places
much reliance on the foregoing and on the Report of the Executive Directors on

the ICSID Convention of 1965, according to which: '*the creation of an institution designed to facilitate the settlement of disputes between States and foreign investors can be a major step toward promoting an atmosphere of mutual confidence and thus stimulating a larger flow of private international capital in those countries which wish to attract it*' (Exhibit C60, at paragraph 9). [. . .] The Claimant also points to the *Maffezini* decision in which it is observed: '*dispute settlement arrangements are inextricably related to the protection of foreign investors, as they are also related to the protection of rights of traders under treaties of commerce*'. Such statements are as such undeniable in their generality, but they are legally insufficient to conclude that the Contracting Parties to the Bulgaria–Cyprus BIT intended to cover by the MFN provision agreements to arbitrate in other treaties to which Bulgaria (and Cyprus for that matter) is a Contracting Party. [. . .]

[. . .]

195. It is true that treaties between one of the Contracting Parties and third States may be taken into account for the purpose of clarifying the meaning of a treaty's text at the time it was entered into. The Claimant has provided a very clear and insightful presentation of Bulgaria's practice in relation to the conclusion of investment treaties subsequent to the conclusion of the Bulgaria–Cyprus BIT in 1987. In the 1990s, after Bulgaria's communist regime changed, it began concluding BITs with much more liberal dispute resolution provisions, including resort to ICSID arbitration. However, that practice is not particularly relevant in the present case since subsequent negotiations between Bulgaria and Cyprus indicate that these Contracting Parties did not intend the MFN provision to have the meaning that otherwise might be inferred from Bulgaria's subsequent treaty practice. Bulgaria and Cyprus negotiated a revision of their BIT in 1998. The negotiations failed but specifically contemplated a revision of the dispute settlement provisions [. . .]. It can be inferred from these negotiations that the Contracting Parties to the BIT themselves did not consider that the MFN provision extends to dispute settlement provisions in other BITs.

[. . .]

198. In the view of the Tribunal, the following consideration is equally, if not more, important. [. . .] Nowadays, arbitration is the generally accepted avenue for resolving disputes between investors and states. Yet, that phenomenon does not take away the basic prerequisite for arbitration: an agreement of the parties to arbitrate. It is a well-established principle, both in domestic and international law, that such an agreement should be clear and unambiguous. In the framework of a BIT, the agreement to arbitrate is arrived at by the consent to arbitration that a state gives in advance in respect of investment disputes falling under the BIT, and the acceptance thereof by an investor if the latter so desires.

199. Doubts as to the parties' clear and unambiguous intention can arise if the agreement to arbitrate is to be reached by incorporation by reference. The Claimant argues that the MFN provision produces such effect, stating that in

contractual relationships the incorporation by reference of an arbitration agreement is commonplace. In support thereof, the Claimant relies on Article 7(2) of the UNCITRAL Model Law on International Commercial Arbitration of 1985. The Claimant adds that in treaty relationships the importation of the arbitration agreement through the MFN provision operates in exactly the same way.

200. Article 7(2) of the UNCITRAL Model Law provides:

> *The reference in a contract to a document containing an arbitration clause constitutes an arbitration agreement provided that the contract is in writing and the reference is such as to make that clause part of the contract. (emphasis added)*

Thus, a reference may in and of itself not be sufficient; the reference is required to be such as to make the arbitration clause part of the contract (i.e., in this case, the Bulgaria–Cyprus BIT). This is another way of saying that the reference must be such that the parties' intention to import the arbitration provision of the other agreement is clear and unambiguous. A clause reading '*a treatment which is not less favourable than that accorded to investments by investors of third states*' as appears in Article 3(1) of the Bulgaria–Cyprus BIT, cannot be said to be a typical incorporation by reference clause as appearing in ordinary contracts. It creates doubt whether the reference to the other document (in this case the other BITs concluded by Bulgaria) clearly and unambiguously includes a reference to the dispute settlement provisions contained in those BITs.

The Claimant contends that the MFN provision in the Bulgaria–Cyprus BIT is a broad provision and is in contrast to other types of MFN provisions, such as Article 1103 NAFTA:

> *Each Party shall accord to investors of another Party treatment no less favorable than it accords, in like circumstances, to investors of any other Party or of a nonParty with respect to the establishment, acquisition, expansion, management, conduct, operation, and sale or other disposition of investments.*

[. . .]

203. This shows that in NAFTA [. . .] the incorporation by reference of the dispute settlement provisions set forth in other BITs is explicitly excluded. Yet, if such language is lacking in an MFN provision, one cannot reason *a contrario* that the dispute resolution provisions must be deemed to be incorporated. The specific exclusion in the draft FTAA [Free Trade of the Americas] is the result of a reaction by States to the expansive interpretation made in the *Maffezini* case. That interpretation went beyond what State Parties to BITs generally intended to achieve by an MFN provision in a bilateral or multilateral investment treaty. The Tribunal will examine the *Maffezini* decision in more detail below.

204. Rather, the intention to incorporate dispute settlement provisions must be clearly and unambiguously expressed. This is, for example, the case with the UK Model BIT, which provides in its Article 3(3):

> *For avoidance of doubt it is confirmed that the treatment provided for in paragraphs and (2) above shall apply to the provisions of Articles 1 to 11 of this Agreement.*

Articles 8 and 9 of the UK Model BIT provide for dispute settlement. The drafters of the UK Model BIT rightly noted that there could be doubt and expressly neutralized that doubt.

205. The expression *'with respect to all matters'* as appearing in MFN provisions in a number of other BITs (but not the Bulgaria–Cyprus BIT) does not alleviate the doubt as pointed out in *Siemens v. The Argentine Republic.*

206. Doubt may be further created by the scope of the dispute settlement provisions in the other BITs. A number of them refer to disputes arising out of the particular BIT. It appears to be difficult to interpret the MFN clause as importing into the particular BIT such specific language from other BITs.

207. Conversely, dispute resolution provisions in a specific treaty have been negotiated with a view to resolving disputes under that treaty. Contracting States cannot be presumed to have agreed that those provisions can be enlarged by incorporating dispute resolution provisions from other treaties negotiated in an entirely different context.

208. Moreover, the doubt as to the relevance of the MFN clause in one BIT to the incorporation of dispute resolution provisions in other agreements is compounded by the difficulty of applying an objective test to the issue of what is more favorable. The Claimant argues that it is obviously more favorable for the investor to have a choice among different dispute resolution mechanisms, and to have the entire dispute resolved by arbitration as provided in the Bulgaria–Finland BIT, than to be confined to *ad hoc* arbitration limited to the quantum of compensation for expropriation. The Tribunal is inclined to agree with the Claimant that in this particular case, a choice is better than no choice. But what if one BIT provides for UNCITRAL arbitration and another provides for ICSID? Which is more favorable?

209. It is also not evident that when parties have agreed in a particular BIT on a specific dispute resolution mechanism, as is the case with the Bulgaria–Cyprus BIT (*ad hoc* arbitration), their agreement to most-favored nation treatment means that they intended that, by operation of the MFN clause, their specific agreement on such a dispute settlement mechanism could be replaced by a totally different dispute resolution mechanism (ICSID arbitration). It is one thing to add to the treatment provided in one treaty while more favorable treatment is provided elsewhere. It is quite another thing to replace a procedure specifically negotiated by parties with an entirely different mechanism.

210. The Claimant has relied on a number of cases that it believes support its interpretation. It is to be noted, however, that in none of these cases was it held that the dispute settlement provisions in the basic treaty are replaced *in toto* by the dispute settlement provisions contained in the other treaty through operation of

the MFN provision in the basic treaty. Indeed, the Respondent contended that no tribunal has ever done what the Claimant is requesting this Tribunal to do in the present case.

[. . .]

212. In the Tribunal's view, the lack of precedent is not surprising. When concluding a multilateral or bilateral investment treaty with specific dispute resolution provisions, states cannot be expected to leave those provisions to future (partial) replacement by different dispute resolution provisions through the operation of an MFN provision, unless the States have explicitly agreed thereto (as in the case of BITs based on the UK Model BIT). This matter can also be viewed as forming part of the nowadays generally accepted principle of the separability (autonomy) of the arbitration clause. Dispute resolution provisions constitute an agreement on their own, usually with interrelated provisions.

[. . .]

216. In *Emilio Agustín Maffezini v. Kingdom of Spain*, the question arose whether the requirement set forth in the dispute settlement provisions in the Argentina–Spain BIT of 1991 that '*domestic courts [be given] the opportunity to deal with a dispute for a period of eighteen months before it may be submitted to arbitration*' was inapplicable by reliance on the dispute settlement provisions in the Chile–Spain BIT (which does not impose such condition) through operation of the MFN provision in the Argentina–Spain BIT. The arbitral tribunal in that case answered the question in the affirmative.

217. In *Maffezini* the tribunal relied on *Case Concerning Rights of Nationals of America in Morocco, Anglo-Iranian Oil Co. Case*, and *Ambatielos Claim*. However, the foregoing review of those decisions shows that they do not provide a conclusive answer to the question.

218. The tribunal in *Maffezini* also noted that in other treaties the MFN provision mentions '*all rights contained in the present Agreement*' or '*all matters subject to this Agreement*,' in which case, according to the tribunal, '*it must be established whether the omission [in the Argentina–Spain BIT] was intended by the parties [i.e., Contracting Parties] or can reasonably be inferred from the practice followed by the parties in their treatment of foreign investors and their own investors*' (Decision, paragraph 53). The present Tribunal considers such a basis for analysis in principle to be inappropriate for the question whether dispute resolution provisions in the basic treaty can be replaced by dispute resolution provisions in another treaty. As explained above, an arbitration clause must be clear and unambiguous and the reference to an arbitration clause must be such as to make the clause part of the contract (treaty).

219. The tribunal in *Maffezini* further referred to '*the fact that the application of the most favoured nation clause to dispute settlement arrangements in the context of investment treaties might result in the harmonization and enlargement of the scope of such arrangements*' (Decision at paragraph 62). The present Tribunal fails to see how

harmonization of dispute settlement provisions can be achieved by reliance on the MFN provision. Rather, the 'basket of treatment' and 'self-adaptation of an MFN provision' in relation to dispute settlement provisions (as alleged by the Claimant) has as effect that an investor has the option to pick and choose provisions from the various BITs. If that were true, a host state which has not specifically agreed thereto can be confronted with a large number of permutations of dispute settlement provisions from the various BITs which it has concluded. Such a chaotic situation— actually counterproductive to harmonization—cannot be the presumed intent of Contracting Parties.

220. The *Maffezini* tribunal was apparently aware of this risk when it added:

> [T]here are some important limits that ought to be kept in mind. As a matter of principle, the beneficiary of the clause should not be able to override public policy considerations that the [C]ontracting [P]arties might have envisaged as fundamental conditions for their acceptance of the agreement in question, particularly if the beneficiary is a private investor, as will often be the case. The scope of the clause might thus be narrower than it appears at first sight. (id.)

The examples given by the tribunal are: (1) exhaustion of local remedies condition; (2) fork in the road provision; (3) 'if the agreement provides for a particular arbitration forum, such as ICSID, for example, this option cannot be changed by invoking the clause, in order to refer the dispute to a different system of arbitration'; (4) 'if the parties have agreed to a highly institutionalized system of arbitration that incorporates precise rules of procedure' (referring as example to NAFTA). (Decision at paragraph 63).

221. The present Tribunal was puzzled as to what the origin of these 'public policy considerations' is. When asked by the Tribunal at the Hearing, counsel for the Claimant responded: '*They just made it up.*' [D2.134]. The present Tribunal does not wish to go that far in its appraisal of the *Maffezini* decision. Rather, it seems that the effect of the 'public policy considerations' is that they take away much of the breadth of the preceding observations made by the tribunal in *Maffezini*.

222. In *Maffezini* the tribunal pointed out:

> It is clear, in any event, that a distinction has to be made between the legitimate extension of rights and benefits by means of the operation of the clause, on the one hand, and disruptive treaty-shopping that would play havoc with the policy objectives of underlying specific treaty provisions, on the other hand. (Id.)

223. The present Tribunal agrees with that observation, albeit that the principle with multiple exceptions as stated by the tribunal in the *Maffezini* case should instead be a different principle with one, single exception: an MFN provision in a basic treaty does not incorporate by reference dispute settlement provisions in whole or in part set forth in another treaty, unless the MFN provision in the basic treaty leaves no doubt that the Contracting Parties intended to incorporate them.

224. The decision in *Maffezini* is perhaps understandable. The case concerned a curious requirement that during the first 18 months the dispute be tried in the local courts. The present Tribunal sympathizes with a tribunal that attempts to neutralize such a provision that is nonsensical from a practical point of view. However, such exceptional circumstances should not be treated as a statement of general principle guiding future tribunals in other cases where exceptional circumstances are not present.

[. . .]

226. In light of the foregoing review, the Tribunal need not examine the decisions in *Técnicas Medioambientales Tecmed v. United Mexican States* and *Siemens AG v. The Argentine Republic* as both decisions are partially based on the *Maffezini* decision. Actually, the *Siemens* decision illustrates the danger caused by the manner in which the *Maffezini* decision has approached the question: the principle is retained in the form of a 'string citation' of principle and the exceptions are relegated to a brief examination, prone to falling soon into oblivion (Decision, at paragraphs 105, 109 and 120).

227. For the foregoing reasons, the Tribunal concludes that the MFN provision of the Bulgaria–Cyprus BIT cannot be interpreted as providing consent to submit a dispute under the Bulgaria–Cyprus BIT to ICSID arbitration and that the Claimant cannot rely on dispute settlement provisions in other BITs to which Bulgaria is a Contracting Party in the present case.

[. . .]

The *Plama* award was not the last word on MFN and jurisdiction. Numerous cases and hundreds of pages of commentary later, there is still no true majority approach to speak of. A particularly interesting case from 2013 demonstrates the continuing divide. In *Garanti Koza v. Turkmenistan*, the majority of the tribunal allowed an MFN clause to override the BIT's language granting consent to arbitration under UNCITRAL rules, thereby allowing the claimant to access ICSID proceedings. The dissenting arbitrator emphasized what she regarded as the more important value—balanced treaty relations among sovereign states.

CASE

Garanti Koza LLP v. Turkmenistan[88]

17. Article 8 of the U.K. –Turkmenistan BIT deals with 'Settlement of Disputes between an Investor and a Host State.' It provides:

> (1) Disputes between a national or company of one Contracting Party and the other Contracting Party concerning an obligation of the latter under this Agreement [. . .] shall [. . .] be submitted to international arbitration if the [investor] concerned so wishes.
>
> (2) Where the dispute is referred to international arbitration, the [investor] and the Contracting Party [. . .] may agree to refer the dispute either to:
>   (a) the [ICSID]; or
>   (b) the Court of Arbitration of the [ICC]; or
>   (c) an international arbitrator or ad hoc arbitration tribunal to
>   be appointed by a special agreement or established under the
>   [UNCITRAL Arbitration Rules].
>
> If [. . .] there is no agreement to one of the above alternative procedures, the dispute shall [. . .] be submitted to arbitration under the [UNCITRAL Arbitration Rules] [. . .].

[. . .]

68. The provision of the Switzerland–Turkmenistan BIT on which the Claimant relies is Article 8 of that treaty, which provides:

> 1. For the purpose of solving disputes [. . .] consultations will take place between the parties concerned.
>
> 2. If these consultations do not result in a solution within six months from the date of request for consultations, the investor may submit the dispute for settlement to:
>   (a)[ICSID]; or
>   (b)an ad hoc-arbitral tribunal [. . .] under the [UNCITRAL Arbitration Rules].
>   [. . .]

69. Specifically, the Claimant seeks to apply the MFN provisions of Articles 3(1) and 3(2) of the U.K.–Turkmenistan BIT to give it the benefit of what it considers to be the more favorable treatment accorded by Turkmenistan to Swiss investors in Article 8(2) of the Switzerland–Turkmenistan BIT, insofar as a Swiss investor

---

88 *Garanti Koza LLP v. Turkmenistan*, ICSID Case No. ARB/11/20, Decision on Jurisdiction (July 3, 2013) (footnotes omitted).

may choose to submit a dispute that cannot be resolved within six months of consultations with Turkmenistan either to ICSID Arbitration or to UNCITRAL Arbitration. [...]

70. The Respondent argues that, while an MFN clause may possibly be used to overcome a qualifying condition, such as a waiting period, in the dispute resolution clause of a BIT, as was the case in *Maffezini v. Spain*, it may not be used to 'import' the State's 'consent to a different arbitration system' from one treaty into another. The Respondent cites statements from both *Maffezini v. Spain* and *Plama v. Bulgaria* to this effect:

> [I]f the agreement provides for a particular arbitration forum, such as ICSID, for example, this option cannot be changed by invoking the [MFN] clause in order to refer the dispute to a different system of arbitration . . . because these very specific provisions reflect the precise will of the contracting parties. It is also not evident that when parties have agreed in a particular BIT on a specific dispute resolution mechanism, . . . their agreement to most favored nation treatment means that they intended that, by operation of the MFN clause, their specific agreement on such a dispute settlement mechanism could be replaced by a totally different dispute resolution mechanism (ICSID arbitration). It is one thing to add to the treatment provided in one treaty more favorable treatment provided elsewhere. It is quite another thing to replace a procedure specifically negotiated by parties with an entirely different mechanism.

[...]

73. [. . . T]he majority of this Tribunal is inclined to agree with the Claimant that importation of a provision for ICSID Arbitration from one treaty to another by operation of the MFN clause of a treaty should not be considered conceptually more difficult than the incorporation by reference into a contract of a provision for ICSID Arbitration from a treaty that has not entered into force. In either case, the consent to ICSID Arbitration is written in one instrument and imported into another by virtue of a provision in the latter instrument to which the State has agreed. The State has expressed its consent to ICSID Arbitration, in writing, in one instrument, and has agreed in a second instrument to look, under certain conditions, to the terms of the first instrument. Whether looking to the terms of the first instrument is accomplished by means of an incorporation by reference or an MFN clause does not appear to be a material distinction.

74. [. . .T]he MFN provision of the U.K.–Turkmenistan BIT effectively replaces Article 8(2) of the U.K.–Turkmenistan BIT with Article 8(2) of the Switzerland–Turkmenistan BIT, which requires no such case-specific consent. In the U.K. BIT, the sovereign parties agreed that their respective investors would have the benefits of more favorable provisions of other provisions in other treaties, and specified in Article 3(3) that the investor-state provisions of the BIT were included within the ambit of this protection. Once the requirements of Article 8(2) of the U.K. BIT are

displaced by those of Article 8(2) of the Switzerland BIT, it is sufficient that the investor have complied with the requirements of that provision of the Switzerland BIT.

75. In any event, the essential consent of the State – the consent to resolve disputes with U.K. investors by means of international arbitration – does not in this case need to be imported by operation of the MFN clause, because that consent is contained in Article 8(1) of the BIT. The consent of Switzerland and Turkmenistan to submit disputes between each of them and investors of the other to international arbitration is similarly contained in a separate paragraph of the Switzerland–Turkmenistan BIT, Article 8(3) of that treaty. There is no need for the Claimant to seek to import that consent into the U.K.–Turkmenistan BIT, because Article 8(1) of the U.K. BIT already achieves the same result.

76. The only provision of the Switzerland–Turkmenistan BIT to which the Claimant needs the MFN clause to apply is the provision of Article 8(2) of the Switzerland BIT that provides a Swiss investor a choice between ICSID Arbitration and UNCITRAL Arbitration, which the Claimant argues to be more favorable than the corresponding provision of Article 8(2) of the U.K.–Turkmenistan BIT, which restricts a U.K. investor to UNCITRAL Arbitration. Such an application to Article 8(2) is consistent with the International Law Commission's observation that the beneficiary of an MFN clause not only has 'an "either/or" choice, but might also be in a position to opt for the cumulative enjoyment of all, some, or parts of the various treatments concerned.'

77. The Respondent argues that Article 8(2) requires a specific agreement between the Claimant and Turkmenistan to submit a dispute to ICSID Arbitration. Article 3, the Respondent argues, is an agreement between Turkmenistan and the United Kingdom, and cannot satisfy the requirement of an agreement between the Claimant and Turkmenistan. But, as noted above, the effect of the MFN clause is not *to satisfy* the requirements of Article 8(2), but *to replace* those requirements with a more favorable provision from another treaty, in this case Article 8(2) of the Switzerland–Turkmenistan BIT, which does not require a separate agreement between the Claimant and Turkmenistan in order to commence an ICSID Arbitration. We adopt the observation of the *Renta 4 v. Russia* tribunal that:

It is not convincing for a State to argue in general terms that it accepted a particular 'system of arbitration' with respect to nationals of one country but did not so consent with respect to nationals of another. The extension of commitments is in the very nature of MFN clauses.

78. [. . . T]he consent requirement is not bypassed by this interpretation: Turkmenistan consented to international arbitration in Article 8(1) of the U.K.–Turkmenistan BIT, and the State Parties to the BIT opened the door to a search by a U.K. investor for more favorable terms in treaties entered into by Turkmenistan with other states by choosing to make the MFN clause of the BIT applicable to

the investor-state arbitration provisions. It is the State Parties to the BIT, not the present Tribunal, that decided that the MFN clause should apply to the investor-state arbitration article.

79. The majority of the Tribunal concludes that, where Turkmenistan: (a) has expressly consented in the basic U.K.–Turkmenistan BIT to submit investment disputes with U.K. investors to international arbitration, (b) has provided in the same BIT that U.K. investors and their investments will not be subjected to treatment less favorable than that accorded to investors of other States or their investments, (c) has expressly provided that the MFN treatment so accorded 'shall apply' to the dispute resolution provision of the BIT, and (d) has provided investors of third States, specifically Switzerland, with an unrestricted choice between ICSID Arbitration and UNCITRAL Arbitration, there is no reason why Turkmenistan's consent to ICSID Arbitration in its BIT with Switzerland may not be relied upon by a U.K. investor, *if* the provision for ICSID Arbitration or an unrestricted choice between ICSID Arbitration and UNCITRAL Arbitration provides treatment more favorable to the investor than the treatment provided by the base treaty.

Dissent by Arbitrator Laurence Chazournes de Boisson[89]

2. My Dissenting Opinion deals with the Respondent's first objection to jurisdiction in the present case, i.e. the objection for lack of consent. Throughout the jurisdictional phase and during exchanges with my esteemed colleagues, I have always kept in mind the need to preserve the exact balance of rights and obligations negotiated in the U.K.–Turkmenistan BIT. Such a concern stems from the desire to ensure that the rights and legal interests of *both* disputing parties are unaltered. [. . .]

4. The objective of my Dissenting Opinion is to determine the conditions for resorting to ICSID arbitration under Article 8 of the U.K.–Turkmenistan BIT, and whether or not consent to ICSID arbitration can be *established* via the MFN clause contained in Article 3(3) of the same BIT. There is no doubt that these are the two provisions at stake at the present stage of the proceedings and that form the real legal dispute between the parties. A tribunal has a duty 'to isolate the real issue in the case'.

5. It is crucial to stress from the outset a fundamental legal safeguard governing the issue of consent before international courts and tribunals, in general, and ICSID tribunals in particular: consent to jurisdiction in international adjudication must always be *established*. First, this is a necessary prerequisite to the exercise of the international judicial function. The principle of *compétence de la compétence* as defined under general international law, and under Article 41 of the ICSID Convention, empowers an arbitral tribunal or any other international court to

---

89 Footnotes omitted.

determine *proprio motu* the extent and limits of its jurisdiction. At the same time, the principle of *compétence de la compétence* requires an arbitral tribunal or any other international court to *establish* the extent and limits of its jurisdiction objectively, i.e., on the basis of the title of jurisdiction that is conferred to the said tribunal, and not to go beyond it.

6. The trust and confidence in third-party adjudication is dependent on the respect by international courts and tribunals of the limits to the jurisdiction conferred upon them. Tribunals should not create a *de facto* system of compulsory jurisdiction, which in the present stage of positive international law remains the exception. The international legal order still rests largely on a system of facultative jurisdiction, and because of that essential characteristic, a tribunal should never attempt to impose its jurisdiction and adjudicate the merits of a dispute when the parties have not consented to its jurisdiction. The ICSID arbitration system is not an exception to that approach. BITs were never concluded by sovereign states with the idea that a third-party adjudicator would then empower himself or herself with the authority to embark on 'consent shopping'.

7. The MFN clause regardless of its formulation in a BIT does not vest such authority in a tribunal. The interpretation of MFN clauses is *mutatis mutandis* subject to the principle of consent4 as enshrined both in general international law as well as in treaty law (the ICSID Convention in the context of the present dispute). It would create a dangerous precedent to formulate new approaches that go against these fundamental rules and principles of international adjudication.

8. Despite the repetitive use of the verb 'import' by both the Claimant and the Respondent, the Tribunal should not be misled and consider that the question in the present arbitration is whether consent can be *imported* from one treaty to another treaty. I consider that the real question that the Tribunal should address first and foremost is whether consent to ICSID arbitration is or is not *established* under the U.K.–Turkmenistan BIT. Indeed, such consent exists or does not exist, and cannot be based on presumptions. Lack of consent cannot be remedied by the so-called 'import' of consent.

[. . .]

16. The majority has persisted in considering that Article 8(1) deals with 'Turkmenistan's consent to participate in international arbitration with U.K. investors and the conditions attached to that consent', and that Article 8(2) deals with 'the arbitration systems that may be used if the conditions of Article 8(1) are met'. Contrary to the interpretation of the majority, Article 8 of the U.K.–Turkmenistan BIT does not divide the question of consent to participate in ICSID Arbitration into two parts. Elementary rules of treaty interpretation invite to interpret Article 8 as *a whole* and not as composed of segmented and fragmented provisions as the majority has chosen to do. The whole mechanism of Article 8 relates to consent to international arbitration. Article 8(1) does not invite the Tribunal to look first at whether the host state has consented to participate in international arbitration at

all (under Article 8(1)), and second, at whether it has agreed to ICSID arbitration (under Article 8(2)).

[. . .]

19. Articles 8(1) and 8(2) are two sides of the same coin. The coin—Article 8—encompasses the provisions governing consent to international arbitration under the U.K.–Turkmenistan BIT. One side of the coin—Article 8(1)—shows the general pre-condition(s) under which a foreign investor can initiate international arbitration against the host state; the other side—Article 8(2)—fixes the strict conditions under which the foreign investor can pursue one specific venue of international arbitration (e.g. ICSID arbitration) rather than another (e.g. UNCITRAL arbitration).

[. . .]

38. It is not within the ambit of the present dissenting opinion to give a detailed analysis of 38.MFN provisions and their meaning under general international law. It is sufficient to recall that the function of an MFN provision is to guarantee balanced and coherent treaty relations between the members of the international community. More specifically, what an MFN provision allows in the context of BITs is the following: to *extend* treatment of foreign investors that is more favourable under a BIT to treatment of foreign investors that is less favourable under other BITs. Therefore, because of the MFN provision contained in Article 3 of the U.K.–Turkmenistan BIT and its application to dispute settlement issues, a foreign investor of British nationality can invoke more favourable dispute settlement provisions embodied in other BITs concluded by Turkmenistan. Since Article 3(3) is part of a *whole*, i.e., the U.K.–Turkmenistan BIT, it is necessary to read and interpret its terms in light of the other provisions of the BIT (the context of the BIT) and, especially, Article 8(2).

[. . .]

40. *Relationship between Article 3(3) and Article 8(2).* To give effect to the MFN clause contained in Article 3(3), the foreign investor must first be in a *dispute settlement relationship* with the host state. A problem of *treatment* can only arise when the foreign investor is treated in a certain way while entertaining a specific relationship with the host state. If there is no relationship between the host state and the foreign investor, the question of more or less favourable treatment is not at stake and thus, the MFN principle does not apply. [. . .]

[. . .]

42. [. . .] Article 8(2) of the U.K.–Turkmenistan BIT offers three options to settle a dispute between a foreign investor and a state arising out of the said BIT. [. . .]

43. Option 1—ICSID arbitration—is only deemed applicable under Article 8(2) of the U.K.–Turkmenistan BIT if the foreign investor has *mutually* agreed with the respondent state to have recourse to ICSID arbitration. As long as such a mutual agreement is not established, an issue of treatment—and even less of MFN—does not arise under Option 1 (ICSID arbitration). The MFN principle can, thus, only apply with respect to ICSID arbitration if there is a mutual agreement between the

foreign investor and the host state to settle the investment dispute through ICSID arbitration [. . .]

44. Here, there is simply no issue of treatment under ICSID arbitration that arises, since ICSID arbitration is deemed inexistent in the absence of a mutual agreement. This is the reasonable ordinary meaning that can be given to Article 3(3) of the U.K.–Turkmenistan BIT under customary rules of treaty interpretation. This gives *effet utile* to the wording of *both* Article 3(3) and Article 8(2) of the U.K.–Turkmenistan BIT. [. . .]

[. . .]

62. In conclusion, the MFN clause embodied in Article 3(3) of the U.K.–Turkmenistan BIT cannot bypass the requirement of consent to ICSID arbitration. This is undeniable. If the requirement of consent to ICSID arbitration, as stipulated in Article 8 of the U.K.–Turkmenistan BIT, as well as in the ICSID Convention itself, could easily be put aside because of the interplay of MFN clauses, there would be a threat to the entire system of investor-state arbitration. [. . .]

63. Granting Article 3(3) of the U.K.–Turkmenistan BIT such extensive effect as to allow for consent to ICSID through incorporation by reference in the frame of a treaty that does not allow this, would have the effect of 'replac[ing] a procedure specifically negotiated by parties with an entirely different mechanism or 'system of arbitration'. It would involve a forum-shopping attitude that bypasses the consent requirement of the Respondent while running against the fundamental principles of international adjudication.

[. . .]

d.iii The dispute is a 'legal dispute'

The 'legal' nature of a dispute

Article 25(1) of the ICSID Convention grants jurisdiction to 'any legal dispute'. The requirement of a 'legal' dispute bars ICSID arbitration of purely political or economic disagreements, but has been liberally interpreted by tribunals. Under the widely accepted view of a dispute as 'a conflict of legal views or of interests' set out by the PCIJ in the *Mavrommatis* case,[90] a dispute is likely to be considered 'legal' for purposes of jurisdiction. Thus, as long as an investor's claim is denied by the host, it is likely to be a 'legal dispute'.[91]

---

90 The Mavrommatis Palestine Concessions, PCIJ, Series A, No. 2, 24 August 1924 at p. 11.

91 The tribunal in the 1975 ICSID case of *ALCOA v. Jamaica* reportedly dealt with the question of whether the dispute was 'legal' very briefly. (*See Alcoa Minerals of Jamaica v. Jamaica*, ICSID Case No. ARB/74/2, Decision on Jurisdiction and Competence [July 6, 1975]; not public—excerpts published in 4 Yearbook Commercial Arbitration 206 [1976]). Neither does the International Court of Justice give much guidance in this respect. *See* Mohamed Sameh M. Amr, *The Role of the International Court of Justice as the Principal Judicial Organ of the United Nations* 213 (2003):

As the tribunal in *CSOB v. Slovakia* stated, '[w]hile it is true that investment disputes to which a State is a party frequently have political elements or involve governmental actions, such disputes do not lose their legal character as long as they concern legal rights or obligations or the consequences of their breach'.[92]

The existence of a 'dispute'

More significant is the requirement that there be a legal 'dispute'. There must be a situation in which the investor and the state hold different opinions as to the law or the law's applicability in a particular case. The *Luchetti v. Peru* tribunal repeated the ICJ's definition of what a 'dispute' is:

> [A]s a legal concept, the term dispute has an accepted meaning. It has been authoritatively defined as a 'a disagreement on a point of law or fact, a conflict of legal views or of interests between two persons,' or as a 'situation in which two sides hold clearly opposite views concerning the question of the performance or non-performance' of a legal obligation. In short, a dispute can be held to exist when the parties assert clearly conflicting legal or factual claims bearing on their respective rights or obligations or that 'the claim of one party is positively opposed by the other'.[93]

This reasoning also appeared in *Toto v. Lebanon*, where the tribunal distinguished between a 'breach', a 'problem', and a 'dispute' for purposes of determining whether jurisdiction exists. In looking at whether the disputing parties' differences that began several years before the relevant BIT went into effect could justify the jurisdiction *ratio temporis*, the tribunal found it important to emphasize that there is a legally relevant difference among the phases of party disagreements:

> The Tribunal wishes to reassert in relation to this question that 'breach,' 'problem' and 'dispute' are three different notions. A 'breach' arises when contractual or treaty obligations are not honored. A 'problem' arises when that party's claim is not

---

... although the Court has failed to identify general criteria (rigid or flexible) capable of distinguishing legal from non-legal disputes, it has never rejected a case on the ground that it involved a non-legal issue. It is inclined to take a broad legal perspective of what constitutes a justiciable dispute and to narrow the scope of political disputes. . . . The Court has affirmed that all legal disputes have a political dimension and once the Court finds that a dispute raises a legal issue then it considers that this dispute is within its jurisdiction and it is entitled to proceed regardless of the political aspects of the dispute and their weight.

92 *Československa Obchodni Banka AS v. Slovak Republic*, ICSID Case No. ARB/97/4, Decision of the Tribunal on Objections to Jurisdiction, para. 61 (May 24, 1999), 14 ICSID Rev.–FILJ 251 (1999).

93 *Empresas Lucchetti, SA et al. v. Republic of Peru*, ICSID Case No. ARB/03/4, Award, para. 48 (Feb. 7, 2005), 19 ICSID Rev.–FILJ 359 (2004) (quoting from South West Africa Cases (*Ethiopia v. South Africa; Liber. v. South Africa*), Judgment, 1962 ICJ 319, at 328 (Dec. 21)). *See also ATA Construction, Industrial and Trading Company v. Hashemite Kingdom of Jordan*, ICSID Case No. ARB/08/2, Award, para. 99 (May 18, 2010). Available at: http://italaw.com/documents/ATA_Jordan_Award.pdf.

accepted by the other side, *i.e.*, when the engineer and the contractor have different views which need to be referred for final decision to the employer/administration. On September 12, 2002, Toto [the Claimant investor] requested to be compensated for the additional works and the delay occurred. However, the [Respondent host] did not take a position, so Toto invited it on June 30, 2004, to have recourse to Article 7 of the Treaty ('Settlement of Disputes'). Thus, the dispute, which had been in limbo for months, crystallized then.[94]

Significantly, a dispute may be implied by the complaint of one party when the defendant contradicts the claims or even when it remains silent. The ICJ, however, has cautioned that the 'mere assertion' of a dispute or the existence of opposing interests does not prove that there is a legal dispute: rather, '[i]t must be shown that the claim of one party is positively opposed by the other'.[95]

d.iv   *The dispute arises 'directly out of an investment made in the host Contracting State'*

Even if there is a legal dispute between the investor and the host, the dispute must be one 'arising directly out of an investment'.[96] While clearly intended to ensure that arbitration is focussed on the host's treatment of the investment, the phrase is not very clear. There are two important jurisdictional aspects to this phrase. One is that of whether there is an 'investment' at issue. The second is that of the dispute's relationship to the investment. We look briefly at each in turn.

Dispute arises out of an 'investment': the umbrella clause
We have already discussed the meaning of 'investment', pointing out the views on what characteristics an activity must have to qualify as such. Traditionally, contractual claims have been strictly excluded from investment arbitration. However, IIA provisions known as 'umbrella clauses' have allowed investors to invoke the IIA investor-State arbitration possibility for disputes based on the host's alleged violation of a contract.

An 'umbrella clause' is a BIT provision that extends investor protection to any obligation made by the state with respect to the investment. There are

---

94 *Toto Costruzioni Generali SPA v. Republic of Lebanon*, ICSID Case No. ARB/07/12, Award, 63 (June 7, 2012). Available at: http://italaw.com/sites/default/files/case-documents/ita1013.pdf. *See also Achmea BV v. Slovak Republic*, PCA Case No. 2013-12, Award on Jurisdiction and Admissibility, para. 180 (May 20, 2014) ('allegation of breach not necessary for existence of a dispute').

95 South West Africa Cases *supra* note 93, at 328.

96 ICSID Convention, art. 25(1).

numerous forms of umbrella clauses, with both the language and placement varying from instrument to instrument. The Mexico–Netherlands BIT provides a separate sub-provision in its article on 'Treatment', for example:

> Each Contracting Party shall observe any other obligation in writing, it has assumed with regard to investments in its territory by nationals of the other Contracting Party. Disputes arising from such obligations shall be settled under the terms of the contracts underlying the obligations.[97]

The Swiss–Trinidad and Tobago BIT is different, placing its umbrella clause at the end of the text under 'Other commitments':

> Each Contracting Party shall observe any obligation it has assumed with regard to investments in its territory by Investors of the other Contracting Party.[98]

The Spain–Nigeria BIT is different still, with the following clause in its Article 3 on 'Protection':

> Neither Contracting Party shall in any way impair by unreasonable or discriminatory measure the management, maintenance, use, enjoyment or disposal of such investments. Each Contracting Party shall observe any obligation it may have entered into in writing with regard to investments of investors of the other Contracting Party and which is clearly according to the internal applicable law.[99]

With no uniform wording of such provisions in IIAs, the interpretation of umbrella clauses is also far from uniform.[100]

The interpretation differences are as much a result of arbitrators' views on the proper role of contractual obligations within the ISDS framework as they are a result of textual differences: the main issue an umbrella clause raises is whether the provision should transform a simple contract violation by the host to the level of an internationally wrongful act. Some tribunals say yes, others say no.

---

97 Agreement on promotion, encouragement and reciprocal protection of investments between the Kingdom of the Netherlands and the United Mexican States, Art. 3(4) (Oct. 1, 1999).

98 Agreement between the Swiss Confederation and the Republic of Trinidad and Tobago on the Promotion and Reciprocal Protection of Investments, Art. 10(2) (July 4, 2012).

99 Agreement on the Reciprocal Promotion and Protection of Investments between the Kingdom of Spain and the Federal Republic of Nigeria, Art. 4(2) (Jan. 19, 2006).

100 Katia Yannaca-Small, *What About this 'Umbrella Clause'?*, *in* Arbitration under International Investment Agreements 479, 483 (Yannaca-Small ed., 2010).

The first ICSID tribunal faced with an umbrella clause worried about the effect of extending IIA protection to such a wide number of potential claims. The *SGS v. Pakistan* tribunal made a policy-based decision when rejecting the investor's umbrella clause claim.[101] When the tribunal 'spelled out in some detail' the consequences of extending an openly worded umbrella clause, it highlighted the inequalities between the investor and the host that would result.[102]

> [. . .] On the reading of [the umbrella clause provision of the BIT] urged by the Claimant, the benefits of the dispute settlement provisions of a contract with a State also a party to a BIT, would flow only to the investor. For that investor could always defeat the State's invocation of the contractually specified forum, and render any mutually agreed procedure of dispute settlement, other than BIT-specified ICSID arbitration, a dead-letter, at the investor's choice. The investor would remain free to go to arbitration either under the contract or under the BIT. But the State party to the contract would be effectively precluded from proceeding to the arbitral forum specified in the contract unless the investor was minded to agree. The Tribunal considers that Article 11 of the BIT should be read in such a way as to enhance mutuality and balance of benefits in the inter-relation of different agreements located in differing legal orders.[103]

Subsequent tribunals have often taken a stricter textual view of the open wording of umbrella clauses. The plain meaning view of umbrella clauses permits investors to claim IIA protection from every breach of contract by the host.[104] This, of course, increases investor protection. A tribunal faced with a case very similar to *SGS v. Pakistan* found the policy arguments brought out by the earlier tribunal 'unconvincing'. The *SGS v. Philippines* tribunal upheld an umbrella clause's extension to contractual breaches by the host, reasoning that, by so doing, it remained firmly within the realm of international investment law.[105]

The *Noble Ventures* tribunal took a highly differentiated approach, noting that it is a combination of elements—the particular words of the agreement, the intent of the parties, and the consequences—which should determine

---

101 SGS *Société Générale de Surveillance S.A. v. Islamic Republic of Pakistan*, ICSID Case No. ARB/01/13, Decision of the Tribunal on Objections to Juridiction (Aug. 6, 2003), http://italaw.com/documents/SGSvPakistan-decision_000.pdf.

102 *Id.* para. 168.

103 *Id.* para. 168.

104 To the extent prescribed by the parties' contract.

105 SGS *Société Générale de Surveillance SA v. Republic of the Philippines*, ICSID Case No. ARB/02/6, Decision of the Tribunal on Objections to Jurisdiction (Jan. 29, 2004), 8 ICSID Rep. 518 (2005).

whether contract breaches can form the basis for a claim by an investor against the host.

 CASE

Noble Ventures, Inc. v. Romania[106]

In August 2000, an American company, Noble Ventures, contracted with the Romanian State Owned Fund to take over the management of a privatized steel mill, Combinatul Siderurgic Resita (CSR). Although CSR was heavily indebted at the time, Noble Ventures claimed that the privatization agreement provided for rescheduling of the debts. When a governmental reorganization led to the State Owned Fund's replacement by a new office six months into the contract, problems began. Labour disturbances as well as an alleged refusal on the part of the government to reschedule the debts in a manner acceptable to the company led to CSR's bankruptcy and Noble Ventures' ICSID complaint.

Among the issues facing the tribunal was whether the US–Romania BIT's Article II.2(c) was an umbrella clause that would permit a claim based on a breach of contract.

> 46. Considering that the Claimant's case comprises some claims which concern alleged breaches of contractual relationships purportedly concluded with the Respondent, the question for the Tribunal is whether Art. II (2)(c) BIT is an 'umbrella clause' that transforms contractual undertakings into international law obligations and accordingly makes it a breach of the BIT by the Respondent if it breaches a contractual obligation that it has entered into with the Claimant. Art. II (2)(c) reads as follows: '*Each Party shall observe any obligation it may have entered into with regard to investments.*'
> 47. As indicated by the parties, a similar question arose in other recent ICSID cases. Thus an important case to address the problem was *SGS Société Générale de Surveillance S.A. v. Islamic Republic of Pakistan* (ICSID Case No. ARB/01/13; *SGS v. Pakistan*), which was heavily relied on by the Respondent in the present case. The Tribunal was there concerned with Article 11 of an Agreement between the Swiss Confederation and the Islamic Republic of Pakistan on the Promotion and Reciprocal Protection of Investments (*Swiss–Pakistan BIT*) which reads as follows: '*Either Contracting Party shall constantly guarantee the observance of the commitments it has entered into with respect to the investments of the investors of the*

---

106 *Noble Ventures, Inc. v. Romania*, ICSID Case No. ARB/01/11, Award (Oct. 12, 2005). Available at: http://italaw. com/documents/Noble.pdf.

other Contracting Party'. The Tribunal found that '(T)he text itself of Art. 11 does not purport to state that breaches of contract alleged by an investor in relation to a contract it has concluded with a State (widely considered to be a matter of municipal rather than international law) are automatically 'elevated' to the level of breaches of international treaty law. Considering the widely accepted principle with which we started, namely, that under general international law, a violation of a contract entered into by a State with an investor of another State, is not, by itself, a violation of international law, and considering further that the legal consequences that the Claimant would have us attribute to Art. 11 of the BIT are so far-reaching in scope, and so automatic and unqualified and sweeping in their operation, so burdensome in their potential impact upon a Contracting Party, we believe that clear and convincing evidence must be adduced by the Claimant that such was indeed the shared intent of the Contracting Parties to the Swiss-Pakistan Investment Protection Treaty in incorporating Article 11 in the BIT. We do not find such evidence in the text itself of Article 11. We have not been pointed to any other evidence of the putative common intent of the Contracting Parties by the Claimant' (see paras. 166 and 167 of the Decision). Consequently, the Tribunal declined to regard Art. 11 as an umbrella clause.

48. Another important case to address the 'umbrella clause' problem was *SGS Société Générale de Surveillance S.A. v. Republic of the Philippines* (ICSID Case No. ARB/02/6; *SGS v. Philippines*). That case was referred to by the Claimant in the present case in support of its position. The relevant clause in that case (Art. X(2) of the Agreement between the Swiss Confederation and the Republic of the Philippines on the Promotion and Reciprocal Protection of Investments) reads as follows: *'Each Contracting Party shall observe any obligation it has assumed with regard to specific investments in its territory by investors of the other Contracting Party'.* The Tribunal interpreted the clause by reference to its wording and the object and purpose of the bilateral investment treaty so as to apply it to *inter alia* contractual obligations (paras. 115 and 116) and accordingly found that the contractual commitment was incorporated and brought within the framework of the bilateral investment treaty by Article X (2): *'To summarize, for present purposes Article X(2) includes commitments or obligations arising under contracts entered into by the host State'* (para. 127).

49. A third case concerned with a clause regarded by one of the parties to the dispute as an umbrella clause is *Salini Costruttori S.p.A. v. The Hashemite Kingdom of Jordan* (No. ARB/02/13; *Salini v. Jordan*). The case was decided only shortly before the end of the written proceedings in this case. In *Salini v. Jordan* the Tribunal was concerned with a clause in the bilateral investment treaty between Italy and Jordan which read as follows (Art. 2(4)): *'Each Contracting Party shall create and maintain in its territory a legal framework apt to guarantee the investors the continuity of legal treatment, including compliance, in good faith, of all undertakings assumed with regard to each specific investor'.* Regarding the terms of Art. 2(4) to be appreciably different from the provisions in *SGS v. Pakistan* and *SGS v. Philippines*

the Tribunal found that '*(U)nder Art. 2(4), each contracting Party committed itself to create and maintain in its territory a "legal framework" favorable to investments. This legal framework must be apt to guarantee to investors the continuity of legal treatment. It must in particular be such as to ensure compliance of all undertakings assumed under relevant contracts with respect to each specific investor. But under Article 2(4), each contracting Party did not commit itself to "observe" any "obligation" it had previously assumed with regard to specific investments of the investor of the other party as did the Philippines. It did not even guarantee the observance of commitments it had entered into with respect to investments of the investors of the other Contracting Party as did Pakistan. It only committed itself to create and maintain a legal framework apt to guarantee the compliance of all undertakings assumed with regard to each specific investor'.*

50. With regard to Art. II (2)(c) of the bilateral investment treaty which is of relevance in the present case, it has to be observed that there are differences between the wording of the clause and the clauses in the other cases. Therefore, it is necessary, first, to interpret Art. II (2)(c) regardless of the other cases. In doing so, reference has to be made to Arts. 31 *et seq.* of the Vienna Convention on the Law of Treaties [. . .].

51. Considering that Art. II (2)(c) BIT uses the term 'shall' and that it forms part of the Article which provides for the major substantial obligations undertaken by the parties, there can be no doubt that the Article was intended to create obligations, and obviously obligations beyond those specified in other provisions of the BIT itself. Since States usually do not conclude, with reference to specific investments, special international agreements in addition to existing bilateral investment treaties, it is difficult to understand the notion 'obligation' as referring to obligations undertaken under other 'international' agreements. And given that such agreements, if concluded, would also be subject to the general principle of *pacta sunt servanda*, there would certainly be no need for a clause of that kind. By contrast, in addition to the BIT, what are often concluded concerning investments are so-called investment contracts between investors and the host State. Such agreements describe specific rights and duties of the parties concerning a specific investment. Against this background, and considering the wording of Art. II (2)(c) which speaks of 'any obligation [a party] may have *entered into* with regard to *investments*', it is difficult not to regard this as a clear reference to investment contracts. In fact, one may ask what other obligations can the parties have had in mind as having been 'entered into' by a host State with regard to an investment. The employment of the notion 'entered into' indicates that specific commitments are referred to and not general commitments, for example by way of legislative acts. This is also the reason why Art. II (2)(c) would be very much an empty base unless understood as referring to contracts. Accordingly, the wording of Article II(2)(c) provides substantial support for an interpretation of Art. II (2)(c) as a real umbrella clause. [. . .]

While it is not the purpose of investment treaties *per se* to remedy such problems, a clause that is readily capable of being interpreted in this way and which would otherwise be deprived of practical applicability is naturally to be understood as protecting investors also with regard to contracts with the host State generally in so far as the contract was entered into with regard to an investment.

53. An umbrella clause is usually seen as transforming municipal law obligations into obligations directly cognizable in international law. The Tribunal recalls the well established rule of general international law that in normal circumstances *per se* a breach of a contract by the State does not give rise to direct international responsibility on the part of the State. This derives from the clear distinction between municipal law on the one hand and international law on the other, two separate legal systems (or orders) the second of which treats the rules contained in the first as facts, as is reflected in *inter alia* Article Three of the International Law Commission's Articles on State Responsibility adopted in 2001. As stated by Judge Schwebel, former President of the International Court of Justice, 'it is generally accepted that, so long as it affords remedies in its Courts, a State is only directly responsible, on the international plane, for acts involving breaches of contract, where the breach is not a simple breach. . . but involves an obviously arbitrary or tortious element . . .' [. . .]. It may be further added that, inasmuch as a breach of contract at the municipal level creates at the same time the violation of one of the principles existing either in customary international law or in treaty law applicable between the host State and the State of the nationality of the investor, it will give rise to the international responsibility of the host State. But that responsibility will co-exist with the responsibility created in municipal law and each of them will remain valid independently of the other, a situation that further reflects the respective autonomy of the two legal systems (municipal and international) each one with regard to the other.

54. That being said, none of the above mentioned general rules is peremptory in nature. [. . .].

55. Thus, an umbrella clause, when included in a bilateral investment treaty, introduces an exception to the general separation of States obligations under municipal and under international law. In consequence, as with any other exception to established general rules of law, the identification of a provision as an 'umbrella clause' can as a consequence proceed only from a strict, if not indeed restrictive, interpretation of its terms and, more generally, in accordance with the well known customary rules codified under Article 31 of the Vienna Convention of the Law of Treaties (1969). [. . .]

56. In the present case, in order to identify the intention of the United States and Romania when they negotiated Art. II(2)(c) of the BIT, a key element is provided by the exact formulation of that provision. Indeed, it is the differences in the wording of Art. II(2)(c) of the BIT and of provisions in other bilateral investment treaties that have been relied on as umbrella clauses in other ICSID cases that go far to explain the different positions taken by different ICSID tribunals that have in recent times had to consider such clauses.

57. In *Salini v. Jordan, supra,* it is evident that the obligation laid down at Art. 2(4) of the bilateral investment treaty between Italy and Jordan plainly justifies the conclusion reached by the Tribunal. A provision creating and maintaining a 'legal framework' favourable to investment deals only with the setting of norms and establishment of institutions aimed at facilitating investment by investors of the other Party; it does not entail that each Party becomes responsible under international law for the breach of any of its contractual obligations *vis-à-vis* the private investors of the other Party.

58. In *SGS v. Pakistan, supra,* the relevant provision of the bilateral investment treaty (Art. 11) does not simply speak of a 'legal framework'; and the provision could be interpreted as laying down a kind of general obligation for the host State as a public authority to facilitate foreign investment, namely an obligation to 'guarantee' the observance of the commitments that the host State has entered into towards investors of the other Party, being an obligation to be implemented by, in particular, the adoption of steps and measures under its own municipal law to safeguard the guarantee.

In other words, the formulation of Art. 11 of the bilateral investment treaty in *SGS v. Pakistan, supra,* may be interpreted as implicitly setting an international obligation of result for each Party to be fulfilled through appropriate means at the municipal level but without necessarily elevating municipal law obligations to international ones.

59. By contrast, in *SGS v. Philippines, supra,* the treaty clause was formulated so as to assimilate the host State's contractual obligations to its treaty obligations under the bilateral investment treaty by saying that each Party 'shall observe any obligation it has assumed' with regard to investments made by the investors of the other Party. It is then understandable that, without necessarily having recourse to completely different reasoning, the Tribunal in that case reached a position different from that adopted in *SGS v. Pakistan, supra.*

60. In the present case, the formulation adopted at Art. II(2)(c), which is even more general and straightforward than that in the bilateral investment treaty that fell to be considered in *SGS v. Philippines,* clearly falls into the category of the most general and direct formulations tending to an assimilation of contractual obligations to treaty ones; not only does it use the term 'shall observe' but it refers in the most general terms to 'any' obligations that either Party may have entered into 'with regard to investments'.

[. . . T]he Tribunal proceeds on the basis that, in including Art. II(2)(c) in the BIT, the Parties had as their aim to equate contractual obligations governed by municipal law to international treaty obligations as established in the BIT.

61. By reason therefore of the inclusion of Art. II(2)(c) in the BIT, the Tribunal therefore considers the Claimant's claims of breach of contract on the basis that any such breach constitutes a breach of the BIT.

Regardless of whether every municipal obligation the host has assumed is considered within the scope of the umbrella clause, the tribunal must still ensure that any particular claim of breach stems from a true 'obligation'. Unlike the umbrella clause scope, which is a question of international law, the obligation-existence analysis must be made on the basis of the municipal law itself. The *Micula* tribunal explained, 'whether an obligation has arisen depends on the law governing that obligation [. . .]. In other words, to be afforded the protection of the BIT, the obligation must qualify as such under its governing law.'[107]

Dispute arises 'directly out of' the investment
The tribunal in *Fedax v. Venezuela* addressed the issue of how closely the dispute must be connected to the investment.

 CASE

Fedax NV v. Republic of Venezuela[108]

In this case, the Venezuelan company Industrias Metalúrgicas Van Dam CA was a holder of Venezuelan promissory notes for capital and interest payments. As payment for services rendered to the corporation by the Dutch-owned Fedax NV, Industrias Metalúrgicas endorsed six of its promissory notes over to Fedax. Although the Venezuelan government paid the capital and interest of one note in full, by May 1994, it had stopped paying Fedax the required amounts. Claiming approximately $680 000 in unpaid capital and interest, Fedax brought its dispute to ICSID arbitration.

Venezuela disputed the jurisdiction of the tribunal on the argument that Fedax had made no direct investment and, therefore, there was no 'dispute arising directly out of an investment'. The tribunal answered with the following words:

> 24. . . . It is apparent that the term 'directly' relates in this Article to the 'dispute' and not to the 'investment'. It follows that jurisdiction can exist even in respect of investments that are not direct, so long as the dispute arises directly from such transaction. This interpretation is also consistent with the broad reach that the term 'investment' must be given in the light of the negotiating history of the Convention.

---

107 *Ioan Micula and Others v. Romania*, ICSID Case No. ARB/05/20, Award, para. 418 (Dec. 11, 2013).
108 *Fedax NV v. Republic of Venezuela*, ICSID Case No. ARB/96/3, Decision of the Tribunal on Objections to Jurisdiction (July 11, 1997), 37 ILM 1378 (1998). Available at: http://italaw.com/cases/documents/433.

The *Fedax* tribunal's approach was adopted subsequently by the *CSOB* tribunal facing a claim for damages arising from the Slovak Republic's refusal to pay an obligation it had on a loss stemming from a loan the claimant bank had paid to a company within the framework of an investment. Arguing that the obligation to repay the loan was not an investment, the respondent disputed the tribunal's jurisdiction as lacking the required characteristic of a dispute arising directly from an investment. The tribunal quoted the above-mentioned *Fedax* passage and continued:

> 72. The Tribunal agrees with the interpretation adopted in the *Fedax* case. An investment is frequently a rather complex operation, composed of various inter-related transactions, each element of which, standing alone, might not in all cases qualify as an investment. Hence, a dispute that is brought before the Centre must be deemed to arise directly out of an investment even when it is based on a transaction which, standing alone, would not qualify as an investment under the Convention, provided that the particular transaction forms an integral part of an overall operation that qualifies as an investment.
>
> 73. The Preamble of the Convention confirms the foregoing interpretation. Here, after 'considering the need for international cooperation for economic development, and the role of private international investment therein,' the Contracting Parties bear 'in mind the possibility that from time to time disputes may arise in connection with such investment between Contracting States and nationals of other Contracting States.'
>
> 74. The foregoing analysis indicates that the term 'directly', as used in Article 25(1) of the Convention, should not be interpreted restrictively to compel the conclusion that CSOB's claim is outside the Centre's jurisdiction and the Tribunal's competence merely because it is based on an obligation of the Slovak Republic which, standing alone, does not qualify as an investment.[109]

? DISCUSSION NOTES

1 Should a claimant's defence to a case brought against it in national court by the respondent be found to be the 'same dispute' as its claim in the investor-State arbitration context? The *Texaco* and *Chevron v. Ecuador* tribunal strictly construed the text of the relevant BIT fork in the road provision that provided for no duplication of disputes 'submitted' to different fora.

> [. . .] The raising of a plea in defence to a claim in the national courts [. . .] cannot properly be described as the submission of a dispute for settlement in

---

109 *Supra* note 92.

those courts. The notion of 'submission' of a dispute connotes the making of a choice and a voluntary decision to refer the dispute to the court for resolution: as a matter of the plain and ordinary meaning of the term, it does not extend to the raising of a defence in response to another's claim submitted to that court.[110]

2 Signing a BIT that offers the consent of the state parties is not enough to show that the disputing parties have consented—a state party cannot force consent onto its nationals; the private investor itself must have consented to ICSID jurisdiction (in writing). The tribunal in *American Mfg and Trading v. Zaire*, for instance, addressed this question in the following way:

> 5.17 [. . .] In other words, does the consent of the United States [create] an obligation for its national? Should there not be, in addition to that consent, also the consent by AMT itself relating to a specific dispute? Can the United States impose upon its national the passage of consent to ICSID? Or, better still, in the absence of AMT's consent, will the Treaty signed by the United States of America and Zaire suffice to take its place?
>
> 5.18 The Tribunal holds that this question must be answered in the negative. The requirement of the consent of the parties does not disappear with the existence of the Treaty. The Convention envisages an exchange of consents between the Parties. When Article 25 states in paragraph 1 that 'the parties' must have consented in writing to submit the dispute to the Centre, it does not speak of the States or more precisely, it speaks of a State and a national of another State. It appears therefore that the two States cannot, by virtue of Article 25 of the Convention, compel any of their nationals to appear before the Centre; this is a power that the Convention has not granted to the States.[111]

3 It is not just contract breaches that can trigger umbrella clause claims. Legislation that harms the investor's interests or even unfulfilled, unilateral promises on the part of the host state can also result in a finding of IIA violation. *See LG&E v. Argentina*:

> 171. In many cases it has been considered that the umbrella clause is activated not by obligations set forth in municipal law, but in contracts between the State and the investor. Several of those tribunals have concluded that the breach of a

---

110 *Chevron Corporation and Texaco Petroleum Corporation v. Republic of Ecuador*, UNCITRAL, PCA Case No. 2009-23, Third Interim Award on Jurisdiction and Admissibility, para. 4.82 (Feb. 27, 2012). Available at: http:// italaw.com/documents/ChevronvEcuadorThirdInterimAward.pdf.

111 *American Manufacturing and Trading, Inc. v. Republic of Zaire*, ICSID Case No. ARB/93/1, Award, paras. 5.17–5.18 (Feb. 21, 1997), 36 ILM 1534 (1997).

contractual obligation in a contract between the State and the investor gives rise to a claim under the umbrella clause.

172. The issue of the Tribunal's consideration is whether the provisions of the Gas Law and its implementing regulations constitute, (i) 'obligations', (ii) 'with regard to' LG&E's capacity as a foreign investor, (iii) with respect to its 'investment,' such that abrogation of the guarantees set forth in the Gas Law and its implementing regulations give rise to a violation of the Treaty.

173. In this case, it will be necessary to establish whether LG&E's claims fall under the umbrella clause's protection.

174. In order to determine the applicability of the umbrella clause, the Tribunal should establish if by virtue of the provisions of the Gas Law and its regulations, the Argentine State has assumed international obligations with respect to LG&E and its investment. To this end, it is necessary to remember that the provisions of the Gas Law and its regulation fixed and regulated the tariff scheme ensuring the value of Claimants' investment; that the purpose of Claimants' investment was to increase the value of its shares in the Licensees through a fragile balanced management of profits and costs, represented by the tariffs fixed by Argentina in light of the already mentioned Gas Law and its regulation. In view of the statements above, the Tribunal concludes that these provisions were not legal obligations of a general nature. On the contrary, they were very specific in relation to LG&E's investment in Argentina, so that their abrogation would be a violation of the umbrella clause.[112]

4 Can an umbrella clause apply if the host has not exercised any governmental powers? *Burlington Resources v. Ecuador* considered that an umbrella clause may also apply even if no exercise of sovereign power is involved:

> [. . .] Ecuador alleges that Burlington's claims do not involve the exercise of sovereign power. This requirement, however, has no support in the text of the umbrella clause of the Treaty. Moreover, while different views have been expressed on this matter, in line with other decisions such as for instance *Duke Energy*, the Tribunal considers that umbrella clauses may apply even if no exercise of sovereign power is involved. [. . .] Consequently, Claimant may rely upon the treaty's umbrella clause even if no exercise of Respondent's sovereign power is involved [. . .].[113]

---

112 *LG&E Energy Corp, LG&E Capital Corp and LG&E International Inc. v. The Argentine Republic*, ICSID Case No. ARB/02/1, Decision on Liability, paras. 171–4 (Oct. 3, 2006), 21 ICSID Rev.–FILJ 203 (2006).
113 *Burlington Resources Inc and others v. Republic of Ecuador and Empresa Estatal Petróleos del Ecuador (PetroEcuador)*, ICSID Case No. ARB/08/5, Decision on Jurisdiction, para. 190 (June 2, 2010), http://italaw. com/documents/BurlingtonResourcesInc_v_Ecuador_Jurisdiction_Eng.pdf.

5 How should a tribunal approach a breach of contract between private enterprises that the host does not redress? The *Hamester v. Ghana* Tribunal found that contracts concluded between an investor and a legal entity separate from the respondent state do not fall within the scope of an umbrella clause. The tribunal explained that

> [. . .] the consequence of an automatic and wholesale elevation of any and all contract claims into treaty claims risks undermining the distinction between national legal orders and international law [. . .] this is not a result that is in line with the general purpose of the ICSID/BIT mechanism for the international protection of foreign investments.[114]

The tribunal in *Amto v. Ukraine* similarly refused to find any violation of the BIT arising from a non-state enterprise's breach of contract.[115]

6 Can a claim based on an umbrella clause be made by a non-party to the contract, such as a shareholder? There does not seem to be any agreement on this issue, with some tribunals holding that only parties can claim protection, while others have found that umbrella clauses are intended to protect investments, not just the particular investor party to whom the host's obligation was directly owed. *See* Katia Yannaca-Small, *What About This 'Umbrella Clause'?, in* Arbitration Under International Investment Agreements—A Guide to the Key Issues 479, 479–503 (K. Yannaca-Small ed., 2010).

7 Because a futility exception for prerequisites to arbitration broadens the state's consent, tribunals accepting it have often underlined that the burden of proof of futility rests with the investor. The proof must demonstrate the ineffectiveness not just of the respondent's judicial system in general, but rather prove how particular aspects of the system would have failed in the specific case. The tribunal in *Kiliç v. Turkmenistan* considered the claimaint's argument that it would have been futile to attempt to attain satisfaction through the host's courts. Open to a futility exception in general, it refused to recognize its application to the context before it, noting:

> Claimant's futility analysis is based principally on broad statements and third party studies/reports, to the effect that the Turkmen judiciary lacks independence, and that the Turkmen authorities would have had a particular aversion

114 *Gustav F.W. Hamester GmbH and Co KG v. Republic of Ghana*, ICSID Case No. ARB/07/24, Award, para. 349 (June 18, 2010). Available at: http://italaw.com/documents/Hamesterv.GhanaAward.pdf.
115 *Limited Liability Company Amto v. Ukraine*, SCC Case No. 080/2005, ECT, Final Award, paras. 105 and 108 (Mar. 26, 2008). Available at: http://italaw.com/documents/AmtoAward.pdf.

> to Turkish investors. The Tribunal considers, however, that if a party [. . .] is
> to make a futility argument, it has the onus of showing that recourse to the
> Contracting State's courts would be futile or ineffective, and that requires
> the tendering of probative evidence that goes to the specificity of the issue in
> dispute. It is not enough to make generalised allegations about the insufficiency
> of a state's legal system.[116]

6.2.2 Applicable law

Once the jurisdiction of a tribunal is established, the case may proceed to its
merits. An initial matter, however, is the tribunal's determination of what law
it will apply. Under the ICSID rules, the answer to this question follows the
voluntary nature of arbitration: the 'rules of law' that the parties have agreed
upon as applicable in their arbitration agreement will be applied. Thus, the
parties may select from one of a variety of legal jurisdictions, domestic or
international, to govern their relations.[117]

However, not all parties have an explicit agreement on choice of law. While the
background of the parties' relations can form the basis for a tribunal's finding of
an implicit agreement on the choice of law to apply, in some cases no such agreement can be found. The tribunal in such a case must still resolve the dispute,
so Article 42 further specifies that if there is no agreement on the choice of law,
the dispute is to be subject to the law of the state party together with applicable
international law rules. Article 42.1 of the ICSID Convention reads as follows:

> (1) The Tribunal shall decide a dispute in accordance with such rules of law as may
> be agreed by the parties. In the absence of such agreement, the Tribunal shall apply
> the law of the Contracting State party to the dispute (including its rules on the con-
> flict of laws) and such rules of international law as may be applicable.

Parra notes the significance of the reference to international law at the time
of drafting the Convention. Not only was international law made available as
a source of law for questions not answered by domestic rules, but, '[m]ore
importantly, the provision was seen as authorizing the arbitrators, in their
application of international law, to set aside the applicable domestic law
when it, or an action taken under it, violated international law'.[118]

---

116 *Kiliç İnşaat İthalat İhracat Sanayi ve Ticaret Anonim Şirketi v. Turkmenistan,* ICSID Case No. ARB/10/1, Award, para. 8.1.10 (July 2, 2013).
117 *See* Antonio Parra, *Applicable Law in Investor-State Arbitration, in* Contemporary Issues in International Arbitration and Mediation 3 (Arthur W. Rovine ed., 2008).
118 *Id.,* at 5 (footnote omitted).

Today, however, the second sentence of Article 42.1 has become less critical. This is because most investor-State arbitrations are now based on an IIA. Thus, it is the law of the treaty—international law—that is the parties' choice, making international law the predominant law for tribunals to apply. As the tribunal in *El Paso Energy v. Argentina* explained,

> [...] The advent of treaty arbitration has brought about a departure from the typical situation where the contract between the investor and the host State is the basis for the consent to ICSID jurisdiction. The basis for consent in treaty arbitration is the treaty itself, in our case the BIT, such consent covering as a rule only claims arising under the BIT ('treaty claims,' as opposed to 'contract claims'). The specific context characterising treaty arbitration permits in our case to define the role of the BIT and international law, on the one hand, and Argentina law, on the other.[119]

The domestic law of the state party remains applicable to the extent the dispute addresses issues the treaty provisions leave to national law, but the interplay of domestic and international legal rules is, in most cases, heavily weighted toward the international ones. The *Azurix* tribunal noted the role of domestic law where the BIT formed the basis of the parties' agreement on choice of law:

> [...] the law of Argentina should be helpful in the carrying out of the Tribunal's inquiry into the alleged breaches of the Concession Agreement to which Argentina's law applies, but it is only an element of the inquiry because of the treaty nature of the claims under consideration.[120]

If the parties explicitly agree, the tribunal may also come to an equitable result on the basis of *ex aequo et bono* decision-making.[121]

6.2.3 Costs

Investor-State arbitration is an expensive procedure. The costs for using the selected arbitration forum and the costs and expenses of the arbitrators are additional to the parties' own legal costs. While the attorney fees make up

---

119 *El Paso Energy International Company v. The Argentine Republic*, ICSID Case No. ARB/03/15, Award, para. 129 (Oct. 31, 2011). Available at: http://italaw.com/documents/El_Paso_v._Argentina_Award_ENG. pdf.

120 *Azurix v. The Argentine Republic*, ICSID Case No. ARB/01/12, Award, para. 67 (July 14, 2006). Available at: http://italaw.com/documents/AzurixAwardJuly2006.pdf.

121 ICSID Convention art. 42.3.

the largest portion of overall expenditures, the costs can nevertheless be substantial.

Under the ICSID Convention and Arbitration Rules, the tribunal will decide who will pay the costs.[122] The traditional international law rule of each party bearing its own legal costs and splitting the costs of arbitration has been applied frequently by ICSID tribunals. It is only where the tribunal senses a frivolousness of claims or where the circumstances would make division unjust that the tribunals grant the successful party relief from the arbitration costs.

In *Daimler v. Argentina*,[123] for instance, the tribunal found several of the respondent's claims worthless, but that did not prevent it from continuing the practice of splitting costs, given other valuable arguments:

> 283. Each disputing party has requested the Tribunal to assess the costs of these proceedings against the other party. The Tribunal sympathizes with the Claimant's request in respect of Argentina's first three jurisdictional objections. The first objection was patently groundless while the second and third objections largely repeated objections which Argentina has raised in myriad other cases—each time without success. Nevertheless, the Respondent's assertion of these objections in the context of the present proceedings cannot be said to have been vexatious, particularly considering that it chose to rest on its written pleadings without insisting upon any further discussion of the issues at the oral hearings.
> 284. With respect to the fourth and fifth objections, the analysis of these questions was difficult and complex. The fourth objection concerned a question that is novel in ICSID jurisdictional practice, while the fifth concerned a point on which the existing jurisprudence is dramatically split. Both parties presented sound legal arguments, and each side ultimately prevailed on some points but failed on others.
> 285. In light of these considerations, the Tribunal finds it appropriate for the costs of the arbitration to be split evenly between the parties, with each side bearing its own legal costs.[124]

In determining who should bear the costs, tribunals will often explain their decisions by setting out the circumstances as well as the results of the case. The tribunal in *El Paso Energy v. Argentina* stated its adherence to the feesplitting practice with the following:

---

122 ICSID Convention, Art. 61(2); ICSID Arbitration Rule 28. *See also* UNCITRAL Arbitration Rule 40(1).
123 *Daimler Financial Services AG v. Argentine Republic*, ICSID Case No. ARB/05/1, Award (Aug. 22, 2012). Available at: http://italaw.com/sites/default/files/case-documents/ita1082.pdf.
124 *Id*. paras. 283–5.

750. The Convention and the Arbitration Rules give ICSID tribunals broad discretion in awarding costs. The practice in apportioning costs has sometimes followed the principle 'the loser pays' while in many other cases the decision has been that the Parties were to bear their own costs and share equally the fees and expenses of the arbitrators as well as the charges for the use of the Centre's facilities and services.

751. Regarding the present case, the Tribunal notes that the Claimant has been successful on the jurisdictional issue but only in part as to the merits of the case and the damages claimed. There are therefore good reasons to decide, as is hereby decided, that each Party shall bear its own costs connected with the proceedings as well as half of the fees and expenses of the arbitrators and the charges for the use of the Centre's facilities and services.[125]

 DISCUSSION NOTES

1 Costs can become a contentious issue for the parties because portions must be paid in advance. When one party refuses to pay them, this inaction itself can become part of the dispute. If the claimant is recalcitrant in forwarding costs, the ICSID can suspend the arbitration until the money is deposited. When the respondent refuses to pay, however, the claimant may—under protest—take over the payments due in order to keep the process moving forward. This is what happened in the *Abaclat* case, where Argentina refused to pay the tribunal's costs beginning in June 2012. In a 31 May 2015 letter requesting assistance from the tribunal, the claimants allege that this recalcitrance 'has prejudiced Claimants' fundamental due process rights and endangers the investor-State system by denying investors a fair opportunity to exercise their rights'.

2 Unlike the ICSID Arbitration Rules, the UNCITRAL Arbitration Rules (2013) provide that 'in principle' the losing party should bear the costs of the proceedings. Article 42(1). The tribunal may, however, apportion the costs differently if the context suggests this would be 'reasonable'.

3 In a case decided under UNCITRAL rules, *ICS Inspection and Control Services v. Argentina*,[126] the tribunal found it lacked jurisdiction to hear

---

125 *El Paso Energy International Company v. The Argentine Republic*, ICSID Case No. ARB/03/15, Award, paras. 750–51 (Oct. 31, 2011). Available at: http://italaw.com/documents/El_Paso_v._Argentina_Award_ENG.pdf.

126 *ICS Inspection and Control Services Limited v. Republic of Argentina*, UNCITRAL, PCA Case No. 2010-9, Award on Jurisdiction (Feb. 10, 2012). Available at: http://italaw.com/documents/ICS_v_Argentina_AwardJurisdiction_10Feb2012_En.pdf.

the dispute. As a result, the complaint was dismissed, but costs still needed to be assigned. Performing the task proved to be more complex than a simple application of the UNCITRAL rules. The tribunal looked to general international law as well in coming to this decision, which highlights the interplay between the rules specific to arbitration and those more generally applicable:

337. Article 40 [. . .] contains distinct rules regarding the awarding of arbitration costs and the costs of the parties' legal representation and assistance. The principle governing the awarding of the costs of arbitration, according to Article 40(1) of the UNCITRAL Arbitration Rules, is that the costs shall be borne by the unsuccessful party, in this case the Claimant, unless the Tribunal finds an apportionment of the costs between the parties to be reasonable under the circumstances.

338. In light of the Tribunal's conclusion that it has no jurisdiction over any of the Claimant's claims, there is a clearly successful party, the Respondent, and a clearly unsuccessful party, the Claimant. Given this outcome, the Tribunal finds no reason to deviate from the presumption in Article 40(1) and consequently awards the costs of arbitration to the Respondent. The Claimant shall thus reimburse the Respondent the amount of EUR 180 743.61 in respect of the costs of arbitration.

339. With respect to the costs of legal representation and assistance as defined in Article 38(e), Article 40(2) of the UNCITRAL Arbitration Rules provides that the arbitral tribunal, taking into account the circumstances of the case, is free to determine which party shall bear such costs or may apportion such costs between the parties if it determines that apportionment is reasonable. Article 40(2) thus grants near total discretion to an arbitration tribunal.

340. The traditional position in investment treaty arbitration, in contrast to commercial arbitration, has been to follow the normal practice under public international law (as exemplified in Article 9(5) of the Treaty) that the parties shall bear their own costs of legal representation and assistance. The Tribunal is aware that a number of investment treaty tribunals have opted instead to apply the principle of awarding costs of legal representation and assistance to the prevailing party as with the costs of arbitration. The Tribunal accepts that this developing practice may be appropriate in some cases, but is not convinced that it should be adopted as a rule and prefers to follow the public international law practice unless a more holistic assessment of the circumstances of the case justifies a departure from that practice.

341. In this case, the Tribunal notes once again that the Respondent has been the prevailing party. Nonetheless, the Claimant's arguments can hardly be said to have been unreasonable, having been previously adopted by other tribunals even with respect to the Treaty at issue in this case. [. . .]

342. The Tribunal further notes that it has found for the Respondent and against the Claimant on only one of the various objections to jurisdiction that were raised by the Respondent and argued by the Parties, albeit one that disposes of the entirety of the claims. The Tribunal has made no finding on these other issues and shall not presume that the Claimant's arguments were without merit and would not have succeeded. The Respondent's success is therefore not absolute.

343. The Tribunal thus, despite its finding against the Claimant, decides that the Parties shall bear their own costs of legal representation and assistance.[127]

4 The rule prohibiting unilateral termination of arbitral proceedings by a party is partially justified by the financial impacts such termination would have on the other party. In the *Forminster v. Czech Republic* dispute administered under the UNCITRAL rules (under which only the tribunal may terminate the proceedings), the respondent objected to the claimant's attempt to withdraw one month after it had filed a notice of arbitration. The tribunal agreed with the respondent that this would leave the latter in a disadvantageous position in terms of cost recovery:

> 'In the Arbitral Tribunal's view, if one were to accept in the circumstances of the present case that the Claimant could bring arbitration proceedings to an end unilaterally by withdrawing its Notice of Arbitration and without the constitution of an arbitral tribunal, that would also mean that the Claimant would be given the right to get rid of the Respondent's claim for costs to all intents and purposes. In the Arbitral Tribunal's view, such a consequence would be unacceptable by any standards.'[128]

6.2.4 Challenge and annulment procedures

Arbitral tribunal decisions under ICSID are to be final. Unlike judicial proceedings or proceedings under the dispute settlement mechanism of the World Trade Organization, the ICSID has no provisions for appealing the legal analysis of a tribunal should one of the disputing parties disagree with the tribunal's award. Neither does the losing ICSID party have the possibilities of most commercial arbitration parties of challenging the award on the basis of its enforcement being against public policy.

---

127 *Id.* paras. 337–43.
128 *Forminster Enterprises Ltd. v. the Czech Republic*, UNCITRAL Arbitration, Final Award, para. 70 (Dec. 15, 2014).

If a party is very unhappy with an ICSID award, there is only one possible procedure for challenging it: requesting that the award be set aside completely, or 'annulled'. The request for such a review must be submitted to the ICSID Secretary-General within 120 days of the final award's release. The Secretary-General will then compose a three-person annulment committee from the panel of arbitrators to review the original award's legal analysis.

Tribunals have been adamant in maintaining the distinction between annulment and appeal. The function of an ad hoc annulment tribunal is not to review the original tribunal's legal analysis of the rules of investment law. Rather, it is to decide to lift an award only where necessary to preserve the essential integrity of the arbitration process. As the ad hoc tribunal reviewing the *AES v. Hungary* award explained:

> With respect to Articles 52 and 53 the drafters have taken great care to use terms which clearly express that annulment is an exhaustive, exceptional and narrowly circumscribed remedy and not an appeal. The interpretation of the terms must take this object and purpose into consideration and avoid an approach which would result in the qualification of a tribunal's reasoning as deficient, superficial, sub-standard, wrong, bad or otherwise faulty, in other words, a re-assessment of the merits which is typical for an appeal.[129]

The *SGS v. Paraguay* annulment committee was even more straightforward: '[T]here is a unanimous agreement that annulment is distinct from appeal. The *ad hoc* committees are not courts of appeal and their task is not to harmonize ICSID's jurisprudence [. . .].'[130]

a Grounds for annulment

Article 52(1) ICSID Convention sets out the five reasons for which an award of a tribunal may be annulled:

> Either party may request annulment of the award by an application in writing addressed to the Secretary-General on one or more of the following grounds:
>
> (a) that the Tribunal was not properly constituted;
> (b) that the Tribunal has manifestly exceeded its powers;
> (c) that there was corruption on the part of a member of the Tribunal;

---

129 *AES v. Hungary, infra* note 133 at para. 17.
130 *SGS Societe Generale de Surveillance SA v. The Republic of Paraguay*, ICSID Case No. ARB/07/29, Decision on Annulment, para. 105 (May 19, 2014).

(d)   that there has been a serious departure from a fundamental rule of procedure; or

(e)   that the award has failed to state the reasons on which it is based.

These are the sole grounds on which a tribunal may annul an award. Of these five possible grounds, two have never been addressed by tribunals: 'that the tribunal was not properly constituted' and 'that there was corruption on the part of a member'. The others have been discussed, and with the growth of annulment claims, other questions are arising. A brief overview demonstrates the main approaches to the different standards and an introduction to some of the procedural questions that the committees have had to face.

a.i   *'Tribunal has manifestly exceeded its powers'*

The idea of annulling an award for a tribunal's misappropriation of arbitrary authority rests on the concept of the mutual consent necessary to arbitrate a claim. Thus, where a tribunal has 'obviously' deviated from the parties' agreement, the award may be set aside under Article 52(1)(b). The provision would also cover awards where the original tribunal mistakenly found jurisdiction where an element of jurisdiction was lacking. At the same time, the *failure* to use available competences to find jurisdiction could also be grounds for annulment.

In applying the standard of 'manifestly exceeding its powers', the definition of 'manifestly' is key. While some annulment tribunals view the 'manifest' quality of the error as being a question of whether there was an impact on the award's result, others view the manifestness as a matter of whether the over-extension of power was 'obvious'. The *SGS* tribunal, for example, stated that the excess use of power was 'easily perceived, self-evident and not result from extensive interpretation'.[131] Thus, where a tribunal's decision has chosen between two possible interpretations of a treaty term, it is unlikely to be found to have manifestly exceeded its competence.

Once the applicable law has been identified, even a misapplication of the law cannot justify annulment. As the *Alapli* committee noted: 'the Tribunal [did] not only correctly identified the proper law, but also endeavoured to apply it. This is sufficient, in the Committee's view, to conclude that annulment of the Award under Article 52(1)(b) of the ICSID Convention is not warranted'.[132]

---

131 *SGS v. Paraguay*, Decision on Annulment at para. 111.

132 *Alapli Elektrik BV v. Republic of Turkey*, ICSID Case No. ARB/08/13, Annulment Proceeding, para. 247 (July 10, 2014).

Assessing a claim of a manifestly excessive *failure* to use power requires the same basic test. The following passage demonstrates how one committee approached a claim that by denying jurisdiction, the tribunal manifestly exceeded its powers.

AES Summit Generation Ltd and AES-Tisza Erömü Kft v. Hungary[133]

[. . .]

33. [. . . T]he Committee notes that there is 'widespread agreement that a failure to apply the proper law may amount to an excess of powers by the tribunal', the underlying basis being that the issues put to a tribunal are circumscribed by the parties' consent. [. . .]

However, the Committee again notes the importance of the distinction between *non-application* and mere *misapplication* of the applicable law. Whilst the precise boundaries of these concepts can be difficult to gauge, the Committee is mindful of the criticism that has been levelled against certain *ad hoc* committees for overstepping the line between annulment and appeal. The prevailing, and correct, view in modern investment jurisprudence must be understood as setting a very high threshold. As put by the *Soufraki* annulment committee:

> Misinterpretation or misapplication of the proper law may, in particular cases, be so gross or egregious as substantially to amount to failure to apply the proper law. Such gross and consequential misinterpretation or misapplication of the proper law which no reasonable person ('*bon père de famille*') could accept needs to be distinguished from a simple error—or even a serious error—in the interpretation of the law which in many national jurisdictions may be the subject of ordinary appeal as distinguished from, e.g., an extraordinary writ of *certiorari*. [citing *Soufraki*, para. 86]

34. The Committee therefore notes that in order to annul the Award under Article 52(1)(b) for a manifest excess of the Tribunal's powers consisting of a failure to apply the applicable law, at the very least something more than a 'serious error' is required.

35. Finally, the Committee considers that annulment for non-application of the applicable law is only sustainable where there has been a failure to apply the proper

---

133 *AES Summit Generation Ltd and AES-Tisza Erömü Kft v. Hungary*, ICSID Case No. ARB/07/22, Decision of the ad hoc Committee on the Application for Annulment, para. 17 (June 29, 2012). Available at: http://italaw. com/sites/default/files/case-documents/ita1072.pdf.

law *in toto*. [. . .] This is because a finding of partial nonapplication of the applicable law (*i.e.* relating to a specific provision) is indistinguishable from a finding of erroneous application, the latter constituting appellate review for which the Committee has no competence.

a.ii   *'Serious departure from a fundamental rule of procedure'*

If a tribunal has taken an improper procedural step and the party disadvantaged by such a ruling objects,[134] that party may request annulment on the basis of ICSID Convention Article 52(d) (that there has been a 'serious departure from a fundamental rule of procedure'). The limitation of annulment to 'serious' mistakes of 'fundamental' rules indicates the narrowness of this ground for challenge. Tribunals are not always consistent in separating these elements, but essentially there are two tests: the quantitative (the seriousness of the mistake) and the qualitative (the nature of the relevant rule as fundamental).[135]

To be 'serious', the mistake must have materially affected the party. That is, 'the departure must . . . be such as to deprive a party of the benefit or protection which the rule was intended to provide'.[136]

A 'fundamental' rule of procedure is one that 'concerns a rule of natural justice'. Called a 'due process' guarantee,[137] the significance here is that the departure from the rule had a negative impact on the basic fairness of the proceedings. Thus, a violation of the parties' equal opportunities to present their arguments would be fundamental,[138] while the violation of evidentiary rules may not be.[139]

a.iii   *Failure 'to state the reasons on which' the award 'is based'*

ICSID tribunals not only have to issue an award if they have jurisdiction, they must also give their reasons for deciding as they have. The level at which the

---

134 If the party does not object immediately, it is considered to have waived its rights to bring an annulment proceeding on this basis.

135 *Maritime International Nominees Establishment (MINE) v. Government of Guinea*, ICSID Case No. ARB/84/4, Decision on the Application by Guinea for Partial Annulment, para. 5.05 (Jan. 6, 1988).

136 *Misima Mines Pty. Ltd. v. Independent State of Papua New Guinea*, ICSID Case No. ARB/96/2, Decision on Annulment, at 87 para. 5.05 (Dec. 22, 1989), 4 ICSID Reports 79 (1997).

137 Gabrielle Kaufmann-Kohler, *Annulment of ICSID Awards in Contract and Treaty Arbitrations: Are there Differences?, in* Annulment of ICSID Awards 189 (Emmanuel Gaillard and Yas Banifatemi eds., 2004).

138 *See, Wena Hotels Ltd. v. Arab Republic of Egypt*, ICSID Case No. ARB/98/4, Decision of the ad hoc Committee, para. 57 (Feb. 5, 2002).

139 *See, CDC Group plc v. Republic of the Seychelles*, ICSID Case No. ARB/02/14, Annulment Proceeding, para. 59 (June 29, 2005).

discussion of the basis for a decision is sufficient, however, is one upon which parties may disagree. ICSID Convention Article 52(e) provides parties who are dissatisfied with the level of analysis an opportunity to claim for annulment based on a failure to state the reasons for the decision. As with the other bases for annulment, Article 52(e) has been interpreted so as to provide limited chances for overturning an award.

Past annulment panels have not held tribunals to a particularly high standard of reasoning. It is enough as long as the tribunal sets forth its thought process of applying the law to the facts. Again, the difference between annulment and appeal is important. The *Vivendi* tribunal was blunt: '[I]t is well accepted both in the cases and the literature that Article 52(1)(e) concerns a failure to state *any* reasons with respect to all or part of an award, not the failure to state correct or convincing reasons.'[140]

Further, there is no need for a tribunal to give explicit reasons on every point of its decision. Implicit reasoning suffices.[141] Nor must the tribunal address every legal argument raised by the parties. They are to address each question, but that has been held to be not the same as addressing each argument.[142] The Annulment Committee in *MCI v. Ecuador*, for instance, held:

> According to Article 48(3) of the Washington Convention, '[t]he award shall deal with every question submitted to the Tribunal, and shall state the reasons upon which it is based.' The obligation in Article 48(3) of the Washington Convention to deal with every question applies to every argument which is relevant and in particular to arguments which might affect the outcome of the case. On the other hand, it would be unreasonable to require a tribunal to answer each and every argument which was made in connection with the issues that the tribunal has to decide, as acknowledged in the *Klöckner (I)* decision. This explains why the tribunal must address all the parties' 'questions' ('*pretensiones*') but is not required to comment on all arguments when they are of no relevance to the award.[143]

---

140 *Compañia de Aguas Aconquija SA and Vivendi Universal v. The Argentine Republic*, ICSID Case No. ARB/97/3, Decision on Annulment, para. 64 (July 3, 2002).

141 *Wena Hotels Ltd. v. Arab Republic of Egypt*, ICSID Case No. ARB/98/4, Decision on the Application by the Arab Republic of Egypt for Annulment, para. 81 (December 8, 2000).

142 *Id.* at para. 100; *see, also Enron Corporation and Ponderosa Assets, LP v. The Argentine Republic*, ICSID Case No. ARB/01/3, Decision on the Application for Annulment of the Argentine Republic, para. 72 (July 30, 2010). Available at: http://italaw.com/documents/EnronAnnulmentDecision.pdf.

143 *M.C.I. Power Group L.C. and New Turbine Inc. v. Republic of Ecuador*, ICSID Case No. ARB/03/6, Decision on Annulment, para. 67 (October 19, 2009). Available at http://www.italaw.com/cases/662.

Finally, as the *Alapli* Committee explained, while an award that contains arguments so contradictory that they 'cancel each other out and amount to no reason at all' would be insufficient, 'annulment committees should not be quick to find contraction when in fact what is evident from the award is the compromise reached in an international collegiate adjudicative body'.[144] As long as there is a recognizable logic leading to the result, committees will assume the reasons have been stated consistently.[145]

b   Consequences of annulment

A finding of annulment means that the original award is set aside in all or in part. The annulment award itself does not substitute for the prior decision—it is not a new or repaired award. It is, instead, a decision to nullify the old, leaving the parties in the same position as they had been prior to the claim having been made.

If one of the parties still wants an award on the matter in dispute, it is free to resubmit its claims to the ICSID.[146] A new tribunal will need to be established and the proceedings begin anew.

If an annulment decision partially annuls an award, any portion of the original award that was not set aside will remain valid and is *res judicata*.

? **DISCUSSION NOTES**

Is annulment of an award discretionary? The Annulment Committee in the *Pey v. Chile* dispute determined that a finding of a serious departure from a fundamental rule of procedure mandates a decision to annul. See *Victor Pey Casado and Foundation 'Presidente Allende' v. Republic of Chile*, ICSID Case No. ARB/98/2, para. 269 (18 December 2012). The *Vivendi v. Argentina*[147] annulment tribunal, on the other hand, agreed with Argentina's claims that a member of the original tribunal failed in her duties of disclosure but refused to annul the award. Notice that while the Committee is careful to emphasize that the tribunal was 'functional', it also gave weight to the interests of closing the case:

---

144 *Alapli Elektrik v. Turkey, supra* note 132, at paras. 199–200.

145 *See id.*, para. 201.

146 *MCI Power supra* note 150 at para. 67. ICSID Convention art. 52.6.

147 *Compañía de Aguas del Aconquija SA and Vivendi Universal SA v. Argentine Republic*, ICSID Case No. ARB/97/3, Decision on the Argentine Republic's Request for Annulment of the Award rendered on 20 August 2007 (Aug. 10, 2010). Available at: http://italaw.com/documents/VivendiSecondAnnulmentDecision.pdf.

232. The *ad hoc* Committee thus understands the argument that the Second Tribunal was no longer properly constituted after the board appointment of Professor Kaufmann-Kohler, and that there was a serious departure from a fundamental rule of procedure and considers that this could lead to annulment whenever justified within the context of the case under consideration.

233. Nevertheless, the *ad hoc* Committee must establish whether in this particular case the conduct and attitudes of Professor Kaufmann-Kohler constitute a sufficient ground under Article 52 effectively to annul the Second Award. It is well understood and established that under Article 52(3) an *ad hoc* Committee has here a measure of discretion and may consider other factors. [. . .]

238. In this case, the fact remains, however, that despite most serious shortcomings, Professor Kaufmann-Kohler's exercise of independent judgment under Article 14 of the ICSID Convention was in the circumstances not impaired. The Tribunal was thus functional and operated properly in respect of both parties. Having extensively considered all the arguments, the *ad hoc* Committee, after long deliberations, has come to the conclusion that there is no sufficient ground to annul the Second Award.

240. In so finding, the *ad hoc* Committee was forced also to take into account that it would be unjust to deny the Claimants the benefit of the Award now that there is no demonstrable difference in outcome. Even though the Claimants originally appointed Professor Kaufmann-Kohler and may have felt that it was their duty to defend her in the annulment proceedings, they bear no responsibility for her actions or inaction.

241. Finally, the *ad hoc* Committee also considered the extraordinary length of the present case. The Respondent rightly says that this is not a conclusive argument in itself. In any event, both parties have contributed to it, and the prospect of yet another Tribunal operating in this case is not in itself a valid argument either but only the consequence of the annulment facility in the Treaty itself which *ad hoc* Committees are not called upon to question. Yet, it is an overriding principle that all litigation must come to an end unless there are strong reasons for it to continue.[148]

6.2.5 Recognition, enforcement, and execution of the award

As stated above, ICSID awards are final and binding. Moreover, all ICSID parties are obliged by the Convention to recognize and enforce tribunal awards, even if the award was not issued against them. Article 54(1) ICSID Convention states: 'Each Contracting State shall recognize an award rendered

---

148 *Id.* paras. 232–3, 238–41.

pursuant to this Convention as binding and enforce the pecuniary obligations imposed by that award within its territories as if it were a final judgment
of a court in that State . . . . ' The provision continues with paragraph (3):
'Execution of the award shall be governed by the laws concerning the execution of judgments in force in the State in whose territories such execution is
sought'. This is expanded upon in Article 55: 'Nothing in Article 54 shall be
construed as derogating from the law in force in any Contracting State relating
to immunity of that State or of any foreign State from execution'. The interplay
of these provisions deserves some attention because it has a distinct impact on
whether a wronged investor can enjoy her success at ICSID arbitration.

First it is important to note that many states comply with adverse ICSID
rulings. However, not all losing respondents are willing to pay the investor
the awarded compensation. In such cases, the claimant must attempt to get
both enforcement and execution of the award through national legal processes in a jurisdiction where the host has assets that can be transferred to
the investor. Because a claim for enforcement may be more likely to succeed
if brought outside the host's territory, Article 54 ICSID Convention requires
every ICSID member to recognize an ICSID tribunal's award.

This gives investors great flexibility in seeking enforcement, as they can
choose any jurisdiction where the liable host has assets that can be attached.
Bank accounts, real property, airplanes or boats, or contractual rights to
payment are examples of assets that a state might have placed outside its own
jurisdiction.

The provisions of ICSID Convention Article 54(3) and Article 55, however,
put a practical limit on the investor's avenues for relief when it comes to execution of the award, as national sovereign immunity rules are not affected by the
obligations of recognition and enforcement. National foreign sovereign immunity rules prohibit the attachment of property owned by another sovereign.
Thus, even if an investor can get a court to recognize an award against a host
which owes the investor compensation, the court may not have the competence
to require execution of the judgment due to the host's status as a sovereign.
That is, 'the host State's consent to arbitrate, although a waiver of immunity
from suit, does not amount to a waiver of immunity from execution.'[149]

Although foreign sovereign immunity of property is often limited to non-
commercial assets, investors may find it difficult to prove that state-owned

---

149 Lucy Reed, Jan Paulsson, and Nigel Blackaby, Guide to ICSID Arbitration 33 (2004).

property is truly commercial. Investors therefore may face further litigation in state courts in pursuance of their successful ICSID claim.

LITERATURE

Antonio R. Parra, The Enforcement of ICSID Arbitral Awards, 24th Joint Colloquium on International Arbitration (Paris, 16 November 2007) (footnotes omitted)

[...] The [ICSID] arbitration procedures are often called truly delocalized or denationalized. This refers to the fact that they are governed exclusively by the international law provisions of the ICSID Convention and exempt from the application of the arbitration laws and the control of the courts of Contracting States. Article 53(1) of the ICSID Convention is frequently mentioned in this context. According to its first sentence, an award rendered pursuant to the Convention is binding on the parties and not subject to any appeal [...]. Also frequently mentioned in this context is Article 54 of the Convention. It addresses the enforcement of the awards.

II.

Article 54(1) of the ICSID Convention requires each Contracting State to recognize an award rendered pursuant to the Convention as binding and to enforce the pecuniary obligations imposed by the award as if it were a final judgment of the State's courts. Under Article 54(2) of the Convention, recognition and enforcement of the award may be obtained from the competent court of a Contracting State on simple presentation of a copy of the award certified by the Secretary-General of the Centre. The regime of the Convention does not, however, extend to the execution of the award. Such execution is, in accordance with Article 54(3) of the Convention, governed by the law on the execution of judgments in force in the country where execution is sought. Article 55 of the Convention additionally makes it clear that Article 54 does not derogate from the law of the enforcement forum on sovereign immunity from execution of an award.

These provisions of the Convention have been tested in [several cases]. In the first case, Benvenuti and Bonfant, an Italian company, obtained, from the Tribunal de Grande Instance of Paris, an order for the enforcement of the Convention award against the company's adversary, the Republic of Congo [citing *S.A.R.L. Benvenuti and Bonfant v. Republic of the Congo*, Decision of Jan. 13, 1981 of the Tribunal de Grande Instance, Paris, 108 Journal du droit international 365 (1981)]. The Tribunal [...] made this order subject to the condition that without its prior authorization there could be no execution on assets located in France. The Court of Appeal of Paris struck down this condition. In doing so, [it] explained that Article 54 of the ICSID Convention provided for a 'simplified' enforcement procedure, that enforcement was a step preliminary to execution, and that courts in Contracting States therefore could not at the enforcement phase delve into the execution phase, the second phase being the one in which there might be a question of sovereign immunity.

The second case also illustrates this distinction between the two phases. The Convention award in that case had been rendered against Liberia and in favor of the Liberian Eastern Timber Corporation, a company controlled by French nationals. The award [. . .] on the company's application [was] granted recognition and enforcement by an order of the U.S. District Court for the Southern District of New York [*Liberian Eastern Timber Corporation v. Liberia*, 650 F. Supp. 73 (S.D.N.Y. 1986)]. On the strength of that order, executions were issued on registry fees and taxes due to Liberia from shipowners and agents of Liberia in the United States. On Liberia's motion, the same District Court, having found those assets to be immune from execution [. . .], because they were sovereign [. . .] assets, vacated the executions on those assets.

The company then obtained writs of attachment seizing bank accounts of the Embassy of Liberia in Washington, D.C. The U.S. District Court for the District of Columbia, however, quashed the writs on the grounds that the Embassy's bank accounts were immune from attachment because they enjoyed diplomatic immunity under the Vienna Convention on Diplomatic Relations, [. . .] and also because the accounts were entitled to sovereign immunity [. . .], the funds in the accounts being essentially public in nature [citing 659 F. Supp. 606 (D.D.C. 1987)].
[. . .]

III

It is important in considering the subject of the enforcement of awards rendered pursuant to the Convention also to recall the provisions of its Article 53(1). [. . .] The second sentence requires each party to 'abide by and comply with the terms of the award.' [. . .]

Article 27(1) of the Convention provides that a Contracting State may not give diplomatic protection, or bring an international claim, in respect of a dispute that one of its nationals and another Contracting State have consented to submit [. . .]. [It] also provides that the first Contracting State may nevertheless give diplomatic protection or bring an international claim if the second State fails to honor its obligation [. . .] to abide by and comply with the award. In such circumstances, the first State could [. . .] institute proceedings against the second before the International Court of Justice.
[. . .]

IV

[. . .]
Often brought up in connection with the enforcement (in the broadest sense) of ICSID arbitral awards is the possible role therein of the World Bank. Its Executive

> Directors formulated the Convention and ICSID is a member of the World Bank Group of international organizations. It is sometimes suggested that the leverage of the Bank with a borrowing member country might be applied to secure payment of an award. An operational policy of the Bank indicates that it may refrain from making new loans to a member country in certain extreme cases involving expropriation or external debt disputes. [. . .] [H]owever, such situations have not arisen in connection with performance of an ICSID arbitral award. A role that has been played by the ICSID Secretariat, and occasionally also by the World Bank, when informed of a delay in paying an award, has been to remind the award debtor of the importance of prompt payment [. . .]. In addition, there has been an instance of the ICSID Secretariat agreeing [. . .] to host post-award settlement discussions.

Even if immunity rules bar execution of an ICSID Award, the host state is still in violation of its ICSID obligations. For the unsatisfied investor, the invocation of the diplomatic protection of its home state therefore becomes relevant once again.

? DISCUSSION NOTES

1 The enforcement of non-ICSID ISDS awards (for example, an award from a tribunal applying the UNCITRAL Arbitration Rules) is different from that of ICSID awards. Non-ICSID awards are subject to enforcement under the New York Convention on the Recognition and Enforcement of Foreign Arbitral Awards (1958). Under Article V of that Convention national courts must recognize and enforce binding arbitral decisions unless there was a procedural failing in the arbitral process (Art. V(1)), the law where enforcement is sought would not permit the dispute to be settled by arbitration (Art. V(2)(a)), or if 'recognition or enforcement of the award would be contrary to the public policy' of the country where enforcement is sought (Art. V(2)(b)). When Ecuador attempted to prevent enforcement of the arbitral award granted to Chevron/Texaco, however, the United States' District Court for the District of Columbia refused. Claims to apply the exception for public policy grounds, it said, are 'rarely successful' as a result of the 'extraordinarily high threshold required' to prove that such grounds exist. *Chevron Corporation and Texaco Petroleum Company v. Republic of Ecuador*, Civil Action No. 12-1247 (JEB) (D.D.C.6 June 2012).

2 A non-ICSID arbitration between Malicorp and Egypt demonstrates the difference between recognition and enforcement of awards. As reported by IAReporter, in this dispute, Malicorp won an award from the Cairo Regional Centre for International Arbitration, but Egypt appealed for the award to be set aside. The Cairo Appeals Court granted

> the set-aside. After an unsuccessful attempt to gain enforcement in France, Malicorp claimed for recognition and enforcement in front of the High Court of Justice of England and Wales. There, the judge found that the set-aside must be recognized and that the arbitration tribunal's determination of damages on a legal provision not put forth by the claimant was a 'serious breach of natural justice' and therefore was a ground to refuse enforcement. See Clovis Trevino, Cairo Centre Award in Favor of Investor Against Egypt Suffers Another Enforcement Setback, IAReporter (24 February 2015).

6.2.6 Withdrawal

It is clear that once an investor-State arbitration case has begun, neither party can withdraw its consent to ICSID jurisdiction unilaterally. What happens, though, when an investment has existed, and has been damaged, but since then the government has withdrawn its consent to that jurisdiction by denouncing the ICSID Convention?

The issue of withdrawal from the ICSID system has arisen in the wake of Bolivia's decision in May 2007 to leave the ICSID system. As Ecuador and Venezuela followed Bolivia's example, the question of what the denunciations mean for existing investors became even more relevant. Particularly significant are the facts that many IIAs include a choice of non-ICSID fora in their ISDS provisions and the existence of 'sunset', or 'survival', clauses in many IIAs, granting protection to existing investments for an extended period of time following the termination of the treaty.

LITERATURE

Sergey Ripinsky, Venezuela's Withdrawal from ICSID: What it Does and Does Not Achieve[150]

[...]

Impact on pending and future claims

From a purely legal perspective, withdrawal from ICSID does not offer any immediate benefits to Venezuela. Being second only to Argentina in this respect,

---

150 Sergey Ripinsky, Venezuela's Withdrawal from ICSID: What it Does and Does Not Achieve, *Investment Treaty News*, 13 April 2012 (footnotes omitted). Available at: https://www.iisd.org/itn/2012/04/13/venezuelas-withdrawal-from-icsid-what-it-does-and-does-not-achieve/).

the country currently has 20 cases pending against it at ICSID (ten of them initiated in 2011) and faces the prospect of having to pay billions to successful claimants. These pending cases are in no way affected by Venezuela's denunciation of the ICSID Convention. Furthermore, disgruntled foreign investors will still be able to initiate new cases during the six months between the notice of denunciation and the date when it becomes effective (25 July 2012).

The question whether investors would have a right to continue bringing claims *after* 25 July 2012 has been a subject of some debate due to the unclear formulation of Article 71 of the ICSID Convention. The predominant view is that such claims, when they are based on a bilateral investment treaty (BIT), will *not* be registered, despite the fact that Venezuelan BITs remain in force and retain a reference to ICSID arbitration. This is because BITs are understood to record a country's unilateral *offer of consent to arbitration* which must be 'perfected' by an investor (by submitting a request for arbitration) *before* the country ceases to be a member of ICSID. (By contrast, where consent to ICSID arbitration has been given by the country, for example, in a concession agreement with an investor, ICSID proceedings could be started even after the denunciation takes effect. This is because, unlike BITs, *both* parties to the contract give their advance consent to arbitration.) However, of the 26 BITs in force for Venezuela, only two (with Chile and with Germany) name ICSID as the *sole* arbitral venue available to investors. All other BITs provide, in addition to ICSID, an opportunity to arbitrate under UNCITRAL Arbitration Rules and ICSID's Additional Facility Rules. This means that even after the withdrawal from ICSID becomes effective, investors from the covered countries will still be able to sue Venezuela outside its domestic courts.

[. . .]

Dealing with the BIT regime

To fully dismantle the system of arbitration under BITs, Venezuela would need to terminate—in addition to the ICSID convention—all of its BITs. After such termination it would have to wait for the expiry of the additional period of 10–15 years (depending on a treaty), during which the agreements will continue to apply to investments established prior to the treaty's termination. All of Venezuela's BITs have such a 'survival' clause.

In 2008, Venezuela gave notice to terminate its BIT with the Netherlands thus triggering the sunset period, which will end in 2023. The Dutch BIT must have been a source of particular annoyance to the country as it has served as a basis of at least ten ICSID cases against Venezuela (the Netherlands is often used by firms from other countries for incorporating holding companies and structuring investments). Aside from the Dutch treaty, Venezuela has not moved to terminate any of its other BITs.

[. . .]

6.2.7   Current concerns relating to investor-State dispute procedures

The foregoing description of the investor-State dispute settlement mechanism available to investors does not purport to be complete. There is, of course, much more one can learn about the procedures and methods of dispute settlement that is not covered in this book. It would be unfortunate, however, to end this chapter without a brief discussion of two topics that have occasioned vigorous discussion in investment law. The first is the issue of transparency and, specifically, how much transparency investor-State dispute settlement should afford. The second is the issue of arbitrator independence, a question that disputing parties are raising frequently and on which there are few firm sources of guidance.

a   Transparency

Transparency is a concept that generally implies a method of acting that can be observed and understood by others. Understood slightly differently in different contexts, in law transparency includes making information and procedures accessible to other parties and the public, holding decision-makers accountable for their decisions, and providing avenues for criticisms or complaints to be heard and redressed.

a.i   Dimensions of transparency

In the area of investment, the transparency discussions can focus on either internal or external transparency.

Internal transparency
Internal transparency aims to improve the investors' and hosts' access to relevant information and to increase the foreseeability of the expected standards of behaviour. Such efforts can be taken through international economic organizations, such as the UNCITRAL, the OECD, the IMF, and the World Bank, which encourage host states to make their investment policies and relevant legislation known, to ensure administrative consistency, and to offer information/contact points where potential investors can receive information about the process of investing in a particular sector as well as reporting accurately and frequently about their macroeconomic indicators. Investors, too, are urged to make their finances and corporate structures public. The reciprocal awareness of host and investor policies, in turn, should lead to more and better investment relationships.[151]

---

151 *See generally* R. Gaston Gelos and shang-Jin Wei, Transparency and International Investor Behavior,

Internal transparency is also increasingly a goal for the investment dispute resolution fora. In that context, attempts are being made to make the institutions' practices more foreseeable. The SCC, for example, is making the Board's practices and tribunal decisions on how provisions will be applied more accessible. Analyses of legal reasoning[152] are being put onto the website to let parties more accurately assess the viability of their claims and/or legal defences.

External transparency

External transparency refers to the openness of the investment system to those outside it. Most of the external transparency discussions in investment revolve around the investor-State dispute settlement mechanism.[153] This is due to the differences between the private and public interests pursued in such cases. While the private party can focus solely on protecting its own financial assets, the state, as an entity representing multiple individuals, must respond to a wide spectrum of interests, balancing political, social, and environmental concerns with the economic ones implicated in a particular dispute. As the OECD recognizes, there is a potential problem in using a mechanism developed in the context of private party dispute resolution for resolving disputes between a private party and the state.

> International arbitration can provide the advantage of impartial and competent decision making. A traditional commercial arbitration, between two private companies for instance, may run its course without public disclosure even of the existence of the dispute. Under the existing rules in this area, hearings are treated as entirely private matters and publication of the resulting award often depends on the decision of one or both parties. There are cases in which published awards are edited to obscure the identity of the parties. The policy of confidentiality serves to expedite arbitrations, as well as to protect the confidentiality of information and reputation. There is no mechanism ensuring that the public will ever know about the claim brought, the positions taken by the parties, the decisions issued by the tribunals and the precise reasons for them. The notion that arbitrators (usually three) decide a purely commercial dispute behind closed doors 'does not offend fundamental principles of justice'. That the same three arbitrators may decide in the same way whether the measures taken by a government—which may raise sensitive issues of public policies—are compatible with an investment treaty could be

---

National Bureau of Economic Research Working Paper 9260 (Oct. 2002). Available at: http://www.nber. org/papers/w9260.

152 These articles, under the heading 'SCC Practice', are written by institute members and practitioners. Discussing the tribunals' decisions, the articles maintain the confidentiality of the parties involved in the disputes.

153 The negotiation of investment agreements is another focus of transparency-fostering initiatives.

more problematic. Current arbitration procedures provide for varied degrees of transparency.[154]

Similar to commercial arbitration, investor-State arbitration procedures are based on a strong belief in the need for tribunals to adhere to the parties' agreed-upon rules. In many cases, however, the parties do not agree on how much outsiders should know about their dispute—respondents may be hesitant to be challenged in a way that makes them look hostile to foreign investment and claimants may be reluctant to be seen as complaining about regulations that were implemented to pursue popular policies. In any particular case, one party might want to pursue its claims or argue its defences openly, while the other party would rather stay out of public notice.

More significantly, not only is transparency rarely a goal of arbitration—quite often, the avoidance of public notice itself is seen as an important reason for a claimant's choice of arbitration over judicial proceedings. Thus, the default rule on arbitration transparency is important. If intransparency is the norm, then one party's willingness to open the dispute will not suffice to overcome the other party's unwillingness to do so.

Increasingly, however, critical voices have been raised over the use of intransparent processes to determine the rights and obligations of states in investor-State arbitrations. If governments are to be held accountable to their citizens, arbitral procedures that evaluate a state's measures' consistency with investment protection should, the critics say, themselves be open to scrutiny.

a.ii   *Efforts to increase transparency*

There are two particular issues where efforts are under way to increase the transparency of investment arbitration: in the public's access to documents and in third party participation.

The public's access to documents and proceedings
Modern political thought generally considers a government's openness about its activities a positive trait. When the openness is about the government's potential liability for its past actions or proposed regulatory policies, it might be thought that openness would be even more desirable. Such is not necessarily the case, however, when such potential liability arises in the context of

---

154 OECD Investment Committee, *Transparency and Third Party Participation in Investor-State Dispute Settlement Procedure* (OECD Investment Division, 2005).

investor-State dispute arbitration. Arbitration's traditional emphasis on confidentiality collides with the good governance preference for openness.

The following sketches out several of the areas where public access to investor-State arbitrations are in discussion.

<u>Registration of disputes</u>
One particularly important element of transparency is the very basic issue of whether or not the fact of a dispute is made public. ICSID is particularly advanced in ensuring that the information regarding who is settling disputes with whom is available to the public at large.

The ICSID's Regulation 22(1) of the Administrative and Financial Regulations requires the Secretariat to publish the filing of a complaint.[155] This list, updated daily, is available on the internet, together with a short description of the claim. Even if the award itself is not published (something that requires both parties' consent), the registration's publication will allow those outside the Centre to know who is launching claims, against whom, and about what. This in itself can be valuable information.

In keeping with their operational focus on commercial arbitrations, the rules of other arbitral fora have long emphasized the confidentiality of proceedings. Thus, not only are awards frequently unpublished, even registrations are often not revealed. While neither the PCA nor the Stockholm Chamber of Commerce will publish names of parties unless both parties consent to publication,[156] the ICC does not provide for even a consent-based publication of filings.

Practitioners active in international arbitration often have a good idea about what claims are being arbitrated, despite confidentiality rules surrounding the notification of claims. Until very recently, however, outsiders have had difficulty assessing how many claims, what type of claims, and under what rules claims are being pursued based only on the fora rules.

---

155 The ICSID also administers arbitrations under UNCITRAL rules. In such cases, the ICSID's publication obligation determines that the registration will be notified.

156 PCA Rules Concerning the Organization and Internal Workings of the International Bureau of the Permanent Court of Arbitration, art. V (done at The Hague, Dec. 18, 1900) (prohibiting staff from making known any information about their work to the public). Stockholm Chamber of Commerce Arbitration Rules, art. 46. As of July 2, 2016, 25 out of 72 pending investor-State arbitration cases were listed by name at the PCA. The Stockholm Court of Arbitration website gives statistics of respondents and industrial sectors involved in arbitrations, but not the names of claimants.

Some governments, therefore, have begun to include notification publication clauses in their treaties. The United States was at the forefront of this group, with its Model BIT of 2004 containing a provision 'Transparency of Arbitral Proceedings', which requires 'the respondent' to send the notice of arbitration (*inter alia*) to the home state and to 'make [it] available to the public'.[157]

Public hearings

Beyond publication of the existence of a dispute, a large step toward full transparency in arbitration proceedings is opening hearings to the public. Here, the NAFTA parties have set the standard by allowing not only for the interested public to be invited into the hearings, but also providing for internet viewing. This overcomes the financial and temporal costs of travelling to the site, greatly broadening potential viewership.

Opening hearings, of course, is complicated by issues of commercially relevant confidential information. Such problems, however, are left to the tribunal, which may hold portions of the proceedings in camera where necessary.

The other fora are less transparent in respect of open hearings. The UNCITRAL rules allow parties to agree to open hearings, but will keep them closed in the absence of agreement.[158] ICSID leaves it to the tribunal to decide whether anyone else is permitted to attend the hearing.[159]

Availability of awards

Even more than the notification of a claim, investment arbitration awards are of interest to the public and scholars. Transparency in dispute settlement awards not only provides the interested public with information about what the government's financial liabilities to foreign investors are; more importantly, it is an instrument for accountability—both of the parties and of the decision-makers. Public access, says Van Harten, 'is about the parties and the adjudicators knowing that their views and arguments can be read and picked apart by anyone, so that they will more assuredly consider the implications of what they do or decide for their reputation and for that of the system'.[160]

As investment law itself becomes more widely known, and as the public realize the impacts that the rules of investment can have on their governments, pressure has grown for better access to awards. The 'norm of public access'

---

157 US Model BIT (2012), art. 29(1).
158 UNCITRAL Rules 2013, art. 28(3).
159 ICSID Arbitration Rule 32(2).
160 Gus Van Harten, Investment Treaty Arbitration and Public Law 161 (2007).

found in other areas of public law is now being demanded in international investment law by scholars and civil society.[161]

It appears that final awards are becoming more readily available—certainly there are more awards available overall. This increase is despite unchanged rules regarding award publication in the main fora. The ICSID, more transparency-oriented than the other fora, is taking a leading role in ensuring awards are available to the public.

Under ICSID rules, awards may only be published if both parties agree.[162] Nevertheless, most newly decided cases are available online. This is in part due to governmental efforts to increase transparency through explicit treaty obligations on transparency that are fuelling the growth in award publication. The NAFTA, for example, provides that Canada and the United States may publish any awards to which they are a party,[163] and both countries' Model BIT calls for the publication of 'orders, awards, and decisions of the tribunal'.[164]

In addition, ICSID awards are known because the Centre has taken an active role in promoting their publication:

> . . . the practice of the Centre is to request the parties' advance consent to publication at the time of the first session. If the parties do not consent, ICSID requests their consent when a tribunal issues a specific decision or an award. [. . .] If a party does not consent to the publication by the Centre, ICSID will publish excerpts of the legal reasoning of the award, any decision deemed to be part of the award and decisions concluding post-award remedies proceedings. These are published in the *ICSID Review–Foreign Investment Law Journal* and on the website.[165]

In the other fora, publication of awards is less common. While the parties' consent would be sufficient for the PCA and the Stockholm Institute of Arbitration to publish an award rendered by tribunals using their rules of

---

161 *Id.*

162 ICSID Convention art. 48.5.

163 NAFTA, Annex 1137.

164 Canada Model BIT (2004) art. 38.3 ('all documents . . . issued by the Tribunal shall be publicly available unless the disputing parties otherwise agree'); US Model BIT (2004), art. 29(1)(e).

165 United Nations Commission on International Trade Law Working Group II (Arbitration and Conciliation), *Settlement of Commercial Disputes Transparency in Treaty-based Investor-State Arbitration—Comments by the International Centre for Settlement of Investment Disputes (ICSID)*, A/CN.9/WG.II/WP.167, at 3–4 paras. 11–12 (55th session Vienna, Oct. 3–7, 2011).

procedure, many of the awards from these fora remain confidential. The ICC will not publish awards at all.

Non-publication by the arbitration fora secretariats, however, is not the same thing as secret awards. Even without both parties' consent, arbitration awards may become publicly available on the internet. This is because the parties themselves are permitted to unilaterally publish awards unless explicitly prohibited from doing so through a contractual clause or confidentiality order.[166] That is, while the secretariats of the official arbitration fora may not publish awards without the parties' consent, those same awards may appear on party websites, on the websites of law firms, or on sites collecting such awards for use by other interested readers.

Publication of party submissions

Efforts to require the publication of party submissions in addition to the awards is currently causing significant debate in the arbitration community.

The benefits of accessing party submissions lies in the public's ability to know more precisely the facts behind the dispute, to monitor the progress of the proceedings, and to assess the strength of their governments' arguments.

Given that neither ICSID nor UNCITRAL rules mention party submission publication, tribunals have significant discretion in permitting publication or mandating confidentiality. Governments, therefore, have once again begun to insert provisions into their IIAs to limit tribunals' ability to make such decisions. The US approach, adopted with slight variations by other governments including Australia, Canada, Japan, and New Zealand, requires all party submissions to be published. Differences remain in whether the publication decision can be made only by the state party or by either disputing party.[167]

Currently, the majority of states maintain that party submissions should remain confidential unless both parties agree to allow publication. The majority of the tribunal in *Telefonica v. Mexico* adopted this approach as well.[168] In its opinion, the fact that the applicable BIT provided for final awards to be public meant that other tribunal decisions and orders were to remain confidential. In absence of 'general rules of confidentiality or publicity' in

---

166 Id. at para. 13.
167 *See* Nathalie Bernasconi-Osterwalder and Lise Johnson, *Transparency in the Dispute Settlement Process: Country Best Practices* 5-6 (International Institute for Sustainable Development, Bulletin no. 2, February 2011).
168 *Infra* note 169.

the ICSID Convention and Arbitration Rules for the Additional Facility, the majority opted for confidentiality.

One tribunal member dissented. The majority's de facto presumption of confidentiality, he argued, was both incorrect as a matter of legal analysis, but also goes against the growing recognition of the benefits of ISDS transparency.

 CASE

Telefónica v. Mexico, Dissenting Opinion of Ricardo Ramirez Hernandez[169]

1. I agree with the majority's decision that the legal provisions applicable in this case do not impose a general rule of confidentiality or transparency for these proceedings. [. . .].

2. Although I agree with the criterion stated by the majority, I do not share the manner in which this criterion has been applied in the present case.

3. The majority's decision indeed establishes a presumption of confidentiality by prohibiting the Parties from disclosing: (i) the transcripts or minutes of the hearings; (ii) the documents submitted by the Parties in this proceedings; (iii) the pleadings or written memorials of the Parties and their annexes; and (iv) the correspondence relating to these proceedings (exchanged between the Parties or between the Parties and the Tribunal). The Parties preserve the right to request this confidentiality restriction to be lifted or modified, but any such request must be justified. This presumption clearly responds to a general interest of confidentiality. [. . .] This can hardly be characterized as a 'solution' that protects the interest of both Parties, and much less as a balance struck between the interests of transparency and the interests of confidentiality. [. . .]

5. When adopting a presumption of confidentiality, the majority fails to explain why a transparency request should be justified, whereas a request for confidentiality does not require justification. If, as asserted by the majority, neither the APPRI nor the Arbitration Rules (Additional Facility) provide for an obligation of confidentiality or an obligation of transparency, the need for justification would apply equally to both requests for transparency as well as requests for confidentiality. The absence of an obligation of confidentiality would give rise to an equally legal valid presumption of transparency.

6. [. . .]

---

169 *Telefónica SA v. United Mexican States*, ICSID Case No. ARB(AF)/12/4, Dissent to Procedural Order No. 1 (Unofficial English Translation) (July 8, 2013).

7. Notwithstanding the foregoing, the majority's decision contains no indication whatsoever as to how it took into account the different interests to which the Parties referred. Nor is there any indication of the reasons that led the majority to put the interests of confidentiality above the interests of transparency in this case. The majority's decision simply opts for confidentiality with respect to all other aspects of the proceedings without explaining why confidentiality should prevail over transparency in this case.

8. [. . .]

11. The only two reasons given by the Claimant to reject the procedure proposed by the Respondent were that the procedure was 'onerous', and that the information 'could not be disaggregated'. [. . .]

12. In regard to the first argument, I believe that the Claimant should have explained and justified why it would have been onerous to comply with the procedure proposed by the Respondent. The burden that transparency puts on the parties cannot not be used as a general excuse to reject a transparency request. [. . .]

13. With respect to the alleged difficulties to classify or segregate information, I do not see why this reason must prevail over transparency in these proceedings. The redaction of documents is a common practice in domestic and international proceedings, particularly for international companies that have experienced counsel such as those who appear in these proceedings.

14. Finally, albeit not related to the procedure proposed by the Respondent, the Claimant referred to the fact that the disclosure of information about this arbitration could exacerbate the dispute. I agree that this reason has been used in previous arbitrations to justify the confidentiality of the proceedings. However, I believe that for this reason to apply, one has to prove the existence of a reasonable risk that the dispute will be exacerbated if information about the case is disclosed. [. . .]

15. [. . .] As stated by the Tribunal in Beccara, 'transparency in investment arbitration shall be encouraged as a means to promote good governance of States, the development of a well-grounded and coherent body of case law in international investment law and therewith legal certainty and confidence in the system of investment arbitration. . .'.

16. This reasoning is, in my view, even more relevant today when disputes of this nature are under intense scrutiny by the public. I would like to clarify that transparency does not mean that the right to protect certain information in particular circumstances should not exist. [. . .] I am convinced that Tribunals can adopt mechanisms that protect such information while, at the same time, provide more transparency to the proceedings.

17. The public has the right to know—protecting at all times, of course, the information that is genuinely considered to be confidential—the actions of their governments and investors, as well as the manner in which they are defended.

> For this reason, transparency provides legitimacy to both to the investor's claims and the State's defence. Transparency generates certainty, ignorance, panic. Transparency, therefore, can be a means to pave the way and facilitate a better development of these proceedings and to avoid a situation in which these proceedings are judged by the public in the dark. For all of these reasons, I cannot subscribe a Decision that goes in the opposite direction.

Third party participation: amicus curiae

While rights to information regarding dispute settlement proceedings have implications for the rights of citizens and good governance, allowing third party participation goes much further in removing a proceeding from the exclusive realm of the parties' wishes. The involvement of the state's regulatory framework in many investor-State arbitration proceedings, and the inevitable potential impact on the state's budget, however, may justify individuals' or groups' interest in making their positions known to the tribunal and the parties. The legal tool for informing participants of non-party opinions is the amicus brief.

An *amicus curiae*, or friend of the court, is traditionally a source of information for the judges on a particular matter, helping the court make decisions that are soundly based on a comprehensive understanding of the issues. Amicus assistance can be helpful for understanding technical or scientific aspects that arise in a dispute or can be submitted to focus the judges' attention on the policy implications of a case.

Widely used in common law systems and gaining significance in international adjudication fora,[170] amicus briefs are not allowed, for instance, in proceedings before the International Court of Justice.[171] In investment arbitrations, 'amici' attempt to inform a tribunal of facts to prevent the arbitrators from making a decision that would ignore interests that may not be adequately represented by the parties or to underline the public's particular interest in

---

170 *See, e.g. Karen Atala and Daughters v. Chile*, case 1271-04, Report No. 42/08, Inter-Am. CHR, OEA/Ser.L/V/II.130 Doc. 22, rev. 1 (2008); United States—Import of Certain Shrimp and Shrimp Products, WT/DS58/AB/R, para. 104 (Oct. 12, 1998).

171 ICJ Statute arts. 34 and 66. *But see* Dinah Shelton, *The Participation of Nongovernmental Organizations in International Judicial Proceedings*, 88(4) AJIL 611, 623–4 (1994): 'In the 1950 *South-West Africa* advisory proceeding, the Court advised the International League for Human Rights (until 1976 the International League for the Rights of Man) that it would be permitted to submit information. . . . On March 16, the Registrar responded that the Court was prepared to receive a written statement from the league of information likely to assist the Court in its examination of the legal questions put to it by the General Assembly in the *South-West Africa* proceeding. . . . The league failed to comply with the Court's orders in the *South-West Africa* case, one reason, perhaps, why the Court has not subsequently extended permission to nongovernmental organizations to submit information. . . .'

the results of the dispute. Bringing in such interests often complicates the tribunal's work and diverges from the parties' own views, with the result that they are often not welcomed by any of those involved.

Two specific legal questions thus arise as regards *amicus curiae*: (1) *may* the tribunal permit an *amicus curiae* in investor-State proceedings; and (2) *must* the tribunal permit an amicus curiae in investor-State proceedings?

May the tribunal permit an amicus submission?
In the context of an investment arbitration, the tribunal's assignment is to decide a dispute in accordance with the parties' agreement. Therefore, if one of the parties objects to the involvement of a third party, it is questionable whether a tribunal may ignore the party's expressed wish to exclude *amicus* participation by accepting volunteered submissions. It is even more questionable if a tribunal may accept a submission when both parties voice their disapproval of allowing a third party submission.

In the absence of any explicit rules on these issues, tribunals approached the request for *amicus* submissions differently until 2006, when the ICSID amended its arbitration rules to provide for the possibility of third party participation. The steps toward increased third party participation were summarized in ICSID's statements submitted to the UNCITRAL working group on transparency in investor-State arbitration.

MATERIALS

Transparency in treaty-based investor-State arbitration: Comments by the International Centre for Settlement of Investment Disputes (ICSID)[172]

16. The first *amicus* request was submitted in *Methanex v. USA*, in which the Tribunal accepted such submissions in early 2001 notwithstanding the Claimant's objections. This NAFTA case was administered by ICSID and governed by the 1976 UNCITRAL Arbitration Rules. The Tribunal relied on UNCITRAL Arbitration Rule 15(1), allowing a tribunal to conduct a proceeding in the manner it considers appropriate. This approach was adopted the same year by the Tribunal in *UPS v. Canada*. These cases were later followed by the issuance of guidelines by

---

172 United Nations Commission on International Trade Law Working Group II (Arbitration and Conciliation), A/CN.9/WG.II/WP.167 (55th session, Vienna, October 3–7, 2011), 5–8, paras. 16–23 (footnotes omitted).

the NAFTA Free Trade Commission in October 2003 confirming a tribunal's discretion to accept non-disputing party submissions.

In proceedings under the ICSID Convention, the question of submissions by non-disputing parties was first raised in *Aguas del Tunari v. Bolivia* in 2002, in which the Tribunal rejected a request to file non-disputing party submissions holding that it did not have such power in the absence of consent by the parties. However, in *Suez et al. v. Argentina*, the Tribunal held that it was entitled to do so based on its inherent powers under Article 44 of the ICSID Convention and because the case was deemed to involve matters of public interest. [. . .]

[. . .]

19. In 2006, ICSID introduced a new provision in Arbitration Rule 37(2) which reads as follows:

> 'After consulting both parties, the Tribunal may allow a person or entity that is not a party to the dispute (in this Rule called the "non-disputing party") to file a written submission with the Tribunal regarding a matter within the scope of the dispute. In determining whether to allow such a filing, the Tribunal shall consider, among other things, the extent to which:
>
> a. the non-disputing party submission would assist the Tribunal in the determination of a factual or legal issue related to the proceeding by bringing a perspective, particular knowledge or insight that is different from that of the disputing parties;
> b. the non-disputing party submission would address a matter within the scope of the dispute;
> c. the non-disputing party has a significant interest in the proceeding.
>
> The Tribunal shall ensure that the non-disputing party submission does not disrupt the proceeding or unduly burden or unfairly prejudice either party, and that both parties are given an opportunity to present their observations on the non-disputing party submission.'

20. A similar provision was introduced under Article 41(3) of the ICSID Additional Facility Arbitration Rules.

[. . .]

22. The process to submit a non-disputing party's brief is divided into two stages by ICSID Arbitration Rule 37(2): an application to the tribunal for leave to file a brief under the conditions described above; and the actual submission, if the tribunal has granted the non-disputing party's application. In its decision on granting the requested leave to file, the tribunal is guided, among other things, by the criteria set forth in Rule 37(2). [. . .] A tribunal sometimes establishes requirements or guidelines for the nondisputing party's submission after agreeing to the application. Procedural safeguards are also put in place by tribunals when a non-disputing party is allowed to file a submission in order to preserve the integrity of

the proceedings. Disputing parties are usually allowed to provide observations on the non-disputing parties' applications and submissions. The tribunal's powers to be the judge of the admissibility of any evidence adduced in the case and of its probative value under Arbitration Rule 34(1) extend to the non-disputing party's written submission.

Therefore, it is within the tribunal's discretion to admit into evidence the nondisputing party's written submission once filed and whether to rely on it in its final determination of the case.

23. The right to submit *amicus* briefs does not grant any other procedural rights. Hence, there is no automatic access to documents, nor is there automatic access to hearings. [. . .] So far, the practice has been that the disputing parties bear the costs related to the *amicus* submissions.

Recent cases have supported the position that it is within the ICSID tribunal's discretion to grant the amicus permission to submit a brief as long as the criteria of ICSID Convention Article 34(2) are fulfilled. In the combined procedural order of the tribunals in *Bernhard von Pezold v. Zimbabwe* and *Border Timbers v. Zimbabwe*, the tribunals noted that this discretion is complete: the tribunal may permit a submission it considers helpful despite the objection of one or both parties to the dispute. Given this broad discretion, however, tribunals will need to attend carefully to the petitioner's qualifications and ensure that the criteria for submission are clearly demonstrated.

 CASE

Bernhard von Pezold et al. v. Zimbabwe and Border Timbers et al. v. Zimbabwe[173]

The dispute involved Swiss and German nationals in Zimbabwe who owned farms and forest lands in Zimbabwe. When the government of Zimbabwe violently dispossessed them, the claimants brought proceedings under the German–Zimbabwe BIT at ICSID. An early Procedural Order was directed at the question of whether the European Center for Constitutional and Human Rights (ECCHR) together with several indigenous communities, could make an amicus submission on the questions of indigenous peoples' rights and on corporate responsibility for human rights.

---

173 *Bernhard von Pezold et al. v. Zimbabwe* and *Border Timbers et al. v. Zimbabwe*, ICSID Case No. ARB/10/15, Procedural Order No. 2, para. 6 (June 26, 2012). Available at: http://italaw.com/sites/default/files/case-documents/ita1044.pdf.

Although the respondent was neither in support of nor opposed to the petition, the claimants strongly objected. The NGO, it claimed, was closely tied to the government, and hence not independent; the issues of indigenous rights were irrelevant to the investment dispute; and would not be bringing in any perspectives that were relevant to the tribunal's decision-making. The tribunal addressed these points in its Order.

> The Arbitral Tribunals have the discretion, upon consulting with the Parties, to allow [a non-disputing party, 'NDP'] to make a submission pursuant to Rule 37(2), provided that certain minimum criteria are met. [. . .]
>
> 49. The Arbitral Tribunals agree with the Claimants' observation that an NDP should also be independent of the Parties. This is implicit in Rule 37(2)(a), which requires that the NDP bring a perspective, particular knowledge or insight that is different from that of the Parties. Other ICSID tribunals have also considered this to be a requirement of to admit *amicus* submissions [citing Aguas, *Suez et al. v. Argentina*, Order in Response to Participation as Amicus Curiae, para. 23]:
>
> '*The Suitability of Specific Nonparties to Act as Amici Curiae.* The purpose of *amicus* submissions is to help the Tribunal arrive at a correct decision by providing it with arguments, and expertise and perspectives that the parties may not have provided. The Tribunal will therefore only accept *amicus* submissions from persons who establish to the Tribunal's satisfaction that they have the expertise, experience, and independence to be of assistance in this case. . . .'[. . .]
>
> 50. The Claimants have raised concerns about the independence of the Petitioners from several perspectives. First, the Claimants contend that the interests of the indigenous communities are adverse to their own and aligned with those of the Respondent. Second, they claim that the indigenous communities are effectively organs of the State and therefore cannot be independent of the Respondent. [. . .] The Claimants also argue that whether or not the Petitioners are in fact independent, these circumstances give the appearance that they are not independent.
>
> 51. The Claimants' first contention is based on the allegation that members of the indigenous communities invaded parts of the Border Estate in 2000 and following, as part of the Respondent's Land Reform Programme ('LRP'). The Claimants allege that the indigenous communities 'wish to permanently occupy parts of the Border Estate,' an intent that runs counter to the Claimants' request for relief in these arbitrations, namely that full unencumbered legal title and exclusive control to the Border Properties be restored to them. In the Application, the Petitioners assert that both Parties have responsibilities towards the indigenous communities relating to their alleged rights over or in relation to their ancestral lands.
>
> 52. The Arbitral Tribunals are not persuaded, on the basis of the indigenous communities' desire to have their claimed rights recognized by the Parties or indeed by these Tribunals, that they are 'aligned' with the Respondent; however, as the indigenous communities appear to lay claim over or in relation to some of the lands in

respect of which the Claimants assert a right to full, unencumbered legal title and exclusive control, they appear to be in conflict with the Claimants' primary position in these proceedings.

The Arbitral Tribunals are not persuaded on the basis of the materials before them that the functions of the chiefs of the indigenous communities are functions of the government. [. . .]

54. As regards the Claimants' third challenge to the Petitioners' independence, the Petitioners state that they have received support from the NULC [a local NGO] in the nature of facilitating communications between the ECCHR and the indigenous communities, the production of affidavits and the holding of meetings to discuss the Application. It is unclear from the Application what, if any, involvement Mr. Sacco may have had. The details provided [. . .] confirm that Mr. Sacco is Director of this organization, and that the focus of its activities is 'Awareness Raising/ Development Education and Development Cooperation Projects'. [. . .] The NULC itself does not [. . . .] appear to be closely linked with either Party.

55. The Claimants have, however, alleged that the NULC is the 'alter-ego' of Mr. Sacco and that he has threatened to 'internationalise' his dispute with them regarding the Border Estate's refusal to enter into a Joint Forest Management Project [. . .]. Mr. Sacco's 2005 paper titled 'Peasant Revolution in Zimbabwe' leaves little doubt as to his support for the resettlement of land in Zimbabwe and the Respondent's land reform policies. This paper also confirms that the NULC is Mr. Sacco's creation and that he is a central figure in its activities [. . .].

56. Based on the foregoing, the Arbitral Tribunals consider that the circumstances of their Application give rise to legitimate doubts as to the independence or neutrality of the Petitioners. The apparent lack of independence or neutrality of the Petitioners is a sufficient ground to deny the [. . .] Application. In addition, having considered the Application in light of all of the criteria set out in Rule 37(2), the Arbitral Tribunals are not persuaded that the Petitioners should be permitted to make a submission in these proceedings because they have not satisfied any of the criteria in Rule 37(2).

57. The Petitioners do not propose to make submissions that would assist them 'in the determination of a factual or legal issue related to the proceeding', as is required by Rule 37(2)(a). The Petitioners, in effect, seek to make a submission on legal and factual issues that are unrelated to the matters before the Arbitral Tribunals. The Arbitral Tribunals agree in this regard with the Claimants that the reference to 'such rules of general international law as may be applicable' in the BITs does not incorporate the universe of international law into the BITs or into disputes arising under the BITs. Moreover, neither Party has put the identity and/or treatment of indigenous peoples, or the indigenous communities in particular, under international law, including international human rights law on indigenous peoples, in issue in these proceedings.

58. The Petitioners provided no evidence or support for their assertion that

international investment law and international human rights law are interdependent such that any decision of these Arbitral Tribunals which did not consider the content of international human rights norms would be legally incomplete. . . . The Petitioners refer in particular to Article 26 of the UN Declaration on the Rights of Indigenous Peoples, which they say requires States to give legal recognition and protection to lands, territories and resources possessed by indigenous peoples by reason of traditional ownership or other traditional occupation or use, and other unspecified customary international law norms which they claim are binding.

59. The Arbitral Tribunals are not persuaded that consideration of the foregoing is in fact part of their mandate under either the ICSID Convention or the applicable BITs. The Respondent has not yet filed a substantive pleading in these proceedings. However, it was afforded the opportunity to make observations on the Application, including any observations as to the perspective the Petitioners propose to bring to the factual and legal issues in these proceedings. . . . [T]he Respondent has neither raised as a defence in these proceedings that it has obligations towards the indigenous communities under international law nor has it indicated that a submission from the Petitioners based on their Application may be relevant to factual or legal issues in these proceedings.

60. The Arbitral Tribunals similarly do not consider that the proposed NDP submission would 'address a matter within the scope of the dispute'. The disputes in these conjoined arbitrations arise out of the allegedly unlawful measures taken by the Respondent against the Claimants and their investments pursuant to the LRP. As noted above, the Petitioners propose to make a submission on the putative rights of the indigenous communities as 'indigenous peoples' under international human rights law, a matter outside of the scope of the dispute, as it is presently constituted. Indeed, as the Claimants have noted, in order for the Arbitral Tribunals to consider such a submission, they would need to consider and decide whether the indigenous communities constitute 'indigenous peoples' for the purposes of grounding any rights under international human rights law. Setting aside whether or not the Arbitral Tribunals are the appropriate arbiters of this decision, the decision itself is clearly outside of the scope of the dispute before the Tribunals.

61. Finally, the Arbitral Tribunals find that the Petitioners do not have a 'significant interest in the proceeding'. This requirement must be interpreted in light of the proceeding as constituted, not as the NDP would prefer the proceeding to be constituted. The Arbitral Tribunals note that the ECCHR's expertise is focused on corporate responsibilities for human rights abuses. The Claimants have strenuously objected to the suggestion that they have committed or are responsible for any such abuses. The Arbitral Tribunals do not understand the Petitioners' statement that the Application 'touches upon . . . redress for alleged human rights abuses by corporations' to be an allegation that the Claimants in these cases have committed or are responsible for human rights abuses. Indeed, the reference for this statement is to a general list of business and human rights issues compiled by the Institute for

Human Rights and Business, and the statement itself, read in its entirety, identifies other concerns of this organization, including the negative impacts of land use and acquisition on communities and community consultation relating to land use and acquisition. [. . .] However, the ECCHR's mission and experience do not, in the context of these proceedings, as presently constituted, satisfy the requirement of a 'significant interest in the proceedings'.

62. As regards the indigenous communities, the Claimants themselves recognize that they have some interest in the land over which the Claimants assert full legal title and therefore have historically granted them access to parts of the Border Estate [. . .]. It may therefore well be that the determinations of the Arbitral Tribunals in these proceedings will have an impact on the interests of the indigenous communities. However, as noted above, the Arbitral Tribunals have reservations as to the independence and/or neutrality of the Petitioners, including the chiefs of the indigenous communities. There is a latent tension in the Rule 37(2) criteria which require that an NDP be independent yet also possess a significant interest in the proceedings. Regardless of whether one or both of these criteria are met, however, Rule 37(2) also provides that an NDP submission must not unfairly prejudice either party. In this case, the Arbitral Tribunals are of the view that the circumstances surrounding these Petitioners are such that the Claimants may be unfairly prejudiced by their participation and the Application must therefore be denied.

Must the tribunal permit an amicus submission?

Even where a tribunal recognizes its competence to accept third party submissions, the tribunal may not want to do so. If a tribunal wants to limit its consideration of the legal arguments to the parties' presentations, if it feels the amicus would not be helpful, or if it recognizes the parties' reluctance to have it take the amicus' opinions into account, the tribunal may want to refuse to permit such a submission. Is this permissible or must the tribunal accept and acknowledge the content of the third party's opinion?

Current arbitration rules are clear that tribunals may refuse to permit third parties' submissions even if the amicus petition would fulfil the criteria of acceptability set forth by the tribunal. Under ICSID rules, if the tribunal finds that the amicus' opinion would be irrelevant or would disproportionately burden the arbitration proceeding, it has no obligation to accept it. Other arbitration rules leave the decisions on amicus submissions to the tribunal's discretion as well. A recent arbitration under UNCITRAL rules at the Permanent Court of Arbitration, for example, presumed the tribunal's competence to accept a submission. The decision of whether to exercise this competence, however, rested on the parties' skeptical attitude toward the *amici's* submissions.

CASE

Chevron Corporation and Texaco Petroleum Corporation v. Republic of Ecuador[174]

The Amicus Petitions

7. The Amicus Petitions are submitted to the Tribunal on behalf of two entities (the 'Petitioners'), acting jointly, who identify themselves as follows:

a. Fundación Pachamama (Pachamama) is an Ecuador-based autonomous indigenous organization, independent of political parties, or any State, foreign or religious institution. Since 1997, Pachamama has been working to promote of alternative models of development based on recognition and respect of human rights and the environment in order to generate the conditions necessary for the indigenous peoples of the Ecuadorian Amazon and other groups in the Andean Region to preserve their traditional ways of life and strengthen their processes of self-determination. [. . .]

b. The International Institute for Sustainable Development (IISD) is a Canadian-based international NGO with a mandate to foster local, regional, and international policies and practices in support of the achievement of sustainable development. IISD has been actively engaged in international trade law issues since 1991 and investment law issues since 1998. With respect to investment law, IISD is primarily concerned with the relationship between international investment agreements and sustainable development. The rights of local communities to use domestic courts to help safeguard the environment is a key element in promoting safe investor conduct, and hence directly relevant to promoting sustainable investments. [. . .]

8. The Petitioners, in their submission, 'attest and affirm that they are independent public interest organizations and that they have no relationship, direct or indirect, with any party to this arbitration which might give rise to any conflict of interest. [The] Petitioners have not received any assistance, financial or otherwise, from a party to the dispute in the preparation of this Petition or the attached written submission.'

[. . .]

10. The Petitioners submit that they have satisfied criteria. The Petitioners assert that their interest in the present arbitration and qualification to address matters in a manner that would assist the Tribunal is demonstrated by the identity, experience, and mandates of their respective organizations. The Petitioners propose to address the implications for the investment protection regime that the Tribunal's

---

174 *Chevron Corporation and Texaco Petroleum Corporation v. Republic of Ecuador*, PCA Case No. 2009-23, Procedural Order No. 8 (Apr. 18, 2011). Available at: http://italaw.com/documents/Chevron_v_Ecuador_ProceduralOrder8_18April2011.pdf.

assumption of jurisdiction in this arbitration would have, as well as other issues of public involved in the jurisdictional proceedings, both for the Lago Agrio litigants in Ecuador and other communities in other States.

11. The Petitioners apply to the Tribunal, as follows:

1.2. The Petitioners [. . .] seek the following orders:

1. *Leave to file a written submission with the Tribunal regarding matters within the scope of the dispute. This submission is attached for immediate consideration;*

2. *Permission to attend and present the Petitioners' submission at the oral hearings when they take place, or in the alternative, attend the oral hearings as observers or to reply to any specific questions of the Tribunal on the written submission; and*

3. *In order to make the preceding order effective, access to the key arbitration documents, subject to the redaction of any commercially confidential or otherwise privileged information that is not relevant to the concerns of the Petitioners as non-disputing parties.*

II. The Parties' Positions

12. In response [. . .], the Claimants asserted that 'any submission by ERI is unlikely to assist this Tribunal in deciding the substantive issues before it,' [. . .].

13. In their letter dated 10 September 2010, the Respondent asserted that 'the participation of non-parties on purely legal issues regarding the scope of this Tribunal's jurisdiction is unlikely to assist the Tribunal in a meaningful way. Nor is it apparent that EarthRights International has a particularized interest in this Tribunal's determination of jurisdiction. If this Tribunal nonetheless concludes that acceptance of the proposed submission would materially assist the Tribunal, or would otherwise further the goals of the process, Respondent would defer to the wisdom and preference of the Tribunal'.

14. Following receipt of the Amicus Petition, in their letter dated 11 November 2010, the Claimants stated that they 'oppose the intervention of the *Amici Curiae* at the jurisdictional phase of this arbitration, and in particular, object to their attendance at, and participation in, the jurisdictional hearing.' First, the Claimants argue that the *Amici Curiae* submissions are unlikely to assist the Tribunal in the determination of 'issues [which] are largely legal and exclusively relate to the Tribunal's jurisdiction.' Second, the Claimants allege that 'both Fundación Pachamama and EarthRights International have a longstanding record of asserting baseless claims against Chevron,' and are therefore 'not genuine "friends-of-the-court"'. Third, the Claimants invoked practical considerations in light of the lack of time prior to the Hearing on Jurisdiction and Admissibility. Finally, the Claimants indicated that they 'do not consent to the *Amici Curiae*'s attendance at the hearing.' [. . .].

15. In their letter dated 19 November 2010, the Respondent indicated that it had

no objection to the attendance of the Petitioners but had no comment regarding the substance of the Amicus Petition.

[. . .]

IV. The Tribunal

17. The Tribunal recalls once again the communication by the PCA on behalf of the Tribunal, by which the Tribunal has already declined the Petitioners' second order sought, relating to '[p]ermission to attend and present the Petitioners' submission at the oral hearings when they take place, or in the alternative, attend the oral hearings as observers', in light of Article 25(4) of the UNCITRAL Arbitration Rules.

18. As regards the two other orders sought by the Petitioners, the Tribunal notes that the Parties agree that they do not believe that the amicus submissions will be helpful to the Tribunal and neither side favours the participation of the petitioners during the jurisdictional phase of the arbitration, in which the issues to be decided are primarily legal and have already been extensively addressed by the Parties' submissions.

[. . .]

20. Accordingly, having considered the Amicus Petitions in all the circumstances currently prevailing in these arbitration proceedings, the Tribunal decides to exercise its discretion [. . .] not to permit the participation of the Petitioners as *amici curiae* at this stage of the arbitration.

UNCITRAL Rules on Transparency in Investor-State Dispute Settlement
A major step forward for ISDS transparency was the April 2014 going into effect of the UNCITRAL Rules on Transparency in Investor-State Dispute Settlement.[175] These Rules currently apply to any ISDS proceeding governed by UNCITRAL Arbitration Rules in which the IIA came into effect after 1 April 2014 or in which the parties agree to their application. In order to make them applicable to the large number of existing IIAs, a United Nations Convention has been concluded which would make the Transparency Rules' application automatic to any ISDS under UNCITRAL Arbitration Rules unless the transparency rules are explicitly excluded.

The UNCITRAL Transparency Rules address transparency issues throughout the ISDS process, from notification to award, promoting openness and public access to information and proceedings. While there are exceptions that may be invoked by a party for a prescribed set of interests (confidential

---

175 UNCITRAL Rules on Transparency in Treaty-Based Investor-State Arbitration, adopted by UN General Assembly Resolution 68/109 (signed 16 December 2013, in effect 1 April 2014).

business information, the endangerment of criminal proceedings, or national security, for example), tribunals are given more discretion to permit openness even where a party objects.

Parties to ICSID ISDS may also choose to apply the Transparency Rules. This heightens their potential for altering the ISDS landscape significantly.

? DISCUSSION NOTES

1 The fact that investor-State arbitration is so closely tied to public interests makes exclusion of the interested public problematic. Indeed, most arguments for increased transparency in ISDS are based on the public's interest in information about government activities. Access to information, however, is not the sole aim of transparency, even if it has an inherent value. If access to information is to serve the interest of improving governance, the opportunity to make known one's opinions about the available information is also a valuable consequence of transparency. 'Ultimately,' writes Hovell, 'the relevant overriding characteristic to which transparency and greater deliberation contribute is legitimacy. Legitimacy is best described (and most often employed) as a theory about compliance.' Devika Hovell, *The Deliberative Deficit: Transparency, Access to Information and UN Sanctions, in* Sanctions, Accountability and Governance in a Globalised World 92, 99 (Jeremy Farrall and Kim Rubenstein eds., 2009).

Thus, from the point of view of the effectiveness of investor-State arbitration, the participation of third parties is important—if all interested parties are heard, the tribunal's decision is more likely to be regarded as legitimate, and consequently, more likely to be effective.[176] *See also* OECD Investment Committee, Transparency and Third Party Participation in Investor-State Dispute Settlement Procedures, para. 28 (2005) (referring to the US and Canadian governments' comments that the closed process of NAFTA investor-State arbitration proceedings was harming the public's acceptance of the awards).

2 What is the proper role of the *amicus curiae*? The tribunal in *Suez v. Argentina* saw the role as a limited one:

> [. . .] the role of an *amicus curiae* is not to challenge arguments or evidence put forward by the Parties. This is the Parties' role. The role of the Petitioners

---

176 *See* Thomas Franck, Fairness in International Law and Institutions 7 (1998).

> in their capacity as *amicus curiae* is to provide their perspective, expertise, and arguments to help the court. [. . .][177]
>
> Is this a convincing distinction of the roles? Is there a role for an *amicus* to argue that the arguments put forward by a party are faulty when the opposing party does not?

b   Arbitrator ethics

b.i   Introduction

Professional ethics has traditionally been extremely important in the legal professions. Behavioural rules applying to lawyers and judges aim not only at ensuring that the legal system is administered by individuals committed to the cause of justice, but also at giving the public faith in the legal system as one that is just. Yet, while there is no doubt that both attorneys and judges must perform their jobs ethically, their different roles require different rules to apply to the two in the adjudicatory process. While an attorney must be loyal to her client, pursuing all possible solutions to ensure that the final judgment upholds the client's interests, an ethical judge must approach the adjudicatory process as a neutral decision-maker.

Of course, there are many complexities in the application of the ethical rules of attorneys and judges in particular cases that make for difficulties. There is, however, basic agreement on the general standards that should apply to each.

As arbitration has become more formalized and calls for transparency and predictability have increased, the issue of the ethical rules and practices applying to international arbitrators has captured the attention of commentators. This attention is welcome, but is still in its early stages. Thus, there is much to be done. The following will introduce some of the current issues facing arbitrators in the international investment setting.

b.ii   International arbitration as a different field of ethics

Ethics in international investment arbitration resembles its courtroom cousin in application, but it is a significantly more ambiguous pursuit on

---

177 *Suez, Sociedad General de Aguas de Barcelona SA and Vivendi Universal SA v. The Argentine Republic,* ICSID Case No. ARB/03/19, Order in Response to a Petition by Five Non-Governmental Organizations for Permission to make an *Amicus Curiae* Submission, para. 25 (Feb. 12, 2007), available at http://www.italaw.com/cases/1057.

the conceptual level. International arbitration brings out the difficulties of addressing ethical issues for a number of reasons. First, there is no single multilateral—or multifora—set of ethical standards for international arbitrators. Thus, in the international setting in which investor-State arbitrations take place, there is a question of which (if any) of the different ethical rules of the different jurisdictions represented will apply to the arbitrators. Second, while sometimes there is a lack of rules governing the practice of the particular arbitrators, at other times there are overlapping (and sometimes conflicting) rules to apply. Finally, the role of the international arbitrator in an investor-State dispute is different from both that of the arbitrator of a private commercial dispute and from that of an international judge in public law. Determining whether the same rules of ethics should apply thus depends on how one views the ultimate purpose of the arbitrator in such a role.

b.iii   *Ethical codes applying to arbitrators*

Whose rules?
There is no single set of ethical rules binding on international arbitrators. There are, however, numerous national sets of rules for arbitrators and a number of international codes setting out general and more specific duties to which arbitrators must adhere. Among the most prominent are the 2004 American Arbitration Association (AAA)/American Bar Association (ABA) Code and the Code of the International Bar Association. In Europe, the Council of Bars and Law Societies of Europe extends its Code of Conduct principles to arbitrators[178] and the Arbitration Foundation of Southern Africa has a Code of Conduct which arbitrators must sign to be considered eligible to be on their roster.[179] While these codes may or may not be binding on arbitrators during their time on a tribunal, courts reviewing awards may be able to rely on such codes as evidence of customary usage.

The main investor-State arbitration fora have no separate codes of ethics for arbitrators under their auspices. Nevertheless, the ICSID, the ICC, the SCC Institute, and the LCIA do have provisions in their rules that require arbitrators to fulfil certain criteria. Article 14 ICSID Convention states, for example, that 'Persons designated to serve on the Panels shall be persons of high moral character and recognized competence in the fields of law, commerce, industry

---

178 Charter of Core Principles of the European Legal Profession and Code of Conduct for European Lawyers, 4.5 (as amended 20 Aug. 2007).
179 Further examples of such codes include the Chartered Institute of Arbitrators' Code of Professional and Ethical Conduct for Members promulgated in 2009 and the National Arbitration Forum's Code of Conduct setting out 'canons' to guide arbitrators.

or finance, who may be relied upon to exercise independent judgment'.[180] Such forum rules are applied by the institution itself if there is a challenge to an arbitrator in a case falling within its ambit. National law might regulate arbitrators or investors may have contracts that specify the ethical rules to which an arbitrator of a dispute about that contract is submitted.

Content of the codes
Given the wide variety of possible sources of ethical rules, there is a clear potential for a multiplicity of behavioural limits on arbitrators. This potential, however, has not been realized, and there are currently only two basic principles guiding investor-State dispute arbitrators: independence and impartiality. These standards will be discussed together, with the contours of their application following the definitional explanation.

<u>Independence and impartiality</u>
The widely regarded International Bar Association (IBA) Guidelines on Conflicts of Interest in International Arbitration, Part I sets out as a first paragraph the 'General Principle' of arbitrator independence and impartiality:

> Every arbitrator shall be impartial and independent of the parties at the time of accepting an appointment to serve and shall remain so during the entire arbitration proceeding until the final award has been rendered or the proceeding has otherwise finally terminated.

The IBA's explanation of this provision calls impartiality and independence a 'fundamental principle', and the introduction mentions that it is so widely accepted in national jurisdictions that some do not even set it out explicitly.

The main arbitration fora do contain explicit references to independence/impartiality, though. The ICSID Arbitration Rules, as mentioned above, require that arbitrators be able to 'exercise independent judgement'. The other rules state the obligation similarly: the ICC Rule 11 says '[e]very arbitrator must be and remain impartial and independent of the parties involved in the arbitration';[181] SCC Rule 14.1 says '[e]very arbitrator must be impartial and independent'; and the PCA Rules of Procedure confirm that '[a]ny arbitrator may be challenged if circumstances exist that give rise to justifiable doubts as to the arbitrator's impartiality or independence'.[182] These rules

---

180 ICSID Convention art. 14(1).
181 ICC Rules of Arbitration, 11 (2012).
182 PCA Rules of Procedure, 10.

ensure that challenges to arbitrator appointments can be brought on suspicion of arbitrator bias.

None of these sets of rules contains any further definition of independence or impartiality. Indeed, the exact meaning of independence and impartiality, and those terms' relationship to concepts such as neutrality, are difficult to pin down precisely. In their essence, they are all terms that go to the idea of ensuring that the decision-maker has not prejudged the situation prior to the parties' presentation of their arguments.[183]

Independence has been said to go to the arbitrator's objective relationship to the issue or parties—it's the 'lack of relations with a party that might influence the arbitrator'.[184] Thus, if an investor is alleging an indirect expropriation of a construction project by virtue of a size restriction imposed on the building, and an arbitrator owns a cement company that supplies the construction company, that arbitrator would not be independent. *Impartiality* goes to the arbitrator's subjective relationship to the issue or parties, to the state of mind he or she may have: 'impartiality involves not favouring one party or the other'.[185] So, in the above example, if the arbitrator, rather than owning the cement company, has a different construction project in a different host territory that is also facing size-restricting regulations, that arbitrator would be partial (not impartial).

Although some commentators parse the terms conceptually, others treat the two as a single standard.[186] In the ICSID rules, in fact, while 'independent judgment' and *'garantie d'indépendance dans l'exercice de leurs fonctions'* are used in the English and French versions, respectively, the (also official) Spanish version requires *'imparcialidad'* of arbitrators' judgment. Even where the relevant rules use one or the other or both, tribunals will often use the two terms interchangeably.[187]

---

183 *ConocoPhillips Company et al. v. Bolivarian Republic of Venezuela*, ICSID Case No. ARB/07/30, Decision on the Proposal to Disqualify L. Yves Fortier, QC, Arbitrator, para. 55 (Feb. 27, 2012). Available at: http:// italaw. com/documents/DecisionontheproposaltodisqualificationL.YvesFortier_001.pdf (saying that the purpose of the independence and impartiality requirements would be to 'protect parties against arbitrators being influenced by factors other than those related to the merits of the case').

184 *Id.* at para. 54. *See also Tidewater Inc. and others v. Bolivarian Republic of Venezuela*, ICSID Case No. ARB/10/5, Decision on the Proposal for the Disqualification of a Member of the Arbitral Tribunal (Dec. 23, 2010). Available at: http://italaw.com/documents/Tidewater_v_Venezuela_Disqualification.pdf.

185 *ConocoPhillips v. Venezuela*, *supra* note 183 at para. 190.

186 Catherine Rogers, *Ethics of International Arbitrators* (Bocconi Legal Studies Research Paper No. 200701). Available at: http://papers.ssrn.com/sol3/papers.cfm?abstract_id=1081436.

187 *See Universal Compression International Holdings, SLU v. Bolivarian Republic of Venezuela*, ICSID Case No. ARB/10/9, Decision on the Proposal to Disqualify Prof. Brigitte Stern and Prof. Guido Santiago Tawil, Arbitrators, at footnote 86 and accompanying text in para. 70 (May 20, 2011). Available at: http://www.italaw. com/cases/1141.

Actual or apparent bias

Independence and impartiality, comments one tribunal, 'are states of mind'.[188] The fact that gathering conclusive evidence on a state of mind is impossible means that challenges to an arbitrator's independence and impartiality must be imputed from the arbitrator's actions or from others' actions in connection with the arbitrator.[189] Lack of evidence of actual bias, however, is not the general standard for determining whether an arbitrator is deemed suitable to sit on a tribunal. Rather, the standard is whether the arbitrator demonstrates actual *or apparent* partiality as well as if there is a *risk or potential* of bias. IBA Guideline (2) Conflicts of Interests highlights this double-approach—based on an objective standard of what a reasonable person would think.

Guideline 2 is based on both practical and theoretical considerations. As stated above, as a practical matter, it is nearly impossible to prove (im-)partiality.[190] Indeed, some arbitrators will be unbiased despite a wide range of dependency-inducing relationships. Theoretically, the double-approach responds to the need for the *appearance of a fair process*. Even if the arbitrators are not actually partial, it could damage trust in the arbitration process (either by the party or by the public) if arbitrators appear to have reasons other than those of legal relevance for making their decisions.

The significant questions facing tribunals who have to determine bias challenges to arbitrators are not how to define the terms of independence/impartiality, but rather what level of independence/impartiality is required of the arbitrator. The ICSID rules require a showing of a 'manifest' lack of independence to uphold a bias challenge. Tribunals differ on exactly what this means, but the term itself indicates that there is room for *de minimis* flexibilities in the standard to be applied. Decisions have referred to the requisite level of proof to reach the level of a 'manifest' lack of independence with various phrases: from needing more than a showing of 'mere belief' by the challenging party that the arbitrator is biased,[191] to requiring evidence that 'clearly' demonstrates the bias,[192] or demanding a showing of a 'quasicer-

---

188 *Suez v. Argentina, supra* note 177, para. 30.

189 *Id.*

190 Dependence as a characteristic arising out of professional or commercial relationships is more susceptible to evidentiary proof, but only if defined to be a factual matter rather than a mental state of bias that arises from such relationships.

191 *Universal Compression v. Venezuela, supra* note 187: 'A manifest lack of the required qualities must be proved by objective evidence. A simple belief that an arbitrator lacks independence or impartiality is not sufficient to disqualify an arbitrator.'

192 *OPIC Karimum Corporation v. the Boliviaran Republic of Venezuela*, ICSID Case No. ARB/10/14, Decision on the Proposal to Disqualify Professor Philippe Sands, Arbitrator, para. 45 (May 5, 2011), http://www.italaw. com/cases/779: 'There thus exists a relatively high burden for those seeking to challenge ICSID arbitrators.'

tain'[193] lack of independence to sustain such claims. This heavy burden of proof on the challenging party often stands at odds with the proclaimed standards of avoiding appearances of bias, however.

CASE

Tidewater v. Venezuela[194]

Professor Brigitte Stern is among the leading arbitrators of investor-State disputes. Having participated in over thirty tribunals, she is also one of the most active of the top arbitrators. Yet, it was just this wealth of experience that was challenged as a hindrance to her independence when she was selected by Venezuela as its choice for a tribunal member in the case launched by Tidewater.

Tidewater was particularly wary of the fact that Venezuela had selected Ms. Stern seven times, thrice when it was represented by a single law firm. This multiplicity of appointments, argued the Claimant, has the potential of creating serious doubts about Ms. Stern's independence and impartiality. Moreover, they argued that a number of the factual and legal issues to be decided were the same as in previous cases, leading to a danger of separating them. Urging the remaining members of the tribunal to apply the cautious and objective standards of the IBA Guidelines, Tidewater asked for Ms. Stern to be disqualified.

The Respondent and Professor Stern herself protested that there was no bias stemming from multiple appointments. Venezuela also denied the applicability of the IBA Guidelines to the proceedings.

The tribunal first noted that it would approach the challenge guided by the ICSID Convention rather than by the IBA Guidelines. On this basis, they made the following analysis:

The Convention's requirement that the lack of independence be 'manifest' necessitates that this lack be clearly and objectively established. Accordingly, it is not sufficient to show an appearance of a lack of impartiality or independence.'

193 *Alpha Projektholding GmbH v. Ukraine*, ICSID Case No. ARB/07/16, Decision on Respondent's Proposal to Disqualify Arbitrator Dr. Yoram Turbowicz, para. 37 (March 19, 2010), http://italaw.com/documents/AlphaDisqualificationDecision.pdf (relying on the understanding that manifest would mean obvious or evident).

194 *Tidewater Inc., Tidewater Investment SRL, Tidewater Caribe, C.A., Twenty Grand Offshore, L.L.C., Point Marine, L.L.C., Twenty Grand Marine Service, L.L.C., Jackson Marine, L.L.C., Zapata Gulf Marine Operators, L.L.C. v. the Bolivarian Republic of Venezuela*, ICSID Case No. ARB/10/5, Decision on Claimants' Proposal to Disqualify Professor Brigitte Stern, Arbitrator (December 23, 2010); footnotes omitted.

58. [. . . T]he next question is whether the existence of multiple appointments by the same party would itself lead an objective observer to conclude that the [ICSID Convention] Article 57 standard has been breached. [. . .].

59. The Two Members begin their analysis of this question by observing that the question whether multiple appointments to arbitral tribunals may impugn the independence or impartiality of an arbitrator is a matter of substance, not of mere mathematical calculation. [. . .] Depending on the particular circumstances of the case, either fewer or more appointments might, in combination with other factors, be needed to call into question an arbitrator's impartiality. [. . .]

60. Considering the matter as one of principle, the conflict which may potentially arise from multiple arbitral appointments by the same party is of a different character from other connections to one of the parties, including service as counsel or other professional capacity. The starting-point is that multiple appointments as arbitrator by the same party in unrelated cases are neutral, since in each case the arbitrator exercises the same independent arbitral function. [. . .]

61. Repeat appointments may be as much the *result* of the arbitrator's independence and impartiality as an indication of justifiable doubts about it. This is reflected in the fact that national courts called upon to consider proposals for disqualification on such a ground normally reject them in the absence of aggravating circumstances.

62. In the view of the Two Members, there would be a rationale for the potential conflict of interest which may arise from multiple arbitral appointments by the same party if either (a) the prospect of continued and regular appointment, with the attendant financial benefits, might create a relationship of dependence or otherwise influence the arbitrator's judgment; or (b) there is a material risk that the arbitrator may be influenced by factors outside the record in the case as a result of his or her knowledge derived from other cases. The Two Members deal with factor (b) in Section D *infra*. In the remainder of this Section, they deal with whether, on the facts of this case, it can be said that the three appointments of Professor Stern by Venezuela *ipso facto* call into question her independence or impartiality.

63. Such practice within ICSID as is publicly available supports a cautious approach to a finding of disqualification on this ground. There have been a number of recent unsuccessful challenges to arbitrators in investment arbitration cases on this ground, both within and outside the ICSID [. . .].

64. In the view of the Two Members, the mere fact of holding three other arbitral appointments by the same party does not, without more, indicate a manifest lack of independence or impartiality on the part of Professor Stern. Indeed, the Two Members find no basis to infer that Professor Stern would be influenced in her decision in any way by the fact of such multiple appointments by one party. On the contrary, her conduct has been demonstrably independent of such influence. The Two Members take notice from the Register of Cases publicly maintained

by ICSID on its website that Professor Stern has held or currently holds arbitral appointments in many ICSID cases and so cannot be said to be dependent on any one party for her extensive practice as an arbitrator in investment cases. Moreover, in each of the two cases in which she was appointed by Venezuela, and where she has to date rendered decisions, [. . .] Professor Stern has joined unanimous preliminary decisions rejecting applications made by Venezuela. This fact tends to indicate that Professor Stern has been appointed on subsequent occasions because of her independence, rather than the reverse. Thus, the Two Members conclude that the appointment of Professor Stern on two prior occasions by Venezuela does not demonstrate a manifest lack on her part of the quality of independent and impartial judgment required of an arbitrator under the ICSID Convention.

D. Possibility of decision on related legal issues

65. It remains finally to consider whether this conclusion is affected by the additional factor [. . .] that one of the prior cases [. . .] may raise a related issue of law [. . .].

66. Tidewater does not allege that there is an overlap in the underlying facts [. . .] so that Professor Stern would benefit from knowledge of facts on the record in [the other case, *Brandes v. Venezuela*] which may not be available in the present case. Rather, it alleges a lack of impartiality based upon an overlap between the issues of law raised in the two cases. Specifically, it states, [. . .] that, in *Brandes*, the sole basis for invoking ICSID jurisdiction is the Venezuelan law. It states that some of Tidewater's claims in the present arbitration also rely upon that law as the basis for ICSID jurisdiction, and that '*[i]t is public knowledge that the Republic of Venezuela takes the position that the Investment Law does not express consent to ICSID jurisdiction.*' Since the *Brandes* Tribunal will have to rule on its jurisdiction first, Tidewater claims that ruling '*will amount to prejudging the identical issue presented in this case, without the Claimants having an opportunity to argue the issue before Professor Stern has made up her mind.*' Venezuela observes that a similar argument has been rejected in other recent ICSID cases.

67. In the opinion of the Two Members, the rationale behind the potential for the conflict of interest identified [. . .] relates to cases where, by reason of the close interrelationship between the facts and the parties in the two cases, the arbitrator has in effect prejudged the liability of one of the parties in the context of the specific factual matrix. They agree with the formulation of the French court, [. . .] that there is '*neither bias nor partiality where the arbitrator is called upon to decide circumstances of fact close to those examined previously, but between different parties, and even less so when he is called upon to determine a question of law upon which he has previously made a decision.*'

68. The Two Members note that this view has also been adopted in decisions on

recent proposals for disqualification within ICSID [. . .]. The Two Members agree with the observation made in one such case [. . .] that:

> '[i]nvestment and even commercial arbitration would become unworkable if an arbitrator were automatically disqualified on the ground only that he or she was exposed to similar legal or factual issues in concurrent or consecutive arbitrations.'

69. Neither Professor Stern, still less the present Tribunal as a whole, will be bound in the present case by any finding which the *Brandes* Tribunal may arrive at as to the issue of Venezuelan law referred to. Indeed, at this stage in the present proceeding, it would be premature to make any judgment as to what issues of law may be pleaded by the parties (and thus as to the similarities or differences between the context for the issues of law to be determined in the two cases), since no pleadings other than the Request for Arbitration have yet been filed.
[. . .]
71. So far as concerns Professor Stern's position, the Two Members have no reason to doubt Professor Stern's statement that *'the fact of whether I am convinced or not convinced by a pleading depends upon the intrinsic value of the legal arguments and not on the number of times I hear the pleading.'*
72. Accordingly, the Two Members find that this third ground upon which Tidewater's Proposal for Disqualification is premised is not well founded and must be rejected.

A tribunal member's prior scholarly expressions of opinion formed the basis of complaint in a different challenge.

 CASE

Urbaser SA et al. v. The Argentine Republic[195]

Urbaser is a Spanish corporation which brought claims under the Argentina–Spain BIT. Among its claims was an invocation of the BIT's MFN clause to access more favourable jurisdictional provisions found in another Argentinian investment treaty. Urbaser relied on reasoning similar to that in the case of *Maffezini v. Spain* to underscore its claim.

After two years of attempts to establish a tribunal, the arguments began in 2007. Several months into the proceedings, however, one tribunal member

---

195 *Urbaser SA et al. v. The Argentine Republic*, ICSID Case No. ARB/07/26, Decision on Claimants' Proposal to Disqualify Professor Campbell McLachlan, Arbitrator (Aug. 12, 2010). Available at: http://italaw.com/docu ments/UrbaserArbitratorChallenge.pdf; footnotes omitted.

died, and Argentina appointed Professor McLachlan as a replacement arbitrator.

Urbaser objected to this selection, as Professor McLachlan is the author of an MFN chapter in an investment law textbook. In that chapter, McLachlan wrote that the *Maffezini* tribunal's decision on MFN was 'heretical', and that he agreed with the *Plama* tribunal's criticism of that decision. Urbaser thus argued that Professor McLachlan 'has already prejudged an essential element of the conflict that is the object of this arbitration'. The tribunal had to determine the extent to which an arbitrator's published opinions about a legal issue can disqualify that individual from deciding on a case in which that issue is argued.

II. The circumstances relevant to the Proposal for disqualification and the Parties' position

20. Claimants' proposal for the disqualification of Prof. McLachlan as an arbitrator and member of this Tribunal is based on views expressed by Prof. McLachlan in his publications as a legal scholar on two questions that Claimants consider crucial to this arbitration.

21. In connection with the Most Favored Nation (MFN) Clause, Claimants refer to the statement made by Prof. McLachlan in the book 'International Investment Arbitration, Substantive Principles', published in 2007 by Oxford University Press. [. . .] Chapter 7 was written by Prof. McLachlan. Claimants base their claim and analysis on Chapter 7. Their concerns are focused on an extract that reads as follows:

> . . .[I]t is essential when applying an MFN clause to be satisfied that the provisions relied upon as constituting more favourable treatment in the other treaty are properly applicable, and will not have the effect of fundamentally subverting the carefully negotiated balance of the BIT in question. It is submitted that this is precisely the effect of the heretical decision of the Tribunal on objections to jurisdiction in Maffezini v Spain. In this case, the Tribunal held that the specific provisions of the dispute resolution clause in the Argentine-Spain BIT did not constitute a bar to its jurisdiction in view of the more liberal provisions of the Chile-Spain BIT, which could be applied as a result of the MFN provision. . .
>
> In Maffezini, the Argentine-Spain BIT contained a dispute settlement clause which permitted the submission of the dispute to international arbitration only if it had first been submitted to the courts of the host State and no decision had been rendered within eighteen months. The Chile-Spain BIT merely contained a cooling off period of six months, with no requirement to resort to the host State courts. . .
>
> On that question, the Tribunal found that the protection of the rights of traders by

means of dispute resolution clauses was a matter which fell within the protections
afforded by treaties of commerce and navigation or investment treaties. . . .
[. . .]
The correctness of this analysis was convincingly questioned in Plama. . . .
[. . .]
It is submitted that the reasoning of the Tribunal in Plama is to be strongly preferred
over that in Maffezini. . . .
[. . .]
'The application of MFN protection will not be justified where it subverts the
balance of rights and obligations which the parties have carefully negotiated in their
investment treaty. In particular, it will not apply to the dispute settlement provisions,
unless the parties expressly so provide.'

[. . .]

23. On this basis Claimants draw the conclusion that Prof. McLachlan 'has already
prejudged an essential element of the conflict that is the object of this arbitration'. It is Claimants' submission that the claim presented before this Tribunal
is under the auspices of the Spain–Argentina BIT in the same way as the claim
presented by Mr. Maffezini against the Kingdom of Spain. When describing the
Maffezini decision as 'heretical', Claimants sustain that Prof. McLachlan has prejudged the jurisdiction of this Tribunal. This would appear all the more so as Prof.
McLachlans' position has been taken as support in one recent decision where the
jurisdictional objection raised by the Argentine Republic in respect of the MFN
Clause has been admitted.

[. . .]

27. Respondent rejects all arguments the Claimants put forth as groundless and
lacking legal basis. Respondent notes that the opinions previously expressed
by Prof. McLachlan and on which the Proposal for his disqualification is based
make no reference whatsoever to the instant case. Respondent's position, as
will be further considered below, is that opinions previously published by an
arbitrator do not raise an issue of lack of impartiality or independence when
issued outside the framework of the ongoing arbitration. . . . Respondent highlights that Prof. McLachlan has given opinions on a large number of concepts
of international investment law and they were rendered in consideration of
neither the Argentine Republic, URBASER, nor concerning the dispute in question. . . .

[. . .]

31. Prof. McLachlan's statement dated May 5, 2010, made in regards to the
Proposal for disqualification, in relevant part, reads:

'I have evaluated my own position in the light of the fundamental requirements of
Article 14 of the ICSID Convention. On accepting my appointment on 7 March
2010, I signed an unqualified Declaration. After consideration of the matters

raised in the Claimant's Proposal, I see no reason to qualify that Declaration, nor any reason why I may not be relied upon to exercise independent judgment in this arbitration.

It is important to distinguish the task of the legal scholar from that of the arbitrator. When writing a book or article, the scholar must express views on numerous general issues of law, based on the legal authorities and other material then available to him. A scholar of any standing should always be prepared to reconsider his views in the light of subsequent developments in the law or further arguments.

However, and in any event, the task of the arbitrator is completely different. It is to judge the case before him fairly as between the parties and according to the applicable law. This can only be done in the light of the specific evidence, the specific applicable law and the submissions of counsel for both parties.

I wish to assure both parties that I would approach such a task in this, as in any, arbitration, unconstrained by my prior publications and without having prejudged any of the issues. This is the essence of the role of the arbitrator.'

[...]

III. The legal basis for the consideration of the disqualification proposal

34. The Parties do not dispute that provisions for dealing with the disqualification proposal are contained in Article 57 (first sentence) of the ICSID Convention, including the reference made to Article 14(1). These provisions read:

> 'A party may propose to a Commission or Tribunal the disqualification of any of its members on account of any fact indicating a manifest lack of the qualities required by paragraph (1) of Article 14.' (Art. 57, first sentence)
> 'Persons designated to serve on the Panels shall be persons of high moral character and recognized competence in the fields of law, commerce, industry or finance, who may be relied upon to exercise independent judgment. Competence in the field of law shall be of particular importance in the case of persons on the Panel of Arbitrators.' (Art. 14[1])

When reading both provisions together, Article 57 has the effect of extending the qualities required by Article 14(1) to all members of the Tribunal, whether or not they are designated to a Panel, and of allowing any party to propose the disqualification of any member on account of any fact indicating a lack of such qualities, under the condition that it must be 'manifest'. Because Article 57 of the Convention refers to 'any of its members' it leaves no doubt that the applicable rules and requirements are the same for all arbitrators of a three-member Tribunal.

35. When considering Claimants' disqualification proposal in light of the provisions quoted above, the Two Members of this Tribunal are called to decide

whether the opinions expressed by Prof. McLachlan on the two matters Claimants qualify as crucial to the outcome of this proceeding, this Arbitrator is deemed to indicate a manifest lack of the required quality to be relied upon to exercise independent judgment.

36. Both Parties have rightly pointed to the fact that the Spanish version of the ICSID Convention introduces a variant to the extent that the final words of the first sentence of Article 14 refer to an arbitrator's quality to 'inspirar plena confianza en su imparcialidad de juicio', thus referring to the notion of impartiality instead of independence as in the English and French version, as well. The Convention states in its last final clause that the texts in all these three languages are 'equally authentic'. It does not contain a rule giving preference to one version over the other. Therefore, the Two Members agree that in case of a divergence of wording the respective versions are to be construed as equivalent. Accordingly, both notions of independence and impartiality are to be considered as equally pertinent for the examination of the Proposal to disqualify Prof. McLachlan. As Respondent rightly pointed out, the ICSID Convention says nothing, however, about specific factual circumstances that would justify a challenge.

37. The Two Members are fully aware of a large body of case law, proposals and guidelines rendered or issued with the aim of providing definitions for such fundamental notions as the independence and impartiality of arbitrators. In particular, they have taken a close look to definitions quoted and explained in Claimants' Proposal and in Respondent's Reply, some of which are rightly considered, as Claimants put it, of 'general acceptance' in international arbitration, such as the IBA Guidelines on Conflicts of Interest in International Arbitration.

However, while these texts certainly constitute a most valuable source of inspiration, they are not part of the legal basis on which the decision rendered in respect of Claimants' Proposal is based. This Decision is based on the provisions of the ICSID Convention, as quoted above, which are to be construed and interpreted in the broader context of the objectives and the operation of the arbitral proceedings governed by this instrument.

IV. The content and scope of the notions of independence and impartiality

38. As stated above, both concepts of independence and impartiality are deemed to be of equivalent content and pertinence in the framework of Articles 14(1) and 57 of the ICSID Convention. Therefore, a debate on the question of whether the concepts may have, at least in part, different meanings, becomes moot. In any event, many efforts to discover a manner to divide these notions cannot overcome their inherent redundancy. Indeed, an arbitrator's lack of independence of judgment results in favor shown to one of the parties and thus demonstrates the arbitrator's

lack of impartiality, while an arbitrator's lack of impartiality is a sign of the arbitrator's lack of independent judgment.

39. Claimants, however, focus on the notion of impartiality, which, in their opinion, has a 'strong subjective content' and therefore, is different from the concept of independence. Claimants consider independence as an objective circumstance, implying the nonexistence of a relationship with the parties. Based on these definitions, Claimants reach the conclusion that no doubt exists regarding Prof. McLachlan's independence, however, in their view, the circumstances relating to his publications demonstrate that he 'does not meet the requisite of impartiality since he has prejudged certain fundamental aspects of this arbitration'.

40. According to Articles 57 and 14(1) of the ICSID Convention, the crux of the analysis is whether the opinions expressed by Prof. McLachlan qualify as indicating a manifest lack of the qualities required to provide independent and impartial judgment. This principle, however, requires that an inherent qualification is expressed. No arbitrator and, more generally, no human being of a certain age is, in absolute terms, independent and impartial. Simply put, every individual is conveying ideas and opinions based on its moral, cultural, and professional education and experience. What is required, when it comes to rendering judgment in a legal dispute, is the ability to consider and evaluate the merits of each case *without relying on factors having no relation to such merits*.

41. Claimants' definition of the requirement of independence and more particularly, the concept of impartiality, is broader. Claimants admit that the opinions expressed by Prof. McLachlan do not raise an issue of partiality shown towards a party or related to the outcome of the claims as to their merits. They contend that there is a showing of preference and partiality in favor of the position that the Respondent will undoubtedly assert in this arbitration with respect to the two crucial issues described above. Claimants assert that Prof. McLachlan lacks the freedom to give his opinion and to make a decision solely based on the facts and the circumstances of the case because he has allegedly already prejudged those facts and circumstances, and issued his opinion on these matters. Claimants argue that Prof. McLachlan cannot issue an opinion contrary to that which he published and thus face criticism that he was inconsistent or possibly 'heretical' himself.

42. In support of this latter point, Claimants refer to the IBA Rules of Ethics, which state:

> '3.1 The criteria for assessing questions relating to bias are impartiality and independence. Partiality arises when an arbitrator favours one of the parties, or where he is prejudiced in relation to the subject-matter of the dispute.
>
> 3.2 Facts which might lead a reasonable person, not knowing the arbitrator's true state of mind, to consider that he is dependent on a party create an appearance of bias. The same is true if an arbitrator has a material interest in the outcome of the dispute, or if he has already taken a position in relation to it.'

When arguing that a position taken on a matter of legal interpretation, as is the case with the excerpts published by Prof. McLachlan, constitutes a prejudice 'in relation to the subject-matter of the dispute' and that it reflects 'a position in relation to it [i.e. the "outcome of the dispute"]', Claimants go far beyond the reasonable understanding of these provisions. The 'subject-matter of the dispute' and the 'outcome of the dispute' are the core concepts that these provisions refer to; their content is thus identical or at least very close to the outcome of the proceedings. These provisions are far from clearly supporting the purported interpretation that any position taken on a particular issue to be raised in arbitration shall be considered as an element of bias showing a lack of impartiality and independence. The provisions are even more unclear or totally ambiguous when the issue to be considered is, like in the instant case, the interpretation of legal concepts in isolation from the facts and circumstances of a particular case.

43. The requirements of independence and impartiality serve the purpose of protecting the parties against arbitrators being influenced by factors other than those related to the merits of the case. In order to be effective this protection does not require that actual bias demonstrate a lack of independence or impartiality. An appearance of such bias from a reasonable and informed third person's point of view is sufficient to justify doubts about an arbitrator's independence or impartiality. Claimants refer to the decision made on December 8, 2009, by the Secretary General of the Permanent Court of Arbitration (PCA) upon the challenge of Judge Charles N. Brower. This decision states that a point of view expressed in an interview gave rise to an appearance that this arbitrator prejudged the issue of an arbitration proceeding although he had not given a specific opinion on the outcome of the pending arbitral proceedings. The issue in the instant case, however, is that the appearance of doubt in regards to the independence and impartiality of Prof. McLachlan is directly linked to the statements quoted by Claimants as grounds for their challenge.

44. What matters is whether the opinions expressed by Prof. McLachlan on the two issues qualified as crucial by Claimants are specific and clear enough that a reasonable and informed third party would find that the arbitrator will rely on such opinions without giving proper consideration to the facts, circumstances, and arguments presented by the Parties in this proceeding. Claimants' view is . . . that the opinions expressed by Prof. McLachlan are to be taken as such . . ., absent any evidence that he has changed his opinion in the meantime. . . .

45. The Two Members seized with the challenge submitted by Claimants are of the view that the mere showing of an opinion, even if relevant in a particular arbitration, is not sufficient to sustain a challenge for lack of independence or impartiality of an arbitrator. For such a challenge to succeed there must be a showing that such opinion or position is supported by factors related to and supporting a party to the arbitration (or a party closely related to such party), by a direct or indirect interest

of the arbitrator in the outcome of the dispute, or by a relationship with any other individual involved, such as a witness or fellow arbitrator.

46. Indeed if one would prefer to extend such requirement of independence or impartiality beyond this framework, as supported by Claimants, the mere fact of having made known an opinion on an issue relevant in an arbitration would have the effect of allowing a challenge for lack of independence or impartiality. Such a position, however, would have effects reaching far beyond what Claimants seem to sustain, and incompatible with the proper functioning of the arbitral system under the ICSID Convention.

47. The opinions expressed by Prof. McLachlan are those of an academic. They represent, even when taken together with numerous other opinions expressed by scholars, a small part of all opinions contained in publications relating to arbitrations governed by the ICSID Convention. These opinions include, in particular, the full set of opinions expressed in the awards and decisions rendered under the ICSID system, most of which are published or available through the Internet. The appointment of the President of the Tribunal in the Alemanni case, as reported by Respondent, seems to indicate that an opinion previously expressed in an arbitral decision does not constitute an obstacle for an arbitrator to be appointed in another case raising similar issues. In the Decision on the proposal for the disqualification of a member of the Arbitral Tribunal rendered in the *Suez/Vivendi v. Argentine Republic* cases on October 22, 2007, the Two Members stated that the fact that a judge or arbitrator had made a determination of law or a finding of fact in one case does not mean that such judge or arbitrator cannot decide the law and the facts impartially in another case. They further observed that:

> 'A finding of an arbitrator's or a judge's lack of impartiality requires far stronger evidence than that such arbitrator participated in a unanimous decision with two other arbitrators in a case in which a party in that case is currently a party in a case now being heard by that arbitrator or judge. To hold otherwise would have serious negative consequences for any adjudicatory system.' (§ 36)

48. If Claimants' view were to prevail and any opinion previously expressed on certain aspects of the ICSID Convention be considered as elements of prejudgment in a particular case because they might become relevant or are merely argued by one party, the consequence would be that no potential arbitrator of an ICSID Tribunal would ever express views on any such matter, whether it may be procedural, jurisdictional, or touching upon the substantive rights deriving from BITs. The wide spreading of ICSID awards through publication and appearance on the Centre's website has greatly contributed to dense exchanges of views throughout the world on matters of international investment law. This is very largely considered as a positive contribution to the development of the law and policies in this segment of the world's economy.

It goes without saying that such a debate would be fruitless if it did not include an exchange of opinions given by those who are actually involved in the ICSID arbitration process, whether they are writing and speaking as scholars, arbitrators, or counsel. Such activity is part of the 'system' and well known to all concerned. Therefore, it seems extremely strange to the Two Members to accept Claimants' position that a view previously expressed on an item relevant in an arbitral proceeding should be qualified as a prejudgment that demonstrates a lack of independence or impartiality.

49. The above analysis is not intended to suggest that Claimants' views are not a matter for debate. It is true, indeed, that each arbitrator's personal opinion is of greater weight in a system like ICSID arbitration than in most other systems of judicial adjudication world-wide. In other judicial systems, decisions are based on precedent that all members of the judicial body have to respect or, at least, observe within a usually small margin for possible overruling, under the control of the appellate body. In such a system, the opinion of an individual judge counts for little to the extent that previous precedents have to be followed. This is not how ICSID arbitration operates. Despite many statements made in ICSID awards affirming the necessity or the duty to achieve consistency through ICSID case law, the principle remains that each Tribunal is sovereign in its decision making. This autonomy also applies to decisions rendered by Annulment Committees, which do not have precedential value and are not in practice considered as having such value. This necessarily implies that weight is given to the opinion of each member of an ICSID Tribunal. However, this is not without limits. The requirement of independent and impartial judgment means that an arbitrator's previously adopted opinion, whether published or not, shall not be of such force as to prevent the arbitrator from taking full account of the facts, circumstances, and arguments presented by the parties in the particular case.

V. Professor McLachlan's statements

[. . .]

51. The Two Members wish to emphasize at the outset that Prof. McLachlan has provided the Parties with a clear statement in which he acknowledges the Claimants' concern and ensures both Parties that he will approach his task as an arbitrator unconstrained by his prior publications and without having prejudged any of the issues. The Two Members have no reason whatsoever not to trust this statement. They also note that the opinions referred to by Claimants have been expressed by Prof. McLachlan in his capacity as a scholar and not in a decision that could have some kind of a binding effect upon him. One of the main qualities of an academic is the ability to change his/her opinion as required in light of the current state of academic knowledge. The Two Members have no doubt that Prof. McLachlan reaches such high standard of science and conscience.

[. . .]

54. The Two Members are not able to identify anything more in these statements than an analysis of international law, the relationship between general and customary international law, and the law of the BITs involved in the cases under examination. Even at this level, it is not clear whether the statements made by Prof. McLachlan are relevant in the instant case, especially given that Claimants acknowledge that there is a clear difference between the BIT applied in the CMS case and the Spain–Argentina BIT relevant to the matter before this Tribunal. The statements made by Prof. McLachlan do not contain any element indicating, from the point of view of a reasonable third party, that he will not be capable of giving his full attention and consideration to the positions developed by each Party involved in the instant case as they relate to the legal items he previously examined. . . .

[. . .]

59. This conclusion necessarily implies that Prof. McLachlan's statements on which the Proposal for his disqualification is based do not indicate a 'manifest' lack of independence or impartiality as required by Article 57 of the ICSID Convention.

Tribunals are extremely cautious in disqualifying fellow arbitrators. The proffered justification for denying the calls for disqualification on the basis of a prior decision-making record is that this would restrict the number of available arbitrators (including, inevitably, the most experienced).

Still, there has been disqualification by co-arbitrators even in ICSID proceedings. Challenged on the basis of his serving as arbitrator in a related case, Mr. Bruno Boesch was disqualified by his fellow arbitrators in the *Caratube v. Kazakhstan* dispute in March 2014.[196] The co-arbitrators did not accuse Mr. Boesch of being biased, but rather stressed the objective nature of the independence and impartiality test and the specific circumstances of the particular dispute:

Based on a careful consideration of the Parties' respective arguments and in the light of the significant overlap in the underlying facts between the *Ruby Roz* case and the present arbitration, as well as the relevance of these facts for the determination of legal issues in the present arbitration, the Unchallenged Arbitrators find that—independently of Mr. Boesch's intentions and best efforts to act impartially and independently—a reasonable and informed third party would find it highly likely that, due to his serving as arbitrator in the *Ruby Roz* case and his

---

196 *Caratube International Oil Company LLP and Mr. Devincci Salah Hourani v. Republic of Kazakhstan*, ICSID Case No. ARB/13/13, Decision on the Proposal for Disqualification of Mr. Bruno Boesch (March 20, 2014).

exposure to the facts and legal arguments in that case, Mr. Boesch's objectivity and open-mindedness with regard to the facts and issues to be decided in the present arbitration are tainted. In other words, a reasonable and informed third party would find it highly likely that Mr. Boesch would prejudge legal issues in the present arbitration based on the facts underlying the *Ruby Roz* case.[197]

? DISCUSSION NOTES

1 Does the fact that investor-State dispute resolutions involve public interests mean that independence standards should be more strict or less strict? Rubins and Lauterburg argue that 'the presence of public interest concerns . . . may militate towards a *stricter* view of arbitrator independence and impartiality'. This is due to the fact that

> [. . .] treaty claims are often predicated on a challenge to regulatory and legislative measures that have been implemented by legislatures or other elected officials—ostensibly at least—at the public's behest. In this regard, one might expect that the state's constituents have a legitimate interest in an impeccably independent and impartial tribunal, and that the public at large may view conflicts issues differently than the international arbitration community. . . . From a layman's point of view, a board member of a company that owns or recommends to purchase a share in a party has been asked to decide a multi-million dollar claim against a sovereign government in relation to measures affecting the public interest. Is the public's (perhaps unsophisticated) perception about the arbitrator's independence relevant? In particular, what is '*de minimis*' to an international arbitrator may not seem insignificant to an average citizen of the host State, whose tax money is at stake. How public perception could be taken into account without unreasonably restricting the pool of qualified arbitrators is a more difficult issue.[198]

2 Under the ICSID Rules of Procedure, the fellow tribunal members will decide a challenge to an arbitrator's independence or impartiality. How does this affect the proceedings' appearance of independence and impartiality?

Nationality

Another source of apparent bias can be the nationality of the arbitrator. While the ICSID rules permit parties to nominate arbitrators of the same national-

---

197 *Id.*

198 Noah Rubins and Bernhard Lauterburg, *Independence, Impartiality and Duty of Disclosure in Investment Arbitration, in* Investment and Commercial Arbitration—Similarities and Divergences 153, 168–79 (Christina Knahr et al. eds., 2010).

ity if the other party agrees, the third arbitrator (or the sole arbitrator) should not hold the citizenship of either party. The preference for non-nationals in the ICSID presumes partiality could arise from 'common cultural and legal backgrounds'.[199] This presumption, in turn, reflects the investor's basic interest in using international dispute resolution techniques: to avoid prejudice in national courts that stems from the fact of being foreign. As a result, there is a strong preference for non-nationals as arbitrators in the rules of the various fora.

LITERATURE

Catherine Rogers, Ethics of International Arbitrators[200]

c. Nationality and Other Group Affiliations

Nationality and arbitrator impartiality have a somewhat strange relationship. As one commentator has noted, '[i]t is both the peculiarity and the essence of the arbitration method that allow—in the very same setting—national commonality to perpetuate and nationalistic favoritism to be neutralized.' . . .

Even if parties can and do choose to nominate party arbitrators who share their nationality, however, there is a general presumption against a chairperson or sole arbitrator sharing the nationality of one of the parties (absent contrary agreement) . . . .

In investment arbitration, concerns about nationality have led to more restrictive rules and practices. For example, the ICSID Rules of Procedure for Arbitration Proceedings (the 'ICSID Rules') provide that '[t]he majority of the arbitrators shall be nationals of States other than the Contracting State party to the dispute and the Contracting State whose national is a party to the dispute[.]' Application of this rule means that in a typical two-party arbitration with a tripartite panel, all three of the arbitrators must be from States different from those of the parties. The ICSID Rules allow the parties to override this provision by agreement, but some investment arbitration provisions, such as those in the *Softwood Lumber Agreement Between the Government of Canada and the Government of the United States of America*, completely disallow any member of the tribunal to be a citizen or resident of the same country as one of the parties.

In a globalized world, and especially among a group as internationally mobile and cross-cultural as international arbitrators, nationality and residency are not always an accurate proxy for cultural or political empathies. Particularly in disputes involving parties from certain regions or nations with historical enmities, ethnic or religious affiliations may be more important than national identity. This distinction

---

199 Rogers, *supra* note 186, at 17.
200 *Id.*

is acknowledged in the ICC Arbitration Rules, which provide that in addition to nationality, in making confirmations or appointments, the ICC Court will consider not only nationality, but also 'residence and *other relationships* with the countries of which the parties or the other arbitrators are nationals.' In fact, ICC national committees and other appointing authorities routinely consider such 'other relationships' when making appointments involving parties from regions or backgrounds that may trigger sensibilities. Potential arbitrators themselves should also consider both whether aspects of their background may actually interfere with their ability to act impartially, or may interfere with perceptions of their impartiality.

There are other values at stake in investor-State arbitrations, however, that complicate the arbitrator nationality question. The main one is the desire of hosts to have their arguments heard by a decision-maker that can appreciate the broader socio-cultural context of the investment dispute. While it may be that selecting nationals would be motivated merely by a wish for an unfair 'win', there are substantial legitimate concerns that speak for permitting nationals on arbitral tribunals.

A 'territoriality' issue as much as a 'nationality' issue, the use of non-local arbitrators on investment tribunals may detract from the legitimacy of the process. The population directly affected by the investment and the decision-makers, argues the following author, are too far removed from each other.

LITERATURE

Marc E. Poirier, The NAFTA Chapter 11 Expropriation Debate through the Eyes of a Property Theorist[201]

B. Problems of territoriality

Like the medieval merchant community, the global merchant and investor community is defined not by spatial location governed by a spatially located sovereign, but by professional activity, commercial interest, and various social ties. Yet the adverse environmental effects of their decisions may often be felt most by those in a location far away from the situs of those decisions and unrelated to it. Even within domestic environmental politics, national level groups are often criticized for influencing environmental decision-making in ways that leave out local affected interests. The disconnect is, if anything, even more complete between international commercial interests without a tie to place and locally situated envi-

---

201 Marc E. Poirier, *The NAFTA Chapter 11 Expropriation Debate through the Eyes of a Property Theorist*, 33(4) Envtl. L. 851 (2003); footnotes omitted.

ronmental interests. There is a territorial asymmetry to the conflict between the nomos that is generating property-based claims for investment protection and the nomos that generates balancing between property rights and police power within a geographically defined community. The latter will likely be much more sensitive to bona fide claims for regulation to protect the public health and the environment because these claims are often bound to a specific territory and hence generate a stronger interest in managing the effects of various actions on natural resources and natural services. The notion that there are two nomoi competing for control of the societal dialogue over international regulatory takings issues— one situated territorially, the other an aterritorial community of interest—also leads to reflections on the connection between place and tribunal. First of all, the fact that a NAFTA Chapter 11 arbitral tribunal can convene anywhere in any of the signatory countries may be especially troubling if it is addressing the legitimacy of a regulation that is intended to protect a specific population. In a U.S. regulatory takings case that involves state or local regulation, the proceeding would likely occur within the same jurisdiction where the adverse environmental effects were felt. In contrast, an arbitration under NAFTA Chapter 11 may occur very far away from the local adverse effects. Metalclad is a good example. Vancouver, B.C., which was selected as the site of the arbitration, is thousands of miles from San Luis Potosi, the Mexican state where the hazardous waste facility site would have been located. This is not simply a question of a distance that makes local participation in the arbitration process more onerous (assuming such participation was generally allowed as of right, which it now is not). There are several related issues that make it desirable to have the dispute resolution in the general territory where the adverse environmental effects are felt. This contrasts to the general run-of-the-mill international commercial arbitration, where a prime goal is often to remove a dispute from the territory of either party.

[T]here is also symbolic value to having disputes linked to a region decided by judges or arbitrators with links to that region. This connection helps to legitimate the authority of the tribunal. It physically links the formal articulation of law to the social practices to which it will inevitably be compared. Thus, federal district judges are required to live in the district in which they sit. Federal appellate judges are required to live in the circuit in which they sit, are apportioned by state, and by law each circuit must have at least one judge from each state in the circuit.

In the course of an examination of the regulatory functions of private international law in an era of globalization, Robert Wai gives a succinct analysis of the shortcomings of adjudicators who are not tied to a territorial polity but instead derive from a particular interest community.

> There may be a difference in outcomes between state regulators or adjudicators and non-state arbitrators. State-based private law often includes protection of third parties and social interests among its substantive objectives, but there may

be a tendency for private adjudicators to ignore arguments about the protection of individuals and groups not party to the actual decision in their interpretation of these laws. This may result from a form of 'democracy deficit' in denationalized legal regimes. The nature of the denationalized regulatory regimes is such that they are subject to less pressure from different third-party constituencies than are national regulators, yet their decisions do have an impact on third parties. . . . While territorially-defined jurisdictions also exclude interested parties, in comparison they are more inclusive because of their broader scope of membership and their more widely-understood and relatively non-volitional concept of territorially defined membership. The implication of Wai's argument for NAFTA Chapter 11 disputes is that arbitrators chosen from a particular non territorial nomos are not in fact as likely to act in the general public interest in matters that, like the 'indirect' and 'tantamount to' expropriation issues, combine public and private matters. It is not only a question of who is allowed to participate in the arbitration. Because denationalized regulatory regimes do not include the whole citizenry, they are less democratic than a regime based on a territorially defined membership.

In Spheres of Justice: A Defense of Pluralism and Equality, Michael Walzer gives us some further clues about the importance of territoriality, although because he does so in the context of a discussion of citizenship and immigration, his discussion requires some refocusing. Walzer writes:

> [T]he link between people and land is a crucial feature of national identity. [A nation's] leaders understand, moreover, that because so many critical issues (including issues of distributive justice, such as welfare, education, and so on) can best be resolved within geographical units, the focus of political life can never be established elsewhere. 'Autonomous' corporations will always be adjuncts, and probably parasitic adjuncts, of territorial states; and to give up the state is to give up any effective self-determination. . . . Hence the theory of justice must allow for the territorial state, specifying the rights of its inhabitants and recognizing the collective right of admission and refusal.

Why does Walzer write that issues of distributive justice can best be resolved within territorial units, and that the focus of political life can never be established elsewhere? I believe he does so because of an appreciation that political discourse involves what David Van Zandt has called micropolitical interactions. That is, citizens produce and reproduce to one another the context and substance of their citizenship in an ongoing, pragmatic, dialogic process. Disputes over property, natural resources, and distribution generally are among the issues addressed within this ongoing dialogic context. Indeed, a sense of commonality as citizens helps to contain and defuse the rancor of resource disputes.

There is also a pragmatic aspect to this argument about the importance of locality to communal norm formation and dispute resolution. Typically, and throughout most of human history, the only way to fully engage discourse with others has been to be in their proximity if not in their actual presence. Until the advent of modern telecommunications and transportation, community was in an important sense inherently and inevitably local. It was thus tied to place and presence in a place. 'Where are you from?' is also inevitably a question about who you are and who your community is.

Disclosure

Closely related to the issue of avoidance of actual or apparent bias is that of disclosure. The IBA Rules of Ethics for International Arbitrators set out a duty of disclosure in Rule 4:

> A prospective arbitrator should disclose all facts or circumstances that may give rise to justifiable doubts as to his impartiality or independence. Failure to make such disclosure creates an appearance of bias, and may of itself be a ground for disqualification even though the non-disclosed facts or circumstances would not of themselves justify disqualification.[202]

The IBA Guidelines on Conflicts of Interest in International Arbitration[203] explain further that the approach taken is subjective and precautionary. If the arbitrator's impartiality or independence 'may, in the eyes of the parties' be doubted due to certain circumstances, then the arbitrator should disclose such facts. Contrary to most institutional codes and national laws that allow for objective measures of the need for disclosure, the IBA yields to parties' desire for any potentially relevant information about their decision-makers:

> [T]he . . . objective test for disqualification and subjective test for disclosure . . . are clearly distinct from each other, and . . . a disclosure shall not automatically lead to disqualification. . . . In determining what facts should be disclosed, an arbitrator should take into account all circumstances known to him or her, including to the extent known [of] the culture and the customs of the country of which the parties are domiciled or nationals.[204]

---

202 IBA Rules of Ethics for International Arbitrators, 4.1.
203 IBA Guidelines on Conflicts of Interest in International Arbitration, approved on May 22, 2004 by the Council of the International Bar Association. Available at: http://www.ibanet.org/ENews_Archive/IBA_July_2008_ENews_ArbitrationMultipleLang.aspx [hereinafter 'IBA Gudelines'].
204 IBA Guidelines, Explanation to General Standard 3 at p. 10.

At the same time, the duty of disclosure is meant to avoid unwarranted appearances of bias rather than to act as a punitive rule. The Guidelines emphasize that disclosure is not to be regarded as a step toward disqualification:

> Disclosure is not an admission of a conflict of interest. An arbitrator who has made a disclosure to the parties considers himself or herself to be impartial and independent of the parties, despite the disclosed facts, or else he or she would have declined the nomination or resigned. An arbitrator making disclosure thus feels capable of performing his or her duties. It is the purpose of disclosure to allow the parties to judge whether or not they agree with the evaluation of the arbitrator and, if they so wish, to explore the situation further.[205]

At the same time, in case of doubt, arbitrators are to err on the side of caution and disclose information that might be considered important. The only qualification to this is where disclosure would violate confidentiality rules. In that case, the arbitrator must step down rather than disclose.

Finally, the IBA takes the view that disclosure considerations apply equally throughout the process. Other institutions sometimes use different standards for disclosures prior to an appointment and at the end of a case.

The reason behind the duty to disclose is to ensure that parties know whether or not to challenge an arbitrator on the basis of bias. The duty to disclose itself, however, can be more or less strict. Generally, the disclosure rule only aims to make information known that would look bad if it came out later. This aim has led to the development of the concepts of 'waivable' and 'non-waivable' conflicts, the latter requiring disclosure and the former allowed under consent of the parties.

Under the IBA Guidelines, there are four lists setting out the standards for disqualification of arbitrators, two red, one orange, one green. These lists provide examples of situations in which impartiality and independence can or cannot be remedied by disclosure.

1. Non-Waivable Red: under these circumstances, impartiality and independence are too (objectively) doubtful. The parties *cannot* waive their rights to protest against arbitrators that have such potential conflicts of interest. Examples include an arbitrator that is a representative of a party or if the arbitrator has a 'significant' financial interest in a party or the case.

---

205 *Id.*

2. Waivable Red: these circumstances might lead to subjective doubts about impartiality or independence, but can be remedied by *full disclosure and express waiver* by the parties.
3. Orange List: situations that could lead to subjective doubts (viewed by the parties); here, arbitrators *must disclose* details as soon as possible; if parties don't react to the disclosures within 30 days, *waiver is presumed*.
4. Green List: situations in which there is no appearance/existence of conflicts, and where the arbitrator has no duty of disclosure; this includes orange list situations that are past their relevant time period.

Importantly, many rules allow for substantial discretion on the part of the arbitrator to determine whether or not facts need to be disclosed. This seems to have changed somewhat over time, becoming more objective, but, when put in terms such as 'facts ... which might be of such a nature as to call into question the arbitrator's independence in the eyes of the parties ...', the arbitrator maintains a level of discretion. For any particular arbitrator, determining whether to disclose sensitive information will be a balancing act—disclosure may result in disqualification for the instant case, but non-disclosure might risk a finding in a challenge action that will reflect poorly later. Moreover, some rules would make non-disclosure itself evidence of bias, and can be grounds for disqualification even if the information that was not disclosed would not of itself have been enough for disqualification.[206]

? DISCUSSION NOTES

1 Disclosure obligations can also be imputed to the (New York) Convention on the Recognition and Enforcement of Foreign Arbitral Awards. If a tribunal member has not disclosed a pertinent fact, the losing party can challenge the enforcement of the award under one of two provisions: that the arbitrator's failure to disclose makes the tribunal constituted without the parties' agreement against the law of the seat of arbitration; or that it violates the public policy of the jurisdiction of enforcement.

Duty to investigate
One more question relating to independence/impartiality and disclosure rules is important to point out. That is whether an arbitrator needs to actively seek out whether they have a conflict of interest. Sometimes the arbitrator's lack of knowledge of a potential conflict will be seen as precluding bias in and

---

206 IBA Rules of Ethics, art. 4.1.

of itself. The *Suez-Vivendi* annulment tribunal seemed to adopt this approach, noting that Arbitrator Kaufmann-Kohler's realization of UBS' shareholdings only occurred after her appointment as a tribunal member had ended.[207] Others would argue that arbitrator appointees have a duty to investigate whether they have any relationships that might be perceived as compromising, based on the idea that perceptions of bias as well as actual bias are also to be avoided. Some courts even put a duty to investigate on the parties.[208]

The IBA Guidelines are relatively strict about the duty to investigate. General Standard 7 puts such an obligation on both parties and arbitrators, noting that parties are to make a 'reasonable search' of information that is publicly available about their appointee[209] and that arbitrators are to make 'reasonable enquiries' into potential conflicts.[210] A failure to fulfil the duty of investigation would result in the unavailability of the arbitrator's lack of knowledge of the conflict as an excuse to a challenge.

Tribunal practice may be less rigorous than the IBA Guidelines. In *ConocoPhillips v. Venezuela*, the respondent challenged Arbitrator Yves Fortier's failure to disclose his possible bias stemming from the merger of the law firm for which he worked with a firm that engaged in substantial work against Venezuela in other contexts. Even though Fortier claimed to have no knowledge of the possible conflicts arising for his work as an arbitrator and even resigned his position at the firm to ensure his independence, Venezuela accused him of failing to actively investigate potential conflicts throughout his term as arbitrator.

The tribunal members charged with reviewing the challenge acknowledged that other tribunals had held arbitrators to a 'continuous duty of investigation', but pointed out that those were special cases, inapplicable to the current complaint. Relying on an objective test for disclosure, the tribunal stated simply, '[w]e cannot see that, in the circumstances of this case, there is a sufficient basis for saying that at some point well before 4 October, Mr.

---

207 *Suez, Sociedad General de Aguas de Barcelona SA, and Vivendi Universal SA v. The Argentine Republic*, ICSID Case No. ARB/03/19, and *Suez, Sociedad General de Aguas de Barcelona SA, and InterAguas Servicios Integrales del Agua SA v. The Argentine Republic*, ICSID Case No. ARB/03/17, Decision on a Second Proposal for the Disqualification of a Member of the Arbitral Tribunal, para. 39 (May 12, 2008).

208 Rogers, *supra* note 186, at 17 (saying this puts too much of a burden on parties, who should be able to rely on information given them by the arbitrator appointees).

209 IBA Guidelines 7(b).

210 IBA Guidelines 7(c).

Fortier knew or should have known the information in question and hence was under an obligation to disclose', and dismissed the challenge.[211]

Other elements of arbitrator ethics
Independence and impartiality are arguably the most important ethical standards for arbitrators. There are others, however. While the specific rules may vary, general principles of arbitrator ethics would include the following duties:

- to conduct arbitration in accordance with the arbitration agreement— parties' agreements are basically the last word, if there is one; the only exception is if the agreement would result in a violation of public policy or if it would result in an unenforceable award;
- of competence and diligence—need to have the knowledge and skills for the particular dispute and also to have the time to devote to the case and issue the award;
- of confidentiality—some of the institutions' rules impose confidentiality on all matters, others do not, but parties may expect confidentiality; and
- to propose settlement—some jurisdictions require judges to help parties reach settlement, while in others there is a ban on *ex parte* communications, prohibiting such a duty.

c   Comparing standards of ethics

c.i   Judges v. arbitrators

It is interesting to question why independence and impartiality are important—clearly we probably all feel that impartiality and independence are important for a judge. Why, actually? And is the impartiality and independence of an arbitrator more important?

In courts, judges have a public role: one of ensuring the fair application of laws of the jurisdiction and of showing the public that the laws are being faithfully applied. The signalling effect of court behaviour is extremely important—probably more important overall than the actual decision in any single dispute. In order to ensure that their decisions are accepted, judges are ideally held to standards of strict independence and impartiality—often they are full-time judges, separate from the daily professional contact with

---

211 *ConocoPhillips v. Venezuela, supra* note 183, paras. 67–8.

attorney problems, often randomly assigned to cases, and often required to recuse themselves whether or not the parties object to an appearance of bias.

Arbitrators, on the other hand, are often party-selected and work interchangeably as arbitrator and counsel—sometimes simultaneously—and often away from the public eye. Should this make the ethical strictures on non-bias more or less compelling? Both arguments can be made: some say arbitrators, as people with practical experience in the trade, should be held to looser standards, and that, indeed, parties want arbitrators who are not completely impartial so as to ensure their sympathetic understanding of the matter of the dispute; others have commented that the lack of institutional safeguards and finality of decisions make strict independence even more important.

The difference in approach to independence used by investment arbitration tribunals and courts is interesting. While arbitrators do express concerns for systemic legitimacy, the fear of setting standards that could lead to too many arbitrator disqualifications seems to weigh heavily in the final decisions. Courts, on the other hand, emphasize judicial independence as part of the individual's right to a fair trial.

The European Court of Human Rights, for example, takes a strict view of both the subjective and objective aspects of judicial bias, emphasizing the importance of maintaining public confidence in the judicial system through avoiding any appearance of a lack of bias:

> The existence of impartiality for the purposes of Article 6§1 of the Convention must be determined according to a subjective test, that is on the basis of the personal conviction of a particular judge in a given case, and also according to an objective test, that is, by ascertaining whether the judge offered guarantees sufficient to exclude any legitimate doubt in this respect. . . .
> As to the subjective test, the personal impartiality of a judge must be presumed until there is proof to the contrary . . . .
> Under the objective test, it must be determined whether, quite apart from the judge's personal conduct, there are ascertainable facts which may raise doubts as to his impartiality. In this respect, even appearances may be of a certain importance. What is at stake is the confidence which the courts in a democratic society must inspire in the public. Accordingly, any judge in respect of whom there is a legitimate reason to fear a lack of impartiality must withdraw. . . . [T]he standpoint of the party concerned is important but not decisive. What is decisive is whether this fear can be held to be objectively justified.[212]

---

212 *Pétur Thór Sigurdsson v. Iceland*, App. No. 39731/98, Judgment, para. 37 (Apr. 10, 2003) (ECHR).

c.ii   *International rules v. national rules*

Should ethical rules for arbitrators be international or would national rules suffice? One position is that there need to be distinct ethical rules for international arbitration. Philip Peters supports this view:

> With many arbitrators hailing from the legal profession, national rules for professional conduct might be a tempting starting point for tackling the issue. This approach, however, has repeatedly been identified as incorrect and bound to fail for several reasons.
>
> Firstly, national legislation is often not primarily aimed at contributing to or satisfying international standards and an international system in which the number of nationalities determines the number of different sets of rules is not a system at all. This problem has been approached repeatedly by international initiatives. Rule sets like the Code of Conduct for European Lawyers published by the Council of Bars and Law Societies of Europe seem to have gone more than one step in the direction of a more broadly applicable professional code.[213]

Arbitrators, moreover, are in a different position than counsel. This adds to the need for separate international standards for arbitrators. Peters continues:

> [...] national rules for professional conduct ... are catered towards the more classical role of the attorney as party representative, which limits their suitability for establishing an ethical standard for arbitrators.[214]

While critics might point out cultural differences and infeasibility of enforcement, Peters says work on broad codes of ethics needs to continue, particularly to address the difficult nuances of impartiality, independence, disclosure, and due diligence.

> ... Idealists argue that the answer to questions of ethics should come naturally to the homo moralis. Relativists consider the idea of presuming to define a uniform standard to be illusive, considering the cultural particularities that define ethics. Pragmatists dismiss the idea of an international standard as unfeasible, citing the lack of enforceability as its critical weakness.
>
> Most of these arguments are valid and understandable to some extent. Of course, there is broad consensus on cornerstones or arbitrators' behaviour and a number of

---

213 Philipp Peters, *Can I Do This?—Arbitrator's Ethics*, Kluwer Arbitration Blog (Nov. 9, 2010). Available at: http://kluwerarbitrationblog.com/blog/2010/11/09/can-i-do-this-%E2%80%93-arbitrator%E2%80%99s-ethics/.

214 *Id.*

basic rules will be accepted by most arbitrators as a matter of course. The general ideas of impartiality and independence, duty of disclosure, equal treatment and due diligence will usually not be disputed amongst international practitioners. However, this does not mean that those of us who are not blessed with an unwavering sense of ethics for every situation might not sometimes find themselves confronted with the question 'Can I do this?' when dealing with the finer nuances of these principles. After all, it is often these 'gray areas' in which arbitrators might be most tempted to act inappropriately, sometimes just by omissions, thereby often alienating the parties in an arbitration. In this regard, it is often not improper conduct in the decision making process of an arbitration. Rather, it is the arbitrator's failure to conduct and steer the proceedings in a way that serve the purpose of arbitration.

Of course, cultural differences matter in a world of international business, and it is clear that in an arbitration related context, ethics cannot be universally defined in every detail. However, this does not mean that there is no common ground or minimum standard of conduct for arbitrators. After all, the 'international' in 'international arbitration' is said to shape this tool in a way that goes beyond an accumulation of national standards.

And, of course, in an ideal world, players who violate the rules have to bear the consequences for these violations. But this does not mean that the unbinding nature of transnational guidelines cannot influence arbitrators in considering their own actions. After all, compilations like the IBA Guidelines on Conflicts of Interest in International Arbitration, while not legally binding, and sometimes rejected by national courts and other decision making bodies, have—at least in part—found wide acceptance. It would be hard to argue that they have not influenced 'ethics' in international arbitration to some extent.

Initiatives like the ABA-AAA Code of Ethics for Arbitrators in Commercial Disputes should therefore be welcome. On a broader international level, the IBA Rules of Ethics for International Arbitrators are now more than twenty years old, and even though the discussion about ethics is far from being dead, it seems to have shifted more towards questions of counsel ethics while codes of conduct for arbitrators focus mostly on the questions of impartiality and independence. While it is perfectly understandable that these issues are of utmost concern, keeping alive the discussions on the broader subject of 'arbitrators' ethics' seems to be desirable.[215]

c.iii *Ethics rules for arbitration counsel?*

It is important to remember that the interests behind applying *ethical rules to arbitrators are not the same as those behind having ethical rules for arbitration*

---

215 *Id.*

counsel. Obviously, there are different interests at stake for representatives of clients and for decision-makers, with the latter more clearly affecting the legitimacy of the process from the perspective of the public's interest. Yet international ethical rules need to be established for arbitration counsel as well. Bishop sets out the following hypotheticals as an explanation of this need:

> 1st, with respect to document production, what are the applicable ethical rules for an Italian lawyer handling an International Arbitration in New York for an Italian client when the opposing side requests the production of certain documents that are harmful to his client's case? And to turn it around, in the same situation what are the ethical duties of an American attorney handling an International Arbitration in Italy? Does it matter if the client is Italian or American? It is my understanding that the ethical rules for American and Italian lawyers in this situation may be in direct conflict. 2nd, what ethical principles apply to the preparation of fact and expert witnesses for giving testimony for a British barrister representing an American company in an International Arbitration in Washington, DC, or to German and American attorneys representing opposite sides in an International Arbitration in London?[216]

d Ethics and arbitrators' outside activities

Adhering to the ethical norm of independence can be difficult for arbitrators who are (or become) prominent persons in the business world. Several challenges to arbitrators have been brought on the basis of the arbitrator's complex network of relationships. One of the more difficult roles to balance with that of being an arbitrator is being on a board of directors of a bank that holds shares in multinational corporations that are often the claimant of investor-State dispute proceedings. This was an issue in the *Suez-Vivendi v. Argentina* dispute.

In that case, Professor Gabrielle Kaufmann-Kohler, one of the most frequently selected arbitrators in investor-State arbitration dispute settlements, was selected as claimant's choice for the tribunal in 2004. In 2006, Professor Kaufmann-Kohler was appointed one of the Board of Directors of UBS, a large Swiss bank active around the world. At that time, she informed UBS of her pending arbitrations.

The Suez-*Vivendi* tribunal handed down its award in August 2007, holding Argentina liable for illegal expropriation and for violations of the obligations

---

216 Doak Bishop, *Ethics in International Arbitration*, keynote address at International Council for Commercial Arbitration Conference, Rio de Janiero, Brazil at p. 2 (May 2010). Available at: http://www.arbitration-icca.org/media/0/12763302233510/icca_rio_keynote_speech.pdf.

of fair and equitable treatment and full protection and security provisions of its BIT with France. Argentina was ordered to pay $105 million plus compounded interest and legal fees to the company.

Following the award's publication, Argentina found out that Kaufmann-Kohler was on the board of UBS. Argentina saw a conflict in the roles of arbitrator and of director of a shareholder of one of the parties and challenged the decision in an annulment proceeding partly on this basis.

Although the Annulment Tribunal refused to annul the award, it noted that there is a fundamental incompatibility in holding a directorship at a multinational bank such as UBS and being an international arbitrator. The ethical doubtfulness of such relationships means that directorship entails 'special duties' for the arbitrator. These duties include:

- the need to specifically investigate issues of connection with a case;
- the need to notify parties of directorship roles and possible conflicts;
- the need to continually investigate for conflict possibilities;
- the need to circulate an updated CV to all parties.

? **DISCUSSION NOTES**

Rubins and Lauterburg bring up some interesting comments on the arbitration context that highlight a specific problem in maintaining independence and impartiality: the fact that there are some jurisdictions where the state is omnipresent. In such jurisdictions there may be very few qualified arbitrator candidates who could pass the independence test. For instance, in states where the university system is heavily controlled by government, some of the most knowledgeable individuals might be 'dependent' on the respondent host. *See* Noah Rubins and Bernhard Lauterburg, *Independence, Impartiality and Duty of Disclosure in Investment Arbitration, in* Investment and Commercial Arbitration— Similarities and Divergences 153, 168–79 (Christina Knahr et al. eds., 2010).

Question to an expert: Mark S. Ellis

Mark S. Ellis is Executive Director of the International Bar Association (IBA), a member of the *Council of Foreign Relations*, and Adjunct Professor at The Florida State University College of Law. Prior to his appointment at the IBA, he was the first Executive Director of the Central European and Eurasian Law Initiative (CEELI), a project of the American Bar Association (ABA), Legal Advisor to the Independent International Commission on Kosovo, and actively involved with the Iraqi High Tribunal and also acted as legal advisor to the defense team of Nuon Chea at the Cambodian War Crimes Tribunal (ECCC).

Besides his expertise in international criminal law, Dr. Ellis was a long-time consultant to The World Bank on investment policies in Central and Eastern Europe and the former Soviet Union. A frequent speaker and media commentator on international legal issues, he appears regularly on *CNN International*, *Al Jazeera*, and *BBC*. He has published extensively in the areas of international humanitarian law, war crimes tribunals, and the development of the rule of law and is the co-recipient of the American Bar Association's *World Order Under Law Award*.

How has international investment law changed in light of the changing international investment business environment?

The most obvious advantage of third party funding (TPF) in international investment arbitration is increased access to justice as investors obtain a more equal position vis-à-vis the state. This situation can be reversed in the case of financially weak states being supported by third party funders in proceedings against multinational corporations. An ancillary effect may be improved quality of claims and proceedings. Before entering into a third party funding agreement, a potential funder will thoroughly investigate the merits of the planned action and its chances for success. Such additional scrutiny may decrease the number of patently frivolous claims.

On the other hand, third party funding bears new risks for the investment law system as it becomes subject to the TPF-investor relationship. Specifically, if the funder and investor have divergent interests, shifting control over arbitration proceedings could adversely affect the process. Not only must investors manage their own interests, they must also consider the interests of the TPF. Given the purely financial nature of TPF interests, third party funders may artificially prolong or inflate a dispute as a way to increase compensation, resulting in 'abuse of process.' Similarly, disagreements or strains in the relationship between the TPF and the investor, or unwillingness by the funder to support the proceedings, can stall the process. Moreover, third party funding could encroach on privilege, particularly concerning the exchange of information such as business trade secrets, settlement discussions, and client-lawyer or inter-lawyer communications.

QUESTION TO AN EXPERT: MARK S. ELLIS *(continued)*

While third party funding is a relatively new phenomenon, it represents a fast growing industry and will undoubtedly play a significant role in the future of investment arbitration. Considering its risks, we may see efforts to increase transparency, and regulation in the development of international investment law. This likely will affect cost allocation as well as disclosure of TPF involvement in certain claims. While presently no general system or method exists for the allocation of costs in international investment arbitration, an ICSID tribunal recently issued, for the first time, a decision enjoining security for costs in an investor-State dispute, and, more importantly, considered the presence of a TPF.

7

Investment guarantees: political risk insurance

Up to now, we have been addressing investment protections—the standards a host state has to uphold *vis-à-vis* foreign direct investment (FDI) and about the possibilities for an investor to gain relief from the host state's violations in this respect. Such protections are meant to encourage investment by offering the investor the security of knowing that any losses incurred because of violations of these standards can be challenged in international arbitration.

In reality, however, investor-State dispute settlement (ISDS) procedures do not offer investors easy security. There is a substantial investment of resources (time, personnel, finance) in bringing a challenge, claims do not always succeed, and claimants do not always recuperate their full losses. Further, even arbitration decisions in favor of claimants cannot offer investors a guaranteed protection from loss: hosts may instigate proceedings to set awards aside or may simply refuse to pay the awards.

What can an investor do to gain more reliable protection than the provisions of an IIA? The same thing that anyone might do to avoid facing a large financial loss from the destruction of property through fire or flood: purchase insurance. We turn then, in our last chapter, to look at investment insurance, or investment guarantees, examining in particular the instrument of political risk insurance.

7.1 Investment and political risk

7.1.1 The problem

The introductory chapter noted that the character of foreign investment differs from that of other international commercial relationships because of the long-term nature of the investor's activities in the host territory. The time between putting financial assets into the host and reaping the investment's returns leaves open the possibility that the host state's behaviour will eliminate or reduce the investor's expected profits. Because the host would (at least theoretically) have no political accountability toward the investor, international protections are the investor's most secure avenue for ensuring that its assets remain intact for the long term.

Yet, investors face a number of financial risks beyond the state's regulatory actions. One of the types of threats that has proven particularly significant for investors in developing economy host territories is political disturbance. However, IIAs, offer little protection to investors for losses due to causes beyond the state's control (for example, business interruptions due to civil unrest or regime change). Moreover, even where the state is involved in the losses (in politically motivated expropriations or regulatory changes), the investor may have to bear its financial losses for years before it is compensated, given that IIA protections are enforceable only through post-violation arbitration.

LITERATURE

Dorothee J. Feils and Florin M. Şabac, The Impact of Political Risk on the Foreign Direct Investment Decision: A Capital Budgeting Analysis[1]

Political risk refers to the risk that, (1) political events and processes within the host country, (2) changing relationships between the host and the home country, as well as between the host country and third countries, will influence the economic well-being of the parent firm. Political risk can be classified as macro political risk and micro political risk. Macro political risk is country-specific political risk and will influence all foreign firms in the host country alike. Macro risks include expropriations of all foreign firms in a country, non-discriminatory measures such as changes in tax laws, price controls, environmental regulations, and constraints which affect foreign firms only, such as limitations on the repatriation of capital, restrictions on expatriate employment and foreign ownership, and local content regulations. Micro political risk is specific to a certain industry, firm, or project. Political risk may affect the ownership of the assets, via full or partial forced divestitures, or the operations of the firm. Kobrin contends that while macro risk is more visible, micro risk is of more importance to firms. Within the context of this paper, economic well being is defined in terms of cash flows. Political risk is defined as unexpected changes in future cash flows due to political events

---

1 Dorothee J. Feils and Florin M. Şabac, *The Impact of Political Risk on the Foreign Direct Investment Decision: A Capital Budgeting Analysis*, 45(2) *The Engineering Economist* 129, 129–43 (2000); footnotes omitted.

in the host country. Political risk may thus lead to unexpected increases or decreases in future cash flows.

Political risk exists because there is no legal recourse if the foreign government chooses to expropriate an asset or otherwise increase the cost for foreign firms. The alternatives for host governments to alter the cash flows from foreign operations range from reducing cash flow due to higher taxes to completely eliminating any cash flows in case of full expropriation. Foreign governments will likely choose to do so only if the expected benefits of the expropriation or other cost to the multinational firm exceed the expected costs to the foreign government of these actions. . . .

The benefits of expropriation to the host country are the ownership of new productive assets. . . . The costs to the host country include foregone future investments by foreign firms, loss of skilled labor supplied by the foreign investor, and loss of export markets.

[. . .]

Irrespective of the motive of host governments to impose political costs on the foreign investors, MNEs have to consider these costs when deciding whether to accept or reject foreign investments. [. . .]

. . . [An expected utility approach] concludes that a risk-averse firm will underallocate capital to foreign investments in the presence of political risk. However, the problem of underallocation will no longer exist once it is possible to buy insurance for political risk. Thus, the existence of an insurance market ensures optimal allocation of capital between domestic and international investment opportunities. . . .

7.1.2   A solution

There are several legal vehicles through which investors may secure their planned investment before engaging in activities in host territories that are likely to pose trouble to investors. One is specifically designed to address the problems mentioned above.[2] Under the general heading of 'political risk insurance', these programs work to lessen the investor's likelihood of suffering financially from circumstances in the host territory that are either beyond the host government's control or that the investor is

---

2 National credit-offering programs are another instrument. These are funding mechanisms that grant investors credit for investing in territories which the home state has a political reason for wanting to promote.

unwilling to 'wait out'. There are four main categories of insurance/guarantee instruments:

- national, or 'bilateral', guarantee programs—government owned and operated programs offering insurance to national investors placing investments in eligible countries;
- multilateral guarantee programs—under the World Bank auspices, the Multilateral Investment Guarantee Agency (MIGA) offers investors from member states insurance policies for political risks that affect investments placed in developing member state territories;
- regional development banks offer similar insurance policies;
- and private insurance—commercial players offer investment insurance to any investors for any investments.

7.2   The guarantee as insurance

Defined very generally, the concept of insurance is an agreement by one party to pay another party a benefit upon the occurrence of an event. The party that agrees to pay the benefit upon the occurrence of the event is the insurer, while the party entitled to receive payment upon the occurrence of the event is the insured.

7.2.1   'Insurable risk'

There are, of course, numerous refinements that can be made to the definition of 'insurance', the main one being that the occurrence of the event must have some sort of uncertainty surrounding it. Either the occurrence itself must be uncertain (as in earthquake insurance—maybe the earthquake will occur) or the timing is uncertain (in life insurance, the timing of death is uncertain) or the frequency or amount of damages is uncertain (as in health insurance—although most people with health insurance will visit a doctor at some point in their lives, it is uncertain how often, and the amounts to be paid are unknowable).

The characteristics of the uncertainty, or risk, are distinguished by three basic hallmarks: assessability; randomness; and mutuality.[3] *Assessability* refers to the quantifiable nature of the risk's probable occurrence and the amount of losses likely to result from its occurrence. It is the ability to calculate statistical likelihoods of losses that makes insurance a potentially profitable busi-

---

3 OECD Insurance Committee, *OECD Checklist of Criteria to Define Terrorism for the Purpose of Compensation: Recommendation of the Council* (Dec. 15, 2004).

ness. The *randomness* element means that the risk will occur independently of any factors over which the insured has control. *Mutuality* indicates the possibility of grouping persons facing the same risk into a 'community' for the purposes of sharing the costs of the losses suffered by those affected by the realization of the insurable event.[4] Together with assessability, the ability to offer full coverage of individual losses hinges on the existence of sufficient numbers of individuals facing the same risk and willing to pay into a pooled fund to cover the costs should the event occur.

This concept of 'insurable risk', however, is only partly reflected in the realm of political risk insurance. As one commentator explains:

> Political risks deviate in important ways from this concept of the insurable risk. For example, insured political events may be at least partially under the control of and not 'independent of the will of the insured'—by their actions, international investors may be able to influence the likelihood that insured political events will take place. Furthermore, political risks tend to be quite idiosyncratic (they are influenced by the specifics of the host country political environment, the sector and the investor-State relationship). Thus, it may not be the case that insured investors form a homogeneous 'risk community' over which political risks can be polled. Political events can unfold over many months or years, they take place within a relationship between investor and the host country officials and reasonable people can (and, as the survey will show, do) disagree about whether or not an insurable event has taken place—thus, at times, political risk is not easily assessable. Finally, the perception in the industry is that political risks are cross-correlated (so that insurers are likely to face multiple claims at the same time).[5]

For political risk, then, insurance activities differ somewhat from other branches of insurance. One of the main differences is the specificity of the insurance contract, or policy, to the investor's proposed project.

7.2.2 The insurance contract

Political risk insurance (PRI) policies are highly individualized financial instruments. Because the level of political risk facing an investment will depend on such a large number of criteria specific to the particular host and

---

4 *Id.*

5 Kathryn Gordon, *Investment Guarantees and Political Risk Insurance: Institutions, Incentives and Development,* *in* OECD Investment Policy Perspectives 91–122, 93. Available at: http://www.oecd.org/finance/insurance/44230805.pdf (footnote omitted).

the particular project, each contract must be carefully studied to determine the scope and extent of the insurer's liability. There are, nevertheless, certain elements that appear regularly:[6]

- *Fixed policy duration*: Most PRI contracts have a duration of 3–15 years, with public providers' coverage often longer than private providers' policies.
- *Applicable law*: In case of dispute, courts will regard the insurance policy as a contract, and apply principles of contract law. The provider is therefore restricted from unilaterally cancelling the policy unless there is a serious breach of the contract's provisions, such as a failure of the insured to pay the premium or to meet the eligibility criteria.
- *Deductible*: The insured is often under an obligation to accept a portion of the financial loss. The amount of self-coverage may be in the form of a predetermined sum (a deductible) or a fixed percentage of the total loss (co-insurance).
- *Salvage clause*: The insured may be obliged to forfeit ownership of the insured property to the insurer if the investment is lost. Such a salvage clause allows the insurer an opportunity to mitigate its financial loss by selling off any of the investment's remaining assets.
- *Subrogation clause*: Another typical feature of PRI policies is a provision that transfers the legal rights of dispute settlement to the insurer. A subrogation clause replaces the insured with the insurer as claimant in a dispute with the host. Like the salvage clause, subrogation provisions offer the potential for recuperating losses that stem from having paid the covered claims.

7.2.3 Coverage: definition of political risk

The insurance the investor purchases will cover only losses arising out of events set forth in the policy. In the case of a claim, the insurance provider will carefully examine the events surrounding the losses to determine whether it must reimburse the claimant.

The traditional political risk insurance (PRI) policies for investors covered three basic types of events or situations generally accepted as comprising 'political risk':

---

6 Feils and Şabac, *supra* note 1.

1. confiscation, expropriation, or nationalization of an investment;
2. currency inconvertibility; and
3. damage from political violence, war, or civil disturbance.[7]

More recently, a fourth risk has been added to most policies' coverage: default on obligations, including breach of contract.

LITERATURE

Kausar Hamdani, Elise Liebers, and George Zanjani, An Overview of Political Risk Insurance[8]

Policy coverage

> Political risk insurance provides coverage for investors making direct equity investments in projects as well as those lending to emerging market borrowers. Recently, PRI has been used as a credit enhancement when securitizing emerging market debt.

The political risks covered under these policies are typically classified into three categories:

- *Currency inconvertibility (CI)* coverage protects against losses caused by currency transfer restrictions. Typically, CI coverage applies to the interruption of scheduled interest payments or repatriation of capital or dividends due to currency restrictions imposed by the host government.
- *Confiscation, expropriation, and nationalization (CEN)* coverage protects against losses caused by various acts of expropriation. Coverage usually applies to outright confiscation of property or funds.
- *Political violence* protects against losses caused by war, civil disturbance, or terrorism. Coverage is usually limited to 'politically motivated' violence.

As with other insurance contracts, the coverage trigger hinges on a loss occurrence connected with a specified insurance peril. CI policies are triggered when (i) currency transfer restrictions are imposed and (ii) the borrower has demonstrated the ability to pay by depositing funds in the local account of the insurer.

---

7 Terrorism is sometimes, but not always, placed within the scope of political violence.
8 Kausar Hamdani, Elise Liebers and George Zanjani, *An Overview of Political Risk Insurance*, Federal Reserve Bank of New York (May 2005). Available at: http://www.bis.org/publ/cgfs22fedny3.pdf.

Triggers under Political Violence and CEN coverage are less straightforward.

It can be difficult to determine if a loss was directly caused by an act of political violence. Likewise, difficulties can arise in determining whether CEN coverage is triggered, especially in the case of 'creeping' expropriation— where a government undertakes a series of actions that are, in sum, *de facto* expropriation, even though none of the individual actions is sufficient to trigger the coverage.

Example of cash-flows under typical insured transactions

To illustrate the role of coverage triggers and the cash-flows that ensue, (Figure 7.1) provides a schematic of cash-flows under a typical CI policy covering a crossborder lending arrangement. The example is simplified. In practice, contracts are highly customized and have cash-flows structured to meet the specific needs of the transaction.

In this example, a local market borrower has been funded by an US institution. The US financial institution pays a premium to the insurer. In the event of currency transfer restrictions, a credit event for the local borrower must first be ruled out by his continued payments into the PRI insurer's local currency account. As long as money continues to be deposited into that account, the insurer is obliged to make regularly scheduled payments to the US financial institution on the loan. In practice, there is typically a waiting period of several months before payment to the financial institution begins. This delay is to avoid invoking coverage in the case of transient events that are of too brief a duration to have real economic impact. Cash-flows under CEN and political violence coverage are similar and more straightforward than under a CI policy. Again using the above example, under a political violence policy

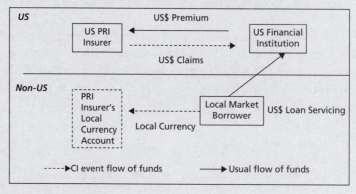

Figure 7.1 Currency inconvertibility event: schematic of cash-flows

the insurer would pay the US financial institution the insured portion of the principal and interest payments in default as a direct result of damage to the assets of the local market borrower caused by war and civil disturbance. In the case of CEN coverage, the US institution would be paid in the event that the local market borrower's real assets were expropriated. As with CI, such payments would only be made after a waiting period, which can range from six months to a year to allow for the documentation and filing of the loss. In addition, the insurer could take ownership of damaged or expropriated assets and could try to recover costs through salvage efforts.

The definitions of the events leading to coverage may differ from policy to policy. This is important to recall, as PRI contracts are often highly ambiguous. Policy-holders need a certain level of ambiguity given the impossibility to foresee all variations of political risks that could lead to losses. At the same time, the provider often makes use of the ambiguity to dispute its coverage of a claim. The intentional ambiguity of PRI policies has the effect of leading to multiple disputes between insurer and insured during the claims process.

In many PRI contracts, however, several risks that clearly do lead to losses are explicitly excluded. Among the most common exclusions is that of losses due to devaluations or economic downturns. Even when such occurrences are the result of political unrest, insurers will refuse to cover exchange rate losses.

7.3 Insurance programs and providers

There are a variety of guarantee programs and insurance providers from which investors can select political risk coverage. The differences in coverage lie mainly in the eligibility criteria, although the maximal length of coverage and the price vary as well. The specificity of political risk insurance policies to the particular project, however, means that the general points set out below may vary substantially for any individual investor.

7.3.1 National insurance programs

Several governments offer political risk insurance to their nationals who are interested in foreign investment activities.

a Features

National, or bilateral, insurance programs do not differ fundamentally from other PRI programs. Certain features, however, are typical and different from the policies of either the multilateral or private providers.

The most defining feature of bilateral programs is that they generally make the insurance only available to nationals. As national political risk insurance is most frequently aimed at increasing domestic firms' competitiveness, many refuse to issue policies to foreign corporations even if the entity has operations in the home state and/or to foreign subsidiaries of domestic companies.[9] Some programs also have lists of eligible host territories, although this seems to be more typical of OECD governments than of non-OECD government programs.

National programs' policies offer longer coverage than other programs—up to 20 years in some cases. The long-term nature of the coverage may reflect an emphasis on building beneficial relationships with the host. Relatedly, while some national insurance programs are budget neutral, others are subsidized. The legal form of the providers, whether as an independent agency or a part of the executive branch or even as a private company, does not afford a clear answer to this issue. One author, for example, notes that the question of whether the US insurance program was subsidized cannot be answered simply by reference to one study's finding that privatization would not be desirable for the clients. The program, she recalls, 'had an exceptional record (relative to the private sector) in claims management (preventing insurable events from happening) and recovery (retrieving the value of insured assets after a claim has been made)'.[10] Yet, she continued, '[i]f cost structures are very different between the public and private sectors, subsidy calculations would also have to account for these costs differentials (thus, low pricing for public sector products cannot be taken as evidence of a subsidy; it might simply reflect a cost advantage)'.[11]

Regardless of the subsidized nature of some national insurance programs, the policies themselves may be more expensive than those of private insurance companies on average. This is because some programs' implementing legislation requires them to be 'lenders of last resort',[12] meaning that investors must have a certain number of rejections from other insurers before they approach their national guarantee authority for coverage. Consequently, the insurer is contracting with the higher risk investments, which in turn increases the costs of the policy.

---

9 Gordon, *supra* note 5, at 118 (Table A2.6).

10 *Id*. at 99.

11 *Id*.

12 *Id*. at 96 (Australia, Japan, and the United States all aim to have their insurers' coverage available to investors that have been unable to find private insurance. This seems to be a part of the effort to encourage small- and middle-sized enterprise (SME) FDI activities).

b   Example: OPIC

The first national insurance program was set up by the United States and became the business model for other national programs as well as for the multilateral investment guarantee agency (which is described below). The Overseas Private Investment Company (OPIC) was established in 1971 to encourage US businesses to invest in countries that were seen as harbouring too much risk for investors. Succeeding the US Agency for International Development (AID), OPIC was created through the Foreign Assistance Act of 1961 and is an important part of the United States government's foreign aid apparatus.[13]

b.i   Goals of the corporation

While the original goals of economic and social development were tied to the Cold War politics of the period (coverage, for instance, was limited to investments planned in 'friendly countries'), today's operations are less pointedly political, aiming '[t]o mobilize and facilitate the participation of United States private capital and skills in the economic and social development of less developed countries and areas, and countries in transition from nonmarket to market economies, thereby complementing the development assistance objectives of the United States . . .'.[14] The challenge of ensuring such activity, however, remains the same as it was in the 1960s when investors were reluctant to place assets in politically unstable markets. Thus, OPIC continues to operate on the assumption that investors will be more willing to invest in developing economies if the political instability common to such states is eliminated as a risk to their financial security.

b.ii   Restrictions on coverage

Because it is a tool for development, OPIC coverage is legislatively limited to certain types of investments:

One set of limitations are those on the eligibility of investors applying for insurance. The OPIC requires investors to be US citizens or legal persons (including partnerships and associations), or foreign legal entities which US persons own.[15]

---

13 *See* Foreign Assistance Act 1961, *as amended*, Title IV (PL 87–195).
14 *Id.*, Section 231.
15 *Id.*, Section 238 and Section 238(c)(3). (If a foreign shareholder owns less than 5 percent of the company, it will fall within OPIC's scope.)

Another set of requirements relates to the investment project to be insured. According to the legislature's intent, the Agency

> in determining whether to provide insurance, financing, or reinsurance for a project, shall especially—(1) be guided by the economic and social development impact and benefits of such a project and the ways in which such a project complements, or is compatible with, other development assistance programs or projects of the United States or other donors; (2) give preferential consideration to investment projects in less developed countries that have per capita incomes of $984 or less . . . and (3) ensure that the project is consistent with the provisions of . . . this title relating to the environment and natural resources of, and tropical forests and endangered species in, developing countries, and consistent with [policies of sustainable development].[16]

Adherence to workers' rights is also a consideration for OPIC's analysis. The proposed host must be at least prepared to initiate programs to ensure international labour rights are protected, and such protections are required by the investor in carrying out the project.[17] As strong as the OPIC's developmental goals are, they are intermingled with national political interests. As a result, further legislative provisions mandate that coverage be refused for projects that would take jobs away from the United States[18] and encourage the OPIC to offer policies to small businesses in the United States to increase their willingness to engage in foreign direct investment projects.[19]

b.iii   Risks covered

Coverage for eligible investors includes the four categories of political risks set out above. As set forth in Section 234, OPIC is empowered:

> (a) . . . (1) To issue insurance, upon such terms and conditions as the Corporation may determine, to eligible investors assuring protection in whole or in part against any or all of the following risks with respect to projects which the Corporation has approved—
>
> (A)   inability to convert into United States dollars other currencies, or credits in such currencies, received as earnings or profits from the approved project, as repayment or return of the investment therein, in whole or in part, or as compensation for the sale or disposition of all or any part thereof;

---

16 Foreign Assistance Act, 22 USC §2151.
17 *Id.* at section 231A.
18 *Id.* at section 231(k)(1).
19 *Id.* at section 240.

(B) loss of investment, in whole or in part, in the approved project due to expropriation or confiscation by action of a foreign government or any political subdivision thereof;

(C) loss due to war, revolution, insurrection or civil strife; and

(D) loss due to business interruption caused by any of the risks set forth in subparagraphs (A), (B), and (C).

Up to 75% of the investment amount can be insured by OPIC for up to 20 years. Maximum coverage for any particular project, however, cannot exceed $250 000.

b.iv   *Dispute settlement*

If an insured investor faces investment losses from political events in the host territory, it must submit a claim to OPIC for indemnification. As any other insurance agent would do, OPIC will evaluate the claim, examining whether the cause of the losses falls within the scope of covered risks, whether the waiting time since the loss has elapsed, and whether there are any other reasons for which payment should be denied. If there are none, OPIC will pay the policy-holder the amount due and proceed to try to recuperate the expenses through pursuing the host government directly.

If the Agency determines that no payments are required or that they do not need to pay for the full extent of the losses, the insured can elect to bring a claim against OPIC in arbitral proceedings. Such tribunals will then examine the circumstances of the claim and analyse the extent of the Agency's liability under the particular insurance policy as interpreted by general contract law and principles of insurance law.

 CASE

Bechtel Enterprises International (Bermuda) Ltd; BEn Dabhol Holdings, Ltd; and Capital India Power Mauritius I Overseas Private Investment Corporation[20]

The following highlights one tribunal's analysis of a claim for coverage based on the host's allegedly expropriatory acts. Here, one of the central points of dispute was OPIC's assertion that §§10.05/10.07 of the insurance policy

---

20 *Bechtel Enterprises International (Bermuda) Ltd; BEn Dabhol Holdings, Ltd; and Capital India Power Mauritius I v. Overseas Private Investment Corporation*, AAA Case No. 50 T195 00509 02, Findings of Fact, Conclusions of Law and Award (Sept. 25, 2003). Available at: http://www.opic.gov/sites/default/files/docs/2294171_1.pdf.

required that the host's courts issue an award for compensation prior to the claimant's request for insurance.

CONCLUSIONS OF LAW

1. *A Total Expropriation Within the Meaning of Section 4.01 of the OPIC Policies Has Taken Place*

   Article IV of the Bechtel and GE policies set out four elements, subject to the exclusions provided for in Sec. 4.03 and the limitations of Sec. 5.04, that must be present for an act or series of acts to constitute a total expropriation. We recite these elements followed by our findings as to each of them:

   a. *The acts are attributable to a foreign governing authority which is in de facto control of the part of the country in which the project is located.*
      Here that element is satisfied as the acts undertaken ... are all either by governmental authorities in control of both the state of Maharashtra and the country of India, agencies of the government, or owned and controlled by the [Government of India (GOI)] or [Government of Maharashtra (GOM)].

   b. *The acts are violations of international law without regard to the availability of local remedies or material breaches of local law.*
      The evidence makes clear that [the government entities] violated each of [the various agreements they had made with the claimants] for political reasons and without any legal justification. ... Indian courts have enjoined and otherwise taken away Claimants' international arbitration remedies ..., all in violation of established principles of international law, in disregard of India's commitments under the UN Convention as well as the Indian Arbitration Act. By its recent consent to [the investment's] Final Termination Notice and joinder in the UNCITRAL international arbitration filing against the India-based financial institutions (IFIs), OPIC has publicly acknowledged that the concerted acts of the lenders with the GOM and GOI have effectively destroyed the investment of Claimants in the DPC, all in violation of international and local law.

   c. *The acts directly deprive the Investor of fundamental rights in the insured investment (Rights are 'fundamental' if without them the Investor is substantially deprived of the benefits of the investment);*
      There is no doubt that [the state electricity board] stopped paying the Dabhol Power Plant (DPC) for the electricity produced ..., and the [government banks], together with the Indian courts, enjoined Claimants from terminating the [contract] in ... and in

this process deprived DPC of its international arbitral remedies under the Project Agreements that were the essential vehicle by which Claimants might have been able to recoup their investment in the Project.

d. *The violations of law are not remedied and the expropriatory effect continues for six months.*

The expropriatory acts by the GOI and its related agencies began in December 2000 when [the government] breached its payment obligations . . ., which have never been remedied, and have continued for over six months.

2. The exclusion [for acts undertaken by the government] does not apply here as the Indian governmental acts were not undertaken in the capacity as '. . . supplier, creditor, lessor, shareholder, director or manager of or purchaser from, the foreign enterprise, or as a guarantor of any payment obligations to the foreign enterprise.'

3. All of the acts undertaken . . . were . . . openly political, and not commercially, motivated, thus eliminating the Section 403(b) exclusion. . . .

4. It also does appear that the GOI has the funds or sovereign resources necessary to generate funds to pay its obligations to DPC.
    [. . .]

5. *Claimants Complied With §§10.05/10.07 Of The Policies*
    Section 10.05/10.07 of the Policies provides for procedures which have to be followed in order for the investors to be entitled to receive compensation in respect of expropriation coverage . . . . The procedures set forth . . . reflect in broad terms most of the procedures required to be followed under the various agreements . . . should Claimants believe that they wished to secure an arbitral award against the Indian entities. During the negotiations leading up to the signing of the Policies, §§10.05/10.07 was submitted to Bechtel and General Electric (GE). They required minor amendments which were agreed to by OPIC and incorporated therein. The evidence indicated that neither Claimants nor OPIC addressed the reasoning behind, or any significant implications to, the insertion of these clauses in any meaningful fashion.

    There was evidence to suggest that they had been inserted in the agreement in order to assist OPIC, in the event it was obliged to pay a claim under the Policies and commence the procedure to recover such amounts from the Indian government, pursuant to the IIA. However, as the evidence was far from clear as to what Claimants or OPIC understood the insertion of §§10.05/10.07 to mean, the Panel has applied certain fundamental rules of insurance contract construction to §§10.05/10.07 and its impact on the contract.

6. In the event of uncertainty or ambiguity, insurance contracts are generally interpreted and construed against the drafting party. Section 206 of the Restatement (Second) of Contracts confirms this position as does Section 83.27 of Couch on Insurance, which provides that 'any ambiguity will be interpreted in favor of the insured and indemnity.'

7. The evidence indicated that neither party had anticipated that the Indian courts would grant injunctions making it impracticable to comply with the provisions in the agreements that triggered computation of the Transfer Amount as contemplated under the contracts. Moreover, neither party at the hearing could produce any evidence which showed there was any precedent for the Indian courts issuing such an injunction. Section 261 of the Restatement (Second) of Contracts provides, *inter alia*, that where a party's performance is made impracticable by the occurrence of an event, the nonoccurrence of which was a basic assumption on which the contract was made, the duty on that party to render said performance is discharged.

8. The issuance of the injunction by the Indian courts rendered compliance with the provisions of §§10.05/10.07 by Claimants to be, at the very least, impracticable, if not impossible, without violating the terms of the court's injunction.

   Moreover, for the reasons set forth above, it was also clear from the evidence that at the time the contract was drafted and §§10.05/10.07 were inserted, it was a basic assumption of the contract and of both parties that the Indian government would not issue an injunction effectively preventing initiation of the procedure to trigger the Transfer Amount.

   [...]

9. In assessing the relative positions of the parties with respect to the interpretation and implementation of §§10.05/10.07, Section 227(1) of the Restatement (Second) of Contracts provides some assistance when it states, *inter alia*, that an interpretation is preferred that will reduce the obligee's risk of forfeiture unless the event is within the obligee's control or the circumstances indicate that he has assumed the risk. As previously stated, neither party assumed or assessed the likelihood that the Indian courts would issue an injunction preventing compliance with the terms of §§10.05/10.07.

   In the absence of clear evidence indicating consensus by the parties on the interpretation of §§10.05/10.07, the Panel is cognizant that to enforce compliance with the provisions of §§10.05/10.07 by Claimants, when the reason for noncompliance was the unforeseen action of a party beyond the control of either Claimants or OPIC, namely MERC and the Indian Courts, would result in forfeiture of Claimants' rights under the insurance agreements.

10. For the reasons set forth above, the Panel finds that Claimants were discharged of their obligation to comply with the provisions §§10.05/10.07. . . .

11. OPIC must pay Bechtel Enterprises International (Bermuda) Ltd. and BEn Dabhol Holdings, Ltd. a total of twenty-eight million five hundred and seventy thousand dollars ($28 570 000).

According to OPIC's 2011 annual report, it has made 291 payments to investors over its history.[21] Of the 28 claims it denied, half were challenged. Even having paid out close to $971 million in claims, however, OPIC's financial stability is intact. Through subsequent recovery efforts, the Agency has managed to retrieve over 92% of the claims it paid out.

c   *Other bilateral providers*

Today, nearly all OECD members have agencies offering investment guarantees, as do a growing number of emerging and developing economies.[22]

Like OPIC, such agencies are frequently also engaged in financing assistance through lending, extending export credit, and providing export guarantees.

A significant difference among the other bilateral providers and OPIC is that most providers are not approaching investment insurance as a foreign policy activity. This has the result that OPIC's goal of supporting host state development is not reflected in most of the other programs. Instead, most of the other OECD and all of the non-OECD program mission statements look to enhancing domestic investors' competitiveness.[23]

7.3.2   Private insurance providers

Beginning in the 1970s, private underwriters began noticing OPIC's financial success. Adopting the same basic formula as their public counterparts, private insurers began offering coverage of the same political risks, but to any interested investor. The companies screen their clients purely on the

---

21 OPIC, *FY11 Annual Public Claims Report – Insurance Claims Experience to Date* (Sept. 30, 2011). Available at: http://www.opic.gov.

22 States with public investment insurance providers include: Austria, Australia, Belgium, Canada, China, France, Italy, Germany (through the private company PwC), India, Japan, Korea, Netherlands, South Africa, Turkey, the UK, and the US.

23 Gordon, *supra* note 5, at 112–13 (Table A2.2).

basis of assessments of whether the claims payouts will be less than the premiums collected. Given that private providers are motivated by profit rather than national policy interests, there are no *a priori* conditions on an investor's eligibility to access coverage. Private providers' policies and prices can also be individually tailored to the insured project. Together with the fact that the accepted investors are often those with less risky investments to begin with, policies from private insurance companies may be less expensive than those from public agents. While profitable, the complexity of PRI activities and the necessary financial capacity to engage in insuring multi-million dollar projects prevents many insurance companies from entering the PRI supply market. Among the current private insurers in this field are Lloyd's of London, Hiscox, Sovereign, Zurich (USA), and Chartis (formerly AIG).[24]

7.3.3 Multilateral Investment Guarantee Agency (MIGA)

a General remarks

Part of the World Bank Group, the Multilateral Investment Guarantee Agency (MIGA) is the largest and most important of the public investment insurance providers. Its establishment followed that of OPIC, coming into existence in 1988.[25] In form, intended function, and methods of operation, MIGA is similar to the OPIC. Similarly directed to assisting in the economic development of host states, MIGA's activities form an important counterpart to its sibling the ICSID.

b MIGA as an international organization: structure and voting power

The Convention Establishing the Multilateral Investment Guarantee Agency sets out its purpose and its structural elements.

Purpose: Article 2 sets forth that the purpose of MIGA is to 'encourage the flow of investments for productive purposes among member countries, and in particular to develop member countries'. This clearly presumes that insurance offerings will encourage investment flows to developing countries.

---

24 The MIGA has a page listing all PRI providers. Available at: http://www.pri-center.com.
25 For a history of MIGA, *see* Ibrahim F.I. Shihata, MIGA and Foreign Investment 31–55 (1988).

Table 7.1 Functions of MIGA bodies

Council of Governors	Board of Directors	President
Representatives of Members • Annual meeting • Other meetings if 5 members or 25% voting power requests one Default powers-holder, may delegate much to board Exclusive competence to: • Admit new members • Suspend members • Determine developing country status • Determine capital, increase contingent liabilities • Amend Constitution and Schedules	12 or more directors, for term decided by council Responsible for 'general operations'	Under control of board; Loyalty to agency Ordinary work of the agency; Head of staff

Structure: Sitting within the World Bank Group, the MIGA has a three-part structure, consisting of a Council of Governors, a Board of Directors, and a President. Table 7.1 summarizes the tasks of these bodies.

Voting: Like the IMF and World Bank, the MIGA uses a weighted voting system that reflects the members' differing economic status. For MIGA, each member gets 177 base votes plus one vote per share owned. Share ownership is based on economic size, resulting in a greater voice for wealthier countries. Most votes are taken on a majority basis, with quorum requirements of two-thirds of the total voting power (for Council) or one-half of the total voting power (Board).

c   Operations: PRI policies

MIGA insurance policies are very similar to those of other public providers. Eligibility is extended to the investors of any member with a planned investment in any developing member host or to investors with an investment in a developing member's territory.[26] The policies' duration ranges from 1 to 15 years (20-year coverage is possible if justifications for the extension are

---

26 Investments made by investors of a developing member may be located in that member's territory if the financing is coming from outside. *See* Convention establishing the Multilateral Investment Guarantee Agency art. 13(c), Oct. 11, 1985, 24 ILM 1605 (1985) [hereinafter 'MIGA Convention']. The host must, however, join the investor in requesting coverage for such projects.

given) and its extent includes a coinsurance requirement.[27] The types of risk, too, include the same ones as other providers' cover. Under the term 'non-commercial risks', 'covered risks' are defined in Article 11:

> Subject to the provisions of Sections (b) and (c) below, the Agency may guarantee eligible investments against a loss resulting from one or more of the following types of risk:

Currency transfer

> any introduction attributable to the host government of restrictions on the transfer outside the host country of its currency into a freely usable currency or another currency acceptable to the holder of the guarantee, including a failure of the host government to act within a reasonable period of time on an application by such holder for such transfer;

Expropriation and similar measures

> any legislative action or administrative action or omission attributable to the host government which has the effect of depriving the holder of a guarantee of his ownership or control of, or a substantial benefit from, his investment, with the exception of non-discriminatory measures of general application which governments normally take for the purpose of regulating economic activity in their territories;

Breach of contract

> any repudiation or breach by the host government of a contract with the holder of a guarantee, when (a) the holder of a guarantee does not have recourse to a judicial or arbitral forum to determine the claim of repudiation or breach, or (b) a decision by such forum is not rendered within such reasonable period of time as shall be prescribed in the contracts of guarantee to the Agency's regulations, or (c) such a decision cannot be enforced; and

War and civil disturbance

> any military action or civil disturbance in any territory of the host country to which this Convention shall be applicable as provided in Article 66. In addition, the Board, by special majority, may approve the extension of coverage under this Article to specific non-commercial risks other than those referred to in Section (a) above, but in no case to the risk of devaluation or depreciation of currency.
> [. . .]

---

27 The MIGA can indemnify up to 90 percent of the investment and 50 percent of the earnings; and up to 95 percent of a loan or loan guaranty principal plus 150 percent of the principal to cover interest due to creditors.

A Commentary is available to further explain these terms. Referring to currency inconvertibility, the comments emphasize that both *de jure* and *de facto* inconvertibility will be covered, although specifics such as how long a 'reasonable period of time' would be for the investor to be required to wait are expected to be set forth in the insurance policy. For expropriation, the MIGA expresses a clear view on coverage of indirect expropriation:

> [. . .] Measures normally taken by governments to regulate their economic activities such as taxation, environmental and labor legislation as well as normal measures for the maintenance of public safety, are not intended to be covered by this provision unless they discriminate against the holder of the guarantee. [. . .] [28]

Not intended to predetermine any arbitral decision on the matter, this comment underlines a strong interest in ensuring host states' policy flexibility. Breach of contract coverage will only be available if the claimant has no other possibility of gaining relief. If court procedures exist and if the host has not unreasonably delayed the proceedings or refused to pay an award, the MIGA will refuse to pay the claim.[29]

Finally, the war and civil disturbance provision has been defined to exclude damages arising from terrorism.[30] Such damages may be covered under a provision 11(b) as an 'other' non-commercial risk, but that is dependent on agreement by a super-majority of the Board.[31]

Despite the familiar definitions of the categories of PRI, there are several particularly interesting aspects of MIGA's insurance for non-commercial risks. One is that, according to Article 12, insurance policies are to be concluded only for 'new' investments.[32] While this generally refers to investments begun after the contract has been concluded, the definition permits both modernization or expansion of an existing investment and subsidiary investments (those financed with money earned through a prior investment within same host) to be covered. It also allows for existing investments to be covered if a new investor purchases them and applies for insurance.

A second aspect of MIGA coverage is that the investment must have a development orientation. This is found not only in the fact that the investments

---

28 Commentary on the Convention Establishing the Multilateral Investment Guarantee Agency, para. 14. Available at: http://www.miga.org/documents/commentary_convention_november_2010.pdf.
29 *Id*. para. 15.
30 *Id*. para. 16.
31 *Id*. paras. 16–17.
32 MIGA Convention art. 12(d).

must be located in a developing member territory,[33] but also in the requirements that the proposed investment have host state approval and contribute
to the host's development objectives.[34] Combined with the requisite compliance with the host state's laws and environmental soundness, the contribution to development provision eliminates the ambiguity of the definitional
debates in investment arbitration for purposes of determining what an 'eligible investment' is for insurance.

Third, in order to be eligible for insurance coverage, the MIGA specifies that
projects should be made where investment protection 'including the availability of fair and equitable treatment' is available. This is clearly an element
to motivate members to agree to investor protection obligations. If making
insured investments will foster capital flows to developing countries, and
if insurance is only available to investments where fair and equitable treatment is promised, then hosts have a self-interest in promising such treatment.
Of course, the requirement also makes it less likely that MIGA will have to
sustain a loss, as political risks will often be susceptible to claims of violation
of FET clauses.

Next, MIGA policies are limited to offering a maximum coverage per project
insured and per host country. Limited by its Convention to insuring only up
to 150 percent of its capital, in 2012, the Agency could insure up to $220
million per project, with a per host limit of $720 million.[35]

Finally, investors must demonstrate that they, their partners, and all of the
persons with whom they have contracts in relation to the investment are free
from allegations of corruption. The MIGA's position as a World Bank entity
is clearly demonstrated with this attention to good governance. The 2006
standards are part of the Bank's own integrity program which aims to raise
the costs of corruption detection.

d   MIGA: dispute settlement

There are several different contexts in which MIGA dispute settlement will
arise, each of which has different procedures.

---

33 MIGA Convention art. 14 ('Eligible Host Country').
34 MIGA Convention art. 12(e).
35 See MIGA website, 'Who We Are', Frequently Asked Questions. Available at: https://www.miga.org/
Pages/Who%20We%20Are/Frequently-Asked-Questions.aspx#con4.

As an international institution based on a convention, MIGA provides for dispute settlement between members and the MIGA should a member disagree with the Agency's interpretations or actions. In such a case, Article 56 applies, providing for a decision to be taken by the Board of Directors, and if necessary, the Council.

Disputes over claims are handled differently. Under MIGA Convention Article 58, the policy-holder must rely on the policy's provisions for dispute settlement.

If there is a dispute between the MIGA as a subrogee of a policy-holder's claim and a member state as host, the dispute settlement is governed by Article 57 in combination with Annex II of the Convention.[36] Following mandatory consultations for 120 days, the provision gives the disputants a choice of initiating conciliation procedures before moving to arbitration (if the matter is still unresolved) or directly beginning arbitration under ICSID procedural rules. Arbitrations between MIGA and a member will result in a final report that is neither appealable, revisable, nor open to annulment.[37]

7.4   A critical assessment of PRI

The idea that 'prevention is better than the cure' has intuitive appeal, and it is this appeal that makes the idea of PRI so strong. Investors, surely, would be better off if they could simply avoid the need for ISDS in the first place—wouldn't they?

It is interesting that, for all of its apparent benefits, PRI remains a relatively rarely used instrument. As one study noted:

> Despite growth during the 1990's, PRI covers only a small fraction of total capital flows to emerging markets. While data are scarce, PRI provided by Berne Union members (which include the major insurance underwriters for U.S. investors) covered only about 10 percent of emerging market FDI in the 1990's. During 2001, Berne Union members insured only $17 billion of investments.[38]

---

36 *See* Who We Are, miga.org. Available at: http://www.miga.org/whoweare/index.cfm. MIGA Convention, Annex II Settlement of Disputes between a Member and the Agency under Article 57.

37 If a party disagrees with the award, it may request an interpretation of the award. Enforcement remains an obligation, however.

38 Hamdani et al., *supra* note 8.

More recent figures indicate higher levels of insurance coverage for developing country investment inflows, but even a rate of 30% indicates that PRI is something of a boutique financial product.

Contrasting the evidence with intuition suggesting that avoiding damages where possible is the more reasonable path, two questions arise: is PRI ineffective, causing investors to feel it is not valuable? And what other considerations may keep investors from purchasing PRI?

7.4.1 How effective is PRI?

According to a 2008 report, only 3 percent of global FDI is insured. At the same time, the report notes that 30 percent of the FDI to developing countries is insured. This difference in levels of insurance would suggest that insurance does, in fact, have a significant positive effect on encouraging capital flows into developing markets. The correlation, however, should be viewed with caution, as correlation is not the same as causation.

a   Moral hazard

Even if the positive effect were to be shown, it is not clear that it is a good thing. PRI, like any insurance scheme, in fact, holds the potential to pose a 'moral hazard' to investors. Moral hazard is the term referring to the effect that the availability of an instrument to protect against losses from risky activities itself supplies an incentive for the protected individual to act in a way that increases the risk of the loss occurring. Recognized as a result of imperfect information,[39] the concept of moral hazard typifies the problems of the insurance industry: once an individual purchases insurance to guard against a specific risk of loss, she has less of an individual incentive to engage in risk-avoiding behaviour. Society and insurers, then, must absorb the costs of losses from riskier behaviour than is socially beneficial.

What is true of the individual insurance purchaser is also true of investors with political risk insurance. Thus, investors may put resources into territories that are likely to face political disturbance or they may be less cautious in maintaining a good relationship with the host. Because the insured will not be bearing the full cost of its behaviour, the moral hazard is toward the community who will be sharing those costs.

While moral hazard is a problem for any type of insurance in so far as the policy-holder has an incentive to act with less caution than is efficient, with

---

39 *See* Benkt Holström, *Moral Hazard and Observability*, 10(1) Bell J. Econ. 74, 74 (1979).

investment insurance, this moral hazard can also apply to the host. To the extent that investor protection is supported as a tool to encourage good governance, reducing the investor's financial interest in whether the host adheres to its protection obligations (because the investor will simply be reimbursed for any losses by its insurer) indirectly harms the international community's interest in accountable, rule-of-law-abiding states. The use of deductibles, or other cost-sharing instruments, lessens but does not eliminate the moral hazard inherent in insurance policies.

b   Halo effect

Counteracting the moral hazard phenomenon for the host is the so-called 'halo effect' of PRI by public providers. The halo effect refers to insurance policies' added effectiveness by virtue of their subrogation provisions. If a host knows that its political actions will harm an investor that is insured by the home state, the host may be less willing to engage in such action in order to preserve its political capital. Insurers' involvement need not even be limited to dispute settlement—if a host is contemplating taking expropriatory actions, for example, MIGA, OPIC, or any of the other insurers' expressions of displeasure may be sufficient pressure to make the host refrain from taking such actions at all. Studies of this effect have supported the hypothesis that public lenders' involvement in investment projects have 'significant risk-mitigating effects',[40] and statistics of these insurers' recovery rates underline their influence.[41]

The following excerpt highlights how public providers can influence hosts' willingness to adjust their behaviour toward an investor.

LITERATURE

Kenneth Hansen, Robert C. O'Sullivan, and Geoffrey W. Anderson, The Dabhol Power Project Settlement—What Happened? and How?[42]

[...]

When OPIC receives notice of a potential expropriation claim, or just an investment dispute involving an insured investor, OPIC consults with the

---

40 Gordon, *supra* note 4, at 94 (citing Wodehouse 2006).

41 *See supra* (OPIC has recovered 92 percent of its claims payments).

42 Kenneth Hansen, Robert C. O'Sullivan and Geoffrey W. Anderson, *The Dabhol Power Project Settlement— What Happened? and How?* (December 2005). Available at: www.infrastructurejournal.com. Link to pdf is www.chadbourne.com/files/. . .40fc. . ./**Dabhol**_InfrastructureJournal12_2005.pdf.

insured investor and may intervene with the foreign government in an attempt to resolve the dispute or avert the claims. These so-called 'advocacy' efforts are nothing new, but OPIC has recently attempted to formalize them by creating an Advocacy Center through which such requests for intervention can be managed. Counterpart agencies of other governments may provide similar assistance, and the World Bank's Multilateral Investment Guarantee Agency (MIGA) has achieved some success in resolving disputes between investors from member countries and governments of other member countries.

Government and multilateral insurers have well-established, open avenues of communication with host country officials and, as investment promotion agencies, can create incentives for resolving disputes. Host country governments perceive such agencies as development institutions implementing mutually advantageous investment encouragement programs, notwithstanding their own financial interest in achieving a resolution that avoids a claim against them, and so they can play the role of honest broker while protecting their own economic interests.

As in any other advocacy situation, it helps to have the facts and the law on your side, and the investor is in a position to help in both respects. Project agreements that create rights and enforceable remedies are a good starting point. The ability to invoke foreign investment laws and investment protection treaties enhances the investor's position. Awareness of 'pressure points' such as the visit of a head of state, the periodic meeting of a joint economic commission, and the opportunity to challenge a country's eligibility for trade or investment benefits or economic assistance contributes to a successful advocacy campaign.

[. . .]

7.4.2 What aspects of PRI keep investors from purchasing it?

According to the Berne Union's statistics, the PRI market has grown substantially since 2010: going from just over $66 billion worth of new business insured to nearly $98 billion in 2014.[43] Still, given the overall amount of FDI, this is not so much.

---

43 Berne Union, Statistics 2010–2014. Available at: http://www.berneunion.org/statistics/.

Why, if PRI is so effective in protecting investors, is purchasing PRI policies not overly desirable for investors? One possibility is that investors are simply less risk-averse than the average person. Clearly, putting large sums of money into any business venture involves a substantial financial risk. Even if the investor's liability is limited to the value of its stocks, putting assets into a project without certainty of return defines the actor as a financial risk-taker. If an investor is willing to put resources into a foreign territory in expectation of making greater profits than those resources could generate at home, then perhaps such an actor is by nature less likely to purchase insurance (thereby definitively reducing the rate of return) to lessen the risk of potential loss of profits.

Another more established factor preventing the more frequent purchase of PRI is the high cost of such policies. Different authors point out that PRI is generally quite expensive. This is because the nature of the risk means that the costs of providing the insurance are high and the costs of covering realized losses are extraordinarily high.

From the assessment of the project risk to the creation of a suitable policy to monitor the investment, PRI requires both time- and expertise-intensive attention. Such time and expertise creates significant personnel-related costs for the insurer. Equally significantly, the nature of political risk requires that providers have very large holdings of equity capital, which in turn makes individual policies expensive. Such holdings are required because if political turbulence threatens one investor, the insurer is likely to face a wide number of claims stemming from the same turbulence or from contagion unrest within a geographic region. Such cross-correlated events can expose the insurer to extremely high levels of liability, and will require sufficient capital to remain viable. Holding such large sums of money is expensive for the insurer, raising the costs for the client as a consequence.

The high costs can create either an unwillingness to purchase policies or an inability to do so. The latter has been referred to as the 'missing markets' phenomenon. In PRI markets, high transaction costs mean that many markets will not be able to be served profitably—that is, there will be missing risk markets (e.g. for smaller clients whose business might not generate enough revenues to cover the high transaction costs).[44]

Public insurance programs may offset the missing market effect to some degree through programs of being an insurer of last resort.[45]

---

44 Gordon, *supra* note 5, at 95.
45 *Id.*, at 96.

Finally, the lack of greater depth in the PRI market may be due to a mismatch between the marketed products and the demand for insurance. This is partly due to some of the absolute caps on the amount of coverage that public providers may offer. Currently the MIGA, as stated above, may not grant coverage for more than $220 million of an investment. Such a policy cannot approach full coverage for most of the investment projects in some of the most active FDI sectors: a single energy sector investment, for example, is often worth more than $1 billion. Even with multiple policies, the investor is likely to be left not fully insured.

More significant than the insufficiency of the amount of coverage, though, is insufficiency in the type of coverage. While breach of contract, the non-honoring of sovereign financial obligations, and even the non-enforcement of treaty-based arbitration awards are now among the PRI offerings, there is still too little innovation in the PRI sector to satisfy wary investors. Because many of the private insurers pattern their activities on those of OPIC and MIGA, which have been highly profitable in the past, product offerings tend to remain those most needed in the Marshall Plan years. Yet, today's investors' interests, for example, in avoiding currency depreciation risk,[46] are left largely unsatisfied. Insurers argue that since new product development would increase the risks for the insurer, this would have to be even more expensive for the client, in turn preventing the wider use of such instruments.

---

46 *Id.*, at 117 (of the public providers surveyed, only India provides coverage for exchange rate changes).

Question to an expert: Markus Krajewski

Markus Krajewski is Professor of Public Law and Public International Law at the Friedrich-Alexander University Erlangen-Nuremberg. An expert in both international trade and international investment law, he has also published in the areas of European Union law and the law of peacekeeping. Among Professor Krajewski's most recent works is *Shifting Paradigms in International Investment Law*, co-edited with Steffen Hindelang (Oxford University Press, 2016).

Should private-sector guarantee agencies also consider the impact of the project on human rights?

In a previous edition of this textbook, I argued that state guarantee agencies should consider the impact of the investment project on the environment and human rights of the population living in the vicinity of the project. This is not a universally accepted proposition, but it is firmly grounded in widely accepted principles of international law.

The question of whether private sector insurance providers should also consider the impact of investment projects cannot rest as firmly on current views of international human rights law, because those obligations bind states, not private parties. At least not usually.

Still, there is growing support to hold companies responsible for their acts affecting human rights. The 2011 (non-binding) United Nations Guiding Principles on Business and Human Rights' 'Protect, Respect and Remedy' framework holds that corporations should—at the very least—avoid violating human rights and help address any harms they have caused. The due diligence standard to which they are held in pursuing this aim means that corporate decisionmakers need to at least ask their business partners and clients about the impacts of their own activities. In the context of political risk insurers, the Ruggie Principles may at least suggest that certain types of projects be excluded from coverage. Here, the OPIC's practice of considering the construction of large dams a 'categorically prohibited sector' if the construction of the dam has *inter alia* a significant and irreversible impact on 'local inhabitants' ability to earn a livelihood'.

The Equator Principles (EP) on environmental and social risk management—a set of soft law guidelines open to financial institution may give PRI providers a good start to thinking about how to determine whether an investment project should be insured. The EP ask its members (financial institutions) to promise to require agreements between themselves and their clients as to the clients' own behavior toward the land and people they affect. If the principles are not upheld, the institution itself can request compensation. Such an approach would allow PRI insurers to continue to play their important role of fostering investment but with the safeguard of promoting human rights-compliance in practice.

Index